The History of Orangeism; Its Origin, Its Rise, & Its Decline

THE

HISTORY OF ORANGEISM:

ITS ORIGIN, ITS RISE, & ITS DECLINE.

BY M.P.

DUBLIN:

M. H. GILL & SON, 50, UPPER SACKVILLE STREET.

GLASGOW : CAMERON & FERGUSON, WEST NILE STREET.

1882.

LOAN STACK

DEDICATION.

TO

IRISHMEN AT HOME AND ABROAD;

TO PROTESTANT AND CATHOLIC ALIKE;

TO THE ORANGEMAN AS WELL AS TO THE RIBBONMAN;

TO THE LAND LEAGUER

AS WELL AS

TO THE EMERGENCY MAN

This Volume is respectfully Dedicated

BY

THE AUTHOR.

INTRODUCTION.

JUST a few words before starting. The history of the Orange Institution has yet to be written. Why this is so might be accounted for by one, or other, or all of many reasons. While demanding no higher qualities than those possessed by every citizen of sense and understanding, who seeks in the present to draw a lesson from the past, it would be affectation to say that the task is not an onerous, in some respects a difficult one. We live in the hurry and confusion of excited times. Every man belongs to a party Every party has a monopoly of virtue, in the opinion of its own members, and, reversing the telescope, can see little or no good in that which is opposed to it. In such a time it may be easily foreseen that qualities of patience and of research, though amongst the humblest, are amongst the rarest to be found, when notoriety is mistaken for distinction, when the ambition that clamours for a place receives censure as the next best substitute for praise, and when to be generally condemned as the leader of an ignorant faction is a gratification second only to being praised as the Tribune of a free people It is no wonder, then, that men who claim no merit but that which industry brings have hitherto shrunk from a painful task which must result in little profit to themselves, and the certainty of their being placed in the pillory of some political faction, an aim for the rotten eggs of political partisans. Why those gentlemen who, from the pulpit, the platform, and the Press, have found it their interest to paint history as they would have it, have not undertaken as a labour of love the details of a lengthened narrative such as this, even in justification of themselves, is, on first sight, a matter of surprise But there are some undertakings at which even enthusiasm and selfishness stand alike appalled. Those who most benifited by the revolution against Charles were most backward in defending the measures which sent their king to the block. They should first grant themselves regicides before proceeding to justification. Those who gained a monopoly by the Revolution of 1688 hurry in silence over the accusation of having called in a foreign Power. Their attempt to right themselves should be preluded by an admission that they were traitors In a like sense may be interpreted the ominous silence which prevails amongst Orangemen in all things that have regard to the history of Orangeism. To gush forth from prostituted pulpits and political platforms to unlettered people requires, fortunately for those who practice it, but little thought and no historical accuracy. The object is gained however. A delusion is continued which had its origin in bigotry, its reward in monopoly, and to which ignorance gives a prolonged existence. Others have thought, and for some time I have thought so too, that the game was not worth the candle. An Institution, they said, born in tumult must wither and die in the very dawn of religious and political freedom. The result is that we have at the present day, even amongst the majority of those who claim an exclusive loyalty and parade their Orangeism, a widespread bewilderment as to what was the origin and what the history of the institution they have sworn before their Maker to uphold. It is the object of its leaders that this ignorance should be perpetuated. Prejudice has no more invincible foe than knowledge, and the reign of one must be the dethronment of the other. To assist as far as I can by the aid of history to let in the light of day upon an organization more dangerous than Nihilism, because it is in the guise of loyalty; more destructive than Communism, because it turns the arms of a people against themselves; more degrading than Ribbonism, being the servile tool of an autocratic conspiracy, shall then be the object to which in these pages I shall devote myself. My weapons may be rusty. They will be not the less invincible. Facts, from the great store-room of history, incidents, the pain of reading which will be lost in the memory of what terror and carnage associated with their enactment, and truths of recent date, best read by the light of past events—these shall be my weapons. Should they compel those interested to stand on their defence my object will be but half accomplished. The end is to bring conviction to upright men of all classes. "No people," says Edmund Burke, "will look forward to posterity who do not often look backward to their ancestors," and in this I find my justification. Whether we blush at their crimes, or feel elated at their heroism, the lesson will be the same. In their errors we may find a warning; in their virtues an example.

THE AUTHOR.

CONTENTS.

CONTENTS.

APPENDIX.

*** ERRATA.—At page 20, end of chapter VI., read "Loughgall" for "Timakeel."

Owing to the hurry with which these pages were run through the Press and the impossibility of the Author reading the proof-sheets some errors have slipped in, for which the writer must claim the reader's kind indulgence.

THE HISTORY OF ORANGEISM;

Its Origin, its Rise, and its Decline.

CHAPTER I.—THE ROMANCE OF ITS ORIGIN:

Those who wish to escape the odium of all transactions connected with the Diamond massacre, and of any movement which might have found its origin in that event have gone backwards into history upon a voyage of discovery in the hope of finding some more creditable auspices as sponsors for the Orange Institution. The first Orange lodge, they say, was founded in the camp of William Prince of Orange, at Exeter, early in November, 1688.* Allowing for the excitement which must attend all declamations upon public platforms, it must still be held that the allusions, however vague, are put forward with an apparent seriousness sufficient to justify inquiry. William landed on the 5th November, 1688, at Torbay, in Devonshire, with a Dutch fleet of 52 men-of-war, 25 frigates, 25 fire-ships, and 400 transports, conveying a land army of about 15,000 men (some authorities say 30,000, but they may be reasonably held as exaggerated), a force not exactly of that character best suited to investigate the birth of the Prince of Wales, which he ascribed as the reason of his coming, and which he affected to consider as surreptitious. He set out for Exeter, where he stopped ten days to refresh his troops, and as Burnet puts it, in the "History of His Own Time," to give the country time to show its affection. It would appear, however, that the display of affection towards the aspirant to a Throne which was not vacant was anything but hopeful.

The rebellion of Monmouth had just terminated ; and the people, disgusted with fighting the battles of men who had little sympathy with their suffering, longed after peace. Dr. Vaughan, in his history of the English Revolution (vol. 3, page 559), says—"Exeter received the Prince with quiet submissiveness." On William's arrival the clergy as well as the magistrates were very timid and exceedingly backward.* The bishop ran away, the dean followed his example, the clergy stood aloof, and only came when the Prince sent for them. But, "the rabble of the people," we are informed by the last-mentioned authority, which upon this point, at least, is not to be doubted, as Burnet was the henchman of the Prince, mindful of favours to come ;† "the rabble of the people came into him in great numbers so that he could have raised many regiments of

---

* This was the contention of a Mr. Beers, D.G.M., at an Orange mee ing in Downpatrick about eight years ago ; of the Rev. Mr. Smith, Armagh in a lecture delivered about the same time ; and has become of late years a matter of frequent reference : upon Orange platforms.

* "Bishop Burnet's History," vol. iii., page 251.
† Bu net was made B'shop of Salisbury by William at the close of the year 1689.

foot if there had been any occasion for them."
And now comes the incident of which Burnet is the
sole authority (Harris, in his "Life of William,"
quotes Burnet), and upon which the Orange leaders
of the present day build their castle-in-the-air of
an ancient pedigree. The reader will please mark—
"After he had staid eight days at Exeter, Seymour*
"came in with several other gentlemen of quality
"and estate. As soon as he had been with the Prince
"he sent for me. When I came to him he asked
"me why we had not an association signed by all
"that came to us since; till we had that done we
"were as a rope of sand; men might leave us when
"they pleased, and we had them under no tie;
"whereas if they signed an association they would
"reckon themselves bound to stick to us.　I an-
"swered it was because we had not a man of his
"authority and credit to offer and support such an
"advice.　I went from him to the Prince, who approved of the matter, as did also the Earl of
"Shrewsbury and all that were with us.　So I was
"ordered to draw it up.　It was, in few words, an
"engagement to stick together in pursuing the end
"of the Prince's Declaration, and that if any at-
"tempt should be made on his person it should be
"revenged on all by whom, or from whom, any
"such attempt should be made.　So it was en-
"grossed in parchment and signed by all those
"that came in to him."†　Now, this passage,
which I have troubled the reader with in its entirety, is the only authority that gives the colouring
of truth to the oft-repeated assertion that the first
Orange Lodge was founded at Exeter in William's
camp.　In it there is no mention of a "lodge," or of
an "Orange institution;" no oath, and none of the
mummeries of inauguration.　These simple, country
gentlemen not being, as the Recorder of Exeter
possibly well knew, of a character that would warrant William depending on their words were ask
to give a written undertaking that they would
support the Prince with their swords.　This they
did with a will, and as their swords had not even
to be drawn on his behalf Burnet's celebrated association fell through, and was never afterwards
heard of. Sir Richard Musgrave, the paid chronicler
and defender of the Protestant cause, himself disposes of the matter.　He says:—"In commemora-
"tion of that victory (the Battle of the Diamond),
"the first Orange lodge was formed in the County
"Armagh, though the name of Orangemen existed
"some time before."

* This Seymour was Recorder of Exeter in 1688.
† "Burnet's History," vol. iii., page 265.

That "some time before" cannot refer to the
association spoken of by Burnet, for he makes no
mention of "Orangemen," and Musgrave,
evidently from the tenor of his remarks, refers to
its existence in the County Armagh a short time
before September, 1795.

That there was an association seems beyond
doubt, but that that association in no way fore-
casted the combination of latter days is equally
reliable.　Lingard says in his history (vol. xiv., p.
243) that soon after the invitation was sent to the
Prince a "secret association in his favour had been
"formed among the officers of the army encamped
"on Hounslow Heath, and a communication estab-
"lished between them and the club at the Rose
"Tavern, Covent Garden."　This cannot have been
the same referred to by Burnet, for the latter
originated after the arrival of William.　The
Orangemen would, therefore, be as justified in
claiming this as their origin.　But they do not.
The secret is they cannot well afford to share the
infamy.　Bad as this silly old monarch may
have been, his soldiers who formed this association
were perjurers and traitors, and to this they added
the crime of inhumanity.　For when James sent
his infant son to Portsmouth to escape to France
Dartmour's fleet was lying at Spithead, and was
ordered by the king—the reigning king, mark—to
give the unfortunate baby conduct to France.　The
admiral would have done so, but was thwarted in
his humane intentions by the "associated officers"
on board.　This is why the incident is not referred
to, and why that other association of which Burnet
speaks of is quoted as the authority.

Another and an effectual way of testing the
question is to see how much of a similarity exists
between the subscribers in the camp at Exeter
under their chief and those who a century afterwards on the field of the Diamond, spattered and
besmeared with the warm blood of their neighbours,
while bestriding the mangled bodies of their
countrymen and kindred, swore before heaven to
continue a war of extermination.

The Prince's Declaration, which his adherents
at Exeter promised to pursue, and which was
signed by him on the 10th of October of the same
year, announced amongst other things "that he
would suffer such as would live peaceably to enjoy
all due freedom in their conscience."　So much for
1688.　Come to 1795.　I am justified by every
reliable authority who has written upon the subject
in saying that this political Rip Van Winkle, the
Orange Institution, revived, as alleged, after a

sleep of a century and seven years has pursued a course of intolerance and of cruel unrelenting bigotry, unexampled in the history of this or any other country.

"A Society," says Coote in his History of the Union, "denominated, in honour of William III., "the Orange Club, laboured with sanguinary zeal "to check the extension of mercy to the rebels and "to multiply the horrors of capital punishment.'

Plowden says, in his History of Ireland (vol. 1 page 53) "It has been asserted by well informed "(though anonymous) authors, that the original "obligation or oath of Orangemen was to the fol- "lowing effect, 'I. A. B. do swear, that I will be "true to King and Government; and that I will "exterminate the Catholics of Ireland as far as "in my power lies.' The frequency and earnest- "ness with which the latter part of the oath has "been acted upon by Orangemen, has rendered the "charge of taking it too credible."

O'Connor, in a pamphlet written by him in 1797, "The present state of Ireland," gives this form of oath as authentic, and the same gentlemen on examination before the Select Committee of the House of Commons, says "it came to my know- ledge that the oath of extermination was admin- istered."

Lord Gosford, Governor of Armagh, addressing the body of magistrates of the County Armagh, on the 28th December, 1795 (three months after the battle of the Diamond) said, "It is no secret that "a persecution, accompanied with all the circum- "stances of ferocious cruelty which have in all "ages distinguished that calamity, is now raging in "this county. The only crime which the wretched "objects of this ruthless persecution are charged "with, is a crime indeed of easy proof. If is "simply a profession of the Roman Catholic "faith."*

"Never did any society exhibit such a glaring "inconsistency; rather such a positive contradic- "tion between its professed principles and its actual "practice. The practice of the society was to "resort to every contrivance to insult, to domineer "over, to offend, to irritate their Roman Catholic "neighbour.—*Edinburgh Review*, vol. clxxxiii.

* "Parnell's Historical Apology," page 18.

Mr. Grattan said in 1796, in the House of Com- mons, "These insurgents call themselves Orange- "men or Protestant Boys; that is a banditti of "murders, committing massacre in the name of God, "and exercising despotic power in the name of "Liberty."

Hay describes their conduct in the County of Wexford as inhuman. Even Musgrave furnishes a negative proof by passing over in silence their acts, or, when he does make reference to them, by attempting to shift the responsibility "to the low classes of Protestants," forgetting that, according to every authority it was "the rabble" who first belonged to the association.

In addition, we have a plain denial of the con- tention in the examination of Lieutenant-colonel Vernor, M.P., before the Select Committee of the House of Commons in 1835 (7th April), question 7. He was asked:—

"Were there any Orange Institution in existence previous to 1795 *in any other form?* None."

Surely this authority must satisfy the Orange- men themselves.

Indeed, whether William had a fixed aversion to all persecution, as Macaulay puts it, whether, as Froude states, "he was studiously lenient," and from inexperience of the Irish character, foolishly attempted to conciliate by indulgent terms, or whether he actually did desire, according to Godkin, to have the Treaty of Limerick restored, one thing is certain—throughout the whole of the Revolution, and during the entire of William's reign no incident is recorded, if we overlook his perfidy, which would justify Orangemen in sub- scribing themselves his followers, or enable them to claim an identity with those who surrounded him even when he had one foot upon the steps of the throne and the lawful king was seated upon it. The alleged connection of Orangeism with the camp of William must then be regarded, in an historical sense, as having no foundation in fact. I account for the claim by that desire found in most mis- guided people not utterly lost to a sense of their wrong-doing which prompts them to seek a parallel in history where it does not exist, or some more honoured name, to bear with them the burden of their iniquity.

CHAPTER II.—THE "GLORIOUS" REVOLUTION, RETROSPECT OF A CENTURY.

An unfounded assertion necessitated my commencing this narrative so far back as the Revolution of 1688 I cannot do better now than continue it in the order of time, particularly as a review of the intervening century will furnish an explanation of the sad and stirring events which are to follow The revolution was accomplished William was on the throne. James was a runaway King and an outcast Than the English there is no nation so calculated to lose its temper when they discover, or think they have discovered, an intended fraud being practised upon them. Burnet's simple story about that dubious warming-pan which was put into the Queen's bed before her delivery, and which he remarked "was not opened that it might be seen that there was fire and nothing else in it," was, with a hundred other foolish pieces of gossip equally unworthy of belief, circulated in the London pot houses, and led to the general opinion that the young Prince of Wales (afterwards called the "Pretender") was surreptitiously being palmed off as a royal body The divinity that had hedged the person of that foolish and weakminded monarch James, now deserted him in his utmost need. His Queen and her baby prince fled, with scarce a decent covering, taking refuge in France, and the poor old man himself, disguised as a servant, having been picked up at Feversham by a few fishermen while attempting to follow, was taken for a priest and put in the lock-up. He probably shed a few tears and told a pathetic tale, for out of his jailers he formed the nucleus of the great Jacobite party. Flinging the Great Seal into the river, where it would have been far better he had flung himself, he eventually crossed to France to seek the aid of his cousin, whose too submissive lackey, it must be acknowledged, he had been. Thus, an event unheard of in the records of governments, since people had been taught to see in kings something more than human and something less than divine, was brought about without a sword leaving its scabbard. By the suspicions of prying and selfish ecclesiastics, who were not ashamed to be caught peeping through the keyholes of ladies' chambers, by the gossip of old women, who believed that Mother Hubbard once upon a time rode to the moon upon a broomstick, by the filthy gibes of debauchees reeking with the

smell of the ale house, and by the nods and winks of enfeebled frequenters of London brothels, who were too happy to make the subject of their obscene jests a woman who was young, and virtuous, and handsome, and a foreigner, a king was dethroned and an entire people handed over to an adventurer. No wonder it has been written "that the revolution succeeded; at least that it succeeded without bloodshed or commotion was principally owing to an act of ungrateful perfidy such as no soldier had ever before committed, and to those monstrous fictions respecting the birth of the Prince of Wales which persons of the highest rank were not ashamed to circulate." [*] It was a successful revolution. Possibly for all parties concerned, Catholic as well as Protestant, it was a revolution not to be regretted, now that we have outlived the ordeal. But there is one thing it was not. It was not a "glorious revolution." Both before and after Englishmen upheld their cause, whether right or wrong, by the strength of their good right arms. In this revolution calumny was the weapon. The lie took the place of the sword; the former did what the latter alone might not have accomplished; and a half-witted King and a virtuous but weak-spirited Queen had to sneak out by the back-door of Whitehall, and give to the valiant English people their room instead of their company. In the whole of the proceeding, as well as much that followed, we trace the clever hands of cunning clergymen.

Before entering upon the subject of our story —Orangeism its origin, its rise, and its decline, its secret workings, and its political consequences —it is essential that we take a retrospective view of the century proceeding it, the events of which culminated in the Battle of the Diamond.' The reader may be impatient. And it will be poor consolation to him to know that that impatience is to some extent even shared by the person who pens those pages. The inevitable consequences of things done in a hurry furnish not alone an excuse but a warning. No history of Ireland in latter times can be read aright without an adequate knowledge of the great events which occurred in that period, bounded on one hand by the Revolution of 1688 and the Broken Treaty, and

[*] Macaulay, "Edinburgh Review," Sept., 1828

on the other by the Irish Rebellion. As this narrative must to some extent partake of a history of Ireland, my readers must set before them this task as an introduction to the interesting details which I promise them will follow.

There is nothing more calculated to relieve the tedium of historical narrative than to speculate upon what would have been the current of events if things, which to us seem to have taken place by chance, had not taken place at all. If Remus had killed Romulus, and Rome had not been built where would have been the Grecian Empire? If William had turned back when the clergy of Exeter ran away, and the aristocracy were "not at home" to him, where would have been England and the Thirty - nine Articles, and who would now be sitting upon the throne? In like manner, if that worthless morsel of royalty, James, had been attached to the Great Seal when it sank in the river; or, to to take a more humane view of it, if James when he went to France had stopped there, had said his prayers like a good old man, nursed the baby, and taught the Pretender his catechism— a branch of instruction, I fear, very much neglected in the early education of this as well as all the other Stuarts—if he had been contented with his condition, and not been hankering after a crown which never fitted him, which he was unable to retain, and unwilling to fight for, what then would have been the current of events? Heavens! what a change! The Recording Angel, at whom poor despairing Byron yelped out his loud guffaw; who

Had it ipped off both his wings in quills,
And yet was in arrear of human ills.

would have been saved much trouble. Limerick would never have fallen. The records of crime would have wanted many of its blackest items. But deeds of heroism unexampled in history would never have been accomplished. If there had been no Limerick and no treaty to break, there would, on the other hand, have been no Landen or Steinkirk; no Ramillies, no Fontenoy; before the conquering arms of William France might have become a province of England, the world would probably have been spared the iniquities of a French Revolution, and have lost the glories of a people who had risen above king-craft. The people might have fared even better in Ireland. The animosities which a century of civil warfare was the occasion of might have settled into toleration, the conquered paying, of course, with their estates the penalty of defeat, and the Irish during the whole of the last two hundred and ninety years have been living upon terms of brotherhood and charity. Anne, who secretly longed after the occupants of St. Germains, might have had in the Pretender, and all subsequent history have been turned topsy-turvy. It was not decreed so. Had it been, this history might never have been written.

The flight of James was taken as an abdication, and William, who had been invited to take the throne before James had relinquished the Crown, was, therefore, chosen. But taking it that James did abdicate the throne, which he certainly did not do,* the Prince of Wales would have been the legitimate heir. If he had no son his eldest daughter, Mary, would have inherited it, and it was the intention of the majority of the Convention assembled to proclaim her Queen, with William as Regent. Lingard and Burnet differ upon the issue. The former says, without quoting his authority, that William would not consent to be a subject of his wife; while the latter relates a personal interview in Holland, in which, though I cannot recollect the exact passage, he says that Mary scouted the idea of her being the superior of her husband. Whether in consequence of any family difference or not, William and Mary were chosen as King and Queen, t being agreed that the former should govern in the name of both. James returned from France landing at Kinsale on the 12th March, 1689. In the meantime Derry had closed its gates against Lord Antrim, the only thing for which this nobleman was ever remarkable,† and the valiant—aye, and noble fellows, as certainly they were, resolved to hold the city for the Protestant cause; and King William. In the meantime the ministers who had left the church at Exeter when the Prince's Declaration was read‡ found they were on the winning side. They came back to share the spoils. In Ireland, then, the army of William took the field, James, believing that the walls of Derry would, like those of Jericho of old, have crumbled before a majestic presence, set out for that place. Finding, however, that he was received with a shower of cannon and musket balls from the ramparts, which killed an officer standing beside him, he took fright, turned pale, and — returned to the capital. The subsequent history of Derry, its determined

* See Burnet, Macaulay, and Lingard.
† Hill, editor of the "Montgomery Manuscripts."
‡ "Dr. Burnet, in the cathedral, read the Prince's Declaration, and the ministers present were so surprised that they immediately left the church. However, the Doctor continued reading to the end."—Burnet's "History of His Own Time."

siege, and its heroic defence, are matters too familiar to be repeated. The same day that Derry was relieved an Irish army under Justin M'Carthy, Lord Mountcashel was defeated by the Enniskilleners at Newtownbutler, which it would seem was occasioned by a mistaken word of command * To the enervating cry of "No Popery," which has so often been the watchword of many a cowardly deed done in the dark, the Enniskilleners fell upon the fugitives, whom they hunted into the bogs and woods with a savage ferocity "that has made even the Williamite historians blush." While James, from whom neither energy nor wisdom was to be expected, was holding his mimic court in Dublin, and strutting about in his pasteboard crown, the wiley foreigners were making their game. Schomberg landed at Bangor (on the 13th August), and with his Dutch troops and French Huguenots and his raw English levies he made for the Boyne. On the 1st July (old style), 1690, was here fought one of the most eventful fights in history, and as to which the conquerors have comparatively little room to boast and the conquered no reason to feel ashamed of themselves. The historians of William† complain of the incompleteness of the victory, and those of James admit that the fighting was done in the main by the Irish. But as this is not a history of William, nor of James, we have but to deal with results. Attended though it was by important consequences the least important to the Irish people was the setting aside of the reigning dynasty. An ungrateful monarch was never a good one. A Stuart never wanted in ingratitude, and James, true to the instincts of his line, blamed the Irish who held the pass of the Boyne, while he himself took care to be out of the way when the fighting was to be done.

Limerick, which Lanzun said he could have taken with roasted apples, was abandoned, and the undivided honour of its memorable defence left to the Irish. There is no seige with which the people of the present day are more familiar. The answer of the garrison, that they hoped to merit the good opinion of the Prince of Orange by a vigorous defence rather than by a shameful surrender, was justified by subsequent events. But the intrepid valour of Sarsfield and his troops, the enthusiasm of the Limerick matrons were of no avail against the indifference of French officers yearning after the gilded salons of Ver-

sailles, and the jealousy of an ambitious commander, who would not sell his country at a low figure, and had not the courage to fight for it. And so Limerick fell. The political existence of Irish Catholics fell with it. The articles were signed on the 3rd of October, 1691 They included a general engagement, independent of the Royal promise of future Parliamentary relief, to protect Catholics from all disturbance, giving them such privileges in the exercise of their religion "as were consistent with the laws of Ireland," or as they did enjoy in the reign of Charles II. It also provided that "the oath to be submitted to such Roman Catholics as submit to their Majesties' Government shall be the oath above mentioned (the oath of allegiance) and no other;" and it further secured the properties, rights, immunities, and privileges (such as in the time of Charles II.) of those who were under the protection of the garrison, but residing in the counties Limerick, Clare, Kerry, Cork, and Mayo* Scarce an hour passed in the long night of persecution which followed without a distinct and shameful breach of this treaty by the English. And here, even beneath the shattered walls of Limerick, do we find the first of that unbroken train of incidents which led up to the Massacre of the Diamond. In conformity with the articles of capitulation the Irish infantry were marshalled on the Clare side of the Shannon, and given an opportunity of choosing between departing for France and remaining at home under the new Government. An Ulster battalion of about 1,000 men entered into William's service, 2,000 accepted passes to return home, and 11,000, together with all the cavalry, volunteered for France. Ships were to be provided in sufficient numbers for the transit of the conquered to France, with their wives and families. The wild cry that went up from the women of Limerick who were left behind was the first protest against the Broken Treaty. In all, about 30,000 men departed the country † The war cost £6,637,000. Two months did not elapse until, according to Harris, that treaty was broken Many Catholics were dispossessed of their property, "to the great reproach of their Majesties' Government." The English House of Commons decreed also that no person should act in the Irish Parliament, nor should hold any Irish office, civil, military, or ecclesiastical, nor should practise law or medicine in Ireland

* Planket MS9
† Story says that only two Irish standards were captured.

* Story, Harris, and Burnet
† O'Callaghan's "History of the Irish Brigade," vol. 1, page 61.

until they had taken the oaths of allegiance and supremacy, and subscribed the declaration against transubstantiation, saving only those lawyers and physicians who were within the walls of Galway and Limerick when those capitulated.

This was the beginning of those Penal Laws which honest Englishmen have learned in the present day to be ashamed of—laws which robbed a people of their inheritance, and sent them in droves to the English shambles, while their own countrymen were aiding in the slaughter or reaping the benefits of it, and fattening upon the blood of their kindred. William was not a fanatic. He was too good a soldier to be cruel. In fact, that he would have restrained the bigotry of those around him is made evident. But he was made King by the Protestant party, and the tenth part of the population of this island were determined, in the words of Gloster, that they would not be called fools as well as villains, and having got the advantage they were resolved to keep it. Accordingly the minority, headed by their clergy, instituted a reign of persecution, for which they cannot even claim the palliation of avarice, seeing that it was carried out with unexampled and unnecessary cruelty. A strange event in the history of nations—one-tenth part of the population set about exterminating the remaining nine. The Irish Peers and Commoners of the Catholic persuasion who attended on the summoning of the next Parliament in 1692 were asked to swear that the Mass was damnable; they left the House in a body, and the political existence of the Irish Catholic became extinct. Mitchel says, referring to this incident, that "thereafter they had no more influence upon public affairs than have the red Indians in the United States." The same monarch who signed the death warrant of the MacIans, of Glencoe, gave his Royal assent to Bills which were a direct breach of faith with the Irish people.

Sarsfield and his Irish exiles were in the meantime fighting the battles of Louis, and on many bloody fields taught the English William what valiant subjects he had lost. "The rights of Ireland and the prosperity of England," says an authority who at least has had the courage of his convictions, "cannot exist together;" and accordingly every defeat of English arms on the Continent was followed by concession towards the Catholics at home. But this period of quiet did not last long. Catholics had been excluded from the Legislature, from Corporations, and from the Liberal professions, and even Darby Ryan, a Papist who subjected Ned Sprag and other coal-porters of Dublin to much inconvenience by employing porters of his own persuasion, received the attention of the Committee of Grievances. A whine went up from the Protestant colonists that they were being unfairly dealt with. Disappointed in the hope of obtaining all the estates of the Catholics, it was proclaimed openly from pulpits that faith should not be kept with Papists, and that the terms made with the Catholics were too lenient. Accordingly, an Act was passed* "for the better securing of the Government by disarming the Papists." By this Act, which subsequently gave a colouring to the illegal proceedings that depopulated Armagh, all Catholics were required to discover and deliver up all their arms and ammunition, and after a certain day search might be made in their houses. Any two justices, or mayor, or sheriff might grant a search-warrant, and compel any Catholic suspected of having arms to appear before them and answer the suspicion upon oath, the punishments being fine or imprisonment, with the pillory, or whipping, at the discretion of the Court. "No Papist was safe from suspicion who had any money to pay in fines, and woe to the Papist who had a handsome daughter."† Not satisfied with the forfeiture of 1,000,000 Irish acres, the colonists should have entire monopoly even in the matter of education. The fourth of William and Mary came next, and placed a ban upon education, Catholics not alone being prevented from instructing their children at home; but prohibited, under the pain of forfeiting all their estates and the guardianship of their own children, from sending them to be educated beyond the seas. It was further enacted, that no Papist should have a horse of the value of £5, or more, with the usual clauses, to induce Protestants to inform and cause search to be made for the contraband horses, the property to be vested in the discoverer. Here we find the first premium held out to that swarm of creeping things called informers, who settled down upon the island and enjoyed its hospitality, that they might learn to betray it. The next step was to enjoin all archbishops, monks, friars, and all other Popish clergy to depart the kingdom by the First of May, 1698, not to return under pain of being guilty of high treason. But it was not the Papists alone who felt the heavy hand of the conquerer.

* 7th William III, cap 5
† Mitchell's History,

English interests now took a fit of jealousy, and on the principle that Irish interests should be subordinate to them, William was compelled, in order to appease his subjects at home, to say, in reply to addresses from both Houses, "I shall do all that in me lies to discourage the woollen manufacture in Ireland, and to encourage the linen trade there, and to promote the trade of England"—rather a strange resolve for one who professed to be a father of all his people. And, accordingly, he did discourage the woollen trade, for by an Act passed in the session of 1689, the duties on Irish woollen goods amounted to prohibition, the woollen trade was destroyed, and forty thousand persons reduced to beggary At the same time they did not encourage the linen trade, and Arthur Young, in his "Tour," quotes the 23rd of George II as a direct breach of the compact. The latter days of William were embittered with disappointment The English Parliament refused to sanction his grant to his favourite, Elizabeth Villiers, created Countess of Orkney, and an Act was passed resuming the forfeited estates of James as public property. William fell from his horse, broke his collar-bone, and went over to the majority on the 26th of February, 1702, only surviving by five months the dethroned James, who died at St. Germains in the previous September, leaving the Pretender the empty title of a king, with none of its emoluments.

To Anne, Haverty says, was reserved the distinction of bringing the execrable Penal Code to full maturity. The colonists did not feel their monopoly secure, and the advent of the Duke of Ormond to the Lord Lieutenancy was the occasion of passing another Bill "for preventing the growth of Popery," though by this time Popery, one would have imagined, might have ceased to be the ghost in the Protestant cupboard. With the assistance of a few other Acts subsequently passed by a servile Parliament, in which there was not one voice to be heard on behalf of toleration or humanity, the Penal Code became perfect. Conceived by the malignant genius of monopoly, they were now well fitted for the debasement and de-degradation of a .people. The common enemy were the Catholics, and every address of every Lord Lieutenant urged union of all sects against them. Then, as now, honest Protestants existed; but they were afraid or ashamed to raise their voices. What could they do, with the Church hounding the dogs of war upon their prey?

The Tory Ministers of Queen Anne were chiefly

occupied during her latter years in preparing to bring in her brother, the "Pretender," at her death, and to this. she lent her sanction. They had not resolution enough. But the Whigs had. And accordingly during her lifetime they invited over "the first of those fools and oppressors called George," put £50,000 as a price upon the Pretender's silly head—a big price for such a worthless article—and sent poor Anne prematurely to her grave, the flickerings of an expiring soul being still visible upon her pallid cheeks while loyal England was ringing with the cry "Long live King George the First." George had packed his portmanteau and come to England, finding there was a vacancy for a Protestant king He put in his credentials and got the situation; not because he was a good Protestant or a good man. He was neither. It is to'd by Thackeray that an agent of the French King once asked the duchess when she lived in her squalid little Court in Hanover of what religion was her daughter, to which she replied, ' of no religion as yet " She was waiting to see of what religion her husband would be.

While Scotland was in arms for the Pretender the Irish remained inactive. A few, when no strangers were nigh and the doors were locked, still secretly drank the health of Louis and to the mole whose mole-hill killed King William But the Catholics in no way aided the Pretender. Still they had to endure all the horrors of persecution as if they were, or had been, in the field. The unthinking Protestants were, however, soon taught that they were but the instruments, and not the principals, of this persecution, and that they too were despised by their English masters. Resulting out of the litigation of Sherlock v. Annesley, an Act was passed in 1719 which had the effect of making the Irish Parliament a mere provincial assembly. Then came the days of "the Patriots," as they were termed—or as they termed themselves; every man of them a bigot, and a bigot without a conscience or a country at their head. Dean Swift could say, "If we do flourish, it is like the thorn in Glastonbury, without blossom, in the midst of winter," he could compare Ireland to a Lapland or an Iceland, but during the entire of his career he had not one word in defence of his Catholic countrymen. He was not the first, and will not be the last, to assume a specious name, and beneath it hide the workings of a narrow mind and a selfish heart.

The revolution opened in England the floodgates

of immorality. By the time of George's death, "religion had long since disappeared, and honour had followed." George II., his successor, assumed the control of a Kingdom, in which millions laboured to prolong and add variety to the debaucheries of the Court; assumed control of a Church in which nothing was thought of by the clergy but the benefices, and by the people but how to minimise them. Primate Boulter, who ruled in Ireland during the early part of this reign, was so solicitous upon the salvation of those poor creatures, whom he actually admitted to be his fellow-subjects, that he endeavoured by all the refinement and dexterity of one who was born to be an executioner, and had a genius for slaughter, to bring them to a knowledge of the true religion. "But" says he, "instead of converting those who are adults, we are daily losing several of our meaner people, who go off to Popery."* The rumour of a French invasion, suggested, it is said, the advisability of getting rid

* Boulter's Letters, vol. II.

of the Papists by a general massacre. It is hard to place reliance upon such general rumours, whether relating to the invasions or massacres. The only particular instance quoted is that where the humane Protestant publican of Lurgan prevented his co-religionists by the aid of a clergyman, from falling upon their Catholic fellow-townsmen in the night time and massacring them. That a general massacre was suggested, according to Curry, by a nobleman in the Privy Council seems reliable, and a conspiracy, says Haverty, was formed in Ulster to carry it out. Priest-hunting had now become a profession; persecution an art: long familiarity with bloodshed and sights of cruelty had blunted the sensibilities of many honest Protestants, and in time, in a country which was a nursery for young tyrants, they too turned into persecutors. We now arrive at that period when secret societies, begotten of bigotry or of persecution, came into existence, and the one which we will find begot in its turn that Cerberus, Orangeism, which is the subject of these memoirs.

CHAPTER III.—THE WHITEBOYS, HEARTS OF OAK, HEARTS OF STEEL, PEEP O' DAY BOYS.

George the Third was King and William Pitt was still Prime Minister. The depravity of a Premier, run riot under the control of an imbecile King, had at last secured its object. The torture which the Catholics of the South had for years been subjected to at length bred the spirit of lawlessness, and in 1760 the great aim of the English Cabinet for half a century was realised—a secret society was organised in Ireland. With laws used only to persecute them, seeing upon the bench only their acknowledged opponents and oppressors "in the interests of Protestantism," the lower classes in the South, upon the first principles of humanity, gathered together, and the outcome was Whiteboyism.* Now, this class of conspiracy is fortunately beyond our present inquiry. We will have iniquities enough to face in the course of this history without intruding upon our neighbours; but lest silence should be mistaken for approval, or even palliation, I must paraphrase of the Whiteboys, that their deeds were alike cruel and inhuman, the only approach towards a defence being that if weighed in the scale

of justice the blood spilled in the name of liberty, and under the spacious guise of law and order, would far outbalance that which followed the acts of a misguided and infuriated people. There were, and always are—for no religion has a monopoly of virtue—a few honest Protestants who did not catch the contagion. With the vast majority, however, anniversary sermons and inflammatory pamphlets had done their work* and the reign of conspiracy, which is ever a reign of terror, set in with earnest. For a period of 20 years, over which we must hasten, the existence of the Whiteboys gave excuse for unheard-of outrages. Musgrave placidly remarks that "all our disgraces and misfortunes are to be found in the history of our Penal Laws, and in the feeble execution of them." It is evident the only thing he regrets is that they were not executed with greater vigour. Have we yet reached the depths of depravity? He must, indeed, be bloodthirsty who could not be satiated with the "energy" and "loyalty" displayed during this

* Prima's Boulter, in one of his sermons, actually regretted the growing to deny towards union which at his time was apparent between Catholics, honest Protestants, and Liberal Presbyterians. "England's influence," he said, "could never exist in the face of such a union." The Most Rev. Primate Boulter is quite right. The cock that never goes is right once in the twelve hours.

* Lord Clare, speaking of this combination, said, "It was impossible for human wretchedness to exceed that of the miserable peasantry in Munster; he knew that the unhappy tenantry were ground down by the butchery of relentless landlords." The scheme of extensive grazing initiated in the South and the high price for cattle were the immediate causes of Whiteboyism." The Act relating to Whiteboyism deals with "all classes and persuasions," but it is must be taken as meaning little.

momentous period. But Sir Richard was not as the rest of men. The Catholic bishops and clergy no doubt hurdled their anathemas at the White-boys, but in vain. It is useless to clean the stream when the fountain is muddy.

People now began to be uneasy in the North. The Sacramental Test Act still remained on the statute book, and led to their exclusion. But commercial restriction of the most depressing kind pressed upon them, and prevented that manufacture which was to take the place of the woolen trade from prospering. Chuckling for a time over the chains their neighbours wore they soon learned that they, too, were chained, and the spirit of rebellion, so dangerous alike to Kings and Governors when cherished by the dogged followers of John Knox, now first displayed itself.

The Hearts of Oak originated in the North, in the year 1762. The lower classes of labourers had learned the impositions that were being made upon them in regard to the repairing of roads, and objected to the practice of many of the gentry who insisted upon private jobs being done for them. They banded together for the purpose of redressing these grievances, put oak leaves in their hats, declared in the County Armagh that they would repair no more roads, and frightened the gentry into subjection. Their immediate grievances were remedied. From the abolition of this compulsory system of road making, known as six day's labour, they turned their attention to tithes, which were at that time pressing upon the people heavily, as they did in after time. The Hearts of Steel originated in the County Down, in 1762. The Marquis of Downshire owned a vast tract of country, but was an absentee landlord. His agent, owing to the extensive traffic in land, occasioned by the success of Northern weavers, determined, like most of his kind, to make the most of the occasion. He initiated a new mode of letting land out of lease by accepting large fines and lowering the rent accordingly. This suited admirably the monopolists of Belfast; but as James Hope, who gave an account of the

proceedings to Madden, stated, it did not suit the occupiers. In Carnmoney a Presbyterian elder was allowed by the occupants to become the purchaser of a townland on the condition that their farms should be re-let on the terms at which he purchased. But the compact being completed he raised the rents exorbitantly. This will give an idea of the cause which led to the combination known as the Steel Boys. *Hearts of oak and hearts of steel as they were, it must certainly be admitted they were very pacific bodies, and their acts in no ways contrasted with the lawlessness and cruelty displayed by the White-boys or Levellers of the South. The former was the outcome of persecution, however; the latter of injustice.

We are now face to face with the father of Orangeism. The Peep 'o Day Boys, or the Protestant Boys, were the begetters of the institution with which we have now to deal. Taaffe says their organisation arose out of a drunken broil in the County Armagh, at Markethill, at which two Presbyterians fell out, and a Catholic foolishly interfering in the quarrel, the party whom he advised was beaten. As on most occasions, where parties meddle in family differences, the defeated party turned upon the generous Papist, and quarrel number two resulted in the "Nappich Fleet" and the "Bawn Fleet," the former being the Peep 'o Day of later times, and the latter the orginators of the Defenders.†

And having at length approached the subject of of our inquiry, let us hope after time not ill-spent, for the prologue has to be studied as well as the tragedy, we may well break the journey and leave the interesting events which immediately follow to the honour of a new chapter.

---

* Those who wish to peruse the history of these combinations further will find details in Taffe's History of Ireland, Madden's History, Teeling's His ory, and Arthur Young's Tour.

† The only reasonable conclusion to be taken from the narrative of Taffe and of Mus rave is that the defeated party turned upon his adviser, and between both the quarrell subsequently lay. From slight events what desperate causes spring !

CHAPTER IV.—THE DAWN OF REASON AND THE NIGHT OF BIGOTRY, PLOTS AND COUNTER-PLOTS.

Gerorge the Third was fast losing his wits. The grass was soon to grow where the Bastile stood. Young America, guided by the immortal Washington, had cast off the old world ways of the parent country, and just tasted the sweets of freedom.

Divine right was doomed. The days when kings were all in all were passing away, and Princes of the Blood now no longer struggled "to hold the shirt of Louis XIV. when his most Christian Majesty thought fit to change that garment." The wave of revolution which arose in the West swept over France, and its influence extended to this remote corner of the world's surface. The Volunteers rose, and though I am far from ascribing to that brief period through which they lived the glory it is the custom to surround it with, they deserve all the credit of being the first amongst us to discover that men were not made to be the sport of princes, nor religion devised that people might prey upon each other. With this most momentous epoch in Irish history we have little to do. It is necessary to note, however, that with the dawn of enlightenment and liberality came hopes for the Irish Catholic—hopes which were too much indulged and too little realised. "The penal statutes," says Barrington,[*] " under the tyrannical pressure of which Catholics had so long and so grievously laboured, though in some instances softened down, still bore heavily upon four-fifths of the Irish population—a code which would have dishonoured the sanguinary pen of Draco, which inflicted every pain and penalty, every restriction and oppression under which a people could linger out a miserable existence." The laws were on the statute book, and it remained at the option of the evil-disposed to put them in execution. Religion was still a crime, and the education of a Catholic child a misdemeanour; the son was still bribed to betray the father, and the house of God had not yet ceased to be a public nuisance. But a feeling of toleration began to show itself which made bigots quake and the despoilers tremble for the safety of their ill-gotten goods. Though the Volunteer period still showed the remnant of the old intolerance—for Catholics were not trusted into their ranks—we must still admire that short-lived spirit, which, being fanned into a flame, flickered and went out before the emancipation of a people was even partially ensured. A few years, and they who had been the terror of England ceased to exist, or existed only in name. With the dispersion of the Volunteers the hopes of Ireland again fell. Still, intolerance had received its death-blow; the spirit of freedom remained, and lived through a period of a dozen years, when it burst out into rebellion.

But if we turn our eyes to one corner of the island we will find that the most degrading page of Irish history has yet to be written. It is still more degrading when viewed side by side with the dawning toleration elsewhere. I speak of Armagh County between the year 1784 and the Insurrection. There is another period, following the Rebellion and cul-

minating in the Union, which may outrival it for the multiplicity of its horrors and the ingenious barbarity of its persecution. But those who have read the history of civil war in all ages, and in all countries, know that it is intestine broil which unbridles the worst passions of mankind, and makes man prey upon his neighbour.

" When Greek meets Greek, then comes the tug of war," is but the heroic rendering of the sad truth that your former friend makes an unrelenting foe. We may, therefore, ascribe the atrocities of the Irish Rebellion to the natural outcome of human passions. But here in the fourteen years that preceded that Rebellion we look in vain for such palliation. On the one hand, we find in a prosperous country a large population, happy if allowed to retain what little had been left them, asking for nothing only not to be persecuted; and on the other, a small gang of needy ruffians, yelling like hungry wolves for another mouthful. The few honest Protestants who were disinclined to join in the sacrifice and share in the spoil stood aloof; for they dare not protest. Disinclined to rob their neighbour, they were compelled to look on while he was being robbed. This, in short, was the condition of the County Armagh during the period under notice. It is a common error to suppose that this was all due to religious enthusiasm or a mistaken zeal for the blessings of an open Bible. There could be no greater error. It was prompted by a greed for other's property and an insatiable desire for monoply. Encouraged by law, this fancy for possessions not their own grew into a passion, and when it was ripe, the Government, ever awake to English interests, availed themselves of it. From the statement of Mr. Longfield in the House of Commons as to the encouragement directly given by the Government to " Capt. Right" and his men at this period, in the County Cork, it is not going beyond reason to credit M'Nevin's statement, that the Peep o' Day Boys were aided and abetted by Government in order to secure what they did secure—a premature Irish rebellion. The fact was the English were becoming alarmed at the action of the Northern Presbyterians, and recollected too well Primate Boulter's warning, that, if the Protestants and Catholics united, they might bid farewell to English interests. Dissention and domestic tumult was their only game. They found the Peep o' Day Boys but willing instruments, too easily caught when something was to be gained. In the early dawn these deluded people visited the houses of Catholics "in order to search for arms," and,

---

[*] Historical Memoirs, vol. 1, page 14.

says Musgrave, the impartial historian, "it is most certain that in so dcing they committed the most wanton outrages, *insulting their persons*, and breaking their furniture." Even in the very next page (54—his "Memoirs of the Different Rebellions") he grants all we have been concluding; for he admits "to exasperate the Defenders, and to induce them to embody themselves from motives of fear, prophecies were frequently made that the Scotch, meaning the Presbyterians, would rise on a certain night and massacre the Romanists, who, being credulous and timorous, posted watches all night to give the alarm. As such reports were constantly made, some time previous to, and during the rebellion, *as devices to inflame the Popish multitude against the Protestants, we may reasonably conclude that the authors of them at this early period, had the same sinister designs.* By a seasonable exertion of the Government this spirit of combination and outrage might have been easily extinguished; but I have been assured that it was fomented by the improper conduct of country gentlemen who espoused one party or another for election purposes." The idea of Protestant country gentle-

men espousing the Catholics "for election purposes," at a time when Catholics were of as much political importance as the Red Indians, is worthy the special pleader of a hostile Government. Catholic historians all agree that this policy was initiated to rouse the Catholics into rebellion, and set those of each creed at the others throats. On the other side, Godkin says the object of the Government a few years later was the mutual extermination of both Presbyterians and Catholics, so that having followed the example of the Kilkenny cats they might leave the island to be divided amongst the Church party.[*]

---

[*] "The Presbyterians were too strong in Ulster for the Government, and fearing them, the Government resolved to make them a political nonentity. The policy was inaugurated by converting the Rebellion of '98 into a religious war. The organisation by which this policy has been perpetuated is the Orange Society, which has always been more or less fostered by the nobility, magistrates, and gentlemen of the ruling classes, and fostered by anniversaries of civil war. The wounds inflicted on a vanquished Church and a subjugated nation were thus triumphantly and tauntingly torn open afresh, two or three times every year." Religious His., page 293.

CHAPTER V.—THE REIGN OF TERROR.

The reign of terror set in. Every effort was made by those in authority to perpetuate and intensify it, and to put the population of the North in hostile camps under the banners of Protestant and Catholic. Taffe assures us that innumerable squibs of an inflamatory character were circulated by thousands. These combustibles fell into the hands of the lower classes, for whom they were intended and so kindled the flame. That the existence of the Peep o' Day Boys gave rise to the Defenders is obvious; one was the natural consequences of the other.

Orange eulogists with more loyalty than logic boldly say the Defenders were the cause of the Peep o' Day Boys. Musgrave, for instance, states "many gentlemen of the North have assured me that the origin of the Defenders, and the excesses which they committed, may properly be imputed to the savage and sanguinary spirit of the lower class of Romanists in the County Armagh, where they are peculiarly barbarous."[*] It is scarcely necessary to point out the blundering dishonesty of this historian when he ascribes the origin of the Defenders to their own acts, which could only prove their existence. Their origin must have been outside themselves. And the existence of the Peep o' Day Boys at this time is strikingly suggestive. There is no reason to discredit the statement of Taffe and Plowden. But that the formation of one followed fast upon the other is quite apparent.

[*] Musgrave's History of Rebellion, page 59.

Musgrave, however, uses this ingenious piece of special pleading in order to excuse the outrages which, strange to say, he does not admit, and for the purpose of narrating a tale of peculiar atrocity, if it be true, to justify the Peep o' Day Boys in all their doings. As I am inclined to hold the balance fairly between these two parties—for their bones lie mouldering during the past century, and reputations of to-day may well take care of themselves—I feel disposed to quote this statement. We will take it even from Musgrave himself, and the matter will be more interesting when we come at a later stage to examine the depositions of a certain member of the Verner family in regard to this event when before the Secret Committee of the House of Commons. Musgrave says[*] that one Richard Jackson, of Forkhill, who died on the 11th July, 1787, devised an estate of about £4,000 a year to the following charitable purposes :—That his demesne, consisting of 3,000 acres, should be colonised by Protestants, and that four schoolmasters should be established on it, to instruct, *gratis*, children of *every religious persuasion*. The trustees, two years afterwards, obtained an Act of Parliament to carry the provisions of the will into execution, and they appointed the Rev. Edward Huston, rector of Forkhill, one of the trustees, as agent to transact the business of the charity. "The Papists," says Musgrave, "who lived in the neighbouring county, a savage race, the descen-

[*] Ibid

dants of the rapparees, declared without reserve-that they would not suffer the establishment to take place; and they soon put their menaces into execution. They fired twice at Mr. Hudson. On one occasion an assassin *was sent from a Popish chapel, when the congregation was assembled,* to the road side, where Mr. Hudson was passing by, and he deliberately fired at him with a musket, from behind a bush, and killed his horse: The new colonists were hunted like wild beasts, and treated with savage cruelty; their houses were demolished and their property was destroyed." He then proceeds to detail the treatment which Alexander Barclay, one of the school masters received " in February, 1791," and he quotes a document signed by the trustees, dated " 1st February, 1791," which states that " on Friday evening, at seven o'clock," a number of villains went to the house of Barclay and stabbed one Terence Byrne, who opened the door for them; put a cord round his neck which they so tightened as to force out his tongue, part of which they cut off. They then cut off the four fingers and thumbs of his right hand. They treated Barclay's wife in the same manner, and also her brother, a boy of thirteen, who had just come from Armagh to see her. The Grand Jury at the ensuing assizes stated that the rage amongst the Roman Catholics for illegally arming themselves was truly alarming, and offered a reward for the conviction of those concerned in the outrage. Musgrave, in the same account, quotes many circumstances as improbable as they are foolish, which show that the " historian" is guided not by reason but by prejudice. It must be mentioned that the nobleman to whom this author dedicated his volume actually refused to accept the honour, as upon all sides the production was regarded as a tissue of falsehoods. There is also upon the face of the document a slight inaccuracy, for while Musgrave says the outrage occurred " in February," the report of the trustees bears date " 1st Feb," detailing an accident which took place " on Friday last." That the transaction is painted in glowing colours there can be no doubt, for the author never touched anything that he did not " embellish." If true, as it must be in part, it is a fact to be regretted, and serves to show the sad results of seeking to force a religion upon the people. That it could justify the long train of atrocities which followed in retaliation would be inhuman to uphold.

In order to make our story consecutive, we may here quote one of the questions asked Lieutenant-Colonel Verner when being examined before the Select Committee of the House on the 7th April, 1835.

At question 29 of the report occurs the following :—

" Can you state from your knowledge the occa-" sion, the origin, and the period of the formation " of the Orange Societies ? The first formation of " the society was in the year 1795. Previously " there were other societies existing; one under " the name of Defenders, exclusively consisting of " Roman Catholics. They were in the habit of " taking arms from the houses of Protestants, and " bodies of men, called Peep o' Day Boys went " generally early in the morning for the purpose of " recovering their arms, and from that circum-" stance derived their name. I think the first " occasion upon which the opinion became general " that there existed a decided hostility upon the " part of the Roman Catholics towards the Protes-" tants was a circumstance which occurred at a " place called Forkhill, in the County Armagh"— and in answer to the next question he therefore proceeds to relate it.

Now, the reader should mark the very nice distinction which Lieutenant-Colonel Verner made between recovering arms and taking arms, and he may form a very amusing picture in his own mind of those conscientious *Peep o' Day Boys,* fearful of robbery, examining minutely in the grey dawn of the morning those arms which they wanted *to recover,* and quietly returning them to their places when they found they had not been 'taken' from them. Again, if they wanted to recover arms which had been stolen from them, where were the police (of those days) and their amiable friends the magistrates, and why, of all things, select the break of day for the recovery of them ? Lieutenant-Colonel Vernor might have honestly held these opinions. I suspect very much, however, that the proceedings pointed rather in the direction of rape, of rapine, and of robbery.

And this view of the case is on all sides held—with the exception of Sir Richard Musgrave.

" From the spoliation of arms the privileged party proceeded to more general acts of plunder and outrage, which were perpetrated on most occasions with the most scandalous impunity"*

" The Defenders had long and frequently complained that all their efforts to procure legal redress against the outrages committed upon them by the Peep o' Day Boys were unavailing; that

* Madden's United Irishmen, First Series, page 99.

their oppressors appeared rather to be countenanced than checked by the civil power, and that the necessity of the case had driven them into counter combinations to defend their lives and properties against these uncontrolled marauders."*

For a long succession of years this persecution continued, the "privileged party" aided and abetted by the authorities. The Catholics were, however, increasing in importance. Nor were they now wanting manly Protestants and Presbyterians to come forward and advocate their claims of being released from years of unexampled injustice and oppression. The Protestant first company of volunteers had long before issued a manifesto condemning the perpetrators of these atrocities, and declared their intention of protecting the Catholics This old spirit still existed. The following may be accepted as an instance:—

"Declaration and resolutions of the inhabitants "of the parish of Tullylish (Co. Down)—George "Law, Esq., in the chair—

"Resolved—That we hold in just contempt and "abhorrence the criminal advisers and wicked per-"petrators of that inhuman, murderous, and savage "persecution which has of late disgraced the County "of Armagh.

* Plowden's Historical Review, page 297.

"That if these barbarities are not immediately "opposed, and some wise, firm, and effectual steps "taken by men in authority to arrest their progress "they will instantly involve this kingdom in all "the horrors of civil war, and deluge our land with "blood.

"That in our opinion the present existing laws "are full adequate to the detection and punish-"ment of every species of offence, in case the civil "magistrate do his duty," &c.

Defenderism had now become formidable, and even alarming to the Government. It had spread through all the Northern counties, and into the adjoining provinces. But the old device of Popish plots had not yet been "abandoned by statesment to aldermen, by aldermen to clergymen, and by clergymen to old women;"* the most absurd stories of massacres were fabricated with a facility which some influential authorities in the pay of the Government conceived it no degradation to stoop to; a Catholic dare not remain in his house; seven thousand had, according to Plowden, been driven from their homes already, and those who remained took to the hillside returning, only under cover of the night. In this state we find the country a few days before the first Orange Lodge was established.

* Macaulay.

CHAPTER VI.—THE MASSACREE OF THE DIAMOND, THE FIRST ORANGE LODGE.

On the 21st September, 1795, the massacre, euphoniously called the Battle of the Diamond, took place. There is yet living one who was present and witnessed the shocking scenes of that eventful day. At my request he dictated to me some few years ago the following:—

"NARRATIVE BY AN EYE-WITNESS OF THE DIAMOND MASSACRE.

"I was born in 1780, and was fifteen years of age at the Battle of the Diamond. My father was a Protestant. He was a well-to-do farmer, living in Loughgall, and had married a Catholic, the daughter of a neighbour. For this reason he met with a great deal of annoyance and persecution from the 'Peep o' Day Boys,' or 'Wreckers,' as we used to call them, and in my recollection his house was wrecked three different times by them. For a couple of years before the Diamond affray occurred, I remember distinctly that it was his habit to keep a loaded blunderbus—a gun three times as big as those you see now—on a table by his side every night while in bed. On Wednesday, I think it was,

the 16th or 17th of September, in the year '95, I was sleeping with a little brother (there were but two of us) in a room off my father's when, about half an hour before midnight, a loud knocking came to the back door. My father jumped out of bed. I got up and found a gun, and then stole to a window overlooking the back, for I had little fear in me at that time, and was up for 'sport,' as we called the sad business of those times. I was able to pull a trigger on my own account. But it was not the 'Wreckers,' as we all expected, for I heard some few pass-words of the Defenders being exchanged with my father, who, on account of my mother's religion, was much trusted by them, though I don't believe he was one of them. They asked him—there were about fifty in all — for any arms he had in the house, as they said the 'Protestant Boys,' or 'Wreckers' were going to attack the house of a one Jemmy Dugan (he lived about a mile off) that night, and they were determined not to let them. After some parley my father gave up the blunderbus, my gun as well together and an old rusty sword, and they went off shouting and cheering. I remember it as distinctly as the doings of yesterday. The next morning we heard there had been a 'scrimmage,' and that two of the Wreckers and one of the opposite party were killed, and their bodies privately disposed of by their friends. Dugan's house had really been attacked that night, and a few days after I saw his body being dragged from 'the field' of the Diamond, for he was amongst the killed. Now, the Diamond was then, as I believe it is now, a place where four roads meet, that is, two roads crossing, where there were a couple of houses, with a rising ground not far off. It is in Loughgall, not far from Armagh City. The Defenders were afraid to return home after the night's business, for the magistrates had got the scent, and one of them a Mr. Atkinson,* was particularly active (in regard to them), so they were sure to be pounced upon. They knew if caught they were certain to be hanged without a trial, as many of them were before, and they remained there, and about the locality, all the next day and the several days following up to Monday.

On Friday a strong party of Wreckers assembled from Portadown and Richhill. They were well armed, with the old Volunteer guns and bayonets ; and they approached the Diamond with shouting and yelling in the hopes of dislodging the Defenders. There was a scrimmage in daylight, actually, for I was looking on from the rising ground, but the Defenders, though their numbers were about the same, beat the Protestants to little bits, and they ran pell-mell for their lives. That night most of the houses belonging to the Catholics were burned, and their wives and daughters came to "the camp" next morning early with the most shocking tales of the usage some of them had received. One fine young girl of eighteen, I saw hide her face in a shawl, and cry bitterly on meeting her sweetheart, a fine strapping fellow. Poor fellow, he little guessed the cause. Her father burst out like a child when his wife whispered to him what was part of the unhappy night's transactions. In fact, she had been shamefully outraged. There were a couple of encounters during the next day, but none on Sunday, for the protestant Boys were too religious to fight upon the Sabbath. I should have said that our own house had been wrecked in the meantime, for some of them had got the scent of my father lending the

* This Mr. Atkinson was amongst the first Orangemen, strange to say.

guns. The house was burned, and my mother, who was with her fourth baby at the time, died soon afterwards from the fright.

The shooting and wrecking continued on Monday, the 21st. Mr. Atkinson and the priest did all they could to make peace, and they succeeded so far that both parties agreed to return home ; and I have heard that a compact was actually signed, but I don't know about that. Both parties left, with the exception of a few stragglers on each side, and I felt rather disappointed to think that all the fun was over. I wish to God it had been, and it would have saved me recollections that have saddened all my life. While they were on their way to their different homes a large party of Defenders from Monaghan, Cavan, and Tyrone—for the organisation had spread over all the adjoining counties, and they had a regular system of communication—as I was saying, these parties came up, for they had heard their friends were in trouble. Like myself some of them were not at all pleased that matters had assumed such a shape, and no wonder, for the truce wouldn't have lasted long, and they would have had the same journey another time. There was then near the Diamond the house of a Protestant named Winters—Dick Winters, I think, they called him. Some of the Monaghan or Cavan men broke some of the windows of Winters' house. His son made off and told the news to the retreating Protestants, and so the murder was out. About "the boys" wheeled, and after wrecking and smashing everything on their way in, took the Portadown direction. This, of course, brought back all the Defenders, and here they stood face to face—neighbours glowing at each other like tigers. The Defenders were of course by this time more numerous, but amongst the whole lot they had only a couple of dozen rusty old guns and my father's blunderbus, the rest being armed with pitchforks, scythes, and all sorts of implements. Few who had guns had ammunition. But the Protestants were well armed with guns, horse-pistols, old sabres, and bayonets, most of which had seen good service since '82.

The fighting recommenced about mid-day. Amongst the Protestants were, I was told afterwards, a number of old soldiers who had seen service—I don't know where ; I suppose in the French wars—and a good many militiamen, and they were directed, too, by some Protestant young men of considerable education and position in the neighbourhood of Portadown. The Defenders were sadly wanting in the matter of drill. As the Wreckers held the side of the hill the Roman Catholics were considerably at their mercy. Their artillerymen, as you would call them, had to keep in front, and besides, they wanted to protect their wives and children who were behind. A good many of them were soon picked down by the old soldiers, while the Defenders' rusty old guns wouldn't half reach their opponents. Those who were left of them soon exhausted their powder before they had inflicted the slightest damage on the enemy. There was a lull, if you could call it a lull, where the air was thick with the screams of the women over their dying husbands and brothers Within forty feet of where I was perched—for I had never got back my gun, or I might have been in the thick of it—and I know which side I would have fought on—within forty feet or sixty feet of me one little girl was shot dead, and the mourning of the poor mother was heartrending in the extreme, but there was a lull in what we might call "the fighting," for want of a better name, and I think there was some notion of trying a hand to hand struggle. It didn't last long for in an instant down swept the Protestant Boys from the hill, shooting as they came, and with their swords and bayonets they spread the wildest confusion, and made terrible slaughter amongst the Papists, on whole side men, women, and children were now huddled up. All that followed was a havoc—a cold-blooded and brutal massacre, the scenes which live in my memory to this day, old as I am, and which has prevented me from associating the place with other than carnage ever

after. Everyone fled, and you could see men dragging their wives and brothers, pulling their wounded sisters after them, leaving their fathers dead on the ground. Even then the rage of these fiends was not abated, and the Protestants cut down men, women, and children, especially women and children, without mercy I suppose I saw the mangled corps of about sixty people lying dead, and there might have been very many others that I did not notice, in the hurry of the route I have heard that the number killed was really more than this, and that their bodies were made away with through fear of prosecution, and of the certain prosecution that would await their families afterwards.

I have read some descriptions in my time, in old newspapers, of the horrible massacre, and was often tempted to send a sketch of it to the papers, for, to my mind, they were all imperfect. I dare say it was not the fault of those who wrote them They would not have been inaccurate if they had been there. Still I am sure I have given a very faint idea of the horrible and deliberate slaughter of that day, and but imperfectly conveyed to you what the massacre of the Diamond was like.

Every hovel belonging to a Catholic in the surrounding neighbourhood for miles was that evening wrecked.

ON THE 21ST SEPTEMBER, 1795, BY THESE MEN, FRESH FROM SUCH A SCENE OF CARNAGE, THE FIRST ORANGE LODGE WAS STARTED IN THE HOUSE OF ONE JAMES SLOAN, AT A PLACE CALLED TIMAKEEL

CHAPTER VII—MORE ABOUT THE DIAMOND.

IT may be interesting at this juncture to call a witness from the Orange side to corroborate, in however prejudiced a manner, the statement already given respecting the Diamond massacre That gentleman is Lieutenant-Colonel Blacker, one whose family had ever been active in perpetuating the discord which prevailed between the Catholics and Protestants of the country previous to September, 1795. First let me say that the Blackers of those days were the intimate friends of the Rev Mr Mansell, of Portadown, and Plowden says of the latter gentleman —"The ascendancy party was worked into an enthusiastic ebullition of renovated fury, by the sermon of a rev divine of the Established Church, Mr. Mansell, of Portadown, who some few days previous to the 1st of July, 1795, had from his pulpit given a very

marked notice to his congregation, that all persons disposed to celebrate the Anniversary of the Battle of the Boyne in the true spirit of the institution, should attend his sermon on that day. This evangelical labourer in the vineyard of the Lord of peace so worked up the minds of his audience that upon retiring from service, on the different roads leading to their respective homes, they gave full scope to the anti-Papistical zeal with which he had inspired them—falling upon every Catholic they met, beating and bruising them without provocation or distinction, breaking the doors and windows of their houses, and actually murdering two unoffending peasants who were digging turf in a bog. This unprovoked atrocity of the Protestants revived and redoubled religious rancour. The flame spread and threatened a contest of extermination." This,

d

which Plowden gives as one of the immediate incidents that led to the Diamond outrage, was prompted by the Rev. Mr. Mansell's blood-thirsty eloquence, the character of which we may very accurately estimate by having regard to recent utterances from the same platform made by a clergyman from the same district. Having said so much, we may now call the Lieutenant-Colonel and allow him to describe the Diamond massacre, in which he was a sharer, in his own language.

On the 1st August, 1835, he was called before the Select Committee and examined as follows:—

You are a Lieutenant-Colonel of the Armagh Militia? Yes.

Are you also Deputy-Lieutenant of the County of Armagh? Not at present; I was.

Have you also held a Commission of the Peace in the County of Armagh for several years? I have.

Did you also fill the office of Deputy Vice-Treasurer of Ireland for some time? For thirteen years.

Are you a member of the Orange Society? I am.

How long have you been so? It wants about six weeks of forty years.

We may rest here for a time. This admission is a highly important one. Lieut.-Colonel Blacker became an Orangeman 39 years and 46 weeks previous to the day upon which he was examined—the 1st August, 1835. A hasty calculation backwards brings us to the 12th September, 1795, as the day upon which he took the Orange oath. The association was not started until the 21st September of the same year, so that if we abide by his evidence he must have been sworn in not as an Orangeman but as a Peep o' Day Boy, confounding the two, a conclusion which if correct would account for his anxiety to supply bullets to his blood-thirsty brethren, as disclosed further on. But, considering his use of the word "about," it would be scarcely fair to bind him to this calculation. We may, however, assume, with all reasonable accuracy, that he was amongst the first that joined the Orange Association when it started; that the Diamond still bore the horrifying marks of the bloody fray, when the future Deputy Lieutenant of Armagh, and Deputy Vice-Treasurer of Ireland, and Lieutenant Colonel, and Justice of the Peace was calling Heaven to witness that he, so far as in him lay, would exterminate his Catholic fellow countrymen. Rather a strange position for such a person to occupy. But the consideration

becomes still more startling when we remember that this man, who had shown himself an accomplice and a partizan, this man who had made bullets for others to fire, and was so wanting both in humanity and self-respect as to give his endorsement to the transaction of the Diamond, was, for a long period of years, to sit and decide upon cases in which party spirit was paramount, and in which Catholics and Protestants were at issue. It contained a lesson to both parties, but one side alone benefitted by it. Catholics soon lost confidence in the constitution of a magistracy in which too many of them were of the same brotherhood as Lieutenant-Colonel Blacker. Protestants failed to see, and are only now beginning to learn, that it has ever been the practice of the Orange gentry to make the bullets while the rank and file fired them; to sit at home and applaud the ruffianism while their own heads were out of danger. To continue—

You, of course, then, are able to give the committee some account of its origin? I think I am.

Can you do so from hearsay or from personal knowledge? Both.

From whom have you chiefly acquired your information? My principal information was derived from a very respectable old gentleman in the County Armagh—*Captain Atkinson*, of Crowhill—who took a principal part in the transaction that led to the origin of the Orangemen, and also from several others of a lower rank in society, *who were mixed up with these transactions.*

Do you consider the information which you received from these persons to be authentic? Perfectly so.

Will you state the amount of it? The amount of the information which I received at different times was, that a large body of persons called Defenders had made an irruption into a district of the County Armagh, near Loughgall; the Protestants of that district assembled to oppose their progress —I believe their principal intention was to disarm the district—the Protestants assembled to oppose them, and there came in to their assistance Protestants from other districts of the country, particularly from the neighbourhood in which I reside.

What neighbourhood is that? The neighbourhood of Portadown.

Is this information derived from others? Yes; it is derived *from the authentic sources above mentioned.*

Can you state the date of it? Monday was the 21st—the *great day*—and I think it began abou

Wednesday before, in September, 1795. The parties skirmished, if I may use the expression, for a day or two without much harm being done. Mr. Atkinson on one side, and the priest of the parish on the other, did their best to reconcile matters, and thought they had succeeded, as the Defenders had on their part agreed to go away, and the Protestants to return to their houses. I believe both parties were sincere at that time in their wish to separate, and that they were going away to their respective homes. At that time, as I understand, a large body of the Defenders, not belonging to the County of Armagh, but assembled from Louth, Monaghan, and, I believe, Cavan and Tyrone, came down, and were much disappointed at finding a truce of this kind made, and were determined not to go home, without something to repay them for the trouble of their march. In consequence, they made an attack upon the house of a man named Winter, at a place called the Diamond, it is a meeting of crossroads, where there are only three or four houses. Word was brought to the Protestants, who were on their way home, of what had taken place. They returned to the spot, attacked the Defenders, and killed a number of them.

Were you yourself at all mixed up with the transactions of the Diamond? I WAS

To what extent? I was a very young lad at the time; it so happened that my father was making some alterations in his house, which occasioned a quantity of lead to be removed from the roof. A CARPENTER'S APPRENTICE AND MYSELF TOOK POS-SESSION OF A CONSIDERABLE QUANTITY OF THIS LEAD RAN IT INTO BULLETS, AND HAD IT CON-VEYED TO THE PERSONS OF MY NEIGHBOURHOOD WHO WERE GOING TO FIGHT THE BATTLE OF THE DIAMOND.

Were you on the spot when the battle was fought? I was not in time to be under fire, but immediately as it was terminating

Can you speak from your knowledge as to the state of the Protestants prior to the battle? I have always understood that they were in the most persecuted state, that they were worried and beaten coming from fair and market upon various occasions

Had this state of things been continued for a long time prior to that event? I understood from those that knew more about it than I did (for I was at school till just before this period) that it was so.

What did you see at the Diamond? When I got up I saw the defenders making off in one direction

and the firing had nearly ceased, I may say had ceased except a dropping shot or two, and I saw a number of dead bodies.

Can you state about the number? No, they were conveying them away upon cars in different directions, so that I could not make an exact cal-culation.

Were there fifty? No, if there were thirty killed that was the outside.

Were there any Protestants killed? None that I could hear of.

How did that happen? The Protestants were in a very commanding situation Winter's house and the Diamond generally is at the foot of a very steep hill, the other party were in that hallow, and consequently the men firing upon them from above could do great execution without being liable to be injured themselves.

Was there firing from the other side too? I be-lieve there had been, but I do not know of my own knowledge.

How were they armed on both sides? With all sorts of old guns.

Which appeared to be the best armed? I should say the Protestants were the best armed, and I will state reason; there were a great number of old volunteer fire-locks in that quarter of the country, and I believe they were almost exclusively Protes-tants.

The Defenders were the assailants, were they? Yes, they were

What was the nature of the fight? I have already stated that the parties who were first at variance had separated, the Protestants were on their return home when they received information that the Defenders from Louth and Tyrone and Monaghan had attacked the house of this Winter in the hollow. They counter—marched at once, they returned in haste, and the road led them to the top of this hill that overlooked the part where the De-fenders were in full work, and they immediately fired on them.

Then the Defenders did not occupy this hill as a military position? They had occupied the opposite hill, from which they descended to the attack at Winter's.

Was there any fire directed against the Protes-tants upon the Diamond? I have no doubt that there was; the fellows did not go away so tamely as that

How long did the engagement last? I do not think the actual engagement lasted about fifteen minutes perhaps.

Was the first Orange Lodge formed then? It was. Where? I understood it was formed in the house of a man named Sloan, in the village of Loughgall.

Have you ever seen any of the original warrants? I have; I think I have one of them with me.

Will you have the goodness to produce it?

[The same was delivered in, and read as follows :—]

"No. 89, Timakeel, July 7, 1796.
"James Sloan.
"To be renewed in the name of Daniel Bulla, Portadown district,".

Now the above, upon close examination, will be found to contain as startling an amount of information as any we have up to the present time met with. Upon the admission of one who subsequently held the position of Deputy Lieutenant for a county, and Deputy vice-Treasurer of Ireland, we find that this ingenuous youth stole his father's lead; cast it into bullets, and conveyed them to those who "were going to fight the battle of the Diamond." This places him not in the comparatively innocent position of having been an accomplice after the fact, but of being an accomplice before the fact—one of the instigators. But lead cannot be procured in an instant, and it takes some considerable time to convert it into bullets. The Blacker bullets were on the facts stated above used at the Diamond by those who were going "to fight" that battle. Now, the Protestants countermarched in hot haste on learning of the attack on Winter's house, so we may reasonably presume that they did not wait, or rather had not to wait until young Blacker had melted down his lead. It becomes, therefore, a question of extreme probability that those bullets had been manufactured a considerable time before the Diamond was fought; that the whole was part of a deliberate scheme in which this junior branch of the Blacker family took anything but a creditable part. Men on their road homewards who hastily turn round to save their comrade's house from being wrecked don't, as a rule, wait for bullets to be cast for them, and there very possibly is a slight error regarding the dates as to when the bullets really were cast.

The fact that this witness had derived his information from Capt. Atkinson, who it is now proven, played the rôle of a partisan upon that eventful occasion ought not to escape the reader's attention, and also that this information was supplemented by accounts from persons "in a lower rank in life"—in other words from the ruffians who shared the ignomy of that day's doings.

This is not the place to deal with the question of the persecution of the Protestants. When the time comes I will produce witnesses of reliability to show, if a doubt should exist even at present upon which side the persecution lay. In the meantime we must pass to the doings of the "first lodge," assembled in Mr. James Sloan's house, in the remote village of Loughgall.

CHAPTER VIII.—AFTER "THE BATTLE."

The instinct of self-preservation was probably that which first prompted the heroes of the Diamond, upon the evening of the 21st September, 1795, to change their name from that of "Peep o' Day Boys" to the more pretentious one of "Orangemen." It is the first device of every wrong-doer, from the pickpocket in the market place to the swindler and murderer. The change was never more necessary than in this instance. Though they had as patrons and protectors some or most magistrates of the surrounding neighbourhood, they still had very good reason to fear, and their latest crimes so far outweighed in magnitude their every day offences, that even a partial Government could not help but interfere. It was, therefore, under the direct advice of justices, whose bigotry made them forget the solemnity of their oaths, that they undertook to appear under a new name as the best method to avoid prosecution. After completing one of the most sanguinary slaughters in the records of civil broils, they returned, flushed with success, to the house of Sloan to slack their thirst and consider upon the next step. The tradition of the neighbourhood is that a prominent magistrate, whose baronial residence was not far removed, and who soon after became prominently connected with the association, sent them to this house a large quantity of liquor to refresh them after their day's exertions. So that Drunkenness joins hands with Murder, Rape, and Rapine in the dance of death round the first Orange Board. This very likely established that custom which, up to the present day, is held sacred—the circulation of the bottle freely at all Orange meetings. We can scarcely hope that those who indulged their worst passions in the bloody excesses of the day were very temperate in their use of intoxicants. On this night was first sworn that oath breathing of murder which subsequently became the test of the society, and which continued so until grave political reasons necessitated a change

THE ORANGE OATH.

The wording of the Orange Oath originally was ·—
"I, A B., do swear that I will be true to the "King and Government, and that I will extermi-"nate the Catholics of Ireland as far as in my "power lies"

Plowden, who quotes this as the original obliga-tion, says it has been asserted to have been so by well-informed, though anonymous authors.[*] The impossibility of otherwise proving it is apparent, particularly when secrecy has been one of the first principles of this institution. Plowden, as I have already quoted, says the frequency and earnestness with which the latter part of the oath has been acted upon render the charge of taking it too reliable.

I must do the Brethren the justice of saying that they have denied this oath ; but the ease with which, in times recent, they have denied facts when their admission was found to be inconvenient throws an air of suspicion over their denial that we cannot pass over in silence. However, unless Lord Clare and the Secret Committee whichacted under his directions had either distinctly known, or had good grounds for believing, that the oath of Exter-mination had been usually taken by Orangemen, they would have scarcely questioned Mr. O'Connor in 1798 as to "whether the Government had any-thing to do with the oath of Extermination"

"Government," said a member of the Adminis-tration, had nothing to do with the Orange Society, nor with the Oath of Extermination," to which Mr. Arthur O'Connor replied, "You, my Lord Castlereagh, from the station you fill, must be sensible that the Executive of any country has it in its power to collect a vast mass of information of every act of the Irish Government. As one of the Executive (of the United Irishmen), it came to my knowledge that considerable sums of money were expended throughout the country, and that the Orange Oath of Extermination was administered ; when these facts are coupled, not only with the general impunity which had been uniformly extended to all the acts of this diabolical associa-tion, but the marked encouragement its members have received, I find it impossible to exculpate the Government from being the parent and protector of those sworn extirpators "[†]

Lieutenant-Colonel William Blacker, when questioned by the Select Committee, must submit to the charge, at least, of prevarication, as the fol-

* History of Ireland, vol 1, page 54.
† Memoir of Examination of Messrs. O'Connor, Emmet and M'Nevin.

lowing extract will show ·—

The oath of the Orangemen was altered, was it not? The oath of the Orangemen was done away with.

Was there not an alteration in the oath when it existed ? I do not recollect that circumstance.

Do you recollect the original oath ? I can hardly recollect it.

Were not the first rules and regulations those adopted in 1799? No ; they were from the com-mencement.

The Committee have no information of any oath previous to 1799, do you recollect the oath taken previous to 1799, when the institution was first formed ? I think I do recollect the oath first taken.

Can you give the substance of it ? The sub-stance of it was this, that they would bear true allegiance to the King, and be true to one another, and not divulge the secrets and passwords.

Do you recollect the Yeomanry oath ? Yes.

What is the Yeomanry oath ? "I do swear that I will bear true allegiance to his Majesty King William the Fourth, his heirs and successors, and to support the laws and constitution of this king-dom and the success on of the Throne "[*]

In this evidence it will be apparent that the gal-lant Colonel entirely ignores, in giving the substance of the original oath, the conditional loyalty which upon all sides is admitted as having been contained therein. It is not denied but actually admitted that the following was at an early but subsequent period the form of the Orange oath —

"I. A. B , do solemnly swear that I will to the utmost of my power support and defend the King and his heirs so long as he or they support the Pro-testant ascendancy"

Now when Lieutenant-Colonel Blacker could ignore that feature in the oath which was con-sidered so important as to necessitate a change, it is equally possible, if not probable, that he conve-niently forgot certain other clauses of the original oath, which could have borne out Plowden and O'Connor, and made the oath one of wholesale extermination of Catholics.

If we turn now to the evidence of the Rev M. O'Sul-livan, who had more reasons than one for justifying his very suspicious conduct in reference to the in-stitution of which he was member, we will find a very important piece of evidence bearing upon this point. At 588 we find—

"Can you state the professed object of the per-

* Minutes of Select Committee, question 9337-9994.

sons who formed themselves into that association? The professed objects of those who formed that association were that they should assist each other for *mutual defence*; that they should assist each other in maintaining the laws; and that they should assist each other in maintaining the Protestant religion; and that they should in all things be faithful and obedient to the King.

"You say that you were bound to be obedient to the King, was there not a condition attached to their allegiance to the King? There was at one time a condition that Orangemen should be in all cases obedient to the King *so long as he maintained Protestantism*; finding that these words were not in *exact* accordance with the oath of allegiance, and that they were *susceptible of an objectionable* interpretation, that oath was discarded and the oath of allegiance substituted."

And further on we find—

"The condition of the oath was that the King should support Protestantism? The condition of oath which had been previously taken was to that effect.

"By Protestantism do you mean the Established Church? *I believe the condition contemplated rather was called* PROTESTANT ASCENDANCY *than the maintenance of the Established Church.* Originally Orangemen were almost exclusively Church of England men; but a number of Presbyterians were induced to join them, and the character of the society became in consequence somewhat changed. I can state, if desired, the circumstances which led to the junction between the different descriptions of Protestants.

You do not conceive that the Protestants of the Established Church merely are identified with the sense in which 'they have used the word Protestants? I do not think that could be the meaning of the Orange Society at any time; certainly *not of late years.*

So that if the King should assent to the total subversion of the Established Church, the Orangemen would not be released from their allegiance? No man, from the circumstances of his being an Orangeman would be released from his oath of allegiance.

From their oath? I would not undertake to say what would be my opinion if I were sitting in judgment upon the oath *previously taken* by the Orangeman.

Now in the above extracts we have the oath of conditional loyalty established; we have it admitted that the condition was the upholding of Protestant Ascendancy and we have the gentlemen who undertook to *give the substance* of the original oath, quietly ignoring these important considerations. Will any man in his senses allow himself to be guided by such prevarication and take it for granted that there was no such thing as an oath of Extermination, as against the calm reasoning of unprejudiced Plowden and the distinct statement of O'Connor as to what came under his own knowledge? As a body of Exterminators, when first constituted, we may therefore take those original Orangemen. We may also conclude that in that same James Sloan's house at Loughgall, from which the first warrant issued, these impious men—besmeared with their neighbours' blood; like the wild beast hungering for more; and besotted and brutalised by whiskey—first went upon their bended knees and swore "to wade knee-deep in Papist blood." This they forthwith proceeded to do.

The attentive reader will find in the circumstances immediately to follow much to strengthen this assumption. The first regular meeting was held on the 27th September, 1795, but before we proceed to its consideration I may occupy the time usefully by turning your attention for a moment to what is the first recorded official act of the Orange Institution immediately following the inauguration ceremony of the 21st September. If we find that in the beginning, the middle, and drawing towards the end, the Orange Society has been always the same, actuated by the same motives, and seeking the accomplishment of the same base purposes, we will have but little trouble in determining whether their deeds were the result of accident or design.

THE FIRST ORANGE OUTRAGE.

The following, which is the first Orange outrage we have upon record, will be read with interest:—Within a mile and a half from the City of Armagh there resided in those days an old and feeble priest named M'Meekin. He had lived through all the persecutions of the eighteenth century, and followed by a few of his faithful flock, had been hunted from hill-side to hill-side in the Counties of Armagh and Down, celebrating Mass now in some lonely glen and again upon the mountain slopes in the wildest parts of the country. During all that time his constant companions were his niece, and her son, now (1795) a young lad of about sixteen years. This young woman had been married to a comfortable farmer and grazier from Dundalk, whose goods and chattels were held in the name of a respectable and large-hearted Protestant neighbour in order to save them from seizure. The son of this Protestant, a scapegrace and a drunkard, turned informer in the certainty of securing a share of the spoils, the result being that the goods were confiscated, and the owner who was transported soon after lost his life on board the fleet where he was compelled to do service. The widow, a young woman of pre-possessing appearance and refined manners, was cast adrift upon the world, and being subjected to many brutal insults, with the fear of worse treatment, at the hands of those who had robbed her of her possessions, she sought a home with the old priest who was himself dependent upon the hospitality of his neighbours. At last, towards the close of the century, the days of toleration dawned, and he with his niece and her orphan boy settled down in the County Armagh, in a district known as Ballymacnab, which had been the place of his birth. Here, in the midst of an increasing congregation—for persecution had created sympathy—he spent the latter days of a useful life.

As a hare whom hounds and horns pursue,
Pants to the place from whence at first he flew.
He still had hopes, his long vexations past,
Here to return—and die at home at last.

And he did die at home at last; and at the hands of the newly created Orange faction, as the sequel will show.

It is generally supposed that this diabolical crime was planned at the same time and place as witnessed the formation of the new association for the maintainance of Protestant ascendancy. The fact that a priest was the object of it; the proximity of the scene to Loughgall, and the occurrence of the horrible outrage on the very night following the starting of the First Lodge give credence to the supposition. At any rate a writer of those days ascribe it to the Orangemen, and his records of many another horrible deed committed as well by the Defenders, as by the Peep o' Day Boys and the Orangemen, show alike his impartiality and his extensive knowledge.

On the night of the 22nd September, 1795 (some two hours before midnight), a party of Orangemen, most of them half-drunk, and "headed by a well-known and infamous character from Portadown" proceeded to the house of Priest M'Meekin. All the family were in bed save the old priest, who was seated in a room opening on to the roadway, piously engaged in reading his office. The Orange party purposed effecting a surprise. The leaders stole noiselessly to the window. See-

ing the old man engaged as described, one of the foremost, with an oath, "damned the Papish w——," and raised his gun to his shoulder to fire. A companion, whose intentions were not quite so humane, insisted that it would spoil sport to "do him right off at once," but the gun went off, and wounded the poor old man in the arm. In went the foremost through the window, the rest of the gang smashing the doors, and thus gaining admission to the house, the only occupants of which were Priest M'Meekin, the niece, her son, and an old woman servant. A dozen of them rushed upstairs to secure the affrighted inmates, who were in bed, while the others secured the old priest, now wounded and fainting from loss of blood. They placed him upon his knees, and threatened to cut him up, joint by joint, if he did not tell them at once where he kept "that damned wafer that he frightened the devil with." Of course, he did not impart the required information. True to their promise, they brutally chopped off the fingers of his right hand. Again the question was asked; but no answer. They were then proceeding to do likewise with the fingers of the other hand. Up to this time they had not noticed, however, that the poor old man held firmly his left hand within his breast. This was now noticed, and they at once tore open his vest, pulling from beneath it the Blessed Sacrament which he had there concealed. Horrible to relate, it was subjected to the vilest and most sacrilegious treatment, spat upon and trampled. During all this time the ruffians overhead had been all but equally as busy as their companions below. This fine young woman was brutally and shamefully dragged from her bed. Her screams attracting her son; he ran to her aid. He was detained, and compelled to look on at the accomplishment of a crime, the bare mention of which freezes up the blood—so foul and brutal as to make, if it were possible, even the Father of Evil turn aside in shameful disgust. The horrors of that night's transactions might now, surely, have been completed. Not so. For the fiend of lust is not so appeased. It will murder what it has destroyed. The young woman, now half dead, was dragged just as she was to the room below, together with the boy and the servant, and here the next act of the tragedy was commenced. In presence of the good and pious old priest, the brutal work of ravishing was repeated. The priest was then subjected to an outrage of the most diabolical kind, and which half a century previous a legislator in the Irish Parliament had been infamous enough to uggest as the best method of ridding the country of priests, and upon which an Irish Parliament actually Jid pass an Act soliciting their English masters to give effect to it.[*]

The boy had then his two eyes put out in presence of his almost irresistible mother. Her sufferings and her shame were, perhaps fortunately, soon put an end to, for those midnight murderers, having divested her of all her garments, stabbed her, and afterwards brutally mutilated her. The priest was then hanged from one of the rafters of his humble cabin, but the old servant managed to escape with the now blind

child, and in the course of her flight, as she turned to take a parting look at a spot which was to her a quiet and a happy home in her old days, she saw flames rising into the sky. By thus setting fire to the house those assassins thought to demolish all evidence of their crime. The old woman died in her hiding-place in the course of a few days, and the poor blind child, whose chief offence was that he "assisted at the Popish Mass," wandered about the country a maniac, and was lost sight of in the rebellion of '98, having possibly fallen a victim to the brutal Yeomanry of those days.[*]

One of those who took part in this outrage afterwards confessed to it, and said he had been forced to join in it against his will. But no prosecution followed. The ringleader was arrested, and discharged two days after.

If asked why do I dwell upon such a loathsome and shocking incident I answer—the necessities of the time demand it. When men pretend ignorance of their history, or know so little of it that they can be taught to glory in it, it is surely time that all delicacy be abandoned, so that murder, rape, and robbery may stand unmasked in their horrible realities.

---

* In 1723 a series of resolution' was agreed upon and reported by the Commons, to the effect that Popery was on the increase, partly owing to the many shifts and devices the priests had of evading the laws, and partly owing to the magistrate's neglect in not searching them out and punishing them. A Bill based upon them was introduced into the Commons. On that occasion one of the most zealous promoters of it, in a lengthened speech, informed the House, "that of all countries wherein the reformed religion prevailed Sweden was observed to be the most free from those irreconcilable enemies of all Protestant Governments—the Catholic priests. This happy exemption, so needful to Protestant interests, was obtained by a who some practice, which prevailed in that fortunate land—namely, the practice of castrating all Popish priests who were found there." A clause to the effect was actually introduced into the Bill. It was passed, and his Grace the Duke of Grafton was requested "to recommend the same in the most effectual manner to his Majesty." His grace did recommend it, but the English Council, influenced by Cardinal Fleury, disapproved of the Bill, and it was not passed into law.—Curry's Review, Plowden's History, and Brennan's Ecclesiastical History.

Mitchell says this was the first occasion on which any penal law met with any obstacle in England.

---

* These facts are taken from an ably-written and now rare pamphlet—"The atrocities that led to the Irish Rebellion," published in 1802, and have been authenticated by some old inhabitants of the district. A very brief account may be found also in the Dublin Journals of the period.

CHAPTER IX.—THE FIRST ORANGE-MEETING, THE FIRST ORANGE LEADER, THE FIRST ORANGE TOAST, THE ORIGINAL RULES AND REGULATIONS.

The first regular Orange meeting was held on the 27th September, 1795. It would appear from the records dealing with those times that, even at the outset, it brought together a considerable number of the lower class of Protestants, chiefly from the Portadown district. Plowden says[a] an apothecary named Gifford, notorious in the annals of Orangeism, has the undesirable reputation of having been the founder of the institution. It appears that this person had quitted the peaceful pursuit of medicine for the then more lucrative one of arms. He became a captain in the City of Dublin militia, and was now quartered in Portadown. Up to this time he had been prominently forward in encouraging the Peep-o-day boys against the defenders, and his zealous exertions were

not left unrewarded. To him are attributed by Plowden the adoption of the title of "Orangemen," their original oath and obligations, and the first regulations by which they were organised into a society. While this gentleman was travelling in a public carriage from Newry to Dublin he met with a Mr. Bernard Coyle, a respectable Catholic manufacturer of Lurgan. In the course of the conversation while driving between Dundalk and Drogheda Mr. Coyle observed that Robespierre was a second Cromwell, to which Gifford in part assented, adding that he would forgive Cromwell everything but one. Coyle asked what that was, and Gifford sharply replied—"His NOT HAVING EXTERMINATED THE CATHOLICS FROM IRELAND," a rather striking corroboration of the existence of the Extermination Oath. Coyle professed himself a Catholic, and insisted upon Gifford being put out of the carriage, but, by the interference of a Mr. Page, Dundalk, and his son, and a Mr. MacLelland (father of Baron

---

a History of Ireland, vol. I., page 21. These volumes it should be recollected, are dedicated to the then Prince of Wales, and his Historical Sketch which was similarly dedicated received the sanction and countenance of the same distinguished personage.

MacLelland), who were fellow-passengers, the quarrel was patched up.

The association was in 'ts earliest stages, composed of the lowest rabble. This is evident, indeed, from the circumstances out of which it arose, but, irrespective of this, most writers are agreed upon the point, however, they admit that in the course of the two following years some gentlemen of property became connected with it Musgrave, for once, "does not attempt to deny that outrages were committed by the lower orders of Orangemen," though he excuses them through "mistaken zeal" Very much mistaken zeal, indeed, did these early Orangemen display. In his "History of the Rebellions" (page 73) this inconsistent historian furnishes an example of the necessity of certain persons having long memories He there says that "the Orange Association should not be confounded with the disgraceful outrages done in the County Armagh by the lowest class of Presbyterians as Peep o' Day Boys and the Roman Catholics as Defenders," as the association was not instituted until the Defenders had manifested hostile designs. If this historian means anything, he must mean that the early Orangemen were not Peep o' Day Boys, or that if they had been the outrages ceased as soon as they adopted the new name, and they should therefore "not be confounded" with their former deeds Take the last interpretation first in the passage I have quoted, he does admit that outrages were committed by the lower orders of Orangemen. If he means that the early Orangemen were not those low people called Peep o' Day Boys, he may be again convicted out of his own mouth. At page 70 of his history he says, "In commemoration of that (the Diamond) victory the first Orange lodge was formed in the County Armagh" The "victory" was "won" by the Peep o' Day Boys, and surely respectable Protestants did not form themselves into an association to commemorate a battle which they never fought! Again he says, at page 71, that "the lower class of Protestants of the Established Church stood forward at this perilous time"—that is that these were the men who fought at the Diamond, and afterwards became Orangemen "in commemoration of their victory." But when he comes to deal with outrages, he conveniently shifts them over to the shoulders of the "lowest class of Presbyterians," with whom he is horrified to think the early Orangemen should be confounded.

I think we have it now that the association was

first made up of the rabble; that of the rabble directed possibly by a few choice souls, the scions of one or two families, since become noted if not famous, the first meeting of the 27th September, 1795, was made up; and that they did then for the first time as Orangemen, and as their successors still continue to do at every lodge meeting, indulge very considerably in intoxicating drinks.

THE TOAST.

Sir Jonah Barrington, who is an authority upon this subject, at least, gives us ("Personal Sketches") the full text of the Orange toast, which he calls "a most ancient and unparalleled sentiment." Considering the times in which Sir Jonah lived, the many opportunities he had of knowing and also remembering the character and social position of the men with whom we are dealing, we are justified in concluding that it was the text of the original charter toast of the society.

The first of July—the Anniversary of the Battle of the Boyne (our authority says)—was the favourite night of assembly "Then every man unbottoned the knees of his breeches and drunk the toast on his bare joints, it being pronounced by his lordship in the following words, composed expressly for the purpose, in 1689, and afterwards adopted by the Orange Association generally, and still, I believe, considered the Charter toast of them all This most ancient and unparalled sentiment runs thus —

"The glorious, pious, and immortal memory of the great and good King William—not forgetting Oliver Cromwell, who assisted in redeeming us from Popery, slavery, arbitrary power, brass money and wooden shoes. May he never want a Williamite to kick the —— of a Jacobite, and a —— for the Bishop of Cork. And he that wont drink this, whether he be priest, bishop, deacon, bellows-blower, g avedigger, or any other of the fraternity of the clergy, may the North wind blow him to the South, and the West wind blow him to the East! May he have a dark night, a lee shore, a rank storm, and a leaky vessel to carry him over the river styx. May the dog Cerberus make a meal of his r——p, and Pluto a snuff-box of his scull, and may the devil jump down his throat with a red-hot harrow with every pin tearing out a gut, and blow him with a clean carcase to hell. Amen."

In later days some low enthusiastic Orangemen in out-of-the-way districts made an "improvement" upon this, rounding the conclusion somewhat in this fashion :—

"May he be rammed, crammed, and jamed into

the great gun of Athlone and blown on to the hob of hell, where he'll be kept resting for all eternity, the devil basting him with melted bishops, and his imps pelting him with priests."

That the above toast was drunk in the Orange lodges of his time Sir John Barrington assures us, and when regard is had to the fact, that the knight was an intimate friend and counsellor of Dr. Duigenan, it is reasonable to conclude that, though not an Orangeman, but the confident and associate of some of the earliest leaders of the Brotherhood, he is here speaking upon a subject, with respect to which, he had means of accurate information, and on a point upon which he may be regarded as an authority. Sir Jonah adds that the extraordinary eal with which this toast was drunk could only be equalled by the enthusiasm with which the blue jugs and the pewter pots were resorted to to test the quality within. Before we pass from this phrase of the question it may said that Barrington jocularly but significantly remarks in one of his notes, that "could his Majesty King William learn in the other world that he has been the cause of more broken heads and drunken men since his departure than all his predecessors he must be the proudest ghost, and the most conceited skeleton that ever entered the gardens of Elysium.

In a letter quoted by Madden in the first series of his United Irishman (page 341) will be found evidence upon this subject. Mr. T. Fitzgerald Geraldine, County Kildare, says "When I was examined before the Council in June, 1798, Arthur Wolfe, the Attorney-General, now Lord Kilwarden, interrogated me if I had not amongst my papers the Orangeman's oath. I replied that I had an oath, which was enclosed under cover to me by post, entitled the Orangeman' oath, and the words were "Rely upon it, sir, the Orange system is rapidly increasing about the town of Athy." The Attorney-General then asked Mr. Fitzgerald do you conceive it possible that any gentleman, or any person of principle or education could take such an oath? I answered, I believed it to be the Armagh oath. The oath I do not recollect nor did I, at the time, understand it; it spoke of rivers of blood, of wading through the Red Sea, and a brotherhood, &c." If we add this to all that is gone before respecting the existence of the exterminating oath we cannot but believe that they who were so ready to take upon them the most fearful and bloody obligations would not have much delicacy of conscience under circumstances not so awful; and that when the punch went round the enthu-

siasm of each member of this banditti was exercised in devising the most novel, and the most original toast to give expression to their bigotry and intolerance.

What were the rules and regulations of the first Orange Lodge? The answer to the question would be alike deeply interesting in an historical as a social sense. From a careful perusal of the point, I am inclined to the opinion that the early Orangemen, like most of the other guerrilla tribes that preyed upon the possessions of honest men, were first banded together and bound together more by verbal than by written agreement. It was not until they found that their association would be olerated by Government, of which more hereafter, that they went to the trouble of placing upon record the regulations by which their association should be bound. Accordingly we find that in the first six or perhaps twelve months of their existence, there was nothing which denoted the objects of their band but a general understanding that they were to do all in their power to harass their Catholic neighbours, and to prey upon them so effectually as to render their remaining in the country impossible. That this was their primary object we have established upon all sides. In fact, it can best be understood by the results. In the County Armagh, in which the association first started, there were then a large number of comfortable and well-circumstanced Catholics, who, even beneath the pressure of the penal laws, had acquired a considerable competency. The Catholics of those days were industrious and frugal, and, paying no attention to matters political, in which they were not allowed to interest themselves, they concentrated all their attention upon improving their condition financially. Their success operated as one of the primary causes of jealousy, the result being a determination to rid the country of them at all hazards. They were got rid of. History says that 7,000 Catholics were driven "to hell or Connaught" out of the county, and tradition assures us that in twelve months after the starting of the institution scarce a Catholic resident was to be found in the entire County of Armagh. But the new association soon extended itself beyond the limits of Armagh, for in the adjoining counties Catholics, too, were beginning to prosper, and there, too, the Defender system was strong and powerful. We must pass for a time—with the promise to return to it—over a considerable period, every day of which left some mark behind of the trail of the serpent, and come to June, 1797, before we find any written law that was looked upon as binding upon the associates. At Lisbellaw, in the County Fermanagh, on the 4th of June of the year mentioned, were framed in a series of resolutions the first general rules of the Orange brethren They are the solemn declarations of the Loyal Boyne and Orange Association, the assembly at Lisbellaw playing then, and for some considerable time afterwards, the part of the now Grand Orange Lodge of Ireland, and on more than one occasion dictating the principles upon which the body of lodges should act. They are embodied in a series of seven resolutions, but as most of them are of a formal character I will trouble the reader with the following only as being those in which interest is alone centred :—

"Resolved—That we hold ourselves bound to our God and to each other, in no less a penalty than our oaths, our lives, and properties, to assist his Majesty King George III., and his lawful successors, against his or her enemies, whilst we reside in his Majesty's dominions, and he and they support, uphold, and maintain the true Protestant religion and ascendancy, as established and declared at the glorious Revolution of 1688 to be the principles for the guide and government of all future monarchs of Great Britain and Ireland."

"Resolved—That, inasmuch as history and experience have truly informed us that the members of the Popish Church will keep no faith with us, whom they denominate 'heretics,' and that they are also bound by the most sacred tie to disclose and make known to their priests at confession all secrets, whether of the State or of ourselves; and also for the reason of their being almost universally disaffected to our good King, that we do declare that no member of the said Popish Church shall have any inheritance in our loyal brotherhood."*

Immediately following these resolutions we find detailed the constitution of the Grand Orange Association, and the names of the grand officers, amongst whom are to be found those of Captain William Blacker, Thomas Verner, and David Verner, names which are already familiar to the readers of this history.

The Grand Orange Lodge was not founded until a year later, as will be seen from the report of the proceedings of that body in 1858, when at a special meeting in Belfast, on the 21st January, a report

* Annals and Defence of the Loyal Orange Institution by O. R. Gowan, late Grand Secretary; published in Dublin in 1835

was read stating that all the books and records remaining in the hands of the late Mr. Swan, D G. Secretary, had been preserved by his widow, and that in 1857 " the Grand Master, accompanied by the Deputy-Grand Secretary, got up from Mrs. Swan, all the books in her possession, *commencing with the foundation of the lodges in 1798*"

The rules and regulations under which the Boyne Society met to pass the foregoing resolutions were the following :—

RULES AND REGULATIONS OF THE BOYNE SOCIETY, COMMONLY CALLED ORANGEMEN

1st. We associate for the defence of our persons and properties, and for preserving the peace and good order of the country.

2nd That we are exclusively a Protestant Association.

3rd. That we will, to the utmost of our power defend and support his present Majesty King George the Third, the laws and constitution of this kingdom, and the succession of the Throne in his Majesty's illustrious house—being Protestant

4th That we will aid and assist all magistrates, and all high and petty constables, in the lawful execution of their office, when called on.

5th That we will upon all occasions aid and assist each other when promptitude and propriety appear to give rise to the necessity of such assistance, and that the same do not exceed the jurisdiction of the laws, or tend to promote insurrection or internal disturbance

6th That we are to be true to all brother Orangemen in all their actions, neither wronging any, nor feeling or knowing them to be wronged, and as far as in our power promote each other's interest and welfare.

7th. That we are not to give the first assault to any person whatsoever.

8th That we are individually bound not only to observe the peace ourselves, but also to be active in preventing all others, of whatever persuasion or denomination (who may come within our knowledge) that *may* have an *intention* to do an ill or riotous act

9th That we are to meet every first day of July (old style) in full body, to commorate the signal victory gained by King William, Prince of Orange, at the Boyne ; who bravely supported our Rights and established the Protestant religion , that on this day we are to walk wherever may be agreed on, *always behaving with propriety and decorum* *

* " The principles of the Orange Association stated vindicated "

Now this looks admirable upon paper. As was shrewdly remarked on the publication of the rules and regulations of the Society, when the Government resolved to dispense with its services, the laws of the Society were so cunningly framed that they showed upon the face of them the utmost concern for the peace and happiness of the country; while at the same time, its constitution was such that it was doing all in its power to mar both the one and the other. But if we even take the published document as it here stands, and ignore, what must be the effects upon an ignorant and misguided peasantry of a combination, the professed object of which was to support the *true* religion, we will find that even in their very earliest regulations they were holding out to ill-minded and misguided enthusiasts a premium for intolerance. The idea of any body of men, however loyal, setting themselves up the judges of what were the *intentions* of other portions of his Majesty's subjects is a suggestion monstrous in itself, and one which must inevitably lead to social disorder, as we will find it did. By the 8th regulation individuals constituted themselves judges not of the actions but of the intentions of their fellow-men, and were " individually bound to be active in preventing all others, of whatever denomination, that may have an intention to do an ill or *riotous* act." Now if we couple that regulation with the resolution of the same lodge given by Mr. O. R. Gowan, and which meant purely and simply that all Catholics were rebels, we will find in it an instruc-

tion to all Orangemen, as they valued their oaths, to prevent all Papists from doing an ill or riotous act—in other words to exterminate them all, as their very existence was a proof of their disposition towards riot. This is a startling fact which has not yet been treated of by any who have briefly dwelt upon the subject, and is a point worthy the calm consideration of all unprejudiced thinkers.

By the 7th regulation they were charged not to give the first assault to any person *whatsoever*, a rule which was entirely unnecessary if the Association were not of a belligerent character and were marked by those desires for law and order, which the advocates of Orangeism claim for their Institution.

Mercutio is made to say to Benvolio :—*

" Thou art like one of these fellows, that when he enters the confines of a tavern, claps down his sword upon the table, and says, *God send me no need of thee* ! and, by the operation of the second cup draws it on the drawer, when indeed there is no need."

It is a fitting caricature of the Orange Society, not as it really was at this period, but as it professed to be ; and finding its professions so full of bluster and braggadacio we may have little hesitation in crediting the tales of its practices. Whether those who walked on the 1st of July behaved themselves " with propriety and decorum" is a question as to which all my readers have ample means of answering by their knowledge of recent events.

* Romeo and Juliet, Act iii,, scene i.

CHAPTER X.—"TO HELL OR CONNAUGHT," THE GOVERNMENT PLOT—IT THICKENS.

WE have now sufficiently studied the rules and regulations of the Orange Association at its start to be enabled to properly estimate the objects for which, under the obligation of fearful oaths, they set out upon their mission of blood and plunder. In keeping quite within this combination we find the County of Armagh at once a scene of terror and persecution, a scene in which the wildest deeds of barbarism, and the most shocking acts of cruelty were perpetrated in the name of religion.

Madden says,* " few of the Orangemen in the North were probably actuated by the motives to which their proceedings are commonly attributed. It is generally supposed that they were animated by a blind, indiscriminate fury against the people, solely on account of their religion. This is not a

* Madden's Lives and Times, first series, page 112.

fair statement, and whoever inquires into the history of these times will find it is not true. These men were impelled, *as their descendants are*, by a simple desire to get possession of property and privileges belonging to a people who had not the power to protect either, and to give their rapacity the colour of a zeal for the interests of their own religion. It is doing the ascendency party a gross injustice to suppose that their animosity to their Roman Catholic countrymen arose from a mere spirit of fanaticism, or of mistaken enthusiasm in their religious sentiments. The plan of converting souls by converting the soil of the old inhabitants of a country to the use of the new settlers is of an ancient date. With this party the matter is one of money, and patronage and preferment, and of property in land, which wears the outward garb of a religious question. The Puritans who sought a refuge in America, when they found the most fertile portion of Massachusetts in the possession of the Indians, did not think of dispossessing the rightful owners of the broad lands they coveted without giving the sanctimonious air of a religious proceeding to their contemplated spoliation. They convened a meeting, *which was opened with all due solemnity and piety*, and the following resolutions are said to have been passed unanimously:—

Resolved—"That the earth is the Lord's, and the fullness thereof."

Resolved—"That the Lord hath given the earth as an inheritance unto his saints."

Resolved—"That we are his saints."

Now, this was practically what the Orangemen of Armagh did immediately after their organisation, as may be seen from the original regulations in the proceeding chapter.

Resolved—"That we Orangemen are the only loyal subjects of his Majesty King George III."

Resolved—"That, as loyal subjects, we are bound to prevent all subjects from acting riotously; and that, by the virtue of our oaths, we are compelled 'to prevent all who may have an intention of acting riotously.'"

Resolved—"That Catholics are universally disaffected towards the King."

Resolved—"That we exterminate the Catholics."

Those who cannot follow, by these easy stages, the argument are afflicted with that worst of all infirmities—the blindness that will not see. The zeal of Orangemen,* in behalf of their religion, cannot impose upon a close observer of its history. The Penal Code was framed for the protection of confiscated property, and the assumed hostility to the religion of the people who were dispossessed was only a practice, in accordance with the purport and pretence of the iniquitous statutes, which had already legalised three general confiscations within a period of 200 years. This legalised system of rapine and proscription has been productive of evils which still are felt; and those who, along with the lands of the proscribed people, obtained all the political privileges that were thought essential to the security of their own possessions, would have been more just than the generality of mankind, if, having the power to protect the spoils they had obtained, or were encouraged to expect, they had not abused their privileges, and did not see in every extension of the people's

* Ibid.

liberties another encroachment on the limits, now daily narrowing, of their power, influence, and political pre-eminence.

Accordingly, we find numerous specimens of notices, generally of a very illiterate character, that were posted upon the doors of the residences of the obnoxious and proscribed Papists, notifying them that they were at once to quit the country under pains and penalties of the most murderous character. These generally took the shape of "To hell, Connaught won't receive you," or the still more laconic form of "Hell or Connaught." The following may be taken as a specimen:—

"TO JOHN HOLLAN, COOPERNACK, GILFORD.

"John Hollan, you are *desired* to abandon *your* house *agen* the 21st March; and if you don't we will *reck* you worse than *never* we did Devlin, and the *resen* is this—that you *pretan* to be a Protestant, and *is* not; moreover, you have a Papish wife. You also harbour at your house one Lenny Lennon, one of the Lisnagade Defenders, who fired a pistol at an Orangeman. We *pipsred* him, and gave him a fortnight's warning, and *sin* he is not gone yet, but if he waits our coming he shall pay double for all his iniquities. Given under our hand this —— day of March, being the second year of the destruction of the Pope, the great scarlet wh—re of Babylon, and his infernal imps, the priests."

Or again—

"TO THE INHABITANTS OF ——

"TAKE NOTICE.—If any person will buy any turf from any Papis in glass moss, that we will *sow* no *feavr* to any person, friend or *stronger*, by any means; for, by the living God, if you will go against my word, that *Captin Recker* will *visit* you when you not aware of him.—BOLD ANTY M'CUSKER, DANNAL HOGAN."

"Morthugh M'Linden, we have *speared* you as long as *possable*, but we will see you shortly; we come unexpectedly. *Now* more at present, but *remains* your humble servant, Captain Recker and brave old Humphy, will be there also."

"Farrell, we desire you to clear *aff*, and if you do not, we will fetch *Captin* Slasher *Raker*, God's *cratur*, and Humphy to you, and *Captin* Slasher wh—re. Go to Hell, *Connat*, or *Butney* Bay. And if *any* one harbours you or your goods, by *Hevens* we will pitch the Thatcher and Glasser to them."

In the present day we may be inclined to smile at such illiterate effervescence of intolerance. But to estimate such notices at their proper value, at the time they were circulated, we must recollect that mob-law was then reigning throughout the country; that if the hand of the Government was not paralyzed, which it certainly was not, cunning legislators were playing a deeply-laid scheme, and were pulling the wires which put selfishness and bigotry in motion, and that above and beyond these there resided in the County Armagh a set of magistrates who were themselves either deeply interested in the success of the plot, or who, prompted by motives generally of prejudice but sometimes of fear, refused to move in the matter, and set the ordinary courses of the law in motion.

In fact, the grand policy of the Government then was to resist the Catholic claims, and so exasperate them as to promote a rebellion that would in all probability, destroy all remaining vestiges of Ireland having been once a nation. But, in addition to this, it saw, with much dread of after consequences, the growing feeling of union and liberality which was now springing up between the Catholics upon one side and the respectable and intelligent Protestants and Presbyterians on the other. The triumphant principles of the French Revolution had made monarchs quake, and George saw in that liberality I speak of the basis upon which his Irish authority rested being gradually but surely undermined. Thus the feeling of losing what was the great source of English revenue operated, and with a view to counteract the effects of this union of different creeds, the Government had recourse to its old and successful trick of division, finding fit and willing instruments in the Orange Institution. " Would it be a rash, though a harsh conclusion," asks Plowden, " that from complacency in the outrages of the Armagh persecutions, Government took to their embraces the associated perpetrators of its horrors. Certainly, upon the actual extermination of the Catholic population from part of the country, Government anxiously propagated them (the Orange Lodges) throughout the realm, and promoted the formation of new lodges, with its power and influence."[*]

Having proceeded so far it may be necessary to refer to the outrages which followed in the track of this institution from its start, and in doing so we must necessarily turn our attention a little backwards.

Curran in his speech in the case of Hevey v. Sirr very truthfully said that " when you endeavour to convey an idea of a great number of barbarians, practising a great variety of cruelties upon an incalculable multitude of sufferers, nothing defined

[*] Plowden's History, vol. 1, page 49.

er specific finds its way to the heart, nor is any sentiment excited save that of a general erratic unappropriated commiseration." Following out the suggestion therein contained it might be well to embody in a short quotation all the atrocities which were committed from the starting of the Orange Institution to the close of the year in which it saw its existence. The quotation is a familiar one amongst those who are interested in the details of this period, but is not so generally read as it should be.

On the 28th December, 1795 (a few months after the Diamond massacre), thirty of the magistrates and Grand Jurors of the County Armagh attended upon summons of the Governor, Lord Gosford, to consider the state of the county.

His lordship then said—" Gentlemen, having requested your attendance here to-day it becomes my duty to state the grounds upon which I thought it advisable to propose this meeting, and at the same time to submit to the consideration of this meeting a plan that occurs to me as most likely to check the calamities that have already BROUGHT DISGRACE UPON THIS COUNTRY, and may soon reduce it into deep distress. It is no secret that a persecution, accompanied with all the circumstances of a ferocious cruelty, which have in all ages distinguished that calamity, is now raging in this country. Neither age nor sex nor even acknowledged innocence as to any guilt in the late disturbance is sufficient to excite mercy or afford protection. The whole crime, which the wretched objects of this ruthless persecution are charged with, is a crime indeed easy of proof. It is simply a profession of the Roman Catholic faith. A lawless banditti have constituted themselves judges of this new species of delinquency, and the sentence they have denounced is equally concise and terrible. It is nothing less than a confiscation of all property, and an immediate banishment. It would be extremely painful, and surely unnecessary, to detail all the horrors that attend the execution of so rude and tremendous a proscription. A proscription, and certainly exceeds, in the comparative number of those it consigns to ruin and misery, every example that ancient and modern history can supply; for where have we heard, or in what story of human cruelties have we read of more than half the inhabitants of a populous country deprived at one blow of the means, as well as of the fruits, of their industry, and driven, in the midst of an unclement season, to seek shelter for themselves and families where chance may guide them. This is not an exaggerated picture of the horrid scenes now acting in this country. Yet, surely, it is sufficient to awaken sentiments of indignation and compassion in the coldest bosoms. Those horrors are now acting with impunity. The spirit of impartial justice, without which law is nothing better than an instrument of tyranny, has for a time disappeared in the country, and the supineness of the magistracy of Armagh is become a common topic of conversation in every corner in the kingdom." His lordship then proceeds to say that he is a Protestant, so that his opinions cannot be taken as in any way biased, and that it cannot be said he was actuated by any other feeling than that of justice, and expressed regret that on "the night of the 21st" (possibly the 21st September) there was no civil magistrate present, concluding by proposing a series of resolutions, of which the following was the chief :—

"That it appears to this meeting that the County Armagh is at this moment in a state of uncommon disorder; that the Roman Catholic inhabitants are grievously oppressed by lawless persons unknown, who attack and plunder their houses by night, and threaten them with instant destruction *unless they abandon immediately their lands and habitations.*"

In resolutions referred to were subscribed to by Lord Gosford, Capel Molyneux, William Richard- son, Arthur Jabob M'Cann, Robert Bernard Sparrow, Alexander Thomas Stuart, Obins, Hugh Hamilton, John Ogle, William Clark, Clarles W. Warburton, William Lodge, William Bisset, Thos. Quinn, Owen O'Callaghan, John Maxwell, Joshua M'Geogh, *James Verner,* Richard Allott, *Steward Blacker,* Robert Livingston, William Irwin, Joseph Lawson, and William Blacker.

Having so far given, upon undoubted authority, a sketch of what was the condition of the boasted County of the Diamond at that period, it might be unnecessary to supplement it even in the least, but that there still remain some few incidents which, for completeness and ingenious atrocity, bearing, as they do, directly upon the Orange Institution, deserve a place in the present history.

CHAPTER X.—(CONTINUED.)—JUST A FEW ORANGE OUTRAGES.

OF course it was, and still is, the object of those who find an interest in upholding ascendancy to deny, in the first instance, all the statements contained in Lord Gosford's address, and to say, in the next, that on his examination before the select committee he recalled most of what he had said. Neither of these positions are justified by fact. As to the wholesale denial, Lord Gosford's words are borne out in the fullest manner, not alone by the solemn statements of writers in those days who detail what knew they from personal observation, but by a long record of horrifying details, which would bring conviction to any capable of examining the subject impartially.

Emmet, M'Nevin, and O'Connor, who gave a succinct account of the Armagh persecutions of these times, say* that the county had been desolated by two contending factions, agreeing only in one thing, an opinion that most of the active magistrates in that county treated one party with the most fostering kindness and the other with the most rigorous persecution. It was stated that so marked a partiality exasperated the sufferers, and those who sympathised with their misfortunes. It was urged with indignation that notwithstanding the greatness of the military establishment of Ireland, and its having been able to suppress the Defenders in various counties, it was never able, or was not employed, to suppress these outrages in that county, which drove 7,000 persons from their native dwellings.* The magistrates, who took no steps against the Orangemen, were said to have overstepped the boundaries of the law to pursue and punish the Defenders. The Government seemed to have taken upon themselves those injuries by the Indemnity Act,† and even honoured the violators, and by the Insurrection Act, which enabled the same magistrates, if they chose, under colour of the law, to act anew the same abominations. Nothing, it was contended, could more justly excite the spirit of resistance, and determine men to appeal to arms, than the Insurrection Act; it punished with death the administration of oaths. . . . The power of proclaiming counties, and quieting them by breaking open the cabins of the peasants between sunset and sunrise, by seizing the inmates, and sending them on board

---

* Memoir o the Irish Union, page 14.

* Here we have corroboration of the statement that such a number of Catholics were driven out of Armagh.

† The Indemnity Act was a measure passed by the Irish Parliament ostensibly to protect the magistrates in the execution of their duty, but had the effect of giving to them an unlimited power in the entry of the houses belonging to Catholics, and legalising all the outrages that were committed under the colour of the law. By it no Catholic could recover for any loss or damage done therein.

tenders without the ordinary interposition of a jury, had, it was alleged, irritated beyond endurance the minds of the reflecting and the feelings of the unthinking inhabitants of that province.

In may be remarked that the right of entry in being limited to the hour between "the setting and rising of the sun" in no way gave protection to the peasants. It rather tended to exaggerate their grievances. In the dark hours alone it was that this armed banditti cared to exercise their terrorism and carry on their work of plunder.

An "Observer on the state of Ireland" (whom Dr. Madden extensively quotes) writing in 1797 gives a long list of successive Orange outrages. This pamphlet, published in London and addressed to the people of England, bears, Dr. Madden says, throughout its pages the eternal marks of authentic statements, wholly divested of exaggeration, and the opinion of a contempory, James Hope, of Belfast, was that this pamphlet contained more truth than all the volumes he had seen on these events. This able writer says that shortly after the peace concluded with America, Ministers perceived they had been playing a losing game in Ireland; the Volunteer associations had materially altered the fall of the country; in many cases the Catholics had embodied themselves into Volunteer corps; a friendly intercourse with their Protestant brethren naturally followed; they felt that as Irishmen their interests were co-equal, hatred on account of religion was banished, harmony prevailed, and, if not an union of affection, at least a union of political sentiment appeared to exist amongst the people. Of this the Administration was well informed, and Ministers trembled for what might be the result. To avert reformation they felt it their duty to create division. Various were the means employed to effect this immoral object; among others they reverted to the old diabolical one of fomenting those religious feuds which had so often consumed the vitals and palsied the native energy of the land. He further states that the Administration taught the weak and credulous Protestant and Presbyterian to believe that if the Catholics who had obtained arms during the war were suffered to retain them they would seize on the first opportunity to overrun the Government, and erect Popery on the ruins of the Protestant religion.

Here then is to be found exposed to the full light of day the objects of the Government and the secret influences which set the Armagh Orangemen and the Armagh magistrates at the throats of their Catholic neighbours. For mark what follows— "This, and other acts equally insidious, had the desired effect on the minds of many persons, *particularly in the County Armagh, where the Metropolitan resided.* Here fanaticism reared her standard, and a number of deluded people entered into combination for the purpose of depriving Catholics of their arms by force. For some time the Catholics remained patient and tranquil under their sufferings, although they declared that all their efforts to obtain legal redress had been unavailing, and that the necessities of the case would oblige them to enter into counter-combination to defend their lives and properties against a banditti of plundering ruffians (the Orangemen), who appeared to be countenanced by authority, inasmuch as they were not punished by the criminal laws of the land. These two parties had several encounters, in which victory was various; but many of the Catholic party, wearied out by continual persecution, fled from Armagh to different parts of the kingdom, particularly to the counties of Louth and Meath."

A banditti of plundering ruffians! Surely, the phrase, coming as it does from such a quarter, is sufficient to strike terror into the hearts of those who boast the name of Orangemen, without exactly knowing the reason why! At least, this account of the early days of the early Orangemen is enough to create a doubt in the minds of thinking and honest men. Granted, for one moment even that the affair of the Diamond had never taken place; or having occurred that the Defenders were all to blame; granted, that it was they got up at early morning and wrecked the houses, and outraged the persons of their neighbours; that most of the burning, the pillaging, the robbing began on their side, and not on the side of the Orangemen to whom they were opposed; that the purity of young and innocent peasant girls was desecrated by—not the Orangemen—but the Defenders, and all of that ilk; that it was they who hunted the priest and hanged the peasant, and drove the unfortunate people from their homes—grant all these, and much more, and surely the evidence of this impartial, and apparently English writer, the evidence of Lord Gosford, and the evidence of Lord Fitzwilliam, without taking into account the testimony of a host of others, in denial of this assumption, is enough to cast a doubt over the minds of all men as to what was the origin and what the objects of the early Orangeman? If it is not the child of bigotry and cupidity, at least it was born of illegality. If the doubt once exists, let them then see whether the tiger has changed his skin, or the leopard his spots. To bring about this wholesome state of mind, and assist Orangemen to see themselves, as others see them, let me proceed to show that this mishapen child of intolerance—as it really is—this offspring of robbery, fostered, from its birth, by designing men in high places, became soon the ignoble tool of a Government faction.

The same author I have been quoting says * that, "led by passion and goaded by persecution, they (the Orangemen) proceeded (like the Peep 'o Day Boys, *who first set the example*, and who never were punished) to acts of felony, by taking arms by force, but they soon fell victims to their folly and their imprudence. This, then, whatever interested and designing men assert to the contrary, was the true origin and progress of Defenderism in Ireland. The tumultuous spirit which manifested itself in several counties could have been crushed on its first appearance with much ease, but the Administration looked on with an apathy which many enlightened men declared criminal. Had the Administration then proclaimed an amnesty to all who might be willing to take the oath of allegiance many lives would have been preserved, and those shocking massacres, which have outraged humanity and tarnished the character of the Government, would not have taken place."

Here we have proof direct of Government complicity in the outrages then being enacted. If the Government can be so charged it becomes a question, what are the charges to be preferred against the actual perpetrators; against those who permitted themselves to be the instruments of a dominant faction; who allowed their avarice, or, if you will, their animosity, to overwhelm all those feelings of friendship and good-fellowship that should exist between those of a common country; men whose interests were identical, however their religions might differ ? Orangemen

call it freedom
When themselves are free.

And this feeling, which first took possession of the Orange faction, will be found, when we come to deal with later periods, to have been perpetuated.

No doubt that in this dark period of our history there is still a relieving feature which should not be ignored. It is to be found even in that complicity which Government extended to Orange intolerance. That Orangemen were intolerant even at the outset there can be no question. But that they

are solely responsible for their crimes is an error into which it is common to fall. It is not justifiable under any circumstances for one section of the community to prey upon the other. But, and especially in the early stages of society, it is natural. We, therefore, find in it nothing but the violent and unfeeling exercise o that prerogative, the grinding spirit of the age, comparatively speaking, only partially civilised, expressed by Scott in

He may take who has the power,
And he may keep who can.

Though the charge of intolerance is grave in itself, there is a blacker and still more iniquitous one to be laid at the door of the Government. With power to restrain and paralyse the intolerance in their hands, the Administration not only failed to perform its first duty to the State, but encouraged' and even counselled, this systematic prosecution, in order that their own hands might be strengthened and Ireland left prostrate at the feet of social dissension. With a strong military force at their command, the Executive could at once have put a stop to such outrages. Intolerance is an epidemic, soon spreads, even in the face of passive encouragement. Those who stand to-day aghast at its horrible enactments learn to-morrow to look with complacency upon them, and soon join in the outcry. Though the body of respectable Protestants still kept loof from the Orange movement, the system found many new adherents. The magistracy found in it a road, however bloody a one, to distinction. The magistracy joined it. The military found coercion a sure way to preferment. The military joined it. Government looked on, and chuckled at the success of its daring scheme.

Accordingly we find a long list of atrocities, for the perpetration of which the Orangemen and the military shared the unenviable distinction between them. Let us take a few instances. In the County of Meath it is told that a number of Defenders had assembled, and a part of the army was sent in pursuit of them. On the first appearance of the soldiery they dispersed with that haste which characterize the disbanding of all organised mobs of the present day in the face of trained troops. But a few of the flying Defenders took refuge in a gentleman's house, where, after securing the doors, they defended themselves for some time, till at length a capitulation was proposed and agreed to by all. The terms were that the Defenders were to deliver themselves up to be conveyed o the county jail for trial at the ensuing Assizes. The doors were opened and the military and yeomanry entered. Instead of abiding by their agreement

---

* View of the present state of Ireland.

every Defender in the house was put to death. The narrator says that the body of each man "killed off" was cast from a window into the street, and for this brutal ferocity the participators were not even reprimanded. In fact the exterminating policy so well initiatiated by the Orangemen had now begun, and seeing their brutal ferocity applauded by their masters, it was but in human nature to continue them, the rank and file leaving to their superiors the task of deciding between right and wrong.

In the County Louth a party of those unhappy men were attacked by a squadron of dragoons, who could have easily made the whole of them prisoners. Still, no mercy was shown them, and those who escaped the sword were driven into the river and drowned. At the head of this military corps was a magistrate of the county holding an eminent seat in the Irish Parliament.* The part that the leaders of the Irish Parliament took in inciting the peasantry to rebellion by encouraging and fostering Orangeism is proven by the various addresses delivered during the recesses of 1795 and 1796, when the resident gentry returned to their seats in several districts of the country. Those who seek further proof upon this point may consult the journals of the day, or find details in the histories of Plowden, Madden, and Gordon.

In Cavan, near the village of Ballnaaugh, a number of troops were ordered out to attack a body of Defenders. On the approach of the military they dispersed. Many of them sought shelter in the village, hiding themselves beneath beds, &c., and the like. From this it is evident that their resistance was not of the most stubborn character, for persecuted as they were that condition had not yet arrive at when they had no choice but to stand at bay. The making of them prisoners would not satiate the fury of this brutal soldiery, or enable them to obey the orders of their commanders, and accordingly we find recorded one of the most brutal scenes that took place during the few years that preceded the insurrection. The magistrates and officers commanding the party of soldiers ordered them to surround the village and set it on fire. This order was obeyed. With one single exception every house in the village of Ballanaugh was burned, and with the guilty many innocent people perished in the flames. What a scene of terror and wild dismay! The Furies would have stood aghast, and bloody Murder and hungry Rapine might have shed a

pitying tear. Mothers, now made widows, running with babes at their breast from threatening death that knew no pity, hoping to find one relenting heart amid a gang of military cut-throats; finding none, and babe and mother perishing together at the hands of those to whom she rushed for succour, and beneath the fiendish jibes and scoffs of organised murderers. Surely Hell itself let loose could not create a scene of such mad confusion as did those brutal soldiery, indulging in slaughter for slaughter sake.

No wonder the writer I have been quoting—after saying that it was unnecessary to mention the barbarities and scenes of horror which took place in Connaught, says :—" The last Parliament, by an Act which disgraced it, and betrayed the rights of its constituents, gave them more strongly to the world than any detailed Act can possibly do. So flagitious, illegal, and unconstitutional was the conduct o the magistracy, that the Administration (yes, the Administration of Ireland) was afraid to let the atrocities which had been committed meet the public eye; and Ministers procured a Bill of indemnity to be passed in Parliament to screen from punishment those officers of the peace, who, at the hour of midnight, tore men from the arms of their families, merely on the suspicion of their being seditious, and dragged them on board loathsome prisonships, transporting them to destructive climates, without examination, without trial, unheard, unpleaded! And for those services and gallant exploits, the man who figured foremost in the scene have been promoted to situations of the first importance in the nation."*

Now, if we recall the eight rule of the Boyne Society, "commonly called Orangemen," as published in the foregoing chapter, we will find that it bound all members by virtue of their oaths "to be active in preventing all others that may have an intention to do a riotous act." The second general declaration of the same society specified all Papists to be disloyal, and therefore riotous. To drag all Papists from their homes, and to either murder or transport them, must have been, as I before indicated, the meaning, and certainly the result of the Orange Society. We have here a striking connection established between the Orangemen and the deeds alluded to by "Observer," and in reference to which he uses such significant phrases as "suspicion of their being seditions," "without examination, without trial, unheard and unpleaded." Here surely is the trail of the serpent !

* Ibid.

* Lord Carhampton.

Notwithstanding the impossibility that existed necessarily in recording one-tenth of the outrages committed by the early Orangemen during the first twelve months of their existence, we have still an abundant store of atrocities, the most horrible, bearing in all instances the impression of truth, and vouched for by some one or other respectable author of those days. Of course a few more can only be selected.

"In January, 1796, a party of Orangemen, headed by Wm. Trimble, came to the house of Mr. Daniel Corrigan, a very respectable citizen in the County of Armagh, parish of Kilmore, and, having before robbed him of his arms, which being registered, he was by law entitled to retain, they demanded a pistol he had subsequently purchased to protect him as he travelled round the country (he being a dealer in cattle), which having obtained, they retired, promising his family protection; but returned in twenty minutes, and forcing the door, Trimble murdered Mr. Corrigan, by lodging seven balls in his body from a blunder-buss, and then destroyed the house and furniture. Trimble was afterwards apprehended, tried, found guilty, and ordered by the judge for execution in forty-eight hours; but through a *certain* influence he was respited. He continued in jail till the ensuing Assizes, when he was again arraigned for having murdered Mr. Arthur M'Cann, as also *for several robberies*; but his trial was put off, and in a few days he was ordered for transportation, when he was only sent to Cork, from whence he was suffered to go on board the fleet like a good and loyal subject."

If I linger longer over this chapter than has hitherto been my custom, I can assure my readers that it is through no desire to pander to that depraved taste which thirsts after everything atrocious. If it is hard to convince Orangemen of the errors of their way even in the present, and if they fail to see in the light of crimes their deeds of but a few months or a few years past, how much more difficult will it be to bring home to their minds the historical fact that the outset of their career is one long record of blood and plunder. A few more instances may, therefore, be necessary, promising, at the same time, to pass over those transactions which were not peculiarly marked for their unnatural atrocity.

Madden (quoting from "An Observer") tells us *that the house of one Bernard Crossan, who in those days resided in the parish of Mullanabrack,

was attacked by Orangemen in consequence of his being a *reputed* Catholic. The reader will recollect that upon the authority of Plowden, Madden, Hay, and "Observer" (already quoted), that these founders of the institution did not confine their attention to Catholics alone. A ruffian, whether to gratify his malice or satisfy his avarice, had but to suggest that his neighbour was reputed a Catholic, that his wife was a Catholic, or of Catholic parents, or that he was accustomed to give shelter to the proscribed of that religion, and forthwith the terrible machinery of the new institution was at once set in motion, the envied or the hated one was subjected to the cruellest persecution, made to quit the country, and chose the customary alternative of "hell or Connaught." There is something deeply significant in the fact that most of those suspected ones were numbered amongst the most wealthy and well-to-do farmers of the county.

When Crossan's house was attacked his son prevented the Orangemen from gaining an entrance by the front door. Their plan was well laid, however, and while defending the premises against the marauders in front, their companions effected an entrance in the back. Mr. Crossan was shot down, as was also his son, and his daughter, after being shamefully used, was then similarly despatched. This was done by professed Orangemen, amongst whom were numbered, no doubt, many of the heroes of the "Diamond."

Upon the same pretence the house of Hugh M'Fay, in the parish of Seagoe, was broken into by a party of armed Orangemen. Mr. M'Fay was wounded by a gun shot, his wife was barbarously outraged, and what furniture was incapable of being removed was totally destroyed.

The same author also assures us that information having been lodged against a few individuals living in the village of Kilrea (County Derry), a party of military were ordered to apprehend them. The men avoided arrest, and about three o'clock in the morning a "reverend" magistrate, accompanied by a clergyman of the same description, and by the commanding officer of the party, ordered the soldiers to set fire to the houses of the accused. The men obeyed, and all was consumed. There were four houses which could not be burned without endangering the whole of the village. They, therefore, gutted them, and, carrying out the moveable furniture, they burned them in the street. The wife of one of the accused men had been delivered of a child the preceding evening.

* First series, page 119.

This woman, in that weak and helpless state which called for the sympathy of all that are mortal, was carried out into the street, and, with her new-born infant, was cast into the snow, while her blanket and wearing apparel were consigned to the flames. Our authority adds that none of those savage violators of the law and humanity were brought to justice; but that, on the contrary, the "reverend" magistrate was afterwards promoted to a larger benefice.

In the month of May, 1779,* a party of Essex Fencibles, accompanied by the *Enniskillen Yeomen Infantry,* commanded by their first lieutenant, marched to the house of a Mr. Potter, a very respectable farmer, who lived within five miles of Enniskillen. On their arrival they demanded Mr. Potter, saying that they were ordered to arrest him, as he was a United Irishman. His wife, with much firmness, replied "that to be a United Irishman was an honour, and not a disgrace," adding her husband had gone from home on business the preceding day, and had not returned. They answered her that if he did not surrender himself in three hours they would burn his house. Mrs. Potter answered that she did not exactly know where he then was, but that if she did know she believed it would be impossible to have him home in so short a time. True to their promise, they set fire to the house, which, it is said, was a very neat one, and only five years built. The servants brought out some beds and other valuables in the hope of preserving them, but those destroyers dashed all into the flames. The house and property, to the amount of £600, were consumed by the flames, and Mrs. Potter, with seven children, one of whom was scarce a month old, were turned out homeless into the fields in the hour of midnight.

Few who have read the history of those sad times but are familiar with the names of the Ancient Britons, a fencible regiment commanded by Sir Watkins William Wynne, and including in their ranks a large number of Orangemen.† The first atrocity that we have upon record in which these ferocious men were implicated occurred in the month of June, 1797. They were ordered to search for arms the house of a Mr. Rice, an innkeeper in the village of Coolavil, in the County Armagh. After making a very diligent search none could be found. Some country people were drinking in the house, and spoke in their native tongue, a matter which was in no way surprising in

* Ibid.
† Vide Plowden's History, from 1801 to 1810, page 91.

the County Armagh, and especially in those days immediately following a period during which the simplest elements of an education was not left within the reach of the Catholic inhabitants. If, therefore, this circumstance were evidence of guilt at all, which it is hard to see, it was evidence of the guilt of successive persecuting administrations. But the Antient Britons were more expert at using the sword upon an unarmed people, than at solving the simplest propositions in logic. They damned their *eternal Irish souls,* swore they were speaking treason, and instantly fell upon them with the most brutal ferocity, maiming several of them desperately. Miss Rice, the daughter of the Innkeeper, was wounded almost to death, while her father "after receiving many cuts from the sabres of those assassins," escaped with difficulty.

In the same month a similar outrage was perpetrated in Newtownards, in the County Down. In an inn kept by a Mr. M'Cormick in that town, some persons, merely casual visitors, who dropped in to refresh themselves, were, it was alleged, overheard uttering sentiments of a seditious character. Having regard to what is seen to have taken place in the County Armagh, where the use of the Irish language was construed into treason, it is not difficult to determine that the grounds of accusation here were probably of the most slender character. M'Cormick was called upon to give an explanation. He denied having any knowledge of them (a statement which was surrounded with all appearances of probability), observing that many persons might enter his house, of whom he knew nothing, and for whom he could not be held responsible. This explanation would not suffice, for the administration of impartial justice would not answer the ends which the Administration and its minions had in view, and accordingly he was taken into custody, and the *next day* his house and an extensive property were reduced to ashes. This was not the only instance of demolition upon *suspicion.* The house of Dr. Jackson, in the same town, was taken down upon the same grounds and "many other houses in the same town and barony were destroyed, or otherwise demolished, by English Fencibles on similar pretexts."

On the 22nd June Mr. Joseph Clotney, Ballynahinch, was committed to the military barracks of Belfast, and his house, furniture and books, worth £3,000, destroyed; as was also the valuable house of Mr. Armstrong, of the same place.

In the month of April a detachment of the Essex

Fencibles quartered at Enniskillen were ordered, under the command of a captain and adjutant, accompanied by the *First Fermanagh Yeomanry*, into an adjoining county *to search for arms*. About two o'clock in the morning they arrived at the house of one named Durnian, a farmer, which without any intimation whatever they broke open, and on entering it, one of the fencibles fired his musket through the roof of the house. An officer instantly discharged his pistol into a bed where two young men were lying and wounded them both. One of them, the only child of Durinan, rose with great difficulty, and on making this effort, faint with the loss of blood, one of the party stabbed him through the bowels. The distracted mother ran to support him, but in a few moments she sank upon the floor, covered with the blood which issued from the side of her unfortunate son. By this time the young man had got upon his knees to implore mercy, declaring most solemnly that he had not been guilty of any crime, when a fencible deliberately knelt down, levelled his musket at him, and was just going to fire when a sergeant of yoemanry rushed in, seized him, and prevented his committing the horrid deed. "There were persons present who smiled at the humanity of the sergeant."

In Newry, information had been lodged that a certain house in that town contained concealed arms. A party of the Ancient Britons repaired to the house, but not finding the object of their search, they set it on fire. The peasantry of the neighbourhood came running from all sides to extinguish the flames believing the fire to be accidental, a fact which is accounted for by its having been the first military one in that district. On coming up they were attacked upon all sides and cut down by the fencibles. Thirty were killed, a woman and two children being included amongst the number. An old man of 70 years, it is related, seeing the dreadful slaughter of his neighbours and friends fled for safety to some adjacent rocks. He was pursued and, though on his knees imploring mercy, a brutal Welshman cut off his head at one blow.

"I have stated," says "an observer," "incontrovertable truths. Months would be insufficient to enumerate all the acts of wonton cruelty which were inflicted on the inhabitants of Ireland from the 1st April to the 24th July, 1797."

That the incidents stated in the last paragraph but one are founded upon fact, may be seen when placed side by side with the following, which I take from Mr. Plowden's authentic history of those times[*] and which will be read with interest:— "In May, 1779, a corporal's guard had been ordered out in the afternoon to search the house of one Hedge at Ballyholan, who was a Presbyterian; for arms; none were found. It happened, however, on this, as on many such occasions that the searchers made free with articles of dress or furniture, as their fancies suggested. Here the search ended in the appropriation of a silk handkerchief, which one of the military purloined. This produced some observation and sarcasm from several of the neighbouring peasants, whom curiosity had brought round Hedge's dwelling during the search. There lived close by one Brennan, a weak, half-witted man, who was a private in the Newry Yeomanry. He ran instantly to town, and gave out, that the party was surrounded, and perhaps cut to pieces. Immediately the trumpet and bugle sounded and the Ancient Britons, some of the Dublin Militia, UNDER CAPTAIN GIFFARD and some of the Newry Yeomanry turned out, and hastened towards Ballyholan, without order, or any special command. For the space of a mile or two the face of the country was covered with military moving in disorder, and acting without any other fixed plan than that of a general massacre and extermination. The Ancient Britons hewed down all the countrymen in coloured clothes they met or overtook; they took no prisoners. The militia fired at some fugitives, but made several prisoners, amounting in the whole to about 26. The Yeoman infantry principally showed their prowess by firing into the thatch of the cabins, and setting fire to them. Upon the first appearance of the military the most active of the peasantry made their escape.

"A party of Ancient Britons came up to a cluster of houses which they set fire to. They had been all abandoned except one which contained an old infirm man, that was bedridden, attended by his

<hr>

[*] Ibid, page 91 and 92. "In this same year the seeds of Orangeism were profusely sown in and about Newry, and promised an early and plentiful harvest. The Ancient Britons, who were mostly Orangemen, and Mr. Giffard, the great apostle of Orangeism, then a captain in the Dublin City Militia, were quartered there; and by far the greater part of the Newry cavalry and infantry Yoemen were also Orangemen. No wonder then that this spot was chosen for a renewal of some of the Armagh scenes of extermination, one of which is submitted to the reader, as it has been narrated to the author, by a gentleman of respectability who, being out with his corps on that day, saw and heard the greatest part himself, and recorded the rest from the confession of the principal actor in that scene, which took place at a distance." The author adds in a footnote that this scene is selected from amongst others, not merely from his possessions of the most undeniable evidence respecting it, as he had evidence of many others which he suppressed, but because it had always been considered as contributing much to the rebellion which took place in the next year.

daughter. She threw herself upon her knees, and, after several refusals, at last obtained leave from the commanding officer to permit her father to be carried out of the house He had scarcely been removed one minute before the roof fell in After the bugle had sounded to rally, and the troops were drawn up in a line in Mr. Hanna's park, one of the Ancient Britons rode up to Sir Watkins William Wynne, their commander, and said the rebels were in the park and the wood adjoining, when they received orders from the commander to spare no one They immediately dispersed. Three of them, perceiving something moving in a thicket, successively fired into it; and one of them shot an unfortunate lad, of about ten years of age, through the left eye. He had been attending some cows on a road, but on seeing the military he had endeavoured to conceal himself from their fury in a thicket. He was shown to Sir Watkins William Wynne by an officer, whose humanity was shocked, and the commander, observing that he was sorry for the mistake, ordered one of his men to take him up behind him and convey him to the hospital.* Another lad, of about fourteen years of age, had been most inhumanly butchered, his head split in twain, and nearly severed from his body. His father and uncle having heard of his misfortune, went after his corpse, and were taken prisoners by the militiamen under Captain Giffard. One man, a revenue-officer, at the risk of his life went up to a gentleman of the Yeoman cavalry, to whom he was known, and entreated him to return to the party, and inform them, that some of Ancient Britons after having killed the lad, had fired into his (the revenue-officer's) house at his wife, who was far gone with child, and he was afraid that he should be murdered himself. He entreated to have the boy brought down to the road, through which the military were to pass, in order, that the commanding officer should see him, and be thereby induced to release the father and uncle. Captain Giffard expressed high offence at the boy's corpse having been brought into sight, and immediately took the

two men, who had brought it to the road, into custody Sir Witkins William Wynne, when he was informed of the circumstance, ordered the father and uncle to be released Two Ancient Britons, one of them by name Ned Allen, had strayed about a mile from from the main body to a farm house of Mr. Robert Maitland Near the gate stood a boy named Ryan, about six years of age, whom they ordered to open it; the child said he would if they would not hurt him. Before he could open it, one of them struck at the child with his sabre over the gate, and broke his arm They still insisted upon his opening it, which the child did with his other hand, and they rode through and cut up the boy with their sabres, and one of them made his horse (though with much difficulty) trample upon him They entered their house, and having taken the key of the cellar, sat down to drink, in the meantime three of the Dublin City Militia came up to the house, and joined them in drinking. The *Ancient Britons gave Orange toasts.* The militiamen gave Irish toasts. They quarrelled and fought, one of the militiamen was killed, and the other two were severely wounded with the sabres of the Ancient Britons. The two Ancient Britons were afterwards tried for murder, and were *instantly acquitted.* About thirty houses were burned, and eleven persons were killed. This closed this unsought day of blood."

In a note to this circumstantial narrative Mr. Plowden says —"Such was the vindictive animosity which the people bore to the corps of Ancient Britons, that after the insurrection had, partly by their means, been made to explode, as Lord Castlereagh boasted, they never came into contact with the rebels without being reminded of *Ballyholan.*

These are but a few of the outrages committed by the early Orangemen.

---

* In a note Mr Plowden adds that the lad's name was Fagan, and that at the time he wrote he was still living in Newry.

CHAPTER XI—A HAPPY LEAGUE, THE CAMDEN ADMINISTRATION—THE MAGISTRATES AND THE ORANGEMEN.

BEFORE we quit this subject for the events more stormy and more interesting, we have still further to pay the penalty so frequently demanded by a due investigation of the truth. We may now take a passing glance over the broad and once fertile

fields of Armagh. There, where there were once comfortable homesteads, where groups of evening gossips might still have assembled to tell of other times and other days, and listened with rural simplicity to the tales of the wandering beggar and the "broken soldier," nought now was to be seen but misery and desolation. Many districts of the county were covered with the blackened ruins of humble cabins that had, at least, afforded shelter to a people whose best riches were "ignorance of wealth." Thousands were wandering homeless and starving, not indeed in the County Armagh, for to be there was death, but in the adjoining counties and provinces, while those whose age prevented them enduring the hardships of the time had, fortunately for them, gone over to the majority, and were saved the fearful trials of the two subsequent years.

It was at the Lent Assizes of the year 1796 that the Sheriff-Governor and Grand Jury of the County Armagh, bethinking them that it would be well to do away with the impressions produced by these horrible events some, and only some of which are recorded in the last chapter, published an address and resolutions. Mr. Plowden says that they were calculated to do away with the impressions generally received by the public upon the ferocious outrages of those exterminators, the Orangemen; but their annunciation of impartial justice, and a resolution to punish offenders of every denomination was rather unreasonable when there remained no longer any of one denomination to commit outrages upon, or to retaliate injuries. Mr. Mitchell, in his history, says that Plowden (who was as much opposed to Defenderism as to Orangeism) "might have added that many of the gentlemen composing that Grand Jury had themselves encouraged and participated in the extermination of the Catholics. But they knew very well that no coercive law of that Parliament was at all intended to be enforced against Orangemen; that the unlawful oaths, 'forbidden under the pain of death,' did not mean to exclude the 'purple oath' of Orangemen to exterminate Catholics, but only the United Irish oath to encourage brotherly union and seek an impartial representation of all the people of Ireland. In fact, no Orangeman was ever prosecuted, nor was any punishment ever inflicted on the exterminators of Armagh Catholics."

The address and resolutions of the High-Sheriff, Governor, and Grand Jury of Armagh above referred to is an important and, indeed, an interesting record, and I therefore think it advisable to transfer it into these pages. It ran as follows:—

"To his Excellency John Jeffreys, Earl Camden, Lord Lieutenant-General and General Governor of Ireland, &c., &c.

"The unanimous Address of the Sheriff, Governor, Grand Jury, and Magistracy, of the County of Armagh, assembled at Lent Assizes, 1796.

"Deeply impressed with the attention which your Excellency has been pleased to show to this county, and sensible of the readiness with which military aid has been afforded, whenever it has been required on occasion of the disturbance that in some places have unfortunately prevailed, we return your Excellency our warmest acknowledgments, and beg leave to express the firmest confidence in the wisdom and energy of your Excellency's Government.

"We have seen with the deepest regret the outrages which, for some time past, have disturbed the peace and interrupted the industry of this prosperous county. And as the Grand Jury of the county have always discharged their duty with that vigorous and impartial justice which is calculated to protect the person and the property of all its inhabitants of every description, so we shall continue to use our utmost exertions to punish offenders of every denomination.

We trust that the peace of the county will, in consequence of the proceedings at this Assizes, be restored universally; but should that unfortunately not be the case we beg leave to assure your Excellency that we must feel it to be our duty and the duty of all the other magistrates of the county to resort to immediate proceedings under the law of the present session of Parliament, however much we must lament the unusual rigor which it will impose upon offenders, and however much we must deplore the burthens as well as the disgrace which such measures must necessarily impose upon the county.

"John Ogle, Sheriff
"Gosford, Governor.
"Caufield, Foreman, for self and fellow-jurors."

Resolved—That the thanks of the Grand Jury be given to our High Sheriff for the care he has taken in making returns of the very enlightened and dispassionate juries that have attended, and for his proper conduct throughout these Assizes.

Resolved—That the thanks of the Grand Jury be given to the Right Hon. the Attorney-General for the very able speech in which he addressed the county, for the candour and unwearied exertions with which he has conducted the prosecutions of this Assizes, and for his readiness in communicating with the Grand Jury on every occasion when applied to.

It will, of course, be noticed that the governor of the county who subscribed to the above was Lord Gosford, who had previously been so outspoken regarding the "banditti of Orangemen.', The fact of his name being attached to such a covert document, in which there is no mention made of the real nature of the outrages, must, having regard to the utterance of the previous December, be taken as evidence of the overwhelming influence of the Magisterial Ascendancy Party of Armagh than as in any way derogatory to his character for strict impartiality. In point of fact, this was but a part played by the magistrates of the county to cloak their iniquity, and partiality in the guise of justice. This excuse the Executive were but too willing to accept, as will be seen from the following answer which his Excellency was pleased to return to the above address —

"I return my most sincere thanks to the Sheriff, Governor, and Grand Jury and Magistrates of the County Armagh for the address which has been presented to me.

"It gives me the greatest satisfaction to observe the anxious solicitude that has appeared during the course of the last Assizes, amongst all descriptions of persons, to extinguish the spirit of outrage which has existed within your county for some time. I lament that those exertions have not hitherto proved totally successful, but I look forward with confidence to the expectation that a continuation of that temper and unanimity which have appeared at the late assizes may render it unnecessary to recur to those powers that have been given by the wisdom and energy of Parliament, which powers, I trust, will be called for with caution, but when granted will be used with effect."

The additional powers of which the Viceroy spoke were, of course, the Insurrection and Indemnity Acts.

The report of the Secret Committee of the Commons shortly afterwards informs us "that in the summer of 1796 the outrages committed by a banditti, calling themselves Defenders, in the Counties of Roscommon, Leitrim, Meath, Westmeath, and Kildare, together with a *religious feud* prevailing in the County Armagh, induced the Legislature to pass a temporary Act of Parliament, generally called the Insurrection Act, by which the Lord Lieutenant and counsel were enabled, upon the requisition of seven magistrates of any county, assembled at a sessions of the peace, to proclaim the whole, or any part thereof, to be in a state of disturbance." There is here

mention of Defenderism which, no doubt, was responsible for many, and even wanton, outrages, for which alone there was the excuse of persecution driving people to despair; while the extirpation of a whole people from one county was mildly set down as "a religious feud," arising between one sect and another, for no other reason than on account of their religion.

Sir Richard Musgrave affords further corroboration of the league between the magistrates and the Orangemen He says[*]—"Lord Carhampton, finding that the laws were silent and inoperative in the counties which he visited, and that they did not afford protection to the loyal and peaceable subjects, who, in most places, were obliged to fly from their habitations, resolved to restore them to their usual energy by the following salutary system of severity —In each county he assembled the most respectable gentlemen and landholders in it, and having, in concert with them, examined the charges against the leaders of this banditti (the defenders), who were in prison, but defied justice, he, with the concurrence of these gentlemen, sent the most nefarious of them on board a tender, stationed at Sligo, to serve in the King's troops." Alluding to this, Mr. Mitchell says in his history[†]—

"There is no doubt that great numbers of people were obliged to fly from their habitations; but then those were the very people whom Lord Carhampton and the magistrates called banditti, and sent to the tender as nefarious. Such is, however, a specimen of the history of those times, as told upon Orange authority."

But this is not the only proof of flagrant partiality on the part of Camden Administration. The *Dublin Evening Post* of the 24th September, 1796, contained the following . — "The most severe stroke made against the character and conduct of the Viceroy, as a moral man, and first magistrate of a free people, who 'ought not to hold the sword in vain,' nor to exercise it partially has been in *Faulkner's Journal* of this day ‡ That hireling print is undeniably in the pay of his lordship's Administration, and what Administration permits it is supposed to prompt or patronize. In that print the blind fury of the banditti which usurps and disgraces the name of Orange in the North is applauded, *and all their bloody excesses justified*

---

[*] History of the different rebellions—page 145.
[†] Cap. xxix, page 224
[‡] Faulkner's Jour l is acknowledged to have been the Government organ, and it was loud in praise of the deeds of the Armagh Orangemen

Murder in all its horrid forms, assassinations in cold blood, the mutilation of members without respect to age or sex, the firing of whole hamlets, so that when the inhabitants have been looked after nothing but their ashes were to be found; the atrocious excursions of furious hordes, armed with sword, fire, and baggot, to exterminate the people for presuming to obey the divine command, written by the finger of God Himself, ' Honour thy father and thy mother,' and walking in the religion which seemed good in their eyes; there are the flagitious enormities which attract the mercenary applause of *Faulkner's Journal*, the literary proof of the Camden administration."

The is no public record of those times extant which affords such full and reliable information of the duplicity of the Camden Government, as the debates which took place in the Commons early in 1796 upon the introduction of the Insurrection and Indemnity Acts before alluded to, and certain resolutions calling for their enactment. Plowden gives his opinion upon it in the following words (His Review, 562) —" This debate is in fact the chief historical source of information for the true nature of the Armagh prosecution. Suppression of the truth on the one hand, the fear of publishing it on the other, confusion, exaggeration, and violence on all sides have left little else upon the subject that can be credited." I will, therefore, venture to place it before my readers seeing that this important record is now hidden away in rare and expensive volumes utterly beyond the reach of those who are mainly interested in it. I will preface it by saying it should be remembered that these extraordinary powers, which these two Acts sought for, had long been in full operation in the hands of both the military commanders and the magistracy Lord Carhampton in Connaught had practically anticipated the powers of the Act by inaugurating a system of martial law wherever he went, and by seizing and sending beyond the seas hundreds whom, without trial, he considered disaffected. For these acts he received the thanks of the Attorney-General, and obtained high favour with the Camden Administration, no doubt, for his having so loyally fulfilled his mission. In the North we have also seen that previous to 1796, the Orange magistrates had acted in a similar manner as Lord Gosford's address proves We may, therefore, take it that Mr. Plowden's conclusion was a reasonable one, that the Insurrection and Indemnity Acts (the latter meant to have a retrospective action), were intended to secure what they

practically did secure; that the chief object of one was to incite insurrection rather than prevent it, and that of the other to place in the hands of the Orange magistracy an effective instrument with which, without fear of consequences, they could the more easily accomplish the diabolical intents of the Government. With the Beresford party at the head of affairs, and a secret understanding between Pitt and his willing henchman to resist Catholic claims, there was nothing too atrocious providing it furthered the ends of this ambitious minister, whose great aim in life was to secure a Union at all hazards.

From the records of Parliament we find[*] that on the 20th of February, 1796, the Attorney General—having previously obtained leave to bring in a Bill for indemnifying such magistrates and others who might have since the 1st January, 1795, exceeded the *ordinary forms and rules of law* for the preservation of the public peace and suppression of insurrection prevailing in some parts of this kingdom—proposed four resolutions to the House, with an elaborate detail of the outrages of the offenders In doing so, he said that the country had been for a series of years disturbed in various parts of it. He did not then enter into the causes of those disturbances, but he should take them up at the period of 1790, when those disturbances chiefly raged in the County Meath. The Defenders' object, then, was to plunder the peaceable inhabitants of their firearms; they associated together, and bound themselves by the solemn tie of an oath. The Defenders, it had since appeared, had their committee men and their captains, whom they were bound to obey, and their object was to overthrow the established order of Government. Seditious emissaries dispersed themselves amongst the people; in one place telling the labouring man that his wages would be raised, and in another working upon their feelings, and enticing them to acts of outrage and of violence. To repress these disturbances, the efforts of the Government were exerted in 1790, '91, and '92, and the consequence was that a great number were brought to justice, and several were transported; notwithstanding these examples the disturbances continued, and proceeded from east to west, and in three counties in Connaught these banditti, in open day, made an attack upon the King's forces; the army always routed them, and in one engagement forty or fifty of these miscreants fell, there were prosecutions in

---

[*] 16 Parliamentary Debates, page 102.

J

the province; that province then was in a state of tranquility (thanks to Lord Carhampton, through whose exertions humanity, and good conduct, quiet was restored). Notwithstanding these examples, disturbances continued in other parts of the kingdom. These wretches associated together by night for the purpose of plunder, murder, and devestation. To prevent witnesses appearing against them on trial they had adopted a system of assassination. The Attorney-General held instanced a transaction said to have taken place about ten days previous, near Lutrelstown, where persons named M'Cormacks, who were to prosecute Defenders on the next day at Kilmainham Quarter Sessions, were inhumanly murdered. Continuing, he said another part of their system was to put witnesses to death after trial, instancing a case where a witness who had prosecuted Defenders at the Assizes of Dundalk, had been murdered after the trial. He instanced many acts of atrocity committed in the County Longford, particularly in the case of Mr. Harman, one of the representatives of the county, and in the counties Westmeath, Cavan, and Meath. Under these circumstances he said some new scheme was necessary to put an end to such enormities His first object was to prevent these risings in future, and in order to do this it was proper to enable Government, on the petition of gentlemen resident in the county where any rising should be, to send a [force to that county, sufficient to quell such rising; another, was, to enable magistrates at sessions to take up at unseasonable hours all persons who could not give a satisfactory account of themselves, and, if they could not find bail at the Assizes, the justices might send them to serve on board the fleet; another was to enable magistrates to search houses, and if the persons were not at home, they might be brought to the Quarter Sessions, and if they could not give a satisfactory account of the cause of their absence from home, they were to be dealt with as persons found abroad at unreasonable hours; but previous to that proclamation should be made, and fair notice given, so that no person should have any excuse to plead; another object was to enable magistrates to search houses for arms and ammunition. It might be spread abroad by evil and disaffected men, that it was the design of the Government to disarm the people; but there was no such design; it was only to take away arms from improper persons. But he said he should introduce a clause in the Gunpowder

Bill to make all persons, great and small, register their fire-arms. He should propose to make the administration *of such oaths as bound the parties to any treasonable purpose* a capital offence. There was another measure, which was that in case of a witness being murdered his written testimony should be competent to go as evidence before a jury. The Attorney-General then read the resolutions, which he afterwards separately proposed, as follows:—

1. "Resolved,—That the spirit of conspiracy and outrage which has appeared in certain parts of this kingdom, and has shown itself in various attempts to assassinate magistrates, to murder witnesses, to plunder houses, and to sieze by the force of arms his Majesty's peaceable subjects, requires that more effectual powers should be given to the magistracy."

2 "Resolved,—That in such parts of this kingdom as the said spirit has shown itself, or to which there may be cause to apprehend its being extended, it will be necessary that the magistracy should have enlarged powers of searching for arms, ammunition, and weapons of offence, and of seizing and securing the same, for the preservation of the peace and the safety of the lives and properties of his Majesty's peaceable and loyal subjects."

3 "Resolved—That from the many attacks which have been made on the houses of individuals by large bodies of armed insurgents, for the purpose of taking money and arms by force, and murdering those who had the spirit to enforce the laws or give information against offenders, it will be necessary that the magistracy should have enlarged powers to prevent such bodies hereafter from assembling or meeting either to plan or execute such horrid purposes.

"4. Resolved—That it will be necessary to give the magistracy further powers with respect to vagabonds, idle and disorderly persons, and to persons liable to be deemed so, or who have no lawful trade, or any honest means to obtain a livelihood.'

A spirit of impartiality could not ignore the importance of these resolutions at such a time. It may be said that they were to some extent rendered necessary to a Government whose first instincts must ever be those of self-preservation. Still, though it must be admitted that affairs at this period in Ireland were assuming a threatening aspect, they were nothing but the necessary outcome of persecution. It was a condition which the Government had desired for years. And even if the Administration sought an effectual remedy they had it in the ordinary powers of the law which were allowed to remain inactive or used only by a prejudiced and malignant magistracy to aggravate the feelings of a people already driven to despair. But the complaint, as will be seen from the debate which follows, and from the incidents I have yet to relate, was not to the resolutions themselves but to the unfair manner in which the Acts based upon them should be administered. It may be interesting to state that the only person in the House who was found to oppose those resolutions was the ill-fated Lord Edward Fitzgerald, and of this opposition Plowden remarks —" His unfortunate end may affix a retrospective import to his conduct, perhaps, before he harboured the dreadful designs which tarnished the latter period of his life.

Lord Edward Fitzgerald said—" Sir, I shall oppose this resolution" [they were proposed separately] " because I think that this resolution will not prevent the crimes of which the right hon. gentleman complains. The disturbances of the country, sir, are not to be remedied by any coercive measures, however strong; such measures will tend rather to *exasperate* than to *remove* the evil Nothing, sir, can effect this and restore tranquility to the country but a serious and candid endeavour of Government, and of this House, to redress the grievances of the people. Redress those, and the people will return to their allegiance and their duty; suffer them to continue, and neither your resolutions nor your Bill will have any effect. I shall, therefore, sir, oppose not only this resolution, but all the resolutions which the right hon. gentleman has read to you except, perhaps, one—that which goes to constitute the written testimony of a dying witness good evidence This, I think, is fair, and likely to facilitate the course of justice, without violently infringing, as all the other resolutions seem to do, the liberty of the subject."

Mr. Vandaleur perfectly agreed with the Attorney General as to the necessity of adopting some strong measures at that juncture With respect to the last of the resolutions—that which related to the investing of the magistracy with new powers—he should not now give any opinion. Of the others he heartily approved, though he could not help expressing a wish that they had taken some notice of the wanton and barbarous outrages which had been committed by the Peep o' Day Boys (or Orangemen), as well as those of which the Defenders had been guilty.

On the 21st, when the Attorney-General's four resolutions were read,

Mr. Grattan rose and said that he had heard the right hon. gentleman's statement, and did not suppose it to be inflamed. But he must observe at the same time that it was partial He did, indeed, expatiate very fully and justly on the offences of the Defenders, but with respect to another description of insurgents, whose barbarities had excited general abhorrence, he had observed a complete silence ; that he had proceeded to enumerate the counties that were afflicted by disturbances, and *he had omitted Armagh.* Of that county neither had he comprehended the outrages in his general description, nor in his particular enumeration. Of those outrages he (Mr. Grattan) had received the most dreadful accounts; that the object of the Orangemen was the *extermination* of all the Catholics. It was a persecution conceived in the bitterness of bigotry, carried on with the most ferocious barbarity, by a banditti, who being of the religion of the State, had committed with the greatest audacity and confidence, the most horrid murders, and had proceeded in robbery and murder to extermination; that they had repealed by their own authority all the laws lately passed in favour of the Catholics, and established in the place of those laws the inquisition of a mob resembling Lord George Gordon's fanatics, equalling them in outrage, and surpassing them far in perseverance and success. Their modes of outrage were as numerous as they were atrocious; they sometimes forced by terror the masters of families to dismiss their Catholic servants; they sometimes forced landlords by terror to dismiss their Catholic tenantry; they seized as deserters numbers of Catholic weavers, sent them to the County Jail, transmitted them to Dublin, where they remained in close prison until some lawyers, from compassion, pleaded their cause and procured their enlargement—nothing appearing against them of any kind whatsoever. Those insurgents, who called themselves Orange Boys, or Protestant Boys—that is, a banditti of murderers, committing massacre in the name of God, and exercising despotic power in the name of liberty—those insurgents had organised their rebellion and formed themselves into a committee, who sat and tried the Catholic weavers and inhabitants when apprehended falsely and illegally as deserters. That rebellious committee they called the committee of elders, who, when the unfortunate Catholic was torn from his family and his loom, and brought before them, in judgment upon his case—if they gave the o liquor or money they sometimes discharged him—otherwise they sent him to the recruiting officer as a deserter They had very generally given the Catholics notice to qu't their farms and dwellings, which notice was plastered on their houses, and conceived in these short but plain words—"Go to hell, Connaught won't receive you—hre and faggot. Wi'l Tresham and John Thrustout." They followed those notices by a faithful and punctual execution of the horrid threat, and soon after visited the houses, robbed the family, and destroyed what they did not take, and finally completed the atrocious persecution by forcing the unfortunate inhabitants to leave their land, their dwellings, and their trade, and to travel with their miserable family and with whatever their miserable family cou'd save from the wreck of their houses and tenements, and take refuge in villages or fortifications against invaders, where they described themselves, as he had seen in their affidavits, in the following manner:—"We ——, formerly of Armagh, weavers, now of no fixed place of abode, or means of living, &c. In many instances this banditti of persecutors threw down the houses of the tenantry, or what they called racked the houses, so that the family must fly, or be turned in the grave of their own cabin. The extent of the murders that had been committed by that atrocious and rebellious banditti we had heard, but had not so ascertained as to state them to the hour, but from all the inquiries we could make we collected that the inhabitants of Armagh had been actually put out of the law; that the magistrates had been supine or partial, and that the horrd banditti had met with complete success, and from the magistracy very little discouragement. This horrid persecution, this abominable barbarity, and this general extermination had been acknowledged by the magistrates, who found that the evil had now proceeded to so shameful an excess that it had at length obliged them to cry out against it. [The speaker, as we find from the debater, here alluded to the remarkable pronouncement of Lord Gosford and to the resolutions passed by the thirty magistrates of the county, which have been already quoted.]

Proceeding Mr. Grattan remarked—It was said by the mover of the resolution that of the Defenders multitudes had been hanged, multitudes had been put to death on the field, and that they were suppressed though they were not extinguished; but with regard to the outrages on the Orange Boys he could make no such boast, on the contrary they had met with impunity, and success, and triumph; they had t-iumphed over the law, they had triumphed over the magistrates, and they had triumphed over the people. There persecution, rebel'ion, inquisition, murder, robbery, devastation and extermination had been entirely victorious. The passing over these offences in the statement introducing the reso'ution, would be of little moment, if they were not also passed over in the resolutions themselves; the resolutions described four different kinds of offences: 1st, attempts to assassinate magistrates, 2nd, to murder witnesses; 3rd, to plunder houses; 4th, to seize by force the arms of His Majesty's subject; but of attempts to seize the persons of his Majesty's subjects, and to force them to abandon their lands and habitations; the resolution said not one syllable, crimes not less great, nor less notorious, and more emphatically calling for the interposition of the State, because they had triumphed over the supineness of the magistracy, and had no chance of being checked, but by the interposition of the Government or Parliament. In the other resolutions, which described that kind of armed insurgency, which the magistracy were to prevent by extraordinary exertions, the crime of driving away his Majesty's subjects is also omitted. The words were—"That from the many attempts which have been made on the homes of the individual by large bodies of armed insurgents for the purpose of taking arms and money by force, and murdering those who had the spirit to enforce the law, or give information against offenders, it will be necessary to give the magistrates enlarged powers," "attempts made on the houses of individuals to rob or take arms," "attempts to murder witnesses" — those were the offences which attracted their notice, but the attempt to exterminate his Majesty's subjects —attempts in part completed, which were very different from seizing arms, or taking money, or murdering witnesses—these attempts and perpetrations, as notorious as horrible, appeared to be neither in the contemplation of the resolutions nor of the member who moved them. Thus the silence of the resolutions might become a hint to the supineness of the magistracy, and where they should have counteracted their partiality, gave it countenance On a further examination of the resolutions he found them not merely defective in describing the offence, but they seemed to have omitted the remedy; certainly the giving magistrates further powers to search for arms and ammunition, or to prevent from assembling or meeting bodies of men assembling for the purpose of taking arms and money, or murdering witnesses; or the giving the magistrates enlarged power to seize vagabonds for the fleet or army, did not go to the case of Armagh, where the subjects complained, that they had been seized as deserters, falsely and illegally, through the supineness or partiality, or connivance of the magistrates; and through the same supineness, to say no worse, had been by force driven with impunity from their lands and habitations. Many of the weavers of Armagh had at that moment sworn against the magistrates. To give the magistrates extraordinary powers as the means of redressing the complaints, seemed to him, however, a remedy for some part of the kingdom, but a very inadequate one for another. In short, the measure of the right honourable gentleman in its present shape, did not go to the whole of the situation of the country. It did not go to redress the North; it was, therefore, a defective measure; it was a partial description of the outrages of the kingdom, and a partial remedy; it proposed to suspend the operation of the Constitution, with a view to produce peace, leaving at the same time, in one great county, violence and insurrection in a state of triumph. It left the families of Armagh, whom a violent mob, and a supaie magistracy had caused to abandon their dwellings —it left them without any certainty of redress, so that they might carry themselves and their families, and tales of woe to their brethren in the other parts of the kingdom, and spread the flames of discontent, and spirit of retaliation, notwithstanding the members Bills and resolutions. On principle, therefore, that it was necessary for the redress of that description of subjects, who had suffered in Armagh, that the magistrates should be called upon to act for the protection of the subject, and that the country should be obliged to pay those inhabitants, who had been aggrieved, full compensation for all their losses, charges, and distress, he had taken the liberty to suggest to the right hon. member amendments which he did not move, because the Attorney-General ought to have moved them, and made them his own measure. The amendments he suggested were, after the words "to seize by force of arms," to add, "and also the persons of his Majesty's subjects, and to force them to abandon 'heir lands and habitations," and in the third resolution, after the words "to murder those

who had the spirit to give information," to add "also attempting to seize the persons, and obliging his Majesty's subjects by force to abandon their lands and habitations."

Sir Lawrence Parsons arraigned the Government for not having timely sent a general officer and a military force to the disturbed parts of the North as they had done to the South, particularly as Lord Camden had avowedly come over to resist the Catholic claims.

The Attorney-General opposed Mr. Grattan's amendment. He said he had, throughout the whole of those resolutions, avoided making any distinction as to persons. They were intended for general good, and persons of every class would partake of their benefits. Were the amendments received, they would have a different complexion.

Mr. Secretary Pelham followed on the same ground. If no general officer was sent to the North, it was because they were all before engaged. An officer, however, was sent, and an experienced officer (Colonel Craddock). Upon this officer the secretary delivered a high eulogium both as to his character and capacity. He further mentioned that Lord Camden did not come over to oppress any part of his Majesty's subjects, but to afford equal protection to all.

Colonel Craddock avowed that he had the most decided instructions from Government to act in the commission, in which he had been employed, with equal justice to all offenders. He had been assisted by General Nugent, end such was the nature of the disturbance that, after repeated consideration, they could see no possible way in which the troops could be employed. He therefore recommended his recall in letters to Government, as he thought that he could be of no use. He admitted that the conduct of the Protestants, called Peep o' Day Boys (the Orangemen), in the County of Armagh, was at that time most atrocious, and that their barbarous practices must certainly be put down, but at the same time he must mention that in September last the Catholics were the aggressors.

Mr. Grattan, in reply, observed that the amendment appeared the more necessary from what fell from an honourable member, a magistrate of the County Armagh, who dissenting from every other person, had spoken of the use of what he called Orange Boys; of the services rendered by these murderers this atrocious landitti; the Northern rebels whose tartarity exceeded re dein times and brought back the reco

E

lection of ancient ferocity and bloodshed. He asked gentlemen who had heard the magistrates apologise for such murderers whether increasing the power of the magistracy would be of itself sufficient to redress the sufferings of the Northern Catholics. He must, therefore, persist in recommending to the right hon. gentleman his amendments, which, if he persisted to refuse, it was vain for him to move them, lamenting, at the same time, that he should have lost an opportunity of so clearly displaying what he must presume he wished—*impartiality* and *justice*.

The Attorney-General presented the Bill, which was read a first time, and ordered to be read a second time the next day.

On the second reading of the Insurrection Bill Sir Lawrence Parsons said he thought that a Bill so severe in its nature should have been preceded by some measure which would evince the disposition of the House to attend as well to the sufferings as to the offences of the people. If the design were to tranquillise the country it would have been right first to have inquired into the cause of the disturbance before such severe measures were taken to repress them. "If," said he, "the root of the evil were once come at, the evil itself would have been easily removed; but by applying merely to the effect, the cause of the evil was left untouched, and the consequence would be that it would continue to germinate new evils." He was willing to admit that the situation of the country was rather improved, but who would deny that the peasantry of Ireland were still miserable to a very great degree. Let gentlemen enter into the cabin of an Irish labourer, and see it without a chimney, often without a fire, and sometimes without food,[*] and then compare his state with the affluence, the elegance, and the pomp with which the casual circumstances of birth surround themselves. Having expressed a hope that no man would impute to him a desire to inflame the popular mind, he said the Bill was unnecessarily severe, was a useless violation of the first principles of the Constitution, and that, instead of doing service, it was likely to produce the opposite effect. He could not

[*] I cannot allow this expression to pass without drawing the reader's attention to the startling fact that in the long interval of nigh a century which has elapsed since these strikingly truthful words fell from Sir Lawrence Parsons in the Irish House of Commons no progress has been made in the condition of the suffering people whose misery he then deplored. In 1831, as in 1796, the peasantry of Ireland are "still miserable to a very great degree;" the Irish labourer knows quite as little now as he did then of the luxuries of a fire or a chimney, while long-continued privation seems to have made him all but superior to the necessaries of life. Yet we boast the progress of this nineteenth century!

bring himself to think that the Irish country gentlemen wished to drive their chariot wheels over the necks of the people; they wished only to restore tranquillity, but certainly they would not surrender the established constitution as an experiment. It was a peculiar quality of the common people of Ireland that they communicated quickly their pleasures and their discontents, and he argued that magistrates having the power, without the form of trial by jury, to send suspected people out of the kingdom would only aggravate the disorders. If this law would probably be a cause of discontent to every quarter of the country, how much more so must it be in the County Armagh? In that county it had been proved on oath that several magistrates refused to take the depositions of the injured Catholics. By some of those magistrates they had been most cruelly prosecuted; others would hear them only out of the window, and some actually turned them from their doors with threats. If such men were entrusted with a power of transporting men at pleasure, what was to be expected but the most gross and flagrant violation of justice? As they were then engaged in a war of which the wisest could not foresee the event, it might become necessary to appeal for assistance against the enemy to those very persons. It would, therefore, be wise to include some clause of amnesty for past offences, excepting murders. To neglect it would be to reduce the Irish peasantry to the alternative of either persisting in guilt and treason or submitting to the halter.

Mr. Archdale, in the course of the debate, referred to the affairs of Armagh; professed habits of intimacy with the noble lord (Gosford), whose letter or speech upon the condition of that county had made such a noise; he declared he thought the letter *incautious*, and such as the noble lord on reflection would not approve of; he finally recommended rather the conduct of that nobleman than his publication as an object for imitation.

At two o'clock in the morning the Bill was read a second time, the young Lord Edward Fitzgerald being found alone in opposing it on the question for committal.

The subject we are now considering is an all important one vitally affecting the question whether the Armagh magistrates countenanced and fostered Orangeism in its extermination of the Catholic inhabitants of that county, and whether their doing so was connived at by, or in obedience to, the Administration of the day. I will therefore take the liberty of quoting one other extract from these important debates.

When the report from the Committee on the Attorney-General's Bill for the better prevention of conspiracies in Ireland, was before the House on the 29th February, Mr. Grattan* asked to have the Bill recommitted as he wished to propose an amendment to compel the country to pay the countryman, whether labourer or manufacturer, full compensation for damages and loss to his person, family, or dwelling suffered in consequence of violent mobs. He was apprehensive that if the compensation were left to the Grand Jury nothing would be done. The Grand Jury would readily present for damages suffered by magistrates or witnesses, but they probably would not, in the County Armagh particularly, give any adequate or indeed any satisfaction for losses suffered by the Catholic weaver or peasant. Government trifled with the Northern weaver, when he sent him for satisfaction to a Grand Jury composed of those very magistrates, whose supineness, or bigotry, or partiality had been the cause of his loss or of his emigration. The Bill complained of violence to magistrate, of the murder of witnesses, of illegal oaths; but of the threats, and force and violence offered to certain of his Majesty's subjects (referring to the Catholics of County Armagh) whereby they had been forced to quit their trades, their lands, and their tenements, outrages of which the governor of a Northern county had complained as unexampled in history, and to which violence and atrocity the magistrates of the county had borne testimony of a formal resolution, there was in Bill complete silence and omission. The Bill, Mr. Grattan, continued, proposes to give extra power to magistrates. This may be very effectual as to certain parts of the country. But what are the grievances of Armagh? That the magistrates have not used the ordinary powers, and in some cases they have abused those powers in such a manner that the subject has not been protected, and that the rioter had been encouraged. The Bill, therefore, punishes disturbance in one part of the kingdom, while it compromises with disturbance in another; it says—if you murder a magistrate you shall pay his representative, but of you drive away whole droves of weavers from Armagh, you shall pay nothing except those persons by whose fault they have been driven away and scattered over the whole face of the earth.

The Attorney-general replied to Mr. Grattan His argument admitted the description of the state

of the County Armagh, given by the hon. member; for he said those offences called papering—viz., the expulsion of persons in Armagh from their lands and habitations, by affixing written threats upon their houses were already made a felony of death by the Acts of the 15th and 16th of George II.* He suggested (no doubt in satire) that the hon. gentleman should bring in a Bill if he wished to amend the existing law.

Sir Lawrence Parsons complained of the unlimited power the Bill gave for encroachment upon the liberties of the Press, as, according to one of its clauses, every printer and bookseller in the kingdom could be taken at the will of any two magistrates, and sent on board the fleet. He continued —Yet that is but a subordinate part of the present Bill. Look at the other clauses; in every one of them the same summary power deposited in the same persons. Now, if the popular disturbances made it necessary to deposit an arbitrary power somewhere, would it not be wise to pause a little and consider where it best might be deposited? Was it with the magistrates? Men, in order to be good judges, should be cool and impartial, but in all disturbed counties the magistrates, instead of being cool are in a high state of inflammation against the objects of that Bill, and it is natural that it should be so. They were not to be reprehended for that, but certainly on that account, they were among the last persons that should be entrusted with an uncontrolable power. And so far from being impartial, it was impossible that they should be so, for they were themselves parties. What was the temper observable in that house? There, from superior manners and education, the human passions were much mitigated, and they saw far more temper and clemency in that house than could be expected from the inferior magistrates in the country. Yet what was the fact? That even there, everything said, however violent, against the disturbers of the peace was received with plaudits, but if anything be said to soften over-charged resentments and mix mercy with punishment it was received with discontent and murmurs. He alluded to the religious feud existing in Armagh between the Orangemen and the Defenders, and said that the result of this Bill would be that a person, without any form of

---

* This was so. But Mr. Grattan's argument was that the ordinary powers of the law had not been used, or were abused. It is peculiarly suggestive that in the whole County Armagh during this period not one person, so far as can be ascertained, was tried or sentenced for this description of felony under the 15th and 16th George II.

trial, without any regular judge or jury, might on the warrant of two magistrates, be torn from the bosom of his family and sent on board the fleet:—for what? Not for being a defender, or any way connected with Defenders, but for being a little too late or a little too early in going in or coming out of his hovel. Gentlemen talk of the mischief of inflaming the people, but he would tell them that one such act unjustly done would inflame them more than what could be said in that House for ages. It was not what they might say, but what they were going to empower others to do that would inflame them.

In this debate not one of the speakers attempted to contradict or even to extenuate the guilt of the Orangemen of Armagh. Mr. George Ponsonby said the enormities committed in the county Armagh had been declared to be beyond any that had ever disgraced a county. If the Administration were sincere they could not hesitate for one moment to adopt the amendment.

After a heated debate the question was negatived without a division. Parliament was prorogued on the 15th April without any other debate of interest.

To add further corroboration to the charge against the Government of complicity with and connivance at the outrages of the Armagh Orangemen, I might quote extensively from the debates of the succeeding session, when Government introduced the Habeas Corpus Act; but relying upon the foregoing and upon the few historical facts that are to follow, I forbear doing so lest I be open to the charge of unnecessary tediousness in corroborating what is now a matter of authentic history. Both in and out of Parliament this serious accusation was levelled at the Camden Administration, the only reply upon all sides being an ominous silence. As to the outrages themselves no one dare attempt to deny them. As will be seen from the debates quoted, the Ministers themselves admitted their existence. Upon the authority of an interesting pamphlet dealing with those times and written by the celebrated "Capt. Rock," the statements contained in the address of Lord Gosford were corroborated by no less a personage than a Mr. Macan, the sovereign of Armagh; but this fact, I am bound to say, I do not find elsewhere mentioned. To substantiate the truthfulness of this address no proofs are wanting. The chief difficulty to a writer upon those times is a judicious selection for the purpose from the mass of facts presented to him.

Three Orangemen voluntary made oath before a magistrate of the Counties of Down and Armagh that they met in committees, amongst whom were some members of Parliament who gave their people money and promised they should not suffer for any act they might commit, and pledged themselves that they should "hereafter be provided for under the auspices of the Government." The magistrate, before whom this startling information was made, wrote to the Secretary of State inquiring how he should act in these critical times; that hitherto he had preserved peace on his large estate, but he wished to know how he should act in future; that if it were necessary for the preservation of the present system for him to connive at or encourage the Orangemen in their depredations, he as *a man* knew his duty. If it were not necessary, he hoped the *magistrates of the county* would be held responsible, and he compelled to act against these depredators.[*] It is further stated that the Executive neglected for several months to reply to this pertinent inquiry, and when at last it did vouchsafe a response it was dictated in such vague terms as to be utterly devoid of reason.

In the spring of 1796 a large number of delegates from the various Orange bodies met in the city of Armagh. Here, at what was possibly the first delegated meeting of this body, they entered into various resolutions which they published in print. One of those resolutions contained a recommendation to the gentry of fortune to open a public subscription in support of the organisation, declaring *that the two guineas per man allowed them by Government was not sufficient to purchase clothes and accoutrements.* These resolutions were published in Mr. Giffard's *Dublin Journal* and also in *Falkner's Journal* of that period, and are sufficient in themselves to show that the Orangemen had not been six months in organisation until they were taken into the secret pay of the Government; no doubt on the undertaking that they would do the behests of a vile Administration of which Pitt and his underling Camden were the dictators. No wonder Mr. Grattan was found to exclaim "That the audacity of the Armagh mob arose from a confidence in the connivance of the Government; under an Administration sent thither to defeat a Catholic Bill, a Protestant mob very naturally conceived itself a part of the State, and exercised the power of life or death, of transportation, of murder, and of rape, with triumph." Had the ascendancy

---

[*] Plowden's Hist. Review, 247.

party of those days not shown a willingness to construe even the inaction of the Government into a sanction of their acts, however bloody, they could not have transmitted the desire that permeates their successors of the present day, and prompts the foolish boasts, an exclusive loyalty, and a right of *entrée* up the back stairs of Dublin Castle.

In those days the star of Dungannon had set. The representative of a bloody faction usurped the seat of the once famous Volunteers. Though these men m have legislated with a view to their particular interests though'; empty pockets may have inspired their patriotism; though their views did not extend beyond those petty measures which they foolishly thought were calculated to replenish them ; though they voted Ireland free, and left five-sixths of her people in bondage, like, as it has been truly said, the English barons of old, who extorted a charter from their monarch, but refused to untie the fetters of their vassals; still comparatively they were men of tolerance, and if they did not free their fellow-men they refused to persecute them. In little more than a dozen years behold the change! The children who in and about this neighbourhood had looked with admiration upon the glancing sabres of the Volunteers, and, emulating them, no doubt played at soldiers as a pastime, who listened to the beat of drum and the blast of trumpet when all mustered for parade, were now in the prime of life arrayed in hostile camps, one side preserving the glorious memories of the past, and foremost in the ranks of the people; the other, wise in their generation, and first amongst their oppressors. It is told by Mr. Plowden that a Mr. James Verner—ominous name!—was nominated for the borough of Dungannon by Lord Northland. He was by profession an attorney, by trade a magistrate, and by commission a Parliament man. He was then, as he continued long afterwards to be, prominently conspicuous for persecuting the Catholics—for, of course, all the Verners were Orangemen, His uncle, also an attorney, had by professional "and other means" realised a very considerable property in those parts' which he devised to the youngest son of Mr. James Verner. "Amongst other exploits of this purple Orangeman he eviscerated the estate of his own son by ruining and exterminating ninety-six Catholic families who were tenants upon it. Mr. James Verner's corps of yeomanry displayed their zeal and prowess on their way to church on Sun-

day by firing into a congregation of Catholics (in a chapel near Tartarahan) whilst attending the rites of their own religion, wounding several, and some mortally." On their return they razed the chapel in the presence of Mr. Obery, J.P., whose two sons were actively employed in it and who, with a thrift, that brands them as plunderers, instead of fanatics, afterwards converted the principal timber into looms for their own use. These ingenious youths were, it is stated by the same authority, in the habit of *selling* written protections *weekly* to Catholics, and upon the black mail not being forthcoming the impoverished weavers were left to meet the general fate of their exterminated brethren. These Verners lived in the County Armagh.

Messrs. Ford, Greer, and Brownlow, three Lurgan magistrates, were next to Mr. Verner, the most conspicuous in fostering and encouraging this Buddha of bigotry, the Orange Association. On their estates they had mostly Catholic tenantry from whom their agents readily obtained a surrender of their arms. No sooner had this surrender been effected than notice was actually given by Mr. Ford, J.P., to the Orangemen of the locality, who, in that district of Armagh, were very numerous, that they would be safe in plundering that part of the country, as the Catholics were totally disarmed. On the Sunday following the day upon which the notice was furnished by this exemplary Armagh Justice of the Peace the Orangemen crossed the River Bann in boats, and indiscriminately attacked, plundered, and destroyed all the property belonging to the Catholic residents. Two of Mr. Ford's most respectable Catholic tenants, whose webs and yarns, with their houses and furniture, had been destroyed, applied to their landlord for counsel, confident of redress. He briefly told them if they would read their recantation and become Protestants they would be protected. The surrender of the arms of Mr. Ford's tenents was made on Saturday, and early on the next morning he set out for Dundalk.* The surrendered arms were put into the hands of the Orangemen by his servants, and were actually employed in exterminating the disarmed owners. "The example," says the narrator, "of Mr. Ford was followed by other magistrates."

The reader will recall the name of Mr. Coile.

* This gentleman was Collector of Customs at Dundalk. From this office he was discharged soon after the incident related above, having been detected in several gross frauds upon the Revenue. It would not be difficult to fathom the depths of this gentleman's "loyalty."

The principal part of that gentleman's property was in the hands of Lurgan weavers, and was at this time destroyed by the Orange rioters, under the sanction of the Lurgan magistracy. He applied for redress to Mr. Greer, one of the famous Lurgan trio, but the "justice" refused to take informations or grant warrants, notwithstanding that there were four persons besides the prosecutor ready to identify the culprits. Mr. Coile, a man of independent mind, but who suffered for his independence, prosecuted Mr. Greer at the Armagh Assizes. He was found guilty upon four counts, so flagrant were the offences and so pointed the direction of the judge. He was sentenced to six months' imprisonment, fined in £200, struck off the Commission of the peace, and committed to Newgate. It may be thought that there was weeping and wailing amongst the Orangemen that this staunch supporter of ascendancy was thus treated by an ungrateful Administration. Not so. In the solemn farce each man knew his part. Greer's fine of £200 was reduced to sixpence. Lord Clare restored him to the Commission of the Peace. While he was a convicted and imprisoned felon he held the sinecure office of General Inspector of Ulster under the Linen Board, and secured, through the interest of Mr. Foster, an additional allowance of £100 per year with leave to take his son as Assistant-Inspector. A conspiracy was in the meantime got up against Mr. Coile, headed by Mr. Brownlow, J.P., resulting in his being cast into prison upon a trumped-up charge of distributing ball cartridge amongst papists. The Rev Mr. Mansell, J P, the bloodthirsty evangeliser of Portadown, before whom

the informations were sworn, induced such of them as were or had been Catholics to read their recantation before being examined * Mr. Coile was confined for eight months in prison vainly entreating and urging to be put upon his trial. Four of the conspirators, touched with remorse, swore before magistrates that they had been suborned to swear falsely against him, some of them stating that they had been rewarded for doing so. Mr. Coile, after eight months' imprisonment, was enlarged without trial, and was prevented from prosecuting the conspirators because "his own trial was hanging over him." Ever after he was a "marked man."

At the Spring Assizes of 1796, more than 100 Orangemen were tried. The witnesses were waylaid and murdered, and the jury intimidated. Eleven of the banditti were found guilty, and one —a Protestant dissenter—was alone executed, the remainder being let loose upon the country to carry on the bloody work of a bloody Administration.

These are but a few of the many instances that could be quoted from authentic sources to prove that the Government, the magistrates of Armagh and the adjoining counties, and the Orangemen were in league; for what purpose their acts best demonstrate.

---

* "The following is a copy of a certificate given to one James Murray on this occasion —' James Murray, of Deryheena, came before me this day and renounced the errors of the Church of Rome, and embraced the Protestant Faith as by law established.' George Mansell, Drum, January 15, 1796."

CHAPTER XII.—THE ORANGE REGIME: ITS EARLY VICTIMS.

I HAVE referred at the close of the last chapter to the case of Mr. Bernard Coile, Lurgan. His sufferings at the hands of an Orange magistracy and an Orange Administration were so acute and so peculiarly harsh that the proofs of them deserve consideration. I, therefore, think it right, his case having been the rule rather than the exception of those times, to devote a chapter of this history to the reproduction of two highly important documents which few of my readers have had an opportunity of perusing. They are to be found hidden away in the musty records of those times. And though we might well afford to pass them over as furnishing what must be considered only corroboration to facts already stated, they are such interesting relics of the past that their existence should not be wholly lost sight of, particularly as I have reason to believe

that with Orange eulogists of the present day their suppression is "a consummation devoutly to be wished for."

Mr. Bernard Coile Lurgan, presented, in November 1796, a memorial to the Lord Lieutenant, in which he stated, "that in the latter end of the year very dangerous riots and tumults broke out, which were fomented by hidden agents, and propagated amongst the ignorant of all persuasions under the pretext of religion; that memorialist, being a professor of the Roman Catholic religion, used every effort to moderate the spirit of his own persuasion, particularly by promoting the printed resolutions of the Roman Catholics of his and the adjoining parish, and enforcing by all his influence the observance of those resolutions, in hopes by setting an example of good will and moderation, to

disarm the animosity of a faction denominated
Peep-o-Day boys, and since called Orangemen,
whose only object was the persecution of the
Catholics. That, notwithstanding this, the most
unheard of cruelty was inflicted upon the Roman
Catholics of the said county by the said
Orangemen, who, in many instances, boasted
of the countenance and protection of magistrates and other persons in power." He
then says that from a sense of duty and pity to the
afflicted he laid before the Court of King's Bench
an affidavit "charging John Greer, Silverwood,
Esq., a magistrate of said County Armagh, with
corruptly encouraging and fomenting the said inhuman persecution," and that at the same time
four other persons respectively made affidavits of
similar facts. It then recites "that immediately
on the service of notice of the said order Patrick
Hamill, one of the above-mentioned deponents, was
beaten nearly to death, his father soon afterwards
was shot in the dead of night in his own dwelling-
house for having dared to complain. One M'Clasky,
another of the said deponents had his dwelling-
house attacked at night, and was driven from
thence by many acts of menace and violence, and
at the same time a conspiracy was also formed to
take away the life of your memorialist by false accusation of the crime of high treason. That being
apprised of this by Andrew Thomas Corner, a
member of the Established Church, who had first
taken part in the said conspiracy, your memorialist
applied to Mr. Brownlow, a neighbouring magistrate, for a summons to bring the parties instantly
before him that he might have an opportunity of
confronting them and preventing so diabolical an
attempt. That this request was made on Wednesday, the 13th January, but the only summons
which Mr. Brownlow was pleased to grant was for
the ensuing Friday.

On the intervening day, Thursday, the 14th of
November, he was warned by some of the neighbours to fly because, however innocent, there was
enough sworn against him to hang, as they said,
one hundred men; but conscious of his innocence,
and relying on the justice of the law of his
country, he rejected this advice with indignation.

Memorialist was accordingly arrested on the said
day (Thursday), and taken before Mr. Brownlow,
who, without waiting for the effect of the summons, which he had granted the day before, or any
further inquiry, together with Michael Obins, Esq ,
another magistrate, committed your memorialist
to the county jail, under the following committal :—

"We herewith send you, the body of Bernard
Coile, a reputed Papist, charged with distributing
a large quantity of ball cartridges amongst a number of Papists for the purpose of destroying the
Protestants, and also, at the same time, swearing
a person to be one of his soldiers, to assist in over-
throwing the King, Government, and the magistrates.

"(Signed) ⎰ MICHAEL OBINS.
          ⎱ WILLIAM BROWNLOW."

Memorialist had not long been in jail until James
Murray, one of the conspirators, came before the
Rev. William Bristow, Sovereign of Belfast, and
made a voluntary confession, which he afterwards confirmed by affidavit before a commissioner,
fearing, as he deposed, to make the same in his own
county, lest he should be put to death; stating
that he had been suborned by persons in his affidavit mentioned, to swear falsely against memorialist to the following effect," &c.:—The memorial further proceeded to detail that one Bernard
Cush* and also one Daniel Kearns made affidavits
to a like effect, all of which he forwarded. It details
his lying in jail until the ensuing Assizes, his bail
being refused, his subsequently being refused a
trial, the adjournment of the cases to the Summer
Assizes, and continues :—

"That in the meantime one Owen Burns, a fourth
of the said conspirators against your memorialist's
life, came forward and voluntarily swore, as the
former conspirators had done, that he had been
threatened by twelve men, in his affidavit particularly named, and by them compelled to swear a
false oath against your memorialist's life; and
further, that he had received a new suit of clothes
from a gentleman of the name of Burke, by profession an attorney, by order of Mr. Brownlow, together with two ruffled shirts; that he was taken
to Dublin in a chaise, conducted and guarded by
two of his fellow-conspirators—George Cull and
John M'Comb—who paid all his expenses; that he
was kept prisoner in Dublin thirteen days, during
which time he was once brought before James
Verner, Esq., a magistrate in said county, in
Dawson Street, who there appointed a day for him
to come again before him and swear something
new against your memorialist, but that said deponent, shocked and penitent for what he had done,

* I have the authority of Mr. Plowden for saying that
this Cush, who belonged to the 5th Dragoons, made oath in
the case of Mr. Coile, before Mr. Secretary Cooke, that the
oath of extermination was that which was tendered to him
on being asked to become an Orangeman. He refused to
swear it; but Cush says that five of the other conspirators
did subscribe to it. On receiving the depositions, the S cre-
tary pledged himself to have the conspirators prosecuted,
Of course, they never were.

before the day appointed came, effected his escape and returned to the County Armagh."

The affidavit then proceeded to detail the particulars already briefly reverted to. The *Press* of November 14, 1798, contains a lengthened narrative of the subsequent interview of Mr. Coile with Mr. Secretary Cooke; the repeated promises made to inquire into his case; the evident desire of the Government to hush up the matter, and their ultimate refusal to grant an inquiry or any other satisfaction to this persecuted man. But the persecution did not end with Mr Coile.

Thomas Hawthorn, a servant of Mr. Coile, a Protestant, made an affidavit at the direction of Mr Secretary Cooke and the Attorney-General, in order that they might prosecute Wm. Brownlow, Esq, J P, M P. *Mr. Brownlow was never prosecuted.* Whether he should or not may be seen from the following —

AFFIDAVIT MADE BY THOMAS HAWTHORN IN THE COURT OF KING'S BENCH

"I, Thomas Hawthorn, of Lurgan, in the County Armagh, servant of Bernard Coile, formerly of Lurgan, but now of the city of Dublin, merchant, maketh oath, and saith that this deponent for two years and upwards, previous to the month of May last, lived in the capacity of servant with the said Bernard Coile. Deponent saith that, on or about the 13th of May last, to the best of deponent's recollection and belief, he was standing at or near the said Bernard Coile's dwelling-house in Lurgan aforesaid, and about the hour of nine o'clock in the evening of the said day, two men, whom deponent did not know, came towards the place where deponent was standing, and one of the said persons having come up to the said deponent, asked him if he would go and take part in a quart of ale. The deponent saith he refused to do so, and gave as his reason for such refusal that he was not accustomed to go and drink with persons he was not acquainted with, or to that effect. Deponent saith he believes that the said persons who spoke to deponent as aforesaid well knew that this deponent had for the period aforesaid, been in the employment of the said Bernard Coile, and consequently acquainted with and privy to all or most of the said Bernard's affairs; that the said person intimated so to this deponent, and told him that it was in deponent's power, as alleging deponent to be in said Bernard Coile's secrets (as he termed it) to make some affidavit against the said Bernard Coile, in order to injure him, and told deponent if he would do so that deponent should never know what want was, or made use of some such expres-

sion, meaning thereby, as deponent verily believes, to bribe deponent to swear some false and malicious affidavit against the said Bernard Coile, who was then confined a close prisoner in the gaol of Armagh for some pretended offence. Deponent saith he refused to make such affidavit, inasmuch as deponent could not make any affidavit whatsoever to the prejudice of Bernard Coile. Deponent saith that on Friday, the 20th May aforesaid, about nine o'clock in the evening, as this deponent, in company with John Lapsay, foreman to said Bernard Coile, and Matthew M'Evoy, servant to Captain Kemmis, were going from Lurgan to deponent's house at Silverwood, in the said county, where deponent's wife and family reside, they were overtaken on the road by a number of persons who assumed the appellation of Orange Boys or Break-of Day men, amongst whom were William Williscroft, George Douglas, John Forsyth, James Doyle, and several other persons, whose names deponent did not then know, to the number of twenty persons and upwards, and amongst them do we verily believe was the person who, on the 13th day of May, attempted to bribe deponent to make the said false oath against the said Bernard Coile, and the said William Williscroft, George Douglas, John Forsyth, and James Doyle, all of the said county, and Francis Johnston, of Kilware, in the County Down; and William Crothers, of Lurgan, aforesaid, without the slightest provocation, whatsoever, or without even speaking to them, or any of them, knocked deponent down, and when down, seized deponent by the hair of the head, kicked, battered, and cruelly beat and otherwise abused deponent, and threw deponent into the gap of the ditch, and leaped upon and trampled upon deponent, with an intention, as deponent believes, to take his life; the aforesaid persons having encouraged each other to kill deponent, alleging that deponent was one of the deluded persons called Defenders, otherwise that deponent would not live with a Papist, the said Bernard Coile, they or some of them having expressed words to that effect. Saith that said John Lapsay and Matthew M'Evoy, having interfered to prevent deponent from being murdered by the aforesaid persons, the said Lapsay and M'Evoy were beat and abused by them, and having battered him in the manner aforesaid they left him lying in the ditch, having, as deponent believes, imagined deponent dead. . Deponent saith that on the next day he went to Wm Brownlow, Esq., a magistrate of the said County

of Armagh to give information against the perpetrators of the said assault, and the said William
Brownlow, having seen the manner in which deponent then was, declared he had never seen a man
more abused, and directed deponent to come to
him on the following Monday with examinations
drawn against the said Wm. Williscroft, George
Douglas, John Forsythe, and James Doyle. Deponent saith that in pursuance of the orders and
directions he received from the said Wm Brownlow he applied to one John Allen, who usually
draws up examinations and warrants for the said
William Brownlow, who drew up an examination
and warrant against the said Williscroft, Douglas,
Forsythe, and Douglas, which examinations deponent, on the 23rd of May, brought to
the said William Brownlow, and the said Willis-
ford and Douglas having then appeared before
the said M.. Brownlow he desired deponent and
others to attend at said Brownlow's house; and
deponent saith that he accordingly attended, as
did the said Williscroft and Douglas; but none of
the other persons concerned in the assault appeared before said Mr. Brownlow. And deponent
swore examinations against the said William
Williscroft, George Douglas, John Forsyth, and
James Doyle, being the only persons whose names
deponent then knew, who had assaulted deponent
in the manner aforesaid, and the said Mr. Brownlow then took bail for the appearance of the said
Williscroft and Douglas to abide their trial at the
next general Quarter Sessions of the Peace, to be
held at Lurgan, aforesaid, in and for the said
County of Armagh; and to the best of deponent's
recollection and belief, bound deponent in the sum
of £10 conditioned to prosecute the said Williscroft and Douglas at the said sessions. Deponent
saith he then requested the said Mr. Brownlow to
give this deponent a warrant against said Forsythe
and Doyle, who had neither appeared or given bail,
in order that this deponent should give the same
into the hands of Wm Coulter, of Lurgan aforesaid,
the high constable, which the said Wm. Brownlow
refused to do, but told Wm. Coulter that he would
deliver same to the said Wm. Coulter. And this
deponent saith that he had been informed by the
said Wm Coulter, which he believed to be true,
that the said Wm. Brownlow never did deliver
same to Wm. Coulter. . . Deponent soon afterwards discovered that Wm. Crothers and Francis
Johnston were two of the persons concerned in
assaulting deponent . . . and had an examination drawn up against them, and offered to swear
same before Mr Brownlow, which the said Brown-

low absolutely refused to take, or to assign any
reason for his refusal Deponent saith he attended
at the next General Quarter Sessions at Lurgan,
with witnesses, in order to prosecute the said
Williscroft and Douglas, who had given bail before
the said Brownlow to abide their trial, and this
deponent employed an attorney for that purpose;
but to deponent's and his attorney's surprise and
astonishment they discovered that the said Mr.
Brownlow had suppressed said examinations, and
neglected to return same to the Clerk of the Peace,
by which means and by the said Brownlow's refusal to take examinations against the said Johnston and Crothers, and by his refusing this deponent a warrant against the said Forsyth and
Doyle aforesaid, or putting the same into the hands
of any constable, the said Williscroft, Douglas,
Forsyth, Doyle, Johnston, and Crothers have seve-
rally escaped from all manner of trial or punishment for the aforesaid assault and unprovoked
attempt on deponent's life."

The conclusion of the affidavit details how Mr.
Coile, "to avoid the rage and fury of that faction
denominated Orangemen," had to leave his place of
residence.

On Friday, the 30th December, 1796, Hawthorn
was attacked outside Lurgan, and had his leg
broken by one Andrew Curry. After being under
the care of a doctor for five weeks, he was wheeled
into Lurgan on a cart, and requested Robert
Douglas, J.P, to take his informations against his
assailant, but this the magistrate refused to do.
The Orange party, seeing that Hawthorn was determined to have justice, for he had intimated to
the magistrate that he would seek justice elsewhere, resolved to take time by the forelock. Accordingly, on the 20th February, 1797, between
eleven and twelve o'clock, a large armed party of
Orangemen attacked his house, there being then no
persons in it but himself, his wife, and three small
children. Hawthorn fired upon them and killed
two, and his wife, with a bravery peculiar to
maternity when the fate of its young are in the
balance, killed one of the ruffians with a spade as
he was entering by a window. After defending his
house for an hour with success, Hawthorn cried out
to his wife that he should surrender to his fate,
when one of his children, concealed beneath a
bed, cried out, warning him of the fate that
awaited them if he did so. Animated with
a new courage he continued to fight against overpowering numbers until his neighbours hearing the
firing came to his assistance His assailants then
and then only retreated. One of them named Harri-

son was arrested by an army major the following day in Lurgan, and overtures were made by Harrison's father to stop the prosecution, and he would pay compensation. This Hawthorn refused to do. But the same end was otherwise accomplished. An Orangeman named Thos. Humphreys swore a false information against Hawthorn, and had him committed at once to the assizes without bail, the result of this trumped up charge being a verdict of not guilty.*

Neither Mr. Coile nor his servant ever got the slightest satisfaction at the hands of the Government, though their cases were taken up by some of the most influential men of those days. In addition, the former was refused rooms in the Belfast Linen Hall, as may be seen from a document which Mr. Plowden quotes at page 127 of his history.

* These particulars will be found recorded in *The Press* newspaper of 1797.

CHAPTER XIII.—AN HISTORICAL PARALLEL.

We have been reading the history of those days chiefly by the light of contemporaneous records. Times of great political excitement, such as those we are treating of, undoubtedly were, when social disorder and tumult reign supreme, and when a community is divided into two hostile camps, the members upon one side seeing little merit upon the side opposed to them, are not, it must be honestly confessed, those best calculated to facilitate the forming an upright and just estimate between contending parties. Such circumstances must necessarily depreciate the value of inferences drawn by contemporary writers where they are not based upon stated facts. For this reason I have as far as possible confined myself to a matter-of-fact record of events from which readers of the present day can draw their own conclusions. Opinions we certainly have had. They are the opinions of men whose works have made them famous in history, whose abilities make them still living examples to those who would leave their footprints behind, and against whose character for integrity and truthfulness not even the breath of suspicion has been entertained. But ability, and integrity, and truthfulness, though some times, are not always bulwarks against prejudice. It might be well before we proceed further in the narrative to seek, as I have already ventured to do in preceding pages, for corroboration under circumstances less calculated to leave room for honest doubt, or even for cavil.

We have to pass rapidly down the stream of time, through no less than two successive generations, to leave behind those scenes of turbulence and confusion, in which the worst passions of men were becoming aroused beneath the darkening clouds of a bloody insurrection; the dreadful melodrama, of which the curtain has been already drawn, fades from our view into a past of nigh forty years, and the groans of the dying—aye, and gallant peasant, and the shrieks of murdered women, and

all that horrible hurly-burly that agitated society to its depths have died away. These scenes are not forgotten; but men's minds have settled into a calm, such as best befits the juror, and they who have lived through those times, and have thought of them and talked of them over many a winter's fire, have learned to apportion to the dread actors in the drama their proper share of censure and of praise. Around a council board some few dozen men are seated, and one whose foot is almost on the brink of the grave—an old man belonging to a noble sect whose character for truth has made the simple assurance of its members equal to the testimony of their fellows, though witnessed by their Maker, a man of sixty-four years who has lived down through all those scenes of horror comes upon the table to leave behind a narrative of preceding events. Mr. James Christie, a quaker, born in 1771, and residing on the borders of the County Armagh since 1793, is before the Select Committee of the House of Commons in 1835 to give evidence.

At 5,566 of the report of the evidence, he says, that the first disturbances that he recollected in the North occurred in the neighbourhood of Churchhill, the residence of Colonel Vernor. Those disturbances were the "wrecking" of the houses of Roman Catholics, and then he proceeds to state how exact were the Peep o' Day Boys of those days in their nomenclature. "Wrecking," he says, "was when the parties broke open the door and smashed everything that was capable of being broken in the house—looms and webs that were probably weaving; they broke the webs and destroyed the yarn and everything, and sometimes they threw the furniture out of the house smashed; and in other cases they set fire to the house and burnt it." This practice which he says spread soon over the adjoining counties, and "after the Catholics were driven, many of them from the county and took refuge in other parts of Ireland—

he understood they took refuge in Connaught. Some years after, when peace and quietness were in a measure restored, some returned again, probably five or six years afterwards; they got some employment; but they stayed out of the county while they thought their lives were in danger, but the property which they left was transferred, in most instances, to Protestants" It occurred within his knowledge that where they had houses and land they were handed over by the landlord to Protestants, in some cases where the former occupants had life leases. Sometimes he heard of twelve or fourteen houses being wrecked in a night, and he pitied the Catholics very much in the straits they were driven to. He was asked—

"Up to what period did it continue? For two or three years; it was not quite so bad in 1796 and 1797 as it was earlier; but after this wrecking, and the Catholics were driven out, what was called the Break-of-Day party merged into Orangemen. They passed from the one to the other, and the gentlemen in the county procured what they termed their Orange warrants to enable them to assemble legally, as they termed it, the name dropped, and Orangemen succeeded to Break-of-Day Men."

That the wrecking "was not quite so bad in 1796 and 1797 as it was earlier" is urged by Orange panegyrists as a consequence of the new association in Armagh. Did a doubt exist we might reasonably afford them the benefit of their special pleading, but we have it upon undoubted authority that so furious was the exterminating system carried on in the latter part of 1795 and the early months of the following year that the county was completely cleared of its Catholic population. The very word "extermination" implies a speedy end Like Alexander, the Orangemen might well have wept, that they had no more Catholics to exterminate.

Mr. Christie proceeds to say, in answer to the question whether the Orangemen were of the same class as those that composed the Break-of-day Men, that he supposed they were; the same people who made use of intemperate language towards the Catholics whilst the Break of-day business lasted, were the same people that he saw afterwards walking in Orange processions. He says he saw three Catholic chapels destroyed. Commencing at 5589 we find the following.—

Were any Protestant or Presbyterian places of worship burned or injured? No; I never recollect hearing of any such thing in the North of Ireland.

Can you form any conjecture of the number of families that were driven from their homes? I cannot form any just idea of it, to ascertain it with certainty; but it was said that several hundreds were driven out of the country, and there must have been from the number of houses destroyed, particularly in the County of Armagh; it was worse there than in any other part of the North of Ireland.

Had you any opportunity of knowing any persons seeking refuge in your own place from the outrage? Yes; my father was living at the time; he and I lived together, the poor creatures, when they apprehended that their houses would be destroyed, my father and I permitted them to stow their furniture in our barn and granaries, and they remained there for a length of time. I have known them myself to leave their homes at night and come to our plantation to be out of the way of being murdered. A man, who took care of my plantation, has told me that they frequently came to his place in the course of the night and took shelter there till morning for fear of being attacked.

Did any murders take place? Yes, there did.

Did any investigation take place by the magistrates upon the occasion? I never heard that there did.

Did you ever hear of a man having been prosecuted or punished for those attacks upon the houses by wrecking and burning, and for the murders that were perpetrated? I do not, I think, recollect any instance of a person being prosecuted at that period for those offences, for no investigation took place; the magistrates were supine and inactive; they did not exert themselves in the manner that I and that many others who wished the peace of the country thought they should have acted

Did you receive any threatening letters? My father received notices, which I saw—threatening letters commanding him to turn off his Catholic servants, and not employ them in his work.

Do you recollect any other circumstance from the period of 1795? Nothing but occasional wreckings and disturbances. There scarcely has been a 12th of July, to the best of my recollection, in any year from the commencement of Orangeism till the present period when a breach of the peace has not occurred, and frequently lives have been lost in consequence of these processions.

You mention that there were processions of the Defenders previous to the processions of the Orangemen? So there were; but not before the Peep-o'-Day men. There were processions of that party previous to the establishment of the Orangemen, but not previous to the establishment of the Peep-o'-Day men.

You state that there were a considerable number of the houses of Catholics wrecked in 1794 and 1795; were there not also a considerable number of the houses of Protestants wrecked by the Defenders? I am not aware that there were; there were none in my neighbourhood; I did not hear of any Protestant houses being attacked and destroyed; I did hear that there were some places in the neighbouring counties where the Catholics had taken arms from the Protestants.

Do you know any of your society that belong to Orange Lodges? No; nothing of the sort; they would be expelled if they did.

Can any member of the Friends' Society belong to a lodge? If it comes to the knowledge of the society he cannot.

Then no Orangeman can be a Quaker? No Quaker can be an Orangeman.

When Orange processions take place, do the magistrates take an active part in preventing them; or what course do they adopt? I think they do not exert themselves to prevent them. Heretofore I saw several going in processions with them, but not of late years.

Did they exert themselves to prevent these processions? Witness stated on the authority of Mr. John Holmes Huston, County Down, how that gentleman had prevented an Orange procession when all the neighbouring magistrates had absented themselves from home. Twenty ringleaders were prosecuted and fined; a subscription was set on foot by the Orange party, and one magistrate of the neighbourhood actually subscribed to it.

Do you regard the punishment of a fine on an Orangeman violating the law as being little calculated to produce any effect? I think under these circumstances it is, but my opinion is that it is not the lower class of the Society that the Government ought to deal with; it is the people of the higher classes that stimulate them to it. I think it is those in the higher ranks of society that are the cause of those processions; and when they were dying away that excited them to it a second time; it is those that have official situations, and probably men that hold commissions;* and I think

* Mr. Christie is, no doubt, here referring to that small tribe of feather-bed warriors, the majors, the colonels, and the captains whose names and the names of whose ancestors have been, intimately associated with Orangeism in the No th of Ireland.

it would subside at the present time, but for the efforts of those who keep in the back ground, and encourage the others on by violent speeches and public meetings. I am satisfied that if the Government . . . would not inflict fines and punishment upon the lower class, who are the tools of others, but take it at the fountain head, the gentlemen of rank and fortune. . . . it would settle these disturbances. . . . I have been an observer of these things for many years, and I have long been of opinion that this party business has been kept up by the supineness of the magistrates, and by their encouragement; walking in the first place in their processions and dining with them at their clubs. . . . I never belonged to any political society, and I think I am pretty impartial with respect to the parties; and I can say that it is not only my opinion but the opinion of the moderate people generally, who are disposed to keep peace in the country, that it is the gentlemen and the people of rank and fortune in the country that have stimulated others to these party processions which tend to keep up party feeling.

What is your opinion of the effect of the Orange Lodges upon the peace of society and the good feeling of the people of the country? I think they have a tendency to keep up a bad feeling, and if anything could be devised to put them down I think the country would be much quieter. It is not the poor people who go into the lodges, but the clergy and the magistrates and the gentlemen of the country; and so far as Government can interfere I think these are the people to lay their hands on. I think no man should hold a Commission of the Peace or any place of profit under the Crown who is an Orangeman.

What is the effect of those Orange processions and lodges upon the minds of the Catholic people with regard to the administration of justice both by magistrates and jurors? Where an Orange magistrate is sitting on the bench the Catholics consider that he is partial in his decisions. . . . I have said before with respect to Orangemen being magistrates in my opinion it is not fit, but when magistrates, men of respectability and intelligence, well-informed and impartial magistrates cannot be got—and I believe there are some parts of the country where they cannot be got. I believe that a stipendiary magistrate in such districts of the country would be absolutely necessary.

For what reason do you believe they could not

be got? Because there are so many completely Orangemen in principle, although not professed Orangemen; they are biassed in their opinion against Catholics so that justice cannot be obtained at their hands.

You yourselves are impartial; do you or do you not think that the Orange magistrates are or are not likely to be biassed? I think they are unsuitable to try questions which originate in party feeling when they themselves belong to a party and encourage party feeling.

From whence do you derive your knowledge of the magistrates? My observations of their conduct and their attending processions when the law was not against it, and for their language to the people at those processions; from the feelings of the Catholics when they are brought before them, and, knowing the circumstances of the case, a person of middling capacity can judge whether a magistrate is doing right or wrong.

Are the committee to understand that the evidence you have given with regard to magistrates is derived from the observations you have stated? From the observations I have made upon the conduct of magistrates, what I have seen, and heard, and known. I have sometimes attended the Quarter Sessions, and I have seen Orange magistrates sitting, and I myself, and many others, were not satisfied with their decisions.

Did you see any act performed that you could say was partial? I thought so.

Can you mention the act? I think the principal thing was in the examination of witnesses; the credit that was given to one witness above another. Where two men of equally good character were brought forward to prove a thing, the one a Catholic and the other a Protestant, the Protestant evidence was admitted as good, and the other was considered as doubtful.

You were understood to say that any feelings of irritation that existed between parties in Ireland are rather between Catholics and Orangemen than between Catholics and Protestants? It is.

Here we find a striking parallel to the facts as related by historians contemporary with the events of which they treated. If in times of peace magistrates can be thus actuated by party motives, it is for the reader to determine whether there can have been exaggeration in the description of their conduct when civil war agitated the community, and when, with all their misdeeds, they took shelter beneath the protecting arm of a patronising Administration.

Are you an Orangeman? If so, and if the inheritance be worthy of possession, it surely is also worth examining into the title-deeds. Go read history for yourself. You will find the doings of your ancestors, the founders of your "glorious" institution, written in every line, frequently between the lines of your country's history. Place those facts side by side with the records of recent years, and the opinions of moderate and impartial men of the present day, and you will find in the coincidence sufficient to bring the blush of shame to your brow; to send a pang to your heart, not, let me hope, because you have allowed yourself to be the tool of a malignant faction, with whom you have nothing in common but a name, but because, blinded by sophistry and captivated by bombast you have worked yourself into the belief that you have an ancient, and an honoured, and a noble ancestry. It is hard, no doubt, to alter those opinions which bigotry, whispering into a young mind, instilled in you when a boy. And it is an easy solution of the difficulty to say that James Christie was a "prejudiced old quaker," a "confounded old rebel" whose statements are not worthy of belief. Mark it, he was as loyal a man as you are; a man who unlike you probably, had. nothing to gain, and much to lose by civil warfare and party strife; and mark it too that he but echoed the sentiments of most writers of that period. Knowing the reluctance with which men alter their opinions, particularly when it implies a change of principle in manhood, I have, in this volume, abstained, up to the present, from quoting many authors whose pronounced views might, with some, have cast a doubt over their honesty, and afforded excuse to those so blind that they would not see. Go you and read the writings of those men who cheated the gallows of its victim—who came safe, I wou'd add honourably, out of the terrible struggle of '98, and lived to tell, in the early part of this century, the story of past abuses. The same parallel will be found. Contrary to what you likely have been taught, you will find this new reservoir of history opened to you full of instruction; principles enunciated in it that are only revolting to those who have not studied them, or even read them; at least, you will find in it the expressions of great and unselfish men, whose chief fault was that they lived a century before their time, in a period when reason and justice in this country were yet in their swaddling clothes, when the sword was mightier than the pen. And you will have the satisfaction of the perusal being rewarded. You will find palliation, not excuse, for misdeeds of your early brethren; that in fact, they claimed a protection above the law, through being encouraged in their excesses by those whose first duty was to administer it.[*] Even seek in the newspaper chronicles of the time for information[†] If your

* MacNevin in his "Pieces of Irish History," page 113, says: "The Peep-o'-Day Boys who had originally pretended onl to enforce the Popery laws by depriving the Catholics o Arms now affected more important objects. They claimed to be associated for the support o' the Protestant Government and the Protestant succession, which the said were in danger, by the increased power of the Catholics in the State, and t ey, therefore, adopted the name of Ora gemen to express heir attachment to the memory of that Prince to whom they owed those blessings. With this change of name they asserted that they had also gained an accession of strength, for the Peep-o'-Day Boys only imagined they were supported by the law of the land in their depredations on their Catholic neighbours, but the Orangemen boasted protection greater even than the law—the connivance and concealed support of those who were bound to see it fairly administered. Thus emboldened and, as they alleged, re nforced, they renewed their ncient persecutions, and not content with stripping Catholics of arms they now went to greater length than they had ever done before in adding insult to injury, sometimes by mocking the solemnities of their worship, and at others even by firing into the coffins of the dead on their way to the sepulchre."

† The Dublin Freeman's Journal (then the Government organ), The Press and the Northern Star (both the advocates of reform) of those days furnish numerous examples of Orange atrocities. For instance, in 1 s issue of 2 th March, 1796, the la t me tioned paper published the following:— "F r several days past r ports were in ustrously circulated that those miscreants the Orangemen meditated an attack on the own of Belfast, and were determined to destroy the persons and property of those in this country who had promoted the union of rishmen; in short all those who reached the Divine doctrine of 'peace and goodwill to all men'," and it proceeds, "the sce unts of the atrocities in the County Armagh had so far corrobor ted this th it Genera Nugent put the garrison of the town in readiness and doubled the guards." In the same las e I al o find the following significant warning:—"In some parishes there a e accounts of unusual d scontent. There are certainly reasons for di content, and let us beware lest by adding fuel to the fire we increase rather than le sen the flame. If an abhorrence of and a wish to defend themselves again t the Genera incursi ns of the Orangemen actuate the districts to which we allude they may rest in peace, for should those daring offenders ever attem t an attack on this country there is force sufficient, civil and mi tary, within the town of Belfast

inquiry be not confined to those journals then knowingly in the pay of the Government and the Orange faction, you can trace in every page—like to the trail of the serpent or that bloody track, such as sometimes providentially connects the murderer with the victim—a continuous chain of circumstances that lead to one irresistable conclusion—that at all events the founders of the "Loyal" Orange Institution were not the honoured followers of the liberal-minded monarch whose memory they pretended to venerate, but a base, bloody, and brutal faction, rocked in the cradle of crime, nurtured by cruelty and lust, moved as much by selfishness as by fanaticism; not the loyal supporters of their King and Constitution, but men who made it a condition of their loyalty that five-sixths of the population should be placed at their feet; men who nominated their blood-money at the maximum amount they could plunder, and the Government secure to them by confiscation.[*] So much, at least, for the founders of the Orange Institution. Let us advance a stage and examine who were the actors on each side of the dread drama now opening upon us.

a'one to annihilate the entire horde." This would indicate that the Orangemen emboldened by the success of their schemes in Armagh, and feeling secure in the connivance of the Government, did at an earl period in their care er contemplate an attack upon Belfast, then the stronghold of reformers.

* When before the Select Committe on the 22nd July, 183, Mr. Patrick M'Connell, solicitor, Tandragee, gave a striking corroboration of the horrible murder described in Chapter X., as having been committed by Trin le, a violent Orange leader, u on Mr. Daniel Co ri an earl in 1796. Mr. M'Connel 's aunt was m rried to Mr Corrigan, the u fortunate. He then states that Mrs. Corrigan who had a large farm had to sell it on such terms as she could and quit the country. An Orangem n bought it. Whle awaiting the trial of Trimble at the As izes Lord Gosford had to afford her protection in his own castle, lest the ordina y mode of preventing prosecution wou d be resorted to.

CHAPTER XIV.—THE YOEMANRY, A LIGALISED ORANGE BANDITTI.

All the Yoemanry who played a part in the bloody drama of '98 were not Orangemen. By far the greater proportion of them were. Some honest Protestants, moved, not by malice or cupidity, but by a strict sense of their duty as citizens, whose allegiance, in their opinion, bound them to defend their acknowledged king against rebels without questioning the justness of the revolt, joined the movement at the outset. And we will find that when these men came to discover, but too late, the despicable part they had to play, when they discovered that they were used not as they thought, to put down an insurrection, but to excite one, they learned to bewail their impetuous loyalty, and repent

even their passiveness in the bloody work of extermination. Still those whose sympathies lie with a struggling people driven to the utmost verge of despair must do this section of the corps the credit of having done according to their estimate no more than their duty. Ascendancy had procured them peace, monopoly, guaranteed them wealth, if it had not already secured it. Two elements so favourable to loyalty could not but have influence upon those who forgot in their own contentment the misery of their neighbours; upon those who, contented with the order of things, were for self-interests opposed to a change. They deserve no blame, unless in a nega-

O

tive sense. They can claim no praise. Self-preservation, the first instinct of man's nature, prompts one to extinguish the fire in his own house first; a higher attribute sends him, forgetful of immediate interests, to the aid of poorer brethren similarly threatened. You cannot condemn the wisdom of the one, but you must applaud the generosity of the other. The very conditions under which the services of such men were obtained were calculated to make their assistance valuable. They were but the units, however. There was another class of men, Protestants likewise, who comprised the vast majority constituting the yeomanry of 1798, but, unlike their co-religionists, their services were obtained under circumstances which " rendered them formidable to everyone but the enemy." This class was the Orangemen. Mr Pitt was nearing the goal of his ambition. The great aim of a checkered life, in the course of which he played many parts, was the accomplishment of a union between the two countries. Gifted by nature, imperious by disposition, haughty and overbearing from an education calculated to fit him as a statesman of the sixteenth rather than the eighteenth century, a great Minister, and a greater tyrant, he was ill calculated to brook defeat, and on the rejection of his commercial propositions in 1785 resolved upon the degradation of Ireland With this view he debauched her under the Duke of Rutland. He re-established her dependence upon the British Minister through the Marquis of Buckingham He weakened her under the Earl of Westmoreland. He tantalised and taunted her by the transit of Earl Fitzwilliam. He exasperated her under the Earl of Camden. He debased her under Marquis Cornwallis. And by continuing the Earl of Hardwicke in his Government he insiduously rivetted by pretending to lighten her fetters. The principles of the French Revolution had extended long since to Ireland Men despairing of Parliamentary reform began to hope that they might transplant its great virtues without reaping its concomitant vices. Mr. Pitt saw the ingrafting of the new plant, and cherished it for a time. He played a desperate game, and like the gamester who had cast his last stake he watched it with desperation.

War! that dread game the world so loves to pay, had no horrors for him, and by an insiduous policy that long accustomed a faction to deeds of blood he had made for himself ready tools to his purpose. An unsuccessful rebellion was the one thing needed. Dissention might secure its failure If this failed persecution could alone cause its premature explosion. He soon found that dissension could not singly accomplish his ends. Since the Volunteer move went the Presbyterians of the North had tasted the sweets of liberty. Republican by religion, reformers by nature, they were men little inclined to forego their rights when once they had established them, men whose busy minds were stirred, too, into revolt by commercial restrictions when persecution and extermination had failed to excite it in a class so long accustomed to suffering as to be all but insensible to it. Between those two classes, of whom we must treat further on, an union sprang up which soon became formidable, and Mr Pitt had to play his last trick or give up the game when nearest winning. Persecution must be resorted to. In the remote County of Armagh a faction in the pay of the Government could carry it on, and minions of the Castle who had forgotten the way to blush could boldly give the lie to any charge arising out of it. But this must be a persecution on an extended scale, which not even a Camden Administration could pretend ignorance of. The English soldiery would not safely answer his purpose, and looking abroad he found the Orangemen, that favourite faction which he had fashioned for his own ends To legalise this banditti was now his object, and accordingly in the autumn of 1793 we find the yeomanry established in Dublin beneath the shadow of the Castle. Some of the anti-Ministerialists did their best to discourage the project, and one of them characterised it thus.—" The manner in which the Administration are about to prepare a force in this kingdom is exceedingly suspicious. Were the liberty of the nation to be destroyed, *its independence or imperial existence to be voted away*, the plan to be acted upon could be no other than that which developes itself. In the metropolis the *canaille de la cour* only are to be armed, we are to have armed pensioners, armed Excise men, armed Revenue officers, from the commissioner to the gauger, armed contractors, armed clerks from all the public offices; every person in the Court, about the Court, or deriving from the Court are to be armed. In the country our little great men known at Court, and none others, are to be armed; their parasites and retainers are to be armed; their domestics are to be armed; their devoted tenants are to be armed; and this piebald mass of incongruous particles, this disjointed piece of patchwork—a just emblem of folly, weakness, and ridicule—is to be called Yeo-manry. See, then, in what situation we will eventually find ourselves. All the partizans of corrupt influence—all those whose interest it is to continue and multiply the abuses of our political system—will have arms in their hands. All those who rely upon their own independent properties, or upon their own industry—the people whom it has become of late the fashion to asperse—will be naked. Thus naked, the people will stand like a fool in the middle, surrounded by a treble army—an army of policemen and pensioners, a mercenary standing army, and an army of militia, officered by the Court."

Mr. Plowden says that the formation of the lawyers' corps gave favour and sanction to the movement in Dublin, and at a meeting in the 16th Sept, 1796, it was resolved "That they held it expedient, with the permission of the Government, to form an armed association for the defence of the kingdom," while immediately following we have this significant sentence, "great efforts were made to fester the soreness of the Catholics, and to inflame the differences between the Protestants and them." The fact is that by the agency of Government an alarm was created in the minds of many honest Protestants that the rebellion (which only occurred two years later as a consequence of excesses) might burst out at any moment. A few Catholics were at first admitted into some of the corps, but the reluctance with which they were accepted, and the cold-shouldering which they experienced afterwards, plainly demonstrated that they were not wanted, and they took the hint accordingly. The Catholics, resenting their rejection, waited upon Mr. Pelham, the dear friend and champion of the Armagh Orange wreckers, and asked for leave to form a Catholic corps They were told to join the corps then being raised by the Protestants Some few individuals, it appears, did join, but the large majority kept aloof

In the North the new movement spread like wild-fire. By this time the Orange weavers and labourers had found that plundering was a paying game, and much more to their metal than honest employment. Out of their dens and hiding-places, from which even yet they seldom ventured to crawl save beneath the cover of night to pursue their depredations, they now rushed forth. Events had shapen themselves much in their favour. While receiving the pay of the Government, armed by Government, and legalised by Government, they could now, and in the light of day, plunder by order of Council; pillage had become a virtue, murder a test of loyalty, and lust one of the corporal works of mercy. The Masters of lodges made fit lieutenents for such a guerilla troop; the District Masters and District Secretaries ranked as captains, and in the Grand Masters of counties, the Grand Secretaries, and that host of conspirators who dealt in the mystic mummeries of the County Grand Lodges we find their colonels and commanders—all, from the bumpkin who had cast aside the plough for the sword, and the weaver who found the blunderbuss a readier instrument than the shuttle with which to secure a fortune, from the understrapper, the miserable tenant, and the bailiff to those needy gentlemen who saw now a means of securing their rents by pocketing the pay of their men, all came swarming out like carrion flies in summer time, but armed with a double power — the right of creating havoc and the privilege of fattening upon it. Forth they went in that autumn of 1796, "Salus factionis suprema lex" their motto, an army of despicable but "loyal" cowards, upon a work which the naked savage in his wilds would abhor, and from which the Author of Evil must have turned aside in disgust, sickening at the thought that he was to be linked to such associates. If prescience be vouchsafed to the doomed, many an unborn babe and many a blooming village maiden, "sweet as the primrose-peeps beneath the thorn," and many an aged parent must have felt the cold shudder of coming death or degradation upon that ominous 14th September.

From the report of Lord Castlereagh to the British Parliament, just after the completion of the Union, I find that the forces in Ireland were 45,839 regulars, 27,104 militia, and 53,557 yeomanry, making a total of 126 500 men, while the defensive and offensive means of warfare were proportionally great in other parts of the kingdom. From the most reliable source open to us, Mr. Madden's interesting series, we find that Lord Edward Fitzgerald when pressing "W. M ' to join the revolutionary movement, said " examine these papers—here are returns showing 100,000 men may be counted on to take the field," to which " W. M." gave this pregnant reply, " 100,000 on paper will not furnish 50,000 in array." With 80,000 disciplined soldiers at their command, with a large reserve force distributed over the United Kingdom, and with ample facilities for transportation to Ireland it is not unreasonable to presume that the Government could have easily suppressed a rebellion of such disorganised forces, as they knew well the United men consisted of, without calling to their aid a body of men inflamed by party feud, and bound by secret ties and oaths of extermination. No doubt their offer of assistance might be too tempting for such a Government as that of Pitt's to refuse, too tempting especially at a time when continental matters were in a state of dreadful and disastrous confusion. But if we recollect, that Administration had in its employ a band of informers, who laid bare before them all the secrets of the organisation, that they had fairly estimated its power, were acqui n'ed with its projects; that they had the names of all its leaders pigeon-holed in the Castle; that with the movement within their grasp they coquetted with rebels in order to tempt a people to their ruin, and neglected to discharge the first duty of a Government under such circumstances, in saving the revolting from the results of their own folly, we will be driven to the irresistible conclusion that the object of the Administration was not, as some honest Protestants thought, to keep down an insurrection, but to foment one that they might suppress it at the cannon's mouth, and so clear the road by blood and extermination for the projected Union For the purpose of extermination we must, therefore, believe they paid those who were sworn exterminators.

With the exception of Sir Richard Musgrave, there is not to be found a writer who does not admit and denounce the outrages committed by the Orange yeomanry of 1798, while at the present day they have taken their place in history as facts which no man dare deny Sir William, with his customary blundering, first denies them and then justifies them.

Lord Holland, in his "Memoirs of the Whig Party," speaking of the reign of terror of Irish Orangeism, and "the clemency" of Lord Camden's rule, says, "The premature and ill-concerted insurrections which followed in the Catholic districts, were quelled, rather in consequence of want of concert and skill in the insurgents, than of any good conduct or discipline of the King's troops, whom Sir Ralph Abercrombie described as formidable to no one but their friends. That experienced and upright commander had been removed from his command" (the fact is he resigned), "even after those just and spirited general orders, in which the remarkable judgment just quoted was conveyed. His recall was conveyed as a triumph by the Orange faction,

and they contrived, about the same time, to get rid of Mr Secretary Pelham, who, thought somewhat time-serving was a good-natured and prudent man. Indeed, surrounded as they were with burning cottages, tortured backs, and frequent executions, they were yet full of their sneers at what they whimsically termed "the clemency" of the Government and the weak character of their Viceroy, Lord Camden. The fact is incontrovertible that the people of Ireland were driven to resistance, which, possibly, they meditated before, by the free quarters and expenses of the soldiery, which were such as are not permitted in civilised warfare, even in an enemy's country. Trials, if they must be so called, were carried on without number under martial law. It often happened that three officers composed the Court, and that of the three two were under age and the third an officer of the yeomanry or the militia who had sworn in his Orange lodge eternal hatred to the people over whom he was thus constituted a judge. Floggings, picketings, and death, were the usual sentences, and these were sometimes commuted into banishment, serving in the fleet, or transference to a foreign service Many were sold at so much per head to the Prussians. Other more legal but not less horrible outrages were daily committed by the different corps under the command of the Government Even in the streets of Dublin a man was shot and robbed of £30 on a loose recollection of a soldier's having seen him in the battle of Kilcally, and no proceeding was instituted to ascertain the murder or prosecute the murderer Lord Wycombe, who was in Dublin, and who was himself shot at by a sentinel between Blackrock and that city, wrote to me many details of similar outrages which he had ascertained to be true Dr Dickson (Lord Bishop of Down) assured me that he had seen families returning peaceably from Mass assailed, without provocation, by drunken yeomanry, and the wives and daughters exposed to every species of indignity, brutality, and outrage, from which his remonstrances nor those of other Catholic gentlemen could rescue them."

Sir Jonah Barrington, writing upon the same subject, says[*] —"This measure (free quarters) was resorted to with all its attendant horrors throughout some of the best parts of Ireland previous to the Insurrection" He adds, "slow torture was inflicted under pretence of extorting confessions; the people were driven to madness. General Abercrombie, who succeeded as com-

* Rise and fall of the Irish Nation, pages 430-1,

mander-in-chief, was not *permitted* to abate these enormities, and, therefore, resigned in disgust. Ireland was reduced to a state of anarchy, and exposed to crimes and cruelties, to which no nation had ever been subject. The people can no longer bear their miseries; *Mr. Pitt's object was now effected.*"

Haverly says (page 743) "The ferocity of the Orange Yeomanry was indescribable; a notion appeared to have generally prevailed among them that the time *to extirpate* the Catholics had arrived, and they acted accordingly; their conduct during the insurrection was that of incarnate fiends. It was a fearful dragonnade, in which the usages of civilisation were set aside; and, such being the case on the part of the Royal troops, it is not wonderful that the undisciplined peasantry should have been guilty of many acts of barbarity. The crimes of the latter, however, were done in retaliation; they were often prompted by private malice, and it should be remembered that they were the work of exasperated multitudes, goaded by injuries and unrestrained by authority."

Lord Moira, speaking on the 22nd November, 1797, in the English House of Lords, said—"I address you this day my lords on documents equally sure and staple. Before God and my country I speak of what I have seen myself. What I have to speak of are not solitary and insulated measures, nor partial abuses, but what is adopted as the system of Government; I do not talk of a casual system, but of one deliberately determined, and regularly persevered in. . . . I have seen in Ireland the most absurd as well as the most disgusting tyranny that any nation ever groaned under. . . . I have seen troops that have been sent full of this prejudice—that every inhabitant in that kingdom is a rebel to the British Government" He then proceeded to compare the *regime* to the Inquisition, to describe the picketings and the torturing, and the half-hanging in order to extort confessions, and added, "No person could say who would be the next victim of this oppression and cruelty."

The Rev. James Gordon, rector of Killegney, Ferns, a gentleman "wholly British by descent," and with "a natural bias on the side of Protestantism and loyalty," as he himself stated*says: "Great numbers of houses were burned, with their furniture, where concealed arms were found, or meetings of the United Irishmen had been

* Gordon's Hist. of the Rebellion, page 65-76.

held, or whose occupants had been guilty of the fabrication of pikes, or of other practices for the promotion of the conspiracy. Many of the common people, and some even in circumstances superior to that class, particularly in the city of Dublin, were scourged—some picketed or otherwise put to pain—to force a confession of concealed arms or plots. To authorise the burning of houses and furniture the wisdom of the Administration may have seen as good reason as for any other acts of severity, though to me and many others that reason is not clear."

To exhaust all the authorities upon this feature of the question were useless. But there is another point which has not been adequately brought before the public in reference to the Orange yeomanry. They were loyal only in profession. Bound by the oath of conditional loyalty, and such a fearful one as the early oath of the Orange Institution, it would be hard to expect it otherwise. Of the feline species, they purred, and were content so long as plunder was permitted and they shared largely in the booty. But rub them against the grain, compel them to be honest men, to abide by military regulations, and to obey the laws, and forthwith they showed their claws. The instances are many in which these same loyal men, these supporters of King and Constitution, mutinied against their officers and refused to serve. Several very notable cases of this sort occurred after the brief rebellion of 1803 had been suppressed, and the conduct of some of the corps, the Armagh corps amongst the number, was so disloyal that they had to be disbanded. Through the year '98 the cases were few, comparatively, for then they were allowed free quarters, but when, a few years later, the work of extermination was done, and a spirit something nearer toleration showed itself, these gallant plunderers in their turn revolted, were censured, fell into disorganisation and into disgrace. As law-breakers they distinguished themselves in refusing to obey such measures as the Party Procession Act, another proof of conditional loyalty,* and by order of the

* Before the Select Committee of 1835 Lord Gosford, the son of Earl Gosford, whose denunciation in 1795 so disturbed the peace of the Orangemen, gave corroborative testimony as to the truthfulness and accuracy of his father's address. He is then at No 3,329 asked "Have the Yeomen taken a prominent part in those Orange processions, or has it appeared from the character and description of the persons that were in those processions that amongst them many of the Yeomanry must have been?" to which he replies :—"I should think so; but not in their dress, or appearing as Yeomen; but that there were men belonging to the Yeomanry corps in these processions I believe there is no doubt." This was after the passing of the Mr. Stanley Anti-Procession Act. In the previous page we find Lord Gosford making use of the following pregnant remark :—"In discharge of my duty as Lieutenant of the County Armagh I have found bodies of them (the Orangemen) resist the law; I have found them resist the law, and refuse to obey the law as Orangemen."

P

Lord Lieutenant many were dismissed. Various peculations have been proved against members of the body. The depth and intensity of their loyalty were measured by their pockets, and accordingly we find numerous instances recorded in which Masters and District Masters (such as Captain Patten, of Tandragee) allowed persons of their own nomination to fill the place of deceased lieutenants and receive their pay without the knowledge of Government; in which majors and captains retaining the pay of their men for rents, debts, &c., and in which men purloined the property of their equals and their superiors when their hands were not otherwise employed. A guerilla troop, these Orange yeomanry possessed all the ferocity of the buccaneer, with none of his bravery; all the brutality of the savage, with none of his nobility; the cupidity of the highwayman, with no relieving dash of courage or of recklessness, the last of the brute, the heart of the slave, and the hand of the assassin,

It is notorious, the real fighting was done without them. They came in at the tail and completed the carnage.

"Harsh words!" Yes; but harsher truths. Some who have learned to abhor the deeds of these men may deem it unwise this "re-opening of an old sore," as they would term it. To this I can best reply in the words of Hamlet—silence "will but skin and film the ulcerous place; whiles rank corruption, mining all within, infects unseen." This embraces a melancholy consideration. But it must be boldly faced. And if, in these pages, I call a spade a spade, I ask my readers to do me the justice of believing that my motive is not to revile the memory of the dead, or to hurt the sensitiveness of the living, but, within the lines of historical accuracy, to mark a canker in our system, so that, looking upon it, all may learn to avoid it.

"I must be cruel only to be kind,
Thus bad begins, and worse remains behind."

CHAPTER XV.—EARLY REFORMERS, THE UNITED IRISHMEN.

THE prejudice against Irish history, prevalent amongst the profusely loyal to British connection, argues more a weakness than a strength in the virtue they boast the possession of, showing as it does a fear to place it in jeopardy by a due investigation of the truth. That prejudice has been the parent of much popular error in regard to the history of the United Irishmen. It has contrived to prolong error, and may be effectual to the end in perpetuating it. Nothing is more common, even in the present day, than to suppose that the United Irish movement was distinctly a Roman Catholic one. Yet nothing could be more erroneous. The ascendancy party has even gone so far as to connect with it the Pope, the College of Cardinals, the Irish Episcopacy, and the Irish priests; a huge ultramontane conspiracy for the overthrow of Protestantism, in which, from the occupant of the Throne of Peter down to the humble Irish curate, all were alike concerned. Those who are responsible for this misrepresentation must bear either the infamy of falsely representing facts or the disgrace of being ignorant of them. Of the grosser charge many, with their minds fixed upon the significance of passing events, will likely hold them convicted. This is but one of the several means by which a clique seeks to divide and conquer. As a matter of fact the United Irish movement found its origin, not in any diabolical Popish conspiracy, but in the broad spirit of enlightenment and reform, which spread amongst the Northern Presbyterians in the latter end of the last century. Of foreign extraction, conquerors in a strange land, estranged from its people by a reformed religion, which laughed at all the cherished dogmas of the ancient faith, the grandfathers of these men—stern, relentless, even cruel, not the children of Fate, but the carvers of their own destiny—had settled down upon the forfeited lands of the early occupiers. Too accustomed to the fortunes of war to feel remorse, and too practical to become elated, they at once made the best of their good luck, and applied themselves to business. That intercourse which the trade of a century ensured had rubbed away the intolerant and despotic manners of the soldier of fortune. With a widening civilisation, we find their successors moderate, liberal, and tolerant, but inheriting the fierce republican spirit of the old Cromwellians, the dogged austerity of the Puritan reformers, which classed crowns and royal sceptres amongst children's playthings, hurried a king to the block, and brought an ancient Parliament Horse with its thousand fond memories and thousand dear privileges, about the ears of its occupants. The interests of these men had become identical with those of their country. As Irish as the Irish themselves, they were not of that mettle to calmly submit to exclusion. They learned to protest against the monopoly and injustice which made Ireland the never-failing source of British revenue, and, in arms against both, they soon came to abhor prosecution as the means by which they were accomplished. England having sowed the wind, had well-nigh reaped the whirl-wind. In the sons of her early Irish settlers she found her early Irish reformers. They were the founders and the directors of the United Irish Society, and the leaders in a rebellion which, but for a succession of misfortunes, might have cost her her Irish dependency.

To say it was a Roman Catholic movement is to pay a compliment to the members of that religion of those days that, in truth, they are not deserving of.* Fettered and degraded by the persecution of centuries, with bitter recollections that every revolt only served to rivet their chains the faster, it is scarcely to be wondered that the National spirit was broken and depressed. Local conspiracies, known here under one denomination, there under another, formed escape valves for long pent-up indignation; but in all cases their objects were purely the redress of local grievances. One society did get so far as to entertain the idea that "something should be done for Ireland;" but what that something was neither they nor their illiterate leaders could suggest. In 1792, when continental politics were in a muddle, the first real remission of the penal code came to Irish Catholics in the 32nd of George III., by which certain restraints and disabilities were removed, and Papists were permitted to become barristers, attorneys, notaries, and attorneys' clerks. Protestant barristers were permitted to marry Catholic wives and bring up their children Papists, and schoolmasters relieved from taking out licences from Protestant bishops. In the following year the difficulties abroad thickened around England, and accordingly an Act was passed to enable Roman Catholics to hold and take degrees for any professorship in any college thereafter to be founded, provided it was not for the exclusive education of Papists, and for a similar reason 1795 brought the Act in relation to Maynooth. The ostensible object of these concessions was to conciliate the Irish people in a time of need, but there was a sinister motive behind them all—to alienate the respectable

* Father Taffe in his history of Ireland, page 94, says, "It is well known that the Catholics, of all others, are the least inclined to rebel, and have borne with persecution when others would have been in arms. Compare the suffering of the Catholics of Ireland with the refractory spirit of the Protestants of the Transatlantic Colonies; the submissive temper of the Catholic provinces of Canada conquered by France, and the stubborn resistance of the Protestant Colonies, united and cherished into growth by England!"

Irish Roman Catholic from the mass of the people, and above all, to separate from them the Irish priesthood. The first object was wholly accomplished, the other only partially, if at all. Accordingly, we find the wealthy Roman Catholic gentry content with small mercies, satisfied that a way had been opened in life for their sons, forgetful of the grievances under which the large mass of the people laboured, and not unfrequently hounding the dogs of war upon their track to show what loyal subjects King George the Third had found in them. Of such men, with an occasional reformer of another religion who looked beyond their programme but dared not declare his intentions, we find that the Catholic committee was made up; men who confined their labours to presenting elaborate addresses to newly-arrived Viceroys, who lost themselves in enthusiasm over the many excellencies which they professed to find in his Gracious Majesty the King, and who a thousand and one times signed themselves as "in duty bound to ever pray" for one of the most rotten Parliaments, made up of the most menial "representatives" that ever befooled an intelligent people or persecuted an illiterate one. This, then, was the position of the Irish Catholics in those days. And being so, who dares say that the United Irish movement was a Roman Catholic one! Who dares pay to selfish respectability and easily purchased loyalty a compliment of which they were not deserving! Who dares rob a sect that was in advance of their fellows of the reputation of being the only intelligent people who contemplated reform, and the people most willing to suffer in its attainment! The rebellion failed for want of leaders. Had the respectable Roman Catholics allied themselves with their reforming Presbyterian and Protestant brethren it is reasonable to conclude it would have been successful; that 1798 had been "a glorious victory, and not a shameful rout;" that it had now taken its place beside the brilliant era of American independence; that Tone would have been our Washington, and that some years hence another free people would have been joining in an universal Te Deum at the centennial celebration of Irish independence.

That the mass of the rebels were Catholic there is no doubt. But they were rebels because persecution made them such, not because Catholicism inclined them to be. Long suffering drove them into revolt, and they in desperation ranked themselves beneath the leadership of men whose religion furnished no reason for doubt, but rather an assurance, that their motives were sincere. The total number enrolled up to February, 1798, was 500,000 ; the available forces counted on, 250,000 Lord Edward Fitzgerald reckoned upon 100,000 men on paper, while shrewd W. M. (William Murphy, of Smithfield) held that 100,000 men on paper meant not half that number (50,000) in the field. From these figures subtract the numbers of the Northern Presbyterians, those men who fought at Antrim, Sain'field, and Ballynahinch, and the residue will make but a poor comparison with more than four millions of Irish Roman Catholics.

There is still another popular error, and a no less grievous one, in regard to this movement. The idea has been long since dispelled that its leaders were men of humble origin, illiterate, and insignificant; but there still remains with many the belief that the movement was that of a political junto, an isolated instance of factious opposition to the Administration of the day; that in the society of United Irishmen were gathered all the irreconcilables of the period, while outside their ranks was to be found, at all points of the three kingdoms, an unbroken calm extending away to the utmost verge of the political horizon. Why, it was the age of reform all the world over. In England it was an age of reform because it was an age of corruption. The scathing sarcasms of Junius had not yet lost their point*, and the eloquent denunciations of Burke and his contemporaries were echoing over the Empire. There were in England such societies as "the Revolution Society of London," the "Whig Club," the "Friends of the Universal Peace and the Rights of Man," the "Westminster Committee of Reform," the "Friends of the Liberty of the Press," the "Society of United Englishmen," the "London Corresponding Society" (seeking Parliamentary reform),† the "Manchester Constitution Society" (Republican); in Scotland some similar associations were to be found, while in Ireland we had the Catholic Committee, the Whig Club,

* This mysterious and able author had used these prophetic words—"The evil lies too deep to be cured by any remedy less than some great convulsion which may bring back the Constitution to its original principles, or utterly destroy it."

† Mr. Pitt who started in life as a reformer attended on 16th May, 1782, "a meeting of members of Parliament friendly to a constitutional reformation," at which delegates were present from several committees of counties and cities. One of the resolutions passed was that the sense of the country should be taken during the summer in order that the members might be able "to lay their several petitions before Parliament early in the next session, when these proposals for a Parliamentary reformation (without which neither the liberty of the nation can be preserved nor the permanence of any virtuous Administration be secure) may receive that ample and mature discussion which so momentous a question demands."

the Political Society of Dublin, and the United Irishmen avowed in the light of day. If the United Men were disloyal in the beginning they were in such good company as the Right Hon. William Pitt and Lord Castlereagh, who surely could do no wrong; if they were rebels in the end, it was their misfortune, not their fault, and they have only to thank the Administration for making them so.

O'Connor, Wyse, and Curry founded the Catholic Committe in Dublin in 1757, the first meeting being held in the Globe Coffee-house, Essex Street, at which but eight persons attended. It is not within the scope of this history to give details of its working, further than to say that they seem to have been for a considerable part of their early career a Vice-Regal Congratulatory Society. After Tone became connected with them as assistant secretary in the spring of 1792, they did assist in preparing the way for reformers of a spirit more in keeping with the necessities of the time. They sought merely to relieve Catholics from the Penal Code. When their claims were taken up by the Presbyterians of Belfast, the Ascendancy Party took fright at what they termed "the exorbitant pretensions of the Catholic Committee." All through the country wherever it was possible, anti-Catholic meetings were called, and elsewhere the Grand Juries did the work. The Grand Jury of Louth, with the Speaker of the House of Commons at their head, declared "that to allow the Roman Catholics the right of voting for members to serve in Parliament, or admitting them to any participation in the Government of the Kingdom, was incompatible with the safety of the Protestant establishment."

The Corporation of Dublin went further. Alluding in their resolutions to the possibility of Government finally acceding to the Catholic claims, they boldly pronounced the doom of Catholics for all time to come in the following significant words:—"That the Protestants of Ireland would not be compelled by any authority whatever to abandon that political situation which their fathers won with their swords, and which is, therefore, their birthright,"and to this threatened resistance against constituted authority they in addition pledged the lives and fortunes of its members. To leave no room for doubt as to what Protestant Ascendancy ment, they put their modest claims thus :—"A Protestant King of Ireland, a Protestant Parliament, a Protestant Hierarchy, Protestant Electors, and Government; the Bench of Justice, the Army, and the Revenue, through all branches and details, Protestant, and this system supported by connection with the Protestant realm of England." Here we may trace the hand of some of those constitutional loyalists who ruled the city with an iron rod a few years afterwards under the auspices of the Orange Institution. Mr. Grattan, when on the 10th Jan., 1793, he moved an amendment to the Address, referred to this resolution of the Dublin Corporation, and said he considered the publication of it as "the act of the Castle; the act of their city delegation; the composition of their city agents."

The "Whig Club," in imitation of that in England, was established in 1790, and amongst its original members were Lords Charlemont, De Clifford, Moira, O'Neill, the Hon. Robert Stewart, Archibald Rowan Hamilton, William Todd Jones, Colonel Sharman, Hon. E. Ward, and Hon. H. Rowley. To give an indication of the objects of this club to those unacquainted with them, it is only necessary to quote a resolution passed by them on the 16th April, 1790—Rowan Hamilton in the chair. It ran as follows:—Resolved unanimously —That when an unmasked and shameless system of Ministerial corruption manifests an intention to sap the spirit, virtue and independence of Parliament, it is time for the people to look to themselves. Plowden says that the most memorable act of this club was the drawing up of a petition to the King at a meeting of the society, held on the 5th April, 1798—Mr. Grattan in the chair—in order to lay before his Majesty the state of the country, and "a vindication of its people against the tradition of his Ministers." He further adds that the Catholic question was not permitted to be discussed in the club.

It will therefore be seen that the necessity for Parliamentary reform was generally admitted so early as in 1790. Dr. Madden, in his first series (page 174), says—"Various political clubs, emanating from the Volunteer associations, had been formed in Belfast, advocating reform and Catholic Emancipation, before either of these questions had gained ground in the metropolis. The Belfast leaders were so far in advance of those of Dublin on both subjects that, long before the change in the organisation of the united Irish societies, ulterior views to those set out with advocating were entertained by a great many of the former." That Belfast was foremost in the struggle against corruption there can be no doubt. Tone, whose pen had, in August 1791, been ably

employed in behalf of the Catholics of Ireland, was invited to Belfast in October of the same year by a Protestant club of volunteers, under the guidance of a secret committee, to spend a few days in order to assist in framing rules and declarations of the first club of United Irishmen, and "to cultivate an acquaintance with those men whom, though he highly esteemed, he knew as yet by reputation."* The persons whom he met in Belfast, and whom he names as "having some reason to esteem himself particularly fortunate in forming connections with" were Samuel Neilson, Robert Sims, William Sims, William Sinclair, and Thomas M'Cabe; these he classifies as "the men most distinguished for their virtue, talent, and patriotism." He proceeds—"We formed our club, of which I wrote the declaration, and certainly the formation of that club commenced a new epoch in the politics of Ireland." The idea of forming the society, the first meeting of which was held on the 18th of October, would seem to have originated with Samuel Neilson, and to have met with the concurrence of Henry Joy M'Cracken and Thomas Russell, while Wolfe Tone acted at the outset in accordance with the opinions of those who had suggested its formation.

They started with a declaration of their principles, read at their first general meeting on the 18th October, 1791:—

"That the great measure essential to the prosperity and freedom of Ireland was an equal representation of all the people of Ireland." It proceeded to say that the great evil was English influence, and continued—"We have no national Government. We are ruled by Englishmen and the servants of Englishmen, whose object is the interest of another country, whose instrument is corruption, and whose strength is the weakness of Ireland." To effect these objects, the declaration states the society had been formed. The following was adopted:—

"We have agreed to form an association to be called the Society of United Irishmen; and we do pledge ourselves to our country, and mutually to each other, that we will steadily support and endeavour by all due means to carry into effect the following resolutions:—

"I. Resolved—That the weight of English influence in the Government of this country is so great as to require a cordial union among all the people to maintain that balance which is essential to the preservation of our liberties and the extension of our commerce."

" II. That the sole constitutional mode by which this influence can be opposed is by a complete and radical reform of the representation of the people in Parliament."

" III. That no reform is practical, efficacious, or just which shall not include Irishmen of every religious persuasion."

That some of its founders, particularly those of Belfast, entertained ulterior views which went beyond Parliamentary reform there can be no doubt, but it is equally certain that they were content at this period to sink those views, to extend their project no farther than the aims set forth in their public declarations, and sought not to engraft their Republican ideas upon the original constitution. That it was therefore a perfectly legal association at the outset there can be no doubt, but the fact that it proposed union amongst all classes of Irishmen was sufficient to appal a Government that formed its strength only in the division of those whom it aspired to rule.

The first petition that ever emanated in Ireland from a Protestant body in favour of Emancipation we owe to them. Early in January, 1792, the following requisition extensively signed was addressed to the inhabitants of Belfast:—

" Gentlemen,—As men, and as Irishmen, we have long lamented the degrading state of slavery and oppression in which the great majority of our countrymen, the *Roman Catholics*, are held—nor have we lamented it in silence. We wish to see all distinctions on account of religion abolished—all narrow, partial maxims of policy done away We anxiously wish to see the day when every *Irishman* shall be a citizen—when Catholics and Protestants, equally interested in their country's welfare, possessing equal freedom and equal privileges, shall be cordially *united*, and learn to look upon each other as brothers, the children of the same God, and the natives of the same land—and when the only strife amongst them shall be, who shall serve their country best. These, gentlemen, are our sentiments, and these, we are convinced, are yours." Then followed a requisition to hold a general meeting of the principal inhabitants at the Townhouse on the following Saturday at noon, to consider the propriety of petitioning Parliament in favour of their Roman Catholic brethren.

Tone and his friend Russell returned to Dublin with instructions to cultivate the leaders of the popular interests there, *being Protestant*, and, if

possible to form in the metropolis a club of the United Irishmen. In the month of November, 1791, Tone, aided by Napper Tandy established a club in Dublin—the Hon. Simon Butler being chairman.[*]

Plowden says[†] that in the month of June, 1791, a paper was circulated in Dublin containing the design of an association to be called the Society of United Irishmen at Belfast, and says that a complete plan and prospectus was published in the *Northern Star* in October following—1791. It is possible, but not probable, that the question may have been discussed in Dublin in June previous to the formation of the club in Belfast in October, but there is certainly an error as to dates, evidently upon Mr. Plowden's part, as we have the undoubted authority of Mr. Madden that the *Northern Star* was only issued in 1792, the first number appearing on the 14th January of that year, Samuel Neilson and eleven others of his townsmen being joint proprietors.

Shortly after their formation the United Irishmen at Dublin issued an address to the Volunteers over the names of William Drennan and Archibald Rowan Hamilton as follows :—

" To be soldiers you became citizens, nor can we help wishing that all soldiers partaking the passions and interests of people would remember that they were once citizens and seduction made them soldiers, but nature made them men."

" In four words lies all our honour—universal emancipation and representative legislature. Yet we are confident that on the pivot of this principle a convention, still less a society, less still a single man, would be able first to move and then to raise the world We therefore wish for Catholic Emancipation without any modification, but still we consider this necessary enfranchisement as merely a portal to the temple of national freedom. Wide as this entrance is—wide enough to admit three millions—it is narrow when compared to the capacity and comprehension of our beloved principle which takes in every individual of the Irish nation, casts an equal eye over the whole island, embraces all that think, and feels for all that suffer The Catholic cause is subordinate to our cause, and included in it, for, as United Irishmen, we adhere to no sect but to society, to no creed, but Christianity, to no party, but to the whole people. In the sincerity of our souls do we desire Catholic Emancipation; but were it obtained to-

* Madden's First Series, page 223.
† Hist. Review, vol. 1, page 83).—

morrow, to-morrow would we go on as we do to-day in pursuit of that reform which would still be wanting to ratify their liberties as well as our own."

Thus was started that society of United Irishmen which furnished excuse to an Orange *régime* for the bloodiest persecution to be found in the records of human cruelties.

It is not within the range of this work to present the readers with a detailed history of the United Irish movement. A brief outline is, however, necessary in order that a fair estimate may be formed of the men against whom the Orange yoemen of Ireland were pitted At the same time, I must say that history furnishes but few examples of interesting narrative like to it. It breathes a spirit of war and daring valour that can favourably compare with the most brilliant days of chivalry. Full of touching domestic love, of romance, and of unselfish patriotism, the history of this movement forms at once the most captivating, the most entertaining, and the most instructive reading that the young Irishman could select for study. What pages could be perused with more interest than Tone's admirable diary, in which his enthusiasm, his hopes, his despair, his bold, ingenuous, and generous nature, all find graceful, striking, and dramatic expression? How his heart bounded as that memorable expedition left the French shore, and the ships of war spread their sails to catch the breeze — "All 'as gay as is we were going to a ball; the wind right aft; huzza!" How he cursed on that unlucky Christmas morning—the last he was ever to see on earth; how he damned the wind, and looked longingly to the shore which he was not yet destined 'to touch, but when to touch only to step upon his grave; and how his heart sank a few days later when the Commodore gave orders to weigh anchor and steer for France! Where is there a passage quoted in the literature of any time and any country breathing more of conjugal affection than that in which a man, his mind busy with daring schemes of revolution, seeks to sustain his wife, whom he loves "ten thousand times more than all the universe" by picturing in his own striking manner the happy rural life awaiting failure—the little patch of land a few miles outside of Paris, the wife milking the cows and making the butter, and, no doubt, Theo. and Mat and Maria tumbling upon the grass. "Who will milk the cows," he asks, "and make the butter if you are not stout?" What tenderness is to be found in that letter, written "to his little daughter Maria"

while standing upon the brink of a fearful precipice! Think of how the heart of the patriot gladdened, and how the tears rushed up from the dauntless soul as he reads the "pretty little letter;" how touchingly he asks, in his reply, if Frank has got a breeches yet; when he tells his daughter to tell mother that "we do defer it most shamefully, Mr. Shandy," when he commands her to take great care of poor mamma, whom he fears is not very well, to kiss her and her little brothers ten thousand times, and "to love me as long as I live." Poor Tone! Poor little Maria! Your father had not long to live when he penned those lines, and in them you might have traced, had you been old enough, the darkening shadow of the coming doom. And tell me, where is there in romance anything more interesting than the intercourse between the young, handsome, truly noble, but ill-fated, Lord Edward and the captivating Pamela? And what more touching or more romantic than the correspondence between poor Emmet and Sarah Curran, the defeated and hunted rebel, risking his life for a farewell interview; Nature's nobleman offering to sacrifice his life without a word that the young girl's name should not be stained by the world's knowledge that her betrothed ended life upon the scaffold; the broken-hearted girl withdrawing from the idle, dancing throng, and singing that plaintive melody which he so loved to hear; the silly crowd gathering round this wreck of woman's love and hushed into reverence, and the young woman finally going to an early tomb, a sacrifice to patriotism and constancy to the last—

> He had lived for his love for his country he died,
> They where all that to life had entwined him,
> Nor soon shall the tears of his country be dried,
> Nor long shall his love stay behind him.
>
> Oh! make her a grave where the sunbeams rest,
> When they promise a glorious morrow,
> They'll shine o'er her sleep like a smile from the west,
> From her own loved island of sorrow.

If you are an Irishman, and have not yet become so respectable as to blush at the name, read the lives of these men; for it is my conviction that by the majority they are either not read at all or merely glanced into. You will come from the study a better Irishman, a better man—aye, and even, a better subject; for you will likely value freedom when you find it, if you have learned to respect the efforts of those who fought for it, and died for it, when they had it not.

It must be particularly borne in mind, through these subsequent pages, that the administration of those times was one of the most notoriously despotic that had ruled the country on both sides of the channel for many years; that Mr. Pitt swayed with the malignity of a pervert and, himself a renegade reformer, initiated a autocracy almost unequalled; that some of the ablest leaders of the English Opposition retired in disgust from their Parliamentary labours; and, that, having placed the Government of this country in the hands of a desperate faction, whose leader was more powerful than the nominal head of the Irish Administration, he gave it, for a purpose, over to a *regime* that destroyed the last vestige of the Constitution, all this calling forth the most eloquent and the most pronounced denunciation from the moderate of all sections. These particulars, forgotten, or proved to be untrue, and the memory of men who loved their country "not wisely but to well," must suffer at the hands of posterity.

The unfortunate men of whom I have been writing gave expression to nothing but the truth when he said, "I must do the society the justice to say, that I believe there never existed a political body which included among its members a greater portion of sincere, uncorrupted patriotism, as well as a very respectable portion of talent."

It would appear that on the society having been formed in Dublin Tone lost all influence in it, in consequence of his advanced opinions, but in Belfast his influence remained unabated. In the latter town Tone, Neilson, M'Cracken, Russell, Hazlett, the two Simms, M'Lornan and M'Cabe, at once applied themselves to carrying out the original organisation. In their praise it must be said that no declaration came from them that did not breathe a spirit of toleration and friendship for their suffering Catholic countrymen. They at the earliest moment applied themselves towards quelling the disturbances then raging in the County Armagh between the Peep-o'-Day Boys and the Defenders, seeing that so long as it continued unity in the North could not prevail. To some extent they were successful, and in the ranks of the Defenders they found many new adherents. The United Irishmen have been accused of stirring up bigotry between the Protestants and the Catholics, but proof of this is no where to be found. In fact their course must have been the contrary, at the outset at all events, did they wish to take the speediest means of securing their object. This certainly could not be furthered by protracting religious dissention. That such was not their endeavour may be seen from the letter of September, 1795, addressed to Tone from Belfast,* to the effect that "Neilson

had been called away by express to settle some dispute in the County Armagh between the Peep-o'-Day Boys and Defenders. Charles Teeling being there before him." The feud then raging in the County Armagh was that which culminated in the bloody massacre of the Diamond, and it was to prevent this that these two left Belfast. Teeling was then a boy of seventeen, but his family had much influence in the county over the Catholic inhabitants, and "learning, with deep concern, that the adverse parties were preparing for a general conflict with the full knowledge and under the very eye of those authorities whose duty it was to have restrained them," he proceeded to the scene in the hopes of opening up "some channel, if possible, for a pacific arrangement, and to preserve the county from a wanton expenditure of blood." On setting out from Lisburn he despatched a letter to Neilson, in Belfast, asking him to meet him in Portadown, but before he had reached Lurgan he learned the news of the Diamond massacre, and retracted his steps, meeting Neilson on the return journey. The United Men favoured the scheme of Catholic Emancipation, but in all the addresses of the Belfast leaders there is noticeable a boldness of speech and a determination for a complete emancipation which are not to be found in those of their brethren of the metropolis.

The Rev. Mr. Gordon's figurative description of the society is possibly the most accurate we have, and certainly the most fitting that could be employed in conveying an idea of its completness in a few words. In his "History of the Rebellion" (vol. 2, page 355), he says—"The United Irish Association consisted of a multitude of societies, linked together and ascending like the component parts of a pyramid or cone, to a common apex or point of union." The members of the society were both ordinary and honorary, but to the latter position none were eligible save those "who had distinguished themselves by promoting the liberties of mankind," and were not inhabitants of Ireland. Candidates were admitted by ballot, having been previously proposed by two ordinary members. Every person elected a member, whether ordinary or honorary, was required to take and subscribe to the following test:—

I, A. B. in the presence of God, do pledge myself to my country, that I will use all my abilities and influence in the attainment of an impartial and adequate representation of the Irish nation in Parliament; and as a means of absolute and immediate necessity in the establishment of this chief

* Tone's Life, vol. 1, page 290.

good in Ireland, I will endeavour, as much as lies in my ability, to forward a brotherhood of affection, an identity of interests, a communion of rights and an union of power among Irishmen of all religious persuasions, without which every reform in Parliament must be partial, not rational, inadequate to the wants, delusive to the wishes, and insufficient for the freedom and happiness of this country."

The seal with which the secretary of the society in Dublin was furnished had upon it the representation of a harp, over which were the words, " I am new ' strung," and beneath, " I will be heard," and on the exergue, the "Society of United Irishmen, Dublin." It is to be presumed that a similar one existed for Belfast, though I have not discovered any mention made of it. A code of rules were drawn up which amply provided for the regular despatch of business

Amongst the original members, both in Belfast and in Dublin, were a number of men of culture, talent, and literary attainments, so it is not surprising that they learned early to resort to the use of the pen as a means of spreading wide their principles. Addresses flowed from them without number to the people of Ireland, to the Volunteers, to the Orangemen, all of which sought to bind all sorts together in more general unity; but those most remarkable for literary merit were from the pen of Wolfe Tone and Dr Drennan. The chief medium for circulating these epistles were the *Northern Star* in the North and by pamphlet in Dublin, for it was not until September, 1797, that the *Press* newspaper was established in the metropolis. An indication of the tone of political opinion then existing in Belfast may be found in the character of the celebration of the French Revolution on the 14th July, 1792, when there was a grand military display, in which the remnant of the local Volunteer corps took part. Many of the mottoes on the flags and standards were of so pronounced a character that to-day they would be classed as seditions. The first toast drunk was "The Fourteenth July, 1789," and then followed such significant sentiments as "The Constitution of France," "The French Army," "Confusion to the enemies of French liberty," and "*May the example of one revolution prevent the necessity of another.*" The Dublin commemoration was a comparatively feeble one.

At this time the Catholic Committee were busy at work, fighting their way to the steps of the

Throne, and awakening the people to a sense of their degradation. Without attaining any very important results they swelled the tide of popular indignation, and helped to turn the attention of the people to this new association which had arisen from the ashes of their former enemies, and was now foremost in advocating their claims. To, the success of the Catholic Convention of 1793 Tone, the chief organiser, largely contributed. In Belfast the delegates chosen to lay the petition, before the King were received on their way to London with public honours Lord Moira gave them the hospitality of his mansion in London, and when the delegates went before the King, his Most Gracious Majesty even condescended to smile. The Catholic cause seemed now to prosper Lord Arthur Wellesley was found inside the House of Commons to advocate the extension of Constitutional rights to those whom the hon member in his maiden speech declared to be "as loyal and as trustworthy as any other of his Majesty's subjects." If corroboration of his statement be necessary, we will find it in the report of the Secret Committee of the House of Lords which sat in this year to inquire into the cause of the disturbances, and reported " that nothing appeared before them that led them to believe that the body of Roman Catholics in this kingdom were concerned in promoting or continuing such disturbances " Lord Portarlington, a member of the committee, said, " if he was not convinced that the Catholic body had no connection whatever in the disturbances created by some of their communion in the North he should not give this (the Catholic) Bill his support." The Act which followed— that of 1793, and of which I have already spoken—is attributed by Mr Plowden ' to the parental tenderness of his Majesty towards his Irish Catholic subjects." The bishops of the long oppressed and reluctantly enfranchised religion honoured the Lord Lieutenant with an expression of thankfulness which did not confine itself to panegyric on his administration,* but virtually contradicted many of the charges which had been preferred by the laity of the same persuasion, and applauded "that spirit of conciliation by which his Excellency's Government was eminently characterised " But the Beresford party still ruled Ireland, and so long Protestant Ascendancy had little to fear. The famous "Captain Rock" (Tom Moore), writing in his memoirs (page 339) upon the effects of this

* MacNevin's Pieces of Irish History, page 11.

Act, says that the influence of the Beresfords was sufficient to neutralise its effect; that the Corporations and other civil bodies were so made up of factions, and the Administration so determined to maintain them, that no benefit was practically derived from it. Such was the "parental tenderness of the King, and such the "sp'rit of conciliation" of his Irish representatives' Administration. It is not without its lesson to Kings and rulers, however. The very pretence of conciliation is with suffering people more effective than the most vigorous coercion. The hope of complete emancipation now became general. Tnough the advocacy of the United Irish Society, and of its organ, the *Northern Star*, was powerful in behalf of emancipation, it is but too apparent that the Catholic Committee, fearful of sinister designs, and of being too closely allied with them, refused, or at least neglected, to give due credit to their influence. It remained, however, to be seen that the advanced party properly appreciated the significance of passing events. Nelson and his friends, who had rescued the Catholic cause "from the cold dull shades of Catholic aristocracy," protested against the slight; but a short time had only to elapse, during which expectation was all on tiptoe, until the hopes of the country were blasted, until the cup was dashed from its lips, just when about to drink deep the draft of comfort, until Lord Fitzwilliam was recalled, until the Beresfords were reinstated, and until a general defection followed from the ranks of the disappointed Constitutionalists to the military organisation that now saw no remedy but by the sword.

About this period there were influences powerfully operating, not alone to multiply malcontents, but even to change their disaffection into the bold and reckless disloyalty of desperate men. For distributing in 1792 an address—an extract of which I have given, and which had for its object the re-embodiment of the Volunteers—Archibald Rowan Hamilton was in January, 1794, prosecuted by the Government. The postponement of the trial which took place was, with much show of justice, attributed to anxiety on the part of the Administration to secure a conviction at all hazards. For this purpose, "the ablest architects of ruin" that Ireland ever saw devised that very ingenious and novel method of jury-packing, which for many years afterwards continued to be one of the cruellest means of legalised torture known to any civilised country. Here we also find the first introduction of those wretches known as informers into the witness box, so that to this trial we owe the inception of two of the worst, two of the most infamous practices that could be resorted to for the "lawful" extermination of a people. Nor is it strange that we should here find figuring the celebrated Jack Giffard (afterwards to distinguish himself as a leading Orangeman), and acting the congenial part of the "Cimmerian zealot" with the proficiency of one long skilled in deception. It was upon this occasion that Curran made that celebrated speech, which in itself would be sufficient to make his name imperishable. "I speak in the spirit of the British law," he said, "which makes liberty commensurate with and inseparable from British soil; which proclaims even to the stranger and the sojourner the moment he sets his foot upon British earth, that the ground upon which he treads is holy, and consecrated by the genius of universal emancipation. No matter in what language his doom may have been pronounced; no matter what complexion incompatible with freedom an Indian or an African sun may have burned upon him; no matter in what disastrous battle his liberty may have been cloven down, no matter with what solemnities his liberty may have been devoted upon the altar of slavery, the first moment he touches the sacred soil of Britain the altar and the god sink in the dust, his soul walks abroad in her own majesty, his body swells beyond the measure of his chains that burst from around him, and he stands redeemed, regenerated, and disenthralled by the irresistible genius of universal emancipation."

A very beautiful piece of oratory no doubt. There is only one thing to be regretted in regard to it—that it was not true. Rowan was found guilty two years after the commission of the offence by a packed jury and on the evidence of informers, who have since been proved to have sworn falsely; was sentenced to two years' imprisonment and condemned to pay a fine of £500.

There now remains no doubt that this was the turning point of the United Irish movement. That they had confined themselves up to this period within the lines of constitutional agitation is equally certain. True, their addresses were bold, fearless, and outspoken; but, whatever they may at that period have been according to the unwritten law of the land, it is clear that they were not illegal, nor could theirs at the present time be classed among seditious writings. But now in one moment all was changed. Men who had been hoping for reform, and would have continued hoping to the end, perhaps, stood confounded on seeing the first right of a citizen—trial by jury—torn from them. As Dr. Madden has forcibly put it, "So long as the people thought that the fountain of justice was moderately pure and did not believe that it had been poisoned at its very source so long was popular discontent kept within bounds." On the 7th of February, 1794, the Society of United Irishmen presented an address to Mr. Rowan, who was then undergoing his sentence in Newgate. It stated that "while they were endeavouring to establish the constitutional rights of their country they found themselves suddenly at a loss for this first and last state of a free people"—trial by jury, and they assured him of their inflexible determination to pursue the great object of their association—an equal and impartial representation of the people.

Such language could not but be distasteful to a despotic Government. The daring manner in which they carried out their schemes—which had now assumed a revolutionary complexion—were no doubt calculated to challenge the Administration to act, and in a few short months brought down the vengeance of the Executive upon them. On the 4th May, 1794, they had assembled at Tailors' Hall, in Back Lane, when it was attacked by a body of police; their papers were seized, and the assembly dispersed. Some of the leaders were successfully prosecuted and imprisoned; others prudently seceded from the society, while the revolutionary element, then a strong one in the body, remained steadfast, and, committing the first and consequently the gravest blunder of their lives, they withdrew from the sight of day and formed what has henceforth been known as the New Organisation of United Irishmen. It was a revolutionary society from that period; a secret society, bound by a secret oath, and connected by secret signs and secret passwords; a society of that character from which the world, now a pretty old one, has derived little benefit; by means of which few of the ills of human kind have been redressed, but through which many of its miseries have been multiplied and prolonged. While we condemn their wisdom, however, we should not be unmindful of their devotion, conscious, as every man of them must have been, of the sacrifice they were making; neither must we forget the character of the times nor fail to bestow a liberal share of the blame, if we do not allot it all, to a Government that left a distracted and tortured people but one dreadful alternative. Their former programme—"the equal representation of the people in Parliament"—now became "a full repre-

sentation of all the people." The civil organisation also underwent a change, and became a military one; a Directory was appointed, with a Sub-Directory for each of the provinces, and an elaborate plan devised for baffling detection and keeping the secrets of the organisation within the body. In all their arrangements, and with all their foresight, they forgot, however, one essential particular, which it had been well they remembered. They forgot that Ireland has been—and I blush to write it, but that the truth must out—that she has been the hot-bed of informers as well as of patriots. Whether we ascribe the cause to weak humanity, or the abundance of English gold, or to the one powerfully operated upon by the other, the effect remains the same. She has had traitors in plenty. Her sons have ever been the executioners of one another. An abundant crop of rascals, the biggest and the basest that ever degraded humanity, has sprung up out of every agitation that went beyond the limits of law. We have too long ignored this fact. They ignored it in the United Irish movement, and many a gallant fellow and many an innocent man paid the penalty upon the scaffold.

The New Organisation of the United Irish Society was completed on the 10th May, 1795. Its objects extending far beyond Parliamentary reform and Catholic Emancipation, the means, keeping pace with the end, went beyond the pale of the Constitution. Some months seem to have been spent in grafting the military upon the civil character, for it was not until 1795 that the officers were elected to their respective grades. Those of the lower rank were selected by the committee, while the higher officers, some of whom were destined to play a prominent part in the subsequent insurrection, were chosen by the executive. A commander-in-chief being now wanted, Lord Edward Fitzgerald was nominated by the Leinster Directory and elected. That election, though the free exercise of a preference in his regard, was still but a matter of necessity; for in him were to be found most of the attributes that qualify for leading an armed multitude. Brave almost to rashness, generous to a fault, with a resolution that levelled mountains into mole-hills, and a vigour that laughed at toil, he brought to the task the experience of a soldier and the enthusiasm of a patriot. However illegal may have been the objects for which they were associated, it must be acknowledged that their motives did credit to their hearts. Rebels as they were, they were unselfish, and self-sacrificing to a degree which modern civiluation would laugh at. Their oath was not an exterminating one, but broad and liberal, and with the exception that it was an oath, and a secret oath, it had nothing to offend the most sensitive moralist or the most constitutional loyalist.

The *Press* of October 9, 1797, publishes the following contrast, which gives the version of the oath as laid before the Secret Committee :—

"THE ORANGEMAN'S OATH.

"I A. B do hereby swear that I will be true to the King and Government, and that I will exterminate, as far as I am able, the Catholics of Ireland "

"Let this be contrasted with the United Irishman's oath, as taken from the report of the Secret Committee, and the people of England will see who are the real traitors to their country, although there are none of the Orangemen hanged or sent to jail.

"THE UNITED IRISHMAN'S OATH

"'In the awful presence of God, I, A. B., do voluntary declare that I will persevere in endeavouring to form a brothe hood of affection amongst all Irishmen of every religious persuasion; and that I will also persevere in my endeavours to obtain an equal, full, and adequate representation of *all* the people of Ireland, and do further declare that neither hopes, fears, rewards, or punishments shall ever induce me, directly or indirectly, to inform or give evidence against any member or members of this or other similar societies for any act or expression done, or made collectively in or out of this society, in pursuance of the spirit of these obligations "

Even previous to this time the United Men had learned to adopt the tactics of their English masters of 1688. The difference was that the English rebels called in the aid of the Dutch to assist them in dethroning their King because he professed the Catholic faith, while the Irish rebels called in the aid of the French to relieve an entire people from an exterminating persecution. With the latter no doubt the blame rests, for their treason wanted that important element, success, which can cover a multitude of sins. "But," said Tone, when before the court martial, that illegaly pronounced his death sentence, "in vulgar eyes the merit of the cause is judged by its success— WASHINGTON CONQUERED—KOSCIUSKO FAILED." That it alters not the moral aspect of the question is a point scarcely worth treating of. Thomas Addis Emmet, one of the shrewdest men of the party, was many years afterwards known to express

the opinion that the expectation of Foreign aid was the ultimate cause of their destruction; that if they had relied upon their own resources there was a greater chance of success. While considering that chance more remote than Mr. Thomas Addis Emmet did, many will at the same time be struck with the apparent truthfulness of the observation. Practically no assistance was derived from France. Up to the time when the dictator Napoleon took the matter in hand several honest but unsuccessful attempts had been made to give assistance. But afterwards, while Tone was living in hopes, the promises and preparation of France—all of which were duly reported in England by males and females whose high birth did not teach them the first principles of morality—produced a decided action amongst the loyalists of Ireland that otherwise would probably not have had to be contended with. Thus the application for foreign aid left the United men in the singular position of having to contend, without that aid, against the repugnance which their application for it had excited. In this sense their appeal did them more harm than good, while their implicit confidence in its final result relaxed that spirit of self-reliance which should be one of the first elements of a people in arms seeking to achieve their freedom.

It was in the few years that intervened between the starting of the Orange institution at the Diamond and the rebellion that the United system obtained a strong hold upon the people of the country, plainly demonstrating that where one secret society exists those opposed to it will, by opposition societies of a similar character, seek to foil their antagonists with their own weapons. The Orange eulogists who appeared to give evidence before the Select Committee in 1835 laid great stress upon the fact that after the formation of the Institution the country became in a comparative sense more peaceful. We have the antonority of the *News-Letter* of May, 1797, that the County Armagh was in almost perfect quiet. But it was the quietness, the silence of the tomb. Elsewhere over Ireland, a period of comparative calm did actually set in, and upon it the Orangemen rest their claim to never-ending fame. Starting with the silly assumption that an entire population stood in awe at a handful of exterminating cowards, who only risked a battle when behind the backs of the king's troops, these people forgot to discriminate between the ominous calm that frequently precedes a great revolution, and the natural calm which always follows one. They ignored the fact, too, that a secret organisation is most determined, and, therefore, most dangerous, when apparently most passive. Whatever is due for bringing about this short-lived quiet the Orange Institution, no doubt, is deserving it. The popular verdict has already been pronounced, and its award is censure, not praise. But if the United Irish Society derived strength from the existence of a bitter opponent, the Orange Society, by the operation of the same law, reaped a corresponding benefit Owing, indeed, to their favourable circumstances their harvest was the richer, having due regard to the limited field of operation. The Insurrection and Indemnity Acts had dubbed them loyal, and their apologists in the House of Commons rightly interpreted for them the significance of those measures. Confined in 1796 to a few Northern counties, they spread in the following year, extending so far as Dublin, and carrying their bloody banner of extermination into many of the intervening counties. Bigotry, after slumbering for a century, was again called into action even in remote districts where the revolutionary movement had not, and, otherwise, might never have reached. Persecution followed. Thus even the natural consequence of the institution suited admirably the proposed object of its patrons in the Government, who sought to secure at all hazards a premature explosion of the rebellion. Finding neither succour nor sympathy elsewhere, with their altars desecrated, their homes laid waste, their substance gone, their wives and daughters ravished, their children butchered, and themselves driven to despair by the refined torture of the pitch-cap, the bayonet, and the rack, they rushed half-destracted from the hell-hounds let loose upon them, straight into the arms of this society of rebels, and determined at last to earn the character, since, under any circumstances, the punishment was theirs. The silence which followed was therefore significant.

When Thomas Addis Emmet was being examined before the Lords Committee in August, 1798, it was shown that the outrages, particularly those in the County Armagh following the affray of the Diamond, were largely instrumental in determining the military character of the organisation, and that it was not until the passing of the Insurrection and Indemnity Acts that the returns to the Society included fire-arms and ammunition.

He says.—"I was then asked as to the military organisation, which I detailed. They asked "when the returns included fire-arms and ammunition?"

Emmet—After the Insurrection and Indemnity Acts had been passed, when the people were led to think on resistance, and after 4,000 persons had been driven from the County Armagh by the Orangemen.

Committee—Was the name of Orangeman used to terrify the people into the United system?

Emmet—I do not know what groundless fears may have been propagated by ignorant people; but I am sure no unfair advantage was taken by the Executive. The Orange principles were fairly discussed, as far as they were known, and we always found that wherever it was attempted to establish a lodge the United Irish increased very much.

Lord Dillon—Why, where was it endeavoured to introduce them, except in the North and in the city of Dublin?

Emmet—My lord, I cannot tell you all the places in which it was endeavoured, but I will name one, in the County of Roscommon, where I am told it made many United Irishmen.

Lord Dillon—Well, that was but very lately, and I endeavoured to resist it.

Lord Chancellor—Pray, Mr. Emmet, what caused the late insurrection?

Emmet—The free quarters, the house-burnings, the tortures, and the military executions in the Counties of Kildare, Carlow, and Wicklow.

Lord Chancellor—Did you not think the Government very foolish to let you proceed so long as they did?

Emmet—No, my lord; whatever I imputed to Government I did not accuse them of folly. I knew we were very attentively watched, but I thought they were right in letting us proceed. I have often said, laughing, among ourselves, that if they did right they would pay us for conducting the revolution, conceiving as I did then, and still do, that a revolution was inevitable unless speedily prevented by very large measures of conciliation.

Dr. MacNeven, when on examination on the 8th August, in answer to the question, "What occasioned the rebellion?" said it was occasioned by "the wrongs, the whippings to extort confessions, the torture of various kinds, the free quarters, and the murders committed upon the people by the magistrates and the army." It was then that Lord Castlereagh made use of those remarkable words— "You a knowledge the Union would have been stronger but for the means taken to make it explode."

From this we see that the Orangemen were made party to the crime; and though you may sometimes find excuse for the men who are induced or driven

HISTORY OF ORANGEISM.

78

into criminality, you can seldom if ever extend pardon to those who, being accomplices by instigation, want the courage, but share the guilt of the actual offenders. In the observations of Lord Dillon we have further proof that the Orange Institution was during those scenes of outrage in full working order in Dublin. Did we wish to seek for further proof that Orangeism played an important part in fomenting the rebellion, being the instrument by which the Castle clique determined to make it explode, we can find it readily at hand.

From the memoir delivered to the Government by Messrs. Emmet, O'Connor, and MacNeven, and furnishing a detailed statement of the origin and progress of the Irish Union, the following is taken:—

"To the Armagh persecution is the union of Irishmen most exceedingly indebted. The persons and properties of the wretched Catholics of that county were exposed to the merciless attacks of an Orange faction, which was certainly in many instances uncontrolled by the justices of peace, and claimed to be in all supported by the Government. When those men found that illegal acts of magistrates were indemnified by occasional statutes, and the courts of justice shut against them by Parliamentary barriers, they began to think they had no refuge but in joining the Union. Their dispositions so to do were much increased by finding the Presbyterians of Belfast especially step forward and espouse their cause and succour their distress. We will here remark once for all what we solemnly aver, that wherever the Orange system was introduced, particularly in Catholic counties, it was uniformly observed that the numbers of United Irishmen increased most astonishingly. The alarm which an Orange Lodge created among the Catholics made them look for refuge by joining together in the United system; and as their number was always greater than that of bigoted Protestants, our harvest was tenfold. At the same time that we mention this circumstance we must confess, and most deeply regret, that it excited a natural acrimony and vindictive spirit which was peculiarly opposite to the interests and abhorrent to the feelings of the United Irishmen, and has lately manifested itself, we hear, in outrages of so much horror"

Even after the formation of the United Irish Society its members still sought to put an end to the dissensions that raged in the North between the Defenders and the Orangemen. Their programme professed to seek the greatest good

for the greatest numbers, and they endeavoured to do this by promoting union amongst all classes of Irishmen. But the absolute necessity of suppressing those outrages, not only for the advantage that union would bring, but from the danger their plans were exposed to of premature explosion, compelled them to keep a strict watch upon Armagh and adjoining counties. For sometime they were successful—after the accession of the Defenders to their ranks—not in quieting the Orangemen or making them more tolerant, but in inducing the Defenders to abandon as far as possible the policy of retaliation. Hundreds who were driven out of their homes sought refuge in Belfast, and were there received with open arms. According to MacNeven, the United Irishmen, having failed in allaying these animosities, determined "to expose the outrages, so that if the connivance of magistrates and higher authorities should succeed in fostering local persecution, at least the horrible atrocities themselves would be exposed beyond the possibility of concealment or denial. By the desire of the Provincial Committee prosecutions were instituted by the Executive against some notorious offenders and some of the most guilty magistrates, but that measure only seemed to redouble the outrages." The witnesses were intimidated, waylaid, or murdered, and where these did not intervene legal artifice prolonged the inquiry and rendered them nugatory. They were ultimately compelled to abandon this course, but thenceforward the Catholics as a body learned to look upon them as their natural friends, to confide in the sincerity of those Protestants who had originated or joined the Union, and "no longer to look with hope of vindication towards the existing law or its remedies."

The years 1795 and '96 marked the progress of the association. Lord Edward Fitzgerald threw in his fortunes with his revolting countrymen, having long since despaired of effecting reforms by constitutional means. Sampson says, and Madden copies the expression, that when he delivered himself of the speech* opposing the Attorney-General's four resolutions, Lord Edward was not a United Irishman, and "did not join for a long time after" Ignoring the date of this debate, Mr. Madden says "Lord Edward was brought into the Union in 1796 by Arthur O'Connor," while Moore states that he was admitted in the beginning of 1796, the usual formalities, as in the case of O'Connor, having been dispensed with. If Sampson made the comment, as he evidently did, to give

* In February, 1796, already quoted.

L rd Edward's utterance in February, 1796, an unbiassed character, he seems to have shot wide of the mark. According to Moore, he became a Unitedman in the beginning of 1796, and we have it an undoubted record that in less than two months after he spoke in the House he proceeded to France on his first treasonable mission. He, therefore, either was in February, 1796, a member of the organisation, or must have become one *very soon after* of O'Connor did act as Lord Edwards' sponsor, this conclusion, it must be observed, is at varia o1 with the statement of Emmet, O'Connor, and MacNeven delivered to the Irish Government to the effect that "none of them were members of the United system until September or October of the year 1796," for if O'Connor were not a member before that time he could not have introduced Lord Edward Fitzgerald "in the beginning of 1796." It is difficult to say where the error lies. The confusion is, however, easily explained by the fact that the sympathies of both these men were for a long time with the society, and the usual ceremonies of initiation having in their regard been dispensed with, the date at which their sympathies and connection took the definite shape of active co-operation may have been even to themselves un. certain.

Mr. Grattan had now retired from Parliament, intimating that having discharged his duty he should trouble the House no more. He, with Lord Henry Fitzgerald, declined longer to sit in Parliament, and Mr. Curran, and Mr. Arthur O'Connor, and Lord Edward followed their example. Though an offer had been made in 1792, and repeated in 1793, on behalf of the French Convention to deposit the pay of 40,000 men for six months in any bank in Europe, and though Jackson had been sent by the French Government to Ireland on a revolutionary mission in 1794 for which he paid the penalty of his life, no "formal or authorised" communication, if we are to believe O'Connor, took place previous to the year of 1796 between the Executive of the United Irish Society and the French Government. Towards the close of that year, as a result of Tone's entreaties and Fitzgerald's and O'Connor's interviews, the French fleet appeared in (but soon after disappeared from) Bantry Bay, and a loyal Catholic straightway ran off with the news to Dublin Castle. If the calling in of foreign aid, proving more distasteful in 1796 than it had done in 1688, augmented the ranks of the yeomanry, it did not pass without a corresponding effect upon the disaffected. Believing that aid from France was now not a visionary scheme, and finding that the French Executive had fulfilled one promise, the Irish were too easily led to believe that they would ultimately fulfil the many they had previously made and broken. Accordingly, they united with those whose negociation had brought this long-looked-for compact about. During all this time, the minions of the Castle were busy at the work of extermination. Continued persecution produced continued accession to the United Irish ranks, and that in its turn begot new and yet undiscovered modes of torture, until, in the end, persecution and disaffection, disaffection and persecution, operating alternately as cause and effect, the people were driven to despair; the peasants preferred death upon the hill-side to butchery in their cabins; they insisted upon immediate revolt; the rebellion "exploded." Lord Castlereagh's wishes were fulfilled; and his day-dream of years brought within the reach of certain accomplishment.

Even at the risk of wanting in that desirable feature of all narrative, consecutive narration, I have paid considerable, but let me hope, not more than necessary attention to the circumstances under which the Orange Institution found its origin, and to the condition and character of the men who through several bitter years of conflict were their dread opponents. The existence of the United Irish Society has been urged by some as an excuse, by others as an necessity, for Orangeism in those times. Not to give a brief history of their movement would, in my opinion, have been secur. ing consecutiveness at the expense of completeness. While the former is only a fault, the latter would be a grievous error.

I will now take my readers back to the Orangemen of Armagh, whom we left a banditti, and trace them as an organisation down their history.

CHAPTER XVI.—CHAOS MADE ORDER, PERSECUTION REDUCED TO A SYSTEM, THE FIRST GRAND LODGE—ITS TESTS AND ITS RESOLUTIONS; THE FIRST "TWELFTH."

THE rise of the Orange Institution dates from that period, when, all the Armagh Catholics having been exterminated or driven "to hell or Connaught" the faction had to seek fresh fields of labour. The Peep o' Day Boy system had been carried into the adjoining counties, and, their name disgraced even in the eyes of their own adherents by the dreadful massacre of the Diamond, those who did not share the crime were still forced into a change of title, lest they might bear the burthen of their Armagh brethren. Henceforth they,too,were known as "Orange-men."[*] For some considerable

time, it would seem, they continued their career without winning over many new adherents, the association being simply the Peep o' Day Boy system under a new and more presumptuous title. The five sons of James Verner, of Churchil, appear, however, with the rising generation of Dean Blacker's family, to have lent the association dignity by joining it at the outset. The future Deputy-Lieutenant, Deputy Vice-Treasurer of Ireland, and embryo Lieutent-Colonel (William Blacker) would seem to have been so hasty in giving in his adherence, that he joined it, if his own dates be correct, some time before it was established.[*] The eldest young Mr. Verner (Thomas) became the acknowledged leader, and with such influence as his family and that of the Blackers, at that time commanded, the brotherhood could not long remain in a dormant state. Tyrone would appear to have been the first county invaded, and a careful perusal of the slovenly compiled statistics of the society shows that the issue

---

of warrants was for a long period confined to Armagh, Tyrone, and Down, in those districts immediately surrounding the locality in which the Institution had its origin. Antrim is far down on the list, and Belfast is the third district named in that county in which a lodge was established. This list can be little relied upon, not alone from the fact that it was admitted in evidence that the documents were all in the most hopeless state of confusion, but that what were called "dormant" warrants or numbers where lodges had ceased to exist were usually given to new applicants, generous rivalry prevailing, no doubt, as to who would get the lowest or first number on the register, that being at first view an appearance of early adhesion to the cause. For this reason we may presume that Loughgall, which should occupy the honoured place of Number One, fell away from its early principles and gave way to Benburb in the County Tyrone wh'ch heads the list on the register of the Committee. Before the Committee of the House of Lords in 1825 Colonel Verner and the Rev. Holt Waring were examined respecting the early constitution of the Orange Society. From their evidence it appears that secrecy was one of the first rules at the outset. From the many versions of those rules that have came down to us in the old pamphlets of the time it is evident that, according to the original custom, the Orangemen of each locality or district usually formed a series of rugged and generally ungrammatical rules of their own chosing for the government of each respective district, the entire being animated, of course, by the one common principle, the destruction of Catholicism. When the means of communication between the brethren in remote parts of the Northern counties became more perfect by the gentry of one district attending at and becoming patrons of lodges in adjoining counties, these local rules were assimilated and formed into one general code the most grammatical and the most plausible version prevailing. I find in a volume of old pamphlets on Irish affairs that have lately come into my possession a roughly-printed document giving, "The early ordinances of the Armagh Orangemen," by a "loyal Protestant." It was prinied in 1801 by King, of Westmoreland Street, and gives the rules under which the Armagh lodges met in the first year of their history. These rules were:—

1st. That we, the loyal and true Protestants of Armagh, calling ourselves Orange—men in honour of the great King William, do promise to uphold

with our lives the property and the lives of all our brethren when they make known to us that they are attached members of our body, and have not abjured its principles; that we will not see the same brother offended for the sake of a penny; neither shall we offend a brother for a penny's sake, but that we will stand by him in the time of need, and assist him, even at our lives' risk, and fight in his cause as though it was our own, all of which we most solemnly declare.

2nd. That we will not admit into our society any member of that superstitious gang of rebels calling themselves Papists, and our association being a secret one, that any Orangeman introducing same, or making known the secrets of our body to such Papists, will be treated by us as a renegade and a perjurer, and in all other respects like to a Papist.

3rd. That our association being an exclusively Protestant association, meant for Protestant purposes, all Papists are not only to be excluded from our community, but we pledge ourselves that we will not sell to such or buy from such, neither will we drink with them, talk with them, or walk with them, but we will treat them as enemies to our religion and traitors to the good Protestant king who holds the succession of the throne in the noble House of Hanover.

4th. "That we will not permit a brother Orangeman to offend or assault a brother Orangeman without interfering in the cause of peace; for 'a house divided against itself cannot stand;' but that we will defend an Orangeman against the insult of a Papist with the last drop of our blood."

5th. "That this Protestant and Orange association of loyal men is, firstly, a religious society for the upholding of the open Bible, and secondly, a defensive one for the protection of our lives, properties, and interests, and that our first principle shall be, therefore, an open Bible, at the 68th Psalm thereof,* and the second a short notice and a sure coming to all our enemies."

The writer then summarises the 6th, 7th, and

---

* "That thy foot may be dipped in the t ngue of thine enemies; and that the tongue of thy dogs may be red with the same!"—69th Psalm, W. J. Battersby, 33, Winetavern Street, Dublin, who wrote and published in 1825 a series of papers, under the heading of the Ghost of the Catholic Association of Ireland, addressing—1st, her Majesty's Ministers; 2nd, the Orangemen; 3rd, the Liberal Protestants; and 4th, the Catholics of Ireland, says, in his "Second Apparition," page 21, "The whole fo ios of the Statu'e Book would not contain the dreadful instances which the Orangemen have given in exemplif ation of adopting the letter of this passage." No doubt, Mr. W. J. Batter by was another of the numerous co spirators for defaming the Orange Institution!

T

8th rules by saying they in effect declared that all Orangemen were bound " to obey the laws ; to make others obey the laws at the risk of their lives ; to punish all Papists whom they suspected of evil designs, and not to allow the lives and properties of Papists to stand in the way of Protestant Ascendancy or of Orange interests."

A series of rude and unmeaning ceremonies, borrowed chiefly from the Freemasons, in which their was a strange contrasting of the open Bible and the loaded blunderbuss, was adopted. Having regard to the remote period and the uneducated men with whom we are dealing, it is not surprising to find in the original ritual much unnecessar mysticism, partaking more of the ridiculous than of the impressive. This is natural. In the early days of conspiracies this mysticism seems to have, in all countries, been the means by which cunning men excited the awe and commanded the obedience of misguided accomplices, and by which it stimulated the curiosity of the uninitiated.

THE FIRST COUNTY GRAND LODGE.

At a meeting held at Richill, the first County Grand Lodge in connection with the Orange Institution, was formed. Plowden tells us of a meeting of Orange delegates held in Armagh City in the spring of 1796, for the purpose of protesting against the inadequate pay of the Government. As this would suppose a condition of organisation, it would argue that the meeting at Richhill took place earlier; likely in the beginning of the same year. But the balance of evidence inclines to the contrary. Colonel Verner when before the committee was asked—

" From the records of the Orange lodge, who was the first Grand Master ?" and he answers, " My eldest brother."

" How soon after December, 1795 did your brother become Grand Master ?" to which he replies, " I cannot state the precise time of the year that he became Grand Master."

" Was your brother Grand Mast   n the year 1796 ?" in reply to which he says, " I rather think the latter part of 1796."

As it is likely the appointment of the first Grand Master must have been the immediate consequence of this formation of the first Grand Lodge, it would follow on the lines of the Lieutenant Colonel's vague reply that the Richhill meeting alluded to must have taken place " in the latter" part of 1796. This is the more probable too, from the fact that the brotherhood seems not to have progressed rapidly within the first nine months.

The Dublin *University Magazine* (referring to this) says* :—" The institution, however, soon received the countenance of the gentry, who, confiding in the principles of the men who had formed it, and perceiving its usefulness as the means of preventing the scattered and unorganised loyalists from being absorbed into the *illegal combinations* which were extending over the country, came forward to enrol their names amongst its members, and to take the lead in its affairs. The five sons of James Verner, Esq., of Churchhill, were initiated in the brotherhood, and Dean Blacker's family were also among the earliest of its associates ; and many of the leading gentry having followed their example, a meeting was held at Richhill, at which the first County Grand Lodge was formed." At this meeting the oath, the local rules, and ordinances were by that delegated assembly made the oath, rules and ordinances of the County Grand Lodge, and, for the first time in its history, the Orange Institution had the requirements of a perfect body possessed of all its members.

The Verners and the Blackers in those days were precocious youths. With much forethought, those gentlemen generously undertook, with their landed acquaintances, to form the *head* of the body, to comprise the " County Grand Lodge" within themselves, and adjourned to commemorate the occasion, while the rank and file dispersed over the country to do the fighting, and place their necks in jeopardy by spilling the blood of unoffending neighbours. And history has many times repeated itself !

It may now be interesting to trace, so far as we are able, the early feats of the brotherhood. Mr. William Simpson, a barrister who in those days had extensive practice as junior with Curran, in the Courts of Law, and who, though in the secrets of the United Irish movement, as was necessary owing to the nature of his professional occupations, was not a sworn associate, wrote and published in 1807 his memoirs, in which he gives many interesting particulars respecting the early Orangemen. From it we find the following :—

* Here is contained an admission that there was a probability of the unorganized loyalists being absorbed into combinations that existed and actually "extended over the country," at that time. The writer cannot mean that the Protestant loyalists would permit themselves to be absorbed by the Catholic Defenders. The Peep o' Day Boys cannot, therefore, have been defunct; and as he says the combinations " extended over the country," the writer must also have been conscious that the Peep o' Day Boy system extend d beyond the County Armagh. Before the Committee there was abundant evidence that immediately after the starting of the Orangemen, the term Peep o' Day Boys subsided.

ORANGEMAN'S ORIGINAL OATH.

"I do hereby swear that I will be true to the King and Government, and that I will exterminate as far as I am able the Catholics of Ireland.

ORIGINAL TEST.

Question—Where are you?
Answer—At the house of bondage.
Q. Where are you going?
A. To the Promised Land.
Q. Stand past yourself?
A. Through the Red Sea.
Q. What is your haste?
A. I am afraid.

Don't be afraid, for the man who sought your life is dead.

Q. Will you hold it or have it?
A. I will hold it.

SIGNS OF THE ORANGEMEN.

"Take your right hand and put it to your right hand, turn round, saying, 'great is the man that sent me;' then take your left hand and say, 'welcome brother, Prince of Orange.'"

The author, who assures us that the above was what was called the "Purple Oath," and what they evidently acted upon, adds "such was the grossness of that faction which now governs both England and Ireland that it was almost incredible."

AMENDED OATH OF ORANGEMEN

as it is said to have issued from the hands of the Grand Master of the Orange lodges of Ulster (*Thomas Verner*):—

"I, in the presence of Almighty God, do solemnly and sincerely swear, that I will not give the secret of an Orangeman, unless it be to him or them I find to be such after strict trial, or on the word of a well-known Orangeman. I also swear that I will answer all summonses for an assembly of Orangemen, eighty miles distance; and that I will not sit, stand by, or be by and see a brother Orangeman struck, battered, or abused, or know his character injuriously injured or taken away, without using every effort in my power to assist him at the hazard of my life. I further declare, that I will not lie to or upon an Orangeman, me knowing the same to be detrimental to him, but will warn him of all dangers as far as in my power lies; and that I will bear true allegiance to his Majesty, and assist the civil magistrates in the execution of their offices if called upon, and that I will not know of any conspiracy against the Protestant Ascendancy; and that I will not make, or be at the making of a Roman Catholic an Orangeman, or give him any offence, *unless he offends me, and then I will use my endeavours to shed*

the last drop of his blood, if he or they be not a warranted Mason; and that I will stand three to ten to relieve a brother Orangeman, and I will not be a thief, or the companion of a thief, to my knowledge.

AMENDED TEST.

Question—What's that in your hand?
Answer—A secret to you.
Q. From whence came you?
A. From the land of bondage.
Q. Whither goeth thou?
A. To the land of promise.
Q. Have you got a pass word?
A. I have.
Q. Will you give it to me?
A. I did not get it so.
Q. Will you halve it or letter it?
A. I will halve it.
Q. March?
A. Delzo, through the Red Sea.
Q. What Red Sea?
A. The wall of the Red Sea.
Q. I am afraid!
A. Of what?
Q. The secrets of the Orangemen being discovered.
A. Fear not for he that sought your life is dead.
Q. Have you got a grand word?
A. I have the grand, I am that I am.
Q. Did you hear the crack?
A. I did.
Q. What crack did you hear?
A. A crack from the hill of the fire.
Q. Can you write your name?
A. I can.
Q. With what sort of a pen?
A. With the spear of life, or Aaron's rod, that buds, blossoms, and bears almonds in one night.
Q. With what sort of ink?
A. Papist blood.

Now, it will of course be said, not alone by the thousands in whom nature, education, and association have implanted that worst of all dispositions, the disposition not to be convinced, but it will be said by many upright men, however misguided they may be, that such records as these are not to be relied upon, and that they prove nothing as against the Orange Institution. To such I can only say that the Orange Institution must be the most villified organisation that ever existed if historical records such as these are not to be depended upon. Nay, more, that there must have existed a huge conspiracy of which the world has not yet heard on the part of historians, both Protestant and Catholic, of orators and statesmen of every persuasion; of judges, magistrates, priests and parsons; of newspaper editors and newspaper reporters, al of whom, from the political writers who swayed a nation by their pens down to the ballad-mongers, who in the streets caught the ears, enlisted the sympathies, and pocketed the halfpence of the gaping multitude, were united together for no purpose under the sun save pure malignity, in blacking the character of this famous institution.

Even by judging the document upon its merits we are likely to arrive at a fair conclusion as to its authenticity. The exterminating oath is sustained by too many corroborating circumstances to deserve further inquiry, but a due examination of the amended oath, as given above, will show that it is deserving of every weight as being possibly the original from which the oath of 1798 (laid before the Select Committee by the Orange Institution) was amended. There are more than one striking resemblance. In the latter there is, as in the former, an obligation to bear true allegiance to his Majesty, to keep the secrets of the association from all but Orangemen; an assurance that deponent never was a Roman Catholic, while the necessity in the original to uphold Protestant Ascendancy is in the latter, or amended form, transferred from the deponent to the Sovereign, the person who takes the oath being thus bound to uphold the upholder of Protestant Ascendancy These are certainly strange coincidents, which the reader would do well to mark, and which, in my judgement, lead but to one conclusion, that William Sampson the suspect, the companion of Curran, and the counsel of many prosecuted United men, has given a document relating to the Orange Institution to the world which is deserving of just the same credit as that submitted by the Grand Lodge of Ireland before the select committee of 1835 The really criminal passage is in the 1798 version, judiciously omitted, for, as will be seen in the following pages, a compact to that effect was entered into before the passing of the Act of Union, by which the organisation was to be moderated in its written law, and made the acknowledged protector of Protestant ascendancy in this country in return for its services in facilitating the passing of that Act That passage, at the close, breathes of nothing but blood, and in every sense corresponds with the exterminating oaths alluded to. By it an Orangeman is not to offend a Roman Catholic *unless the Roman Catholic offends him*, but in such a contingency he swears "*that he will use his utmost endeavours to shed the last drop of his blood*" Now, we have ample means at hand to ascertain what an Orangeman would construe into an offence on the part of a Roman Catholic. Everything short of the existence of a Roman Catholic is offensive to an Orangeman, and, indeed, as all Papists are presumed by him to be rebels, or disaffected citizens, or, at least, opposed to Protestant ascendancy, it might be reasonably concluded that their very existence is an offence. The oath, therefore, in no way fell short of wholesale extermination, and in effect was the same as the fearful vow of the Diamond heroes.

There is something remarkable, if not suspicious, in the fact that neither a copy of the original oath nor of the original rules were produced before the committee of 1835. None of the original records, though asked for, were forthcoming although it was admitted by Lieutenant-Colonel Verner and others in evidence that they were in existence and in their possession. Unfortunately they were always "in Ireland" when inquired after. Lieutenant Colonel Verner, when examined on 7th April, said that he had such documents, but *that he had them not with him* Four months afterwards on his second examination (Lieutenant-Colonel Blacker having crossed to Ireland and returned meantime), he seems to have been in precisely the same condition It is to be regretted that on a point so vitally affecting their reputation they did not take the trouble of refuting "the slanderous accusations." that on all sides had been made for the previous forty years against their association. The rules were in existence. Their simple production would have set the question for ever at rest

THE ORIGINAL WARRANT.

The original warrant. a specimen of which was handed to the Select Committee of the House of Commons. bears the date July 7th, 1793, and the number 89 If we may reasonably presume that at this early period the energies of the secretary were equal to the duties of an office almost a sinecure, it follows that original warrants were issued consecutively, and that the new institution for the first nine months did not make as rapid progress as we are generally led to believe. The document ran as follows:—

"No. Eight-nine—Timakeel, July 7th, 1796.
　　　　　　　　　　　　"JAMES SLOAN."
"To be renewed in the name of Daniel Bulls, Portadown district."

The last line is not belonging to the original document, as we find by the meeting of the Grand Orange Lodge in Dublin, in 1798, that new numbers were "ordered to be printed on parchment," and that for every old number renewed or every new number issued a sum of 5s 51 should be paid. No. 89 was a district claiming a renewal.

THE AMENDED WARRANT.

The following is an exact copy.—

ORANGE INSTITUTION.

Day of   *County of* _____

_____ 18___   *District of* _____

𝔅𝔶 𝔟𝔦𝔯𝔱𝔲𝔢 𝔬𝔣 𝔱𝔥𝔦𝔰 𝔄𝔲𝔱𝔥𝔬𝔯𝔦𝔱𝔶,

Our well beloved Brother ORANGE-MAN *of the* ℑurple Order *(and each of his Successors) is permitted to hold a* LODGE, ℜo.   *in the County and District above specified, to consist of* TRUE ORANGEMEN, *and to act as* MASTER *and perform the requisites thereof.*

Given under Our Great Seal.

(Co. Seal.)   (Great Seal.)

countersigned by ⎫
_____ ⎬
Co. Gd. Master. ⎭

_____ *Grand Master.*
_____ *Deputy Gd. Master.*
_____ *Grand Secretary.*
_____ *Deputy Gd. Secretary.*
_____ *Grand Treasurer.*
_____ *Deputy Gd. Treasurer.*

It is not remarkable to find that Presbyterians were in the few years preceding the rebellion, and for many years after, generally excluded from the Orange society. That they were so excluded will, I think, be granted by those who take the trouble of perusing the journals of those days. Their columns not alone bear ample testimony to the vindictive spirit which prevailed, by the repeated protests against murders, arsons, and robberies of the most outrageous kind, but show that the Northern Presbyterians were not sharers in the disgrace or afraid to denounce the crimes of the dominant faction. Page after page that we turn to discloses some new atrocity and some fresh protest from the local residents. Neither must we forget, however the admission may operate, that Presbyterianism was socially, though not religiously, outlawed almost to the extent of Catholicism. From its ranks, as we have seen, came the leaders of reform, the men of thought, of independence, and of action, and, born with little respect for kings and a great regard for popular rights, the great body of Presbyterians, if they did not assist, must have sympathised in the movement. The *Cork Gazette* of July, 1796, says:—"It is by no means the opinion of the South, as our friends in Dublin imagine, that the Orange murderers of the North are Presbyterians. We are far from thinking that men so enlightened, so early in the field of toleration, so devoted to the liberties of mankind, would cut the throats of their Catholic fellow-countrymen on any score, much less on the score of religion. Those, therefore, who spill the blood of their fellow-citizens cannot be Presbyterians. They may be monopolists of loaves and fishes; of rights and privileges." That there were exceptions to this rule is beyond doubt; but, as after the rebellion, it became the desire for an obvious reason to represent the Presbyterians as having formed the great portion of the Orange body, it is not surprising to find their paid champion, Musgrave, stating that "in the Counties of Fermanagh, Derry, and Armagh, there were 14,000 yeomen, and most of them Orangemen, and much to the honour of the Presbyterians, three-fourths of that were of that order." In Tyrone, so he adds, "there were about 5,000 yeomen, the majority of whom were Presbyterians, and there were about 4,200 Orangemen among them." This is a gross exaggeration. Plowden, alluding to this statement, says "It is unquestionable that the Presbyterians generally abhorred the principles of the Orangemen; but it is also certain that many of them were sworn in to

their society." How it came that these attached themselves to it he reasonably and justly explains by saying that they were mostly of the lower orders, who depended for their subsistence upon the landlords. This is of course quite consistent with the truth, for at that time the Orangemen themselves were of the lower orders, with the exception of those who figured as their leaders, and it is but natural to conclude that as Presbyterians were not likely to be given prominent positions in the Institution those who went into the rank and file were like to be the rank and file of the lower or rather the lowest order. The author I have been quoting mentions, evidently as an excuse for these Presbyterians having joined the Orange Institution, that "several persons of great landlord interest in those parts (Armagh, Down, Tyrone) insisted upon their Protestant (I give the term its wider signification) tenants and labourers becoming Yeomen and Orangemen. Such were the Marquis of Hertford, Marquis of Abercorn, Lord Northland, the Earl of Londonderry, Mr. Cope, Messrs. Brownlow and Richardson, and other possessors of great landed estates in Ulster." This statement is now to be received with greater reserve than when first it met the eyes of the public, for we have directly to the contrary in at least one of those particulars the authority of a person who had every opportunity of knowing the facts. The Earl of Gosford, when examined on the 23rd June, 1835, was asked a question founded upon this statement of Mr. Plowden :—

3657. Is not your lordship aware that the parties who compelled the Presbyterian tenants to become Orangemen were the Lords Hertford, Abercorn, Londonderry, Northland, and the Messrs. Cope, Brownlow, and Richardson; did you not hear that these noblemen and gentlemen compelled their tenants to join the Orange Institution? Never; a great proportion of the persons named lived not in any county that I am connected with, but many of them in the County of Down, and others in the County Antrim; but with respect to one name, Mr. Richardson, whom I knew intimately, a connexion of my own, my own positive belief is that he never did attempt to coerce his tenants to join that society; that is contrary to any communication I ever had with him." The same answer, with a little more reserve, he applies to Mr. Brownlow.

At any rate we may take it for granted that few, if any, Presbyterians of independence entered the society. In the Presbyterians of Belfast the Catholics of Armagh found staunch friends. Through their assistance many of them having been expelled from their homes were enabled to cross over to Scotland, and encouraged to settle in the neighbourhood of Glasgow and Paisley. "This," says Plowden, "was the beginning of that colony of Irish in that part of Scotland, which at this time (1811) is computed to amount to nearly 20,000." In addition, we have also the fact that where Presbyterianism most prevailed the new institution found the greatest difficulty in entering. Belfast was, as I have said, a long time free from the presence of such partisans. It is probable that a lodge was not established in that town before the autumn of 1796. That it was not later than June, 1797, we have an established fact, as an Orange meeting took place in Belfast on the 17th of that month, particulars of which appear in the columns of the *News-Letter.* Previous intimation of their existence in Belfast I have failed to find, and though I must admit, there is a possibility of its having been overlooked—so ill-arranged and ill-placed was the local intelligence of those early days in newspaper literature—a patient search resulting in failure has as a natural consequence given rise to the belief, not formed without much labour, that no such record is to be found. We can, at all events, limit the period within a year. On the 8th July, 1796, the *Northern Star* published the following:—"It is currently reported that an underhand attempt is being made to spread this (the Orange) association into the counties of Down and Antrim — nay more, some say into the town of Belfast. Lest some honest, well-meaning men should be deluded into this association, we think it our duty to lay before them the following test, which we understand is the bond of their association. *Some men of infamous character are prominent in this diabolical business.* They are well known. They shall be exposed." Then follows the Orangeman's exterminating oath as already quoted. This would show that about that time there was a lurking desire entertained by "*some men of infamous character*" to establish a lodge in Belfast. This discovery of the *Northern Star* and its disclosure no doubt had the effect of deferring the establishment of the first lodge in Belfast for some period. That there had been no lodge even secretly established in Belfast up to that time we have satisfactory evidence of in the absence of any demonstration upon the occasion of the first Twelfth of July that occurred in their history, or any mention of Belfast brethren sharing in the ceremonies of that ominous event.

THE FIRST ORANGE CELEBRATION.

Considerable interest must surround any record we have left to us of the first Orange celebration of the 12th July. Though meagre enough they are still sufficient to afford a fair idea of its character and an unpleasantly accurate knowledge of its bloody consequence. There would seem to have been ever in close attendance upon this Orange Institution an Evil Genius that has directed its steps at all times through blood. We have found it the offspring of massacre. Through its various stages of progress, not excepting its first carnival, we shall trace it by means of the bloody marks it has left behind. That in all cases its members were primarily in fault would be hazarding an assertion scarcely in accordance with the natural order of things, but that in the large majority of instances the crime was theirs and theirs only, and that in all instances the sad results were but the natural consequences of such a combination is unhappily but too apparent. The Armagh brethren who justly claim the honour of being the founders of the association have also whatever credit attaches to the first celebration. The numbers who took part in it, as will be seen from the following, were exceedingly small when we recollect the gatherings of subsequent years.

The *News Letter* gave a brief description of the first Orange twelfth, this year, 1796, which contrasts strangely with the innumerable columns in latter days devoted by that organ to the records of the Orange saturnalia, showing the advocacy of the brethren had not yet become a paying speculation. Its issue of the 15th July contains the following:—"We understand that on Tuesday, being the anniversary of the Battle of Augrim, a great body of Orangemen, amounting to upwards of 2,000, assembled in Lurgan and spent the day with the utmost regularity and good order. It unfortunately happened that in the course of the afternoon some words took place between a Mr. M'Murdie, at Ahalee, near Lurgan, and one of the Queen's County Militia, when coming to blows, Mr M'Murdie received a stab of which he died. As the whole business will come before a Court of Justice we would think it highly improper to make any remark on either side of the question."

The *Northern Star* of the 15th July, 1796, thus describes the same:—"On Tuesday last (12th of July · O S.) the gentlemen calling themselves Orange-boys, who have desolated the County of Armagh during the last year, paraded publicly in

large bodies, with Orange cockades and colours flying, through the towns of Lurgan, Waringstown,
Portadown, &c. Their colours, which were new
and costly, bore on one side King William on horseback, and (will it be believea?) on the reverse King
George the Third!!! This banditti, who have
hunted upwards of 700 families from their homes,
and their all, who have put the Catholics of the
county out of the 'King's peace,' paraded in open
day, under banners bearing the King's effigy, and
sanctioned by the magistrates? Irishmen, is this
not plain enough! One of the captains of the
name of M'Murdie was killed in the afternoon in
an affray with some of the Queen's County Militia."

From the *News Letter* of a few days subsequently,
Friday, July 22nd, we learn that "the trial of James
Delaney, of the Queen's County Militia, for the
murder of Mr. M'Murdie, came on at the Antrim
Assizes, before Justice Chamberlain. It lasted
about two hours, and after a great deal of evidence
being adduced on both sides, the jury, having retired for a short time found a verdict of guilty of
manslaughter. He was sentenced to be burned in
the hand, which having been inflicted *in presence
of the Court* he was immediately dismissed."

It will be seen from this that the first Orange
procession did not pass without its quota of
blood. Upon what side the blame rested in this
instance, or whether upon any, we have no means of
ascertaining, but it was likely in a family "quarrel"
the first blood was spilled. Though we have it on
the authority of Mr. Plowden that there were Catholics in the Queen's County Militia it is a fact
that the large majority were of a different religion,
so that the probabilities are two to one in favour of
this view, there being no mention of a party difference In all probability drunkenness was its origin,
for we have it on the authority of the great majority of witnesses examined before the Committee
and corroborated by the experience of later times
that these celebrations have ever been a fruitful
source of dissipation.

The Earl of Caledon, when under examination,
said the first Orange Lodge in the County Tyrone
was introduced on his father's estate in 1795—very
probably alluding to the district of Killyman, which
is destined to play a prominent part in our history.
From Mr. Plowden's History we learn (page 63 of
the 1st vol.) that Tyrone was then rivalling
Armagh for the number of atrocities committed by
the members of this new institution. Indeed, it
would seem that by this time the outrages had become general over the counties Armagh, Antrim,

Down, and Tyrone. One of the most shocking he
instances as being that in which two brothers, industrious tenants of Lord Hertford, Catholics, by
name Branagan, were burnt, with their whole
family, consisting of eight persons, and their house
and furniture, while "the savage Orangemen"
encircled the flames to prevent escape, and made
merry over the carnage. Lord Hertford was then
in Lisburn. Instant investigation and exemplary
rigour were threatened, but, as usual, no punishment ensued. To the bigotry and narrow
prejudice of some members of the Episcopal
ministry is due the advance of the organisation at this period. The Revs. S.
Cupples, Lisburn, and Philip Johnston, Dernagby,
were prominently zealous in evangelizing the new
code. Deputations were sent* from the
County Grand Lodge in County Armagh to
various districts of the country with the object
of "inoculating the new lodges with the genuine
matter and the erruption was exuberant." Besides
encouraging his Orange partizans in their orgies,
the latter rev. gentleman is said to have in one of
his unwonted fits of "loyalty," attacked, with a
large force of newly initiated brethren, the house
of a Scotch Presbyterian named James Cochrane.
He was an industrious man of the most exemplary
character. The outrage took place at two o'clock
in the morning, and the Rev. gentleman "hurried
him to Carrickfergus Jail where he languished
twelve months without even the remotest appearance of crime, merely because *he judged him a friend
to the Catholics.*"

The year with which we are dealing was not an
eventful one in the history of the Institution, and
furnishes little of diversity save the repeated horrors that were now becoming general in the Ulster
counties, and that were by the Yeomanry carried
towards the close of the year into other provinces.
With these I have already dealt, perhaps too fully.
I will request that the reader will bear in mind
that neither through the intervention of Government or of the heads of this Institution was this
bloody persecution put a stop to. In Belfast military despotism had long since set in, and though
many were sufferers in the raids made upon that
town, the spirit and intrepidity of the inhabitants
that saved the thousands from becoming victims to
this "vigour beyond the law." During all this
time, while Republicanism was rampant, and when
loyal men of all persuasions, particularly in the
North, were meeting and passing resolutions con-

* Plowden's Ten Years' History, vol. i., page 65.

demning "the plots of these wicked men," the United Irishmen, the Orangemen as an Institution was not heard of, its attention being, no doubt, confined to those districts in which a display of loyalty could be attended with pecuniary advantage to those taking part in it. The disaster which, fortunately for the British occupation, overtook the French fleet in Bantry Bay in the December of this year was the turning point in the history of the United conspiracy. It was a turning point in the history of our country too. Mr. Plowden says the news created the greatest consternation, and that nothing could exceed it save the loyalty and zeal with which all ranks of the people showed to go out and meet the enemy. The peasantry vied with each other to see who would do service to the troops on their march, and administered to them whatever comforts their scanty means would allow. He adds, "The fortuitous failure of the French invasion was a critical moment for Ireland; it had furnished a very strong and unexpected test of the loyal disposition of the Irish people, and some real patriots fondly augured for it favourable symptoms from Government towards their countrymen. Reports were circulated with credit that measures of conciliation towards Ireland had been resolved on by the Cabinet. Catholic emancipation and temperate reform were now confidentially spoken of, and Lord Camden, whose Administration was pledged to resist these two questions, it was generally expected would resign." The scheme was all but perfected, but the power of the Irish junto prevailed, and intolerance had its sway. The Irish, it will be seen, were not rebels but loyalists at this important crisis. They were shortly to be made rebels. The news arrived in Belfast on Friday, the 29th December, and on the following Saturday a town meeting was called by the Sovereign to consider the propriety of the citizens arming themselves against invasion. By an adroit diplomatic move the United men turned the occasion to account, and, as will be seen by an extended report in the News-Letter of the 2nd of January, 1797, every effort was made for the ventilation of grievances. Strange to say, such men as Arthur O'Connor, Sims, Simpson, and Tennant were appointed on the committee to consider the proposal. On the 5th of January they published a series of resolutions declaring for Parliamentary reform, and calling upon the Government to permit them to arm after the manner of the old Volunteers. To the credit of the Government, it must be said that they at least were not

such fools as harken to the prayer of the revolutions. These resolutions the Sovereign, one John Frown, and a clergyman named Bristow refused to agree to, and they accordingly left the meeting. Two days prior to this, a volunteer corps was started by the Sovereign, and 120 inhabitants of Belfast enrolled their names. This course was adopted like wise in other districts. By the means of these Volunteers the Orange Yeomen now sought the extension of their system, and, armed as they were with the patronage of the Government, it is but natural that they succeeded. As the outcome of this increased loyalty, on the 30th January, 1797, the Northern Star was illegally suppressed, for the law for seizing the materials, &c., was not then in force. Its proprietors and staff were imprisoned. This act, effected as it was, in the most wanton and outrageous manner, by a violent military mob, had the effect of rousing the ill-feeling of both sides into activity.

There is in the declaration of the Belfast Volunteers, published on the 9th of March, something suggestive, to my mind, of the creeping influence of Orangeism in its ranks. According to that declaration it would seem "that erroneous ideas were being formed as to their motives," and they accordingly came forward to protest that their ends remained still the same—the liberty of all. A certain French proverb about the excuser being the accuser will here occur to the reader without its being quoted. That at this period the Orange Institution first obtained anything like a general hold upon the nobility and gentry of the Northern counties is a fact to be admitted in their favour, and had the leaders but the wisdom to dissolve when the clouds of rebellion had passed they might, in the general confusion of those times, have acquired the title of heroes, and their names have come down to us as the self-sacrificing preservers of the English occupation. Sanctioned now openly by the Government, favoured by the nobility, headed by the gentry, and having the perfect machinery of the yeomanry system immediately at their command, the Institution reached its full tide of popular progress, and animated, as in their early days, by the principles of cruel extermination, its members succeeded in swelling the ranks of the malcontents and in driving the populace into rebellion.

ADDRESS OF THE UNITED IRISHMEN OF ARMAGH TO THE ORANGEMEN.

In the month of May, 1797, the following inte

resting address was issued by the United Irishmen of the County Armagh to the Orangemen—and appended is also the Orangemen's reply.—

ADDRESS.

" We have heard with inexpressible sorrow that those men whose wicked designs have already rendered our county infamous through Ireland, are again endeavouring to establish amongst you their abominable system of rapine and murder, persecution and bigotry. To us the motives of their conduct have been long obvious; permit us therefore to explain to you the diabolical principles on which they act, and to contrast them with those genuine precepts of Christianity and reason which influence United Irishmen. The men who have hitherto led you astray are anxious to turn those differences in religion which result from abstruse and perplexed questions in theology into fixed principles of hatred and animosity. What is the ultimate cause of this odious attempt? Is it not that whilst you are employed in idle contentions with your neighbours about heaven, they may enjoy and monopolise the goods things of earth? You quarrel with your fellow-citizens about another world. They and their abettors laugh at the silly dispute, and riot in the luxuries and pleasures of this. Their safety and power is built upon the disunion of the people, and therefore they urge you to commit the most atrocious crimes against society, for matters of as little import to true religion, as that which agitated the Blefuscans and Lilliputians mentioned in Gulliver's Travels, when they slaughtered each other about breaking eggs at the broad or narrow end Brethren, as long as your attention is engrossed with these absurd disputes, which do not originate in religion, but in that bigoted zeal which dares to trammel Christianity in the dogmatic creeds of particular sects, so long will you be ruled with a rod of iron by men who have overwhelmed the people with taxes in support of a war which they detest, who have destroyed our commerce, annihilated our manufactures, placed us under military government, transported our fellow-subjects without trial beyond sea, and when we gently remonstrated against these evils, branded us with the odious name of refractory rebels Have not the Ministry, whose creatures your leaders avowedly are, overwhelmed us with debts and taxes in support of an unjust war, in which Ireland had no natural interest. Do they not persist in maintaining all the corruptions which they have introduced into the Constitution. They obstinately resist a reform in Parliament, because if the people were fairly represented, their abominable, system of corruption must be annihilated. They oppress you with unjust burdens to support their extravagance; and with the very money they tear from you and your families, they are enabled to purchase votes in the House of Commons, and thereby overwhelm you with fresh taxes and fresh impositions. They grudge you the common necessaries of life, and their revenues arise not from taxes laid on articles of luxury, but from matters essential to your very existence. Even salt is not permitted to pass untaxed. Look now at these men who thus scourge the people with scorpions, you will see them and their creatures wallowing in wealth, indulging in the wantonness of unbridled luxury, laughing at your contentions, and fattening on your miseries. The poor starve, that pensioners may riot in excess. Placemen, and the whores of placemen, squander that money for the want of which your wretched families endure hunger and cold. Even Germans and other foreigners feast sumptuously at your expense Is is your business, it seems, to till the ground, it is theirs to enjoy the crop. You labour and feed them, your tyrants use your donations, yet despise and trample on your donors Know that, if union prevailed amongst you and your fellow-citizens, you would discover that the present Ministers and their creatures are your enemies, and not United Irishmen. They wish to engage you in religious battles, for the same reasons that Henry the Fourth wanted to lead his people to the Holy War at Jerusalem—namely, that they may turn your attention from their own misdeeds, and their own unjustifiable assumptions of power. Consider now, on the other hand, what are the objects of the Irishmen—union, peace, love, mutual forbearance, universal charity, and the active exercise of every social virtue. We know that true religion consists in purity of heart, in love to God, and goodwill to men. We persecute no man for speculative opinions in theology, we know the mind of man is free, and ought for ever to remain unfettered. Our principles lead us to wish for a reform in Parliament, because it is to us indubitably clear that the present system of things is inconsistent with your happiness as well as ours, and erected in violation to the common rights of man. Already we have forgiven you the injuries you have committed against us, we offer you the right hand of fellowship, and entreat you to co-operate with us in that great work, which we are able and ready to effect, whether you aid us or not."

" Your plans and schemes are now before the Select Committees of the Houses of Lords and Commons, and such measures we trust will be adopted towards those among you, who penitent for the crimes ye have committed, and the crimes you intended to commit, throw themselves on the mercy of our rulers. The blood of four soldiers of the Monaghan militia, who were shot a few days ago at Blaris Camp; and the blood of the unfortunate wretches who shall suffer for connecting themselves with ye, will at an awful tribunal be demanded at your hands. The unfortunate soldiers took an oath of allegiance to their King at the time they were enlisted; but ye tempted them with a promise of making them officers in your new diocese, and succeeded in making them perjure themselves, and thereby brought them to an untimely end. In future we desire ye will not call us friends as ye have done in your last address. We will not be your friends until you forsake your evil ways, and until we see some marks of contrition for your past conduct; neither do we wish to hold any intercourse with you, for evil communication corrupt good morals as well as good manners. We are satisfied in the enjoyment of what we can earn by honest industry, and neither envy those above us, nor desire to take from them a single farthing of their property; we wish ye to be of the same mind." [May 21, 1797.]

In most centres of Orangeism large meetings were now held, sufficient to indicate the increasing popularity of their scheme. Armagh, Fermanagh, and Antrim were successively the rendezvous of the brethren, and every effort was used to give a more respectable character to the Association. From the *News-Letter* of Monday, June the 5th, 1797, we find that a meeting of the masters of the different Orange Societies in the Province of Ulster was held in the city of Armagh on the 21st May—James Sloane, whose name we find attached to the original warrant, occupying the chair. The resolutions passed were as follows :—" We, having seen our association calumniated and stigmatised, our obligations belied and exaggerated, and ourselves abused and insulted by a coalition of traitors, styling themselves United Irishmen: being determined in this public manner to declare the principles upon which our glorious institution is established :—

" 1st. We associate together and defend ourselves and our properties to preserve the peace of the country, to support our King and Constitution, and to maintain the *Protestant Ascendancy* for which our Protestant ancestors fought and conquered —in short, to uphold the Protestant system and establishment at the risk of our lives, in opposition *to the wicked claims* of rebels of all descriptions.

" 2nd. Our association, being entirely composed of *Protestants*, has afforded an opportunity to people who undeservedly assume the appellation of *Protestant* to insinuate to the Roman Catholics of Ireland that we are sworn to extirpate and destroy them, which infamous charge we most openly deny and disavow. Our obligations bind us to second, not to break up, the existing laws of the land, and, so long as we remain under that obligation, the *loyal well behaved men may fear no injury of any sort from us.*

" 3rd. We earnestly request that the several members of the Administration in this country will not suffer themselves to be prejudiced against us by the unfounded calumnies of *unprincipled traitors* of ambitious dispositions and desperate circumstances, who detest us from no other cause than our unshaken loyalty, and who are using every exertion to increase their consequence, and to repair their shattered fortunes by plunging the kingdom in all the horrors of rebellion, anarchy, and civil war; and we likewise request the nation at large to believe our most solemn assurance that there is no body of men more strongly bound to support, or more attached to the Government of the Empire than the Orangemen of Ireland.

" 4th. We further warmly invite the gentlemen of property to reside in the country in order that we may enroll ourselves as district corps under them, *and as two guineas (Government allowance) is not a sufficient sum for clotheing (sic.) a soldier,* we entreat gentlemen to subscribe whatever they may think proper for that necessary purpose ; *many an honest fellow having no personal property to contend for or any other object than the laudable patriotic ties of our association.*

" ABRAHAM DAVIDSON, Secretary."

That the association was in the pay of the Government at this period was evident from the above, and from the statement of Mr. Plowden regarding a similar complaint made at a similar meeting in the same city in the spring of 1796, we may presume that the brethren in Armagh were determined to have their services adequately remunerated. But this is not the important consideration which forces itself upon us from reading this document. Even foregoing the conclusion that should follow from binding by oath a number of men of the lowest classes in society to uphold Protestant ascendancy, and how their efforts in support of it would naturally be directed—foregoing this and many other minor considerations, we come to the fact that this body of arrogant men assumed to themselves the prerogatives of dispensing justice and mercy, and of dealing out punishment to those who did not support the existing law. Their obligation was such that "all well-behaved men might fear no sort of injury" *from them*. Then, those who were not "well-behaved" or "loyal" might, as a natural consequence, fear injury from them. But the question suggests itself, how was the ill-behaviour or the disloyalty to be determined. Not by the known and legally established methods of the Constitution, for the Government and not the Orangemen would then be the chastisers of offended justice — the expression being, "fear no injury from us." Having no form of trial save the rude caricature of legal formality which is said to have been in those days attempted within some lodges the question of ill-behaviour could then be merely a matter of opinion in which each individual, prejudiced by assumptions of exclusive loyalty, was bound to judge, and, according to his obligation, to act for himself. So far as that opinion led the individual Orangemen to think his neighbour ill-behaved or disloyal that neighbour had much reason to fear injury from him. It appears likewise by the third resolution that those who did not agree in the theory that the Orange Institution was a model of magnanimity and loyalty, and who gave expression to these sentiments, were nothing but "unprincipled traitors," which affords a fair idea of who they were who were considered to be ill-behaved and disloyal. In fact the very exclusive Protestant nature of the association itself would without further aid sufficient in lica tion of the opinions of Orangemen in this respect. This is nothing more or less than a justification of the Armagh outrages, and it should be borne in mind that these arrogant professions of loyalty and these promises of an impartial dispensation of justice were made by men whose name had not yet become known to history save by the exterminating policy of their brethren in Armagh.

On the 4th June, of the same year, a meeting of the Orangemen of Fermanagh was held at Lisbellaw, at which a series of resolutions, already quoted, were passed which, it would appear, were up to the starting of the Grand Lodge in Dublin, looked upon as the general written law of the Institution. References are made to them in more than one of the numerous pamphlets of the time in defence of the principles of Orangeism.

That the association had by some mischance acquired a bad name throughout the country is evident from the repeated protests and declarations we find recorded about this time. At a meeting of the Orange Lodge of Belfast, held on the 19th June, 1797—the "Right Worshipful James Mont-gomery (master") in the chair—the following series of resolutions were passed:—

"1st. Resolved—That at this critical juncture we feel ourselves called upon, collectively and individually, to declare our sentiments in the most public manner."

"2nd. Resolved—That we will with our lives and fortunes support and maintain his present Majesty, King George the Third, our happy Constitution, and the succession to the Throne in his Majesty's illustrious house."

"3rd. Resolved—That we will aid and assist, to the utmost of our power, all civil magistrates in the execution of their duty."

"4th. Resolved—That we will use our utmost endeavour to suppress all riot and disorder, and support and maintain our most ancient and honour-able society in its truest interest and meaning."

"5th. Resolved—That we do recommend all lodges to enter into similar resolutions."

JAMES MONTGOMERY, Master.

John Brown, Past Master.

JOHN GALT SMITH, Secretary.

In addition to these numerous declarations of the most loyal intentions, an accomplishment for which the brethren have been from their earliest existence remarkable, resort was also had to the old policy of Popish massacres, to assassination committees,* and various other vague generalities likely to spread alarm amongst the Protestant inhabitants. That the large body of re-spectable and liberal-minded Protestants of

---

* Some individuals, who can only measure their own loyalty by the acrimony with which they calumniate their country, have, upon the strength of this (the Committee of the Lords' report) specifically charged the United Irishmen with holding regular committees of assassination. But no evidence whatever is offered by the Lords even to support their loose inuendo or charge of systematic assassinations. The private murders, though numerous and bloody, rather rebut than substantiate the charge of any organised system of that atrocious nature.—Plowden's Hist. Review, vol. ii., part i., page 572. In the memorandum delivered to the Government the leaders gave distinct denial to this charge. They solemnly declared that they believed such a committee never existed, and there is no proof that it ever did.

Ireland were little affected by the outcry is without question, but in the minds of many these concoctions did not pass without receiving credence, thus to some extent fulfilling the ends for which they were intended. The attention of the founders was now directed to a new field of labour. The Yeomen were all their own with the exception of a few members in odd corps ; but the militia had not yet been experimented upon and a move was now made in that direction. When we consider the case of a large body of men subsisting by the pay of the Government, with promotion and pension an object of their lives, we cannot, recollecting the fact that the Orange Association was now openly patronised by Government, expect that as a rule it would be received otherwise than with favour by those whose persuasion made them admissible. With the Administration it had become a test of loyalty and as such by the militia it was now considered. There was also powerfully operating both in the military as well as in the civil character of the Institution the fact that it allowed men of the lowest grades, who quailed beneath the glance of an ignorant country squire, or a tyrant village attorney, to meet with superiors if not always in education at least in fortune, to sit with them in their lodges, to drink at the same board, to cuddle their secrets and their mysteries and in all respects to meet with them on terms of equality. The first warrant that appeared to have been granted to a military regiment was No. 47, which was issued to the Monaghan militia in 1797. It would appear from the statement of Mr. Baker, a gentleman who occupied the high position of Deputy Grand Treasurer of the society, that this warrant was issued in consequence of a branch of the United Irish Society existing in that regiment The exact date of the issue we have not. It would be important to prove priority. Any further evidence we have on the point goes to corroborate the statement, as four members of the Monaghan militia were shot in this year for such an offence. Both civil and military departments now spread far and wide, and, beneath the patronage of a cruel Administration, that was false to its duty in refusing Catholics protection and rights which the Constitution entitled them to, the outrages increased as they went, the Orange contagion being taken up and passed from county to county. It is not, therefore, a matter of surprise that the next Orange celebration we find upon record was treated as a much more auspicious event than that which had preceded it.

THE 12TH JULY, 1797.

At Lurgan upon this day General Lake, commander-in-chief of the northern district, with General Knox, reviewed a large body of Orangemen, whose numbers are variously estimated at 12,000, 20,000 and 30,000. Colonel Blacker says the Orangemen numbered 15,000. The review took place in Lurgan Park, in presence of Mr. Brownlow, its proprietor. Generally speaking, those in the park were unarmed and without uniform. The yeomanry who took part in the demonstration were small in number. A similar demonstration took place in Belfast on the same day The following description of the event is taken from the *News-Letter* of July 14th, 1797 —

"BATTLE OF THE BOYNE.

"Wednesday being the anniversary of the Battle of the Boyne, conformable to the old style, a very great number of the inhabitants of this town and neighbourhood, denominating themselves Orangemen, assembled at an early hour in the morning to celebrate the return of the auspicious day. The different detachments moved from their respective places of rendezvous, and paraded through the streets, with music playing, drums beating, and colours flying. On the last were different devices, a painting of King William on horseback, &c. A large party of the Artillery and Monaghan Militia, as also a numerous body of yeomanry, drew up side by side, with a very numerous body who had assembled for a similar purpose as those of this town. As soon as General Lake had set off, the corps in Linen Hall Street marched in grand procession through High Street, &c., and the other parties took different routes. It is estimated that between six and seven thousand were present Previous to this procession being resolved upon by the parties, a deputation from their number waited on General Lake to obtain his permission. The General very politely granted it, under the express condition that they should conduct themselves with the strictest decorum and preserve the most respectful demeanour. This they pledged themselves to maintain, and we have it to say to their honour that they punctually and faithfully adhered to and fulfilled what they promised ; not the smallest indiscretion was observable, and the most exact regularity prevailed After the procession was concluded the several corps marched to their respective districts and then separated highly gratified with the exhibition of the day, heightened by the peace and good humour which prevailed.

w

It was novel and pleasing to observe numerous groups of girls range themselves in the ranks, and walk in procession, many of whom had come from distant parts of the country for the sole purpose.

Every person in the procession wore orange and blue cockades or ribbons, on many of which were imprinted *a crown*, and under it *God save the King and Constitution*, and others *a crown and harp*, and under, *the glorious, pious, and immortal memory of King William.*

the procession was still more numerous than here; not less than 12,000 were present. Flags, with similar devices, were flying, and orange and blue ribbons worn by the company bearing inscriptions of like import. General Lake and his suite were received with every mark of respect and honour. The processions of the day were conducted with great decorum, and concluded with much mirth and innocent festivity.

CHAPTER XVII.—CENTRALISATION, THE FIRST LODGE ESTABLISHED IN DUBLIN, EXTENSION SOUTHWARDS.

Flushed with its success in the Northern and Midland counties, the Orange Institution now directed its attention towards centralising its influences, that it might the more effectually operate all over the country. The first lodge was established in Dublin in the year 1797, and rules and regulations drawn up for its guidance. Unfortunately they too are lost to history, for Colonel Verner when asked for them happened to have them—*at home*. The date of its formation was the 4th of June. It appears that it gathered round it at its formation a large number of noted, or soon to be noted, individuals. As many of the names of its original members are familiar to most of my readers or likely to be so it may not be uninteresting to give a complete list. Mr. *Thomas Verner* was chosen master. The following were the members·—*Hamilton Archdall*, Earl Annesley, Earl Athlone, John Armstrong, *James Armstrong*, Richmond Allen, Thomas P. Ayres, F. owe Armstrong, Thomas Babington, Henry Brooke, Rev. Henry Bruce, Matthew Bathurst, William Bathurst, Christopher Bowen, *Jonah Barrington*, George Barnes, Marcus Blair, Charles Bury, *Rev. Charles Beresford*, Henry Brabazon, James Bathurst, Rev. Mr. Brickle, Captain Caulfield, Henry Colclough, Robert Conwall, George Carr, Hugh Cochran, Lord Corry, Cottingham, John Conroy, Henry Coddington, Hans Caulfield, Wm. Corbett, Wm. Ii. Cowan, *Patrick Duignan*, Stephen Draper, Frederick Darley, Wm. Darley, John Sakbey Darley, Edmund Darley, James Eustace, *Captain Henry Eustace*, Francis Fardley, T. Emerson, E. Emerson, Henry Faulkner, Robert Frazer, John Burke Fitzsimons, John Ferns, Wm. Ferns, Hon. Captain Ginchell, Walter Giles, Cornelius Ganton, Geo. Hill, Andrew Higginbotham, David Hay, Wm. Stewart Hamilton, Thomas Johnston, Arthur Jones, James Johnston, Rev. John Keating, Arthur Kelly, Elliott Knipe, Rev. Thos. Knipe, Thomas Knot, Benjamin Lucas, Richard Lucas, John Lindsay, Charles Leslie, John Leslie. William Large, Samuel Montgomery, Rev. Henry Maclean, Geo Vaughan Montgomery, Geo. Moore, Edmund Alexander M'Naghtan, Sir John Macartney, Wm. Mills, Hamilton Maxwell, Wm Newman, George Newman, Thomas Norman, Luke Norman, Thomas Orley, Charles Oulton, William Ormsby, Samuel Pendleton, James Poe, Andrew Price, Godwin Pilsworth, S W Plunkett, *Alderman Poole*, R. Powell, J. S. Rochefort, Rev. H. Roper, Wm. Roper. Thomas Reid, *Captain Ryan*, William Rawlins, William Stanford, Hon Benjamin O'Neale Stratford, Hon. John Stratford, John Steele, *Major Sardys, Charles Henry Sirr*, Richard Sayne, John Stanlan, Captain Shanley, Nathaniel Sneyd, *William Bellingham Swan*, Richard Carpenter Smith, Thomas Townzend, Francis Thomas, Urquhart Thompson, *James Verner, David Verner, John Verner, William Verner,* Alexander James Vance, Henry J. Worthington, Joseph Worthington, Thomas Worthington, William Wilcon, James Warren, Roger Wetherall, and Thomas White.

From this list it will be readily seen that though we find here many of the Browns, Joneses, and Robinsons of the metropolis, there was a considerable sprinkling of men high in position and authority who played important parts in the governing clique, or who afterwards were destined as their minions to enjoy unenviable notoriety. This lodge was afterwards divided into two lodges, and *Mr. John Claudius Beresford* made Master of the second.

The Dublin lodge was no sooner founded than it gathered together the most prominent members of the noted Beresford clique, who now, meeting in midnight conclave under the security of an oath of secrecy, found a means by which their reign of terror could be secured and prolonged. In the course of a few months various lodges were opened. Through a dispensation of Providence, the wisdom of which we dare not scrutinize, it generally happens that wicked men are endowed with those qualities which fit them for their wickedness. The professional duellist has a quick eye and a dexterous hand making death sure and sudden to his unfortunate victim; the highwayman, an athletic form and a vigorous constitution to face the mischances of the road and overcome its hardships; the burglar, an expertness, activity, and daring that laugh at bolts and bars; the pocketpicker, a sleight-of-hand, with an instinct that scents alike the presence of a purse and the proximity of a policeman; the informer, a bloodless countenance, which nature has forbidden to blush, a glib tongue and a long memory; and the selfish politician, a knavish duplicity, which perplexes his contemporaries and not unfrequently convinces himself he is the purest of patriots. Amongst the founders of the first lodge in Dublin there were many men of shrewdness and ability. They were in power, and the main question was how to prolong it. At this time it must not be overlooked the Orange Association had not anything that could be termed a good name. Notwithstanding the labours of its friends in the Government, and its representatives in both Houses of Parliament, notwithstanding the unceasing efforts of Mr. Pelham and Mr. Duigenan to dress it up in a respectable appearance, the name of Orangeman was damned before the country; nor could its apologists succeed before the eloquent denunciation of Grattan, the plain matter-of-fact reasoning of Parsons, the unlooked for admissions of General Craddock, and the annihilating testimony of Lord Goxford, in whitewashing it in the eyes of humanity. The early efforts of the Dublin brethren were then directed towards making a respectable appearance before the country. The advantages which politicians derive from the assumption of a virtue readily enable men in public life to dispense with that self-congratulatory reflection which first rewards the possession of it. By the people the Orange Society was held in abhorrence. *They resented the Orangeman's proscription of above four millions of their fellow-subjects as objects of distrust and enmity. They retained a lively sense of the atrocities of Armagh. They knew them sworn to secrecy, and were convinced of their oath of extermination. They were indignant at the aggravated provocation of Government encouraging them to assume the tone and function of affording protection to the great population of the country, whom they swore to exclude from their societies as unworthy to unite with them in their boasted loyalty—men to whom they, with peculiar inconsistency, proffered protection while designating and excluding them as rebels.' Sensible of the popular impression, and staunch to their original spirit of deceit, five of the leading members of the Orange Society put forth in the newspapers of 1797 a solemn manifesto of their order, by way of an address to the public, disclaiming the imputations of their enemies and speaking language of refined loyalty :—

"TO THE LOYAL SUBJECTS OF IRELAND.

"From the various attempts that have been made to poison the public mind, and slander those who have had the spirit to adhere to their King and Constitution, and to maintain the law—We, the Protestants of Dublin, assuming the name of Orangemen, feel ourselves called upon not to vindicate our principles, for we know that our honour and loyalty bid defiance to the shafts of malevolence and disaffection, but chiefly to avow those principles, and declare to the world the objects of our institution.

"We have long observed with indignation the efforts that have been made to foment rebellion in this kingdom by the seditious, who have formed themselves into societies under the spacious name of *United Irishmen.* We have seen with pain the lower orders of our fellow-subjects forced or seduced from their allegiance by the threats and machinations of *Traitors.* And we have viewed with horror the successful exertions of *miscreants* to encourage a foreign enemy to invade this happy land, in hope of rising into consequence on the downfall of their country.

"We therefore thought it high time to rally round the Constitution, and there pledge ourselves to each other, to maintain the laws and support our good King against all his enemies, whether rebels to their God or to their country; and by so doing, show to the world that there is a body of men in this island, who are ready in the hour of danger, to stand forward in defence of that grand paladium of our liberties, the Constitution of Great Britain and Ireland, obtained and established by our ancestors, under the great King William.

"Fellow-subjects, we are accused of being an institution founded on principles too shocking to repeat, and bound together by oaths at which humanity would shudder; but we caution you not to be led

---

* Plowden's Ten Years' History, vol. i., p. 76.

away by such malevolent falsehoods For we solemnly assure you, in the presence of Almighty God, that the idea of injuring any one on account of his religious opinions, never entered our hearts. We regard every loyal subject as our friend, be his religion what it may, we have no enmity, but to the enemies of our country.

"We further declare, that we are ready, at all times, to submit ourselves to the orders of those in authority under his Majesty; and that we will cheerfully undertake any duty which they shall think proper to point out to us, in case either a foreign enemy shall dare to invade our coasts, or that a domestic foe shall presume to raise the standard of rebellion in the land. To these principles we are pledged, and in support of them we are ready to shed the last drop of our blood."

"Signed by order of the several
  lodges in Dublin for selves and
  other Masters.

  "THOMAS VERNER.
  "EDWARD BALL
  "JOHN CLAUDIUS BERESFORD.
  "WILLIAM JONES.
  "ISAAC DE JOUCOURT"

This spacious address, Plowden says, tended to irritate the great body of the people proscribed from the society It certainly was a discovery of which the world had not previously heard that the English Constitution, which has been justly said to have "broadened down by slow degrees from precedent to precedent," was obtained by those of our ancestors who lived under William In a debate in the Commons which followed shortly after, this address was referred to by Dr. Duigenan as "breathing nothing but loyalty," an expression which, if it ended there, would have been nothing but the truth. But he was tempted further. It showed, he said, a desire to "protect" all descriptions of persons that should behave themselves in a neighbourly and peaceable manner, as well Catholics as others. He wondered that any charge should be made against Orangemen in that debate, "particularly as whatever excesses might formerly have been committed by them, and which certainly could not be justified, however they might be extenuated, by a spirit of loyalty from which they sprung, were now at an end." Mr. Pelham, in the same debate, said that "with respect to the Orangemen and Defenders whom an honourable gentleman had in the inadvertence of debate called rebels, he did not, for his part, think that either description of these men

deserved the epithet." If the Defenders were not rebels how could that persecution which Dr. Duigenan admitted, but extenuated, spring from a spirit of loyalty? If, in Armagh, the Orangemen persecuted those who were not rebels, was t unreasonable for the people of the South to receive with suspicion the specious offer of protection which they now made. Such protection the wolf gives the lamb. This address was issued in the after end of 1797 Mr. Plowden says; in 1798, says Lieutenant-Colonel Verner, but from a pamphlet —"The defence of Orangemen," — containing a number of those productions, this one is given first pl c, and immediately precedes "a declaration of the loyal inhabitants of Ulster, styling themselves Orangemen," of February 15th, 1798, so that it likely saw the light in the latter part of '97, or very early in the following year as the subsequent addresses follow in order of time.

Dublin having been so far thoroughly organised the association, pushed further South. In the neighbourhood of Wicklow they found a large class of landed proprietors who had ever been foremost in opposition to Catholic claims. The question of tithes was then regarded by the peasantry as a great injustice, and now, examined by the light of a broadening spirit of toleration, there are few who would venture to deny that, peasants though they were, they had a fairer sense of justice than the educated classes, and lived three-quarters of a century before their time. In Wicklow this agitation was deep-seated, and was a sure precursor of any association that had as its result the fostering of enmity between classes. While the landlords favoured the introduction of the Orange system, and furthered it in every way, the peasantry, little disposed towards constitutional agitation at a time when conditional loyalty was practised by heads of Government, soon followed the example of their betters They went over to the United Irish Society, outraged as they were by the military then quartered amongst them. So towards the close of 1797 we find in all those counties embraced between Wicklow and Derry a complete network of Orangeism, prompted by one common object—the extermination of Catholicism, euphoniously styled "Protestant ascendancy."

During all this time County Wexford was in comparative peace. It is true that its population had, as in the adjoining County of Wicklow, been stirred into discontent by the unhappy legislative enactments of a few years previous—enactments which still remained on the statute-book; that the determined opposition which its landed gentry gave to every measure of reform made more galling the condition of servitude in which a community, almost universally Catholic, was placed, and that circumstances, in spite of which a thrifty and intelligent people became comfortable if not opulent, tended to aggravate their feelings in so far as they made them more sensitive to inferiority, more qualified to detect, and more capable to resent injustice. Here the t the agitation found determined adherents. The Catholic clergymen of the district are accused by some historians of having advised this opposition, but whether in justice or not it would be difficult to say, for we have no proofs save the assertion of authors not altogether unprejudiced upon such points. At all events, if we would judge such advice by the spirit of our own time, the general verdict would be that however illegal it might have been, it was neither opposed to justice or humanity. The fact that the weekly gatherings at chapel in country districts was taken advantage of in some cases for administering oaths against tithes is likely to have given rise to the supposition—a supposition which, in the absence of further evidence, would be wholly unfounded. Though this agitation gave rise to some tumultuous assemblies, the condition of the country was peaceful and law-abiding. That the United Irish system had not spread into this country to any appreciable extent is admitted upon all sides; that the inhabitants had to endure all the hardships and indignities that incipient rebellion could scarce tolerate, is equally undeniable. The petty magistrates of the country, who in most instances reaped the benefits of the abominable tithe system, received with exultation their increased powers which the spirit of the law had intended for other counties. These powers they exercised with cruel vindictiveness.* The system of accusation and espionage necessarily admitted, but not sufficiently limited by Government, made ample room for the exercise of private malice and malignancy of disposition. Magistrates and military officers were empowered to receive information, but keep the names of the informers profoundly secret, and to proceed against the accused according to their own discretion. Mr. Gordon, a benevolent clergyman, profoundly confident of the honesty of human nature, says that "to suppose any magistrate should so abuse his great trust as to feign information for the indulgence of private spite would be invidious,"

* Rev. Mr. Gordon's History, vol. ii., p. 360.

but he admits that "some gentlemen vested with these powers were led into most grievous errors by *false* informers, *whose names, notwithstanding, have never been divulged.*" The latter admission would be sufficient with men having more limited confidence in their kind to show that the supposition would be in no way invidious. At all events, these measures gave ample grounds for suspicion to a peasantry already disposed to scrutinise closely, and possibly uncharitably, every act of those in power. The trial of some men for connection with the united system, and their conviction upon the evidence of notorious informers of the most degraded character, served the purposes of the united men in this county, in so far as it showed to a community that had hitherto kept aloof from the movement how needful were the measures of reform proposed. At the time these men were being charged there was little proof to support the arrogant assumption.* It would be contrary to the truth to say that there were no United Irishmen in the County Wexford, but from every statement worthy of credit it appears that their numbers were comparatively fewer in this than in any county in Ireland, and such as were of that description seemed to have been sworn in privately in an undetached, unconnected way, before the society had assumed the forms of a regular organisation.

Whether intentional, by "designing men," or simply the natural effect of the general alarm which the Armagh atrocities occasioned in the minds of the Catholic body, it is certain that rumours of the most startling character were spread abroad, to the effect that the Protestants would rise in a body and massacre the Catholic inhabitants; Plowden says that reports of this nature were spread by some United Irishmen in Wicklow, and gave the character of a religious war to the contest in that district; so that if it were done in one county, it may be presumed to have been done in another. Judging events as we are now able to do, with the light of three-quarters of a century, to read them by, the probable conclusion, and likely the right one will be, that rumours of this kind were spread by some incautious local leaders (for the Dublin leaders were then seeking to restrain their country associates), but that in general the terror caused amongst the inhabitants of Wexford, and the subsequent evacuation of their houses, arose from the widespread fear which atrocities and house-burnings elsewhere had oc-

* Hay's History of the Rebellion in Wexford.

x

casioned. That the fear of Orangemen riding knee-deep, or where it was possible saddle-deep, in Papist blood was grounded upon extreme probability, is best judged from the subsequent persecution. That persecution having followed as a consequence upon the introduction of the Orange system, it is reasonable to conclude that the dread of it was caused not by any deep-seated conspiracy to excite the minds of the Catholics, but by the natural effects of its intolerance upon a people who had little to hope for in the way of protection from the governing classes. That they did quit their houses is established upon all sides. As this movement must have created a corresponding alarm amongst the Protestants the natural current of events was so fashioned as to prepare in the county the way for Orangeism. When it did enter, no county in Ireland, particularly during the brief period of the rebellion, but in a lesser degree, for many long years after, experienced—as the County Wexford did—the intensity of Orange cruelty, or so deeply drained the dregs of Orange despotism.

It was not until the beginning of April, 1798, that the Orange system made any appearance in the County Wexford. It was introduced by the North Cork Militia (commanded by Lord Kingsborough), in which regiment there was a large number of Orangemen, who were zealous in the making of proselytes. In their public parade they displayed Orange decorations upon their bosoms, and flaunted their colours and emblems tauntingly in the face of the inhabitants. Hay says that previous to this period there were few actual Orangemen in the county, but soon after all those whose opinions were inclined that way, finding themselves supported by the military, joined the association, and publicly avowed themselves by assuming the devices of the fraternity. Orangeism soon after became prevalent throughout the county, and was strengthened by the accession of almost every Protestant in it. This, says Hay, was forwarded by the received prejudice that no man could be loyal who was not an Orangeman. Dr. Jacob, a captain of a yeomanry corps, did not at first deem Orangeism an essential to loyalty, and refused to become a member, but he was soon induced to alter his opinion. By a resolution entered into by the majority of his corps—*that they would resign if he did not join the Association*—they absolutely compelled the captain to take the oath, thus affording an instance of how readily their exuberant loyalty could be turned aside at a most critical period. The Association became at length so general and indiscriminate that their members could by no means be considered capable of constituting a select assembly. Multitudes of them were of the lowest, and most uninformed vulgar, and, of course, subject to the weakest passions, prejudices,

and frailties of human nature." By similar means the Association was carried further southwards, and was productive of the same unhappy consequences. We now find the whole of Ireland covered with conspiracy, comprised of two secret societies, whom the intriguing of Government had placed at deadly enmity. One the child of reform and advanced thought, but of whom a system of cruelty had made a rebel; the other the outcome of monopoly, which immunity had fashioned into an absolute tyrant; the United Irish embarked in that desperate game in which, all the odds being against them, few men engage without some desperate cause; the Orangemen resolved to resist them, and to maintain their monopoly, full of that fierce determination which the tiger can command when something unforeseen imperils his plunder, deluded by self-interest into a belief of the righteousness of their cause, convinced by guilty Government patronage that they were loyalists, determined to suspect all who were not Orangemen, and to treat as rebels all who were Papists.

That some prominent members of the society at this time were actuated by more liberal principles it is my pleasure to acknowledge.* In the worst conspiracies that selfishness or passion has called into existence, we do find men to whom we can point with satisfaction, not as proof of the blessings of such associations, but as solitary examples of generous natures rising superior to their contaminating influence, making more marked the lines which divide them from their criminal associates, and by contrast rendering more revolting the pernicious principles which neither their presence nor example was capable to control.

* On the 15th February, 1798, the Orangemen of Ulster presented Lord Camden with an address of loyalty, " signed by several thousand loyal inhabitants," in which we find the following :—" We have no doubt of the sincerity of such declarations, and that the Catholics of Ireland, sensible of the benefits they enjoy, will not suffer themselves to be made the dupes of wicked and designing men for the most diabolical purposes, and we flatter ourselves that such declarations will be embraced, and have the happiest effects in other parts of this kingdom. Such conduct must be acceptable in the eyes of God and man. We declare most solemnly that we are not enemies to any body of people on account of their religion, their faith, or their mode of worship. We consider every peaceable and loyal man our brother, and they (sic.) shall have our aid and protection." Their practices having been at all times contrary to their professions, we must regard, if not with suspicion, at least with credulity, all documents of such a nature that issued from the Orange body. While we must contemplate with pity the disposition of those arrogant men who could at that time speak of Catholics being sensible of benefits, it is only by the most overwhelming testimony we could be driven to the sad conclusion that all were alike concerned in making professions which they did not believe, for the rendering of their power more effective. The more generous, and possibly the more rational construction is, that some few were sincere in their declarations, while the general body little inclined to be bound by trammels that would disarm their vindictiveness, regarded them as so much waste paper. And it is also likely that intolerance was so inevitably the consequence of an exclusively Protestant conspiracy in Ireland that no amount of good intentions on the part of a few men could divert it from its allotted end. Such views alone would reconcile the above declarations with the persecution of Catholics in subsequent years, and with the malignant hatred and barbarous cruelty (the former cherished where the latter was impossible) that ever characterised the Orange Association, handed down as they have been an inheritance to all succeeding generations of Orangemen.

CHAPTER XVIII.—EXPLODING THE REBELLION.

There is no class, save one, who would dispute that the rebellion of 1798 was "exploded" by unnecessary and unrelenting cruelty That class is the Orangemen of the present day. Their opinions —considering the utter ignorance of the great majority of all things relating to Irish history, and also the light in which early prejudices have taught them to read it—are indeed of little moment English statesmen have learned, and are by modern legislation continuing to acknowledge, that Ireland has been treated with shocking injustice by the governing monopolists. And there are men who, judging from the beneficent enactments of late years, would be inclined to say that had it suited the purposes of Administration a few wise concessions granted even on the eve of that unfortunate explosion would have saved an immensity of blood, and the blackest record of cruelty which man, when before his Maker, will ever have to account for. A little conciliation, and the reformers of '92 would have been the Oppositionists of '95, and might have been directors of an Administration in 1798. At this time but two alternatives remained to Government. By concession they might have made loyalists of the malcontents; by persecution they could have made rebels. They chose the latter, and while those who, seeing in the union between the two countries much commercial advantage, may not question the wisdom of the selection, all must agree in questioning its humanity. From end to end of the island we find practiced the most inhuman barbarity; tales of outrage and untold crime which, if they came to the ears of the civilised English multitude of to-day, would arouse the indignation, and call aloud for the sympathies of all. That there were cruelties upon the side of the rebels no one dares deny. But the apologists of the English occupation have fallen into the very grave mistake when dealing with them of entirely ignoring the fact that the greatest and most wanton outrages were committed by the Orangemen and soldiery previous to the rebellion, and for the purpose of exploding the rebellion; while the outrages upon the other side were committed during the rebellion and were but the natural results of an ignorant and desperate multitude in arms. Macaulay has said, I think in his essay upon Machiavelli, that it is an established principle, and one, in his experience, without an exception, that the violence of a revolution is always equal to the injustice which has created it. If we judged the rebels upon this principle they would be in no measure accountable for their acts, and might be considered but rude implements of chastisement in the hands of an offended Providence

There is no blacker page in Irish history than that which details the multiplied horrors of the few months that preceded the rebellion of '98. Bloody persecutions we have had in plenty, but none so degrading as this. When that Deputy of Munster, obedient to Queen Elizabeth, put the suspected Irish to the rack, and "to torture when he found it convenient," he was putting in practice political principles prevailing in England 300 years ago. When, under the milder reigns of a few subsequent generations, Ireland again was quivering beneath the lash, there was one consolation still remaining to her in her sufferings—the torture was alone inflicted by her conquerors But '98 came, and brought with it all the accumulated horrors of previous persecutions with none of their consolations, making it at once the darkest and most degrading epoch in our sad calendar. Now the torture was multiplied ten fold, but worse still the instruments were prepared by those of our kindred and our country; the lash was applied with redoubled vigour, but it was wielded by the strong and willing arms of fellow-countrymen, while familiar voices in shrieks of savage laughter aggravated the pain a thousand fold. The pitch-cap, inhuman at any time, was made more galling by the recollection that it was an Irishman invented it, or rather borrowed the invention from the devil, and that the hands of neighbours formed, fashioned, and applied it to the head of unfortunate victims. Et tu Brute. The Orangemen were the executioners of these days. Wherever an Irishman—take the presumptions against him and call him a rebel if you will—was to be placed in the rack, whether by half-hanging, picketing, or "crucifying," an Orangeman was not wanting to put into practice those ingenious and barbarous contrivances that shocked the humanity of the English soldiery. If there is anything which makes this consideration more saddening it is that I speak upon authority which permits of no other conclusion; which leaves no room for rational doubt. Cruel as the English soldiery were, they were not much more so than, as a rule, soldiers of fortune are in a conquered land, and even in their wildest freaks of passion and drunken debauchery we find revealed occasionally traits of a better humanity. But the Orangemen exhibited no such weakness. Theirs was a double game—extermination as well as plunder. They came to the persecution with more freshness because they carefully avoided the dangers of the field. The Orangemen were the walking gibbets of those days, the mutilators of the honoured dead, the ravishers of female chastity, the dread enemies of women and of children—in the absence of their natural protectors—and the willing instruments of torture for making rebels of an entire people It would be a most surprising feature in the consideration of these events if the brethren of the present day were not, in this respect at least, convinced of the iniquity of their ancestors.

The acknowledgment of error being at all times disagreeable, it would be unnatural to expect that the admission of guilt would come more easily The public are, therefore, wise in concluding that the silence which prevails amongst them is prima facie evidence of admission, and in construing the occasional protests of platform orators more as an effort to catch the crowd than to convince the reasoning. And still it does seem strange that intelligent men should at the present day, for such a purpose, or for any purpose, seek to divert history to other ends than that for which it is intended The object of these craters—reverened and otherwise—is apparent, and the more to be regretted because it will partially succeed with a confident, and unhappily an unlettered, people. And yet this can be only effected by the suppression of the fact that history is bristling upon all sides with proofs of Orange atrocities   I do not now speak of the bloody deeds done during the rebellion, but of those enacted previous to it, and of which the rebellion was but a consequence.

All those who have written upon the subject admit—because they dare not deny—that the Rebellion was hastened, if not actually caused, by the cruelty of the Orange Yoemanry. Hay, Plowden, Gordon, Barrington, Sampson, and Madden are at one upon the subject; the newspapers of the time are teeming with horrible details of nameless outrages and unheard-of crimes, and the records of Parliament and reports of trials of subsequent years amply corroborate them. Too often the torturing seems to have been indulged in for torture's sake; the scourging, the half-hanging, the mutilation appear to have been often inflicted to afford

amusement to the merry crowd of drunken yoemen who laughed at the groans of an unoffending fellow-creature; too often the pitch-cap was applied for no better reason than to see how the victim would conduct himself under the pangs of this newly-invented and hellish mode of torture. A ready pretext was found for these proceedings—the victim would not confess—and seeing that this was a condition that could as easily belong to a loyalist as to a rebel, if there were nothing to confess, the pretext was of the greatest convenience, and applied under every possible circumstance That it was taken advantage of largely is evident from the shocking disclosures that came out upon the trial of Wright against the celebrated Thomas Judkin Fitzgerald, High Sheriff of Tipperary. Fitzgerald's inhuman and unjustifiable conduct became subsequently the subject of discussion in Parliament, where he was vigorously censured, *John Claudius Beresford* defended the High Sheriff's conduct. There is reason to suspect that the defence by this notorious Orange leader was prompted by selfish motives, as well as by brotherly love. If Judkin Fitzgerald, for his half-hangings and scourgings, did not receive the protection of indemnity, where would end the responsibilities of this scourger-in-chief of the Marlborough Riding School, this director of that infamous pack of exterminators who swarmed the metropolis during that period? It is not the intention to disgust my readers and weary myself by giving a detailed chronicle of the cruelties perpetrated by the Orange Yoemen, and which brought about the rebellion of 1798. I confess I did at one time intend it   I thought it would indeed be a gratification and a public benefit to silence those mouthing demagogues who seek to justify their intolerance by a reference to those times   But these men are playing too deeply laid a scheme to justify our considering them fools. As they are not fools, they can read history as well as others   If they can now command the effrontery to ignore the overwhelming evidence spread widely through the writings of the period, and contributed to by many authors of their own way of thinking, bigotry would still furnish an excuse, or villiany a justification to overlook any accumulations of such proofs that I could offer in these pages. One of the most silly and laughable replies to these charges of atrocity on the part of the Orange Yoemen was made by an Orange witness before the Committee of Inquiry in 1835—that the United Men dressed themselves in the garb of Yoemen and committed the outrages. It is an important admission coming from such a quarter that outrages were committed at all. Whether it is a reasonable explanation of them I leave my readers to judge. It was also stated before that Commission that many of the United Men became Orangemen previous to the rebellion, this being, of course, meant to indicate the extraordinary benefits the institution conferred upon the State. Any such must have first been perjurers, for the terms of the oath bound them to swear—"I am not and never was a United Irishman."

That the atrocities were knowingly permitted and connived at by the Administration is evident. They could not plead ignorance of it. General Abercrombie put them in possession of the facts in one brief sentence—"The very disgraceful frequency of court-martials and the many complaints of irregularities in the conduct of troops in this kingdom having too unfortunately proved the army to be in a state of licentiousness which must render it formidable to every one but the enemy, &c." This commander resigned in a few short months because he would not be allowed to curb the inhuman practices that prevailed.* But there are still remaining even more substantial proofs that Government connived at this system in order to explode the rebellion and disconcert its leaders. The Northern Star having been suppressed—for in the North the Government's work was now done—the prospectus of The Press was published in Dublin on Thursday, the 28th Sept., 1797. In its very first issue it bristled with sedition, and all its subsequent issues were such as to afford secret gratification to a Government that sought to excite the people to rebellion. With the best intentions, its contributors told plain truths and sought for no mild language in conveying them. Even Tom Moore, then a young student of Trinity, did not hesitate to contribute secretly an address to his fellow-students urging them to join in a rebellion in which, if not unwilling, he was at

least unable to take part as well from his youth as from his natural effeminacy of character. For six months this publication was allowed beneath the shadow of Dublin Castle to disclose the most horrible crimes, to beard the perpetrators of them, the Orangemen, and dare them to a denial which never came, and to urge the people to prepare for armed resistance since they found no other protection but in the rifle and the sword. When the people had prepared it was then suppressed by Orangemen under Mr. Maxwell, an Orange leader, and the insurrection burst forth in all its venom. On Saturday the 25th November, 1798 (No. 26) The Press published the following, which as an interesting record I venture to transfer into these pages:—

ORANGEMEN v. UNITED IRISHMEN.

"At a moment when the rulers of this country profess loudly to hold no wish amidst the struggle of parties, but the preservation of peace and good order, and the maintenance of the laws; at a time they would impress on Ireland and the world, a belief that they side with no class of partisans; that they held all in equal abhorrence; that the denominations of United Irishmen and Orangemen, are to them equally obnoxious; that the cruel and sanguinary expulsion of the Northern Catholics from their peaceful industry, and humble lots, had not their sanction; at a time when every man who ventures to profess a wish that Ireland was United against every foreign or domestic influence inimical to prosperity, is harrassed by prosecution and persecution; but even in his own dwelling, his house and property burned about his ears, his wife and daughters violated, and himself and his sons hanged, shot, or hunted through the country like beasts of prey—will it be believed that in the narrow vicinage of a Northern village, Lisburn, no less than fourteen societies of illegal associators under the denomination of Orangemen, and numbered from 138 to 354, which proves that so many other societies of the same kind exist, avow themselves in a public advertisement, which appeared in the Evening Post of Thursday, publicly addressing a Mr. Johnson as their chairman, and publishing their resolutions, publicly entered into at a meeting held on the Sabbath Day, at the parish church of Derryaghy.

"The world are no strangers to the oath of the Orangemen, any more than to that of the United Irishmen. They have been publicly contrasted in this paper, that the world might fairly judge of their comparative deserts or demerits—and the world has seen that the former is an oath of

* See the general orders of February 26th, 1798, to be found in extenso in Plowden's Appendix, or a summary of which can be seen at the end of Madden's series. Writing in the Edinburgh Review upon Sir John Moore's services at this time in Ireland, Major-General William Napier says, "What manner of soldiers were then let loose upon the wretched districts which the ascendency-men (the Orangemen) were blessed to call disaffected? They were men, to use the Venerable Abercrombie's words, who were 'formidable to every body but the enemy.' We ourselves were young at that time; yet being connected with the army, we were continually amongst the soldiers, listening with boyish eagerness to their conversation—and we will remember, and with horror, to this day, the tales of lust and blood and pillage—the record of their own actions against the miserable peasantry which they used to relate."

intolerance, bigotry, patricide, persecution, civil warfare, and extermination to their Catholic fellow subjects.

"The other—a solemn vow of unity, peace, charity, and christian tolerance with all sects, in the common prosperity of their country.

"If oaths then be the tests of principle, let the world judge between the two parties — and if impartiality, peace and national prosperity, be the professed wish of the ruling powers, let the world judge of their sincerity, when Orangemen, openly and avowedly professing and practising their principles—are not only unmolested, but cherished and caressed; while the very suspicion of a connection on the other side is tantamount to felony of death. Nay, the Orange party go so far as to assemble by thousands, in arms by day and by night, with Orange ribbons at their breast , and cockades of the same colour ; while a green ribbon or a green handkerchief even accidentally worn, being suspected as an emblem of affection to Ireland—subjects a man to imprisonment—transportation — the rope or the bayonet —and exposes women to the brutal insults of the common soldiery.

Such things, however, cannot be deemed *new* in a country where so much pains have been taken by the English party to *deter*, or erase every symptom of the *amor patriæ*, from the bosoms of the inhabitants. The modern *sham* of tolerance to the antient religion, and revival to ancient prosperity of Ireland, backshaded as it is by the persecution of fire and sword—cannot erase from the minds of the insulted Irish, the memory of those laws heretofore passed to destroy their religion, to annihilate the language of their country, and blot out for ever the family names of their ancestors ; nor can they be unmindful that such is the ruling system now received under different forms.

"Facts are too palpable to be veiled in the flimsy texture of pretence—those that run may read—and the people of Ireland are not such *dolts* as to mistake the evidence of their senses.

"If military generals were legally considered as *gaolers*, gaols would be ambulatory; as every flying camp would become a prison, with the assistance of summary proceedings, and a few *walking gallows's*, the commissioners of Oyer and Terminer, would have little business to transact on circuit."

If we had not the evidence of Lord Gosford to show that the Rebellion became a religious war by reason of the outrages of the Orangemen we have indicating it a plentiful supply of facts, precisely stated, and vouched for over the names and ad-

dresses of the writers, showing how fermented was the public mind in consequence On the 23rd of January, 1798, the *Press* published an able letter over the signature of Vincent. It was addressed to the Orangemen of Ireland and expressed concern at the horrible idea entertained by them of exterminating the Catholics of Ireland—sorrow that the Protestants, Presbyterians, and Catholics of Ireland had not been melted down into one great and indissoluble mass of Irishmen—and called upon them to forsake their cruel practices and unite with their fellow-countrymen in a peaceful agitation for reform. Scarce a page of this paper you turn over but discloses some new act of Orange inhumanity and some direct charge of perfidy against the Administration. That it was tolerated as a means for exploding the Rebellion is evident from the statement of Thomas Addis Emmet before the Secret Committee—"I know we were very attentively watched , but I thought they were right in letting us proceed." Two direct and powerful influences we therefore find urging the people forward to the awful brink of insurrection—before the tempting hopes held out by the reformers ; behind the advancing bayonets of Ascendancy.

The chosen instruments of torture—cruel, barbarous, and unrelenting—these Orange yeomen prosecuted their bloody task with a vindictiveness that all but brutalised our kind, that left an indelible stain upon our character as a nation, and inflicted a wound upon the great majority of the population, the degrading scar of which even centuries will not be able to remove. Yet to Orangemen of the present day "the gallant Orange yeomanry who fought in Ninety-eight" are upheld in rude poetry and in ruder prose as patterns of all that is good, and loyal, and just, and generous in humanity—as fitting models to men who, fortunately, can imitate their example only in so far as the principles and the conspiracy they inherit from them prompt them so to do. They are as profoundly ignorant of the deeds as they are unconscious of the infamy of their ancestors.

As a fair specimen of the poetry I allude to, the following (sung at Orange boards after the mysteries of the lodge have been disclosed) may be taken as a fair specimen—that it is authentic is best shown from the fact that it is from a volume of Orange poetry published in the interests of the Grand Treasurer of Ireland, and edited by our present distinguished Inspector of Fisheries, William Johnston, M.A., of Ballykilbeg :—

THE ORANGE YEOMANRY OF '98.

Air—"*Partant Pour La Syrie.*"

I am an humble Orangeman—
My father he was one ;
The mantle which the sire once wore
Has fallen to the son ·
He ranked with those who quelled their foes—
The foes of Church and State—
The gallant Orange Yeomanry
Who fought in Ninety-eight !

The light which led their spirits on
O'er battle-field did shine,
Each breast was Freedom's temple pure,
Each heart was Freedom's shrine ;
As sinks the day in glorious ray,
Some sunk—and bright their fate,
The gallant Orange Yeomanry
Who fought in Ninety-eight !

Behold the Orange peasant, or
The Orange artizan,
Go view his home, observe his ways ;
You'll find it is his plan,
Through woe or weal, with godly zeal,
True men to imitate—
The gallant Orange Yeomanry
Who fought in Ninety-eight !

To guard the faith which Luther preached—
The rights which William won,
The Orangeman relies upon
His Bible and his gun,
He prays for peace, yet war will face,
Should rebels congregate ;
Like the brave Orange Yeomanry
Who fought in Ninety-eight.

"Who fears to speak of '98 ?"
This was the silly note
Of one who was afraid to put
His name to what he wrote ;
He was afraid—they're all afraid—
They know we'd gag their prate,
As did the Orange Yeomanry
Who fought in Ninety-eight !

In peace, like watchful silent stars,
Can Orangemen remain ;
In war, their energies are like
The surges of the main ;
And each true-hearted Orangeman
Would smile, though death await,
As did the Orange Yeomanry
Who fought in Ninety-eight !

Little wonder that Orange outrages follow fast upon Orange Lodge meetings, where such blasphemous productions, are rendered more exciting by deep potations, are permitted to arouse the religious frenzy of ignorant fanatics.

CHAPTER XIX.—1798.

This is not a history of the rebellion. Its subject —Orangeism—is so intimately interwoven with all its surroundings, and was so prominently a cause in promoting the rising, that a patient and laborious effort was required to show in what light Orangeism was connected with it. Having traced its working to the fearful threshold of insurrection we will follow it no further in that direction. Happily we can, with consistency, pass over in silence this awful chapter of horrors. In excuse for some of the French Revolutionists it has been urged by a noted writer that the most peaceable and amiable citizens know not what passions they possess until they find themselves whirled amid the vortex of a great revolution. When contending elements arouse the passions of men in arms, particularly of men engaged in civil warfare, to form an estimate of their character would lead to an exaggerated opinion which those of sense and moderation are ever anxious to avoid. That it was a sanguinary war between the Orangemen on the one side and the United Irish and Catholics on the other is but

too apparent. Towards the close, and particularly in the Counties Wicklow and Wexford, where the Catholics were most numerous, it became a war of extermination, for the outrages of the Orange yeomanry were met with reprisals on the part of the rebels, the one party ingenious in its modes of extermination, the other, if not as inventive, at least as reckless in its species of retaliation. "Among the loyalists," says Gordon, "whoever attempted to moderate the fury of his associates, or prevent the commissions of wanton cruelties on defenceless prisoners or helpless objects was generally browbeaten and silenced by the cry of *croppy.*" And again "to suppose that the insurgents were all alike sanguinary or prone to cruel deeds would be as little conformable to truth as to probability. Many of even the lowest were men of humanity ; but amid so wild an agitation, so furious a commotion, the modest and feeble voice of compassion was drowned by the loud and arrogant clamour of destruction to enemies ; *revenge on the bloody Orange dogs*" The same author assures us that even some officers in the army were ahy to restrain the sergeants and others under their command from the commission of cruelties, lest they should be charged with "croppyism," adding, "When this was the case under a regular Government and established military discipline, what was to be expected from tumultary bands of ignorant peasantry suddenly starting into action without order or subordination ?"

We may close the account of the fearful transactions of the rebellion. Nor can there be a doubt upon which side the sacrifice is made. The desperate and inhuman retaliation of Scullabogue and the blood spilled by an infuriated mob upon Wexford Bridge may well be blotted out before the savage massacre of the Enniscorthy invalids, the conflagration of and slaughter at Carlow — in the midst of which, Cox says, an Orange trumpeter was seen parading with a crucifix stuck upon his bayonet, crying "behold the wooden Jesus"—the cool, deliberate massacre of Kilcoomney, the slaughter at the Gibbet Gate of Kildare, the dreadful havoc made by the Ancient Britons in the Counties Wicklow and Wexford. In one respect, which deserves to be recorded, the rebels did not imitate the practices of the yeomen and soldiery ; not an instance is to be found, and Gordon himself admits it, where the person of a female was violated,

Lord Camden was recalled, having executed the work for which he was sent, and on the 20th of June Lord Cornwallis made his entrance in the capital, bringing with him hopes of a milder administration. As the one had been sent to create a rebellion the other was commissioned to allay it. It would be tedious and scarcely in keeping with the above intimation to detail the horrors which followed in the course of a few months succeeding the suppression of the rebellion. But there is one incident of more than passing importance, which, as it serves to illustrate the intimate connection lasting to this day, between a certain noble family and the Orangemen, deserves some attention. In the early part of October a circumstance occurred of singular notoriety and importance to the welfare of Ireland. The Earl of Enniskillen, who ranked as a colonel in the army, had ever been prominently zealous for the system of coercion and severity. "It is to be hoped," says Plowden, "that few of his colleagues, associates, and co-operators in those measures supported them by the same infamous injustice and profligacy he notoriously did. It is to be feared from the common cause which most Orangemen made with this nobleman's

disgrace and punishment that the sympathy of that association with the noble lord's disposition and conduct was lamentably too general." Lord Cornwallis was now in power. Disliked at first this benevolent nobleman became after the incident I am about to relate henceforward execrated by the Orangemen. They villified him and lampooned him wherever they found it possible, and attempted to blacken his unstained character by the opprobrious application of "Croppy Corny." In fact every evidence was afforded that the Orangemen of those days were alone loyal to their own nominees and to that Administration which permitted them without question to carry out their plundering intolerance. On the 13th of October, 1798, a court-martial, by order of Lieutenant-General Craig, was held, at which an Orange yeoman named Hugh Wollaghan, of Middlewood, County Wicklow, was charged with having on the 1st October murdered Thomas Dogherty. The circumstances of the murder, which will be found disclosed in the following, were of peculiar atrocity. The President of the court martial held upon this Orangeman was the Earl of Enniskillen, and the other members of it Major Brown, Captain Onge, Mr. Leslie, Fermanagh ; Capt. Irwin, Fermanagh ; Captain Carter and Lieutenant Summers of the 68th. It is an instructive example given us of what will inevitably be the result when an Orangeman is put upon his trial before his brother Orangemen. The prisoner, on being arraigned, pleaded not guilty. It appeared from the testimony of Mary Nulty, of Delgany, that the prisoner came to her house and demanded "If there were any bloody rebels there," to which she replied that there was no one in the house save a sick boy who was then lying in bed. Woollaghan went over to the bedside and asked the boy "If he were Dogherty's eldest son." The boy sat up and said he was, Wollaghan then said, "Well, you dog, if you are you are to die here." To this the boy replied "I hope not. If you have anything against me bring me to Mr. Latouche and give me a fair trial, and if you get anything against me give me the severity of the law." Wollaghan replied, "No, dog. I do not care for Latouche, you are to die here," at the sametime levelling the gun. The mother threw herself between her son and his murderer, and asked him for Heaven's sake to spare his life and take hers. To this piteous appeal the "gallant Orange Yeoman" had no reply save "no, you bloody whore, and if I had your husband here I would give him the.

same death." He then snapped the gun, but it missed fire, again snapped it and again it missed, upon which a yoeman named Fox rushed in and "damned his gun" that there was no good in it. While making the third attempt to shoot the boy the mother caught hold of the gun and endeavoured to turn it aside from her enfeebled son, but it went off grazing the boy's body, the ball lodging in the arm; he staggered; leaned on a form; turned his eyes towards his distracted mother and said, "Mother pray for me," upon which he fell senseless into her arms. Wollaghan then left the house, but in a short time he returned and asked, "Is not the dog dead yet?" The mother replied, "Oh yes, murder was set up on the ground that *it had been done under the order of the commanding officer.* It was sworn by several witnesses, some of them Orangemen, that *Captain Armstrong,* of the Queens County Militia, who commanded, gave orders that if any yoeman on a scouring party (then scouring parties occurred daily) met any person whom they *knew or suspected* to be rebels *they need not go to the trouble of bringing them in—they might shoot them off-hand for convenience.*

* This is no exaggeration. Such was the distinct and precise orders of the celebrated Captain Armstrong. It was an order that the Orange Yeomanry availed themselves of to the utmost. The Orangemen facetiously called these scouring excursions "Partridge shooting," and they actually did employ dogs to scent out parties who lay concealed in the woods and thickets to avoid their fatal cruelty. When a "rebel" (the "rebel" might be and often was a decrepid old man, or a feeble child, or perhaps a female) when a "rebel" was started the gallant Orange Yeomanry without condescending to investigate commenced at rifle practice. Most shocking of all bets were actually made as to who would bring down the fugitive first.

After some deliberation, the Court acquitted the prisoner, and Hugh Wollaghan walked forth an unstained soldier and a better Orangeman, while his hands were actually wet with the blood of a defenceless and unoffending boy.

The minutes of evidence having been forwarded to the Lord Lieutenant, his Excellency "utterly disapproved of the sentence acquitting Hugh Wollaghan of the cruel and deliberate murder of which, declared in the evidence, he appeared to have been guilty." But now comes the incident which has linked the fortunes of the Enniskillins with that of Orangeism for all time, for the simple fact that it made them fellows in misfortune. The president of the court-martial was disgraced. By order of Lord Cornwallis, the Court was dissolved immediately, and Hugh Wollaghan, the Orangeman, was dismissed the service, and disqualified from entering any other in the kingdom. A new court martial was also ordered to be immediately convened for the trial of such prisoners as might be brought before them, and by express orders Lord Enniskillen and other members of the former Court were prohibited from being members of it.

This was an instance in which an Orange murderer was acquitted by sympathising Orange judges and Orange jurymen. Plowden remarks upon it that the profligacy was too rank not to be stigmatised—for the Union was yet an awfully uncertain distance.

CHAPTER XX.—AFTER THE REBELLION, AN INAUGURAL CEREMONY, THE GRAND LODGE IN DUBLIN, THE AMENDED RULES AND REGULATIONS OF THE SOCIETY.

The rebellion was suppressed. Havoc was abroad over the land. Destitution was everywhere. Starvation and misery stared the unhappy people in the face. Lord Edward had fought his last fight, and death had happily conquered. Wolfe Tone had given up his young life, and hundreds of others had made a like sacrifice to swell the roll of martyrs to a noble but losing cause. A handful of hunted rebels remained still in the fastness of Wicklow—but they, too, were soon compelled to give way to hunger and superior force, and the last remnants of the rebels of '98 soon found in some desperate death-struggle a welcome release from all their sufferings. The ferocious soldiery and brutal yeomanry, having accomplished their work of extermination in the country districts, now gathered into the towns and, more brutalised by their late unrestrained excesses, pursued a course of shocking and overbearing despotism, in the exercise of which they paused not to distinguish between the loyalist and those sympathising with the rebels. To dwell on the sad propensity to extortion, cheating, pilfering, and robbing acquired or encouraged by a temporary dissolution of civil government; on the practice of perjury and bribery in the accusation and defence of real or supposed criminals; and of perjury in claims of losses, even by persons who might be supposed superior to such meanness, laying aside religious considerations, would be attended with more pain than utility. Even dissipation which might reasonably be expected to be checked by the calamities attendant upon this cruel commotion seemed to revive with augmented force on the subsiding of the Insurrection. Collected in towns in the following winter many of the lower sort of loyalists spent the days in drunkenness, and their superiors the nights in late suppers and riotous conviviality. It was a time peculiarly suited for the rooting of Orangeism into our social system. While affording men the secret pleasure which is derived from the possession of something (if it be only a name) which is not shared by the majority; it congregated its members in the taverns and rude ale houses of the towns and villages, and having excited their enthusiasm by mysteries which were the more effective in proportion as they were bewildering, it soothed their feelings by a liberal indulgence in strong drinks. Ever ready to put a generous construction upon the motives of its members, and never disposed to a literal reading of its rules, the Orange Institution was not then inclined to be over delicate in the promotion of its ends and little likely to scrutinise where meetings, beginning with mystery, were continued in revelry and ended in debauchery. The means which lodges thus afforded for the gratification of the loose passions of the period was a sure stimulus to Orangeism, while it at the same time served to gather together the scattered forces which the rebellion had partially dissevered. Dublin having now become the great centre of Orangeism the importance of making it literally so was soon made evident. It was the only place where its prominent leaders, the members of the Beresford clique could with facility or advantage assemble. Accordingly the Dublin Grand Lodge was established. From the fact that it assumed the title of the Grand Lodge of Ireland it is evident that higher powers appertained to its members than those retained by the Grand Lodge of Armagh the existence of which was for a time tolerated.

RULES OF THE SOCIETY, 1799.

The first rules and regulations that we have under the authority of the society are those which were revised immediately at the close of the rebellion, and presented to a meeting of the Grand Lodge of Ireland in Dublin. At this meeting,* held on the 20th November, 1798, and of which Thomas Verner was Grand Master and Chairman, and J. C. Beresford Grand Secretary, Messrs. Harding, Giffard, and S. Montgomery presented the following :—

REPORT.

Having been honoured by the Grand Lodge with

* See appendix 3 to second report on Orange Lodges.

instructions to revise and select a proper system of rules, for the government of Orange Lodges, we beg leave to make a report of our progress.

We are happy in being able to say, that in our duty upon this occasion, we received the greatest assistance from the experience of the Grand Master of Ireland, and his Deputy Grand Secretary, who did us the honour of imparting to us their sentiments.

Encouraged by their help, we have ventured very materially to alter the shape of the confused system which was referred to us, preserving the spirit, and, as much as possible, the original words, except where we had to encounter gross violations of language and grammar.

The general plan of our proceeding has been this we have thrown what are, in our opinion, very improperly called the Six First General Rules into one plain short declaration of the sentiments of the body.

Next in order, we have given the qualifications of an Orangeman, selected from the Antrim Regulations; and the rather, as it breathes a spirit of piety, which cannot be too generally diffused throughout an institution whose chief object, whatever political shape it may assume, is to preserve the Protestant religion.

After this comes the obligation of an Orangeman, from which we have struck out the word "Male," as we learn from the Grand Master that it is an unauthorised interpolation, and as it might lead to unnecessary and injurious cavils.

The secret articles are as nearly as possible in their original shape; they have, however, been a little improved in point of language, and two of them, which were mere matter of private economy, are placed among the bye-laws.

The marksman's obligation is, on the suggestion of the Grand Master, here introduced.

Then follow the master, treasurer, and secretary's obligations.

We have endeavoured to reduce the general rules for the regulation of lodges into a degree of method; and we hope we have at least given hints, in our arrangement, which may be adopted.

For the same reason which we have given for adopting the qualification of an Orangeman, we have recommended the insertion of two prayers, for opening and closing the lodge; they are to be found in the Antrim Regulations. We confess, however, that we think the first of them rather too long to have a good effect; but this not being exactly within the line of our knowledge, we beg leave to transfer the duty of abbreviating it to some of our clerical brethren. [It was accordingly referred to the Rev. Mr. Knipe, and the prayer is here inserted in the abridged form.]

Samuel Montgomery.
Harding Giffard.

Nov. 20, 1798.

RULES AND REGULATIONS, &c, &c.

General Declaration of the Objects of the Orange Institution

We associate to the utmost of our power to support and defend his Majesty King George the Third, the Constitution, and laws of this country, and the succession to the throne in his Majesty's illustrious House, *being Protestants;* for the defence of our persons and properties, and to maintain the peace of our country; and for these purposes we shall be at all times ready to assist the civil and military powers in the just and lawful discharge of their duty. We also associate in honour of King William the Third, Prince of Orange, whose name we bear, as supporters of his glorious memory, and the true religion by him completely established; and in order to prove our gratitude and affection for his name, we will annually celebrate the victory over James at the Boyne on the 1st day of July, O.S. in every year, which day shall be our grand æra for ever.

We further declare that we are exclusively a Protestant association; yet detesting as we do any intolerant spirit, we solemnly pledge ourselves to each other, that we will not prosecute or upbraid any person on account of his religious opinion, but that we will, on the contrary, be aiding and assisting to every loyal subject of every religious description.

Qualifications Requisite for an Orangeman

He should have a sincere love and veneration for his Almighty Maker, productive of those lively and happy fruits, righteousness and obedience to his commands; a firm and steady faith in the Saviour of the world, convinced that he is the *only Mediator* between a sinful creature and an offended Creator. *Without those he can be no Christian.* Of an humane and compassionate disposition, and a courteous and affable behaviour, he should be an utter enemy to savage brutality and unchristian cruelty; a lover of society and improving company; and have a laudable regard for the Protestant religion, and a sincere regard to propagate its precepts; zealous in promoting the honour of his king and country; heartily desirous of victory and success in those pursuits, yet convinced and assured that God alone can grant them; he should have an hatred of cursing and swearing, and taking the name of God in vain (a shameful practice); he should use all opportunities of discouraging it among his brethren; wisdom and prudence should guide his actions, honesty and integrity direct his conduct, and honour and glory be the motives of his endeavours. Lastly, he should pay the strictest attention to a religious observance of the Sabbath, and also of temperance and sobriety.

Obligation of an Orangeman.

I, A. B., do solemnly and sincerely swear, of my own free will and accord, that I will, to the utmost of my power, support and defend the present King, George the Third, and all the heirs of the Crown, *so long as he or they support the Protestant ascendancy,* the Constitution and laws of these kingdoms; and that I will ever hold sacred the name of our glorious deliverer, William the Third, Prince of Orange, and I do farther swear that I am not nor was not a Roman Catholic or Papist; that I was not, am not, nor ever will be, an United Irishman; and that I never took the oath of secrecy to that society; and I do further swear, in the presence of Almighty God, that I will always conceal, and never will reveal, either part or parts of this that I am about now to receive, neither write it, nor indite it, stamp, stain, nor engrave it, nor cause it so to be done, on paper, parchment, leaf, bark, brick, stone, or anything so that it might be known; and that I am now become an Orangeman without fear, bribery, or corruption.

SECRET ARTICLES

1. That we will bear true allegiance to his Majesty King George the Third, and his successors, so long as he or they support the Protestant ascendancy, and that we will faithfully support and maintain the laws and Constitution of this kingdom.

2. That we will be true to all Orangemen in all just actions, neither wronging one or seeing him wronged to our knowledge, without acquainting him thereof.

3. That we are not to see a brother offended for 6d or 1s, or more, if convenient, which must be returned next meeting, if possible.

4. *We must not give the first assault to any person whatever that may bring a brother into trouble.*

5. *We are not to carry away money, goods, or anything from any person whatever, except arms and ammunition, and those only from an enemy.*

6 We are to appear in ten hours' warning, or whatever time is required, if possible (provided it is not hurtful to ourselves or family, and that we are served with a lawful summons from the Master), otherwise we are fined as the company think proper.

7. No man can be made an Orangeman without the unanimous approbation of the body.

8. An Orangeman is to keep a brother's secret as his own, unless in case of murder, treason, and perjury, *and that of his own free will.*

9. No Roman Catholic can be admitted, on any account.

10 Any Orangeman who acts contrary to these rules shall be expelled, and the same reported to all the lodges in this kingdom, and elsewhere.

God save the King.

Marksman's Obligation.

I, *A. B.*, of my own free will and accord, in the presence of Almighty God, do hereby most solemnly and sincerely swear that I will always conceal, and never will reveal, either part or parts of this which I am now about to receive; and that I will bear true allegiance to his Majesty King George the Third, and all the heirs of the Crown, so long as they maintain the Protestant ascendancy, the laws and constitution of these kingdoms, and that I will keep this part of a marksman from that of an Orangeman, as well as from the ignorant, and that I will not make a man until I become master of a body, nor after I am broke; and that I will not make a man, or be present at the making of a man, on the road, or behind hedges; and that I will be aiding and assisting to all true Orange honest marksmen, as far as it in my power lies, knowing him or them to be such, and that I will not wrong a brother marksman, nor know him to be wronged of anything of value, worth apprehending, but I will warn or apprize him of, if in my power it lies. All this I swear with a firm and steadfast resolution, so help me God, and keep me steadfast in this my marksman's obligation.

General Rules for the Government of Orange Lodges

1. Each lodge is to be governed by a master, deputy-master, treasurer, and secretary; the master appointed by the Grand Lodge; and the deputy-master, treasurer, and secretary, by the Master, with the approbation of his own lodge

2. These officers, upon their appointment, shall take the following obligations —

Master, Secretary, and Treasurer's Obligation.

I, *A. B.*, do solemnly and sincerely swear, that I am not, nor was not, a Roman Catholic or Papist, that I am not, was not, nor ever will be, an United Irishman, and that I never took the oath of secrecy to that society.

For the Master and Deputy-Master, add,

That I am not now made a Master for any private emolument or advantage; that I have not a sitting in my house for the purpose of selling beer, spirits, &c., and that neither I, nor any other person for me, will admit anyone into the society of Orangemen who was, or is a Papist, or has been a United Irishman, or has taken their oath of secrecy; and that I will use my authority *to keep proper behaviour and sobriety in this lodge,* and that I will not certify for any person without having first proved him, and knowing him to be of good character. So help me God.

For the Secretary, add,

And that I will keep safe the papers belonging to this lodge; and that I will not give any copy of the number of secret articles, or lend them to make an Orangeman out of the lodge I belong to, or lend the seal, so that it may be affixed to any forged paper, or irregular Orangeman's certificate So help me God

For the Treasurer, add,

And that I shall fairly account for all the money I have, or shall receive, for the use of this lodge, when called upon by the master of this lodge. So help me God.

3. That a committee be appointed to conduct the affairs of each lodge, to consist of the master, deputy master, secretary, and treasurer, and five members, the first of whom is to be nominated by the master, the second by the first, and so on until the number five be completed.

4. That in the absence of the master, the deputy master shall preside, and in his absence, the senior committee man who shall be present.

5. That each candidate for admission shall be proposed by one, and seconded by another member at one meeting, and admitted or rejected at a subsequent one.

6 That one negative shall exclude.

7. That any person wishing to become an Orangeman must be admitted in the lodge nearest his abode (except in cities or great towns), or have a recommendation from that lodge, that he is a proper person, before any other lodge can accept him.

8. That the names of persons rejected in any lodge shall be sent by the master or secretary to the district master, with the objections to such per-

sons, in order that the district master may communicate the same to other lodges, as those who are unfit for one lodge must be so for every other.

9 That each member on admission shall pay——

10. That all Orangemen shall be considered as members, but none to vote in any lodge except the particular members thereof.

11. All members to be subordinate to the master or person presiding for him.

12 Any dispute arising, not provided for by the rules, is to be decided by the committee, and the parties must abide by their decision, on pain of expulsion.

13. That each new resolution shall remain on the books from one meeting to the subsequent one, previously to its being adopted or rejected by the majority of the members then present.

14. That no election or other business do take place unless ten members at least be present, provided the lodge consist of so many, if it do not, then two-thirds of the lodge must be present.

15 That no business be done in any lodge after dinner, supper, or drink have been brought in, but every motion shall be previously decided.

16. Any new member attending intoxicated cannot be admitted at that meeting; any old one so attending to be fined

17. The secretary is to read out, before the books are closed, the names of those persons proposed for the next night.

18. A person is to attend on the outside of the door while business is going on; that person to be nominated by the master, or whoever presides at the time.

19 The master to have full power of fining all disorderly persons to an amount not exceeding ——

20. No gentlemen are to be ballotted for unless the person proposing or seconding him be present, or some reasonable excuse for his absence be offered.

21. Order of business for each night:—1. Lodge to open with a prayer (members standing) 2. General rules read. 3. Members proposed 4. Reports from committee. 5 Names of members called over. 6 Members ballotted for. 7. Members made. 8. Lodge to close with prayer (members standing).

Prayer for Opening the Lodge.

Gracious and Almighty God, who in all ages has shown thy mighty power in protecting righteous kings and states, we yield thee hearty thanks for so miraculously bringing to light and frustrating the secrte and horrible designs of our enemies, plotted and intended to have been executed against our gracious King, our happy Constitution, and the true religion established by our glorious deliverer, William the Third, Prince of Orange.

Vouchsafe, O Lord, to continue unto us thine Almighty protection; grant to our pious King long life, health and prosperity; let thy providence ever guard our happy Constitution, and enable us to transmit it to our latest posterity, unimpaired, and improved by our holy religion. Bless, we beseech thee, every member of the Orange institution with charity, brotherly love, and loyalty. Make us truly respectable here on earth, and eternally happy hereafter. These, and all other blessings, we beg in the name, and through the mediation of Jesus Christ, our Lord and Saviour. Amen.

Or this.

Almighty God, and Heavenly Father, who in all ages hast showed thy power and mercy, in graciously and miraculously delivering thy Church, and in protecting righteous and religious kings and States from the wicked conspiracies and malicious practices of all the enemies thereof, we yield thee hearty thanks for so wonderfully discovering and confounding the horrible and wicked designs of our enemies, plotted and intended to have been executed against our most gracious Sovereign Lord King George, and the whole estates of the realm, for the subversion of Government and established religion. Be thou, O Lord, still our mighty protector, and scatter our enemies that delight in blood; infatuate and defeat their councils, abate their pride, assuage their malice, and confound their devices Strengthen the hands of our gracious Sovereign, and all that are in authority under him, with judgment and justice to cut off all such workers of iniquity as turn religion into rebellion, and faith into faction, that they may never prevail in the ruin of thy Church amongst us; but that our gracious Sovereign and his realms, being preserved in thy true religion, and by thy merciful goodness protected in the same, we may all duly serve thee with praise and thanksgiving. And we beseech to protect the King, Queen, and Royal Family, from all treasons and conspiracies; preserve him in thy faith, fear, and love; make his reign long, prosperous and happy here on earth, and crown him hereafter with everlasting glory. Accept also, most gracious God, our unfeigned thanks, for filling our hearts with joy and gladness, by sending Thy servant, the late King William, for the deliverance of these nations from tyranny and arbitrary power.

Let truth and justice, devotion and piety, concord and unity, brotherly kindness and charity, with other Christian virtues, so flourish amongst us, that they may be the stability of our times, and make this our association a praise here on earth. This we most humbly beg, in the name and for the sake of Jesus Christ, our Lord and Saviour. Amen.

Form of Prayer to be used at Closing.

O Almighty God, who art a strong tower of defence unto Thy servants, against the face of their enemies; we yield Thee praise and thanks for our deliverance from those great and apparent dangers wherewith we were encompassed: we acknowledge Thy goodness that we were not delivered over as a prey unto them, beseeching Thee still to continue such Thy mercies towards us, that all the world may know Thou art our Saviour and mighty Deliverer, through Jesus Christ. Amen.

Resolutions of the Grand Orange Lodge of Ireland.

Resolved,—That new numbers be printed on parchment, and stamped according to the specimen produced, and that any lodge wishing to get them instead of their old numbers, shall have them on paying half a crown.

Resolved,—That for all new numbers issued on parchment the sum of 5s 5d be paid, half a crown for the Grand Lodge of Armagh, and half a crown for the Grand Lodge of Ireland.

Resolved,—That after the date hereof, every old number renewed, and every new one granted, must be signed by the Grand Master for Ireland, or Grand Secretary for Ireland, and countersigned by the Grand Secretary of Armagh, and that no other shall be valid, and that the Grand Secretary of Armagh do issue them to the Grand Master of counties, and to no others, save and except to the Grand Lodge of Ireland, and that he do receive the fee of 5s 5d, as before directed, for each number so granted, and shall make a monthly return to the Grand Lodge of the numbers by him granted, and to whom.

Resolved,—That in a county where there is no Grand Master appointed, an application for a number must be made to the Grand Lodge of Ireland.

Many persons having introduced various orders into the Orange Society, which will very much tend to injure the regularity of the institution, the Grand Lodge disavow any other orders but the Orange and Purple, as there can be none others regular, unless issuing from and approved of by them.

Resolved,—That the secretary of the Grand Lodge do write to Wolsey Atkinson, Esq., Grand Secretary of Armagh, enclosing him these resolutions, and requiring him to make a return of numbers granted up to this time, and that he do not issue any new numbers until he has the parchment numbers, signed by the Grand Master and Secretary.

Resolved,—That the thanks of the Grand Lodge be and are hereby given to S. Montgomery and H. Giffard, Esqrs., for their great trouble in revising these Regulations.

Ordered,—That the foregoing Rules and Regulations be printed, under the directions of the deputy-secretary, and by him dispersed to Orangemen only.

The Grand Lodge will meet, the first Tuesday in every month, at Harrington's, in Clifton Street, at seven o'clock in the evening, and the third Tuesday in every month, at three o'clock in the afternoon, at the same place.

Form of Summons.

Orange Society, No.

Sir and Brother,—You are requested to attend a meeting of your Society, at   on the   day of   at the hour of   o'clock.

Fail not as you are an Orangeman. Signed by order of the Master,

Secretary.

Form of Certificate.

Loyal Orange Association, No.

We, the Master, Deputy-Master, and Secretary of the Loyal Orange Association, No.   held at   in the kingdom of Ireland, do hereby certify that Brother   has regularly received the degrees of a true Orangeman, in this our Association; and that he has conducted himself, during his stay amongst us, to the entire satisfaction of all our Brethren. We, therefore, request that all the regular associations of the universe do recognise and admit him as such.

Given under our hands and the seal of the Society, this   day of   17

Master.
Deputy Master.

MAKING AN ORANGEMAN.

THE FOLLOWING IS THE RITUAL OF THE ORANGE INTRODUCTION:

The applicant shall be introduced between his two sponsers: namely, the brethren who proposed and seconded his admission, carrying the Bible in his hands, with the book of rules and regulations placed thereon. Two brothers shall precede him. On his entering the room, a chaplain, if present, or in his absence a brother appointed by the master, shall say the whole or part of what follows :—

O Lord God of our fathers, art Thou God in Heaven? And rulest not Thou over all the kingdoms of the heathen? and in thine hand is there not power and might, so that none is able to withstand thee?" 2 Chron. xx. 5.

"Who is like unto Thee O Lord among the Gods? Who is like Thee, glorious in holiness, fearful in praises doing wonders? Thou in thy mercy hast led forth thy people which Thou hast redeemed; Thou hast guided them in thy strength unto thy holy habitation." Exodus xiv. 11, 13.

"Lord, Thou wilt ordain peace for us; for Thou hast wrought all our works in us. O Lord our God other lords have had dominion over us: but by Thee only will we make mention of thy name." Isaiah xxiv. 12, 13.

"Wherefore, glorify ye the Lord in the fires, even in the name of the Lord God of Israel in the isles of the sea." Ibid. xxiv. 15.

[During the reading of these the candidate shall stand at the foot of the table, the brethren all standing also in their places, and strictly silent.]

The Master shall then say—Friend, what dost thou desire in this meeting of true Orangemen?

And the candidate shall answer—Of my own free will and accord I desire admission into your loyal institution.

Master— Who will vouch for this friend that he is a true Protestant and loyal subject?

[The sponsors shall bow to the master and signify the same, each mentioning his own name.]

Master— What do you carry in your hand?

Candidate—The Word of God.

Master—Under the assurance of these worthy brothers, we will trust that you also carry it in your heart. What is that other book?

Candidate—The book of your rules and regulations.

Master—Under the like assurance, we will further trust that you will study them well, and that you will obey them in all lawful matters. Therefore, we gladly receive you into this order. Orangemen, bring to me your friend.

[The candidate shall then be brought by his sponsors before the master; the two brothers standing at each side of the centre of the table; during this the chaplain or brother appointed shall say]—

"Many shall be purified and made wise, and

tried; but the wicked shall do wickedly, and none of the wicked shall understand; but the wise shall understand. Blessed is he that waiteth, and cometh the thousand three hundred and thirty days. But go thou thy way, until the end be; for thou shalt rest and stand in thy lot all the end of thy days." Daniel xii. 10, 12, 13.

[The Candidate shall then kneel on his right knee; and the Master shall invest him with the decoration of the Order—an Orange sash. Then the Chaplain or Brother appointed shall say :—]

"When thus it shall be in the midst of the land among the people, there shall be as the shaking of an olive tree, and as the gleaming of the grapes when the vintage is done. They shall lift up their voice; they shall sing for the majesty of the Lord; they shall cry aloud from the sea." Isaiah xxiv., 13, 14.

"Then the mountain of the house of the Lord shall be established in the top of the mountains; and it shall be exalted above the hills, and the people shall flow unto it." Micah iv. i.

"And this shall be for a token upon thine head, and for a frontlet between thine eyes; for by strength of hand the Lord brought us forth out of Egypt. Thou shalt therefore keep this ordinance in his season from year to year." Exodus xiii. 16, 10.

Then the Master shall say —

We receive thee, dear Brother, into the religious and loyal Institution of Orangemen; trusting that thou wilt abide a devoted servant of God and true believer in his Son Jesus Christ, a faithful subject of our King and supporter of our Constitution. Keep thou firm in the Protestant Church, holding steadily her pure doctrines and observing her ordinances. Make thyself the friend of all pious and peaceable men; avoiding strife and seeking benevolence; slow to take offence and offering none, thereby so far as in thee lieth, turning the injustice of our adversaries into their own reproof and confusion. In the name of the Brotherhood I bid thee welcome; and pray that thou mayest long continue among them, a worthy Orangeman, namely —fearing God, honouring the King, and maintaining the Law.

[Then the Master shall communicate, or cause to be communicated, unto the new Member the Signs and Pass-words of the Brotherhood, and the Chaplain or Brother appointed shall say :—]

"Glory to God in the highest; and on earth peace, good-will towards men." St. Luke ii. 14.

[After which the Brother shall make obeisance to

the Master, and all present shall take their seats; the Certificate of the new Brother being first duly signed and registered]

The ritual for the introducton into the Purple Order is in most respects so similar to the above as not to need quotation The same misterious mummery prevails, with an evident effort to make the impression upon the mind of the applicant more lasting by the influence of the supernatural.

The reader may be inclined to smile at the holy arrogance—the pious hatred expressed in almost every line of the foregoing. The feeling, however, must be that of pity and mournful contempt Religion has been a cloak for some of the greatest crimes done in the history of mankind Without stopping to consider how often the qualifications of an Orangeman were forthcoming; how often (in 1798), the members were "righteous," "obedient," "humane," "courteous," "affable," "temperate," " sober," opposed to cursing and swearing—possessed of all those qualities calculated to make him quite an angelic being—we pass to another and more important consideration. If there be anything that the Orangemen of to-day make boast of it is that they are loyalists to the core, and that the institution has ever been founded upon loyalty. This is not true. From the above rules and regulations it is plain that the institution was as illegal and unconstitutional as any that ever existed in the State. By the common law of the land allegiance—absolute, unqualified, and perpetual allegiance is due from every subject to his Sovereign. An oath binding the deponent to give allegiance only "so long as he (the King) shall support Protestant ascendancy" is conditional, qualified, and temporary, and is of a treasonable character. It should be borne in mind that the oath did not stipulate that the King should be a Protestant, but that he should support and maintain Protestant ascendancy, which are conditions widely differing. This illegality, however, need not surprise. We will find through all its subsequent history, where it did not ignore Acts of Parliament, all its efforts were directed towards evading them, and in a manner which shows extreme inconsistency and absence of honesty in persons wont to boast of their loyalty to the Constitution. As a proof, the association was made felonious by the 47th Geo. III, section 3, cap. XIII, which enacted that every person who should administer, or cause to be administered, to any person in Ireland any oath or engagement importing to bind the person taking

same to be of any association formed "to disturb the public peace, or to injure the property of any person or persons whatsoever, or to do, or omit, or refuse to do any act or acts whatsoever, under whatever name, description, or pretence, such association, brotherhood, committee, society, or confederacy, shall assume, or pretend to be formed or constituted; or any oath or engagement importing to bind the person taking the same to obey the orders, or rules, or commands of any committee or other body of men not lawfully constituted, &c, *shall be adjudged guilty of felony, and be transported for life*" No 5 of the Secret Articles is a plain contravention of this Act, as it specifically binds the members to carry off arms and ammunition from an enemy—enemy, no doubt, meaning Catholic—and the whole constitution of the society was directly opposed to the intention and meaning of the Act It is needless to say that none of its members were transported for life; neither did the " loyal" Orange institution then cease to exist.

It is unnecessary to point out the immorality and the disastrous consequences likely to ensue from an exclusive combination under the above rules. The secret articles, which for a long time were kept hidden from the world and then disclosed only by virtue of a Parliamentary Committee, afford a plain and matter-of-fact sanction to the waylaying and the robbery of Catholics. The brother was by No 4 not to give the *first* assault to any person who might bring a brother into trouble—a very discreet provision, which implied that the first assault might be given under all other circumstances. No. 5 literally lays down robbery of Catholics as a duty. Reasonable men can easily understand how far a mob of ruthless Orangemen, after breaking into "an enemy's house" in the stillness of the night would be inclined to discriminate between arms or ammunition and other but more valuable property. They will incline, I am sure, to the opinion that the precise terms of No. 5 of the secret articles, would under each tempting circumstances, be for the moment forgotten.

The illegality of those articles were admitted by the Orange Grand Secretary before the Select Committee (1835), though he was unable to show by his books that they had at any time been repealed by the brethren. For all we know they are at present existing, and are certainly implied by the present rules of the institution. By this witness the term Protestant ascendancy was specifically defined by his saying that he looked upon a banner with " equal laws" upon it as a party flag, and loyalty to the king therefore rested upon the very questionable condition of justice not being vouchsafed to the Catholic inhabitants of these countries. The opinion of most of the witnesses examined, that the practices of Orangemen were, in most instances, diametrically opposed to these rules (Lord Gosford, 4536), is of little moment when dealing with this period of their history, for we find in their rules not only a justification for intolerance, but a solemn avowal of illegality because of provisional loyalty. The expediency and lawfulness of Secret Article No. 6, which bound a large mass of men with arms in their hands to appear on receiving ten hours notice at any specified spot, is too apparent to need comment. It was in the power of any master, whether drunken or otherwise, of a private lodge to send out such a summons A very dangerous power this is at all times, but particularly so in the hands of irresponsible and uneducated men, and when dealing with such inflamable material.

As in most secret societies of the kind, which have at intervals for their object the working out of schemes which would not only not bear the light of day, but into the secrets of which it would not be safe to admit the great body of humbler associates, the Orange Society consists of two orders—the Orange and the Purple. Colonel Verner admits that the latter, which is the higher grade, was devised for the "purpose of excluding improper persons" (471), a phrase which must be taken to mean persons who could not be trusted with the more important secrets of the body. If it means anything else, it means that all outside the Purple order are improper persons—an interpretation which now would find many adherents, seeing that it includes the vast body of Orangemen There can

be no doubt, seeing the use which was afterwards made of it, that this Purple order was intended for keeping the secrets of the body within a small clique of leaders This it was well qualified for doing It was, and is yet, carefully guarded by an exclusive system of signs and passwords unknown to the general body.

During the period intervening after the Rebellion and before the Union the progress of Ascendancy and the significance of the compact between the faction and the Government were sufficiently indicated by the periodic processions of the Orangemen military and Government officials round the statue of King William in Dublin. These insulting displays in many instances led to riot, but the fact that they were offensive to their Catholic citizens was one of the chief reasons for the Orangemen persevering in them.

About this time the Institution received a check at the hands of Lord Hardwicke, Colonel of the Cambridgeshire Militia. It appears that the brethern were very active in obtaining recruits from the English regiments, and having become a vare of the fact the Earl of Hardwicke issued, on the 17th April, 1797, regimental orders prohibiting any of his men from joining the Orange Institution, which he pronounced to have been formed "for party and other mischievous purposes." Plowden regrets that when two years later the Earl was appointed Chief Governor of Ireland, and when the purposes of the society were in no way changed, he did not follow up this condemnation. The colonel could honestly condemn what was pernicious and subversive of the discipline of his regiment, but the Lord Lieutenant dared not disapprove of what was prejudicial to the best interests of the country.

CHAPTER XXI.—THE UNION.

Amongst the most discreditable transactions of the leaders at this time was the sale of the brethern generally to Mr. Pitt for the purposes of the Union. The machinery of the Purple Order was put into motion for the purpose This sale was transacted for certain considerations, that can easily be guessed at guaranteed to the Beresford and Verner clique. Mr. Pitt was about perfecting his project of a legislative union, for the purposes of which he had sacrificed thousands of lives, and he made overtures to Mr. Beresford and Mr. Verner to aid him in the disgraceful trick. The

large majority of Orangemen in the country were then strongly opposed to the measure, for they foresaw in it the certain downfall of ascendancy in the transfer of the legislative machinery to the other side of the channel. Mr. Pitt had his schemes deeply laid Mr Beresford could not be convinced of the necessity or the advantages of the Act of Union until he crossed to London. When there, his opinions underwent a change, and he came back to Dublin with such indisputable arguments that the Grand Lodge were but too willing to consent to the proposal. Feeling that the general

2

opinion of the body would be against them, the Grand Lodge issued "general orders" that the question of the Union was not to be discussed by them as Orangemen, and to this Thomas Verner, as Grand Master, and John C. Beresford, as Grand Secretary, subscribed their names. This had the effect of disarming the brethren against any agitation of the question. For the purpose of seducing them to political emasculation, the Lord Lieutenant, in a Viceregal tour during the year 1799, exercised all his personal and private influence in promoting the plan of the English Minister. To the Catholics he held out the allurement of emancipation. They trusted him and were deceived. To the Orangemen he pledged amnesty and favour.* But the discussion of the Union was in some districts persisted in, and was likely to disconcert the plans of those who had effected the discreditable sale of such a large body of men. The result was that Thomas Verner, Esq, Grand Master of all the Orange Lodges of Ireland, sent in his resignation. This, together with the revealing of a portion of the Government compact, had the desired effect, the Grand Master was asked to recall his resignation, and with much condescension he undertook to do so. That portion of the compact to which I allude and which concerned the brethren generally, for the remainder affected only those who betrayed their associates, was that the term "Protestant Ascendancy" should be made an established condition in the affairs of this country. Thenceforth they were allowed to use it not only as the bond and test of their union but as the condition and measure of their allegiance. In return they undertook to abstain from opposition to the Union and to so model and moderate the rules and regulations of their society that no Protestant should in future be shocked with the oath of extermination or "deterred from entering into their society by any pledge, obligation, or oath, unpalatable to the most tender Protestant conscience.† It was thus by the selfish duplicity of a few and the blind bigotry of the masses that the entire body was bundled up and disposed of wholesale to that cunning political trickster William Pitt Who pocketed the purchase money the pension list will tell.

This compact having been so far completed, the Grand Lodge met in Dublin on the 16th January, 1800, and again revised the rules and regulations

There is a material difference to be found in the general declaration as revised on this occasion. Instead of abiding by their former declaration that they "would not persecute or upbraid any person on account of his religious opinion," we now find an important change, which makes the sentence read, "That we will not persecute, injure, or upbraid any person on account of his religious opinions, *provided the same be not hostile to the State*," &c, a reservation which gave the members full scope for injuring, upbraiding, and persecuting all Catholics, seeing that then, as now, that religion is regarded by Orangemen as "hostile to the State."

These revised rules further provide, in a more formal and precise manner than those of the preceding year for the government of lodges. The only important one we find introduced in the following.—

14. "That, as *regiments are considered as districts*, the masters of all regimental lodges do make half-yearly returns of the numbers, names, and rank of the members of their lodges to the secretary of the Grand Lodge, but that they shall not make an Orangeman except the officers, non-commissioned officers, and privates of their respective regiments; and that they do remit to the Grand Treasurer of Ireland the half-yearly subscription, as well as that which is immediately to take place."

This was a point upon which the institution in latter years underwent considerable question, and wisely incurred not a little condemnation by those who saw in it a means of putting an end to all that discipline which is the first requisite of an efficient military body. It was also specially provided that Masters of cities and counties divide their respective cities and counties into districts and regulations were made for the election of District Masters and other officers. The Grand Lodge was also reformed.

* Plowden's Tryers History, vol. 1, page 139.
† Ibid, page 119.

CHAPTER XXII.—AFTER THE UNION, PROTESTANT ASCENDANCY AND ITS EFFECTS.

Had we not already a surfeit of shocking and barbarous outrages, for which Orangeism and Orangemen alone is responsible, we could find in the pages of Plouden, Hay, Gordon, and others revelations of the most inhuman deeds perpetrated by the brethren upon the disarmed and cowed Catholics of Ireland during the four or five years subsequent to the Union. Outrages such as the exhumation and desecration of the corpse of James Redmond, in Wexford, in 1801[*] (where the Orangemen dug up the body, maltreated it and placed it on the site of Monamolig chapel, which they had burned, so that the worshippers would meet with it at their Sunday devotion); such as the cannabalism at Naas,[†] where the Orangemen declared that "Paddy ate sweet;" such as the barbarous outrages committed upon women in the Counties of Wicklow and Wexford, vouched for by Plouden and Barrington.

"Of comfort no man speak; let us talk of graves, of worms, and of epitaphs."

The Catholics of Ireland had previous to and during the days of the rebellion drunk deep of the cup of misery. They were now draining it even to the dregs at the hands of an intolerant and dispicable Orange faction. But there was another phase of refined misery awaiting them, and to which they were destined to be subject for a much longer period. After the brief rebellion of 1803, which revived for a time the old and bloody system of extermination, and when the ordinary machinery of the State for the administration of justice was put into something like working order the Catholics were made to feel if possible more bitterly than before the degrading condition to which they had been reduced. The Government being distinctly and unblushingly composed of an Orange faction for a change of Ministers only brought to them a change of executioners, all departments of the Irish Government had within it its Orange nominees. Not only were they to be found in the Senate and the Bar but even the Bench in its superior grades boasted its Orange adherents. It may then be easily understood how and why Orangeism predominated amongst the Irish magistracy. Those country squires, being mostly ignorant, uneducated, and prejudiced men, did not even take the trouble to

conceal their partiality. No wonder the fountains of justice were not clean since they were poisoned at the very source. When we come to examine the letters and correspondence of Mr. Wilson, a magistrate of the County Tyrone, who reveals the shocking state of the magistracy at that time we will find disclosures that could scarce be credited, but that they are founded on the most indisputable testimony. As showing that their excesses were of the most varied kind, and included the affording of protection to murderers, I may give the following incident as a fair specimen of the Orange justice of the day, and how the Orangeman endeavoured to awe the Government into acquiescence with their misdeeds:—

In July, 1806, an Orangeman named Saunders or Alexander Bell, a yeoman of Colonel Blacker's corps, committed, near Portadown, an unprovoked attempt at murder upon a Catholic named James Birmingham. That the crime was one of peculiar atrocity is proved by documentary evidence, bearing the signature of the Judge of Assize. Bell received a notification from one of the magistrates (the account does not say that it was not Colonel Blacker) that the law would be put in motion, and he escaped. In those days it required but a little effort for an Orange culprit to elude the vigilance of sympathising Orange magistrates and Orange yeomen. That he remained in the district is evident from the fact that the same man made a second attempt upon Birmingham's life nine months after the commission of the first offence. Notwithstanding the fact that a warrant was the for the arrest of Bell, that he remained in the neighbourhood of Portadown, and that his presence there was known to both the magistrates and yeomanry no earnest effort was made to arrest him. In those days the district of Portadown was disturbed by an Orange faction that made life almost a burden to the Catholics of the locality, and outrages were daily committed upon them without any attempt to afford them protection. Though there existed a desire on the part of one or two magistrates, such as Mr. Brownlow, to put a stop to this species of terrorism, they found themselves helpless in the face of the fostering sympathy of the Messrs. Verner, Blacker, & Co., who had the Orange Yeomanry under their complete control, and who

* Hay's History, page 301.
† Sampson's Mems, page 438.

feared to forfeit their good-will by the bare exercise of justice when it ran counter to their prejudices. Bell was accordingly not arrested. In the
year 1807 Colonel Blacker's regiment was in Tuam,
and—how strange is the coincidence—Bell turned
up there too * He actually offered himself for
re-enlistment in his old corps. It must be recollected that, though then a prosecuted felon, he was
an Orangeman and a member of Colonel Blacker's
corps. The offer of Bell was politely declined, and
the Orange felon was allowed to depart in
peace to the knowledge of Lieutenant-Colonel
Blacker, who says—"I believe he continued a
considerable time in the town of Tuam, and I think
when we left it he remained there." Certainly
the Lieutenant-Colonel seemed to have been accurately acquainted with the movements of the
would-be murderer. At last, after an interval of
three years, Bell was by accident arrested, and
tried in Armagh. The Orange jury finding the
evidence most convincing, and believing that the
Government dared not execute an Orange yeoman,
returned a verdict of guilty which verdict they
understood would mean no more than many
similar verdicts against Orangemen meant at the
time—a gentle reminder not to do it again if he
could conveniently avoid it The judge, however,
to the surprise of all, ordered Bell to be executed On
leaving the court Lieutenant-Colonel Blacke- and
another magistrate waited upon the judge, Baron
M'Clelland, and asked him to save the prisoner's life.
They did not ask the Government through the judge
to exercise clemency, which was within his power
to do, but simply put it to him that the Government dared not execute him, as it would lead to
the certain murder of the prosecutor and those who
had given evidence in the case, also, representing
that they feared he would be rescued by his companions in the Yeomanry. This threat the judge
wisely refused to regard, and Bell was brought up
for execution at Portadown, on the 7th August,
1807. In order to resist the expected attempt at
rescue on part of the "loyal" Orange Yeomanry, a
large number of troops, consisting of a regiment of
infantry, two troops of dragoons, having five pieces
of artillery, were drafted into the district. Lieutenant-Colonel Blacker was present inside the
circle in regimentals, and was the last to speak to
the prisoner words of encouragement He was
executed, and owing, no doubt, to the strong force

* See Lieutenant-Colonel Blacker's evidence the before
Select Committee of 1835, question 9,309

present, no attempt at rescue was made. In
justification of the above facts I may quote the following letter from Baron M'Clelland, who tried the
case, replying to the Government as to whether the
memorial of the Orangemen of the district should
be complied with.—

"Annaverna, 1st August, 1809.

"I have the honour of receiving your letter this
morning, in which you request I would acquaint
you, for the information of his Grace the Lord
Lieutenant, whether it would be proper to comply
with the petition from the inhabitants of Portadown which you enclosed to me. The convict
alluded to in the petition is a person of the name
of Alexander Bell, who was found guilty before me
at the last Assizes on two indictments—the one
charging him with having stabbed James
Birmingham with a bayonet, in July, 1806, *with
intent to murder him*; the other indictment charging him with having wounded him (same person)
on the head with a hatchet, in the month of
March, 1807, *with intent to murder him*. The case
on the trial appeared to be one of *peculiar atrocity*,
and the prisoner *was convicted on the clearest
testimony*. It appeared on the trial that for three
years the prisoner had set the law at defiance,
appearing publicly in the neighbourhood where
the crimes were committed, and effectually resisting any attempt to take him in that neighbourhood (*which the petition represents so peaceable and
quiet*), although on one occasion the military were
called in aid of the peace officers. He lately
ventured to a fair at some distance from
Portadown, and was there arrested. In a
few minutes after the trial was over, *two
of the magistrates who have signed the petition
Mr. Lofty* and *Major Blacker*, applied to me in
favour of the prisone, and requested I would have
his life saved and his punishment reduced to transportation, and assigned as a reason for the application that the prosecutors and those who had assisted in the prosecution would be murdered by
the friends of the prisoner, if the prisoner was
executed. I informed these gentlemen I could not
comply with their application, and that the reason
they assigned for saving the prisoner's life rendered
his execution indispensable as an example and a
warning to that riotous and disorderly neighbourhood. Immediately after a counter application was
made to me by some of the most respectable gentlemen of the county, and in particular by Mr
Brownlow, who stated to me that in his opinion
he peace of that part of the country depended on

the execution of Bell, and that it would have the most salutary effect to order the execution to take place in the vicinity of the place where the crimes had been committed, and that Portadown was the fittest place for that purpose. I accordingly ordered the execution to take place at Portadown on Monday next. On my leaving court, Mr. Dawson the assistant-barrister for the county, waited on me and laid before me several informations sworn before him and other magistrates, whereby it appeared that the district immediately around Portadown had been of late much disturbed by a combination of the landholders against their landlords, limiting the rent of lands and preventing any stranger from taking lands in the neighbourhood. On the next day I called the attention of the Grand Jury to this important subject, and gave them such advice as I thought would enable them to check this dangerous combination. Several of the Grand Jury then stated to me that they had great hopes that the execution of Bell at Portadown would have the desired effect of quieting the neighbourhood, and that they would consider it their duty to attend at the execution and admonish the people who would assemble there, and caution them against such illegal combinations. For the reasons above mentioned, I am of opinion that it would not be advisable to comply with the petition.—I have the honour to be, &c,

(Signed)

"JAMES M'CLELLAND.

"To Sir Charles Sexton, Bart."

It is worthy of remark the Lieutenant-Colonel in his evidence (see third report) admitted a confidential interview with the culprit Bell, represented him as the mildest type of Christianity, insisted that the attempted murder was all moonshine, that Birmingham had fallen accidentally upon Bell's bayonet while the latter was cleaning it, but at any rate the affair was the effect of a sudden impulse for which he was not responsible. It is a very suspicious circumstance that Birmingham at the time the cowardly attempt was made upon his life had called upon Bell to execute the summons of a magistrate. To suppose that the Lieutenant-Colonel's representation was correct would also necessitate supposing that nine months afterwards the hatchet fell accidentally out of Bell's hand upon Birmingham's head, or that Birmingham had awkwardly knocked his head against it. Can any sensible man doubt it—this Orange magistrate, Orange major, and Orange leader, protected an Orange felon for three years from the just

punishment of the crime committed upon an unoffending Catholic?

No more powerful indictment was ever made, and so successfully sustained against the Orange Institution than that contained in the correspondence and narrative published in 1807 and 1808 by Richard Wilson, Esq., a Protestant and a magistrate for the County of Tyrone, and at one time a member of the British Parliament. An Englishman, a resident of Tyrone, just across the borders of Armagh, and a neighbouring Justice of the Peace to the Verners and the Blackers and all of that ilk it can be distinctly understood that his lot was cast just in that quarter in which best to be made acquainted with the proceedings by which the Orangemen maintained Protestant Ascendancy. His narrative, I think I am warranted in saying, is the most unparalleled record of audacious crime that stains the pages of our history. The only regret in connection with the subject is that the pamphlets, which ran through no less than five editions, are now placed beyond the reach of most readers, and, fortunately, (hitherto) for the already shattered reputation of our Loyal Orange Institution, copies are to be found in but few libraries in the kingdom, and then only where the collectors have had a partiality for the political pamphlets of the past century. Through the kindness of Dr. Kavanagh, of Kingstown—a gentleman as eminent in his profession as he is distinguished for literary taste and antiquarian lore—I have been enabled to obtain the use of the pamphlets I refer to. For the purposes of our history, their importance cannot be exaggerated or their value too highly prized. That they are well worthy of reproduction I have not a doubt. To do so in these columns would be cumbersome as well as beyond the issue, I will, therefore, content myself with extracts such as will be sufficient to give the reader an idea of the times in which the author lived. It should first be mentioned that Mr. Wilson, finding that he could not obtain the relief of Catholics, or bring the Orangemen to justice by the ordinary means at his disposal as a magistrate, opposed as he was by the Messrs. Verner and the Orange magistracy, found it necessary to write to the Secretary of the Lord Lieutenant—with full assurance that there his efforts would at least be seconded. An Orange Government was in power, however, and an Orange faction directed it. The result was that justice was not obtained, and, as will be seen in the sequel, Mr. Wilson was dismissed the magistracy, it being

3

no doubt found that he was a very inconvenient and a much too honest person to administer justice upon the Irish Bench. The failure of Mr. Wilson to secure any justice for Catholics, even in cases of murder and robbery by Orangemen, led to the publication of his correspondence with Government, which constituted the first pamphlet (printed in 1807, by John King, 2, Westmoreland Street), and th s was followed in the following year by a second pamphlet, styled "A Narrative of the Various Murders and Robberies committed in the Neighbourhood of the Relator upon the Roman Catholics by a BANDITTI DESCRIBING THEMSELVES ORANGEMEN."

Taking up the story in the order of events, we first have to deal with the correspondence. It is styled—"A correspondence between Richard Wilson, Esq , a magistrate of the County Tyrone, and late member of the British Parliament; the late Right Hon. Wm. Elliott, Principal Secretary to his Grace the Duke of Bedford, and the Right Hon. George Ponsonby, Lord High Chancellor of Ireland, relative to the persecutions of the Roman Catholics in his district by a certain description of Orangemen, and the manner in which the laws are administered with regard to the former class of people; with a short introduction in which allusions are made to former communications and conversations which Mr. Wilson had with Mr. Wyndham, Lord Eldon, Mr. Wickham, and Sir Evan Nepean, upon the above-mentioned subjects. *Inritus ea vulnera attingo, sed nisi tacta tractaqus sanari non possunt.*" which simply says it was with unwillingness he touched those wounds, but that unless they were touched and handled they could not be healed

The author (who it may be stated was related to one of the highest families in the kingdom), in his introduction, admitted that he subjected himself to the resentment of those who might consider themselves glanced at by our observations, upon which head he was perfectly at ease, as he challenged the production of a single instance in his political life of a factious or interested nature. He further—and the italics are not mine—says .—"Soon after I had settled in Ireland fifteen hundred young Roman Catholics, inhabitants of the parish I reside in, offered, through me, their services to the Government to be employed in any part of Europe, *provided I was placed at their head.* The address I conveyed to the then Irish Secretary Mr. Wickham; the answer, however, he wished me to convey to the addresses was to the following

purport .—That Government had already received from other bodies of the Roman Catholics many similar offers, but, that, as no decision had as yet been made upon those previous ones it could not accept of this present one, and, therefore, could only thank the Roman Catholic inhabitants of Clanfeale for their loyal offers of service, &c. Sometime after this Mr. Wickham was replaced by Sir Evan Nepean. With that gentleman I was well acquainted, and called upon him in consequence of the following circumstance. A poor diminutive Roman Catholic tailor saw a huge Orangeman unmercifully beating an acquaintance of his, who appeared unable to resist him; he implored the Orangeman ' to spare his friend." This *out ageous provocation* was punished by instantly attacking the little unarmed tailor, whose skull was soon fractured and he was carried off without any prospect of his outliving the night. Indeed it would have been happy for the poor wretch if he had died, as he now lives, or rather exists in a state nearly approaching to idiotcy ! . A few days after this (and during the time the surgeon who attended the poor man had little or no hopes of his recovery) his savage assailant was seized *in my presence as a murderer.* Whilst I sent to enquire into the state of the tailor's health, I committed this alleged murderer to the charge of a constable, who, whilst he was conveying him to a place of safety, *was attacked by two Orangemen in military dress, who, drawing their swords, and presenting a pistol at his breast, swore " they would put the contents of it into his heart if he did not deliver up his prisoner ".* The constable was obliged to yield him to them, and he was carried off in triumph ! I applied to the then Commanding Officer of the Benburb cavalry to assist me with a party to seize these fellows ; he answered me that "he was sure none of the Yeomen would stir, as they were not upon permanent duty." I do not think, however, he made the experiment ; the truth is, he knew there was a more forcible reason " than their not being on permanent duty " What that reason was the reader may guess, when I inform him that the Benburb Cavalry are to a man, I believe, Orangemen.

When I related this business to my friend, Sir Evan Nepean, he appeared both shocked and irritated ; he, after mentioning many acts of tyranny *within his own knowledge,* exercised by the Orangemen against the Roman Catholics, declared " *his determination that nothing on his part should be left untried to bring these villains to punishment ;*" he desired me, "on my return to the country, to transmit to him the necessary documents, with the deposition of the constable, &c., &c., in order that he might be enabled to carry into execution his and my wishes." I did so, but although I wrote to my right hon. friend three official and as many private letters, from that day to this (the 12th December, 1806) I never heard one syllable from him upon the subject, nor was ever a single step taken to punish the aggressor or his rescuers! Here ends my intercourse with the late Irish Administration. I shall now proceed to my correspondence with the present one. I must, however, just observe, by-the-bye, that *at this very moment* a man of respectable rank in life is assisted by *two* magistrates (one of them bred an attorney) in opposing my execution of the law, when he himself absolutely insisted upon my punishing poor people *who violated it through ignorance*, and the *supreme conduct* of the acting magistrate of the district—*one of the above-mentioned two* !"

His correspondence with Mr. Elliot, the Chief Secretary to the Lord Lieutenant was based upon a statement contained in a letter bearing date 11th April, 1806, from the Rev. Dr. Conwell, parish priest of Dungannon and Killyman, relative to the persecution and ruin of one Constantine O'Neill. The Rev. Dr. Conwell's letter ran as follows:—

"DEAR SIR,—Constantine O'Neill, the bearer, is an honest, industrious man, who has often suffered great injury, but has been totally ruined within this week past. It was heretofore useless for him to make application for redress, for Government was considered as encouraging these proceedings for political purposes, which was evidently the case. But from the great providential change that has happened lately, and from the consideration that no wise policy can direct apathy or encouragement of such measures at present I now begin to think that the men who have been ruining this country by fire and sword these ten years would now experience a check. This poor man was a hatter by trade, and lived by his honest earnings, and was every way independent, for he was out of debt and had saved some money. But on Saturday night, which was a meeting night of the Orange lodge, this banditti, who are generally Yoemen, and armed, came to his house, which was a thatched cabin, burned it, and all his property to ashes, except what was carried upon their backs. They fired several times at himself and his wife, who both providentially escaped

with their lives, which are all that now remains to them, for their wearing apparel were also destroyed. I request you will be so obliging and so charitable as to give him instructions how to be redressed. The magistrates I know ought to be applied to in the first instance; but this measure will be unavailing, for the magistrates abetted these proceedings from the beginning, and this man lives in the County Armagh, and accordingly not within the limits of your jurisdiction as a magistrate. Hence your charitable advice is all that is wanted, which I am convinced you will not refuse to give him. His situation in life is too humble for his address to be attended to with effect, *for the men against whom his charges would be directed are men of some importance as having high authority*, and there is no good to be got from applying to any magistrate except yourself in such cases as this. I have the honour to be with sentiments of esteem and respect your most obedient servant,

"HENRY CONWELL."

Mr. Wilson says he examined the bearer O'Neill, and found his narrative so simple and affecting that he without hesitation promised to lend assistance towards prevailing upon some Armagh magistrate to take his examinations, O'Neill having solemnly assured him "that he durst not apply to any of them lest his application would come to the ears of the Yoemen and Orangemen which would be attended by certain loss of his life." He met O'Neill by appointment in Armagh, and applied to a Mr. Lawson, J.P., who, though he lived near the scene of the outrage, pretended ignorance of the whole transaction, appeared much astonished, and advised him to apply to the barrister then sitting. Before there was time to draw up the depositions, the barrister had left the town, and Mr. Wilson sent O'Neill to the resident magistrate, who had him turned out of doors, with a threat that he would be kicked out if he did not be off. The resident magistrate afterwards confessed to Mr. Wilson that the reason for his conduct was, "He could not take examinations against his particular friends the Messrs. Verner !!!"

So far unsuccessful in getting justice done to this poor man, Mr. Wilson transmitted a memorial of O'Neill's to the Lord Lieutenant's Secretary, Mr. Elliott, with a letter in which he said, "I have taken great pains to satisfy myself as to the truth of what is stated in the enclosed papers, and from a thorough inquiry into the character of the unfortunate subject of them. I learn that his only crime is that he is a Roman

Catholic, a crime which in the minds of certain men makes him undeserving of the protection of the laws It is with great concern that I feel warranted to declare that where an Orangeman and a Roman Catholic are concerned, a most disgraceful partiality in favour of the former governs the proceedings of nine out of ten of the magistrates in the part of the kingdom I reside in. The numbers of affecting incidents of this nature that I met with on my arrival in Ireland (with the earnest entreaties of the people in my neighbourhood) induced me to take out a Commission of the Peace, which from the part I take, has subjected me to great personal fatigue, expense and obloquy. I have, however, the great satisfaction of knowing that I have often prevented tyranny and oppression and to a certain degree tranquilized the district which formerly had contained a nest of villains who harrassed the poor without redress or opposition. . . . I had determined to confine myself whilst I remained in Ireland to private efforts towards ameliorating the condition of the oppressed, insulted, deceived, and basely misrepresented people (the Catholics.) Nothing could have induced me to depart from this determination but the conviction that justice in its common course could not be obtained by O'Neill. I broke through my resolution with the more reluctance as I had once occasion to treat with some severity the father of the two alleged aggressors (the father of the Messrs. Verner) on account of his attempt to prevent the operation of the law—merely because an Orangeman was the delinquent—which materially affected the public revenue as well as the morals of the people " After paying a compliment to the Lord Lieutenant, which, from the ultimate issue, seemed anything but justified, he ended by saying, " I cannot conclude this letter without particularly and distinctly declaring that if the system with respect to the Roman Catholics is not ma terially altered, and that the Irish gentlemen (the magistrates particularly) do not adopt very conciliatory conduct towards them there cannot exist a hope of cordially attaching them to the Government, and sure I am if they were properly and humanely treated their hands and hearts would unite to support British independence."

The result of this letter was that Mr Sergeant Moore, one of the Law officers of the Crown, was instructed to repair to Armagh for the purpose of "fully investigating" the grave disclosures contained in O'Neill's depositions. Sergeant Moore, accompanied by Mr. Hamilton, Crown Solicitor, waited upon Mr. Wilson at his residence, Ownа Lodge, Dungannon, where the sergeant and his companion expressed the same opinions as those contained in the above regarding the treatment of the Catholics by the Orangemen and Orange magistracy, and regretted that such proceedings on the part of both should be allowed to pass unpunished. ·Attention should be paid to such expressions of opinion in order the better to understand how far the public and the private conduct of these gentlemen differed. The first day of the inquiry held in Armagh, Mr. Moore seemed anxious to get at all the facts of the case, and adjourned to visit the scene of the outrage upon O'Neill (in close proximity to the Verner Mansion), it being understood that Mr. Wilson, would in the meantime, make out a list of all the "inaccuracies" of the local Orange magistrates Mr. Moore, on his return, refused to receive Mr. Wilson's written statement, made out at his (Moore's) own request, and refused to hear further evidence. The cause of this sudden change is thus stated by Mr. Wilson. Mr. Sergeant Moore, after great cortiveness, allowed it to be drawn out of him that on his arrival at the appointed place, he called upon the elder Verner in order to learn from that gentleman how he would get at the particulars of the outrage. Mr. Verner kindly undertaking to allow his two sons (who were actually the persons charged with directing the attack on and the burning of O'Neill's house) to assist in bringing forward evidence This Mr, Moore consented to. In other words he allowed the criminals to select and direct the evidence for the prosecution of themselves. The result of this inquiry was he found O'Neill's house was burned at all events, but that it did not transpire who were the culprits. Of course not And if the culprits had been discovered the young Verners were less ingenious youths than their father took them for Upon the singular conduct of Mr. Moore the author comments very strongly, and says he actually did observe to that gentleman upon the absurdity of employing the offenders to collect evidence to bring them to the gallows. Dr Conwell who was present expressed the same opinion, upon which this impartial Commissioner said, "If you want to thrust the two young Mr. Verner's into jail you certainly are mistaken; but that I suppose is the only thing that will satisfy you " To this Dr. Conwell made the very pregnant reply—" By no means, that he only wanted such an investigation as might be the means of permitting his people to live in peace, but that it was well known that the inhabitants in Mr. Verner's neighbourhood stood in such dread of that gentleman and his yeoman and his Orangemen that they would not dare to state anything which could affect him or his party." The result of such an inquiry may be anticipated And there was joy in Israel, and bonfires at Mr. Verner's !

Mr. Wilson had a formal interview with the Secretary and Chancellor, both of whom declared "that the conduct of Mr. Sergeant Moore met with the entire approval of Government. As showing how corruption had permeated the magisterial body at that time, it may be said that, in the course of the conversation, Mr. Wilson r commended the issuing of a new Commission for the entire magistracy of the county as the only remedy of a grievance, the existence of which the Lord Chancellor admitted.

The event which led to a renewal of his correspondence with Government was an application made to him "by certain Yeomen and Orangemen," who were unable to get their pay from their officers, and unable also to get any magistrate to take a matter in hands, which Mr. Wilson, upon investigation, found "to rest upon grounds which warranted the complaint." He accordingly wrote to the Chief Secretary (letter dated 1st July, 1806, page 31 of pamphlet) in which he condemned the policy of the Government towards the Catholics and their sanction of Orange outrages upon Catholics as a most infatuated one, and said he should "make one effort more to draw the attention of Ministers to the *hourly increasing tyrannies* exercised against these unoffending creatures." He then alludes to the significant change in Mr. Moore's conduct after his visit to Mr. Verner, and closed by stating that since the abortive investigation "many daring and atrocious violences have been committed against these poor people by a banditti calling themselves Yeomen and Orangemen, who, with arms in their hands, bid defiance to the law and its ministers," adding, "You may be told 'I exaggerate;' I wish it was not in my power to give repeated instances, and recently, too, of the certainty of this statement." He then requested to be placed upon the Commission of the Peace for the County Armagh (upon the borders of which he lived), as before he could get an Armagh magistrate to back his warrants the culprit was in consequence able to escape. This request was distinctly refused.

Upon the 12th July of this year Mr. Verner caused great rejoicings in his neighbourhood amongst the Orangemen by way of celebrating the acquittal of his two sons, and with his consent and approval Mr. Wilson's effigy, together with that of the Pope's, were burned. A party of the most rabid ruffians of the locality paraded past his house offering insult and threatening an attack on the return journey. Hearing of their approach the same evening, Wilson, with more bravery than discretion, ventured out alone to request them to proceed by some other route, when the five hundred fell upon him and beat him almost to death, his life being saved only by the interference of a servant of his, who was also an Orangeman. These facts were, together with several subsequent attempts to murder him, brought under the notice of the Government, as will be seen from the following interesting and important letter —

"THE RIGHT HON. WILLIAM ELLIOTT.

"Owna Lodge, August 16th, 1806

"SIR,—Five weeks have elapsed this day since I acquainted you with the daring and wanton outrage which had been committed upon me the preceding evening; and somewhat more than a month since I received your reply to my information, 'lamenting that disorderly and tumultuous transaction, with your intention of laying my letter before the Lord Lieutenant.' Your silence leaving me in ignorance of his Grace's opinion upon that disgraceful business, I hold myself just fled in demanding why I have not obtained that "opinion" long before this, peculiarly and dangerously situated as I am ? It rests with you, sir, to show, why justice and humanity should be so far apparently violated as to have their operation withheld in protecting the life of a magistrate in the performance of his duty, when the meanest subject is constitutionally entitled to the prompt, active, and vigorous exertion of them, when either his life or property is endangered ?

"In consequence of the observation in your letter of the 16th July, I wrote to the Chancellor, 'to rectify the error you apprized me of having committed in not applying to his lordship, instead of the Government, to extend my magisterial power to the adjoining County of Armagh ' In my letter to his lordship I took leave to state, 'that I had been attacked a second time on the 19th of the above-mentioned month ;' the particulars I did not then, nor shall I now, enter into—the limits of a letter, indeed, would not permit me, even was I disposed (which I confess I am not) so to do, having much important matter independent of what relates to myself, that ought to be submitted so grave and deliberate consideration. When I perceive Government disposed to afford that to my communications, I will cheerfully, but personally, detail them, in the meantime, I am to observe that I am prepared to prove that the laws (as I, in my first letter to you, intimated) are most partially and carelessly (I wish to speak mildly) administered with regard to the Roman Catholics—that I have instances, within these few days, of robbers, assassins, forgers of bank notes, and public disturbers being protected, and their prosecutors frightened from following up their complaints—also of examinations being either secreted (by those who ought to have been brought forward) or withheld from the Clerk of the Crown, or, if given to him, his being prevailed upon not to form bills of indictment upon them ! All this, sir, I say, I am prepared to prove, and call upon the Government to put me to the proof—If I fail (provided I am enabled to bring forward my witnesses and assured of their personal protection then and hereafter, also that my judges shall not be prepossessed) let me be held out to the public as the very opposite to what I have dedicated my life to substantiate—a man devoted to its interests, its happiness, its tranquillity and its freedom ! In my letter to the Chancellor I hinted that there was an idea rather too prevalent with a great part of the public, that "Government was either unable or unwilling to protect the oppressed." If the outrage committed against me continues unnoticed, and the means denied me of bringing forward the charges I have declared myself to make good, you cannot, sir, be surprised at my being confirmed in this opinion, not only with regard to the Roman Catholics, but also with respect to those who are bold enough to stand forward as their advocates, and venture to vindicate a conduct, which, instead of procuring the thanks and support of Government, has excited a vindictiveness which, unless I speedily desert my residence, will not be allayed until I fall its victim !

"The Chancellor not replying to my letter, I confess, a good deal puzzles me, as whatever opinion his lordship may please to form of my representations and objects, I cannot bring myself to believe him deficient in the politeness of a gentleman —I have the honour to be, &c,

"RICHARD WILSON."

The result of these communications was that Mr.

Wilson was told to seek the ordinary mode of remedy open by the law, and *was dismissed the Commission of the Peace.* That "the ordinary modes of justice" were not open to him in such cases was I think admitted by the Government sending down Sergeant Moore to investigate O'Neill's case, and to it no better answer could be given than that of Mr Wilson that " if he put himself to a couple of hundred pounds expense to retain counsel and bring up a horde of witnesses to Omagh he should have for his pains a host of gentlemen to appear to the character of the accused parties, which would have obtained for them expressions of esteem and honourable acquittal by the jury "

So frequent were the attacks now made upon his life that Mr Wilson dared not appear outside his door in day light, and in the whole narrative there is good reason to suppose that this Orange persecution—if you would not give it a stronger name—was directed by their leaders, the Verners He was finally compelled to leave the country —"Nor have I anything now more at heart since my hopes of proving myself a really useful member of the community have failed than to quit a country where oppression and injustice are formed into a system, and where true patriotism meets with obloquy, instead of honour, gratitude, and protection "[*]

These disclosures, it must be borne in mind, have as their author a gentleman of high birth, of education and of unblemished character, an ex-member of Parliament, a magistrate, and *Protestant*

Mr WILSON's narrative furnishes a striking proof of how unmixed an evil must be the result of any exclusive combination for the upholding of the ascendancy of a class. An exclusive Catholic Association formed in Ireland now or at any other time in our history, for the sole purpose of upholding Catholic ascendancy, for preserving all the places, honours, and emoluments of the country in the hands of Catholics, for having the Bench, the Bar, and the Senate open to none but Catholics, and for the maintaining of an exclusively Catholic magistracy would meet with the strenuous opposition of every intelligent and right-minded man, whether Catholic or Protestant, in the community. If that Catholic association were bound by a secret oath and connected by secret signs and passwords, the evil would be greater and the necessity for its suppression in a tenfold degree more apparent It is a pleasing consideration that in those days, when village despots ruled the land, when honours were

[*] Mr Richard Wilson to the Right Hon. Wm. Ellie t, Aug. 23, 1836.

heaped upon men in proportion to their iniquity, when Protestant intolerance was sure to receive reward and favour, there were some men who, without conceding one iota of true Protestant principle, could afford to condemn the sway of a faction and despise the means by which they prolonged their intolerable reign. It may strike some of my readers as strange, that the Orange Institution has found its bitterest and most determined opponents amongst the ranks of Protestantism. Than their own co-religionists no men were more likely so soon to discover how hollow was the cry "Protestant Ascendancy," which meant not the triumph of Protestant principles, but that all the good things of the earth should be showered upon those who made of them an empty profession, without caring as to their practice. By them it was felt that this boastful Institution was calculated to retard Protestantism rather than advance it. The very questionable aid which it proffered to enforce the survival of the fittest, looked in their eyes not alone as bombast, but as a blasphemous insinuation of the insufficiency of Providence. Amongst this class, at present a numerous one, including the vast body of reflecting Protestants, the Orange Society found even at this early stage of its career many strenuous opponents not ashamed to express their convictions. Of that class the Earl of Gosford was the first exponent. Mr. Wilson followed a dozen years afterwards, and amply corroborated his statements.

The entire pamphlet breathes a spirit of hopelessness on the part of a brave and just man struggling against intolerance without effect. The object for which it was given to the public was to prove those statements which he was not allowed to substantiate before a Government inquiry."That there was scarce an outrage, however flagitious, which could be committed in his quarter of the kingdom against a Roman Catholic, by an Orangeman, that by some means or other did not generally pass unnoticed, but always unpunished to the extent of its enormity; that in matters of dispute between Roman Catholics and Orangemen a most disgraceful partiality in favour of the latter governed the proceedings of nine in ten of the magistrates in his district; that the murderer, the forger, and the felon were, when Orangemen, protected and screened from justice by the Orange magistracy, and bills of indictment suppressed or smothered by Orange officials; and lastly, that the man who had hardihood sufficient to protect a Roman Catholic subjected himself not only to

obloquy but to personal danger." These are grave charges, and the reader will, by a calm perusal of the following be enabled to see whether they are established by facts. The painful history of Mr. Wilson's persecution proves but too plainly the latter, which is certainly not the least grievous indictment.

He first gives the history of a Roman Catholic, a blacksmith, residing near Dungannon. During the rebellion he had been arrested on suspicion of making pikes. The two facts combined, a Roman Catholic and a blacksmith, were in those days a hanging matter, and the surprise is that he was not summarily disposed of. Reasonable suspicion is likely to have pointed quite the other way, when we find that this Roman Catholic blacksmith living in '98 was not hanged but imprisoned. It should be mentioned that he had been ordered to be hanged by a neighbouring Orange magistrate, but the edict was not carried out. There being no proof of guilt he was discharged. The blacksmith's business was ruined, and he opened a public-house with the proceeds, of which he supported his wife and family. Being cottier to an Orangeman who desired to repossess his house and field, his landlord—seconded by the hanging magistrate before referred to—prosecuted him in the most illegal manner in order to drive him out of the country. Not succeeding as he desired, he got the magistrate to cancel his licence, then to fine him £10 for selling without a licence,he then arrested him, then to grant a warrant for the recovery of the £10, and, finally, the landlord became a special bailiff, broke into the house in the absence of the owner, destroyed everything he could capable of destruction, and, in his hurry, appropriated five guineas that were carefully placed by. Mr. Wilson, on hearing the facts, granted a warrant for the arrest of the Orange burglar. As the constable, who was charged with the execution of it approached, the landlord judiciously made off—the constable said he dared not follow—and the narrator states he was not a little surprised on seeing him present himself at his (Mr. Wilson's) own house "determined that no man should take him.' Two stout servants took him into custody, Mr. Wilson made out his committal, and they conveyed him to Dungannon. On the route they met the constable who took charge of the prisoner, and conveyed him to the friendly Orange magistrate who liberated him (notwithstanding he was charged with robbery and burglary), on the ground that from "his knowledge of his respectable character he was incapable of the crimes." Mr. Wilson referring to this says—"If the prisoner is not foully belied this robbery was a feather to the other crimes which he committed" He says the landlord appeared at the bar in Omagh but that no bill was found against him, and he continues.— "Query, why was this bill of indictment smothered? The aggrieved parties were Roman Catholics and the aggressors an Orangeman and a Yeoman—reverse the case and would the issue have been similar? I boldly answer it would NOT."

Having thus dealt with the protection of robbers, the author proceeds to justify his assertion regarding the cloaking of forgers because they happened to be Orangemen. detailing several glaring cases that came directly under his own knowledge and quoting the expression of the prosecuting solicitors on the failure of justice in one instance "that there was no use to attempt convicting at Omagh a man charged with forgery, however strong the proofs"

In this pamphlet (page 14), the author distinctly charges the Administration with "scandalous encouragement of the abuses he called upon it to redress, by the neglect of its constitutional duty in disregarding representations which he had bound himself to confirm by irrefragable proofs" In a letter, dated June 12, 1807, to the Chancellor, Lord Eldon, with whom he had been on terms of intimacy, he warns him that the existence of the Administration depended' upon its pursuing measures pointed by the reverse of those of the preceeding one, relative to this country, and that it ought to direct its powers to the amelioration of the condition of the lower classes in general, and the curbing the licentiousness and profligacy of a set of men who are protected in their oppression of the Roman Catholic poor" After bringing many cases of the character he alluded to under the notice of the Administration, he received the curt official reply that the ordinary remedy at law was open to the afflicted parties, a statement which, as I have before remarked, was not founded on fact, seeing that Government had undertaken to supersede it by a commission of inquiry.

Addressing Lord Eldon as to the policy he should pursue regarding the Catholic people, and the means he should adopt for affording them protection from the armed Orangemen, our author says—

"The consistent language you and most of your friends have held with regard to the Catholic question augurs to me a hope (whatever my private opinion upon that great point may be) that you will leave nothing untried—oh! heaven how have

I been deceived!) short of yielding it—'o conciliate the great body of people interested in it. My intimate knowledge of the real grievances which the lower orders labour under enables me to point out the most probably effectual means towards their conciliation. Without a moment's delay or hesitation you are to convince the general body of Catholics that though you resist their great political object, yet you are determined (I need not observe that I am now speaking of administration when I say you) to afford them every relief short of that; you will free them from the insults of the armed Orangemen; that you will take care that the law shall in future be administered with vigour, justice, and impartiality; that juries shall not be packed to screen their oppressors (to my knowledge sometimes their murderers); that the magistracy shall be placed in the hands of honourable, just, and independent gentlemen; that some favourable modification with regard to tythes shall be adopted; that the Lord Lieutenant shall take into his councils men who have a thorough knowledge of the state of the country, that he shall depute persons (fully competent to the duty) to pervade every part of the Kingdom, and examine into all sorts of abuses, and report them with boldness and integrity, that he shall set his face against every species of jobbing; that he shall rid himself of the swarm of locusts who at present devour the bread of the industrious poor—I mean the Castle Crew who some way or other never fail thrusting themselves into office about the Viceroy, whoever he may happen to be. Gloriously and wisely has my friend availed himself of these hints, as will appear in the following pages."

Accompanying this letter he enclosed affidavits, proving that a shocking outrage had been committed upon the person whose cause he had undertaken to lay before the Chancellor. The case is thus stated by him.—"I shall now return to the case I sent the Chancellor for his lordship's consideration As it is very long, I will extract from it all its material features, leaving the technical rubbish where it ought to be—on the lawyer's shelf, M——'s deposition states that on the 29th of April, 1807, after he was in bed, his house was forcibly broken open by H—— Y——, accompanied, as he verily believes, by his brother-in law, H—— H——, both of B—— C—— in the County of Tyrone, that he was most violently assaulted, beaten, stabbed, and knocked down, and kicked under his bed by Y——, who, having lighted a candle, robbed him of his silver watch, breeches, and some money, with several other articles, such as shirts, a bed-quilt, wearing apparel to the value of ten pounds and upwards, which articles the said Y—— put into a sack, whilst his accomplice A—— (whom he confidently believes, as aforesaid), assisted and held the candle, after which they made off with the plunder. M—— further deposes that he verily believes, from strong circumstances, that S——, a pedlar who frequented Y——'s house, was the man who guarded the window without and talked to the robbers. He further says that he has good reason to believe that A——, sen, of B—— C—— aforesaid was head plotter in said robbery. Said M—— deposed that he had lodged examinations to the above effect, before Mr. F——, on the 1st of June inst., and that he was prevented from prosecuting said Y—— and A—— the last Assizes for the following reasons :—For fear of his life through the threatening of said Y—— and A——, and also of A——, sen., and M——, of C——; also from his bad state of health through the injuries he had received when he was robbed; that he was rather induced to withhold his prosecuting the robbers through the flattering speeches and promises of A——, sen, who said he would free M—— from every fine and trouble that might attend his non-appearance at Omagh, &c., &c , &c.

Sworn before Richard Wilson, Esq., March 20th, 1807.

I desire not to be understood as assigning the above affidavit as a ground for troubling the Chancellor; no, I was induced to endeavour to interest his lordship in this unfortunate man's behalf on account of the following statement of his persecutions through the immediate means of the villains who had abused and plundered him. His statement is upon oath, and sworn before me. It is to the following purport:—That, having been deceived through promises of the father of the robbers and his associate, M—— was thereby prevented from prosecuting. He attended at the Easter Assizes, and took out a Bench warrant for the said A—— (the person who, he verily believes, was the accomplice of Y——, and who had so cruelly abused him); that the Clerk of the Crown desired him to deliver it to M——, of said county, to have it executed; that said M—— refused taking it in the presence of the Rev. Mr. Lowry. (N.B.—Mr. Lowry confirmed this fact to me). M—— states he was made prisoner on the 30th of April last by the robber himself accompanied by one G—— who hurried him away to jail for a fine as they said of £50 for prosecuting the said Y—— (now turned into a constable; a tolerably natural transition). When on the road they met the above-mentioned M——, the H C., who gave one of the constables a paper and desired him to deliver it to the jailer; that he verily believes they had no warrant or order to take him until then, and that he is persuaded they were not constables (indeed I know they are not, for they constantly refused showing deponent their authority for taking him prisoner). He further goes on to state that on the 3rd day of May, inst., he was pressed to take some liquor (by persons whom he had good reason to believe were in the confidence of the parties who had injured him, particularly of A——, the father of the robbers); that he had gone to his bed in prison and slept for some time, that on his awakening suspecting some treachery he examined his pocket and found it had been picked of the warrant which M—— had refused to take; that he made great cry of distress but to no purpose; he further deposes that he has good ground to know that the above-mentioned prisoners were the persons who robbed him of his bench warrant againt A—— the younger, &c., &c.

In another deposition of M——'s, which I sent to the Chancellor, he enters into the particulars of the means which were pursued to prevent his prosecuting the fellows who robbed him; that he was cajoled to go before a magistrate by A——, sen, and persuaded also by his parish priest, when he said he would give up the prosecution, but that the magistrate can certify he said he did give it up through fear of his life, of this he mentioned many proofs in the various depositions I sent to the Chancellor, but as I believe I have stated sufficient to prove that this poor old man has been most cruelly treated (with the addition of his lying several months in jail until discharged on account of his poverty) and that examination into his case and into the conduct of the H. C., as well as the persons concerned in the robbery and assault would not have reflected any discredit upon either the Lord Chancellor's justice, humanity, or dignity, although his lordship was not the immediate and exact channel through which the investigation should be set on foot. I must not omit that this old man is a Roman Catholic, and that his persecuters and plunderers are of the loyal school of Orangemen.

I cannot refrain from mentioning a circumstance which will tend to show the accuracy of the magisterial gentry of my part of the county, although it took place some months previous to M——'s robbery. On the evening of which the Orangemen had made the attempt to assassinate me, (mentioned in my correspondence with the late administration) a very respectable Roman Catholic was driving his cow towards his house, when he was overtaken by a straggling party of the assassins who were, of course, extolling their exploit in having nearly murdered Papist Wilson, &c., &c. The man incautiously desired them to speak respectfully of a gentleman who had done so much good since his residence in the country. He was immediately knocked down, and would have been despatched but that some of the party knew him to be a Freemason, and rescued him before the spark of life was extinguished. He was, however, beaten most dreadfully, in so much that his life was considered in danger. I was informed of his situation, and not being well enough to go abroad from the abuse I myself had received on the same evening, I advised his brother-in-law, who is a tenant of mine, to go to an M.P., the magistrate who is the agent of the estate the injured man lived upon, bringing with him an authenticated state of the man's health, abuse, &c. This was done. The magistrate's clerk or stewart, although acquainted with the object of their interview with the magistrate, and of the very precarious state of the man's health, and that there was but very little hopes of the man surviving any length of time yet the clerk or servant refused acquainting his master as he was then dressing to go to dinner with Lord C——" his employer!!!

The man, however, did recover. Some of the persons who abused him were sworn to by a person who happened to be on the road, but nothing was, or indeed could be done, for the Orange party to whom this detached one belonged, had commenced a prosecution against me for beating 500 of them, though unarmed and unsupported. Little, therefore, could be expected from his informing until the issue of the prosecution against me should be known, lest he with equal consistency might have been proved to have commenced the affray, &c. This prosecution, I must observe, still hangs over me, and has been carried on by an open subscription, under the legal advice of a Mr. Pettigrew, who utrumque paratus officiates one day as a magistrate the next as an attorney!

I shall now proceed to give a detail of some atrocious murders and violations of justice—I might say even of the common forms of justice—which have occurred near me since the entrance into

office of the present Administration. The first act of this kind to which I shall advert was one committed near the town of Ballygawley, a few miles from my house, last spring. I do not mention it as having been occasioned by any party dispute, but as a proof of the laxity of our administration of justice. Two men had some altercation in the fair, but it was supposed to be too trifling to predict any serious or future consequences, however, as one of the disputants was returning home, at a little distance from the town, he was overtaken by his adversary, who without saying a word dashed out his brains with, I believe, a spade he had purchased in the fair! I never learned that the murderer was even put in the way of punishment! I will not insult the understanding or attempt to excite the indignation of my reader by a commentary.

The next murder I shall relate is still more atrocious in its circumstances as well as more momentous as to the effect which it has produced.

On the 25th December, 1806 (I must here anticipate an objection that this murder was committed previous to the present people's coming into power, by observing that the trial took place just about the time of their entrance into office, and therefore that their predecessors could not be charged with any blame, if there was any blame in the mode of carrying on the prosecution, or the means which were adopted to obtain an acquittal of the murderer), as one D——, accompanied by one M'G——, was returning home after having conveyed a young woman to her master's house, who had spent the evening with his family, and passing by the house of one S——, two shots were fired at him by S—— without him or his companion having given the smallest provocation to S—— either then or before, whereupon the deceased went forward to S——, and declared himself to be F. D——, and that he was Dr. B——'s servant, and that he had no intention to hurt his person or property, upon which S—— opened his door and leaning upon the underpart of it (being a divided door), fired his third shot which instantly deprived D—— of life. This is the substance of what was proved at the inquest, which was held upon the body of D——. The verdict was wilful murder against said S——. There were two magistrates, one of whom (as he himself informed me) was for sending the murderer to gaol, but the other insisted upon taking the murderer under his own protection until he could get another magistrate Mr. A——, of Dungannon, to join him in taking bail—he did so, and the murderer was at large until it was necessary he should appear in the dock at the ensuing assizes—he was there convicted of manslaughter, as it appeared to the jury from the testimony of his captain, that he the captain had put the murderer upon his guard shortly before the murder on account of his having received some intimation that a riot was expected on the night that the murder was committed!!! I will only add that the murderer, the magistrate, the witness and I firmly believe most part of the jury were Orangemen, and the murdered man an unfortunate Roman Catholic! However, the judge, I suppose, saw into the real state of this nefarious business, and though he could not alter the verdict of the jury, he, I understand, punished the murderer as far as he could by imprisonment, which I have since heard great interest has been made to free the murderer from. I beg the reader will bear in mind the mode we have of punishing murder in our country, and contrast it with the punishment for an affray which I shall presently advert to, where the convicted party had Orange witnesses, magistrates, and jury to contend with, and was himself, the vile wretch, a Papist. The next murder, or rather murders, for two were perpetrated almost on the same instant, took place on the 30th day of March last (1807). A man of a most excellent character and inoffensive manners was at the fair of C——, and without even an indication of previous resentment on the part of the assailants, beaten down and stabbed by a party of Mr. P——'s yeomen. He lingered, I believe, a day, and expired. A principal in the murder was advised to surrender himself and turn King's evidence. He did so, but none of the other murderers having been taken (for reasons which may be accounted for through the sworn documents which I shall insert of the murdered man's brother) he was discharged, and now quietly enjoys himself under the patronage of his Orange commander. The deposition of the murdered man's brother is as follows. He commences it by stating that he firmly believes that due means were not taken towards seizing the murderers of his brother for the following reasons—first, because the magistrate confessed he was acquainted with certain of the murderers against whom examinations were lodged, yet would not grant warrants against more than three of them, whereas seven were sworn against, exclusive of W——, the King's evidence; that upon application of said brother to the deceased on the 15th July following the magistrate did the

grant a warrant against the whole party, dating said warrant as on the 4th April; that said magistrate was heard to say in his office to one B—— (one of the accused persons) that he B—— might go home, as he had enough against him, thereby appearing to caution him to keep out of the way. He further deposes that he believes said magistrate was well acquainted with all the circumstances of the murder, as well as with the persons who had committed it, before W——, the King's evidence, was examined, from what he, said magistrate had observed to deponent upon his application to him, deposes that said magistrate gave directions for the Yeomen to appear who had their arms and clothing to be inspected, yet, to this day the 23rd of July, there never was an inspection of their arms; though several of the Yeomen did come in to the magistrates as ordered—that deposed then applied to another magistrate, brother to the other—for a guard to take up certain persons suspected of the murder; said magistrate positively refused, saying it was nonsense, how could he allow him a guard? Said magistrate was commander of the Yeomen, many of whom were suspected of the murder; said magistrate asked deponent at the same time whom he suspected. Deponent replied, his own Yeomen and no others. Deponent afterwards applied to the first mentioned magistrate to sign deponents description of the persons sworn against, in order to have it published in the newspaper; said magistrate refused, saying it was an odd sort of production, and he would have nothing to do with it; but deponent is persuaded that the magistrate's objection arose from deponent's describing the person as C—— Yeomen, with their names and occupations. All the persons alluded to deponent believes to be Orangemen. Deponent and his brother were Roman Catholics. The above facts I am ready to prove if called upon

("Signed) R. M.

"Various persons appeared ready to corroborate the above statement and have left their names with me. "RICHARD WILSON."

The other murder committed on the same day at the same fair and by the same party, had little to distinguish it from the foregoing, I do no not think it necessary to detail it; he was also a man of fair character, who had gone to the fair accompanied by his wife, and niece, and was murdered (as appears by the confession of one of the party) merely because he was a Papist, and that none of his sect were to escape that night. Several other persons (R. C.'s) were grossly abused on the above day, and who had been prevented from informing against the Orangemen (as they positively swear) for fear of the sharing the fates of M—— and M'S——. I will insert one deposition to prove that the attack upon the R. C.'s was a preconcerted one   "W—— showeth that on the night of the 30th May, 1807, M——, the deceased, was in the inn of R—— of C—— when W—— (the King's evidence), and P——, with others, came to said inn and demanded in a peremptory manner to send or put out the Papists, or that the above mentioned would pull down his sign-board and destroy the house. Further, that P—— on the evening of said day drew out a pistol and presented the same at W——, but was prevented firing it by a young girl who was in his company."

These somewhat startling details are interrupted by the insertion of a correspondence between the author and the Lord Lieutenant relative to the dismissal of Mr Wilson from the magistracy. He seems to be a man very much given to calling a spade "a spade," for without the slightest attempt at inuendo he charges the Government for this act with direct complicity in the crimes which he attempted to prevent; that they objected to his endeavours to serve the great mass of the afflicted Roman Catholics, then suffering at the hands of the Orange faction, and warned them that this act would be construed by those most intimately concerned as "having originated in principles hostile to their interests and protection." From his narrative it would seem that this must, indeed, have been a trying time upon any person who ventured to raise his voice in favour of the afflicted. Not alone was Mr Wilson's property pillaged, his person insulted, and his character villified by a paper "notoriously in the pay of the Orange faction," but attempts upon his life were applauded, and "public rejoicings recommended for Richard Wilson, Esq., of Owna Lodge, having been deprived of the power of any longer committing acts of injustice and oppression," with "acknowledgments of gratitude to the Lord Chancillor for his removal of him" This, which at such a time, and under such circumstances, meant neither more nor less than an organised attack upon Mr. Wilson, an attack likely to end in blood, calls forth the following exclamation from the author —"Merciful God! I an oppressor! If in my ministry one single act of oppression, injustice, or partiality appears—nay, on the contrary, if my accusers can shew that I ever even omitted an oc-

casion to prevent oppression, restrain violence, and promote tranquillity, then I will confess that the Chancellor and those who advised the late measures are justly entitled to the eulogy of the Orangemen of Tyrone, and the gratitude of the country" It may be, he added, that his removal from the Justiceship of the Peace discloses a piece of political duplicity seldom equalled. All his demands for an opportunity to justify his conduct were refused.

Mr. Wilson's personal sufferings at the hands of the Orangemen are thus partially recounted by himself·—"A person whom I had employed by contract early in the summer of 1806 to make some alterations and repairs in my house, having for near a year and during the whole of the ensuing winter neglected to finish the work he had begun (and thereby occasioned considerable injury, not only to the house itself, but also to the furniture through the defective state of the gutters), I found myself obliged, after repeated efforts to get him to finish his job, to commence an action against him for breach of contract and the injury I had sustained, both with regard to my furniture, as also with respect to my loss in not being able to advertise my place for a tenant, which last was my principal view in the repairs and alterations I had contracted with him to complete. Alarmed at this step, he began about the middle of last summer to proceed in the repairs, &c. After various delays, he at last told some of my servants that he had finished. Upon examining, however, I found that no one part of his contract was completed, and that the rain still made its way through the leads of the gutters. However, I sent him a message that I was ready to have the work examined by proper and competent judges and then submit to them the injury I had received through his neglect, leaving them finally to settle the business, and in the meantime I would withhold my prosecution, &c. Instead of complying with this offer, he consulted an attorney who he knew had before succeeded (by means which, for the sake of some persons whom I venerate, I will forbear to state) in obtaining a verdict against me for a claim of a person whom I had never any dealings with, and who I proved had confessed he had no demand whatever upon me, having entered upon the work about my place before I had settled in the kingdom, upon the credit of my steward, to whom only he should look for payment. This steward, however, having fled the kingdom (on account of frauds committed against others as well as me), he had been advised

to make his claim upon me. I mention this circumstance to give an additional weight to any declaration of false debts being sworn against me. I could give several more instances, but this one, I trust, will be considered as sufficient to establish the fact. The measure (as the man himself told me) he was advised to pursue to get payment of his bill was to arrest me. Accordingly, two fellows forced past the servant who had opened the door to them, and made into my study, where I was writing. Seeing a man with a most savage countenance bursting open the inner door of the room, I was immediately struck with the idea that he came to assassinate me (repeated attempts having been made with that intent). I instantly seized him by the throat, and certainly had nearly choked him, but upon his telling me that he was a bailiff and come to arrest me, and another man at the moment coming to his assistance, I let him go. I rang my bell, and the servant who attended was threatened with instant death if he did not quit the room, two pistols being held at his head. I implored the officers not to injure the man, my only object being to send him for persons who would be answerable for the supposed debt. (they having at first consented that they would be satisfied with security till I could give bail). Two of my tenants, men of substance, soon after were brought, but the bailiff's tone was changed :—No, I must either pay the money or go to gaol. Upon this I requested them to permit me to send to Dungannon to the sheriff, as my state of health (not having been beyond my own gate for near five months), was rather delicate, and riding then might be attended with the most dangerous consequences. After some objections, this request was complied with, and I sent my groom to Dungannon with a note to a friend there to secure the sheriff in a debt of £49. About this time a servant of mine, to whose gallantry and fidelity I twice before owed my life, came into the room. As soon as he appeared the man who was the chief spokesman of the bailiffs addressed himself to him as follows.—(I am to entreat the readers will pay due attention to this conversation, for I have entered into this circumstantial detail chiefly upon its account)

Pray, Mr. Moore, are not you an Orangeman?

Moore—I am.

Bailiff—Then I desire sir you will leave this room, you have no business here.

Moore—I will not leave the room—I am doing no harm, nor mean any, and I think it my duty to remain with my master placed in the situation I see him in.

Bailiff—If you do not go when I order you I tell you you are a perjured man and no Orangeman.

Moore—I am an Orangeman, and do not think I act unworthy of one [in staying to protect, if necessary, a master who has been a father to me and my family.

Bailiff—Well, you shall answer for this another day.

Moore did not leave the room, nor did the bailiff again insist upon it. In the course of conversation, sometime after the bailiff observed, on my making a remark upon the baseness of the attack upon me, that I had brought it upon myself, for it was universally allowed I was the best and justest magistrate in the county, and this would never have happened if I had not fallen out with Colonel (so the bailiff denominated that gentleman) Verner and protected the Papists!! Though I had before suspected the motive that had induced the advice which made the tradesman adopt this method of getting payment of an unjust demand, and to stop my prosecution of him I was now convinced. In the meantime the second-bailiff had been collecting some Orangemen about the house, armed with swords, &c. As soon as they conceived there was no danger of their being overpowered (in case of their attempting any abuse of my person), I was told that I must prepare to set off to Dungannon, as it would soon be dark, and that possibly a rescue might be attempted. I observed that there was not time yet for the servant to go to Dungannon and return, even though the sheriff and my friend should happen to be in the way, which possibly might not be the case, as there was a fair at Moy, where most of the people in business attended. I said it was impossible for me to go to Dungannon without risking my life, unless I had a carriage, as I was not able to put on a boot, to say nothing of my catching cold from the dampness of the evening, and my not having for several months ventured abroad. To this was answered — that that was not their affair. If I could not walk, which he did not see but I was very well able to do, they would get me a horse, but go I must. They accordingly sent one of their attendants for a horse. As soon as the horse was procured, my room was filled with their attending Orangemen. I was ordered to get up and quit the house. I remonstrated again, and told them that I would not be accessory to my own death, which I conceived I should be if in my state of health I encountered the night air, and, therefore, though I would make no resistance, yet I would not move, and that if I must go they should carry me. I will not vindicate my mode of reasoning at that time; others have condemned it, and, perhaps, they may be right. I, however, thought otherwise. Upon this the chief bailiff ordered me to be taken off my chair. I was then placed upon the carpet, and two of the savages seized me by the feet and dragged me through the adjoining room, hall, and down the stone steps, with my head beating upon the ground as they proceeded (for no one was permitted to touch me but those persons who dragged me by the heels). I was then laid upon the wet gravel upon the terrace, my clothes from the dragging having left my back quite uncovered, where I remained for at least twenty minutes, until a servant, who was acquainted with one of the assistants, prevailed upon him to allow me to sit on a chair, which had been brought out in the meantime. My faithful orange servant was imploring the bailiff to let me return to the house, and he would instantly send for a carriage to carry me to Drangannon, appealing to him as a man and a christian not to murder me, which most likely he would do if he insisted upon me going to Dungannon such an evening (it was then raining). All was in vain. Four pistols were held at his breast, which, with horrid imprecations, they swore should be fired into it if he offered to lay a hand on me, as there were enough present to prove he meant to rescue me. I called out to Moore, for his own sake as well as mine, to make no further efforts to protect me from those men. Their object was plain that they only wanted an excuse to murder me, which they would find in what they might call a rescue; that my death one way was certain, in the other by God's assistance it might be preserved. Moore upon this ceased to interfere further than by entreating leave to have a horse of my own prepared, which with great reluctance was permitted. I was then mounted and, attended by a strong guard, carried off. When we came to a village upon the road entirely inhabited by Orangemen, one of the bailiffs who was next me called out "Now, see this is for your conduct to the Orangemen." The motive for this remark at that spot was obvious, but it failed of its object, for not one of the inhabitants showed even the appearance of exultation, much less made use of a term of abuse; on the contrary, I perceived rather an expression of sorrow at the treatment I was receiving. This I think a tribute due to the villagers. Upon our arrival in Dungannon, I

asked the bailiff's permission to go directly to the Sheriff's house, as it was late, and the only hope I had of being preserved from the effects of the rain and cold would be by getting home as soon as possible. The answer was completely of a piece with what had before taken place—"No, by God; I'll leave you in the properest place for you, the body of the jail." I said, as he liked, and turned my horse to the prison. Upon entering the prison, to the honour of the jailor be it told, he appeared shocked at the treatment he understood (from the servant who had attended me) I had received, and turned the bailiff instantly out of the room. He went off immediately to the Sheriff, saying he was convinced the Sheriff knew nothing of the situation I was in, &c. In as short a time as possible, he returned expressing his regret that the Sheriff was not to be found. However, he at once proved that he possessed, whatever his superior did, humanity, and liberated me, upon a most worthy and truly respectable friend of mine (a Quaker) saying he would be answerable for my appearance, but had not this friend interfered, I feel perfectly convinced the jailer would not have detained me a moment after. I had warmed myself by an excellent fire, which his wife placed me before. I then got on my horse, attended by my two servants, and rode home as fast as I could. I confess, I thought that the consequences would be very fatal, but so far from the effect this outrage threatened, I have been daily getting strength, and am at this moment (Dec. 14) in better health than I was for six months before, though I have taken up too much of my pamphlet already with this attack upon my life, I am persuaded that was more the object of the advisers of it, than the forcing an unjust debt for a knavish tradesman, although I am far from saying that, too, had not its share, as the ruining me in a pecuniary way has long been, with success, resorted to (of which I shall have occasion to hint at one or two more instances before I conclude yet, I have a few more words to add upon the above business which are not altogether unimportant, as they will tend to corroborate the opinion already expressed of the motives of my persecutors.

"On the day appointed to give bail to the sheriff I attended with two of my tenants as my securities, whom I had fixed upon as they were the fathers of two of my domestic servants. One of them had a freehold worth a profit rent of £25 per annum for his life, the other one of £15, also for his life. I confess I imagined these were sufficient securities for a debt of £40. I was mistaken. The sheriff said he did not know them (he knew me, however, very well) and he must take care of himself, the men replied that he ought to know them, for he himself had registered their freeholds, and if he would look at his books he would be convinced. No, that would not do, I must get somebody else. I accordingly sent for my friend the Quaker, the sheriff having also refused the security of an officer settled in Dungannon, a man of the most honourable character (but in that town unfortunately of a most independent mind). I very well knew that though my friend would willingly pay the money, if necessary, yet that he did not like entering into any legal disputes. However, as there was no alternative but my going to jail, he signed the bail bond for which the sheriff, or rather under-sheriff, thought proper to demand two guineas, which I paid him. I had before, as may readily be believed, satisfied his jailor. I leave it in the hands of the under-sheriff's superiors to examine into that. I shall now finish this detail by stating that the two bailiffs, all their assistants, and the under-sheriff, were Orangemen. The latter, indeed, is in a high office amongst them, I learn, Grand Secretary."

Mr. Wilson continues—Though I think I might rest my declarations upon what I have already stated, yet I will take leave to detain the reader a little longer by acquainting him with our mode of hearing cases and deciding upon them at our solemn sessions meetings. Before I begin this part of my narrative, I am to entreat the reader to be assured that I do not mean to make reflections upon the private honour of our magistrates or to throw out a hint that they may not be, as far as I know excellent husbands, fathers, &c., and faithful stewards to their masters, but this I cannot help thinking, that gentlemen, however mentally endowed or independent they may be in their fortunes, who accept of the office of a steward and have large estates to manage are not the properest persons, if only for that reason, to regulate (at such times as these particularly) the policy of the country, and it is a certain truth that there is not one magistrate within several miles of my house, with the exception of my Lord Northland (now I have been dismissed), who is not either the steward of some absent possessor of an estate, a practising attorney, or retailing shopkeeper, and that every man of them, as far as I can learn, are at the head of, or belonging to, yeomen corps and Orange parties.

The author then proceeds to detail the particulars of a correspondence which took place between himself and Lord Northland, in reference to a court tial issued by Mr. Wilson against a celebrated Orangeman, who had been guilty of a disgraceful crime, which was one of a long calendar of similar offences. Lord Northland used the significant expression, on learning of the incarceration of his brother, that "he (Mr. Wilson) would never have it in his power to imprison a man again." His Lordship indirectly denied the charge of having used the expression, and to prove that he did use it, Mr. Wilson produced numerous affidavits, which placed the matter all but beyond doubt. He next narrates the usual course of procedure by the Orange magistracy sitting in Petty Sessions, when a case in which an Orangeman and a Catholic were opposed to each other. The Catholic was invariably a perjurer and a ruffian, and the Orangeman a model of truth and magnanimity.

"What! would you believe what that rascal would say? I never saw such an ill-looking dog in my life," were the phrases he has heard addressed to Roman Catholic witnesses. In short, from his narrative it would appear that inside, as well as outside the Courts of Justice the Catholic was by the Orangeman regarded as an outlaw, beyond the pale of the law, and deserving no protection from it.

I am tempted to apologise to the reader for having thus so extensively quoted from this pamphlet. The interesting statements it contains, and the hope of not having them altogether lost to history, is, I think, an ample excuse. Mr. Wilson concludes:—

"I shall now conclude with showing that the hostility of the Orangemen to me did not altogether arise from my falling out with Mr. Verner (I beg his pardon, Colonel Verner), and protection of the Papists. It had, if possible, a more irreconcilable ground, powerful as these others would have been. I refused becoming a member of their body! This I am the rather led to trouble the reader with a mention of, as some pains have been taken (amongst other equally true motives which have been assigned for the line of conduct I have pursued since my residence in Ireland, such as disappointment, a desire of becoming the head of a party, &c.) to account for my resentment against them, because they refused to admit me amongst them. Before I enter upon this part of my subject I must take leave to set the repectable part of the Orangemen right with regard to my sentiments of them. I am, therefore, to observe that Orangemen who act up to the principles which were assigned for their original institution have my most unqualified respect and approbation. but when I see those principles degenerating into party, and the institution made a plea for cruelty, injustice, and oppression: when I see a set of narrow-minded men, of mean extraction and vulgar manners, without education or any one qualification to entitle them to distinction, save what the strange caprice of fortune has bestowed upon them, when I say I see such men misleading the Government for the purpose of ingratiating themselves with it, affecting to take a lead encouraging a spirit of discord amongst the lower classes under the pretext of loyalty, harrassing, persecuting four-fifths of the population of the country, and not only paralysing its great physical strength but as it were forcing it into a rebellion as its last refuge for preservation—then, indeed, to such Orangemen am I a professed and irreconcilable opponent. I am now to show the reader how well founded the charge of the Orangemen is of their having refused to admit me into their society. A rev gentleman, who is at the head of the Northern Orange district—I really forget the title which distinguishes his office—but we will call it president, having heard me frequently mention acts of atrocity committed in my neighbourhood by men who described themselves as Orangemen, wished to give me an opportunity of judging of the respectability of that body by dining with him at the next general meeting in Dungannon. To this invitation I very readily acceded, and accordingly attended him at the next quarterly Orange dinner. With the exception of the rev. gentleman himself, the secretary (the person before mentioned as the present under Sheriff of Tyrone), and one other person, I never had even seen any of the company. After the cloth was removed and the usual toasts were drunk, a gentleman at the lower end of the table rose up and in the name of the company begged leave to return the president thanks for his having introduced Mr Wilson to the meeting which would be proud to receive Mr. Wilson amongst them as a member, and, therefore, hoped he (Mr. Wilson) would permit him to propose him as such, persuaded that then there would not be one dissentient voice. I confess I was a good deal startled at this address, for it was entirely unexpected. However, 1 recollected myself sufficiently to reply to the following purport that I felt much

honoured by the mark of respect intended me. I was, however, obliged to decline availing myself of it as I had, for reasons which it was not then necessary to explain, formed a determination never to enter into any party or political association whatever. After some expressions of regret on the part of the proposer and a hope that I might be induced at a future period to break through my resolution from a more intricate knowledge of the national benefits arising from the Orange institution, the rev. president observed that he would expect to see me at their next dinner, of which he would give me timely notice how the matter rested. The rev president, however, did not remind me of his invitation. I trust the reader is satisfied that my hostility to the Orange system did not arise from having been refused the honour of becoming one of its members. I must say a word or two about the rev. gentleman whose guest I had been at the Orange dinner. Our acquaintance commenced at the houses of two of the most particular friends I had in Ireland. The rev. gentleman was good enough to honour me with some marks of distinction; he even invited himself to partake of my humble hospitalities, yet at the very moment of friendly intercourse this rev. gentleman, forgetful of the duties imposed upon him not only by his present but former profession, descended to become the associate in calumniating me with one of the most despicable reptiles that ever disgraced the clerical function! Of the former rev gentleman I will say no more. My affectionate regard for those persons through whom I became acquainted with him withholds further allusion to the rancour, duplicity, and dereliction of honour which he has exhibited in his persecution of me Or the reptile it would, indeed, have been a degradation to have noticed him at all. His wretched phillipic I should have disdained to notice, had it not been calculated (and unhappily but too well succeeded) to ruin an unfortunate person and three children whom humanity, honour, religion and morality ought to have taught him to pity and protect.

"It is now necessary for me to wind up my narrative. I cannot, however, conclude it without slightly adverting to some other instances of outrages committed against the Roman Catholics by the Orangemen, which these wretched victims of oppression dared not apply to the laws for redress of. O'Neill (the man who was the cause of my correspondence with Messrs Elliot and Ponsonby), was lately attacked on a market day in the streets of Dungannon by a party of Orangemen, who beat him almost to death. I understand that they thought they had killed him. The person who informed me of this cowardly attack was himself an Orangeman but not one of the assailants. He also confessed that O'Neill had not given any sort of offence then to the party—the beating had been long promised him, and he was well off in escaping with his Life. I have reason to believe that O'Neill has not dared to apply for redress, experience having shown him that legal interference only increased his calamities. A young man who formerly lived in my service (and lately returned to it), was in the course of last Summer overtaken by a party of Orangemen as he was returning home to his father's. They asked if he had not lived with that rascal, Papist Wilson. He replied he had, and was idiot enough to speak of me in terms of respect The consequence was that they fell upon him, and had not some people appeared at a short distance, there is little reason to doubt of his sharing the fate of his brother Catholics, who were but shortly before murdered at Caledon. Since I left the country I have heard that a tumultuous assembly of Orangemen, on the 5th inst., had endeavoured to provoke the Roman Catholics to some act of violence by insult and invective, but as this proceeding was described to have happened in a neighbourhood which, on O'Neill's memorable trial in Armagh, appeared to be a quiet and respectable one, through the conciliating manners and undeviating exertions of Colonel Verner and his sons to prevent all party disputes and distinctions, I am apt to think that my information is erroneous. However, I do know that, notwithstanding the efforts of that truly patriotic and conciliating gentleman, yet a most scandalous outrage was committed since O'Neill's trial by some of his Orange friends, who destroyed a part of the chapel of Dr. Conwell, situated in his vicinity.

" It is a matter of some consolation to me, though a very melancholy one, to find that others feel themselves warranted to speak not only hardly of Orangemen in their private capacities, but also in their judicial ones. A learned gentleman lately accounted for the acquittal of an Orangeman (who had been proved to be a most abandoned villain as well as robber) through his being acknowledged by an Orangeman to be an Orangeman, and from his having the good fortune to be tried by a jury of twelve Orangemen ' I myself was a witness of a similar instance where a set of Orangemen were acquitted of a most

wanton assault upon a Roman Catholic, they afterwards, through a direct perjury, had the unfortunate injured party put upon his trial when, by a dexterous manœuvre in getting an Orange friend upon the jury, they absolutely convicted the unhappy real sufferer. His punishment, indeed, was not very severe, from the circumstance, I am thoroughly convinced, of there being two Orangemen implicated with him in his supposed transgression.

" I must mention one more proof of the impunity with which Orangemen or Yeomen may commit the most atrocious offences. A poor man in the parish of Killyman was nearly murdered and robbed of a three-guinea note by one of these villians. I took the man's examinations. He said he could only know the thief by his voice, as it was dark, but that he had no doubt of his being the person who abused and robbed him. However, he, a few days after, was thoroughly convinced by the thief himself who came to his cottage whilst he lay without hopes of life, and told him that if he offered to swear against him he would finish the work he had begun and murder him outright. The man was too ill to go to the ensuing assizes. In the meantime the robber entered in the artillery corps of Charlemont, and was sent of to Dublin.

" I will not exhaust the patience or irritate the feelings of the reader with but very few instances more of the vindictiveness of my, as well as the Roman Catholic persecutors

"I must mention one instance more of the candour and liberality which the directors of the Dungannon newspaper exhibited against me. It was stated in this print that Dr Conwell was making a collection to support me for my exertions in favour of the Roman Catholics. As I have not seen that gentleman for at least these eight months, nor have had any sort of communication with him on any subject relative to Catholic persecution, I cannot pretend to say what steps he may have pursued towards enabling me to bear up under the calamities I have subjected myself to through my endeavours to prevent it That rev. gentleman is now called upon by me to prove or disprove the following statement In consequence of the various expenses I had been vexatiously harassed with, I certainly did apply to Dr. Conwell and three or four other persons of respectability to borrow for me a few hundred pounds on the most unquestionable security only. I made my application to him particularly and his friends, having reason to know that in consequence of the prominent part I had taken n the Catholic cause I had no chance whatever of obtaining a loan through a Protestant channel. I will do Dr. Conwell the justice to acknowledge that I have reason to believe that he used his endeavours to procure me the loan. That he failed I had fatal experience to know. This circumstance, which I certainly took no pains to conceal, gave occasion to the Orange directors of the Dungannon paper to distort it in the manner above recited. In alluding to a false representation, I feel myself called upon to relate a true one.

"A short time after Dr. Conwell's disappointment to assist me, one of my own tenants sent me a message that he wished to speak to me on particular business. When the man came into the room he drew out of his pocket a canvass bag as it appeared to me(and as it really was) filled with money and notes, he said that the poor people in the country hearing of my difficulties and late disappointment, had made a collection amongst themselves to extricate me from the distress my protection of them had occasioned me, that the persons who had been entrusted with collecting the money were without, and requested permission to see me. This unequivocal proof of gratitude and generosity for some moments deprived me of utterance. When I had recollected myself sufficiently, I desired the man to take up the money and restore it immediately to the generous owners, and at the same time, assure them how very sensible I was of their kindness ; that it was true I had solicited and really did want a loan, but never thought of extricating myself by any other means. That as to my seeing his friends, I must be excused, as also from a knowledge of the persons who had contributed to the intended gift, I could not answer for my impartiality in case any of them should hereafter be brought before me in my character as a magistrate, when I recollected their generous and grateful dispositions towards me. I need make no observations upon the true character of the people, who could feel and act under all their oppressions and poverty as these men did, but it would not be unwise, I conceive, to give them a more enlarged field for a display of their natural benevolence and generosity.

" I must here add that though I did not not receive any assistance to defend myself against Orange prosecutions, yet it is a well-known fact that a man of the name of George actually pervaded the whole country to collect money amongst his Orange brethren to enable them to carry on a suit against me for having assaulted and abused five hundred of them (though unarmed even with a stick, and entirely unsupported) at a preceding Orange procession. Mr. Pettigrew, an attorney and magistrate, (as the case might be) actually served me with a subpœna on this charge, and it still hangs over me. This is the outrage I stated in one of my letters to Mr. Elliot to have been committed upon me in consequence of my endeavours to prevent these Orange gentlemen from persevering in the insults which in the early part of the day they had directed against the Roman Catholics, lest a riot might be the issue.

" "I shall now finish my narrative with observing that the late attempt to murder me, and the Duke of Richmond's resolution not to afford me any protection but such as I could obtain from my persecutors, determined me to abandon my place to enable me to remove and discharge my pecuniary engagements. I advertised a sale of my effects, but such was the virulence of the party that my advertisements was pulled down as soon as they appeared.The consequence was that few people attended the sale, and those who did attend took care that nothing should be sold ; two gentlemen only purchasing some trifling matters at a fair price. The auctioneer gave notice that on a future day he would distribute regular catalogues; but this man (for what cause I don't pretend to say) never after came near me. The consequence was that I was obliged to set off, and leave my property under the care of my gallant and faithful Orangeman (who I know will honourably discharge the trust I have reposed in him) to sell it upon certain terms of credit to such people as might be induced to become purchasers through that inducement. I have not heard, however, that even upon that condition he has disposed of anything. I should not have alluded to a matter so uninteresting to the public but for the purpose of showing that every means are resorted to for he purpose of ruining me, the public's unvariably faithful

"RICHARD WILSON.

" Dublin, December 19, 1807 "

To comment upon such statements coming from such a quarter is unnecessary. Mr. Wilson speaks chiefly of the district of Verner's Bridge, Dungannon, and Killyman. Allowing for the fact that in this locality the notorious leaders of Orangeism resided, we have sufficient in the narrative to show that the country elsewhere, where Orangeism prevailed, was in a like state of lawlessness, and that " Protestant Ascendancy" had for its effects the fostering of crime, and the encouragement of pillage, robbery, andmurder.

CHAPTER XXIII.—"NO POPERY."

It was over the notorious veto question and the Catholic claims which called it into existence that the "No Popery" cry became the watchword of the Orange party. The No Popery administration of the Duke of Richmond was in power; No Popery had placed them in office, and No Popery kept them there. During the previous administrations of the Earl of Hardwicke and the Duke of Bedford, if ascendancy in its most violent forms were not practically discouraged, a spirit of toleration had set in which found many adherents. It is not easy to ascertain actually the cause, but it is more than probable it was the result of disgust created by the systematic ruffianism of the Orange yeomanry, who, now let loose upon the community, their occupation gone, too lazy to work, and unwilling to beg, exercised unexampled despotism over the defenceless Catholics. This, too, so paralysed trade that those with a stake in the country felt its injurious effects. The desolation which followed the triumph of Ascendancy in its early career was a natural check to ferocity. The hewers of wood and drawers of water being exterminated or driven from the land, those who had hitherto been taught to consider themselves the equals of men of substance were little inclined to do the drudgery. The expulsion of the enemy was as with the Egyptians of old, but a waste of substance, bringing innumerable and unexpected difficulties in its train. Plowden says that the destroying bands did not choose to hold and cultivate the lands as the former tenants had done, but if any of them took farms they claimed the reduction of half, and frequently two-thirds, of the former rents as the price of their meritorious devastation. The consequence was a partial discouragement of Orangeism by those who did not reap an immediate benefit from its monopoly. This was the first sign of that breach to-day widened into a broad gulf between genuine, respectable Protestantism and Orangeism. The Catholics, who had for some time previous been discussing in private and brooding in silence over their wrongs, now came forth in the light of day and began that remarkable agitation which ended, as we all know, in their emancipation. Many of nature's noblemen who had fought in the vanguard of the people, in the debased assembly of the Irish House of Commons during its latter years, and in the equally corrupt Imperial Parliament,

had now gone over to the majority or had become grey in the service of their country. A guiding spirit was wanted; some man equal in genius to those who had gone before, but possessing more invincibility of purpose, more scornful indifference to English opinion, more perseverance, and in whom were allied the highest mental powers with the greatest capacity for physical endurance. Young O'Connell leaped forward to the helm. In him the necessity of the time found its man. The question of Emancipation then became a tangible thing. In proportion as the Catholics felt their growing strength, so was it dreaded by their enemies, who then were with few, if any, exceptions, the Orangemen.[*] Intolerance now concentrated itself in "those deep and pestiferous dunghills in which the serpent's eggs were hatched undisturbed."[*] So much undeniable truth had lately been brought before the public concerning the Orange Institution, and so glaring was the illegality and mischief of the system, that it had now become fashionable even for the Orange aristocracy to disown the organisation, to affect to disclaim everything objectionable in the system, and while winking at it with both eyes, to throw all that was blameable in it upon the incorrigible ignorance and bigotry of the rabble. While disclaiming it they did not fail, however, to foster it in private. Some honest men in office were outspoken enough to condemn it. Baron Fletcher, in his charge to a jury in a case where William Todd Jones (who had been arrested at the instance of the Orangemen under the Earl of Hardwicke's Administration) was plaintiff, used these remarkable words:—"I cannot entertain the disrespectful idea, in viewing the whole process of Mr. Jones's arrest and confinement, that any *Government of Ireland* could have known of or countenanced such an imprisonment. I take it for granted that Mr. Jones was arrested under the very unhappy ferment of the hour in Dublin at the vulgar instance of some secretary's secretary's secretary, some understrapper's understrapper's understrapper, who, *in a drunken paroxysm of party* or personal spleen, signed an order for Mr. Jones's committal, which, when sober, he forgot having done, and never afterwards recollected till Mr. Jones's printed letter to Mr. Wickham entreating for trial refreshed his memory, and informed him where he lay." This was aimed directly at the

* Plowden's Ten Years History, vol, iii., page 749,

Orange clique of the Castle then in power. For Jones had in 1802 fought a duel with the noted Orange historian, Sir Wm. Musgrave, and proved himself too formidable an opponent to be at large.

With the advent of the Richmond Administration the Institution received new life and vigour, and with foresight not unjustly described as duplicity the exterminatory programme was softened into perpetual warfare; "massacre and conflagration lowered to proscription and oppression, and the whole lacquered over with the treasonable varnish of conditional allegiance." In England many of these regiments which had been largely augmented by the Irish Orangemen during the period of the rebellion were now quartered, and under the old warrants of the Irish Grand Lodge they continued to hold their meetings. Regiments received civilians into their lodges, and these regiments left on their removal to other towns the seeds of Orangeism behind, which ultimately gave rise to the English establishment. Lodges were held amongst the milling population of Lancashire during the year 1807, and in the latter portion of that year a County Grand Lodge was formed in Manchester, with Colonel Samuel Taylor of Moston as Grand Master.* The idea was then entertained of forming a Grand Orange Lodge for England, a circular letter having been received from an Orange Lodge in London (the only one then in existence there) suggesting the same, and requesting delegates to be appointed for the purpose of proceeding to London to consider of its advisability. Mr. James Lever, Bolton (le Moors), and Mr. R. Nixon, Manchester, were nominated, and the result is thus described by the latter gentleman—"On our arrival in London we were disappointed to find the society neither so numerous nor quite so respectable as we anticipated, or as the nature of such establishment requires we, therefore, deemed it prudent to withhold our countenance to the measure, and the meeting dissolved without adopting anything whatever towards the plan." From this and a subsequent letter we find that the Irish Grand Lodge, though in the words of Mr. Verner it had "almost ceased to exist," had practically set their face against the establishment of

* Mr. Nixon, secretary, writing from Manchester, on September 3, 1808, to John Verner, Esq., says:—"I beg respectfully to direct your attention to my letter of the 2nd of December, wherein I apprised you of the establishment of a County Lodge, which establishment you were pleased to approve of in a subsequent letter to Colonel Taylor."

the Grand Lodge in Manchester, fearful, no doubt, of finding in it a rival for patronage. The English brethren persisted, established their Grand Lodge, and in the year 1808 set actively to work, calling in all the old Irish warrants, and granting new English warrants in their place. The systems, both as regards the lectures, the signs and passwords, were the same, and no practical difference existed in the rules, which were mostly based upon those of the parent institution. From the correspondence appended to the English report, it appears that their first work was to set the regimental lodges on a firm footing, this being a branch of the Institution in which the leaders, even from the outset, evinced a peculiar and abiding interest. A strong condemnation of the Orange system, as applied to the army was contained in the General Orders of General Cockburne in 1810 to the brigade then quartered at Chelmsford, in which the officers of all regiments were directed "to confine any man who dared to wear any ribband or emblem which might create dispute amongst the men." "It must be evident," the order continues, "that this order applies chiefly to the Irish soldiers. The mischief which all such party divisions occasion to the state is unfortunately too severely felt in Ireland; nothing of the kind can be allowed here. Soldiers have no concern with such matters. They should serve his Majesty and their country with unanimity, which it is impossible for them to do if the spirit of party be allowed in a battalion." The 11th Infantry, amongst whom were a large number of Orangemen, recruited from Ireland, formed part of this brigade. Notwithstanding this order, and many subsequent orders of a like nature, the Loyal Orange party continued to increase and multiply in regiments, much to the inefficiency of his Majesty's forces.

The Catholic question, under the influence, now not yet under the guidance of O'Connell, was now making itself felt, and only in the Orange Societies did it receive anything like strong opposition. Actuated by honest motives, Lord Grenville in the House of Lords and Mr. Grattan in the House of Commons, in moving the reception of a petition from the Catholics of Ireland, gave grounds for the supposition that emancipation would be acceptable even on condition that the King had a veto upon the appointment of Irish bishops. O'Connell saw plainly that the enemies of Catholicism were not likely to appoint as bishop those best fitted to be its directors, and that the purity of religion would not alone.

le thus tampered with, but that in the compromise Ireland would lose the most patriotis advocates of their cause. He saw more. He descerned an u'timate abandonment of that Catholic creed in substituting for Papal supremacy the supremacy of an English king. While the English Catholics, represented by their Board, were willing to purchase concession at almost any cost, the Irish Catholics, labouring under far heavier penal restrictions, decidedly refused to purchase concession at such a price. The proposition was received with general indignation. That it was a cunning device to effect in Ireland what the sword could not accomplish there was no doubt. In the meantime the Orange associations were busy in opposition. While the Catholic bishops were assembled to oppose the veto the Orange Association deputies, with a representation by delegates from seventy-two English lodges, assembled on the 15th September, 1808, in Dawson Street, to consider what steps should be taken against "the alarming growth of Popery." The business was conducted with closed doors, but Plowden, who gives the names of the leaders present and particulars of the proceedings, says that expressions were used by Mr. Giffard to the effect, that he so fondly anticipated the distructive powers of the Royal Veto upon Catholic purity, that he would be the first freeman of Dublin to propose Emancipation upon such terms. To the confusion of Orangemen the proposal was refused and the Veto question for ever put at rest. That the important change from the extirpatory programme was made at this meeting, Mr. Plowden seems convinced, and he is so far borne out in his assumption by the evidence of the Rev. Mortimer O'Sullivan, when before the Committee of Inquiry, who admitted that about the year 1810 the oath of conditional loyalty was done away with. Plowden asserts that refusal to take the new oath was the cause of many being expelled the society, and, amongst the historical documents which he alludes to as proving this statement, he refers to a cancelled Orange certificate of June 29, 1809, which he himself saw as evidence of expulsion for such refusal.

In the Corporation of Dublin we find the most remarkable evidence of growing liberality. In 1810 a petition against the Catholic claims was negatived by a majority of five, and but a few months afterwards we find them petitioning Parliament for a Repeal of the Union. Such rapid progress spread dismay amongst the Orange body,

more particularly as they saw they broad-minded, intelligent Protestants of the country joining in the Catholic movement. Some of the most prudent and least factious brethren saw even at this early stage of the agitation the necessity of accepting the inevitable. The Veto question was violently opposed by the Catholics. Opposed to all things Catholic a portion of the Orange party thought it wise to favour it, and urged the Government to grant redress of grievances to the Catholics on the lines laid down by Lord Grenville. At a county meeting in Tyrone, held at Omagh, and called on the requisition of Earl Belmore and other leaders of the Orange party, resolutions were passed to this effect. These declarations were received by the general public as signs of returning sanity, but Mr. Plowden, writing a few years afterwards, refused to give that credit to the promoters which the public had awarded. He seems to see beneath it the hand of Mr. Giffard, the Orange leader, who, on his own alleged statement, hoped for the total destruction of Catholicism.

In the ranks of the Yeomanry the "No Popery" cry enlisted the great body of sympathisers. The large majority sworn Orangemen, every man of them with Government arms in their hands, they were not inclined to look on peaceably at the Government granting, even if it were never so well disposed, any measure of equity to the Irish Catholics. The doctrines they had learned had taught them to consider not alone equal laws, but a relaxation of penal restrictions on the Catholics as aimed directly at their downfall, and in their action we find the first glaring example of conditional loyalty, of how little they regarded loyalty even to the House of Brunswick, when their immediate interests were only apparently in jeopardy. The instances are innumerable in which we find the yeomanry not alone in mutiny against their officers, but in which they actually threw down their arms and deserted that loyal cause to which they proclaimed themselves so much attached, rather than parade beside a few Catholics of loyalty much less questionable than theirs. The first remarkable instance of this kind occurred at Bandon, where the whole body of Yeomanry, amounting to 600, on the 6th July, 1800, mutinied. His Grace the Duke of Richmond was about making a viceregal tour through Munster, and it seems to be thought on some sides that an order had gone forth to discourage Orange displays as much as possible in the ranks of the Yeomanry. The Bandon Yeomanry were in the habit of making

8

great demonstration on the 1st July, and Brigade-Major Auriol, with the officers, thought fit to curb this offensive display as much as possible, ordering the parade to take place on the 6th. Fearful of fatal consequences, Captain Kingston, however, paraded them on the 1st July. "in order to gratify them in moderation, knowing that they would have assembled without orders otherwise. They paraded were permitted to fire a *feu de joie*, and proceeded to march, decked with orange lillies through the town. The officer, "expecting there would be some disturbance and insult offered to the Catholic inhabitants,' got before them and gave the order to dismiss. This they refused to do, but at the moment Lord. Bandon came upon the scene, addressed them upon their want of loyalty, and the necessity of putting an end to such foolish demonstrations, and succeeded in dismissing them. That night a shot (a musket ball) was fired into the room of Capt. Kingston, from which a lady, who slept in it narrowly escaped with her life. For the discovery of the offender a reward of £586, subscribed by the officers and the principal inhabitants, was offered. The attempt to discover the ringleaders in the breach of military discipline was resisted, as also the attempt to bring the would-be murderer to justice. "In order to show their defiance" (the words are those of Lord Bandon), "they all wore orange lilies on parade on the 6th." On seeing this further breach of discipline, their commanding officer lectured them upon the impropriety of it; said such conduct was not becoming to loyal men, and told them either to take the orange badges out of their caps or throw down their arms. *They threw down their arms.* The only punishment that followed this act of mutiny, which under existing statutes was a felony, was that the Bandon Yeomany were disbanded. But they were within a year afterwards reorganised. One William Roberts, an Orange Yeoman, lodged a complaint against Colonel Auriol with the Commander-in-Chief of the Forces in Ireland, which had no other result but to give to the world Lord Bandon's opinions of the want of loyalty of these same Yeomanry. The conduct of Captain Connor, of the Ballyaueen Yeomanry, and a violent Orangeman, in refusing to pay Colonel Auriol the salutation due to his position, was also the occasion of the latter contributing some interesting correspondence which shows the disorganisation and bigotry of the Yeomanry at that period.*

A similar instance of the results of the "No Popery" cry upon military discipline was found in September, 1810, in the County Down, when—on the 12th of that month the Bann and Upper Iveagh Corps, in the latter of which there were six Catholics — the Upper Iveagh men conspired with the Bann men to refuse to parade, believing that by this means they could get the six Catholics dismissed. On the official report of Brigade-Major Wallace we find that the meeting was a most violent one, and that almost all the infantry, together with the cavalry, laid down their arms, leaving alone the six battalions who ultimately retired from the field. "Every argument," says Brigade-Major Wallace in his report, "was used by Captain Reilly and myself, and also by several gentlemen present, to convince the men of the enormity of such behaviour, as an armed body, and the fatal consequences to the public service, as well as the great illeberality and impolicy of entertaining such sentiments and feelings for our Catholic fellow-subjects; that great part of the army and navy was composed of such men; that his Majesty was pleased to accept and authorise the services of all his loyal subjects; and that it was their bounden duty to yield implicit obedience. At length, after much advice and, I may add, entreaty from me that they would reflect on their disgraceful behaviour and atone for it in some degree by an immediate return to a state of order, they complied at my request (as they said), resumed their arms, and mounted their horses. Some, however, seemed to retain their prejudices and wished to make stipulations not to parade with the Catholics. Captain Reilly would not pledge himself to any such terms thinking them unreasonable with his duty and opinion, and that he would not wish to command men *who would hesitate to do their duty* by co-operating with their fellow-subjects in defence of their King and country." One man was dismissed. No further punishment followed. A similar instance occurred in the Moira corps under the command of Mr. W. S. Crawford, M.P.

In the case of the King at the prosecution of

---

* In the narration of the above circumstance Plowden has fallen into a few errors, but such as were only natural, seeing that he had not the official correspondence before him. It is well to state this fact, however, since he attributes most of he blame to the officers for opposing the demonstration. The fault lay with the men, since, from the above, they were allowed to demonstrate "in moderation," which fact Plowden does not admit. It is right to say that this author takes Roberts' side, and says it is no wonder the yeomanry did not believe in Colonel Auriol's anxiety on the part of the Government to put down Orangeism, which had been encouraged the previous year. He looks upon it as a bait thrown out to catch the Catholics, and that it took. "Long privation is apt to engender voracious credulity."

Butler *v.* Howard (a yeoman), for murder tried at the Kilkenny Assizes in 1810, Mr. Burrows, counsel for the prosecution, elicited from one of the witnesses, also a yeoman, that by the nature of the oath he had taken he felt himself absolved from his allegiance should the King grant emancipation to the Catholics. Counsel asserted, in open court, that such an oath was treasonable, and challenged the judge and Crown counsel to deny it. Both were silent.

In the County Fermanagh, at Derragonally, on the 11th July, 1811, an instance occurred which helps to illustrate, amongst other things, the use to which the arms of the yeomanry were turned by the Orangemen. A riot occurred, in which sticks were used freely. The Catholics had the best of it. Beaten at the sticks, the Orange yeomanry retreated for their guns and fired upon the people, "which was the common way of concluding the fights in those days." One, Denis Murvounage, was killed, and the father of the deceased went from magistrate to magistrate without avail seeking for some one to take the necessary depositions. All refused, and Kitson, the man charged, escaped to America. Justice was so completely defeated that at the ensuing Assizes Justice Osborne gave the magistrates, one and all, a severe reprimand, and ordered them to make what little reparation lay in their power by then taking the depositions. The rioters on the occasion were tried by an exclusively Orange jury; all the Catholics were convicted; all the Orangemen acquitted. When Kitson returned to the country the Grand Jury found a true bill. He was also acquitted.

"There were many Catholics and many Orangemen tried? Yes.

"The jury was exclusively Orange and Protestant? Yes; and the Catholics were convicted and the Orangemen acquitted.

"Kitson was acquitted though he had absconded? Yes; he had absconded. I thought I would try the conduct of the magistrates, and I sent the father of deceased from magistrate to magistrate until everyone of them had refused.

"What is your observation generally as to the administration of justice? *In all cases, civil and criminal, between Protestant and Catholic justice is positively denied to the Catholic.*"*

* See Mr. Kernan's evidence before the Select Committee of 1855 (page 75, question 7313), in which the facts are recorded. He says it was a constant practice with the Orangemen to lodge their arms in some convenient place in order to be prepared for such emergencies.

We have more than one instance recorded in which the Yeomanry absolutely refused to obey the orders of their superior officers where the latter had signed petitions in favour of Catholic emancipation. The most notorious is that in which the Yeomen of Armagh threw down their arms and refused to serve unless Lieutenant Burns were dismissed for having signed such a petition. The men who had thus offended were dismissed by Lieutenant-General Mackenzie, and the remainder of the corps reassembled. In an historical memoir of the City of Armagh, written by James Stuart, an Orangeman, we find it stated "The corps was reassembled, and the officers used every argument which *prudence* and *loyalty* could have suggested to bring the malcontents to a due sense of their misconduct. Every effort proved abortive." The greater part of the privates made common cause with their brethren, and the corps was disbanded.

But the ramifications of Orangeism extended beyond the yeomanry at this period. They cannot be better described than by an extract from the evidence of Mr. R. Kernan, a barrister of note, who had wide experience of the administration of justice in the times we are dealing with and for a long period subsequently.

Commencing at question 7213, in vol. 3 of the Report of the Select Committee of 1835, we find the following :—

What has been the effect of the society, as to the administration of public justice? I think it has injured it very materially.

Have the goodness to state how the administration of public justice is affected by the existence of the system? In the first place, the returning officer at the assizes and sessions, the high sheriff generally, and sub-sheriff always, are both Orangemen, and I conceive that for the last 30 years to the best of my recollection, there has been no jury (in Fermanagh at least) consisting of other persons than Orangemen; I think the administration of justice has been most materially injured in that respect; and the reason I think so, because the verdicts were generally in all cases between Orangemen and Catholics contrary to the judge's charges as well as contrary to the evidence; that is my impression, and I can state several cases in proof of the fact.

Do you recollect any instance in which the judge expressed his disapprobation of the verdict I do.

Will you state it? I recollect the case of the King against Hall, an indictment preferred by the parish priest of the town of Enniskillen against the prisoner Hall, for breaking and entering the chapel, and taking thereout the vestments and carrying them away, this case was tried before Mr. Justice Fletcher.

About what time? I think in 1810 or 1811; the evidence given to sustain the indictment was very short, and therefore I shall mention it briefly. It was given by the provost of the town of Enniskillen, William Stewart, Esq, he is deceased; the evidence consisted of the admission and confession of the charge by the prisoner to the provost and another person.

Was the provost a magistrate? He was *virtute officii*; the judge I recollect told the jury that they had nothing to try; that the prisoner's admission and confession as aforesaid, was sufficient in point of law to warrant his conviction, the issue was sent up to the jury; the prisoner was called upon for his defence, but declined to examine witnesses; he gave no evidence whatever. In a few minutes afterwards, the jury returned a verdict of "Not Guilty," the judge expressed great disapprobation. He said he *thanked God it was their verdict and not his*, and he then turned round and said—"Gentlemen, I will not treat you in this case as my highly esteemed departed friend Judge Fox treated a jury of this country, I will not placard your names on the session house or grand jury room door, you shall not have an opportunity of dragging me before Parliament, but I will immediately order the sheriff to discharge you from doing any further duty at these assizes," and they were discharged accordingly by the sub-sheriff; the prisoner was also discharged, and on his going into the street I did not see what followed, but I heard the noise, he was hoisted on the shoulders of Orangemen and carried through the town of Enniskillen in triumph

Was that man, the prisoner, an Orangeman? He was, I recollect he had an orange riband in his breast on the day of his trial, when he was in the dock; that is frequently the case.

You do not think that an uncommon thing in the County of Fermanagh? No; one of the Grand Jurors, Mr D'Arcy, seldom is seen in the grand jury box at Assizes without appearing with orange ribands or lilies, without a bunch of orange riband appended to his watch.

Of what description of persons were the jury composed? Of rather respectable persons.

The question refers to the jury who tried that man? They were respectable men, freeholders of Fermanagh, they are very respectable, highly respectable before these societies were established

I do not think there was a happier set of people in any county than the people of Fermanagh; it is merely that unfortunate fiend of dissension which destroys the peace of the county; there are not better men any where than in that individual district, with the exception of their conduct as members of the Orange Lodge

What was the religious persuasion of the jury? They were all Protestants

Were they deemed Orangemen? I think they were Orangemen.

You have never heard that disputed? I never heard it disputed, and I have seen most of them in procession.

Do you think the verdict would have been different had not the system of Orangeism prevailed, the jury being composed of Orangemen, and this man who was tried being an Orangeman? I cannot doubt it, seeing what the evidence was.

The case was so clear? The case on admission and confession; he brought one of the witnesses to the place, influenced by feeling compunction after he committed the act, he had the vestments dug out of the ground, and by his own particular desire they were handed back to the parish priest, to whom they belong.

The man confessed this guilt? Yes, his admission and confession were the only evidence on the trial

You stated that the man confessed his guilt? Yes; not on his trial, but before the provost, of which the provost gave evidence

It was proven that the vestments he had stolen from the chapel he had restored to the priest to whom the chapel belonged, and whose property of right they were? Yes.

The priest appeared on the trial to identify the property that was stolen, and the provost who was also a magistrate of the County of Fermanagh, gave evidence of previous admission and confession, the evidence was clear and conclusive to such a degree, that the judge told the jury they had nothing to try   Just so.

The jury found a verdict of acquittal in what time? Immediately.

They found a verdict of acquittal under such circumstances for this man? Yes.

That man you say was a reputed Orangeman Yes.

The jury were deemed Orangemen? Certainly.

Had not the jury been Orangemen and the system prevailing, the verdict you say must necessarily have been otherwise Certainly, it must have been so; there could be no other conclusion

You mentioned a case that occurred in 1810; have you had an opportunity of observing the administration of justice since that time? I have had.

Do you think the same feeling which produced a verdict so illegitimate in 1810, has prevailed from that period to the present, and still operates on the administration of justice? Yes; I positively swear it does to that extent from my own knowledge as a professional man, as between Orange and Catholic parties.

You stated that the sheriffs and sub-sheriffs are generally Orangemen? Yes, they have been as long as I can recollect, with a few instances excepted, as referrible to high sheriffs.

Do you mean in all cases, or are there not exceptions where the sheriffs are not Orangemen? Not to my knowledge, there may be exceptions with respect to sub-sheriffs.

You speak of Fermanagh? Yes, and the County of Donegal; there are exceptions in Donegal.

Who is the present high sheriff of Fermanagh? A Mr. Lendrum; he is an Orangeman; the present sub-sheriff of Fermanagh is a Mr. Dean.

Is he a reputed Orangeman? I have not the least doubt of his being one.

Is he violent as such? No, indeed; I never saw him violent, nor heard of his improper conduct; but he is an Orangeman.

Is not Mr. Auchinleck an Orangeman? He is, I think; and he has been an Orangeman for many years past.

Has not he been repeatedly sub-sheriff of that county? Yes, he has been four, or five or six years in succession.

He is deemed an Orangeman? There is no doubt of that.

Do you recollect any sentiments expressed publicly by that Mr. Auchinleck with respect to the composition of juries, how he had acted, and how he would act? I was not present at the meeting, but I have heard and I believe it, that he has made declarations; if they be not evidence I will not state them.

Have the goodness to state them? It was reported in a newspaper published in Enniskillen, in a speech he made.

What were those sentiments? He said in his speech, as reported by Mr. Duffy, and by one of the other papers, that he never would impannel any Catholic on a jury on any occasion whose conscience was in the keeping of his priest; I think that was his expression; and in the last four or

five years that he has been sheriff I do not think that he ever impannelled a single Catholic freeholder.

Are there many Roman Catholics in the County of Fermanagh who would be entitled from their property and condition in life to be upon juries? A great many.

Can you state the relative proportion between the Catholic and the Protestant population? Not very well; there is a majority of Catholics; there are many respectable of both classes, and very competent jurors of juries of each.

Your evidence is that the sheriffs generally speaking were Orangemen, and the sub-sheriffs Orangemen in the County Fermanagh? Yes.

And in many other counties in the North of Ireland to which you go circuit? No doubt.

And yet the result of this was, the composition of juries in your County of Fermanagh is almost exclusively Orange? Yes, I have hardly a recollection of an exception; I have heard of one or two instances.

Have you any recollection of a Catholic being on a jury? Yes, I have only one or two.

Do you mean to say that in your experience as a barrister for nearly 30 years you recollect but one or two Catholics on juries in that county? I do say so, neither in the civil court nor for the Crown court.

Were there any other instances besides that you have mentioned in which the judge reprimanded the jury? I do not know any other; but I can state a very remarkable case tried by Chief Justice Bushe in the County of Tyrone of a verdict given against his charge and against evidence.

Can you state the date? I cannot give the date precisely without referring to my notes; it was about ten years, or from ten to twelve, it was an indictment for murder by the son of the deceased.

Do you recollect the name of the party? I do; the name of the party was M'Cabe; M'Cabe against Robinson and others.

Who was the prosecutor? The son of the deceased, a man residing near Portadown of the name of M'Cabe, I think.

Was he a Roman Catholic? He was.

Were the defendants Orangemen? They were, for it was in the lodge room the conspiracy by the prisoners was hatched.

Where was the trial? It was at Omagh, either the first or second time the judge went that circuit.

Under what circumstances did it appear that M'Cabe had met his death? It appeared in

9

evidence that at the lodge room held near the town of Portadown, the persons who committed the murder proceeded directly from the lodge room to the deceased man's house and perpetrated the act, and killed him.

Who were the persons who committed the murder? One of the men was, I think, Robinson.

Then the case was the King, on the prosecution of M'Cabe, against Robinson and others? Yes.

Have the goodness to state the facts? The prisoners and several other men in the Lodge, it appeared in evidence, proceeded from the lodge room, and went to the deceased M'Cabe's house and there committed the murder; the judge charged the jury very strongly, indeed, for a conviction against the prisoners; the jurors found a verdict of not guilty. Immediately after they returned their verdict I left the court, and soon after the judge sent for me; on receiving the message from the Chief Justice I went and spoke to him, and this has been the reason I am not so accurate in respect of dates or names of the prisoners; he said, in substance, "Kernan, you are the only barrister in court who I have seen taking a full note of this trial." I said I had a full note of, he then said, "Do you intend to publish it?" I said, "Certainly sir, I do," and gave him my reason. He said, "Kernan, my dear fellow, do you think its publication would tend to pacify the country and establish peace in this country to have this made public?" Said I, "I cannot tell that, but it is at present the chief remedy the Catholics have to bring these cases before the public, and expose such outrages; but, however, if you think it would excite a feeling to disturb the peace on the part of the Catholics, I shall submit my opinion to your better judgment, and will not give it publication." I did not give it publication; it was the strongest case of unprovoked homicide I ever recollect in my professional practice.

What do you mean by the strongest case you ever recollect in your professional practice? It was the clearest case for conviction, and the Chief Justice was of the same opinion who recommended me not to publish it.

In the face of such evidence, could any more pregnant reply be given to the following question (4,973) than that of Mr James Sinclair, J.P., D.L., after forty years experience of the magistracy:—

"One of the rules (of the Orange society) is that they will not admit any one into their brotherhood not well known to be capable of persecuting or upbraiding any one on account of his religious opinions? That is ridiculous.'

Or could anything appear to have more evidence of justice than the opinions of Lord Gosford, Mr. Hancock, and others, that if such were their rules their practices were exactly the reverse?

Government had raised a spirit which, if they would, they could not lay. They had to abide the issue. But they had raised more spirits than they had bargained for. The formation of all such illegal and exclusive associations is the sure precurser, not alone in Ireland, but all the world over, to the starting of opposition societies as a counterpoise to their influence. The peasantry, of course, the vast majority Catholic, had borne the yoke too long. The Ribbon lodges now started into existence; and if, in many instances, the r members exercised a wild spirit of revenge, they have at least the palliation due to those who seized in desperation the only means of redress at their command, the use of which in their opinion justified the end.. If among their enemies they spread dismay, they unconsciously spread confusion amongst their friends.

From the evidence of Swan, the secretary of the society, we find that the records of the institution were not forthcoming from the 11th July, 1810, to the 20th November, 1817, and he accounts for the absence of them by saying that perhaps the Grand Lodge was not sitting during those times. The omission is not without some significance, as we find not only that the Grand Lodge did sit during that period, but that they made in the year 1814 a very important alteration in the rules and regulations. Omitting the secret articles, they in the declaration, "We shall not prosecute any one on account of his religion," inserted, "provided the same be not hostile to the State;" and Mr. Swan, when questioned as to whether he thought the Catholic religion hostile to the State, honestly answered, "I do" The oath also underwent a change about the year 1814, the condition to support the King "so long as he would maintain Protestant Ascendancy," being substituted by the phrase, "being Protestant," which, read between the lines, means but one and the same thing—No Popery, even at the sacrifice of loyalty.

The significance of this phrase, "being Protestant," is easily understood when we recollect that it has ever been the custom of Orangemen to put an interpretation upon the term "Protestant" widely differing from that in which it is generally understood. It does not suffice with them to absolutely endorse the Thirty-nine Articles. Nor does even an earnest profession and a steadfast practice of true Protestant principles, entitle one to be considered a Protestant in the eyes of this institution. Luther himself, did he walk the earth in our time, and venture to oppose even the most violent schemes of Orangemen, or indirectly from whatever motive to discourage the Orange Institution, would be pronounced "a Papist" by the members of the society with as little hesitation, and as much confidence in its accuracy, as if the term were being applied to the head of the Holy Roman Empire himself. Prejudice, when cherished in the minds of ignorant men, has oftentimes worked novel inconsistencies. Mr. Wilson, of Dungannon, the generous-hearted English Protestant, was "Papist Wilson;" Mr. Handcock, Lurgan, himself a staunch Protestant, and the representative of a long line of Protestants, was "Papist Handcock;" while Lord Gosford, of whom it may be said that the mantle of the father descended to the son was stripped of his titles and distinctions, and plainly designated "Papist Gosford." In connection with this feature of the subject, a circumstance occurred in the year 1832 which it might be well briefly to anticipate, for the purpose of further illustration. In the prosperous days of the English Orange Institution, a Mr. Chetwoode Eustace Chetwoode was the Grand Secretary of the Institution. He enjoyed the honoured companionship of dukes as Grand Masters, while marquises, earls, lords, and men of high degree swelled the roll of D.G.M.'s. Mr. Chetwoode Eustace Chet-

woode somehow got into disgrace with his brethren. He was not a chicken-hearted Orangeman, but quite the reverse. But his accounts got into disorder. Amongst numerous charges which we find from the report of the Grand Lodge of England were made against him, was a distinct indictment "that Mr. Chetwoode, the late Deputy Grand Secretary, was no true Orangeman, but a Papist," the latter following, of course, as a natural consequence, of the former. The Grand Lodge, of which Field-Marshal H.R.H. Prince Earnest Duke of Cumberland, K.G., &c., &c., was President and Imperial Grand Master, received this charge against their D.G.M. without a smile, and with all earnestness proceeded to investigate it. A Committee of Inquiry was actually appointed to give the matter their consideration, and at a subsequent meeting they reported their decision "that Mr. Chetwoode Eustace Chetwoode be expelled, thinking it "their duty at the same time to state" that they consider no charge had been made out against him as being a Papist." "Being Protestant" was, therefore, a very shaky foundation, upon which Orange loyalty had to rest. When Orangemen could charge their trusted leaders with being Papists it would have required but a very trifling act of conciliation towards his Catholic subjects for a Protestant king to be regarded as a Jesuit in disguise. Loyalty and allegiance were, then scattered to the winds, and we would stand face to face with a tumultuous armed assembly of " No Popery" rebels.

CHAPTER XXIV.—WORDS OF WARNING.

The dark clouds of social disorder, which for so long had hung ominously over Ireland, were now beginning to break. The unlimited sway of faction which prevailed was going down for ever but not without a struggle on the part of ascendancy. The violent efforts which they made at this period to prolong their reign of despotic tyranny called forth public attention, and set inquiring minds to investigate the causes which gave rise to such tumult and frequent outrage. A band of conspiring ruffians, "broken tools which tyrants fling away by myriads," was to be found in every village of the land. Attention was directed in high places to them by men who read aright the writing on the wall, and saw the bane of a country's happiness.

In the House of Commons on the 29th June, 1813, Mr. William Wynne rose pursuant to his notice to bring before the attention of the House the forma-

tion of societies which existed in direct contradiction of the law.* The existence of Orange societies, he said, was directly in opposition to a specific Act of Parliament, 39 George III., cap. 79, which was passed in the year 1799 for the very purpose of putting down societies meeting for political purposes, and bound to each other by oaths and tests. This Act expressly

* A large number of petitions were during this and the previous sessions presented to Parliament praying for the suppression of the Orange societies. In the Dublin Monthly Mag.um for September, 1814, a number of "Belfast resolutions" are published, in which the first is thus worded—"That, as the evils of the Orange system still remains unabated, we will renew our petitions to both Houses of Parliament in the ensuing session." In this year the Duke of Sussex presented petitions in the Lords from a number of Protestant and Catholic inhabitants of Ireland against Orange societies, and they were allowed to lie on the table. In the Commons some members who saw the evils of the system were still more active, but no results followed their activity. The Orange societies were encouraged though declared illegal, while the Catholic Board was suppressed.

mentioned divers societies existing, where unlawful oaths were administered, and where members bound themselves to secrecy and fidelity, and knew one another by signs. It then proceeded to prohibit meetings of these societies, and of all others the members whereof should be required to take an oath, test, or declaration not authorised or required by law, or which should be composed of different divisions acting separately from each other. By this statute those oaths were to be considered unlawful, and severe penalties were to be imposed on persons becoming members of such societies, who, in certain cases, were liable to transportation There was a particular clause omitting the Freemasons from the operations of the Act on condition of them registering themselves with the Clerk of the peace, but that was extended to no other denomination of meeting. It did not matter, he said, what might be the professed objects of the society; if there was a secret oath, and members were bound together by a secret system of signs and pass-words, it was capable of being perverted to the worst purposes. For the first time it was proposed to establish these societies in England, and certainly it was impossible to conceive an institution more ill-timed in itself or more mischievous in its operation. (Hear, hear) In delivering himself of what he had to say upon the question, he wished to divest himself of every feeling that could have the remotest reference to the question of Catholic Emancipation Everyone should see that if these societies were permitted they should give rise to others of a similar character, and thus one part of the country would be arrayed against the other with all the jealousies of political faction and hatred.   He said he was saved from much he had intended to say, by the distribution in the lobby of a pamphlet containing the rules and regulations of the Orange Socie'y At the time when he gave notice he had founded his ob'ections upon another pamphlet, containing an account of the laws and regulations of the Orange Society, and at the end of which it was announced that a smaller and cheaper edition would soon be published. But there was a great difference between the two pamphlets, for the former contained in the oath a condition of allegiance, "only so long as the King should support Protestant ascendancy," and the latter omitted it.   What could be thought of such an oath?   Conditional allegiance!— loyalty depending upon the maintenance of the Protestant ascendancy! terms hitherto unknown in

that country. What construction would necessarily be put upon this oath. Would not every man put his own, and in that case might not everyone consider himself as discharged from his allegiance supposing the Royal assent should be given to a Bill for the relief of the Irish Roman Catholics. Such would infallibly be the case upon weak and extraordinary minds. He next alluded to the oath of the marksman in which the House would recognise no salvo was made for inquiry in a court of justice. Another instance in which the two pamphlets differed occurred in the secretary's oath, for while in the former the oath merely related to keep ing safe the papers belonging to the lodge, &c , in the latter the oath included a declaration that he (the secretary) "would not give any copy of the secret articles of the lodge, &c"   Here, again, was manifestly an illegal oath, as it openly set aside the authority of the law and the power of a court of justice, and avowe l that there *existed further regulations than those now printed and communicated to the public*. He next alluded to the regulations for the establishing of military lodges, in which non-commissioned officers and privates were to meet on a footing of equality. He warned the House to check the evil in its growth, said it was its duty to make further inquiry, remarked that the existing law would be found sufficient to suppress those illegal associations, said if not the hands of the Government should be strengthened to put down this *imperium in imperio*, and concluded by moving "that a committee be appo'nted to inquire into the ex stence of certain illegal societies under the denomination of Orangemen" Mr. Bathurst was prepared to go the length of saying that the Orange societies had rendered themselves amenable to the law as it stood, and that the House might take up the subject as tending to a breach of the principles of the Constitution It was impossible to say to what purpose such societies might be perverted if allowed to proceed. With respect to the army, if such societies were carried into effect one must see from the practices in another country to what dangerous consequences it might lead. As he had no doubt the Orange Societies were amenable to the law, he did not see any occasion for the interference of Parliament. Mr. Stuart Wortley thought the subject was not to be contemplated as a mere breach of the law, which was punishable, but that the principles of the society ought to be condemned with the utmost severity. He was in doubt whether the better mode would not have been to have treated these Orange lodges with silent contempt, and their *intemperance would have soon put an end to their existence.* The same speaker severely censured the proceedings of the Catholic Committee, and pronounced as disgraceful the resolutions of the Catholic bishops respecting the *veto.* Sir Henry Montgomery read a letter, dated 4th June, 1813, from a resident magistrate in Donegal, describing an outrage that had recently taken place at Carrowkeel, arising out of a dispute in which two Orangemen were concerned. The fight, friends on each side joining in, led to the loss of nine valuable lives, which might have been lost in a better cause. He said Donegal had been ever in perfect quiet until the revival of the Orange clubs among them. In the year 1809 about fifty Protestants of a very low description resolved to "walk in procession" with the orange flag and paraphernalia of the society through the populous town of Letterkenny, several miles distant from their habitations; a town which was chiefly inhabited by Catholics, and in which there never had been before an Orange procession. All the Catholics of the town—men, women and children—m t them in the suburbs of the town, and after much blood had been spilled the Orangemen were obliged to return home. Since that period all confidence between both parties was at an end. Sir Henry said, a nobleman lately appointed to the high office of Lord Lieutenant, had an arduous duty to perform. He had not the advantage of high birth and exalted rank to support him; but he trusted he would show an example of sobriety to the country, and that when he visited the interior of the kingdom they should not hear of "*midnight orgies" of songs and toasts* tending to inflame one part of his Majesty's subjects against the other. Mr. Peel, with considerable warmth, protested against the unfounded insinuations on the character of the nobleman at the head of the Government. Mr. M'Naughten insisted on the absolute necessity of the Orange societies, and thought it would be extremely severe if the 39th Geo. 3, pas ed against traitors should be applied to the liege subjects of the king. If the act was to be applied to Orangemen, why was it not applied to Friendly Brothers and Freemasons, to both of which societies he belonged. Whether he was or was not an Orangeman after what had been said he dared *not confess.* Mr. Whitbread alluded to statements of persons of high rank being connected with these societies—it had been imprudently said that the Prince of Wales and the Duke of York were at the head of them; referred to the insiduous publication of two distinct sets of pamphlets for the purpose of misleading; pronounced these associations worse than illegal—as outrages upon common decency and common sense, and asked were the robes of a peer to be proof against the sword of justice, or was there a magic charm about the great which bewildered the understanding and made that appear in them a virtue which in others was an unpardonable crime. He challenged Mr. M'Naughten, who had spoken of signs and passwords, which were meant only to distinguish associates, to point out what members on the Opposition side of the House belonged at any time to Orange Associations. Mr Preston thought the Orange Society equally illegal without the oath as with it. Mr. Canning taought it was consolatory to reflect that amongst all the digressions the evening, no one had branched into any such of anomaly as to stand up in defence of the innocence of the Orange Institution; nor had anyone denied that those who entered into its full design were guilty of an attempt against the peace of the empire Was the Act of 1799 founded on avowed intention? No. The Revolution Society, the Constitution Society, bore on their *faces* no intention to destroy, but to preserve and purify the Constitution. Nor was it in the profession, nor even in the design, of the Orange Soc ety that the danger existed. He referred to the modest assumption of the institution vesting in itself the care of the pub'ic safety, and saw that this presumptious, this stupid proceeding, but for the contempt it excited, would call not only for inquisitorial but vindictive proceedings. He hoped that this soc ety need only be noticed to sink into oblivion. He thought that the decided sense of the House and a declaration (which he did not doubt would be given) from one of his Majesty's Ministers that the law would be recurred to if the association were persisted in, would put an end to this despicable society which, if suffered to exist, might shake to its foundation this noble country. Lord Castlereagh concurred entirely with Mr Canning, and expressed his obligations to Mr Wynn for the temperate manner in which he had discussed the subject. He pronounced such associations dangerous particularly so in Ireland, where if there had formerly been some cause for them they had survived the danger. Such associations, he said, were very dangerous but particularly so in military bodies. He felt it was unnecessary to press the subject as he was convinced that the good sense of the people would prefer the empire of the law to the domination of clubs and associations. Mr. Wynn said the unqualified disavowal and disapprobation of the society rendered reply unnecessary. He hoped his Majesty's ministers would be alive to every attempt to carry the plan of these societies into execution, and withdrew his motion.

Whether the Government of the day feared or cared not to act up to their expressed opinions is not worth inquiry It is possible that both feelings equally influenced their non-interference. With the result we have to do. The appeal of a Minister to the good sense of the people, who would prefer the empire of the law to the empire of faction, was made in vain. With this new letter of credit, for it was interpreted as such, the Orange Institution went on its way rejoicing

On the above declaration of illegality reaching Ireland, the Dublin Grand Lodge met and issued a proclamation to its members, calling upon them to resist the feeling of the Government, and not to be intimidated by it. The meeting was held on the 12th July, 1813, and on that same day (how strangely consistent were the events!) a horrible tragedy was enacted in Belfast. Six or eight lodges met in that town to celebrate on the Twelfth a triumph which had been gained a century and a quarter previously. The lodges marched out of town, and on the return journey they marched through North Street. A crowd collected, and on their reaching the house of a man named Thompson mud and stones were thrown, by whom the record does not say. The result was a riot in which five persons were shot, three fatally The shooting must be laid at the doors of the Orangemen, for the person who took a prominent part in it was a member of an almost exclusively Orange corps. The *News-Letter* of the following day gives particulars of the riot, and, in a tone in no sense parallel with its later pronouncements, it condemns the foolishness of such displays and the illegality of such associations It says—"It is much to be regretted that any circumstance should have been permitted to take place yesterday that had a tendency to excite party spirit A few days only have elapsed since the politics of Orange societies drew the attention of the Legislature. The topic was discussed in a most deliberate and dispassionate manner. The illegality of such associations was declared and admitted by the most distinguished characters in the British Synod. Mr. Wynn, who introduced the subject, exhibited the unconstitutional nature of all such societies, and declared that he could not imagine an association that was more pregnant with alarm. Mr. Canning

and Lord Castlereagh expressed their opinions in the most explicit terms that *they were illegal, and ought to be suppressed* In fact the House was most unanimous in reprobating them. With such a recent expression of the sentiments of the Synod, we certainly did expect that some deference would have been paid to it by those societies, and that they would not have thus so soon manifested their opposition to the declared opinion of Parliament by this public parade. When this intelligence reaches London how will it be taken up, and what severe animadversions will it give rise to against this town, which was so long the theme of eulogium, alike distinguished by its internal peace, its opulence, and its industry? All those high and honourable' qualities are thus thrown into the shade by an *idle parade* having enkindled those animosities and heartburnings which should have for ever sunk into oblivion" (See *News-Letter*, July 13th, 1813) Strange language for an organ now the acknowledged representative of the Orange party and its defender upon all occasions, even at the risk of truth. The class is, unfortunately, a numerous one who would pay such a forfeiture to have their bread buttered on both sides.

The disturbance and fatalities were not confined to Belfast this year, for in various parts throughout Ulster riots occurred of the most unseemly character, and we have it on the authority of the report of the Select Committee that in one village in which a large force of military were drafted for the preservation of the peace, that the Orangemen were received by some members of a dragoon regiment with open arms, that they drank with them in the house in which their lodge was being held, deserting their post in the meantime, and that some of them who had not been already initiated into the system, returned to their post full blown Orangemen.

On July 18th, 1814 on the introduction of the Peace Preservation (Ireland) Act, Mr. Peel referred to such societies as the "Thrashers," the "Carders," the "Caravats," as necessary to be suppressed, but made no mention of the Orange societies. Sir Henry Parnell, commenting upon this, exposed the Orange system in the course of an able speech. Mr. Peel defended it, and said their outrageous conduct was "the exuberance of loyalty;" admitted that he would not encourage them, but in no way attempted to reply to the charges made against them.

From the Irish Bench words of warning to the same effect were heard one year later. In August,

1814, the Hon. Justice Fletcher, when opening the Assizes in Wexford, delivered an able and lengthened address to the members of the Grand Jury, in which he dwelt at length upon the evil effects of Orangeism. He congratulated them upon the fact that the county was then in the same condition as when he knew it thirty years previously. He regarded it as a moral curiosity. When other parts were lawless and disturbed, it had a peasantry, industrious in their habits, social in their disposition, satisfied with their state, and amenable to the laws; cultivating their farms with an assiduity which assured a competency. This led him to dwell largely upon "the exaggeration of misrepresentation" that had gone abroad about the extent and causes of disturbance. He declared unhesitatingly, after lifelong experience, that he had never observed any serious purpose or settled scheme for assailing his Majesty's Government, or any conspiracy connected with internal rebels or foreign foes. "But," he continued, "various deep-rooted and neglected causes, producing similar effects throughout the country, have conspired to create the evils which really and truly do exist." One of those causes he said was the existence of Orangeism. He had found those societies, called ORANGE SOCIETIES, had produced most mischievous results, and particularly in the North of Ireland. They had poisoned the very fountain of justice, and even some magistrates, under their influence, had in too many instances *violated their duty and their oaths*. (Is it necessary to remind the reader of the charges made by Mr. Wilson, and of the corroboration which these words convey?) He referred to the conduct of the Orange Yeomen in terms which meant to brand them as nothing but murderous exterminators, who took occasion of every fair and market to carry out their bloody work, and said that where legal prosecutions had followed such had been the baneful effects of these factious associations that under their influence petty juries had declined to do their duty. "These facts," I give his own words as reported in a periodical of the day, and the accuracy of which has been accepted by the Orangemen themselves, "have fallen under my own view. It was sufficient to say such a man displayed such a colour, to produce an utter disbelief of his testimony; or when another has stood at the bar, and the display of his party badge has mitigated the murder into manslaughter." His description not alone of the evils of Orangeism but of the state of the country consequent upon its existence is heartrending, and creates a feeling of amazement that such a state of things could have existed in a civilised land. But his lordship agrees with Mr. Wilson in more respects than one, if he does not even outstep him in the bold honesty of his language and in the fearless eloquence with which he condemned existing abuses. He recommended, as Mr. Wilson had done to the Lord Chancellor seven years previously, a complete reformation of the magistracy, without which all expectations of tranquillity or content were vain. Some were over-zealous, others over-supine. Distracted into parties, they were often governed by their private passions to the disgrace of public justice and the frequent disturbance of the country. He described "a hideous but common picture," in which poor innocent people were ruined in health and morals by the flagrant acts of injustice of the Orange magistracy, and how the industrious cottager was converted into a beggar and a vagrant. "There are," he says, "parts of Ireland where, from the absence of gentlemen of the country, a race of magistrates has sprung up who ought never have borne the king's commission. (For expressing similar sentiments, or rather for proffering to justify them, Mr. Wilson was dismissed the Commission of the Peace). The needy adventurer, the hunter for preferment, the intemperate zealot, *the trader in false loyalty*, the jobbers of absentees—these he recommended should be expunged from the magistracy and replaced by gentlemen of property and consideration. Should their number be inadequate he recommended the appointment of clergymen long resident on their benefices, more inclined to follow their Divine Master's precepts by feeding the hungry and clothing the naked Catholic—*not* clergymen who, "in a period of distraction, perusing the old testament with more attention than the new, and admiring the glories of Joshua (the son of Nun) fancied they saw in the Catholics the Canaanites of old; and at the head of militia and armed yeomanry wished to conquer from the promised glebe. He cautioned the gentlemen of the grand jury to discourage Orange and Green associations. Suffer them to prevail, and how can justice be administered? 'I am a loyal man,' says a witness, that is, "gentlemen of the petty juries believe me, let me swear what will.' When he swears he is a loyal man, he means '*gentlemen of the jury, forget your oaths and acquit the Orangeman*.'" Such men, the learned judge described, as mere pretenders of loyalty; men who were loyal in times of tranquility; men who were attached to the present order so far as they could get anything by it; men who maligned every man of different opinions from those whom they served; men who brought their loyalty to market, exposed it for sale, and were continually seeking for a purchaser. (See appendix.)

Such was the warning voice of one of the ablest and most upright judges that ever sat upon the Irish bench. It was not heeded. An incorrigible perversity seems to have been implanted in human nature by which, as by the slime of some crawling thing, we can trace man's track through rolling ages —here his misdeeds, there his mistakes—until we find him in his original state, bent upon plunder, deaf to the warning voice of conscience, smiling at the hissing whispers of the serpent; the weak, covetous imbecile, swallowing the apples which she could not pocket, the infatuated fool rushing to wrong-doing even when he recognised it, and both fixed upon perpetuating a race- having perversity in evil and insensibility to advice as their sad inheritance. As with a man, so with a nation. It is painful to look back and mark the numerous errors of the past. Still it is wholesome. One of the greatest errors in this country's past was inattention to those who said, "There lies the canker in your wound; you can cure it if you will." By many a dreadful holocaust and a sacrifice of countless lives we have had to atone for that perversity.

On July 4th, 1815, Sir Henry Parnell moved an address to the Crown, praying for a Commission of Inquiry into the proceedings of the Orange societies in the North of Ireland, which was supported by the Knight of Kerry, and opposed by Mr. Peel and the Ministerial party. Mr. Peel said since the illegality of such associations was borne out by Mr. Justice Fletcher and Judge Day (who in Dublin, in 1813, on the trial of Dr. Sheridan, also pronounced them illegal) there was no need of an inquiry. Twenty members voted for the motion and eighty-nine against it, and it was thus lost by a majority of sixty-nine. Men's minds were not yet ripe for such a measure. They preferred fostering their prejudices amid doubt and uncertainty to dispelling them by hard but unpleasant truths.

The five subsequent years in our history present no feature worthy of comment. With the dissolution of the Catholic Board those who, but a few months previously, had been moved to enthusiasm, and resolved upon obtaining redress from the reign of a cruel faction, now returned to a state of apathy and despair. They bent with resignation to the lash of their prosecutors, and only resumed an upright posture to bend again. The tales of horror which followed our social life during these five years, particularly in the course of those periodic displays when men seemed to have lost their reason — to have divested themselves of their humanity, are all amply recorded in the current history of the time. Novelty in crime there could not be. Cruel invention had exhausted itself. Into these five years a multiplicity of horrors, committed by a handful of tyrants upon a population accumulated not by thousands but by millions, was compressed with an ingenuity that bespoke a most barbarous persistency. In lethargy the body of the people submitted until, by the arrival of the King in 1821, they were momentarily aroused, and soon after hurried on in that unbroken whirlwind of events which ended in their emancipation, and the overthrow for ever of ascendancy.

CHAPTER XXV—THE ENGLISH INSTITUTE.

We have seen in a previous chapter how the dying embers of intolerance—not Protestant intolerance, for those concerned had little in common with that creed, save the name—we have seen how they were stirred up and fanned into a flame. On the other side of St. George's Channel the brethren had no circumstances of necessity by which to justify their existence. To be sure they worked on the prejudices of party, if they did not absolutely create them, and cried " wolf, wolf," by times, to keep up a show of self-defence. For the first few years of their existence in England the lodges afforded a rendezvous for all the intolerant old fogies who had played a part in the late rebellion in Ireland, some of whom had found the island too hot for them, even beneath the laxity of its administration, and most of whom had left their country for their country's good. But bigotry had no part to play. They were all in a greater or lesser degree of a mind. There were none to oppress. The Orange Institution, as a natural result, became first an association for the distribution of patronage, and in years afterwards ripened into a huge conspiracy, of which the humbler members were content to divide the loaves and fishes, whilst its leaders secured political power, beneath which lay concealed the diabolical intention of changing the succession The first effort towards insinuating itself with those in power is seen in a letter from Mr. R. Nixon, the Grand Secretary at Manchester, to the celebrated Mr. J. Giffard, at Dublin, in 1811, in which he asked, "If the Duke of Cumberland had ever been initiated an Orangeman," and if it was likely " His Royal Highness would countenance and support the Institution" by becoming its Grand Master? Whether application was then made, or whether, if made, the reply was favourable we have no means of ascertaining, but we have for a guidance, though possibly not a safe one, the statements of the newspapers of the time to the effect that the duke and his brother had been initiated into the Orange Society. Lord Kenyon and the Earl of Yarmouth were, about the year 1813, made members, and on the 4th August of that year a committee was appointed for the purpose of altering their rules to enable them, as the Grand Secretary bluntly put it, "to elude the grasp' of the law. The advisability "of framing some suitable instrument as a substitute for the old form of warrant" is, by the secretary, suggested; the necessity "of calling the masters, sub-masters," in order to get rid of the idea of delegation is hinted at, the question of legality or illegality of the oath (fac-simile with the Irish oath) is left to the committee, but under no consideration can he see how the signs and tokens "can be dispensed with."[*]

In this year one-fifth part of all the lodges in England existed in regiments, an important but very unpleasant fact admitted by Mr. Nixon in a letter to Sergeant James Green, of the 4th Garrison Battalion at Guernsey, with whom he condoles over the meddling propensity and erroneous conception of his superior officer, Major Doyle, who prohibited lodges in his regiment. In the face of the most direct evidence, that this clique within a clique was opposed to the wishes of commanding officers, and with knowledge that wherever the existence of lodges in regiments came to be known they were forthwith suppressed, the officials of the English institution, with a chivalrous anxiety persisted, they saw that the Constitution was in danger, that those charged with the care of it were sleeping at their post, and accordingly proceeded to increase and multiply in regiments with the utmost indifference to constituted authority. So pertinacious were they in this particular that one would be inclined to pay them the compliment of greater foresight than

they were possessed of, and to suppose they foresaw even at this early date the "moral weight" which would be available in the plundering of a throne, with half the standing army were their sworn confederates. Up to the year 1820 the society seems to have been feeling its way secretly in the English commercial centres, dependent upon the humbler classes chiefly, but gaining proselytes here and there from the ranks of the aristocracy by the promises of political power which it flaunted before their vision. Stealthily, silently, within closed doors, every "brother" a sworn accomplice, and every accomplice a conditional loyalist, these men pursued their devious and designing course, occasionally vaunting their loyalty, feeling tolerably certain that the profuseness of their declarations would in the nature of things preclude the probability of question. Rubbed against the grain, their caution forsook them, their ire rose, they bristled all over, bid defiance to all law, cast aside all authority, and stood boldly forth, outlaws to all order which did not bend itself to their infatuation, and a menace to that Constitution which in their meeker moments they affected to support. In 1819 the Loyal Orange Institution of Great Britain, at a meeting of the Grand Lodge, resolved, on a subscription, to prosecute Sir John Tobin, Knt., Mayor of Liverpool, and the magistrates, for interrupting in the interest of peace an Orange procession on the 12th July of that year. Lord Kenyon was a large subscriber to the fund. To this purpose the funds of the institution have often been applied, both in Ireland and England. It evidences little inclination to bend before the symbol of constituted authority.

Communication seems to have been kept up between the Grand Lodge of Ireland and that of Great Britain, though only at long intervals, from an early period, and from this correspondence we are enabled to see that the Irish Institution fell a prey at this period " to one of those fatalities to which all human institutions are liable." In other words, a number of persons had been admitted as loyal brethren who were proceeding "to initiate rebels into the secrets of the institution in order to facilitate their treasonable and murderous plans." This, in simple terms, meant that some few Orangemen, convinced of the necessity of granting emancipation to the enslaved Catholics of the kingdom, had the courage of their convictions in the face of the anathemas hurled against them by the institution. Expulsion followed. An immediate change in the signs and passwords was made, and the

---

[*] See appendix to English Report, page 179—Mr. R. Nixon writing to the Earl of Yarmouth.

brethren, expelled, for a liberty of conscience in advance of their kind, were excluded from both the Irish and English systems.

On the 14th March, 1820, Lord Sedmouth presented a dutiful address from the Grand Master, officers, and members of the Loyal Orange Institution of England, which his Majesty was pleased graciously to accept.

On the death of Colonel Taylor, the Grand Lodge was, on the suggestion of Mr. Chetewoode, removed to London, and the Duke of York, with the sanction of a member of the Ministry, accepted the office of Grand Master, Lord Kenyon being appointed as his deputy, and the first meeting was held on the 21st April, at the house of Lord Kenyon, in Portman Square, the Deputy Grand Master occupying the chair. On this day it was resolved that no communication, written or printed, of the proceedings of the Grand Lodge be made without the special orders of the Grand Lodge, Grand Master, or Deputy Grand Master, and ever afterwards this resolution binding all the confederation by virtue of their oath to secrecy, seemed to have been acted upon. The acceptance by the Duke of York of the position of Grand Master was conveyed in a letter dated "The Horse Guards, 8th February, 1821." On the 22nd June following, a question regarding the acceptance of the office having been previously asked in the Commons, his Royal Highness writes that he had learnt "that the Law Officers of the Crown and other eminent lawyers were decidedly of opinion that the Orange Institution, under the oath administered to their members, was illegal, and he accordingly withdrew from the association. Lord Hertford, Lord Lowther, and others also resigned But the confederates were playing too high a game to be thus foiled by constitutional restrictions. Instead of forthwith dissolving as an illegal body, bound together by an illegal oath, they submitted a case to Mr. Serjeant Lens and Sir Wm Horne, by whose advice they hoped to devise some means of more successfully "evading the law" than the first Secretary, Mr. Nixon, had done. The rules and regulations having been revised, the Orange oath omitted, and oaths of Allegiance and Abjuration substituted, 1st William and Mary, c. 1, s 8; oath of supremacy, 1st Anne, c. 22, s. 1; and of Abjuration, 6 Geo. III., c. 53; substituted, a case was submitted for the purpose of ascertaining if the society violated the common law or any existing statute, particularly the Acts of the 37th Geo. III, c. 123, 39th Geo. III., c. 79, and 57th Geo. III, c. 19, which referred to *traitorous* conspiracies

inconsistent with the public tranquillity and calculated to endanger the Constitution. "To evade the law" (the words now are those of the members of the Select Committee) "the word 'warrant', was substituted for 'lodge;' the original form was to grant a warrant to hold a lodge in a particular house or place; and by the alteration it was given to the person to hold a lodge wheresoever he pleased." Thus, no doubt the professed object, was but a technical evasion for the new authority answered, and was applied to the same end as the old.

The opinions given upon this submitted case in no respect differ from those of all lawyers. Indefinite, obscure, and wanting in that bold, blunt honesty which commends man to man the opinion of Mr. Serjeant Leno was that the institution could not be deemed a violation of the statutes referred to. But that it was opposed to the principles of common law and to the unwritten code of the Constitution, in his opinion we may see from the following extracts:—"I think, therefore, that this society if it be objectionable at all must be so on the principles of common law and not as falling within the particular penalties of the statutes. It is rightly remarked that the denomination of 'loyal' or any other epithet which a society affixes to itself, and pleases to announce as the objects of its institution will not decide or alter the nature or legal description of it. No one will, in this case, suspect the society of that declaration, or that any other purpose is in view than that which is exhibited, but it must be observed that an institution of the extent and influence which must from its constitution, belong to the present, may be made the engine of great power if it should be capable of abuse in its application. It must also be observed that its object is not distinctly defined as to the nature of what is to be done. 'Its affairs' are mentioned in general terms, but the affairs are not specified, nor are the particular functions or duties which the Grand Master has to execute anywhere defined. The Grand Orange Lodge is, I presume, to be composed of *all* the members"—which presumption was wrong, thereby adding to its illegality by the fact of its being a delegated assembly—"and there is to be no separate division inaccessible to the general body"—also wrong; the purple order was rendered inaccessible through a separate system of signs and pass-words to those of the Orange order —"and in that and other respects it is clear of the particular objection made to such societies in sec.

2 of 39 George III., chap. 79. The secrecy of the signs and symbols, which may be changed from time to time, I cannot help thinking is objectionable, and, if any question were hereafter to arise on the legality of any of its proceedings, might be urged as a circumstance of great suspicion. It is also to be remembered that the societies known as regular Freemasons' Lodges are particularly and specially exempted from the operation of the Acts only under certain conditions to be observed in future." Only the wilfully or woefully blind could construe the above into a sanction of legality. But when we find that the opinions of other eminent lawyers were taken upon the same issue, and that "they were less favourable than the opinion of Mr. Serjeant Leno,"* we see the Orange Institution face to face with the dilemma, gross illegality, or dissolution.* They selected the former. They did not dissolve; nor does it appear that they went to further trouble in so altering their rules and constitution as to cheat the law with more certainty of success. That the Institution—meaning both the English and the Irish branches—had at this period two distinct sets of rules was stated openly in the House of Commons, without receiving denial. That there was a secret and probably unwritten code of laws is fairly to be implied from those laid before the Committee. Their reproduction here would scarce be interesting. So far as the general management of the body was concerned, they were similar to those existing in Ireland, and precise provisions were made,it would seem contrary to the wishes of the Duke of York, for the conduct of lodges established in regiments. "It has been alleged (says the committee) by some of the officers of the Institution that the orders of the Commander of the Forces of 1822 and 1829 were merely confidential recommendations and not General Orders published from the Horse Guards. Your Committee are desirous of removing that error by referring to the evidence of Major-General Sir J. Macdonald, the Adjutant-General of the Army, who on the 6th August stated to the Committee of the Orange Lodges in Ireland that the confidential letter of

July, 1822, was embodied in the edition printed in the year of the General Regulations and Orders of the Army; that it is the duty of the colonel or commander of every regiment to have one of those books; that every regimental officer is directed to supply himself with a copy of it; and that every regimental orderly-room ought to have a copy. Of the orders of the Duke of York Sir J. Macdonald adds no officers ought to be ignorant." Of very doubtful loyalty under statute law, plainly illegal by common law, and directly contrary to the regulations of the Horse Guards, by which the army was regulated, the Orange Institution still continued to exist and multiply. Writing a year subsequently to a military brother in Woolwich the secretary, Mr. Chetewoode, uses those pregnant remarks which he, no doubt, at the time of writing them, believed would never see the light—"All masters of warrants are, according to the present rules, members of the Grand Lodge, and entitled to sit therein, but from many considerations it is highly objectionable for any brother to attend in uniform, and it is earnestly hoped that none will think of appearing but in coloured clothes." Though this will serve to illustrate the irreconcilable ignorance which the Grand Master affected when brought to question upon this point by the House of Commons it cannot rid him and his associates of winking at the offence, and of so wilfully closing their ears to the correspondence from military lodges, as to render ignorance a matter of their own selection. All was not at this period open and above board on the part of this institution. Mr. Blount, at a meeting of the British Catholic Association, held in London in November, 1825, read warrant 99, which bore only the signature of Kenyon as Deputy Grand Master, and he remarks—"A Peer of the Realm is their Deputy Grand Master and no name appears of the Grand Master himself. He must, of course, be some illustrious person who towers above the Peerage, but whose name it is thought imprudent to divulge."

From the year 1825 to the year 1828 the Orange Institution being dissolved in Ireland by an Act of the Legislature, the English brethren came to their aid, enabling them to evade the law. Though dissolved and presumed to be not in existence, the Irish lodges secured warrants from the English Grand Lodge, under which lodges were held in Ireland as before the passing of the Act. "And the objects and intentions of the law were thus frustrated," say the committee of the

* "Do your lordships recollect whether they were to the same purport, or whether they differed from these? I think I should say, upon the whole, during the earlier period their opinions were less favourable than the opinion of Serjeant Leno. I am not sure whether it was precisely the same case or not. I think, I recollect, in the opinion of Mr. Dallas, he wished very much (being connected with Government at the time) to abstain from giving any opinion as to the course to be pursued by a society not considered strictly legal, with a view to that society rendering it self legal.—" Lord Kenyon's evidence before the Select Committee of 1835, English Report, question 2,417."

House of Commons in treating upon this manœuvre. The stratagem was an audacious one, strangely inconsistent w.th the professions of men who not only boasted exclusive possession of loyalty, but whose every act of intrigue was glossed over with a sanctimonious surface, and who in their public utterances pretended they held the key of all the cardinal virtues in their pock ts. Not for a trifl? do men in high places off and against the law or enable others to frustrate its intentions. Was the stake so high a one as to demand such a risk and recklessness?

It now became indispensable for the brethren to set their own house in order. A shockingly irreverent reforming spirit was abroad. With religious horror, eyes upwards; with a sickly prayer to Heaven to stay its avenging hand for the wickedness of the times; that at least its thunderbolts would only be directed against those traitors to the Constitution who proposed to emancipate vile Catholics; with a

> "God conf und their stubborn face,
> And blast their name,
> Wha bring thy elders to disgrace
> And public shame."

they met—button-holeing the Deity—and resolved upon wha'?—simply to amend their rules and regulations. All societies bound by oaths were now, under the law, illegal. The English Orange Inst - tution dropped the oaths, for even the legality of others than magistrates administering those of allegiance, supremacy &c was now denied. Members claiming admission required to produce evidence of their having taken those oaths before the regular authorities, and were called upon to make the following declaration against Transubstantion :—

"I, A. B, do solemnly and sincerely, in the presence of God, profess, testify, and declare that I do believe that in the Sacrament of the Lord's Supper there is not any transubstantiation of the elements of bread and wine into the body and blood of Christ, at or after the consecration thereof by any person whatsoever; and that the invocation or adoration of the Virgin Mary, or any other saint, and the sacrifice of the Mass, as they are now used in the Church of Rome, are superstitious and idolatrous. And I do solemnly in the presence of God profess, testify, and declare that I make this declaration and every part thereof in the plain and ordinary sense of the words read unto me as they are commonly understood by the English Protestants, without any evasion, equivocation, or mental reservation whatsoever, and without any dispensa

tion already granted me for this purpose by the Pope or any other authority or person whatsoever, or without any hops of any such dispensation from any person or authority whatsoever, or without thinking that I am or can be acquitted before God and man, or absolved of this declaration, or any part thereof, although the Pope or any other person or persons, or power whatsoever, should dispense with or annul the same, or declare that it was null and void from the beginning" To the above declaration add the solemn mummery of the initiatory ceremony, the Bible in the one hand, the rules and regulations in the other, here a dash of religious frenzy, there some mystic ceremony calculated to excite the awe of the new brother, and it will be easily seen how readily the Orange Institution could do without their oath and at the same time accomplish all the ends which they could with the oath.

"The effect of the religious ceremonies and forms has been to enforce, with the apparent obligation of an oath, secrecy on the members admitted; as the Deputy Grand Master of England and Wales, and all the Orangemen examined by the committee (with one exception) refused to communicate the secret signs and passwords of the institution, and it appears that a disclosure of the system by a member would subject him to expulsion"*

A committee was appointed in October, 1826, for the purpose of forming a new system of signs and passwords for both the Orange and the Purple order, which committee completed their labours in the February of the following year. Thus armed against busybodies, and independent of the Con. stitution, Orangeism set out anew on its career. The rules of 1826 remained in force till 1834 Attention was at this period (1826) about being paid to the Colonies, to which a large number of the Irish brethren, experiencing beneath the sway of grinding land'ordism the common lot of cultivators of the soil in Ireland, had emigrated † But it was

---

* See Report of Select Committee (English), page vii, paragraph 5

† That the majority of Ulster landlords, when the question was £, s d, treated their Orange w th as much h rshness as they did their Catholic ten nt , is now a matter upon which all sides are p etty much agreed. T is w s one of the bitterest delusions that awaited the brethren in the North who saw, as the outcome of the confederacy in which they were engaged with their landlords as leaders, leases in perpetuity at o.e-third the market value of the land. Blessed a e they w io expect not (from the landlords) for they shall not be i appointed H w miserably mistaken were these Orange ten nts histo y has proved. They knew not the renth of landlord villainy They believed that when as a magistrate the r G M polluted the stream of just ce and defouled the bench in their behalf he won das a landlord make pecuniary sac ifices to sec re their monopoly, forgetting all th ime this essent al difference—the one requ red but a sacrifice of

interrupted in its earlier stages. In 1827 the Duke of York died, and at a meeting of the English Grand Lodge, held at the residence of Lord Kenyon on the 15th February, it was resolved to commit the consideration and management of appointing a substitute to Lord Kenyon, who, " with his usual urbanity towards the brethren and zeal for the institution, most kindly undertook the same." Generous Lord Kenyon! It is sweet to be liberal with other people's property. Here was a throne to be given away, and the noble lord kindly undertook to bestow it. The Duke of Cumberland "consented" to be Grand Master. The prefix IMPERIAL, now added, gave an air of sovereignty and a suggestive significance to the title. There was soon observable, not to the outer world, and but indistinctly to the rank and file of the Orange order, a stealthy and subdued bustle in the world of Orangeism; some great project was on foot; the lodge doors were well watched, were opened quietly at midnight, and—sure enough the tyler was there! not sleeping! and the road clear!—closer still over their deep potations—and a stage whisper went round that a Great Deliverer was coming to fetch them out of the land of Egypt, out of the house of bondage, one who would feed them wit manna in the desert and could give them milk and honey when beyond it; the Duke of ——, but hush! not a word more; and away at cockcrow, out of the hells, the public-houses, the public liquor-brothels of the Kingdom, scattered those intoxicated King-makers, drunk with their own conceit, their own selfish greed, their fantastic fanaticism, and doubly drunk from a liberal indulgence in bad liquor; away to dream of the millenium, when they could reap abundantly where they did not sow, when work for them would be no more, when an Orange King would sit upon an Orange throne, dispensing favours and royal bounties to his Majesty's right trusty and well-beloved brothers, the country squire, ignorant as debauched, the village ruffian, again the village tyrant, the Orange tinkers, the Orange tailors, the Orange cobblers of the Kingdom, and when the entire of the Government, with all its honours, places, and fat pensions—particularly the pensions—was to be comprised within one mighty Grand Orange Lodge, in which all the officers, from the bailiff to the King, were to be sworn brothers and true Orangemen. A novel conception, truly! Not too novel for a drunken fanatic to conceive. Not too novel for the scatter-brained directors of this Institution, men with the hearts of conspirators and the heads of school-boys, to seek, during a period of eight years' plotting, to realise to its fullest.*

honour, the other a sacrifice of money. Writing upon this point, Thomas Moore, under the title of "Captain Rock," says. " Notwithstanding all his (the Orangeman's) crimes, I cannot help pitying him ; he is the victim of unprincipled men ; and could he divest himself for a moment of his prejudices I would convince him that his antagonistic position is not a prudent one. He has only to recollect the events of the last ten years ; within that period, how many thousands of h s brethren have from poverty been compelled to emigrate? His answer to this question, if honestly given, will involve in it matter for serious consideration. The result would be, I am convinced, that Orangeism has been beneficial only to the designing few."

* The "Dublin University Magazine" (of 1835), an acknowledged and devoted advocate of Orangeism, speaks with the utmost contempt of the "absurd vagaries" of Lieutenant-Colonel Fairman, the silly successor of Mr. Chetewoode as Grand Secretary. It goes further. It throws all that was discreditable upon the English Institution, thus seeking to shift the blame from the shoulders of the Irish Institution. " When rogues fall out, &c."

CHAPTER XXVI.—THE IRISH QUESTION, PLOTS AND COUNTER PLOTS.

THE period over which, in the course of the last chapter, we have passed covers many outrages in the history of the Irish Institution. It would seem, indeed, as if about this time the forces of the organisation were being concentrated towards a combined effort to establish monopoly and intolerance upon a permanent footing. George the Third died in 1820, and in the following year the hopes of the Irish Catholics were excited by the idle pageantry of three weeks, during which his successor, the last of the Georges, paraded to the edification of his Irish subjects. It is easy to delude an expectant people. They see in every trifling occurrence out of the ordinary routine of events some reason for grounding a hope that a change for the better is at hand. That George the Fourth came with a message of peace to the persecuted Catholics was believed in by some who boasted more than common political shrewdness. The consequence was that all sections of the Irish united in making the Royal tournament as brilliant as possible. Fearful of disturbing the equanimity of the Royal bosom, the Catholics withheld all complaint. No lamentation of grievance, no petition for redress, was heard during the whole of the period of that Royal visit. Everything looked happiness, harmony, and good order. The Catholics, with a temperance (it has been given a worse name) that was the astonishment of all Europe, refrained from the slightest allusion to their oppressed condition. The fraternal embraces of Mr O'Connell and Alderman Bradley King are not yet forgotten * The silly monarch so paraded his affection for " his faithful people" that he pressed their national emblem to his bosom, dropped a few crocodile tears, and, on his departure, addressed a fraternal epistle to them, in which he "trusted that every cause of irritation would be avoided and discountenanced, that mutual forbearance and good will would be observed and encouraged, and a security be thus afforded for *the continuance of that concord amongst themselves which was no less essential to his happiness than to their own"* If concord amongst the Irish was essential to the happiness of George the Fourth, his Majesty took very little trouble in securing peace and contentment to the Royal bosom. What an unhappy monarch he must have been too ' No change took place. The same men continued in office. Nothing was done to raise the Catholics out of their depressed condition—nothing to depress their enemies. The letter was regarded, says Mr Wyse, as an idle proclamation for temporary purposes, the Protestant laughed at the credulity of the Catholic, and scornfully assumed his ancient ascendancy ; the Catholic, ashamed and indignant at the deception, sank at once into his former lethargy.

The Orange magistracy continued to exercise their despotic sway without intermission. A writer in the *Edinburgh Review* of January, 1836, analysing the evidence before the Committee, remarks upon the state of the Irish magistracy, and gives from Mr Kernan's evidence an intelligent summary of an outrage that took place in 1821, which I cannot do better than utilise The writer says —

" We shall less wonder at the proceedings of these magistrates, when we learn who and what some of them are For this purpose, and as an exemplification of the unequal and savage state of society consequent upon a long indulgence of party feelings and factions, we know of no case more instructive than that of Lieutenant Hamilton. We shall, therefore, make no apology for the length of our extracts

' This was a trial for murder The transaction out of which it arose occurred on the evening of

the fair day of Dromore. Mr. Hamilton, the reputed murderer, was a lieutenant of yeomanry, of which his father, also a magistrate, was the captain. In the morning all was perfectly quiet, and, as it appeared, in evidence, ' Lieutenant Hamilton came marching into the fair in the evening with a party of his own company of yeomanry. They were armed with their guns and bayonets; the country had been disturbed a good deal with party feuds. The corps assaulted several Catholic persons as they came into town.' It was also stated that stones had been thrown at the yeomanry. ' They were armed, and marched through the fair. When they arrived opposite the house of a man of the name of James Kelly, a publican, Lieutenant Hamilton ordered them to halt, and immediately after that, he gave them the word of command to prime and load, and fire into the house, which order they obeyed Several persons that were then taking refreshment in the house were wounded by the shot, and the deceased, Michael M'Brian was killed. According to custom, of course, the next day Kelly and several others came to consult me upon the business, in the town of Enniskillen, and I advised them to go to Lord Belmore, who was a magistrate of the counties of Tyrone and Fermanagh. Lord Belmore received them, and listened to their case, and told them he would meet them at a meeting of the magistrates, in a day or two afterwards, at Omagh. In the interim the friends of the deceased, and the party who were assaulted at the fair by the yeomanry, heard that Hamilton intended to fly the country; and, without waiting for the meeting of the magistrates, they made a prisoner of him, and brought him before two magistrates. The Rev. Mr. Stack was the name of one, I have not the name of the other magistrate ' The father of the prisoner, who was also a magistrate, came, and attended before them ' The people applied to those magistrates to grant a warrant for the purpose of committing Lieutenant Hamilton for trial, and the magistrates refused—saying they would take his father's security for the son's appearance; and they did take his verbal security for his appearance at a future day at the town of Omagh, where Lord Belmore was to meet the magistrates, and where his lordship did attend. Informations were taken by Lord Belmore against Mr. Hamilton and against the whole corps of yeomanry, but young Hamilton thought proper to forfeit the verbal bail taken by the magistrates He fled from the country, and did not return for some years afterwards, but is now returned, and *he is a justice of the peace of the County of Tyrone.'* Mr. Kernan then goes on to state, 'that the person aiding and assisting—in fact, all the yeomanry that were of the party—were, after much delay, in consequence of the absconding of Lieutenant Hamilton, tried at the Summer Assizes for murder, convicted of manslaughter, and sentenced to nine months' imprisonment' The committee then asked if Mr. Hamilton was ever tried. Mr. Kernan replies, 'that he believes not; but he knows he is now a justice of the peace in that county, in which he was charged with committing the murder, that there is no doubt he commanded his yeomanry to fire the shot which killed the deceased; and the chief defence of the yeomen was, that they, in firing the fatal shot, acted by command of Lieutenant Hamilton, their officer, and that, therefore, they were not liable; and it was by that means that the jury found them guilty of manslaughter, and not of murder.' (7326 to 7332) Here is a deliberate murder, in broad daylight, in the presence of hundreds. The homicides scatheless, and roaming the country. The friends of the murdered man fleeing for justice to a noble lord, who tells them he will meet them in a day or two. As a further proof of the low state of even the sentiment of law, we may add that Mr. Kernan attaches no blame to Lord Belmore for this remissness—but, on the contrary, expresses his praise, adding, that but for Lord Belmore's interference, not one of the delinquents would have been brought to justice —(7421, and Foot Note) The principal offender charged with the murder, and an attempt to abscond—admitted to bail by two magistrates, on mere verbal security The principal absconding from this bail—the accessories to his crime tried and found guilty of the minor offence of manslaughter, on the plea of the superior guilt of the principal. That principal returns, and is not tried for felony, but made a justice of the peace in the very county in which the widow of Michael M'Brian lives under the protection of the laws !!"

In connection with the above it may be well to state that Lieutenant-Colonel Blacker gave it as his opinion (9078) that the yeomanry then doing permanent garrison duty in the country did good service, an expression strangely contrasting with that of Sir F. Stovin, the Inspector-General of Police, who says (4778) "For the past ten years the yeomanry were useless, and more than useless, in my opinion. *I think they are dangerous and more than dangerous.*"

About this time appeared in Dublin a series of ably written pamphlets under the head of "The Ghost of the Catholic Association of Ireland, addressing, first, His Majesty's Ministers, second, the Orangemen, third, the Liberal Protestants; fourth, the Catholics of Ireland," the publisher, and I have good reason to believe the author, of which was Mr. W. J Battersby, 33, Winetavern Street, Dublin. In the second of these pamphlets the author, addressing the Orangemen of Ireland, says—

"It is evident that the Government is determined to abolish your associations, that his most gracious Majesty has expressed his disapprobation of them, that the great body of the nation are opposed to them It is likewise evident, that your supporters have become ashamed of you; that your best friends have scorned to vindicate you; and, that some of your own body, have betrayed you into the hands of your enemies, by making known those signs, passwords, and oaths, which kept you together.

"Sacrifice, then, on the altar of Christian charity, on the altar of the peace of your country, your prejudices and your folly, let justice triumph over the combined machinations of servile interest and malicious bigotry, prefer the peace and happiness of a nation, to the futile forms of a worthless confederacy.

Say not that a love of the established religion has induced you to uphold your Association, or to contaminate genuine loyalty, with worthless faction or party spirit. This is a libel on the Protestant Religion.—Is the Protestant Religion under the necessity of being supported by intolerance? Is its creed composed of calumny, virulence, and falsehood? Is bigotry entwined in the essence of its nature? Does it require the co-operation of injustice and uncharitableness? Does it consist in misrepresenting the principles and practices of Catholics? Are you, who are always declaiming against the Catholics, convincing them by your example, that the principles of your Religion inculcate that you should hate your neighbour, and detest your brother? Oh ! how by your actions, can you answer all this? He then narrates in a foot note the following incidents—'In Brownlow's county of Armagh, in 1822, at Creekvekenagh, a James Gormley, the only son of aged father, was shot to death by an armed party of Orangemen—and the only crime laid to his charge was being present at one of their meetings. His cousin-german Catherine Gormley, happened to be with him at the time—she fled, they pursued her, although a woman, she escaped barely with her life,—she saved her life, but lost her senses—and is still a maniac The two leaders of this Orange party were the sons of the Rev. Mr Smith; they were tried and acquitted. But though they made some efforts to stop the murderers in their course, neither of them attempted to arrest one of them. The murderers were tried, and of course acquitted, for the Sheriff, the Jurors, and witnesses were all Orangemen. And is it to be doubted that the heart-rending prayers, the disordered cries and shrieks of this wretched maniac, will plead powerfully to the Almighty.

Upon the 12th of July, 1823, as usual there was an Orange procession at which a Catholic was murdered A person named Hamilton fired the shot, and after this deed of horror was pepetrated, the Orangemen marched back to their Lodge-room, at Hamilton's house, and spent the remainder of the evening in a species of festivity suitable and accordant with the deeds which they executed during the day That blood has fallen on the ground unrequited and unrevenged ! ! ! There was another murder committed as horrible, if possible, more horrible, than those which I have related. Patrick Hughes, a Catholic, was way-laid and murdered on his way from the fair at Cade, in March 1823 He was shot dead, without any pretence of having given offence. The Orange murderer lay under a hedge; another of his companions was posted near him, and cried out. " There goes old Hughes, shoot him!"

It is not alone that the Catholics are liable to be murdered by Orangemen in their habitations, but even in courts of justice as Jurors they are determined to shew no justice to Catholics."

For a further illustration of this statement we may again revert to the evidence of Mr Kernan (7275). It will be amply verified in the details of the King by M'Cabe v Robinson and others, tried at Omagh Assizes, before Chief Justice Bushe. The murdered man M'Cabe the prosecutor's son, was a Catholic, and the parties implicated, about five in all, were Orangemen. That the particulars of the murder were arranged in the lodge room is shown by the facts appearing in evidence There had been a lodge meeting held near Portadown, and the Orangemen selected for the perpetration of the cowardly deed went directly from the lodge-room to the house of the deceased man and there committed the murder. The prisoners were directly connected with the deed, being traced from the lodge to the actual commission of the crime. With

this evidence before him, the judge charged the jury so strongly for a verdict of guilty as to amount to a direction. The jurors, all of whom were Orangemen, returned a verdict of Not Guilty "Immediately after they returned their verdict I left the court," says Mr. Kernan, "and soon after the judge sent for me, and he said in substance, ' Kernan, you are the only barrister in court whom I have seen taking a full note of this trial ' I said I had a full note of it; he then said, ' Do you intend to publish it?' I said ' certainly, s r, I do,' and gave him my reason. He said, ' Kernan, my dear fellow, do you think its publication would tend to pacify the country and establish peace in this county to have this made public ?' Said I, ' I cannot tell that, but it is at present the chief remedy the Catholics have to bring these cases before the public and expose such outrages ; but, however, if you think it would excite a feeling to disturb the peace on the part of the Catholics I shall submit my opinion to your better judgment and will not give it publication.' I did not give it publication , it was the strongest case of unprovoked homicide I ever recollect in professional practice. I have not the slightest doubt that the prisoners were acquitted because the jury were Orangemen and through party feeling."

The case of the King on the prosecution of M'Custer against Alexander Coulter, and others, exhibits an Orange magistrate, a Mr. William Gabbet, peremptorily discharging a party of Orange Yeomen, who had been duly committed by two other magistrates on a charge of capital felony, at Tempo, in which the aggrieved persons were Catholics. "For this," says the Edinburgh Review, " he would have been removed from the Bench but for his connection with the great Orange chieftain, Lord Enniskillen," and the evidence amply bears out the statement. Mr Gabbet, in the following year, expiated on the Catholics his lenity towards Orangemen, for Mr. Blackburn, the Attorney-General, having been officially sent to Enniskillen, found, on examining the jail, eighteen or twenty Catholics who had been confined for three weeks, without any committal or cause whatever assigned for their imprisonment For this good deed he was again reprimanded, and Mr. Blackburn ordered the immediate discharge of the persons thus illegally confined.

On the 12th June, 1823, we find from the Annual Register that a fight of a party nature took place at Maghera, in the County Derry, between the Orangemen and the Ribbonmen, who had now become a power in the country, particularly in the Northern province where Orangeism most prevailed. The result of the quarrel was that the yeomen were driven "into their barracks," where, after providing themselves with arms and ammunition, they returned to the scene of their recent defeat and fired repeated volleys upon the country people, "of whom," says the record, "some were killed and from 1 to 30 persons wounded. "The Orange triumph was afterwards celebrated by an attack on the houses and windows of the Roman Catholics." I quote this not as possessing any isolated interest in itself, but because it is a case illustrative of the conduct of the Orange party all over the country at this particular period. Their outrages now were even in excess of those committed in previous years, as the efforts of the Catholics towards emancipation and the advocacy of their claims by many distinguished minds exasperated the Orange party and drove them to the utmost desperation in those remote districts of the country where the law could not or would not follow in their bloody track.

Speaking recently with a prominent member of the legal profession in the North of Ireland, a gentleman whose business made him familiar with some of the worst deeds of Orangeism in its latter days, I was reminded by him of the fact "That as it is the unwritten code of Orange laws is the worst so the unwritten history is the blackest" The statement is pregnant with meaning. It is the murders concocted within the secret assemblies of the brethern, and done at midnight by desperate and often times chosen accomplices (as we have seen in at least one of the above instances) with no ear to hear the faltering accents of the victims as they died away upon the lips of the unoffending Catholic, no eye to mark the last deadly blow administered to one whose greatest offence was (as Lord Gosford expressed it), because he was a Catholic; it is these, and such cases as these, that would form the blackest record in the history of this institution. But the wisdom of a higher power so decreed that even the machinations of the lodge-room should sometimes be revealed by the members themselves, and at this period we have recorded, upon undoubted testimony, one of the most glaring cases of conspiracy to murder ever yet attempted, in which the victim was none other than the REPRESENTATIVE OF MAJESTY ITSELF. Lord Wellesley came to this country "to administer the law and not to alter it," and he certainly set out upon that administration with conscientious vigour and impartiality, notwithstanding

the adverse opinions held by the contending parties of those days. His administration was not palatable to the Orangemen. His Excellency took too much to do with the Executive. He did not leave the work of governing Ireland to the Secretary, and the Secretary's secretary, and the Secretary's secretary's secretary. But, so far as the law of the time permitted, he endeavoured to save the Catholic from assault and from insult. The consequence was that he, aided by the Lord Mayor of Dublin, put a stop to those disgraceful and offensive displays which periodically took place in the Metropolis on the dressing of the statue of King William. Lord Wellesley was, according to the wont of the Orangemen, called "Papist" or "Popish" Wellesley. To "necessitate his resignation" (in plain terms to murder him or frighten him out of the country), and to give such an expression as would lead the Government to believe that his administration was not a popular one was then the object of the Orange party. An occasion was not long wanting which, on being taken advantage of, resulted in the bottle riot in the Theatre Royal, Hawkins Street, on Saturday, 14th December, 1822. His Excellency was engaged to witness a performance at the Theatre Royal. On the Friday night previous a lodge meeting (No. 1612) of which Robert Fletcher was Grand Master, was held in Peter Daly's public-house, in Weyburgh Street. Purple men alone were present. At this lodge meeting, the diabolical scheme was hatched of assaulting the Lord Lieutenant—the subsequent indictment arising out of it called it a conspiracy to murder, and there are more features than one in connection with the transaction which leaves it open to this construction. That a premeditated assault upon the person of the representative of Majesty and upon the Lord Mayor was was in this lodge arranged there is now no doubt. A subscription was proposed by the Grand Master to defray expenses. In this other lodges of the city joined, and it was determined that those who could not buy tickets for themselves should, by aid of the common fund, "be sent" to the gallery of the house. "It was not necessary to secure tickets to any other parts of the house, as there were plenty to go there at their own expense"—the expression is an extract from the evidence of John Atkinson, a Deputy Grand Master, an Orangeman since the year 1818, and one who admittedly took a prominent part in the conspiracy of the night, one who had in his ex-

13

mination said "he had taken the oath of allegiance, and yet had not done anything to prevent this huge conspiracy against the Government, but had actually furthered it." That there were ninety Orangemen (armed with sticks, &c.) in all, we have proven in evidence, but from another and not less reliable source upon the point—the *Irish Protestant* —we find, "There were hundreds of Orangemen present in the theatre that night—we recognised many of them." Forbes, one of the parties present, and subsequently a prisoner, made use of these expressions—" The devil mend him (Lord Wellesley), I don't care if I be transported, so as I can raise an Orange Lodge wherever I go"—a phrase which, coupled with another of the conspirator's advice, " Be wicked, boys," and read by subsequent events, afford a fair idea of the desperate nature of the plot, and how reckless were the conspirators of consequences. " Look out" was agreed upon as the pass-word for the night. It was arranged that the assault should begin after the Royal Anthem was performed, and that they should insist upon " The Boyne Water" and "The Protestant Boys" being played by the orchestra immediately afterwards; otherwise the programme was not to proceed. The doors of the theatre were surrounded an hour previous to the opening, and when the time arrived a rush was made by this band of " loyal" desperadoes upon every part of the house. The respectable members of lodges took their places in the pit and stalls, and the hired assassins occupied the gallery These men were, as stated by the witnesses at the inquiry, all tipsy, and *had drink with them*, with which they drank to " Protestant ascendancy." When the Lord Lieutenant appeared in the theatre he was received with loud hissing and groans, cries of " Popish Wellesley," " No Popish Lord Lieutenant," " No Popish Government," " Out with the bloody Papist Lord Lieutenant," and the like expressions. The performance, amidst this unseemly disturbance, proceeded. At a stage in the performance when the curtain was down the signal was given, and the preconcerted disturbance was pushed to the highest pitch, in the midst of which a quart bottle was thrown from the gallery at the Viceregal box, and a stick was cast at the Lord Mayor. For the simple reason that the person who fired the bottle had finished its contents, his greed alone defeating his diabolical purpose, the bottle fell wide of the mark; but the second missile, though missing its object, was better directed, and struck the side of the Lord Mayor's box. (" Amid

cries of no Popish Lord Lieutenant they drank ' the Glorious Memory, and ' Protestant Ascendancy, and ' the Boyne Water to-night, when the gallery is ours' "—evidence of Christopher Morans, which accounts fully for the empty bottle) The result was the greatest confusion, in the course of which the Viceregal guard made their appearance and arrested several of the conspirators. The prisoners were James Forbes and William Graham, of lodge 1660; William and Henry Hardwick of lodge 780; and George Brownlow, of lodge 1612, in which the attack was planned George Graham, also an Orangeman, but whose lodge the witness, an Orangemen, could not specify, was also amongst the prisoners. Henry Hardwick was distinctly identified as having thrown the bottle; George Graham as having thrown the stick; Forbes, Brownlow, and Wm. Graham as accomplices and persons of good position. Deplorable as was this outrage, the means taken of thwarting justice were more to be condemned. The Grand Jury was packed by Sheriff Thorpe, a noted party man, who had supplied him a list of men from the Merchants' guild, all of whom were certified as " good men in bad times." He boasted that he had taken measures to have the Grand Jury all true Orangemen, and said there need be no fear of the result. The result was that the Grand Jury ignored the bills; and on the application of Attorney-General Plunkett *ex-officio* informations were filed against the prisoners. The case was tried in February of the following year in the King's Bench; and of it "The Annual Register" says that " the political connections of the prisoners lent the trial importance." Here we also find recorded that "Sheriff Thorpe exchanged smiles of recognition with some of the traversers" as they entered court; that "fifteen counsel appeared for them;" and " that there was no Roman Catholic on the jury" The prisoners were charged with riot, with conspiracy to riot, and with *conspiracy to murder the Lord Lieutenant*, but the latter charge was subsequently withdrawn. The Attorney-General, in his opening statement, described the conspiracy as the foulest he had ever heard of, and did not hesitate to say that its intention was to murder the Lord Lieutenant. The evidence given was to the effect already stated, the plots of the lodge-room having been divulged by Orange witnesses and distinct evidence having been given of identification. The jury disagreed, were locked up for the night, still disagreed, and were ultimately discharged, the Attorney-General saying that he would bring for-

ward the case again. "But it was not thought
prudent to carry the contest with the Orange party
any further," says the authority already quoted,
"and a nolle prosequi was entered upon the informations."

This incident was not allowed to pass without
comment. The Orange plot was discovered, and
the conspirators had no means of defence but by
the old, worn-out cry of a Popish plot, which has
so often brought a smile to the face of sensible
men. Sir Harcourt Lees wrote a pamphlet which,
for villainous vituperation and bigotry, exceeds
any production of the sort I have seen. He justified
all that the Orangemen did, and then proceeds to
say that it was a ruse of the bloody, abominable,
perjured, and murderous scoundrels—the Pope, the
Papish prelates, and ruffianly priests, who hired a
Ribbonman sitting near the orchestra to fling a
"flask" bottle, and not a "quart" bottle, as the
Irish Protestant admitted, over the footlights. Such
a production as this pamphlet is useful. It affords
us evidence of what was the extent to which Orange
violence could reach in those times.

In Parliament the matter received attention.
The charge of jury-packing was investigated by a
committee of the House, and evidence produced by
the Right Hon. Mr. Plunkett of the most convincing nature. Sir Abraham B. King, an Orangeman
since 1797, who was one of the jury, was questioned
as to the signs and oaths of Orangemen, and threatened with the displeasure of the House, but refused
to divulge them. It is not surprising that the
House of Commons was satisfied with regard to the
inculpatory allegations of the Attorney-General.
As then constituted Houses of Commons were
easily satisfied upon such questions. But while
recording this fact, the Annual Register admits that
the inquiry "had another and a more important
issue, for it showed how familiar corruption in the
administration of justice was to the minds of the
Irish people." One would be inclined to think that
the inquiry could not well show the latter and
justify it without proving the jury-packing alle-
ga'ions of the Attorney-General.

Owing to an Act passed in 1823 affecting societies
bound by an oath and using signs and pass-words,
and declaring them illegal, the Orangemen at
their half-yearly meeting in Dublin "dissolved,"
graciously altered their written code of resolutions,
and again reappeared upon the scene, consoling
themselves that they had acted a noble part.

The Parliamentary history of the Institution from
1823 to 1825 is one continued wail against its

existence in spite of its declared illegality. In the
House of Commons on the 5th March of the former
year Mr. Abercromby brought forward the subject,
on motion of an address to the King, regarding the dissensions created in Ireland by this
secret organisation. A lengthened debate followed,
in which Mr. Goulburn, Sir John Newport, Mr.
Dawson, Mr. Fitzgerald, Mr. Peel, Mr. J. Grattan,
and Mr. Canning took part. The Association was
denounced even by the prominent leaders of the
House as an illegal and dangerous conspiracy, and
the prevalent opinion was generally and in a high
degree adverse to it. Scarce anyone attempted to
speak in its justification. The motion was withdrawn.

A few months later the Duke of Devonshire
said in the Lords, "The whole of the Government of Ireland demanded a prompt and
thorough examination." His Majesty's Ministers
had defended their Irish policy by saying that
their object was not to give a triumph to any
party, and the result was that the Government of
Ireland was completely in the hands of the Orangemen. He moved a resolution expressive of regret
at the spirit of violence which existed to an alarming extent in Ireland, and that extra powers were
required as the laws had not been sufficient to
eradicate the evil. The motion was negatived
by a majority of 135 to 59.

On the 30th of March, 1824, on the presenting
of a petition to have the Freemasons exempted from the workings of the Act before
mentioned, Mr. Hume called attention to the
Societies, and demanded Government to remove
from the Commission of the Peace those magistrates who lent their names to party processions,
then illegal in Ireland. *While Mr. Brownlow
referred the House to a recent charge of Baron
M'Clelland where he pointed out that many
murders and other outrages were the result of
those processions. Though an Orangeman himself

* In February, 1825, the Grand Society of Ireland announced by circular to the brethern that on the opinion ɔ
the most eminen counsel the Orange Societies, as then constituted, were legal, and did not militate against the law of the
land or that if anything could cause even an approach to its
doing so it should be a deviation from the rules. Processions, the fruitful source of outrage and of murder, were at
the same time being held all over the country. Remarking
upon this the Dublin University Magazine of April, 1835, condemns the sins of the Orangemen and says—"It i not
strange that they should not widely acquiesce in the legislative enactments which suppressed with a high and haughty
rigour of the Administration, the good-feeling which were
wont, by their periodical returns, to be kindled up in their
enthusiasm of their hearts, &c." Strange expressions for
the organ of the Grand Lodge. It smacks much of the suggestive defiance of all law, particularly when the brethern
were actually defying it.

he condemned these processions. Mr. Abercromby followed, denouncing Orange Societies, with all their alterations of rules, as an illegal conspiracy, but no result followed.

We find from a statement of Mr. John Smyth in the Commons on the 4th May following, on presenting a petition against Orange societies, that they had largely increased in consequence of the law which intended to suppress them; while Sir John Newport called the attention of the House to the judicial remarks made on the last circuit to the Grand Jury " that if they allowed Orange societies, they must be prepared for Ribbon societies, one of which created the other." Later on in the session —in June—Sir John Mackintosh presented the petition of Mr. John Lawless, Belfast ("Honest Jack"), praying to have an end put to these Orange displays, and following immediately in the pages of Hansard, we come upon an old acquaintance, Mr. Bernard Coile—rising as if from the grave, but still outliving the turmoil, a breathing example of intolerance in the past quarter of a century—petitioning the House for redress of his grievances at the hands of the Orange faction. Sir James Mackintosh, who presented the petition, said the outrages mentioned in it were so cruel, and abounded with expedients so calculated to degrade our nature and to revolt public feeling, they formed such a combination of menaces and malice, they were so miserable, and yet for the base objects of vexation and cruelty so nefariously operative that he would not disgust the House by repeating them. The petition, so revolting in its horrible details that the hon. member dared not read them, was withdrawn on the guarantee that the matter would be investigated on the opening of the next session.

The Catholic Association had now become a power in Ireland. Moved by the one impulse—redress of grievances, and aided from the outside by a large mass of respectable and liberal Protestants, who felt for their fellow-creatures woe, the organisation moved forward, with O'Connell in the lead, the prelates and priests of Ireland ably supporting him, but more than all, the people, the great power—the people, without whom no agitation can succeed, and with whom none can fail of ultimate success, pushing them on to fearless assertion of their rights. No popular organisation in Ireland can be said to be nearing success until the English Government directs its powerful and convenient machinery towards the suppression of it. The time had now arrived for the suppression of the Catholic Association, and

the clamour of the Orange faction who feared its power afforded a pretext to the Government. But a strange dilemma presented itself. If the Catholic Association, with their meetings open to the Press and public, were to be suppressed how was Government to deal with those who were on its own admission conspirators? It was endeavoured to be solved in this fashion. Mr. Goulburn obtained leave in 1825 to introduce a Bill "to amend certain acts relating to unlawful societies in Ireland." the Attorney-General assuring them it was intended to apply the Act to the Orangemen as well as to the Catholic Association; and a month later, on-March 3rd, Mr. Brownlow presented a petition praying for inquiry into Orangeism. There is something here suggestive of the adroit move, notwithstanding that Mr. Brownlow said " he did not apprehend that after the Bill before Parliament passed, the Orange Association would continue in Ireland," when we recall the fact that two years previously the Orange leaders vigorously opposed all inquiry, and did all in their power to prevent inquiry into what they now voluntarily offered to disclose. Both Mr. Abercromby and Mr. Secretary Peel expressed pleasure at hearing that there was soon to be a complete end to Orange Societies in Ireland. The inquiry was not granted. The Bill passed. The Orange Societies as well as the Catholic Associations were illegal in Ireland. Did they cease to exist? Not a bit of it. They had been too long exercised in the work of evasion. They "dissolved" (in the Orange sense) the Irish branch of the Association, and in the few cases where they could not meet the expenditure of securing English warrants they simply did without them. All over the country the lodges were rampant as ever, and equally capable of evil.[*]

The Relief Bill of 1825 was thrown out by the Lords. The Bill of suppression, the Algerine Act alone passed both Houses. The most subtle Act of Parliament is but a feeble restraint upon the ex-

[*] See question 7063, and read also the carefully-worded circular of "dissolution" at question 17 of the Select Committee's Irish Report. In the circular the Grand Secretary says: "Parliament have considered it necessary that all political societies should be dissolved. Of course our society is included. We were pledged to the principles of Orangeism, which are inviolable, and we shall feel ple sure in inculcating them to our neighbours and others and in instilling them into the infant breasts of our children, so that they may grow with their growth and strengthen with their strength, and so be handed down entire and unimpaired from generation to generation." Rather inconsistent language from the society of an illegal association when declaring an intention to dissolve! Positive proof I am, and I think my readers will be inclined to take it, that this vaunted association was only a name which, wrapping up the organisation in even more secrecy, withdrawing it more from public scrutiny, and deceiving the people into a false confidence, made the institution more powerful for evil,

pressions of a suffering people. No legislative enactments can repress the troubled elements of a persecuted community. "Junius" has wisely said that "clearing the fountain is the best and shortest way of purifying the stream." Press down the foul and stagnant waters here; there they will ooze to the surface as foul and pestilential as before. To draw them off by precautionary measures is the only effectual remedy. The truth of this hygienic principle the Commons had partially acknowledged. But the born legislators, the hereditary rulers of their species, refused with their usual obtuseness to see it, and the foolish work of repression proceeded. The statute in all its bearings was examined by O'Connell and found to contain numerous absurdities, many inconsistencies, a long catalogue of incoherencies of which the Catholic Association, now put upon their metal, were not slow to take advantage. The Association was reformed. They made no pretence of being anything but strictly legal. They boldly took advantage of the many chinks in the armour of an hostile assembly, and boarding the Legislative power they met openly in the light of day. The Orangemen acted otherwise. The question is not before us for consideration whether the Catholics acted wrongly. It is simply did the Orangemen act rightly, or had they even legality to atone for any indiscretion? Of the two charges they stand convicted, and of an additional one surpassing both in gravity in the estimation of honourable men. They acted wrongly by continuing their institution in the face of such adverse opinions expressed as well by their friends as by their enemies; they acted illegally by ignoring the precise terms of the measure which declared them dangerous conspirators; and they played their old trump card of deceit in pretending to the world they had dissolved, while the fact is established that they did nothing of the kind. They met in secret in the garrets of Orange pot-houses, and shot their poisoned arrows out of the window at the thousands of men who boldly defied coercion and took the consequences, into the vast multitude who pressed forward for complete emancipation. We have in the evidence of Mr. Richardson Bell the fact that the Orange Lodges continued to meet during this period in the neighbourhood of Dungannon with the same frequency and the same regularity (7063), and that the processions were of precisely the same character as previous to the passing of the Act; that on the usual occasions for display "they marched through the town and behaved in a most ridiculous manner; so much so, that none but low Orangemen would

associate with them." On the authority of the *Belfast News-Letter* of July, 1826, I find that on the 12th July of that year there were Orange processions at Aghalee, County Antrim; at Dromara, at Lisburn, at Lurgan, &c. In the issue of the same journal for 10th July, 1827, we find the following:—"We are happy to learn that *it is the determination of the several Orange lodges of Belfast* not to have any procession on the 12th July. This will have the effect of preventing those scenes of riot which frequently take place upon the returns of this day." In its issue of two days' subsequent to this, it commends the propriety of the Orange lodges in not holding a demonstration. Again, on the 12th of July, 1828, we find in the *News-Letter* the following:—" The Orangemen of Belfast resolved to have no public demonstration. The lodges accordingly met *in their respective rooms*, and passed the evening in unobtrusive hilarity. A small party went off to Lisburn. . . . Arches were formed across the principal streets." It further states that demonstrations were held in Lisburn, Hillsborough, Dungannon (where 170 lodges met), and where the cavalcade was headed by several protestant gentlemen of rank, who "appeared to countenance the procession, dressed in costumes suited to the occasion," in Dromore, in Kilmore, in Saintfield (forty lodges met here), in Portadown (where between thirty and forty lodges met), in Lurgan (where eighty or ninety lodges assembled), in Ballymoney (with 28 lodges), in Ballymena, Antrim and Coleraine. How in the face of this testimony the Orange Institution could boast (with truth of course, for with them boastfulness is built upon slender foundations) or how they could unblushingly assert that they had dissolved in deference to the Act of Parliament is one of those undefinable questions which each party must solve for himself. Of those demonstrations the *News-Letter* remarks—"Everything has been peaceably and orderly conducted, and though the simple fact of having a procession for a specified purpose *may* be an infraction of the existing statute, yet does it not carry in it some redeeming qualities when not a solitary departure from propriety has occurred in all the *numerous* assemblages to which our extracts of correspondents refer." That it was a deliberate and wilful breach of the law cannot be gainsaid as we find by the opinion of Attorney-General Plunket and Solicitor-General Joy given in 1827, that the Orange Association and processions came within the provisions of the 3rd section of the 6th,

George IV., cap. 4, and that as they did not come within any of the exceptions in section 8 of that statute such societies were illegal That this net-work of conspiracy still continued over the country, and with the knowledge and connivance of respectable and titled wirepullers, who fulfilled all the purposes which they had previously avowed, is placed beyond doubt. Regeneration for the illegal demonstrations of July would otherwise have been a work difficult of accomplishment upon such an extended scale and within such a brief period. The report of the Select Committee saves us all trouble of drawing conclusions on this head

As the constitution in no way changed neither did its immediate consequences. Indeed, the latter are so numerous and so fearful during this period that we might reasonably accept them, tracing for the effect the cause as proof in themselves that the Orange Institution was full of life and activity As in the case of the Bottle Riot, where the Orangemen sought by their desperate attempt to frighten his Majesty's representative out of the country, and make his Ministers believe the faction was sufficiently powerful to be feared, so now we find over the country the dread results of the last efforts of a faction whose light was soon to be put out, like to the redoubled exertions of some noxious thing who scented danger in the air; of some beast of prey, doubly dangerous through seeing approaching a superior force to pare its claws; of some venomous reptile spreading death indiscriminately around, hoping to avenge itself in anticipation of hastening doom; the last efforts of a band of bigots, their strength in their intolerance, their power in their recklessness, who, knowing too well how often the braggart is mistaken for the hero, how slowly a whole people perceives the ears of the jackass protruding through the lion's skin, ran stark mad into the community, kicking and belching round about, leaving many murders in its tract, no doubt, but withal, having an air of sanctimonious greatness—the giant presumption of the frog in the fable, who would be an ox; the silly pretensions of a body, whose folly outstripping its discretion, gives to mankind an object of shame and of ridicule, and, who'ly blind to the world's smiles or its frowns, boastfully

Assumes the god,
Affects to nod,
And seems to shake the spheres.

It must be borne in mind that the morning of emancipation had dawned. Like to the tiger when disturbed at his prey, a wail went up from the Orange community upon discovering that they were no longer to be allowed to persecute the Catholics. Upon this persecution they had lived and fattened, as we have seen in the foregoing, and the idea of emancipation was to them a sacrilegious wrong Anxious to stem the advancing tide of intelligence and liberality, they assembled in their lodges, and reorganised that system of guerilla warfare which in the days of the Rebellion had been so fruitful. No longer to be allowed to persecute the Papists! It was an irreverant innovation. The wail which went forth was justified if not by reason at least by precedent For purposes of extermination, William Pitt had created the Orangemen; and when his successors in the Administration objected to their domination, the fault of being no longer useful was not alone theirs. Isolated, disregarded — a broken tool which tyrants cast away without respect the Orangemen gathered together, and in a huff struck out at all institutions which appeared to favour the advance of liberty. Orange lodges were by law prohibited A show of combination was necessary as well for the appearance of strenght as to afford a mouthpiece to the organisation. Conservative Clubs were thought of, and the idea seeming to require all the requirements of the body, 'Brunswick Clubs" were started all over the country. Wherever an Orange lodge "had been' there started up a "Brunswick Club," and under the latter title all their utterances were put forth. That they were regarded as Orange lodges purely and distinctly appears from the debates in Parliament at the time, and from the general expression of opinion recorded in the newspapers of the time. Under the title of a brunswick Club the leaders of Orangeism in Dublin issued their orders, and managed the affairs of that association, which Government, no doubt in their blindness had thought it wise to do without. The alteration in the name in no way affected the character of the association. Somehow outrages still continued and multiplied. Their recurrence had succeeded in uniting more firmly the large mass of Catholics together, and the Orangemen now sought by the same means to oppose the outcome of that unity which their own intolerance had greatly furthered No more striking example of their conduct and inconsistency could be had than that detailed before the Committee of the House of Commons by Richard Bell, of Killymuddy, near Dungannon. In 1827 a Catholic, a butcher, named

Thomas M'Crory, was returning from a fair with his wife and daughter. He was brutally murdered by an Orangeman named Richey, who, with two others, set upon him. To get an Orangeman out of the meshes of the law was then no difficult task. A note from his clergyman to the effect that A. B. was not a likely person to commit a murder answered all the purposes of an alibi, and forth the murderer walked fresh for further slaughter. In this instance the Rev Mr. Brydge, or Bridges, was applied to for a character for Richey. Believing that Richey was about to quit the country, he gave him such a character as would help to disarm suspicion in the interval. Confident of an acquittal, Richey did not leave the country, and to the rev. gentleman his friends applied for a second character. In stricter terms, they appeared with a written *acknowledgment of his innocence*, which they requested him to sign When questioned as to who were the murderers, the mother of the culprit Richey said that two of the murderers, whose names she gave, were known. The name of the third she refused to give until after a subscription had been raised by the Orangemen for the defence of her son. The Rev. Mr. Bridges naturally concluded that Richey was number three murderer and refused to sign the "character." A verdict of wilful murder had been returned against him, and at a subsequent trial Richey's attorney requested the clergyman to stop away, as any character he could give would only militate against him The agent of the estate upon which Richey's father lived left the court just before a character was called for. Strange to say, Richey was found guilty, and stranger still, considering that the Brunswick Clubs were powerful in Dublin, Richey was hanged. But now comes the moral of the story. The leaders of Orangeism, with Mr. Verner at their head, took it into their silly brains that their brother was hanged, not because Richey murdered a Papist, but because his clergyman had refused him a character. All the lodges in Tyrone were set in motion, and a person was selected from amongst them to murder the Rev. Mr. Bridges Upon a certain Sunday contingents from all quarters of the country appeared—to attend an interesting sermon at the Episcopalian church—Mr Bridges' meeting-house was besieged by an organised mob of Orangemen, an attack was made upon his person, and an effort made not alone to interfere with the course of worship, but to do personal injury to the clergyman himself. He succeeded in escaping with his life, but for three successive Sundays

this work continued, efforts being made each day by deputied parties to murder him. The result was that he had to fly from his residence, and despite all the entreaties of the Synod the Orangemen, headed by the Episcopalian clergy of the place, continued irreconcilable to the last. For refusing a certificate of innocence to a murderer, Mr. Bridges was compelled to fly the locality. Mr. Crossley, J.P , *agent to Colonel Verner*, played a prominent part in this prosecution.

Instances such as this are too numerous for quotation, but the above may be taken as a fair indication of the character of the Association. With all, they did not, nor could they stop the march of events. Waterford election had been won by the Catholic freeholders, and Clare followed in rapid succession. The South was under the complete control of the Catholic Association, and O'Connell seemed to hold the reins of Government in his hand, so great was the revolution that had taken place. Onward the great current of emancipation swept, carrying with it Brunswick Clubs, Orange Lodges, Conservative Associations, and all those feeble barriers which prejudice or ignorance had opposed to it.

The North, says Mr. Wyse in his history of the Association, was* not yet ripe for this measure, nor was it to be expected that a delegate or deputy of the association could I carry it so immediately and quietly into effect, as the inhabitants themselves, in possession of superior knowledge of local difficulties, and of the means by which they might most easily be obviated; but, besides this, the moment selected was more than ordinarily inauspicious. The lately established Brunswick Clubs had pervaded every part of the country. The yeomanry, so far from having been disarmed, had considerably augmented their military resources. The entire country had been roused to the utmost degree of excitation by the invectives and denunciations of the Orange party. An open and shameless cry for the blood of their fellow-citizens, and a direct avowal of an anxiety to bring back the scenes of 1798, had been heard from even the ministers of the Gospel at several of their late meeting. The association and its leaders in all these harringues had been pointed out in precise terms, as the prime source, the fertile principle, of the existing distractions of the country , and the vengeance, sometimes of the

* History of the Catholic Association by Mr. Wyse, vol I , page 400.. Mr. Lawless had just been chosen as a delegate to extend the Catholic Association in the North.

Legislature, sometimes of the population, been repeatedly invoked against them and their proceedings. To send them a member of that body, and in the authorised character of its representative, to such men and at such a moment, was little less than a direct provocative to open combat, an immediate signal for civil war. Many of the most considerate Catholics deprecated this unadvised intrusion on en the territory of their enemies, and regretted that their voice had not been consulted, or had not been allowed to be heard, in a matter of so much public moment. Nor was Mr Lawless the person precisely the most calculated for such an adventure. His sincerity, his ardour, his perseverance, are beyond all impeachment; his popular talents have been felt—the enthusiasm which he felt himself, and knew so well to communicate to an assembly of his countrymen, were better testimonies to his efficiency than any commendation of mere phrase. But Mr. Lawless is more sparingly gifted with other qualities of a less shining nature, but far more important, for the judicious discharge of the delicate functions with which he was entrusted. A nice discrimination of time and place; a keen perception of the innumerable shades of public feeling; a calm and even cold judgment of popular excitation; a prospective regard to consequences, and an exceeding discretion in the management of popular resources, are qualities which we require even in an ordinary diplomatist. In the diplomacy just noticed, they were more than especially necessary. Mr Lawless would have made a good Commissioner to the Departments, under the French Republic Had it been necessary to stimulate, to kindle, to force into immediate action a slumbering province, or to call out on a sudden emergency a levy en masse of fierce and determined men, no person, I am persuaded, would go through "such a labour of love" with higher spirit, more success, or greater physical and moral intrepidity But the task here was of an opposite description, and Mr. Lawless either mistook the character of his mission, or, with the best intentions, found nothing in his nature which was calculated to second the intentions of the association. Had it really been his purpose to organise the North, it would appear to a reasonable man, that the most obvious mode which, under the circumstances, could have been adopted, would have been to have gone at once to the North, and in a manner the most private and unostentatious possible. In such a country, as little notice, as little delay, as little crowd as possible, was the obvious policy of the as

sociation Mr. Lawless, personally objectionable as he undoubtedly was to very many, even of the most moderate of his antagonists, adopted every expedient which could most inflame their animosity. He hovered for several weeks on the borders of Ulster, and though it is not to be denied, that in those places he did much good, and with as much alacrity as could reasonably be expected, yet the very good which he did, the time which he spent in doing it, the excitation which accompanied, and the lofty terms in which he announced it to the association, and through that body of course to the entire country, put it altogether out of his power to execute the really important part of his mission, when the period arrived for its accomplishment. All this time was spent in preparation; when the contest came, his enemy was also prepared. But this want of political generalship was likely to have produced consequences far more fatal than mere personal defeat. Mr. Lawless was inadvertently on the point of involving the two great contending parties in instant conflict, and by no very strained inference suddenly plunging both bodies, and perhaps both countries, into civil war.

Mr. Lawless had now addressed several successive meetings in the different parts of the country through which he had passed, Kells, Dundalk, &c., with his characteristic eloquence, and had everywhere been received with the loudest acclamations. The rent was established as he moved along, and hopes were indulged that the representations hitherto made to the association of the state of the Catholics of the North were false, or grossly exaggerated. In every chapel where he appeared crowds came to meet him, and many even of his opponents joined the people, and returned with favourable impressions. As he proceeded the usual results of such assemblies became perceptible. Meetings had never been frequent in that part of the country, and the people were fresh and easily affected by such appeals. The exertions of Mr. Lawless were indefatigable, His success exceeded his anticipations. The numbers of the auditors augmented as he had advanced—a corresponding enthusiasm grew up with their numbers Throughout all this, too, the temper and order of the populace were marvellous. They had studied with success the lessons of Waterford and Clare. Though thousands and tens of thousands were grouped around him a single violation of good order had not yet taken place These were emphatic proofs that the spirit of organisation as well as agitation had spread through every part of the country. But

Mr. Lawless was carried away, no extraordinary case, by his own victories. The time now seemed arrived for the subjugation of the "black North." Mr. Lawless determined to enter it at Ballybay. He was accompanied, it is said, by one hundred and forty thousand peasants, all well clothed, and, it is added, well armed; but their arms, on closer inquiries, have been reduced to a certain number of bludgeons and pistols, concealed under their freize coats. This was of itself imprudent, but it was without the cognisance of Mr. Lawless. There were circumstances which rendered it infinitely more so. The Orangemen were alarmed at the hostile incursion, and prepared for defence. They were impressed with an idea that Ballybay was devoted to destruction by the Papists, and their allies were summoned for every part of the country to support them without delay. Three thousand Orangemen, who soon increased to five thousand, took possession of the hill immediately above the town. They every moment expected reinforcements. The next day it is very probable they could have counted a force of from ten to twenty thousand men. The two armies, for literally they were such, were now very near each other, and no sort of disorder had yet marked the conduct of either. It was a singular sight, in the midst of perfect peace, and a general in her Majesty's service, General Thornton, standing close by. In a happy moment, ere it was quite too late, Mr. Lawless perceived his mistake. He had trusted too far to his sway over the multitude. To a certain point such rule is omnipotent—beyond it, it vanishes into air. The people, as long as they are not attacked, will not attack others; they are orderly, if not provoked. Even a certain degree of provocation they can bear; but this forbearance has its limits, and these limits are easily passed in the North. The men here brought into collision were not like the men he had lately been witnessing—the men of Clare—neither were their wrongs, nor their quarrel, nor their hatreds, as theirs. This was not a question between an old friend and a popular leader, between Mr. O'Connell and Mr. Fitzgerald; but it was a deadly and inextinguishable national feud between two parties, the one masters, the other servants; one oppressors, the other oppressed—burning with mutual detestation—heated by remembrance of centuries of injury, and closing gradually on each other in the full conviction that they could not separate without blows. That the Catholic party had any intentions of vengeance or outrage, it would perhaps be unjust to

assert; that they could never have entered the town, and preserved their tranquillity and good order, is now beyond a doubt. Their dispositions might have been the most peaceable—their intentions the most pure—their peace and their purity no longer depended upon themselves. A single man with difficulty bears an insult—a hundred thousand men would certainly not bear even its shadow or intimation. The alarms of the Orangemen would have produced the same results as the confidence of the Catholics. A collision would have been inevitable: a single shot would have been enough. It was easy to begin, but where would it have ended? The entire North in four-and-twenty hours would have been up. But would the South have remained quiet? In the meantime Mr. Lawless adopted the only best course to that of not having appeared there at all. The people took his entreaties to peace and order, as words of course, plausible pretexts for the better concealing of real intentions, and were for the most part persuaded that he intended heading them in military array against their enemies. They hurried him on in his carriage to within a very small distance from the town. In a moment the difficulty and the danger flashed upon him. He rushed with a sudden effort from his carriage, mounted a grey horse, instantly dashed through the crowd—and fled. In the very moment of his escape a partisan of his own is said to have presented a pistol to his breast, indignant at the failure of the expedition. It happily missed fire. Another leader was to have taken his place. What the consequences might have been it is not very difficult to conjecture. Ballybay might have been entered, but a rebellion that very night would have commenced in Ireland.

It is sometimes as courageous to retreat as to advance, and, unquestionably, the flight, as if really was, of Mr. Lawless from Ballybay was one of those exceptional instances. Popular excitement was at its highest point. The Catholic element was aroused to a pitch never before exemplified, and the slightest spark would have fired the breasts of those one million five hundred thousand Catholic associates who met in their respective chapels, in January, 1828. That the Orange body, comparatively few and insignificant, could have coped single handed with such an outraged multitude, men who felt their grievances and their power to redress them, is an idea that cannot be retained for an instant. It verges into the ridiculous. We must pay them the credit of not even entertaining this thought. But their object, as acknowledged by their platform orators, such men as John Claudius Beresford, the Master in Chancery, Mr. Ellis, Sergeant Lefroy and others, was as brutal as it was nefarious. To bring back the bloody days of 1798 was now the only means by which Catholic Emancipation could be successfully resisted. From an Orange platform in Dublin the design was made known Could a collision be brought about between the two contending rties' Government could scarce allow them to fight t out without interfering, and there was little doubt upon which side English influence would be exerted. It was this design that called forth the memorable, though somewhat indiscreet, challenge of Mr O'Connell—"Oh! would to God that our excellent Viceroy, Lord Anglesey, would but only give me a commission, and if those men of blood should attempt to attack the property and persons of his Majesty's loyal subjects with a hundred thousand of my brave Tipperary boys I would soon drive them into the sea before me" But Government could not afford to stake their existence upon such a trial of strength. The army was in great part Catholic and Irish, and the events of the Clare election rendered it doubtful that the arms of the soldiery would be used in shooting down their Cathol c fellow-countrymen.

The Brunswick Clubs had continued the system of exclusive dealing which had been long recognised as one of the regulations of the Orange Society. This reprehensible conduct had—but chiefly in the North—very disasterous consequences in many instances. A resolution recommending similar conduct on the part of the Catholics of the South was proposed in the Catholic Association by some of its most violent members and summarily negatived, Mr O'Connell and The O Gorman Mahon being amongst its strenuous opponents Upon this occasion it was Mr. O'Connell said, "Whether the death of a human being be hastened by the horrors of starvation or by the gun of the Orangeman or the yeomanry bayonet the crime is equally detestable in the eye of God and in the opinion of every good man. Yes, I repeat it, a persecution of this nature has been carried on by the Brunswickers, and the "backing" system has by them been acted upon to a frightful extent."

That emancipation was bound to come was beyond question. Still it is questionable whether it would have come so soon but for the praiseworthy action of the Liberal Protestants of Ireland, who had kept themselves aloof from what they honestly characterised as the violence of the Catholic party,

and were too broad-minded and too loyal to mix themselves up with the machinations of the Orange Society, then known as Brunswick Clubs. "The neutrals bring about revolutions," and they who so long had stood carelessly, at any rate listlessly, watching the two parties confronting each other now joined in the contest. A few went over to the Brunswick side, but the vast majority, says Mr. Wyse, thinking that the hour of action could no longer be deferred, declared for the Catholics and for Ireland. The celebrated Protestant declaration in favour of Emancipation, the remarkable pronunciation of Lord Morpeth, the verbal puzzle which Wellington sent for Dr. Curtis and Ireland to unravel, the bold, out spoken, and manly declaration of the Viceroy, Lord Anglesey, that emancipation could no longer be denied, all now followed in rapid sucession, and are matters having more to do with the general history of Ireland than with our unassuming story. The sudden recall gave room for high hopes in the Orange bosom that the old days of intolerance and of blood were about to come back again, and from many quarters came the empty toast that the Government dared not emancipate the Catholics for fear of the Orange party "Papist" Anglesey was abused and vilified, and Wellington and Peel idolised as "true Orangemen" and Protestant heroes. Great was the jubilation. The nest of vipers in the Castle, who, by garbled reports, had been poisoning the mind of each successive Viceroy, had been rooted out by Lord Anglesey, and they now hoped for a return of the old misrule. A secret alliance between the Government and their faction they openly proclaimed, and, ever loyal to those whom they thought favourable to their own prejudices, they called on their clubs "to support the hands of his Majesty's Government" On the other hand, there was over the Catholics a sorrow, which was the more significant from its expression by a silence, almost unbroken save at the departure of Lord Anglesey from Dublin. It was a demonstration of the most affecting kind, resembling that which took place on the memorable departure of Lord Fitzwilliam By those who witnessed it the two occasions were likened, and an inference by no means comforting drawn, that the same terrible results would follow.

---

* Mr W Sharman Crawford, M P., in his examination before the Select Committee, in 1 35, gave it as his opinion that the Catholics did not take any step to secure emancipation which the circumstances did not warrant "They proceeded mildly in the first instance, until their patience was tried, and until no resource remained but a bold and determined assertion of their rights."

Before the occurrence of these events the Orange Society had openly avowed their existence. The statute of 1825 lapsing in 1 28, they could now with safety acknowledge themselves. Ernest, Duke of Cumberland graciously condescended to extend his imperial sway and to become Grand Master of the Irish Institution, the Earl of Enniskillen, Colonel Wm. Verner, and Robert Hedges Eyre acting as deputies. Read by the light of subsequent results, we will find the "annual" of this year, that is the password to all the lodges of the Institution, pregnant with meaning. We have it on the authority of Mr. Swan, who this year joined the Society and shortly afterwards filled the place of Deputy Grand Secretary that the "annual" for this the year of "revival" of the Orange Association was "ERNEST" The word suggests plots, dark designs, and revolution; a faint streak of light, by following which we can unearth the traitors. The rules, which in little sense differed from those of 1824, were submitted, and received, we are told, the sanction of legal authority. The Orangeman's oath being omitted, the applicant was required not alone to take the oaths of allegiance, supremacy and abjuration, but had to subscribe to the declaration against transubstantiation, and to "solemnly and sincerely, in the presence of God, profess, testify, and declare" that the sacrifice of the Mass was idolatrous, superstitious, and damnable, as well as the invocation of the Virgin Mary. In the face of this declaration the Grand Lodge of Dublin, meeting in November, 1823, had the effrontery to issue an address to the Protestants of the Empire in which, after speaking about their religion being menaced by Popery and infidelity, they said they rejected from amongst them an intolerant spirit, and only accepted as brothers those whom they knew to be incapable of persecuting, injuring, or upbraiding anyone on account of his religion. This epistle ends with a threat which is in itself an acknowledgement that the Institution had not been dissolved during the three previous years. "The Orange Institution cannot be suppressed but by means which would subvert the Constitution of Great Britain, and erase the name of the Prince of Orange from among her sovereigns. After that"—no, not the deluge, but something akin to it—"the Brunswick dynasty would soon follow, the liberty of these realms, our religion, and our monarchy would again be placed under Papal darkness and despotic oppression." How far this prophecy was true we in the present

are able to judge. The Orange Institution was suppressed not many years after as we shall see. What followed? Not the Brunswick dynasty. Neither was the liberty of these realms, their religion, or their monarchy placed under "Papal darkness or despotic oppression."

How far the Grand Lodge was sincere in imploring the brethern over the country to respect the law, and refrain from processions may be seen from the following rule inserted this year —

"21. In as much as a popular error prevails respecting the landing of King William III. of glorious and immortal memory, that happy event having taken place on the 5th and not the 4th of November, as generally supposed, the former day being recognised by law, and a solemn prayer appointed to be used in all churches—viz., for the happy deliverance of King James I. and the three estates of England from the most traitorous and bloody-intended massacre by gunpowder, and also for the happy arrival of his Majesty King William III. on this day, for the delivery of our church and nation, the members of the Orange Institution will henceforth *celebrate* the 5th of November as the grand *era*, the same to be observed by *the brethern at tending Divine Service in their respective churches*"

With such a rule inculcating processions it would be difficult to attach blame to the ignorant masses when they wantonly broke the law. Though the Secret Articles were omitted from the rules they had not been repealed, so that all who had been sworn in previous to 1824 were bound by them. Secrecy was still the motto of the institution. At all their lodge meetings the tyler, the guardian spirit, presided outside the door. Up to this year (1828) the Trinity College Lodge met within the walls, and it is now for the first time that we find the young law student, Isaac Butt, who, in years, after, learned to repent the follies of his early days, figuring as an Orangeman. At a meeting of the Grand Lodge, held in the Merchants' Hall, he made a violent Orange speech, which was thought sufficiently bigotted to receive the praise of the Orange organ, the *Evening Mail*. Mr. Butt soon after was raised to a place of distinction in the order.

The association was now used in every possible shape for the purpose of thwarting the generous intentions of his Majesty's Ministers. Mr. James Christie in his evidence before the Committee (5691) says—"I have known and seen instances in which the Orangemen have been collected and stimulated to assemble and march in order to the church; I saw them go into one church to sign a petition against Catholic emancipation, and the church was kept open and they marched in procession, and I was myself in a gig with an Orangeman who reprimanded them for so doing ; he said they were *ordered* in, but not to go in a procession. They were ordered in by the District Masters, as I understand."* This leaves little room for wonder that there were presented to the House of Commons 2013 petitions against the Emancipation Bill, as compared with 955 in favour of it. The petitions in the Lords' were—against, 2521; in favour, 1014. Had the Orangemen confined themselves to the constitutional course of petition, even signed under circumstances of menace, there would be little room to quarrel. But they sought by every possible means to terrorise those who differed from them from adopting the same course, and by many acts of outrage endeavoured to show how fierce and bloody would be their resentment if the Bill became law. Mr. W. J. Handcock ("Papist" Handcock) says (7913) that a violent and most disgraceful riot took place in May, 1828, in Lurgan. A rumour was raised that the Catholic Bill had been thrown out by the Committee, and in the evening flags were hoisted on the church of Holt Waring, a reverend and venerable Orange firebrand of those days, and the church bells were rung. An Orange mob paced the streets, shouting "Verner for ever," and sending the Pope and "Papist" Handcock to hell. From house to house in which Catholics resided they proceeded, smashing and wrecking as they went, until at length Mr. Handcock read the Riot Act, and sent for Mr. Forde, a neighbouring magistrate, to assist him in restoring peace. Our police system was not then so perfect as in latter years. The yeomanry, every man of them Orange about Lurgan, were presumed to be the *peace preservers* in time of tumult. Desirous of preserving order, the magistrates sent for George Douglass, the permanent sergeant of the yeomanry corps, and the person in whose care were the yeomanry arms, to see if the assistance of the yeomen could be relied upon. This course, though no doubt necessary on the part of the au-

thorities, seems silly in the extreme, seeing that the very persons upon whom reliance was placed for preserving order were then actually engaged in wrecking their neighbours' houses. Douglass was a true Orangeman—much more loyal as an Orangeman than as a yeoman. He accordingly refused to assemble the yeomen to aid the magistrates, approved the action of the rioters, and told Mr. Handcock, J.P., "he cared no more about him than he did about the tail of a scallion." The conduct of Douglass was such as to induce the magistrates at once to take measures to have the arms removed from his custody, and after some difficulty this was accomplished. In the meantime the riot proceeded, the drums beat to arms with "Croppies lie down" and the "Boyne Water," and after satiating their frenzy by house-wrecking and burning to their entire satisfaction, the "Loyal Orange Yeomen" retired from the scene. Nine of the rioters were arrested, and the sergeant of the yeomanry waited upon them and urged them not to give bail. By two magistrates they were committed formally and legally, and sent under an escort to Portadown, the the Orange bands undertaking to cheer them on their march by discoursing the tunes before mentioned. When they arrived at Portadown, Curran Woodhouse, J.P., actually set at nought the committal of the two Lurgan magistrates, and released them on bail. Douglass, the yeomanry sergeant, was one of the securities. The incident will suffice to illustrate where and how the yeomanry secured their arms.

Indeed, the entire North was about this time a scene of violence and outrage. Towards the close of the year riots of a serious character took place in Monaghan, and many upon both sides were arrested. An Orange jury was packed, who acquitted all the Orangemen and convicted all the Catholics (7,355), the verdict being so flagrantly unjust that the barrister discharged the convicted on payment of a nominal fine. Mr. R. Kernan, B.L., who defended the Catholics, narrowly escaped assassination at the hands of the Orangemen, for, on the night he was supposed to be returning from Monaghan, the Belfast coach was stopped, attacked and wrecked, and a clergyman in mistake dragged out by the would-be assassins. Mr. Kernan had stopped to dine with a friend, and so escaped.

Meantime, the associates in Dublin were arranging to break up the great Liberal Protestant meeting in the Rotunda. That the arrangements fell through was not on account of their forbearance or from any

---

* The *News-Letter* of Tuesday, January, 27, 1829, contains the f llowing :—" ORANGEMEN OF LONDONDERRY.— On Wednesday last, the 21st inst., the city district of Orangemen was reorganised by the County Grand Master, under the authority of the Grand Orange Lodge. On the ensuing morning at seven o'clock the lodges of the Newtown'amivady district assembled in great numbers at Ballykinly for t e purpose of signing their petitions against Papish ascendancy in Ireland. At nightfall they adjourned t their lodge-rooms in Newtownlimavady, where they occupied the evening in affixing their signatures to the rolls of parchment, which, being short, another fold was lent to them by the Brunswickers of the barony of Kenaught, the great majority of whom belong to their body."

wise counsel imparted by Mr. Beresford. The amalgamation of the Catholics with the Liberal Protestants by means of the "Society of Friends of Civil and Religious Freedom" now made the quarrel, not one between Catholic and Protestant, as it unhappily had been, but between Ireland on the one side and England on the other.

The year 1829 must be for ever memorable in the history of Ireland. It was the year of Catholic Emancipation. And Catholic Emancipation broke the spine of Protestant ascendancy. The speech from the Throne on the 6th February announced the introduction of a Catholic Relief Bill, but this was to be preceded by an Act intended for the suppression of the Catholic Association, but extending to every species of political associations in Ireland. This announcement, notwithstanding the coercive measure accompanying it, was received with delight all over the country. Before the Act of suppression was passed, the Catholic Association, after many years of earnest work, seldom unaccompanied by danger, and in its early days cold-shouldered by friends, and sneered at by enemies, voluntarily dissolved, and contemporaneously with it the "Society of the Friends of Civil and Religious Freedom." A few days later the Royal assent was given to the Suppression Bill, and on the same evening in the House of Commons Mr. Peel brought in a Bill "for the relief of his Majesty's Roman Catholic subjects." The Bill was passed in the Commons by a majority of 180 on the second reading and in the Lords by a majority of 105. On the 13th April 1829, the Royal assent was given, and there was placed upon the statute book an Act which has not been unjustly termed THE NEW MAGNA CHARTA.

CHAPTER XXVII.—AFTER EMANCIPATION, "NO SURRENDER."

IT has been truly said that it was not the Duke of Wellington who originated the measure of Emancipation. It was the stern hand of necessity. He admitted it. To the degenerate successors of the Orangemen of this period it will bring little consolation to know that the action of their fathers accelerated the emancipation of the Catholics by, at least, a quarter of a century. Had the South American slave drivers been kinder to their species they would, in all probability, have been driving slaves to-day. Had the Orangemen of the Diamond been less blood-thirsty, or had their successors learned wisdom and moderation in time, Protestant ascendancy would have been rampant for another quarter of a century. They, fortunately for our time, played the part of the ass between the two bundles of hay. They would have all. They retained none. They would concede nothing. They were left nothing to concede. An Act of Parliament had, however, no magic in it to exercise the evil which had for so many years held undisputed sway over the affairs of Ireland, and for so long given forth with the arbitrary power of usurper the decrees of life or death. The snake was scotched; not killed. The wound inflicted, it gathered itself up, and crawled into those infamous holes so numerous over the United Kingdom, there to hatch new treason. The "Glorious Constitution, as established by William of immortal memory" had been violated beyond a doubt. There was no disguising it, even to themselves. Into their lodges they crept. In every filthy tavern of the country they were to be found—these men, once the boasted exclusive loyalists!—there they brooded in sullen silence over their plans, and in muttered, in whispered phrases communicated their guilty intent's the one to the other: "The Constitution has been betrayed!" "The King has betrayed it!!" "Ernest is our Imperial Grand Master!!!" "ERNEST SHALL BE KING!!!!"*

The management of this wide-spreading conspiracy to alter the succession fell, as a matter of

---

* It must be recollected that at this time the "first gentleman"—and the biggest fool—in Europe was giving token of approaching dissolution. That he was fast losing what little wits he ever had, and had prematurely arrived at second childhood, was shown by the great partiality he had, though always his failing, of weeping upon all occasions of perplexity. The occasion seemed, therefore, an opportune one, but the early demise of the last of the Georges perplexed the conspirators, and did not give them time to gather their forces against the popular Duke of Clarence. I wish to guard myself from being misunderstood. The conspiracy was not against George IV., although had he long survived he would in all probability have been made the object of it. But the King having, in the opinion of the Orangemen, betrayed the Constitution of 1688, these men thought themselves justified, no doubt, in conspiring to alter the succession, anxious to place upon the throne the head of their faction, and fearful lest the legitimate heir, an acknowledged and broad-minded Liberal, should succeed. It may be said that the conspiracy would not have been exerted against the then reigning monarch, that George the Fourth opposed Emancipation. Well, possibly it would not. But George really did not oppose Emancipation. He made a show of doing so, blubbered a great deal, spluttered out that he would run away to Hanover, or drown himself in some of the German baths. But he did nothing of the sort. M. Guizot, in his life of Sir Robert Peel, said that this weeping was all dumb show to please the prejudices of the English people. At any rate, shedding tears was not the opposition that the Orangemen wanted from the King against Catholic Emancipation. Shedding blood would have been more after their heart, and would possibly have been the course adopted by their "dear and venerated monarch George III." In the eyes of Orangemen the King had, therefore, betrayed the Constitution.

course, to the English Grand Lodge. Before entering upon this important feature of the subject we
have to do first with the Irish Grand Lodge, and
what were the more immediate effects of Emancipation in this country. It is worthy of inquiry how
the brethren respected the laws of this land which
gave to Catholics the right of every free-born
citizen. The Relief Bill was received with deep
thankfulness by the Roman Catholics, by the
wholesome advice of their clergy they abstained
from demonstration of any kind. The result was
that the first day of Emancipation passed in unbroken quiet. No outward expressions of joy were
indulged in lest they might, by a hostile party, be
construed into appearances of triumph. Wanting
an excuse the Orangemen contrived to do without
one. All over the entire country, from April to
the latter end of July, we have one continued record
of excitment and outrage. The lodges were let
loose upon the community, and stimulated by
strong drink nightly administered in the lodge-
rooms, all of them tap-rooms, they commenced a
system of warfare upon the Catholic inhabitants
which nothing but the most unholy hate
could prompt * We find from the minutes
of evidence before the Irish Select Committee that on the 6th May, of this year,
a boat belonging to Mr. Peter Clarke, a
Roman Catholic, was proceeding on the canal from
Portadown to Newry with a cargo of potatoes,
when it was attacked by a large party of Orangemen armed with yeomanry rifles, who fired upon it,
and compelled its inmates to take refuge on the
opposite side of the shore Such instances of outrage were numerous, and spread terror all through
the north, which in no sense was calculated to be
quieted by the feeling that the Orange celebrations
of July were approaching. So fearful was the
alarm that the Lord Lieutenant, now the Duke of
Northumberland, thought it necessary to issue
specific instructions against all party processions,
and to warn, by circular, the officers of yeomanry
against permitting their men to take any share
in such demonstrations The Irish Grand Lodge
was equal to the occasion. The records of the day
gave them credit for desiring to stop processions
on the 13th July (the 12th was a Sunday), but from
our reading of their doings in the present day we
must be disposed to give them credit for a knavish
duplicity which was well calculated to befool their

contemporaries. The Imperial Grand Master,
early in July, addressed a letter to the
Earl of Enniskillen, ' dissuading the Orangemen of Ireland from having any process-
sions on the anniversary of the Boyne ;" and
the Irish Grand Lodge issued an order recommending the same. This order was signed by the Earl
of Enniskillen, Colonel Vernor, and all the grand
officers of the Irish institution. If it were really
intended to produce the effect which it professed
on the face of it we are driven to the conclusion
that the Grand Lodge of Ireland have little power
in controling the mischievous disposition of the
institute over which they are presumed to preside.
But, from the terms of the circular, it is more than
likely that they did not wish to do so, that it was
part of the desperate game from the consequences
of which they wished, as far as possible, to secure
themselves. The circular did not lay stress upon
the fact that processions were contrary to the law,
that they were an express violation of the proclamations of the Lord Lieutenant; that they might
lead to murder and anarchy; it mildly suggested
not to nail the ears of the Catholics to the pumps,
and the Grand Lodge having first offered up a
prayer that heaven might pardon those
traitors to the Constitution, the Duke of Wellington, and Mr Peel, they departed their several
ways to stimulate their blind brethren in the
country districts to set at nought the very advice
which they pretended to have given. If we pay
the Orangemen the compliment of being better
skilled in the interpretation of circulars of the
Grand Lodge than are those without the pale of
Orangeism, we are driven to no other conclusion
from the unanimous and general action which followed than that the circular was intended to produce what it actually did produce. All through
the North the Orange Lodges, in spite of statutes,
proclamations, and circulars, met that year in their
strength. All throrgh the North the 13th July,
1829, was one scene of bloodshed and confusion.

Orange processions were held in Belfast, Newry,
Portadown, Lurgan, Lisburn, Derriaghy, Tandragee, Richhill, Armagh, Moira, Waringstown, Caledon, Strabane, Banbridge, Glasslough, Killelea,
Monaghan, Aughnacloy, Coleraine, Magherafelt,
Maghera, Castledawson, Randalstown, Castlewellan, Kilkeel, Rathfriland, Ballybay, Cloner,
Newtownstewart, Newtownbutler, Enniskillen,
Dungannon, Stewartstown, and, indeed, if all the
districts in which a lodge could muster sufficient
numbers to beat a drum, blow a whistle and suffi-

* "Mr Peel, after Emancipation, left the Orangemen
still in full power in I e a rd." M Guizot's ll e of Sir Robt.
Peel, page .6.

cient cash to steep themselves in intoxication. In Belfast a meeting of the magistrates was called, at the request of the Marquis of Donegall, and sworn informations having been made that serious result might follow a procession, the magistrates issued a proclamation prohibiting it. Proclamation piled upon proclamation, and statute upon statute would have had no result with those "loyal" men. The lodges of Belfast met in Chichester Street, formed into procession, marched and counter marched to the lively airs of the "Boyne water," and "Croppies lie down," and defied the Municipal authorities to their face. Nor were the expectations of serious consequences without foundation. A fearful affray took place in Brown Street, the Orange locality; many houses were wrecked, shots were fired; one man was killed, very many wounded, and the rioters dispersed at the point of the bayonet.

In Enniskillen a desperate riot took place, in which large numbers were killed, the ultimate result being that 500 Catholic families were left houseless, and driven for refuge to the mountain side, where they were compelled to remain encamped for many weeks.

A similar tale came from Strabane, where the havoc was dreadful. The *Derry Journal* of a few days later records the particulars, and adds, "We have rather fearful anticipations of accounts of some similar disturbances in the town of Donegal."

In Monaghan the riots were of an alarming nature, and in Stewartstown and Coalisland the *News-Letter* admits that a party of drunken brethren —"heated with drink" is the mild expression— caused the wholesale sacrifice of blood in that locality. So general was the action on the part of the Orangemen in the latter district that upon the same authority we have it all the ammunition in Moy and Armagh was purchased at an early hour, and every evidence was given that the Diamond tragedy was about being enacted anew. Portadown, Comber, Maghera, &c., all offered up their sacrifice of blood in atonement for the outrage on the Constitution by the emancipation of the Catholics.

The Macken case, recorded in the evidence so often referred to (7,428), furnishes us with similar proofs of the desperation of the Orange party and the excitement prevalent amongst the Catholics. Macken is a village in the County Fermanagh. An Orange demonstration was about to take place there on the 13th July of this year; and a large number of Catholics assembled to prevent it. Lord Enniskillen, the Deputy Grand Master,

was in the district, and proceeded to the Catholics, requesting them to disperse. This they undertook to do, provided he prevented the Orange procession through the district on that day, and that he would order them to take down the flags which were flying all round the country. This Lord Enniskillen undertook to do, and the people quietly dispersed. Lord Enniskillen fulfilled his part of the engagement, but in the evening the Orangemen got tipsy, armed themselves with their yeoman rifles, and proceeded to the village, fired three rounds of ball cartridge, and a desperate and bloody encounter ensued. A large number of Catholics were arrested and but one Orangeman, though it appeared that the Catholics suffered most loss on the occasion. The petition of the nineteen Catholic prisoners, which was given in evidence by Mr. R. Kernan, shows, if it is to be believed, and there is nothing contrary to reputation upon the face of it, how gross was the partiality displayed by the sub-sheriff and the exclusively Orange jury who tried them. Hanging and transportation for life awaited the poor Papists!

This state of excitement and outrage continued during the month, displaying itself at intervals. The result was that the Lord Lieutenant had to issue a private circular to magistrates, in which he expressed regret that such demonstrations were countenanced and abetted by persons of respectability, and pointed out how illegal they were, and how obvious was the necessity of suppressing them.

During the remainder of the year the Irish Grand Lodge, allowing their humbler brethren to demonstrate as far as possible to the Government "that the balm of Catholic Emancipation had not soothed as it was intended," turned its attention to furthering the Institution in the army,* and towards perfecting a scheme for the Protestant colonisation of Ireland.

The summary wiping out of the forty-shilling freeholders had little of that effect it was intended to have. They were sacrificed to the injured feelings of the Irish Orangemen. Such an immolation went a short way to appease them. The sudden change of front on the part of Tory Ministers, the emancipation of the Catholics, carried through fear of a civil war by one who had lived his life in camps and fought more battles than any man of

---

* That many warrants were renewed and new warrants issued in the army appears by the records before the committee. Progress in this direction now became important if a hope was to be entertained of a change in the succession. With the navy the legitimate heir to the throne was a special favourite. Hence this movement

his time, was a still grievous sin for which there was no redemption. It must be admitted that the very circumstances under which the Act of Relief was granted were calculated to aggravate the resentment of the Orange party. Under other conditions the granting of emancipation might have shown advancement in a general desire for freedom But conceded through fear, its concession now plainly demonstrated to the Orangemen the invincibility of the Catholic cause Though we find in this no excuse for their subsequent violence, we might see some palliation were we not dealing with men who boasted entire subjection to, and undeviating respect for, the laws But for "the betrayal of the Constitution," the outrages of the nine months following the passing of the Act might have been sufficient to appease the offended dignity and the disregarded prejudices of the Orange party. Both sides would then have settled down peaceably to enjoy the blessings and make the most of the advantages the new Constitution bestowed A deeper plan was, however, on foot It was not meet, therefore, that the wounds of Ireland should be immediately healed by the application of this new salve. The Orange leaders in the Lords and Commons had prophesied that emancipation would produce results quite contrary to those hoped for; that turbulence and not peace would be its product. It was the prophecy of men who first predicts what the desire and then exerts their utmost to bring about their prediction Some people would call it a threat Towards the close of the year the Duke of Cumberland pointed, with a smile of Satanic satisfaction, at the dire consequences which had followed it To directly undo the measure must have appeared even to men steeped deep in bigotry an impossible task. But they were not unmindful of the fact, for they had many instances of it in their experience, that the best of measures may be neutralised by concomitant evil ones. No act is good but in the just administration of it. Nor were they blind to the strong current of reform setting in in all directions, threatening to wash away the last stronghold of monopoly Agitation was, therefore, kept alive by the most disreputable and guilty contrivances; by disgraceful and inflammatory harangues from Orange platforms; by the filthy outpourings of unknown scribes, whose productions had a money value set upon them in accordance with the number and character of the libels they contained; by the incentives to blood of men who forgot alike the iniquity of their calling, the sacredness of their mission, and that the ground whereon they trod was holy, but, above and beyond all else, by those private circulars of that huge compound of hypocrisy—the Grand Lodge of Ireland. From the opinions taken relative to the legality of proces si ns, we see that secret preparations were made for a grand demonstration all over the country on the 12th July, 1830. The result was that the embers that these men were busily engaged in fanning prematurely burst into a flame in several localities, and had the effect of warning the authorities. For instance, we find that Crossgar, in the County Down, was during the months of May and June in a most excited state. That district lying between Saintfield and Downpatrick had been given over to a species of civil warfare. The drumming parties of the night became the shooting parties of the morrow, and for many weeks Protestant and Catholic, little recking loss of blood upon either side, contended for the mastery. In May a Roman Catholic was shot at Crossgar, in one of those shooting parties, and many persons were wounded. The Rev. Richard Curoe, parish priest, Crossgar, made an information before the magistrates of Saintfield, in which he swore that he was convinced that party processions on the part of either Protestants or Catholics had been attended with deplorable consequences, and that he was fully persuaded that the peace of society in that part of the kingdom could not be preserved unless such processions be effectually stopped upon both sides. The Rev. High Green, parish priest of Saintfield, made a similar declaration. The consequence was that the magistrates issued a proclamation prohibiting all such demonstrations. The Right Rev. Dr. Crolly, Catholic Bishop of Down and Connor, had, on the previous 17th March, succeeded in preventing any Catholic demonstration taking place in Crossgar; this, as we shall see, in no way induced the Orangemen to abandon their display of July. In Armagh, in the beginning of July, we find twenty-seven magistrates, amongst whom were Colonel William Verner, James S Blacker, and other leaders of the Orangemen issuing an address "to the peaceable and wel - disposed citizens of the County Armagh. The proclamation did not forbid processions, but said that the magistrates having met to deliberate upon the best measure to be adopted, were unanimously of opinion that they 'might rely on the good sense and good disposition of the majorit ● th population not to countenance or   in any c lebration of any day in any manner which may be construed, *however erroneously*, into the intention of giving offence to any person or persons whatsoever." Whether " the great majority of the population" were wanting in good sense or in good dispositions it would be difficult now to say. Possibly the result was due to failure in both respects. At all events the address by no means prevented the holding of a demonstration on the 12th, which did not pass off without many unpleasant consequences. The Grand Lodge now became conscious that they were pushing their offensive policy too far, and, alarmed for their own safety, they, in an address issued to the brethren on the 26th June, 1830, recommended them to abstain from party demonstrations on the 12th July, because "the public processions were likely to lead to great loss of life, and prove injurious to the Orange Association," and might " in all likelihood be made the groundwork of some legislative enactment for the suppression of the Orange Society." Too late! Goaded into activity by that very body which now sought to restrain their violence, the vast body of bigots over the country overleaped the traces, broke away from all control, and making light of the reins which had too long been used not as a check, but as an incentive, less for retarding than for guiding, they rushed madly forward to blood and to their own ultimate destruction. The demonstrations of this year are full of instruction. They are all the more significant, seeing that they occurred while the nation had on all " the trappings and the suits of woe" for the demise of the King. The light of the last of our Georges had been put out, and the popular Duke of Clarence, amid the acclamation of the people, ascended the Throne under the title of William IV.

On June 23rd, 1830, the eve of the Feast of SS. Peter and Paul—a day generally regarded as a festival by the Catholic Irish—a number of boys and girls assembled in a field, by leave of its owner, about a mile and a half from Tandragee, in the County Armagh.* There this merry group, heedless of the impending danger, spent their evening in those rustic sports peculiar to their time. But in Tandragee there was once upon a time, and, for all I know, is still, an orange hall. Close by lived the Rev. Dean Carter, the most violent Orange firebrand of his time, and one who placed much less reliance upon the open Bible than

the sword. In Dean Carter's employment there was a certain Deputy Grand Master named Wm. Murphy. On this evening, whether by accident or design, the Tandragee lodge held its meeting. And for the sake of our humanity, let us suppose that the liquor distributed upon the occasion was worse, or more plentiful than usual. The Orangemen, their meeting over, assembled at the lower end of the town, under the lead of Murphy, and, with fifes and drums and colours flying, they marched to the tune of " Croppies lie down," by a circuitous route to the field in which the party was enjoying themselves. By a manœuvre which suggests the presence of yeomanry, they surrounded the field in all directions. The " Protestant Boys" was then struck up, and a determined attack made upon the crowd of amazed villagers from every side. The owner of the field remonstrating, was knocked down. One Samuel Gault drew a dagger from his sleeve and mortally wounded a Catholic named Peter M'Glade. Several others were stabbed and wounded. At the inquest upon M'Glade a verdict of wilful murder was returned against Gault, and also against his accomplices, Wm. Murphy (Dean Carter's man), Wm. Ford, and James Hagan. They were all arrested. Gault and Hagan " escaped," while Murphy and Ford were tried for the murder at the Armagh Assizes in the following spring, before Mr. Justice Johnston. They were acquitted of murder by a jury of Orangemen, and found guilty of riot and assault, and sentenced each to 12 months' imprisonment. Ford, on his release, was taken into the police, on the recommendation of Dean Carter. Murphy was at the same time admitted a member of Dr. Patten's Orange yeomanry at Tandragee. What an impartial body of men the Armagh police of those days must have been, since the murdering of a Catholic was regarded as a proper preliminary examination ! Dean Carter also refused to receive informations sworn against other parties concerned in this murder.

Fearful of an outbreak, the magistrates of Down had issued orders, as we have seen, against processions in Crossgar. The Executive had been communicated with, and the Duke of Northumberland, the Lord Lieutenant, in Council, sent down a proclamation to the same effect, which was extensively posted in the district. Setting aside at the same time the advice of the Grand Lodge and the proclamation of the Lord Lieutenant, the Orange party assembled on the 12th July. Instructions were sent to Mr. Sharman Crawford to be present, and from his sworn depositions

---

* See question 6,389 in the Irish report of the Select Committee on Orangeism. Mr. P. M'Connell, who details the circumstances, says there was no distinction of party or sect, and that he believed both Protestants and Catholics were concerned in it.

made a few days afterwards, and his evidence before the committee in 1835, we find that on his arrival in Crossgar he found there a force of twelve police, under the command of Chief-Constable Fielding Giveen. An orange arch had been erected at the Cook Public-house, about a mile distant from Crossgar, and Mr. Crawford detached a party of four men, under the chief constable, to take it down. Mr. Giveen reported on his return that from the threats and violence of the persons assembled he did not think it prudent to attempt the removal of the arch. By this time the Orangemen had assembled in large numbers in procession, with fife and drums and colours. They had gathered into Crossgar, a Catholic locality, from Protestant districts distant ten miles and more, a fact which made Mr. Crawford believe that the demonstration was intended as an insult to the Catholics. Some individual in the procession carried short poles or halberts, with pikes on the ends of them, while in some instances drawn swords were carried by persons at the head of the lodges. Pistol shots were fired, and a determined disposition exhibited to resist the civil power. Mr. Crawford met the first lodges in the procession, stopped them, read to them the proclamation of his Grace the Lord Lieutenant and commanded them to disperse. They laughed at him, and proceeded. He attempted to stop other lodges, but with the same result. They forcibly marched on, says the deponent, Mr. Crawford, apparently defying the civil power. An express was despatched to Downpatrick for further assistance, and in the meantime Mr. Crawford* "procured the attendance of Mr. Hugh Taylor, the District Master of Saintfield, and a few other masters of lodges, in a house in Crossgar, read to them his Grace's proclamation and commanded them to disperse, and stated every consideration in his power to induce them to do so. They treated the communication with respect, but said they had warrants for marching *bearing the authority of Government*, and that they considered themselves justified in marching until these warrants were withdrawn. They produced to informant some of these warrants, bearing, as well as informant recollects, the signature of his Royal Highness the Duke of Cumberland"—the Imperial Grand Master be it recollected—" Lord Enniskillen, and some other individuals. Informant endeavoured to impress upon them that they were acting under a wrong impression, but without effect, in saying

* Mr. W. Sharman Crawford's evidence before the Select Committee, question 4,313.

that the Duke of Cumberland's name being attached to the document was an authority equal to that of the Government of the country or greater. I argued the point with them; they stated to me that *the Duke of Cumberland is a greater Duke than the Duke of Northumberland.* I attempted to remove this delusion, but without effect. They said they had a warrant from Government, though it appeared, when I came to investigate it, that they had no warrant from Government but those warrants." Here, truly, is "something more than natural." A number of intelligent men, not wholly blinded by passion, for they could receive the magistrate's communication "with respect," defended the defiant and lawless attitude of their brethren, in which the proclamation of the representative of the reigning monarch was set at nought by saying their Grand Master, "the Duke of Cumberland, was a greater duke than the Duke of Northumberland," by alleging the warrant of the Grand Lodge superior to an order in Privy Council. The sad consequences which might result from such an opinion being seriously entertained count as nothing when compared with the traitorous designs of which it gives us an indication. When we come to examine the political aspect of affairs in England we will find that at this time the duke who was esteemed greater in Ireland than the Viceroy was an aspirant to the throne, of which he was not the legitimate heir. An additional force arrived from Downpatrick, and by the temper and vigilance of the magistrates, and the wisdom of the Catholics, a violent outbreak was averted. Taylor was arrested and liberated on bail, and in the evening he re-appeared upon the streets, riding about amongst the multitude, his horse decked with orange ribands.

It would be wearisome to wade through the many proofs furnished this year of the conditional anallegice of the Orangemen. All over the North and in many places, at the sacrifice of life, they set the law at defiance. In Dungannon, County Tyrone, they assembled, contrary to proclamation, erected arches, and were so menacing that the magistrates would not permit the chief constable, Captain Duff, to remove the decorations, although he offered to do so at the risk of his life. This procession of loyal law breakers was headed by six gentlemen of position, one being a lieutenant of yeomanry. In Magherafelt, County Derry, the Orangemen on the same day assembled while the Barrister was sitting, broke into the jail, and rescued several prisoners from custody. For a few days previous to this the Ribbonmen and Orangemen were engaged at skirmishes on the adjacent hills.

In the face of these outrages the Orangemen still persisted in holding their processions. The Grand Lodge, which appeared to be so anxious, previous to July, about the bloody consequences that *must* follow such demonstrations, found their former friends in the Government more earnest than usual, resolved to have the best legal advice to aid them in their difficulty. Their taking the opinion of counsel, as they did in October, 1830, as to the legality of processions, savours very much of an inclination to continue them. The Grand Committee caused a case to be laid berore two eminent barristers Mr. Serjeant Pennefather and Mr. Holmes, both of whom gave it as their decided opinion " that under existing circumstances, and the present state of the law, Orange processions are *not only decidedly illegal but dangerous*." The Grand Committee, therefore, made a virtue of necessity, and felt called upon " to recommend to the whole body at once *voluntarily* to give up all processions, and publicly to make known their intention of doing so."

We now come to one of the most shocking incidents in the history of Orangeism; an outrage which has made the name of the " Killyman Wreckers" noted to this day. On the 19th Nov., 1830, a party of Orangemen from Killyman passed, with drums and fifes playing, and colours flying, through the village of Maghery, in the Co. Tyrore, inhabited by Catholics (within a short distance from Churchhill House, the residence of Colorel William Verner) to attend what is denominated a " Black lodge meeting" of Orangemen in the neighbourhood. This "black" sitting, as its name indicates, was an assembly of brethren, constituted after the fashion of a formal court, for the purpose of trying and passing sentence upon some person who had been so unfortunate as to incur the resentment of Orangemen. The result in many places in the North was that the brethren, thus banded together, permanently united under a separate or " black" warrant, and combined to execute the decrees of the Court. On Saturday, 20th November, the Orangemen returned through Maghery. The Catholics refused to let them pass unless they played " Garryowen," a request which, having complied with the previous day, they passed unmolested. The Orangemen replied by playing the "Protestant Boys," and a scuffle ensued in which some of the Orangemen were knocked down and wounded, and their drumheads broken to the extent of ten shillings worth.

Their wounds, however, were not serious, nor did the Orangemen care much for the damage to their drums or the loss of their caps, six or eight of which they left behind in their hasty retreat from the village. It was the complete route which galled them. On Sunday following, if they read their Bible, which is questionable—though an open one (at a very significant passage) is their motto—they also cherished their resentment, and at daybreak on Monday, the 22nd November, the drums of Killyman beat to arms, and the brethren assembled to march on Marghery for revenge. They were armed with guns (the Rev. Mr. Donaldson swore he counted 49),47 muskets, bayonets, swords, &c., and with drums beating and fifes playing they marched along the road "with the declared and avowed intention of taking revenge upon the inhabitants of Maghery for the affair of Saturday." The alarm spread. Mr. Boretree, a lieutenant in Colonel Verner's yeomanry, having heard this, rode after the Orangemen and remonstrated with them in vain. He then hastened to report to Mr. Jackson Lloyd, Captain of the Killyman yeomanry, and to Colonel Verner, Captain of the Churchhill yeomanry and Justice of the Peace for the Counties of Armagh and Tyrone, "that the Killyman boys were armed and coming over the bridge to wreck Maghery, and that if Col. Verner could not stop them by shutting the iron gates on the bridge over the Blackwater, nothing could stop them." Col. Verner, his captain, his lieutenant, and a sergeant of police met them at the bridge, the gates having been locked by the order of Colonel Verner, and a parley ensued in which the magistrate, without taking the slightest means to disperse, arrest, or identify any of them, engaged to send two ambassadors to the village of Maghery from this illegal assembly, demanding of them to pay 10s for the missing caps and the broken drumheads. It was engaged that the Orangemen should await at the gate the return of the embassy, and not attempt to pass it—a wise precaution having been made by the gallant colonel that the police should be sent on with the deputation to the village. Unfortunately for the people of Maghery, it was now breakfast hour at Churchhill House. The colonel and the captain returned to Churchhill to enjoy what was no doubt a substantial repast, leaving an armed and tumultuous assembly of Orangemen bent upon revenge to be restrained by one man—the keeper of the toll bridge. But gatekeepers have to breakfast, too, and this particular one seems to have hungered for it quite as much as did the colonel or the captain. The gatekeeper went to his breakfast, and the Orangemen commenced to climb the gate. Mr. Boretree, who was absent for his horse, on returning found them making the attempt. He proposed to them to go back to a public-house a quarter of a mile distant, and he would treat each man to a glass of whiskey They went back. They got the whisky, Mr Boretree, the lieutenant of yeomanry, having paid for it, rods off to Dungannon, leaving the Orangemen drinking it. It is no wonder that Mr. Serjeant Perrin, in his report to the Government on the occurrence here breaks out into a sort of exclamation. "It is here to be observed that neither Col Vernor, nor Lieutenant Boretree, Mr. Murray, nor the police sergeant, nor the gatekeeper can tell the name of any one of those who spoke or took a part, or had arms on the occasion, and Captain Lloyd is almost equally uninformed !" None blind as those who will not see ! When the breakfast was over at Churchhill, the drums were heard approaching, and the refreshed Orangemen seen proceeding on the road "They bad," says Mr. Serjeant Perrin, "passed the bridge and through the gate, which had been thrown open by the gatekeeper, who went into the lodge to eat his breakfast." Captain Duff reports that they burst through the gates, shouting that "Bloody Wellington would not stop them," and that "they would shoot him if they had him" Very probable, indeed ! Colonel Verner, who was in the midst of his own tenantry, and his own yeomanry, a hundred of whom he could have assembled in half the time he took to eat his breakfast, contented himself with putting the Riot Act in his pocket, and with writing the following note to his lieutenant, a Mr. O'Neill —"I am afraid there will be bad work in Magbery. Jackson, Lloyd, and I are going down to prevent it. Will you have a few steady men ready in case I should need your or their assistance" According to the official report, he wrote this fearing there might be opposition in Magbery, so that the force seems to have been meant more for the protection of the Orangemen than for the defence of Magbery or its Catholic inhabitants Colonel Verner, with his friends, rode after the Orange party, which by this time were augmented largely by their brethren of the locality—no doubt the yeomanry of Churchhill. They overtook them at the entrance to the village. The people of Maghery had escaped, with exception of the old and decrepid, who were compelled to abide the fury of the Orangemen. The Killyman boys had

their own way of it this time. Just as they were about commencing operations, the colonel pulled the Riot Act out of his pocket, and—one can almost imagine there was a smile on his countenance at the time—he proceeded to read it. "He might as well have read Dens' Theology." He had indeed remembered the Act, but, with a supernatural want of judgment, had neglected to provide the means of enforcing it; consequently twenty-eight houses belonging to Catholics, were wrecked, all their owners' little wretched furniture, and clothes, and tools, were broken and destroyed, and the few inhabitants who could be caught were beaten and abused. One unhappy widow, within eight days of childbed, was knocked down with an infant in her arms, whilst her half-witted son was shot at (the ball pierced his coat), and every article of furniture torn from her. These proceedings lasted for nearly an hour, at the end of which time Colonel Verner persuaded the Orangemen to move off. They did so with colours flying and drums beating, wrecking also two or three houses by the way; Colonel Verner, Captain Lloyd, and Lieutenant O'Neill, who joined the party after the Maghery wrecking was over, marching either with these ruffians, or following in the rear along the high road through a populous country ! What Colonel Verner's feelings on this occasion may have been, we do not pretend to guess; we know only that he followed the Killyman boys as far as the gate of his own demesne, when he turned in, "never having" (we copy his own deposition, App. 154) " called upon any of the persons mentioned by him to arrest or stop any of the party, nor did he on his return desire them to do so." Captain Lloyd, in the same manner, continued with them only until he reached his own house beyond the Blackwater. They were then left alone, and were so met by Captain Duff and a party of police that he had collected and brought to Dungannon on hearing a report of the threatened riot. He stopped and questioned them, but they had the wit to say that everything had been settled by Colonel Verner. Finding no one with them, or following them, to give a contrary statement, he passed on to Verner's Bridge, where he first heard the state of the case. He immediately went to Colonel Verner for orders. The answer was, "Colonel Verner was reporting the affair to the Castle, and had no orders to give." Mr. Perrin's report declares these wreckers "to have been guilty of felony," and concludes —"I am further of opinion that Colonel Verner appears not to have performed his duty as a magistrate at Verner's

Bridge, in order to disperse (as he was bound and required by Law) the persons there tumultuously and unlawfully assembled, and compel them to depart to their habitations. That he did not take the measures and precautions proper for that purpose, which he was empowered and required by law to take, and which the result evinces to have been necessary for the preservation of the peace and the threatened breach thereof, and that he is liable to be prosecuted at the suit of the Crown by information for such (as it seems to me) *criminal neglect of his duty.* I do not deem it within my province to observe on the non-exertion of Captain Lloyd and Lieutenant Boretree, or of Constable Crawford, not being, as I apprehend, the subject of legal cognizance."

It will be asked, what were the consequences of all these outrages, and of this criminal neglect of duty? Was Colonel Verner prosecuted? On the contrary, he and Colonel Blacker were selected as the two magistrates to whom the informations were specially forwarded by the Crown (Mr. Blackburn was then Attorney-General) for the institution of prosecutions (8687). But the Maghery men and the wreckers of their village were tried. The result is instructive. Mr. Perrin's report names and specifies ten persons as spectators, more or less active, besides Colonel Verner and his officers, six others as countenancing, and twenty-nine (eleven Armagh and eighteen Tyrone men) as armed, and engaged in the outrages of the Monday—that is, fifty persons are named as present. Informations were laid, and true bills found against many of them. But when the first seven were successively acquitted' the trial of the others was thrown up. It appeared, that out of all these depredators with whom there had been so much communication, both on the Saturday and on the Monday, not one could be recognised in the dock, either by Colonel Verner or his companions (8697). Other witnesses, the sufferers themselves, did recognise and identify some of the prisoners (8705); but their testimony was overborne by Colonel Verner's (8678). All were acquitted (8678). Up to this hour, not one person has suffered for the Maghery outrage. But not so the Catholics of Maghery. They indeed had broken drum-heads and hats on the Saturday to the value of ten shillings, according to the estimate of the Orangemen to whom they belonged. This had been done in a chance-medley scuffle, which those Orangemen had provoked as they were illegally returning from an illegal or black Orange meeting. For this offence those Catholics were tried, con-

victed, and sentenced to three months' imprisonment! and possibly this may have been a *mitigated* sentence, in consideration of the *trifling* loss of their houses and property on the following Monday. The constitution of the Bench on the Maghery inquiry was so remarkable as to need mention. Capt. Atkinson, who was at the Diamond, and was an Orangeman from the commencement, was the senior magistrate; Colonel Verner, an Orangeman, occupied a place on the bench, *not in the dock,* where he should have been; Mr. Ford, an Orangeman; Mr. Woodhouse, an Orangeman; Mr. Hardy, subsequently suspended by Lord Chancellor Sugden; Col. Blacker, an Orangeman ;* and Mr. Hancock were the magistrates who took upon themselves to inquire into this Orange outrage. Little wonder that none of the Orange party were brought to justice, and that the huge farce ended in the incarceration of the Catholics only! Lord Charlemont subsequently obtained their release.

Towards the close of the year we find the Orange brethren banded against Parliamentary Reform; applying, as against Emancipation and the Tories, all the secret machinery of their institution towards retarding the measure to which a Whig Ministry, reading aright the signs of the times, attached their fortunes. They were, of course, not less an enemy of Repeal, and many brethren who identified themselves with the movement were summarily dismissed by the Grand Lodge. In truth much dread seems to have filled the Grand Committee at this period, the records of this year laid before Parliament showing a giving in at various points along the line. The results were that the efforts of the District Masters were, in compliance with the request of the Grand Lodge, redoubled for the purpose of keeping alive and vigorous that old spirit of bigotry, without which the occupation of the Grand Committee was gone. For "uniting with the Papists" and hoisting a green and orange flag on a platform at Randalstown half a dozen brethren were dismissed, while a court of inquiry formed to consider the conduct of certain Orangemen of Sligo who voted for a reform candidate at the recent elections, reported against the brethren for having the effrontery of exercising

* Colonel Blacker voluntarily undertook to supply a report of the transaction, which is full of the most glaring inaccuracies, and seeks to throw a cloak over his friend Verner, whom, he says, "used every exertion to stop the outrage," and the Churchhill Yeomanry. Mr. W. J. Hancock, conscious that there were two ways of telling the truth, would not trust Colonel Blacker, and him self reported to the Government. Mr. Hancock's report, with that of Mr. Serjeant Perrin, inculpate Mr. Verner and his gallant Orange Yeomanry.

the franchise otherwise than as the Grand Lodge directed. They were dubbed "Papists" and dismissed. This must be regarded as a most trying time for the institution. While from the outside they were subjected to the stern criticism of O'Connell, of the celebrated Dr. Doyle and party; there was not wanting within its ranks many who for selfish if for no other reasons sympathised with the great tithe agitation then beginning to move the country.

About this period we find some of the brethern, for the first time in their eventful history entertaining a vague suspicion, if not becoming actively alive to the fact, that while on the one hand the organisation might be used for the furthering of political schemes far outside the reach of their interest, it was on the other being utilised by the numerous landlords who appeared at its head as a means for exacting oppressive rents from their tenantry. The Orange tenant had enlisted under the Orange standard of his Orange landlord in the firm belief that while he would be free to persecute and drive hence the neighbouring Papist his leader and sworn accomplice would not be so unbrotherly as to call upon him for the payment of such a paltry thing as rent. In the progress of the great cause of ascendancy, and where, too, the great, glorious, and immortal memory was at stake, such thrash, he not unnaturally expected, would be overlooked. To men bound together in such a holy cause, possessed of common secrets, united by the same mystic ties, and sworn in "heart, pocket, and hand" to befriend each other, it would be an indignity to mention such a thing as rent! The word had an odious and rebel ring about it as well, and recalled horrid phantoms of the O'Connellites and the Catholic Associations. Thus the Orangeman reasoned, and thus was he betrayed into that false security which was rudely shattered by a notice to quit, a sheriff's sale, and the subsequent horrors of the emigrant ship. The humble yeoman had yet to learn in the bitter school of experience how selfish were those above him; how hard were the task masters whom he had chosen in fitful spleen to lead him against his countrymen. To such men Protestant ascendancy was not in itself a good. It was only esteemed a blessing for the advantages it brought, the powers it gave them of strengthing their grasp upon possessions which their consciences told them were not their own. Given to exaction, and having now no opportunity of sacrificing those, the persecution of whom could be done in the name of the Lord,

they soon failed to recognise any essential difference between a Papist and a brother, where their interests were at stake. The rents in various parts of the North were now doubled, in some places actually trebled. Emigration on a wholesale scale followed, while amongst those who remained behind we find springing up a secret society, an association within an association, under the title of the "Tommy Downshires," who for a long period carried on in the most notoriously Orange districts of Ulster an inveterate war against rents and tithes.

In their struggle against rack-renting those men still preserved their hatred to the Catholics, and wherever occasion offered they resorted to their old game of robbing them of arms. They were of the lowest order of Orangemen and Protestants. It was but natural. The poorest being first to feel the extortion of tyrannical landlords, would, in the order of things, be the first to resist. A large force of soldiers were, at the request of the magistrates, drafted into Lurgan and Banbridge, and a reward of £200 offered to any person who would discover upon persons calling together those illegal assemblages of the dreaded "Tommy Downshires." In their raids for arms upon Catholic houses lives were in many instances lost. At a meeting of the magistrates of Down, Lord Dufferin expressed his surprise at drafting in soldiers when they had the yeomanry to fall back upon. His lordship evidently had little knowledge of the men with whom he was dealing. The very yeomanry of Lurgan and thereabouts were themselves, in a large measure, augmenting the forces of these marauders. Mr. Handcock, better acquainted with the circumstances, laughed at the suggestion, and said the Orange yeomanry could not be depended upon, a remark which, when reported to the Castle by his lordship, brought about a searching investigation into the constitution and character of the Lurgan yeomanry. Lieutenant-Colonel Molyneaux reported that they could not be relied upon, that they were in a most disorganised state, that some looked upon their captain, Mr. Handcock, as a rebel and a Papist, and would not obey his orders; and that Douglas, the permenent Orange sergeant, of whom we have before heard, had been guilty of many peculation. The Lurgan yeomanry were Orangemen with the exception of Mr. Handcock; meet successors of "loyal Orange yeomanry, who fought in '98."

On the 11th February, 1831, the Committee of the Grand Lodge passed a resolution, in which they called upon the Government to afford encouragement and support to to the loyal Protestants of I eland, urging that the only means of giving confidence to the Protestant mind was by the immediate embodying, augmenting, and arming the Protestant yeomanry of Ireland; and stating that they felt it imperative on them to hesitate in yielding an implicit confidence (obedience), or in forming any resolutions of unreserved support, so long as yeomen were dismissed for appearing in Orange processions. In the following April the Grand Committee renewed their protest against the Emancipation Bill, and gave expression to great apprehension at the introduction of the Reform Bill which was "fraught with consequences the most dangerous both to the empire at large and to Ireland in particular."

The Grand Orange Lodge of Ireland were by this time fully aware of the illegality of processions. Inclined, as they might have been, to conveniently forget it, the activity of the Executive authorities were not disposed to allow them. Accordingly, we find the circulars of the previous two years re-issued, and proclamation after proclamation flooding the country to try and rid the land of the periodic effusion of blood now near at hand. What were in 1831 the consequences of this knowledge of the law? What the result of the half-hearted injunctions of the Grand Lodge? From the official return,* we find the astounding fact that in the province of Ulster alone there were this year not less than fifty Orange processions representing attendances in each case of from 5,000 to 1,000 persons, and these headed and countenanced by Orangemen in high civil station and authority, as well as by members of the Grand Lodge who had prepared the anti-procession injuction of 1830.

In Tandragee, we learn that a procession of 10,000 assembled on the 12th July of this year; that they were armed with not less than one thousand guns and an equally unpleasant number of pistols and side-arms; that they were preceded and followed by carts holding amunition (ball, not blank cartridge); and that a demonstration, insulting as it was cowardly, took place, in which all authority was set aside. At the same time that this body of desperate men were parading in arms at Tandragee, to the terror of his Majesty's subjects, and in open defiance of the law, a like body of Orangemen were assembled at Dungannon, headed by two officers of the yeomanry — Lieutenant Thomas Irwin, Moy corps, and Lieutenant Francis Irwin,

* Irish Report, appendix 3, page 98.

Dromara corps—both of whom were dismissed from the yeomanry for their conduct on the occasion. Captain Harpur, Moy Infantry, was at the same time dismissed for a similar offence. Fifteen of the Lurgan yeomen were likewise dismissed. In order that the yeomen could plead no excuse the orders of the Government forbidding their appearance in Orange processions were repeated in the most precise terms. They were prohibited from taking part in processions "in any garb or in any way." The breach of orders was in each case, therefore, a deliberate act of disloyalty.

The Orange organ of Ulster, after calling attention to the proclamation of the Lord Lieutenant, had reminded the brethren that no *respectable* Orangeman would walk in procession on the 12th July. If we take them at their word, and apply the opposite term to all those who did walk in procession, it leads us to appalling conclusions. Bloodshed followed the meeting of 10,000 Orangemen that year at Portadown; murder (of four Catholics) was the result of a numerous meeting at Rathfriland, rioting and house-wrecking resulted from a demonstration held in Belfast, in spite of Government proclamations, magisterial orders, and the counsel of literary advisers.

But while these scenes of turbulence were proceeding in Armagh and Tyrone, we find a dreadful tragedy, unsurpassed for its cold-blooded brutality, being enacted in the neighbourhood of Banbridge, County Down. In this district preparations on an extensive scale had been made for the celebration of the 12th July. As in the case of the Orangemen of Maghera on the previous year, challenges passed between both sides, the one party threatening to walk in the face of the other's determination to prevent them, and both resolved upon risking their lives in the issue. Upon the morning of the 12th the Orangemen assembled to the number of several thousands. The Catholics had also congregated, though in much smaller forces, to prevent their passage through Tullyorier, a townland in the parish of Gariaghy, in the barony of Upper Iveagh, through which the river Bann flows. How the belligerents escaped each other in the morning of this eventful day does not appear upon the face of the depositions, but upon the return journey in the evening, a number of the Catholics having by that time left in security for their homes, the Orangemen, the majority of whom were armed, came up with a crowd of unarmed villagers, who had assembled on the roadside in the neighbourhood of the Bann. A volley from the guns of the Orangemen was the first notification of an attack. Implements of war were hastily improvised, and an opposing force, though of no formidable kind, made its appearance upon the ground A determined struggle ensued, in the course of which we are told 400 shots were fired, and many persons lost their lives Amongst the victims was a bedridden old woman named Strain, who was killed by a bullet which passed through the window and struck her as she lay upon her bed. The story is but half told, however. The result naturally to be expected when an armed force of yeomen and a motley group of unarmed villagers come into collision followed. The Catholics were routed and pursued with vindictiveness by the Orange yeomanry Those who took to the fields were deliberately shot down by the skilled marksmen, and the only hope of refuge from certain death lay, therefore, in the waters of the Bann Into it they ran in hundreds—men, women, and children, the Orangemen following and shooting at them as the unfortunate victims were actually struggling with death, which threatened in another though less formidable shape. Four unarmed Catholics, Peter Farrell, Peter Byrnes, Patrick Macken, and Bernard M'Lenan, none of whom appeared to have taken any active part in the day's proceedings, were deliberately shot at while in the river. One Gilly Logan, a District Grand Master of an Orange lodge, and his brother Robert approached to the edge of the Bann, deliberately loaded their muskets, fired, loaded and fired again, repeating their cowardly act so often as one of their victims rose to the surface. The four persons just named were, with many others, either shot or drowned and as each one of the "Papists" sank to rise no more, Gilly Logan "threw up his hat and shouted there's another Kiln-cant gone"

That "challenges" were frequently issued between the Orangemen and the Catholics previous to these dreadful occurrences need not surprise But they were of a description not altogether implied by the name. It is evident from the elaborate arrangements of the Government to prevent those celebrations that house-wrecking, riot, and bloodshed were their natural consequences. On their approach the Catholics of the North in those districts in which the demonstrations were threatened saw nothing but ruined homes and remorseless havoc staring them in the face. A determination consequently followed to prevent such scenes, which is the more excusable, seeing that law and order were upon their side. But the determination

of the Catholics was usually followed by the reckless resolve of the Orangemen to march, and hence we have upon the face of the depositions of those days so many references to the challenges that were given. That the Catholics outstepped the boundaries of the law there is no question That in many places those lawless bands of malcontents, the Thrashers and Slashers and Crashers of the North—bands of men whose existence argue something wrong in the social state, frequently lent their aid to their co religionists, there is no doubt, but that all this was due to the presence in their midst of an armed band of conspirators, who without the power to gratify them, had all the exterminating propensities of their ancestors, is equally undeniable.

The days of adversity had indeed set in The very alliance of the Orange party seemed to bring with it nothing but disaster. Did a Government weary of office it had only to ally itself with the Orange party. Did any measure of reform need to be passed the opposition of the Orangemen furthered its progress and made its success a certainty. The Emancipation Bill was proposed. By them it was vigorously opposed. In the face of that opposition the Emancipation Bill was passed. The Reform Bill was suggested. Parliamentary reform was by the Orangemen scouted as an impossibility. "One hundred thousand loyal Orangemen, every one a good man and true, were ready to lay down their lives rather than permit it to become law and allow the representation of Ireland to pass into the hands of O'Connell." But the Reform Bill passed. On the 16th December, 1831, there was found in the Commons a majority of 162 in its favour.[a] The truth was that the unrelenting hostility of the Orangemen to all things Catholic and Irish opened the eyes of Liberal English statesmen to the fact that where there was so much bigotry there must needs exist much injustice.

If the "hundred thousand loyal Orangemen" were wise enough in their generation not to risk an appeal to arms, they were not loyal enough to passively submit to this act of the Legislature. An appeal to arms did not follow; but the old muskets were burnished up, the rusty bayonets were put in order, and secret preparations made throughout the land "to defend Protestantism against Popish

---

[a] The King, in his speech at the opening of the session, had recommended the measure of Reform to his faithful Commons. The fulfilment of his commands was a double betrayal of the Constitution as established by King William T us reasoned the Orangemen Herein they found a double justification of their treason!

aggression"—which in other terms meant to assist at the first opportunity in placing upon the Throne the Royal libertine whose fortunes were identified with the cause of Orangemen, and whose name figured as their Imperial Grand Master.

In Dublin a great Orange meeting was held, at which all the leaders of the Institution assembled. Here it was resolved to form a Protestant Association to repel the advance of Liberal reform. "In order to effect the views of the founders of the Association the Orange system was adopted at the meeting, and it was resolved to recommend and to spread that system as much as possible throughout the country."* The grafting of this new association upon a semi-military establishment such as the Orange Association was, particularly at this period, a sufficient indication of the means by which the associates sought to accomplish their ends. But there is another, and possibly a more reliable proof at hand. At this meeting Lord Viscount Mandeville, an Orangeman of the belligerent type, proposed the following resolution, every word of which breathes war to the knife:—"The Irish Protestants (Orangemen) are no paltry faction as they have been represented, but a gallant people possessed of *physical and moral energy which no power can crush*, comprising the vast proportion of the property, education, and industry of Ireland, the descendants of brave men who won their privileges and rights, and which their posterity must not forfeit by indolence or neglect." This, unmistakably, alludes to a resort to those dreadful means towards preserving their privileges which their fathers had employed for obtaining them; a means which the hoary old tyrant J. C. Beresford, who, like the skeleton at the feast, was present at the meeting, right well understood. It meant armed resistance. It meant treason. Read by the light of events occurring just then in England, it meant much more—it meant the usurpation of the Crown, the stealing of the precious diadem from the shelf and lodging it in the stronghold of the Grand Orange Lodge of the Three Kingdoms.

Before the year was out, we have furnished to us further proof of the desperate intents of this treasonable faction. On the 28th December, a meeting similar to that of Dublin was convened by the High Sheriff of Armagh, and held in the Court House of that city. Here we again find that amiable sprout of the old nobility, Lord Viscount Mandeville, at the same good work of "awakening

the Protestants to the abominations of Popery, and arousing them to "the necessity of arming themselves for resisting its encroaches." The third resolution passed at the meeting is almost as significant as that adopted by the Orangemen of Dublin :—"Resolved—That the alarm now agitating the minds of the Protestants of Ireland is in our opinion *amply justified* by the spirit which appears to influence the counsels and dictate the measures of the King in this part of the United Kingdom." Then it was that Lord Viscount Mandeville, in vulgar parlance, let the cat out the bag. In a speech of the most violent nature he said it was the wish of the King's Government to eradicate Protestantism from Ireland and to establish Popery; that the Government had mistaken for apathy and indifference the determination of the Orangemen to defend their rights, and warned the authorities that *the lion of the North had been aroused*. A voice from the crowd here called out "*give us guns,*" and, impulse getting the better of discretion, his lordship replied in these significant words, "*I will give you as many as I can ; but you have your watch and clock clubs, why not have your gun clubs as well.*" This expression was what led to the starting of gun clubs in connection with the Orange Institution. The brethren were not slow to take the hint given by the Grand Master of Armagh, and Deputy Grand Master of the Orangemen of Ireland. Very probably they had already got advice in plainer terms within the privacy of their lodge rooms. As a result, we find soon after gun-clubs covered the entire province ; a vast net-work of secret organisations, constituting the armoury of the Orange lodges in their respective localities, wherein busy preparations gave fearful warning of some approaching struggle. Children and fools may play with edged tools But men of intelligence and position like Lord Mandeville do not handle them for nought. It was not for mere amusement, then, the Orangemen were playing at soldiers. Their arming and their parading were alike significant of their purpose.

A hint is afforded us also as to against whom those arms were to be used by the following pas-

* Mr. W. Stratton, a police constable, from Pointspass, in his evidence before the Select Committee (Irish) directly attributes gun clubs to this speech. At 4545, Sir F. Stovin, Inspector-General of Police, on examination is asked "Are the majority of the gun clubs Protestant," to which he answers, "As far as I have heard they are ! I have heard that a great number of the landlords of the highest class are encouraging their tenantry to arm." Lord Gosford gives evidence, showing that these clubs existed to an alarming extent in the North shortly after the delivery of Lord Viscount Mandeville.

* *Belfast News-Letter, 16th December, 1831.*

19

sage, taken from Lord Mandeville's speech on this occasion :—"Dr. Doyle told his people not to pay tithes, and the King's speech and the King's Government echo the same.

In the course of his examination before the Irish Select Committee, the great spokesman and ethical expounder of Orangeism, the Rev. Mortimer O'Sullivan, laboured earnestly in defence of Orange exclusiveness and intolerance to prove that Dr. Doyle, as representing the Catholic bishops of Ireland, was a traitor to the King and a menace to our Constitution. It is due to the position and calling of Mr. O'Sullivan to give him the credit of sincerity, however incomplete his proof. He spoke the opinions of the Grand Lodge. If the Deputy-Grand Master of Ireland, Lord Mandeville, found in the King's Speech nothing but an echo of principles enunciated by Dr. Doyle, he must have seen in the King himself a traitor to the Protestant principles of 1688 and in his prerogative a menace to the Protestant Constitution as then established. The maxim that the King could do no wrong, had, since the revolution which placed William upon the Throne, taken its place amongst the nursery legends of the period. It answered admirably as the head-line of a copy-book. But, if it really ever were a principle of the Constitution the theory, now, was at variance with the practice. A betrayal by the King's Ministers meant a betrayal by the King, and the shout of "treason," which went up from the Orange platforms, penetrated both Houses of Parliament, and vibrated at the foot of the Throne. Those measures, which the Orangemen of that time looked upon as treason, the world has since learned to regard, not alone, as necessary acts of justice, but as the dictates of political wisdom and foresight.

CHAPTER XXVIII.—AT BAY.

WE have, after the exercise of not a little patience, arrived at a period possibly the most interesting, certainly the most instructive of any in our unpresumptive history. A dense mid-night of doubt, had to cortemporaries, surrounded all things Orange But with the morning of 1832 a fierce sunlight broke in upon its affairs and revealed the conspiring band in all the naked deformity of rebel to that authority which it had pretended to uphold. We now find the heroes of the Diamond, the exterminators of the few years preceding the rebellion, the bloody runaways of 1798, the dictators during the first years of the Union, the exclusive loyalists up to 1829, and the opponents of Emancipation, chased into those dens wherein massacre and treason had been hatched, and standing at bay at the doors of their lodges yelping out a fierce defiance at law and all constituted authority. It did not require Mr. Stanley's Anti-Procession Act of 1832 to make Orange processions illegal. At common law they had again and again been declared so. But common law failing, statute law was resorted to with a no more salutary effect. January we find ushered in with the murder of some Catholics in the neighbourhood of Armagh, while the criminal records of Cavan and Monaghan were being stained by the records of atrocious crime. Under the date of 29th February a sum of £20 is devoted by the Grand Orange Lodge of Ireland to "the defence of our brethren about to be prosecuted at the ensuing Cavan Assizes in the case of the King v. Beckett, Souddon, and others;" while on two subsequent dates sums of £59 17s 9d and 45 guineas are applied to the like purpose, making in all a grant of £125 for "securing justice" to "Beckett, Souddon, and others."* Costly justice, beyond a doubt ! Not a pleasant prospect for those numerous Catholics who had not £125 to throw away. At an early period of the session it became evident that Government was determined to stop party processions at all hazards; the consequence being that the leaders of Irish Orangemen determined at an early stage to demonstrate their determination to resist, hopeful of the old results of temporising legislation.

So early as the 27th April, 1832, Captain David Duff reported a procession of Orangemen in Dungannon. That official report is headed, "Orange processions, headed by Colonel Verner and others, magistrates, &c., wearing orange and purple in Dungannon." It appears that at mid-day on the date mentioned, between four and five thousand Orangemen marched in regular procession, carrying twenty-four stands of colours into Dungannon, the bands playing the "Protestant Boys" in front.

* This is quite customary not alone on the part of the Grand Lodge but also on the part of the County Grand Lodges. In 1833 I find that a large sum of money was voted by the Grand Lodge for the defence of an Orangeman named Beith, charged at Dundalk Assizes with murdering a Catholic with an oyster knife. By judicious swearing and an adroit manipulation of the jury panel the murder was reduced to manslaughter, of which the prisoner was found guilty. The gentlemen of the Grand Orange Lodge were not the less aiders and abettors of the murder by this transaction.

The police inspector says (7864) " I observed the following gentlemen decorated with orange and purple:—First, Lieutenant-Colonel Wm. Verner, a Deputy-Lieutenant of this county, as also a magistrate for it and the County of Armagh; second, Mr. Joseph Greer (a Grand Master) also a magistrate for the Counties Tyrone and Armagh, and captain of the Moy corps of yeomanry; third, Mr. Jackson Lloyd (the Marghery hero), a captain of the Killyman corps of yeomanry; several other gentlemen of this neighbourhood also accompanied the procession." Some insulting language was used towards them "by four or five Roman Catholics on which a riot ensued, stones thrown by each party, the Roman Catholics retreated, and when on their retreat, either two or three pistol shots were fired by the Orangemen, one of which took effect and broke the left arm, close to the elbow of a man named Peter Tully, a Roman Catholic." The Inspector further reports that "on the procession halting in the centre of the town, the several masters of lodges, forty in number, together with the gentlemen before mentioned returned to the *Courthouse* where a private meeting was held for upwards of two hours, the object of which was for making the necessary arrangements for the 12th July, as I have since heard, as also for the purpose of forwarding petitions against Reform, and the Education System." The belief was well founded; for the meeting subsequently published their resolutions, in one of which thanks were voted to Colonel Verner for his attendance. Here two resolutions were passed in favour of Protestant colonization for the preservation of a Protestant population, with, at its head, an aristocracy truly Protestant. It was a sickly effort to bolster up a rotten system:—"That such of us as are tenants will endeavour to merit this encouragement, and, that such of us as are landlords, pledge ourselves to give it, seeing no reason why Protestant colonization should be attempted on lands *that are reclaimed* as well as on lands that are not reclaimed"

Lieutenant-Colonel William Verner was now in a difficulty. He was called on by Government for an explanation. He found one at his fingers' ends The gallant colonel pleaded an alibi. He was not in the procession at all he said, he was not decorated. This was his justification to the Lord Chancellor, and also to Lord Caledon, the Lord Lieutenant of the county, who felt it his duty to take cognisance of the matter. In the face of this

denial we have the resolutions at the meeting in the court house before referred to, and to be found at 8056 of the report—"That the thanks of this Grand Lodge are eminently due, and are hereby given to Brother William Verner, Brother James Verner, and Brother John Ellis, Esqs, *for their attendance* here this day." These records were then locked up in the archives of the Institution, however, and in the face of Mr. Verner's denial, Capt. Duff was called upon by Sir Wm. Gosset, on the part of the Executive, to verify his statement upon oath. This he did without hesitation, forwarding at the same time the affidavits of one sergeant and two privates of the constabulary, "who not only observed Colonel Verner in the manner reported by Captain Duff but saw him distinctly take off his hat and cheer the procession he was leading These affidavits the magistrates of Tyrone (all Orangemen) refused to have sworn, the result being that the deponents had to proceed to Dublin and swear them before Major D'Arcy. In a letter to Sir William Gosset, Captain Duff stated that he was prepared to prove that Colonel Verner not only headed the procession through the streets of Dungannon decorated with an orange scarf but that he "pledged" himself to do so some four or five days previous to the procession of the 27th April taking place, "stating at the same time that he was regardless of consequences." There is no getting over the fact. The gallant Colonel was convicted of lying. It can, in truth, be pleaded in his favour that many a gallant colonel lied before.

Lord Caledon, when on examination before the Irish Select Committee, was asked (at question 5,473) the following:—

What is your lordship's opinion as to the effect of those processions and drum-beatings and party tunes as it respects the peace of the country? I think the processions are very mischievous; but I should, as regards the other part of the question, that is what I think of the effect of the Orange system, prefer with the permission of the Committee to read the extract of a letter which I addressed to a gentleman who, I believe, belongs to the Committee, and who is a member of Parliament. An Orange procession took place on the 27th April, which led to a correspondence between me and Colonel Verner, and I find by reference to that correspondence I wrote what follows—"It is hardly necessary for me to add that I neither did nor can subscribe to your position that the word Orangemen means Protestants generally. I believe there are few who value the Protestant population of Ulster more highly than I do, but when a portion only of that body become members of a political society, I cannot consent that such portion should assume to itself the right of being considered the Protestant body at large   I look upon the Protestants as the main support of the British connection, as the most industrious and intelligent part of the community ; but I consider the Orange system as tending to disunite us when our religion alone should be a sufficient bond for our union;" that is the opinion I entertained on the 5th July, 1832, and which I still entertain

Mr. Greer, J.P., was called upon by Lord Caledon immediately after the occurrence at Dungannon for some explanation of his conduct.   His reply I have not been able to lay my hands upon, but from the records of the Grand Lodge, I find that "it was so manly, straightforward, and spirited" as to deserve the thanks of the gentlemen in Grand Lodge assembled.

Mr. Stanley's Act was now before the House, where the Orange representatives used every effort to protract the debates in order to prevent the passing of the Anti-Procession Bill before the 12th July All over the country secret preparations such as those unearthed in Dungannen were made for such a display this year on the Orange anniversary as might terrorise the Government into inaction, or paralyse their measures of restriction   The Grand Lodge of Ireland, it was known, was in favour of the demonstrations.   The Duke of Cumberland— whether from the dictates of a sounder political wisdom or fearful that the desperate game in which he hoped to be the winner might be spoiled by the silly trifling of children, few of whom had brains enough to conceive they were playing for a throne —the Duke of Cumberland now addressed a letter to his Irish brethren, whose precipitate rashness threatened to spoil the sport.   It is dated "St James's Palace, June 21st, 1832," and ran as follows —

"As Grand Master of the Orange Institution in Great Britain and Ireland, honoured as I feel myself in being so placed in a station, the more flattering because wholly unsolicited by myself, as the successor to my beloved brother the Duke of York, and fully inheriting his Orange feelings and attachments, I think myself called on to give proof of such principles and attachment, even at the risk of doing what my zealous and warm-hearted Irish brethren may disapprove   We are now assuredly in an awful crisis. We know not in whom to place confidence for our security from reprehen-

sion, even when influenced solely by the most loyal sentiments of attachment to our gracious Sovereign, and to that sacred Protestant cause; or, to express the same thing in other words, that Orange cause, to maintain which our family of Brunswick were called to the throne, and which I for one will never abandon. Bound as we are, all of us, by every religious and loyal principle to support the true Protestant cause (for in its support are involved, alike the altar and throne of our country) bound to that united, and I pray God it may ever be indissoluble cause, still determined resolutely to maintain that union to the last hour of our lives, we must beware that we do not let our passions (praiseworthy and honourable as they are) mislead us into acts which, however laudable as they undoubtedly are in their design, may yet by artful and wicked men be construed into illegality, and which it seems the intention of the Government to declare by statute illegal.

Under these circumstances we shall best consult the dignity and promote the objects of our institution by voluntarily abstaining from all public demonstrations of feeling. With regret, therefore, but with full conviction of the wisdom of my advice, I call upon you, one and all, to make the sacrifice of declining this year to attend the Orange processions usual on the glorious 12th July.

" In making this appeal to your self-denial, I desire to be understood as recognising to the same extent as ever the sacred duty of co-operation for furthering the Protestant cause. I call upon all Protestants, without distinction, throughout the United Kingdom to combine peacefully, but firmly, for the defence of our common liberties, our common religion, and our one Protestant King ; for it is by union alone, not in processions, both in heart and mind, that we can hope to escape the encroachments and the tyranny of our enemies.

"ERNEST, G.M."

If this document were intended in the light in which it appears to the ordinary reader, if there were no private directions given in lodge to ignore it, if sundry winks and nods did not hint that it was not intended to be acted upon, but merely to act as a justification and a cloak for the Imperial Grand Master, certainly a result followed such as might be expected if in all particulars the contrary were the case. It was treated everywhere as so much waste paper. On the 2nd July the Grand Lodge of Ireland met to arrange for the celebrations of the 12th. It was there resolved— " That under the existing circumstances, and the present excited state of the public mind, it will be in expedient to put forth the address of the Duke of Cumberland, written under the impression that the Procession Bill, then passing through the Commons House of Parliament, would be passed into law. That an address from the Grand Committee be prepared to the Orangemen of Ireland, impressing upon such of our brethren as intend celebrating the coming festival of the 12th July the strict observance of order and decorum, and the absence from all demonstrations calculated to insult their fellow-countrymen or lead to the violation of the public peace." This was plainly recommending the carrying out of their programme to the fullest. The honesty of recommending the celebration, and in the same breath advising an absence from all demonstrations " calculated to insult 'heir fellow-countrymen," must certainly be questioned. No one knew better than the Grand Orange Lodge of Ireland that these demonstration not only were calculated to insult the Catholics, but were absolutely organised for that purpose. Blood here, blood there, blood everywhere in the track of these demonstrations told how offensive and how dangerous they were.

The address of the Grand Lodge followed, and left no doubt that they meant to beard the Government on this question of processions. They recommended them,* and stated their determination to uphold and protect those members of their body who joined in them, concluding thus, " You now have leaders whom you can trust. Watch, obey, and co-operate with them, and by your own exertions, under the help of the Most High, you will overturn your oppressors, secure your own rights, and render the country prosperous and the people happy ;" a production quite as blasphemous as that hackneyed Orange refrain, " Put your trust in God, my boys, keep your powder dry !"

All over the country these preparations excited the utmost consternation, in which the members of the Administration were sharers.

On July 9th, in the House of Commons, Mr. Hume called the attention of the right hon. Secretary for Ireland to the fact that the Orange Lodge of Ireland had assembled on the 2nd inst. to arrange measures for celebrating the 12th July. It was said, he remarked, that the Lord Lieutenant of a county presided at the meeting, and that several

magistrates were present. He wished to know whether the Government intended to strike the names of those persons out of the Commission of the Peace ? Mr. Stanley said, in reply, that Government had certainly received information that the Orangemen were preparing to celebrate the 12th July by processions. Government had made their arrangements for preserving the public peace, and would mark with proofs of their disapprobation any person under their control who would encourage or attend those processions.* While the Government was taking every precaution in the re-issuing of circulars of instruction to the magistrates and others, the Catholic clergy were upon their part doing still more effective work in cautioning their people from all interference. To the wise counsels of the clergy and the forbearance of their followers must be attributed whatever saving of life was this near effected.

The action of the brethren on the 12th July, 1832 evinced not only a decided hostility to the Government but a determination, too fully persisted in, to be bound by no enactment of the legislature at variance with their prejudices. Not a district in which a lodge was known to exist failed to swell the clamour, and for weeks the entire of the North was again given over to scenes of menace and confusion. It is needless to dwell in detail upon them, but one incident reported by Captain Duff to the Government cannot be passed over. On the 12th July at Dungannon a great Orange procession took place at which 9,000 Orangemen with sixty stand of colours were present. "230 of them," says Captain Duff, " were armed with muskets independent of concealed arms." Further—" it was headed by several gentlemen of respectability and property, and amongst others by Hon. A. G. Stuart, Deputy-Lieutenant, as also a magistrate of this county, and captain of the Killyman Corps of Yeomanry, his horse decorated with Orange and purple but none on his person ; Mr. Greer, a magistrate for this county as also for Armagh, his emblem of his office of Grand Master of the county suspended from an orange ribband around his neck. Thirdly, Mr. Lowry, jun., Captain of the Cameroy Corps of Yeomanry, decorated with an orange and purple scarf. Fourthly, Mr. Lloyde, second captain of the Killyman Corps of Yeomanry. Also, that the Earl of Castlestuart, headed the procession in his own neighbourhood. His second son, the Hon. Charles Stuart, was decorated, and marched in the procession from Mr. Lowry's to Mr. Greer's.

* Lord Rod n appears to have been the only exception. He wrote previous to the passing of the Anti-Processions Act and before the 12th July, 1832, strongly condemning demonstrations, and advised the brethren to abstain from them.

* Hansard's Debates for 1832,

Several clergymen of the Established Church also attended." Mr. Greer was soon after dismissed from the magistracy for signing an Orange document, inconsistent with his character as a magistrate. Two days before the passing of the Anti-Processions Act he headed, with the Hon. Mr. Stuart, an Orange procession into Dungannon. Lord Caledon asking him if he still intended, notwithstanding the passing of the Act, to attend processions, which were now made a misdemeanour, received the reply, from Mr. Greer, that he would give no promise whatever, and was ready to take the consequences.

Mr. Stanley, in the House of Commons, while condemning the proceedings and the menacing attitude of the Orangemen this year, admitted that the peace was kept owing to the praiseworthy conduct of the Catholics and to the manner in which they followed the excellent advice of their pastors. That the Catholics were willing, if allowed, to live on terms of amity with their neighbours, was placed beyond a doubt by their general conduct. In fact their efforts towards conciliation went, in some places, beyond mere passivity. Mr William Crossley, in the report, supplied the Government, relative to an Orange procession in Maghera, County Derry, notes the fact that the Rev. Mr. Quinn, P.P., and his niece displayed large bunches of orange lilies in their breast in Magherafelt, and the Orangemen determined, it may be supposed, not to be outdone "spent the evening in a Roman Catholic public-house." This unfortunately was but an isolated instance of good fellowship. Elsewhere over the country a deep-seated rage took possession of the Orangemen, and revealed the conditional loyalists to the Government and the country. Mr. Blacker's description of the state of the country and of the feeling of his brethren, which, it may be said, he rightly understood, is anything but reassuring. For playing the role of an Orange partizan on the Portadown Petty Sessions bench he was called upon by Government for an explanation. This production opens with the following words, which if they did not threaten armed rebellion give, at least, a very significent hint of its proximity.—"Subsequent to the Assizes (of 1833) the country was in a state of excitement such as my recollection car not parallel. It was not a transient effervescence, a momentary ebulition of popular feeling, or confined to the rabble, or unthinking portion of the people; it was a fierce, stern exasperation, in which men of sober minds and religious habits evinced an extensive participation; it was

general, it was deep-rooted, springing, as it seemed, not from ordinary party feeling, but from a wide-spread alarm of endangered liberty—endangered by the statute prohibiting the manifestation of political sentiments." If I read the signs of the times correctly, it was, in plainer terms, a rebellious spirit such as the Orangemen had often menaced the Government with before and since, and arising out of dissatisfaction at the "betrayal of the Constitution" by the King and his Ministers. As subsequently found to be, it was dogged determination to secure in the person of royalty, by a change in the succession, a partisan who would, if not re-establish the old Constitution, at least secure to the Orangemen the remnants of ascendancy that had been left them in the new one.

During the subsequent winter and the intervening spring of 1833, efforts were made to strengthen their hold upon the army. In many regiments new lodges were secretly established. That the Grand Lodges were aware of the dangerous ground upon which they were treading is seen in their refusal to send Orange initiatory documents to the Sappers and Miners, then quartered at Ballymena, unless "under cover" to some faithful brother "who could be depended upon." Mr. Andrew Crosbie, saddler, was thereupon chosen as the "faithful" medium through whom Orange documents could be smuggled into one of his Majesty's regiments without the knowledge of its commanding officers. The resolution of the Grand Committee in Dublin touching this proceeding is "that the Committee would most willingly forward all documents connected with the Orange system to any confidential person in Ballymena, as prudence would not permit that documents should be forwarded direct to our military brethren." This resolution bears the signature of Mr. William Swan, the then Grand Secretary for Ireland.

It may be thought that party demonstrations now being a misdemeanour, the Orangemen bowed obediently to the law. Not so. They had been again and again declared illegal at common law, and were now rendered doubly so by statute. It mattered little. Orange turbulence could make light of either. The Executive sent out its circulars; large forces of military were drafted into the North, and every effort made to preserve the peace. The Orangemen utterly ignored the law, and walked in as large numbers as on previous years. At Portglenone the Riot Act was read, and the intervention of a large force of military alone prevented the usual scenes of riot and disorder.

At Cootehill the Orangemen walked, and an affray took place in which several persons lost their lives. A verdict of wilful murder was found against some persons unknown, and a similar verdict returned against one John Allen, an Orangeman, who was subsequently acquitted. In Garvagh, County Derry, a like scene took place. The Riot Act was read, but at the words, "Our Sovereign Lord the King chargeth and commandeth all persons here assembled immediately to disperse themselves," the brethren simply responded by striking up "No surrender" and "The Protestant Boys" on their drums, an intimation that their Sovereign Lord the King was a personage of very little consequence indeed. At Killieandra a demonstration took place. The entrance gate to the glebe of the Protestant curate, the Rev. Henry Marten, had been decorated with an Orange arch, which the chief-constable had removed lest it might lead to a breach of the peace. The family subsequently left the house, unmistakably winking at the illegal proceedings of the Orangemen, for immediately afterwards the Petty Sessions Clerk, who acted also as agent to one of Mr. Marten's brothers, actually redecorated the gate. At Ballyhagan, near Portadown, a serious attack was made by a procession of Orangemen upon a few Catholics assembled on the roadside. Shots were fired from the procession, and several persons wounded. The Catholics issued summonses against their assailants, but, being naturally reluctant to appear before Colonels Verner and Blacker, at the Portadown Bench, they petitioned the Government to assist them, stating at the same time that their lives had been threatened if they persisted in the prosecution. The case subsequently went before the Portadown magistrates. Colonel Blacker suggested the withdrawal of the prosecution, upon which Mr. M'Connell, who appeared for the Catholics, agreed to do so if the Orangemen promised not to insult and assault his clients in future. Colonel Blacker refused to allow the Orangemen to enter into such a condition, and the proposal was received with a loud shout of "No surrender" in court, in leading which Mr. Harvey John Forter, the moral agent of Lord Mandeville who occupied a seat on the bench, took the chief part.* The reason why Colonel Blacker would not allow the compact to be entered into is fully explained. He said in court to Mr. M'Connell that the Anti-Procession

* See Mr. M'Connell's evidence before Select Committee Irish Report, 6412.

Act " was a law made by the Whigs, and that they made many laws as well as that that ought not to be obeyed."

In July, 1833, there was an Orange procession in Lurgan. The parties engaged in it had no excuse in pleading ignorance of the law, for Mr. Hancock had at the Petty Sessions taken the precaution of reading and explaining that law to those assembled. There was no rioting, and it appears from the letters of Mr. Hancock that "This was in great measure to be attributed to the exertions of the Roman Catholic clergymen," who had on the previous Sunday "used every exertion to prevent the people of their congregation from attending the market for fear of some collision arising between the parties." But the law had been publicly defied. A great number of arrests were made, and Mr. Hancock and Mr. Brownlow committed the most prominent leaders to jail on their refusal to give bail. Great excitement prevailed, and as a rescue was feared, the thirteen prisoners were marched to Armagh after midnight. The trial took place before Mr. Justice Moore, and the jury, after a considerable time, found three of the prisoners guilty and acquitted eleven on the ground that they were ignorant of the law, notwithstanding the fact of proclamations and notices having been issued and had been notorious for years. The judge discharged there three without punishment. Justice Moore even told them, "I concur in the verdict which the jury have returned. It does just as well as if every one of you had been found guilty." So, indeed, it did! The worthy Judge concluded, after flourishing about obedience to the laws, by discharging the men upon their own recognizance to appear at the next Assizes if required. As might be expected, the prisoners exclaimed in court, "Thank God, we have so mild a judge!" The natural result of this was, of course, that there were riots, with flagrant breaches of the peace, immediately afterwards. The Orangemen, to the number of 3,000 dressed with sashes, &c., and headed by that same moral agent of Lord Mandeville, marched in triumphal procession from Armagh to Lurgan, escorting the acquitted and their unacquitted brethren. Colonel Blacker awaited them upon the steps of the hotel in Lurgan, and cheered and waived his hat as they passed. On reaching "Papist" Hancock's house, a desperate attack was made upon it, under the able and reverend direction of Mr. Kent, the curate of the parish. Mr. Hancock, his wife and family, were relieved from their just terrors by the timely arrival of a party of the 52nd Regiment.

Lieutenant-Colonel Wm. Blacker makes use of some very strong language in writing upon these arrests. In a letter dated "Carrick, Portadown, July 18, 1833," he throws all the blame for the excitement which followed upon the Government for passing the Anti-Procession Act and upon the two magistrates for putting it in force. The law breakers seemed in his eyes to have been acting a noble part. He threatens Government that if they persist in this they will have three processions where they had but one. He disavows an intention to ask the Government to yield to clamour, and in the following sentence hints that it is necessary to do so, winding up a most nonsensical effusion thus —"Much allowance must be made, and I am sure will be made, by a person of Lord Anglesey's high mind for the long-cherished and hereditary feelings, to say nothing of their being fostered and encouraged by Government after Government for so many years; and I feel confident, from my knowledge of the country and its people (the Orangemen), that it will effect more with them than all the laws the Legislature could enact or all the force Great Britain could supply to support them. I am a Christian, and I wish for 'goodwill among men,' and both there I unhesitatingly aver have been placed in greater jeopardy by the events of this day than by all the celebrations of these forty years put together" Remarkable language from a Deputy-Lieutenant of a county upon an incident in which the law was put into fo ce and the peaceable inhabitants protected.

There is an incident in connection with this celebration worthy of note. On the 12th July in Lurgan an unfortunate man named Devlin who was in the market on business was so unhappy as to obstruct the Orange procession with his cart, which he had left inadvertently standing in the street The poor animal was beaten unmercifully. On the subsequent Thursday, the 18th July, the Rev. Mr. Kent, who had witnessed the obstruction of the 12th, was in the town of Lurgan, and left his mare standing in the street without any one to hold it. The mare ran away, and the identical Devlin succeeded in catching the mare, but, for his services, he received from the rev. gentleman a sound rating for having obstructed the procession a few days previously. Mr. Hancock, who came up, took Devlin's part, and said he was in the market on lawful business, and had no right to leave the way for people who were breaking the law. The Rev. Mr. Kent replied—

"Orangemen have as good a right to walk in procession as the Catholics on St. Patrick's Day, and the Government is composed of a set of base, cowardly rascals, not fit to govern any country." Mr. Hancock, a Justice of the Peace, very naturally replied to this—"I warn you Mr. Kent, I hold his Majesty's Commission of the Peace and will not permit you or any other person to speak contemptuously of his Majesty's Government in my presence." "Oh," said Mr. Kent, "I did not intend what I said to be personal, but since you take it so I repeat what I said before, that the present Government is composed of a base, paltry, and cowardly set of poltroons, unfit to govern any country." Mr, Hancock—"Not so base, so cowardly as you and such as you, who skulk in safety yourselves, but put forward ignorant deluded people to break the law by walking in processions when you dare not head them yourselves." The Rev. Mr. Kent—"You are a damned liar." Mr. Hancock replied to this by a blow upon the left cheek, which some say put down the Orange cleric Ample apology was afterwards made by Mr Hancock for his hot headedness, but the very natural results were used by the Orange clique for blackening Mr. Hancock's character before the committee of the House of Commons before whom he was examined.

But the Orange triumphs of the Armagh ascendancy men were drawing to a close. Lieutenant Colonel Blacker on this 12th July, countenanced and encouraged an Orange procession of 2 000 in Portadown. In the words of Captain Patton "He and his brother magistrates acted as if no such law as the Anti-Processions Act were in force." He received the brethren in his demesne, the entrance of which was decorated with orange; entertained them at his residence; appeared at his window beside the members of his household, who wore Orange decorations; and after addressing an eloquent harrangue—what did think you? Send for the police to take them into custody ! Not likely. He quietly sat down while the brethren were in retreat from his lawn, and wrote a report to the Castle which is about the most remarkable example of the effects of light and shade to be found in the history of these doings Riots occured in Portadown in which some of the gentlemen to whom Lieutenant-Colonel Blacker had addressed himself were concerned. The names of the offenders were taken and sent to the Castle. The Attorney-General ordered informations to be taken and the parties returned for trial. Mr.

Blacker refused to take those informations, and prevailed upon the other magistrates to follow him, showing a disposition to frustrate the operations of the law, as well as to screen those Orangemen who had violated it. An inquiry was instituted into Lieutenant-Colonel Blacker's conduct, and—the " Fabian Colonel" was dismissed.

Misfortunes came not now in single file. Dean Carter had by this time also got into disgrace. The acquittal of the brethren arrested in Lurgan at the instance of Mr. Hancock and Mr. Brownlow was too inviting an incident not to demand special commemoration In the following week Lord Mande ville provided tar-barrels and timber to the Orangemen surrounding his demesne to burn in honour of the acquittal of their brethren. Beer was supplied by his lordship in large quantities, the impartial distribution of which his " moral agent," Mr Porter superintended. We find from the description given of the rejoicings by Lord Gosford that the Orangemen dressed up a figure as an effigy of " Papist Hancock," the magistrate who had incurred their displeasure by proceeding, under the Anti-Procession Act, to commit the Orangemen who had marched contrary to law. This effigy had a rope tied around its neck, and was hoisted up on a pole, or gallows; the tar-barrels were set fire to, and the effigy was consumed amid the shoutings and hurrangs of the people assembled about it. This compliment to a brother magistrate was got up by Lord Mandeville's agent. During the gaiities of the evening this agent, Mr. Porter, was chaired around the bonfire by the mob. But the hero of the day was Dean Carter, a reverend magistrate, who, having dined with Lord Mandeville came forth from his lordship's gates, attended by Lady Mandeville, her ladyship's children, and some ladies of their suite They took their stand upon an elevated postion opposite the bon-fire, and joined in the proceedings with evident zest. Cheers were given for the Dean and the lady, as well as groans for " Papist Hancock," and the worthy and reverend justice joined in the unseemly demonstration. Mr. Crampton, the Solicitor-General, in his report, rightly expressed surprise at " a magistrate countenancing, accrediting by his presence and by his approbation the indecent exhibition of an Orange triumph over an Act of the Legislature, coupled with the infliction of on infamous punishment upon the effigy of a brother magistrate." Dean Carter was dismissed from the Bench also, and that gentleman, whom in

describing the occurrence, a writer in the *Edinburgh Review*, calls the Marcellus of the party, Colonel Verner himself, the Deputy-Master of Armargh, threw up his commission as a magistrate in indignation at this invasion of Orange rights and privileges.

To exaggerate the outrageous conduct of the Orangemen of Ireland during the greater part of the year 1834 would be simply impossible. Not alone did they conceive themselves not bound to pay allegiance to the King's ministers, but they demonstrated their hostility by crimes as brutal as they were unprovoked. To a Whig Government the Orangemen owe no allegiance; to a Tory they owe only a conditional obedience, founded upon the quid pro quo principle, to which they rigidly adhere. At the period we are treating of they certainly acted as if they owed no allegiance to the Government. They assumed hostility to all men who did not actually belong to their body. It would be practically impossible to embody within the compass of a small volume even a brief summary of all the outrages which found during this year their origin in Irish Orangeism. To the minute inquirer I would recommend the Parliamentary Blue Books dealing with the subject, and if in the particulars there stated he does not find, within the brief records of nine months, sufficient reasons for judging the institution an evil to society he has read indeed to little advantage. In fact, for all practical purposes we may now denominate the Orangemen of the United Kingdom as the rebels of the time. The Ninety-Eight movement had gone out; the Forty-Eight reaction had not come in, and during the brief reign of the reformed Parliament the Orangemen occupied the position which had been deserted by the disaffected Irish, and appeared boldly and unblushingly in the light of rebels to the Crown and Constitution. The Repeal movement, under the guide of O'Connell, was still making strides amongst the Irish peasantry, and in the beginning of this year its veteran leader became serious in his projects for a dissolution of the Union. The result was a reaction on the part of the Orangemen who, though belonging to a professedly non-political association, offered every opposition to the movement both within their councils and outside Mr Scott, the Sheriff of Dublin, was expelled the association for being favourable to repeal. It appears he was present at a breakfast at which Mr. O'Connell was the guest which gave dire offence to the gentle-

21

men of the Grand Lodge. It was only on the part of the Grand Lodge that this virtuous indignation was at all apparent. Elsewhere many of the brethren seriously lent the repeal movement their support, which only had the effect of making the Orange autocracy and its minions more determined and more pronounced in its opposition. Indeed there is no better proof of the gross illegality of the association than that afforded this year. Oaths and solemn ordinances had long bound the brethern together, and when their existence was put to the test both were conveniently denied. A simple declaration on the part of any person entering a society at this time was by Act of Parliament rendered illegal. Yet we find the Orange Grand Lodge at which were present most of the dignitaries of the institution, adopting a declaration for the admission of brethren, which was manifestly illegal. This declaration was circulated amongst the brethern, and when attention was privately called to it Mr. Ward, the solicitor of the Grand Lodge, adopted the simple method of scratching the record of its existence off the books of the institution in order to make amends for the glaring illegality. A communication had been received from Trinity College Lodge respecting this declaration and a resolution adopted in reply. That reply was of a nature admitting the existence of the Orange declaration. It was quietly scratched out behind the back of the secretray and the words inserted "resolved that Brother Swan will *orally* make known the opinion of the Grand Committee upon the subject of their communication" While making the erasure in one book the brethern ignored the record in another, and they have only to blame their own obtuseness for the fact of the glaring illegality of the association becoming thus revealed. From the same book, which gave a record of the daily proceedings of the Grand Lodge in Committee, we find that three leaves had been torn out before it was submitted to the inspection of the Committee. The supposition may have been an unwarrantable one. It was a supposition, however, which found credit at the time, that these three missing pages had reference to matters relating to the succession of the Crown, which had better be hidden away in the strong box of the Institution. These pages were missing in the minute book of the Grand Lodge for February, 1834. Mr. Ward, solicitor, could not account for them; Mr. Swan, the secretary, could not account for them; Mr. Blacker never saw them; Colonel Verner shook his head whenever he was asked for them, and the existence of the three pages remains wrapped in mystery to the present day.

The existence of the conspiracy was now a subject of question in the House of Commons, and, as appears upon the pages of Hansard, the leaders of the Institution took care to disarm suspicion. A pamphlet, professedly containing the rules and regulations of the Orange Society, was distributed amongst the members of both Houses by the Orange body; but when a comparison was made between them and those actually in circulation amongst the Orange body, it was found *that the declaration had been omitted.*

On the 17th March the Catholics abandoned their display, which they were bound to do by law.

The Orangemen, instead of following their example, verified the truth of Colonel Blacker's solemn warning to the Government—That so long as the Party Processions Act existed the Government would have not one but three processions on the part of the Orangemen to deal with. The most trifling opportunity was taken advantage of now for an Orange demonstration. If the magistrates were less supine than usual the result of their vigilance was disastrous. The parties arrested for breaking the Anti-Processions Act were invariably brought to trial before an Orange jury, who acquitted them. On their release they were received in triumph outside the very court of justice by their brethren, who made heroes and martyrs of them, and improvised Orange demonstrations homewards in their favour. On the homeward route it may naturally be supposed that the brethren would not be in the best of moods, and the result was house wrecking, pillage and murder, in which the Catholic inhabitants as usual were the sufferers.

With the Anti-Procession Act in force the demonstrations of the 12th of July were as numerous as ever. Not alone did the Orangemen demonstrate all over the Province of Ulster as usual, but they exhibited a wanton and reckless defiance of authority such as brands them unmistakeably as rebels to the Government of the day. At the same time the inner workings of Orangeism were such as to lend a more tragic import to their proceedings. In the County of Wexford a handful of Orangemen made a sally at midnight from their lodge, and murdered three Catholics who were passing upon the road In Cavan a shot was fired from the window of an Orange lodge, and a Catholic farmer was shot dead upon the spot. Fermanagh was at that time a scene of midnight outrage, in which the brethren played a conspicuous part., In a remote village on the borders of the county a midnight attack was made by the members of the Black Lodge upon the houses of a few Catholic inhabitants. The latter were brutally ill-treated, while their residences were burned to the ground. We find about the same date a Black-Lodge located between Lisburn and Lurgan, at a place called Maralin, taking an active part in outrages upon unoffend'ng Catholics, all of which, owing to the constitution of the magisterial benches, were duly allowed to go unpunished. In fact, the Black Lodges never made themselves more conspicuous than at this particular period, and, after being allowed to carry on a sanguinary warfare for the space of ten months, the Grand Lodge, in November, 1834, quietly got rid of all the odium connected with their murderous proceedings by declaring that they should no longer acknowledge the existence of such lodges in connection with their institution.

But the proceedings of July revealed the Orange party more vividly than ever in the light of rebels. If before they had defied the law, they now menaced, intimidated, and outraged its supporters and administrators. On the 1st July Counsellor Costello arrived at Dungannon to discharge some legal business. It was rumoured that the Catholics from Coalisland would draw his carriage into the town, but whether this was entertained or not we have the fact that Mr. Costello entered the town by an unfrequented route, with the object, it appears, of avoiding outrage at the hands of the Orange party and to give the slip to his Catholic admirers. The incident did not end there. The Orange Yeomanry were at midnight called to arms and paraded the town for hours. Mr. Stronge, a magistrate, directed an Orange arch to be taken down, a proceeding which at the time rendered him exceedingly unpopular, and for which he subsequently was nearly forfeiting his life. It secured for him the term "Papist Stronge" ever afterwards.

On the 12th July, at Portglenone, the Orangemen of the Counties of Derry and Antrim united in forcing their way through a large force of military drawn across the bridge leading to the town. The Riot Act was read, and also the Dispersion Act, but with no effect, and the entire military force were paralysed by the 3,000 armed Orangemen who paraded. In Dungannon, a great demonstration took place of Orange Yeomen, which passed into the town in spite of all efforts on the part of the authorities to the contrary. At Stewartstown, a village about six miles distance from Dungannon,

a lodge was sitting on the same evening, when by chance a Catholic was passing, and he was fired at from the window of the lodge. The would-be-assassin was a fair marksman. He shot his finger off. In consequence, both the Dungannon and the Stewartstown corps of yeomanry were ordered to be dismissed. It would be tedious to go minutely into the various demonstrations, notwithstanding that the effort would be mere or less justified by the intimate connection which they had with outrages of the most shocking description. It is sufficient for our purpose, however, to say that the records supplied the Government show that in this year, with the Anti-Procession Act in force, there were little less than fifty Orange demonstrations over the Province of Ulster, most of which were attended with violence and bloodshed.

This state of things was prolonged through the whole of the subsequent autumn, with little less disastrous effects. The clamour of the Orangemen were not without results—results which, however gratifying at first, still lead to a more speedy dissolution.

In a sham fight near Keady on the 5th November the military were alone prevented from asserting the law through fear of blood being shed.

In the second week of November the death of Earl Spencer took Lord Althop from the Lower to the Upper House, and on Lord Melbourne waiting upon his Majesty for his commands respecting the appointment of a new Chancellor of the Exchequer, William. IV. expressed disapproval of the conduct of the Government in regard to the Irish Church question, and by the advice of the Conservative chief, the Duke of Wellington, Sir Robert Peel was sent for to form a Ministry. This act of his Majesty gave rise to high hopes that the Orangemen of Ireland were about to have back the old *regime* of intolerance. But those days had gone, and for ever. There was, however, in the change of Ministry enough to give rise to a feeling of triumph over the downfall of the Whig reformers, and meetings were at once called at various centres throughout the country "to thank his Majesty for dismissing his late advisers." At a meeting of the Royal Luther Lodge (No. 1483), in Dublin, on the 2nd December, at which most of the leaders of the Irish Orangemen were present, an address of thanks was voted to the King after the delivery of speeches breathing of extermination to all things Catholic and Liberal. On the 8th December a "grand concurrent Orange meeting of the County and City of Dublin" was held in the Merchants' Hall for the purpose of "addressing the King relative to the late dismissal of his Ministers." The Lord Mayor, who a few days subsequently entertained the Viceroy, took the chair at this meeting. From the report of the *Evening Mail,* I find that one of the most important resolutions passed upon the occasion was—

"That we will shed the last drop of our blood in defence of our Protestant Institution."

During the proceedings, a violent Orange bigot achieved a brilliant success by the introduction of a blasphemous production, which is attributed in Orange poetic publications to the pen of Colonel Blacker. As this sanguinary rhapsody was such as to warrant the exclusive attention of the House of Commons, its transfer into these pages may not be out of place —

The night is gather'ng g rowly, the d y is closing fast—
The tempest flaps its raven wings in loud and angry blast
The thunder clouds are d iving athwart the lurid sky—
But, "put your trust in God, my boys, and keep your
    powder dry."

There was a day when loyalty was hail'd with honour due,
Our banner the protection wav'd to all the good and true
And gallant hearts beneath its folds were link'd in honour's
    tie.
We put our trust in God, my boys, and kept our powder
    dry.

When TREASON bar'd her bloody arm, and maddened round
    the land,
For king, an law, and order fair, we drew the ready brand
Our gathering s ell was William's name—our word was
    "do or die"
And still we put our trust in God, and keep our powder
    dry.

But now, alas! a wondrous change has come the nation o' r,
And worth and g llant services, remembered are no more,
And, cru.h d beneath oppression's weight, in chains of grief
    we lie,
But "put your trust in God, my boys, and keep your
    powd r dry."

Forth starts the spawn of Treason, the 'scap'd of nicety-
    eight,
To bask in courtly favour, and seize th helm of state;
E en they whose hands are re king yet with murder's
    crimson dye—
But ' put your t.ust in God, n y boys, and keep your
    powder dry."

They come, whose deeds incarnadin'd the Slan y's silver
    wave—
They come, who to the foreign foe the hail of welcome
    ga e;
He comes, the open rebel fierce he comes the Jesuit sly;
But "put your trust in God, my boys, and keep your
    powder dry."

They come, whose counsels wrapp'd the land in foul re-
    bellion's flame,
Their hearts, unchastised by remorse, their cheeks un-
    ti g d by sh me
B still, be still, indignant heart—be tearless, too, each eye,
And "put yo r tr.ist in God, my boys, and keep your
    powder dry."

The Pow'r that led his chosen, by pillar'd cloud and flame,
Through parted sea and dese t waste, the Pow'r is still the
    s me
He fails not—He—the loyal he.rt that firm on Him rely—
So "put yo r tru t in God, my boys, and keep your
    powder dry."

The Pow r that nerv'd the stalwart arms of Gideon's cho
    few
The Pow'r that l d great William, Boyne's reddening tor-
    rents through—
In his protecting arm o fide, and e ery foe defy
Then " ut your trust in God my boys, and keep your
    powder dry."

Already are the Star of Hope emits its orient blaze,
The cheering b acon of relief, it glimme s thro' the haze;
It tells of better days te come, it tells of succour nigh
Then "put your trust in God, my boys, and keep your
    powder dry."

See, all along the hills of Down, its rising glories spread,
But brightest teams its radience from Donard's lofty head.
C anbrassil's vales a e kindling wide, and Roden" is the
    cry—
Then "put your trust in God, my boys, and keep your
    powder dry."

Then cheer ye heart of lo alty, nor sink in dark despair,
Our banner shall again unfol l its glories to the air,
T e storm that aves th wildest the sooner passe by
Then "put your trust in God my boys, and keep your
    powde dry."

For ' happy homes," for "altars free," we grasp the
    ready sword
For Freedo n, Truth, and for our God's unmutilated Word
These, these the war cry of our march, our hope the Lo d on
    High;
The "put your trust in God, my boys, and keep your
    powder dry."

We are told by the *Evening Mail* that this production was received with the most deafening cheers. It expressed the sentiments of the assembled brethren, who overlooked the blasphemy in its violence. It did not pass without remark in the House of Commons, in the course of the debate which this gave rise to, that the Duke of Wellington had recalled Lord Anglesea because he had dined with Lord Cloncur y, a member of the Catholic Association. Clamour for a brief interval was supreme, and no recall followed this coalition between Viceroyalty and Orangeism.

A meeting was held on the 19th December at Dungannon, and by a series of successful manœuvering on the part of the Orangemen of the county Lord Caledon, who was decidedly opposed to the Institution, was prevailed upon as Lord Lieutenant of the county to call the meeting. Under colour of a Protestant demonstration to address the King an Orange demonstration and procession was organised, and the evidence before the committee justified the supposition that Verner, Blacker & Co. had been busy at work behind the scenes. At midnight on the night previous to the meeting a violent Orange circular was sent out to the following effect.—"Will you desert your King? No, you will die first. The King, as becomes a son of George III, has spurned from his Council the men who would have overturned the most valued institutions of your country, *and would have led your monarch to a violation of his Coronation Oath.* Your Sovereign has done his duty; will you abandon yours? If you will not; if you will maintain the liberties which your fathers purchased with their blood, you will be found at the great Protestant meeting to be held at Dungannon on Tuesday, the 19th inst, at twelve o'clock, and your cry will be—the King and the Constitution, the Altar and the Throne."

So complete were their arrangements that it was not until Lord Caledon had actually taken the chair that thousands of armed Orangemen came trooping in, with flags flying and drums beating, surrounding the platform. A scene of the greatest violence followed. Lord Caledon had to leave the chair prematurely amid cries of "Pap st Caledon," and Mr. Stronge, J.P., who had on the 1st July ordered the removal of an Orange arch, was subjected to the grossest treatment, had to fly for his life from the meeting, and was finally compelled to steal by a back way out of the house in which he sought refuge.

Sir Frederick Stoven, the chief of the police, was upon the same occasion fired at by the Orangemen while outside his own house, the ball passing within a yard of his person. Sir Frederick had, like Capt. Duff, incurred the displeasure of the Orange party "for doing his duty," for such are his words, like him he was called Papist Stoven, and such were the speedy means they adopted in getting rid of him. In the course of his examination before the Select Committee, and immediately after the reading of Captain Duff's report of this outrage to the Government, we find the following :—

Is that a correct report? Yes, two or three of the gentlemen called upon me, one of them a clergyman, with very strong opinions. I went to the gate with him, from which I could look down the street, and they were hurrahing and drinking at public-houses, and shots firing in all directions; and I walked up and down before my house, and certainly to my great surprise a shot came within a yard of me, close by my ear and struck the house.

Did you observe whether it struck the wall of your house immediately behind you? Yes.

Do you take for granted that the shot was fired kill me, and it was a very long distance that it was at yourself? Yes, I do not say that they wanted to fired from.

Had you any reason to apprehend mischief at that meeting, from any intimation made to you or any other person, previous to that meeting? No, I was very much surprised at this shot, and I went

* Sir F. Stoven's evidence before the Select Committee of the House of Commons—ques ion 4573.

down to the magistrate who lived within a hundred yards of me, where the orange flags and things were standing close to the magistrate's door at a public-house opposite, and I went to Mr. Murray and said "Why Mr Murray you may call this keeping the peace of Dungannon, but I never saw anything so bad in my life, I have just been shot at, if you do not stop this firing I think it is the most disgraceful thing I ever saw," however the firing was not stopped, but I was a good deal surprised at the shot, because, though I do not conceal my ideas upon this subject, I have never made myself offensive, I believe, but the following Sunday, a lady, the wife of the chief constable, Mr. Duff, went to church; she had not been to church the previous Sunday, and when she opened the prayer-book a paper dropped out, and she saw it was a curious sort of thing, and she gave it to Mr. Duff.

Have you the paper here? I have, Mr Duff looked at it and saw what is was and put it into his pocket and brought it to me, and asked what he should do with it; I said as to myself I did not care, but it was a most disgraceful thing to put a threatening notice into a church, particularly into the cover of a lady's prayer-book, and this is a copy of it.—"Sir,—As this is the last day to be in this rotten town, I send you this advice, tell Robinson that he and that damned scout Strong, will do very little on Friday at the Protestant meeting; that Duff and Sir F Stoven had better stay in the house or they may get an orange ball which may cause them to stay at home on the 12th July. Tell Duff that he and Strong, that they will not be able to stop the meeting nor the walking on the 12th, tell them to kiss my —— and suck my—— I remain yours, something, Dodd, Amen" This was clearly put into the prayer-book the Sunday before, but it was not found in consequence of Mrs Duff not having gone to church till the following Sunday, I said he might do what he pleased with it, and he sent it to the primate, what was done I cannot say, but I believe Mr. Horner, the rector of Dungannon, took some pains to endeavour to find out the author. But Mr. Duff, by my advice, sent it to Mr. Jones the secretary of the primate, and this is his answer :—"Dear Sir,—I cannot say how greatly the primate was shocked at the disgraceful notice put into Mrs Duff's prayer-book, his Grace has written to Mr. Horner to use all the means in his power to detect the person who placed it there; I write in a great hurry," and what was done I do not know,

But the author of it was not found out? No.

Had you ever before reason to suppose that the Orangemen had any spite against you? No, I never came into collision with them, except in this instance at Dungannon, where I happened to be living.

Have you heard that Lord Claude Hamilton was made an Orangeman at that very meeting? Yes, it is notorious.

Had you an particular account of it? No, I had no account of his being made an Orangeman, except that I know he was made one in the afternoon of that day about three o'clock.

Was it at the meeting itself that he was made, or in a public-house? In a public-house.

Do you know what public-house? A man of the name of Lilburn.

Must not Lord Hamilton have witnessed all this scene that occurred? I suppose so.

And heard the shots firing? No, perhaps not at the time of the meeting on the hustings I do not believe there were any shots firing; it was after the meeting had terminated in the afternoon.

Lord Hamilton was witness of course to all these colours and the scarfs and the colours, and everything of that kind at the meeting? He must have been.

Did you receive any information, or did you observe yourself, as to the yeomanry arms being amongst the arms used upon the 19th of December? None whatever.

We also find from the evidence of Captain Duff that about that time an attempt was made on the life of Inspector Crofton—called Papist Crofton—in the County Down, ample proof of which the witness proffered to bring before the Committe. *

At the races, in Armagh, a faction fight took place, in which, from the evidence at hand, it seems both parties were implicated. The results, as disastrous as they were dreadful, was the subsequent burning—three months after—of an entire village, while the Orange party surveyed from an adjacent hill the terrible ruin their handiwork was accomplishing.

I an giving Lord Mandeville and his Orange contemporaries all credit that they sought for in taking it that the burning of Annahagh, on the 17th January, 1835, was the result of the Armagh races—race held more than 3 months previously, in which they allege a Protestant named M'Whinney was beaten. It must strike even the ordinary reader, however, that we might with as much rea on regard the Belfast riots of recent years as the immediate result of the 1688 revolution. But granted that in this instance cause and effect were so widely sundered none but an absolute bigot could find in a simple assault palliation for so brutal, cold-blooded, and fiendish a crime as this which stains the criminal calendar of Orangeism. For the assault at the races four Catholics suffered transportation, a fact which needs to be borne in mind, until we come to consider what fate awaited the destroyers of Annahagh. This, coupled with the fact that M'Whinney survived the assault, and we see little to justify the giving of a whole village to flames. But while Lord Mandeville connects this outrage with the race accident, Lord Gosford, the Lord Lieutenant of Armagh, more reasonably connected it with *the election of Colonel Verner* for the county, which took place exactly two days previous.

Though the Whigs had been put to confusion by the recent exercise of the Royal prerogative the Reform Party was still powerful in the Commons. In the face of this, Sir Robert Peel could not afford to break with the Orangemen* Since the splitting up of Lord Liverpool's Administration, which was the close of their long reign, all had been with the Tories make shift. They were too weak to stand alone, and they knew it. With one hand leaning upon Orangeism they beckoned with the other to a faction of the Liberal party. Though Sir Robert Peel might hint a fault when pressed upon Orange matters, he still was compelled to give "very gracious answers" from the Throne to their addresses, and seats on the Bench, in the Treasury and the Cabinet to their leaders and abettors. There was now, therefore, a substantial coalition

---

* The Grand Lodge of Ireland were not alone aware of these flagrant breaches of the law but actually returned the brethren over the country their thanks for illegally assembling, to the terror and danger of his Majesty's subjects The books of the Grand Lodge contain the following, under the date of November 12, 18 :—"And las ly, we beg to call the attention of the G and Lo ge, and through them return our heartfelt thanks and *congratulations* to our brethren through the various parts of Ireland, who in the late meetings of 3,000 in Dublin, 5,000 at Bandon, 3,000 at Cavan, and 7,000 at Hillsborough, by their strength of numb r, the rank, respectability, and orderly conduct of their attendance, the manly and eloquent expressions of every *Christian* and loyal senti ent vindic ted the nobly this character of our institution against 'he aspersions thrown on it s 'the paltry remnant of an expiring faction' And we ardently hope that our brethren in the other parts of t e Kingdom, who have not as yet come forward to do so (sic) and no forget the hint given to us in our Sovereign's last most precious declaration 'to speak out.'" To say that the Grand Lodge did no countenance these illegal demonstrations is, then, not founded upon fact. Not alone did it countenance them, but, as proved by the foregoing, it furthered them in all possible ways The days of William IV. were numbered as they knew. They needed to be on the alert. And so they were.

* *Edinburgh Review*, No. CXXVI., page 522.

between the Tories and the Orangemen. The latter were enraptured at what they considered the revival of the old ascendancy days; the former, satisfied so long as the exultation of the Orangemen could afford the colourable excuse of "vigour beyond the law" and both parties agreed to coalesce, without caring to enter very minutely upon either side into the precise terms of the coalition. More than one of the elections had, during the close of the preceding year, been largely influenced by the menace, intimidation, and even the active violence of armed Orangemen—instance the elections of Drogheda and Trim *

The Armagh election took place on the 15th January, 1835. In the evening an Orange party chaired Colonel Verner on his return, and as the electioneering contests of those days were, without exception, attended by a liberal distribution of cash, it is reasonable to conclude that "Brother Verner" was more than liberal in his treatment of his brethren. Inflamed with drink, they passed to their homes late at night, and on their way attacked the houses of two Catholics, in one of which, belonging to a publican named Hughes, it was alleged the persons who had committed the assault three months before on M'Whinney had previously been drinking. The houses were wrecked, the furniture broken, and what liquor could not be consumed was allowed to run off.

Election times were then not a season for active or earnest labour. With nothing particular to occupy their attention, the Orangemen of Killyman, alias the Killyman Wreckers, resolved on the 16th to burn down the village of Annahagh, situate between Armagh and Charlemont, and in this resolve they were ably seconded by their Armagh brethren. Preparations on a vast scale were made. Three church bells were kept ringing the entire of the day in Killyman, one of these being that in which the Orange firebrand, the Rev. Mortimer O'Sullivan, officiated. In Loughgall, and

also in Charlemont, the powder vendors' stock ran short, and the Orangemen were therefore compelled to fall back upon the supplies in the King's stores. In obtaining it, both powder and ball cartridge, they experienced little difficulty, and absolute proof of its distribution is found in the evidence of Sir F. Stovin, Inspector-General, of Captain Duff, Inspector of Police, and Charles Atkinson's (Chief Constable) report to the Government, all of which are faithfully recorded. Captain Duff says that one George Weir, the yeoman sergeant at Charlemont, gave gunpowder out of the King's stores to Captain Clarke's yeomen prior to the Annahigh outrage, making use at the time of the expression "I would be sorry to see Colonel Verner's boys lost" (8104). On the 17th January the Orangemen assembled at midday on the Hill of Kinuego to the number of several thousands. They were all armed, and so regular in their movement as to lead Sir Frederick Stovin to describe them as resembling "a regiment of soldiers on parade, previous to their falling in line." While the main body remained on guard upon the hill, a detachment was dispatched to the village to execute their fearful mission. All of the inhabitants who could fly fled. And wise were they in so doing. In half an hour the whole village was in flames,* and the detachment returned to the main body on the hill to join in the fiendish dance of death. A military force arrived from Charlemont under the command of Sir Fred. Stovin in time to see this Orange detachment joining the main body, and to see the conflagration they had made. One old man named Moore, who was bed-ridden, was carried out of his house and placed at his own door in the snow to contemplate the ruin of his humble homestead. Death soon released him from his misery. How many more victims were added to the black records of that day's doings it is impossible to say, for, upon the authority of Sir F. Stovin, we are assured that the Catholics were so intimidated that they were afraid to come forward to give evidence. In this affair several of the Armagh police were implicated and punished. They refused to assist Captain Duff and another constable in pointing out where several of the Orange party lived. "They did not know," they said, although the parties "wanted" resided not more than a mile and a half from their station.

An investigation was held by Lord Gosford on the

* Dr. Robert Mallen gave evidence before the committee of the House of Commons that 2 armed Orangemen collected from the neighbouring counties of Kildare, Westmeath, and Ca an marched in o T im on the day of the election. On stating that they were headed by the Rev. Mr. Preston, the witness was asked this significant question by a member of the committee—"Had he a crucifix in his hand?" to which this equally significant answer was given—"No, he had a pistol in his hand" (6101). This Orange mob was actually lodged in the old county jail and supplied with bedding by the Sheriff. On their way back they marched through Kells, where they murdered a Catholic named Henry in cold blood. And yet these were the men whom the Orange candidates, Mr. Wade and the Hon. R. Plunket (the latter of whom was a high dignitary in the Institution), could thank "for their services." As it was proved that not one of them was a voter, it is not difficult to imagine what was the nature of the services rendered.

* Lord Gosford, in his evidence, says that as far as the subsequent investigation afforded information all the houses burned, numbering sixteen, were those of Roman Catholics.

28th January, which resulted in the stern condemnation of the Orange party and the implication of more than one person of position. It was proved that a Mr. Hardy, J.P., aided and abetted in the transaction. He was dismissed the magistracy. It was also proved that a Mr. Obree, a landed proprietor and a Deputy Grand Master of Armagh, headed about 150 Orangemen on their march through the Loughgall district. From the 17th January, 1835, to the present date not one single Orangeman has been punished for his part in that outrage.

It was evident that the criminals were not unknown to the district Grand Lodge of Armagh. In the House of Commons attention was called to the transaction. Lord Mandeville, moved by a fit of desperation, defended the Orangemen in a manner, which in his calmer momen's, he must have regretted. He wildly and fiercely attacked Lord Gosford for the manner in which he had cors'i tuted the Bench (which was not constituted by him at all, as it was an *ex-parte* inquiry in which he was absolute). He stated that it was not proved the Orangemen were concerned in the outrage and, what was much more, that *he knew* they were not concerned. Dr. Lushington, an English member, here interfered, and said that the matter should be inquired into, that Lord Gosford's character should be cleared of the imputations, or the reverse. He called the attention of the House to the words of Lord Mandeville; if *he knew* that the Orangemen were not there he must be in a position to prove who were there; and he might, therefore, be in a position to ass'st the Crown. *Lord Mandeville was silent.*

Is it any wonder that O'Connell wrote almost coincident with this transaction in his letter to Lord Duncannon, " their (the Orangemen's) souls are so hardened in guilt, and so accustomed to an avowed desire of practical cruelty that they do not affect to conceal their wishes to render Ireland once more a desert, and to irrigate her plains with the blood of her inhabitants;" or, viewed in connection with the foregoing, in connection with the Rev. Mr. Preston, with his pistol where the crucifix ought to have been, with his band of Orange desperadoes following close upon his heels ready for anything from the pillaging of a public-house to the murdering of a Papist, is it any wonder that O'Connell was at this time denouncing the Orangemen in such terms as the following :—" the Orange faction are in point of intellect and understanding the most despicably degraded that even excited the contempt or scorn of mankind. Then, as to their

moral guides, what are they? They preach up wholesale proscript'en, massacre, and extermination. They call themselves Christians! They preach up doctrines almost too bad for the eternal enemy of mankind ta suggest to human depravity. Bayonets and blood—bayonets and blood—bayonets and blood form their *text* and their *commentary*. Their laymen vie with their parsons in ruthless audacity, and it becomes doubtful which of the two are the more ready to preach rapine, murder, and desolation. An infernal spirit of religious persecution reigns over the whole, and renders Irish Orangmen the most depraved, as well as the most despicable of the human race.*

It will be recollected that on the occasion of the great Dungannon meeting Lord Claude Hamilton was made an Orangeman. The initiation of this nobleman into the Orange system took place in a common public-house. Whether one of the unwritten laws or not, it has certainly been the usual practise with the Orange body to promote to the Bench, and, indeed, into all high places, as many of their brethren as possible. An Orangeman on the Bench becomes doubly armed in the cause, and those who are in a position to occupy such a place, and who refuse to avail themselves of it *for the benefit of the brethren* are as black sheep in the society. The honour of the magistracy may not have been coveted by Lord Claude Hamilton; but, since he was Lord Claude Hamilton and an Orangeman, he had no option but to assume it, if for nothing else, at least " for the benefit of his brethren." Accordingly, we find him a few weeks after his initiation (in this low public-house), applying to the Lord Lieutenant of the county for the commission of the peace. This application gave rise to the following interesting correspondence :—

" Dublin, Feb. 9, 1835.

" Sir,—As Lord Claude Hamilton has requested me to recommend him for the Commission of Peace, it becomes necessary for me to mention, for the information of his Excellency the Lord Lieutenant, the *difficulty* I feel in complying with his lordship's wishes.

" Since I had the honour of being named Lieutenant of the County of Tyrone, it has been my study to suppress party feeling; and I had the satisfaction to know that my exertions had been so far successful as to prevent the display of it upon all periodical occasions, except in the town of Dungannon.

" On the requisition of the *custos rotulorum*—

* See O'Connell's letter to the people of Ireland in 1824

Lord Abercorn, Lord Castle-Stuart, and nineteen magistrates, in addition to several clergymen and county gentlemen—I convened a meeting of the county on the 19th December, for the purpose of addressing the King on his Majesty's assertion of the Royal Prerogative; and it was upon this occasion, I may say, *in the face of the country, Lord Claude Hamilton was initiated into the Orange Society, was decorated with Orange emblems and was publicly chaired through the town by a large body of Orangemen who were assembled on that occasion.*

"This open and avowed adhesion to a particular party, and this disregard of what I consider the spirit which guides his Majesty's counsels, has been very painful to me, and places me in the embarrassing position which I attempt to describe.

" When I consider how my hopes of tranquillising the country have been counteracted, and knowing, as I do, that the conduct of Lord Claude Hamilton had caused increased excitement, *I cannot offer this recommendation to the Lord Chancellor without exposing myself to animadversion.*

" On the other hand, when I reflect that he has been elected member for the county, and that his rank and station fully qualify him for the appointment, I know not how to withhold my recommendation, more especially as I do not believe that the act of which I complain was in itself illegal—and, above all, when I am willing to hope, that, if appointed to the magistracy, his decisions will not be biassed by party prejudice.

" Under these conflicting considerations, I lay the case before his Majesty's Government, and if I find no objection is taken on their part, I shall submit his lordship's name to the Lord Chancellor. —I have, &c,

" Signed   "CALEDON."

———

" Castle, 9th Feb , 1835.

" MY LORD,—I have laid before the Lord-Lieutenant your lordship's letter of this day's date, and I am desired by his Excellency to say that the sentiments you express, and the judicious conduct you have always observed in the county of Tyrone, in suppressing all party feelings, meet with his Excellency's entire concurrence.

" The line you have pursued is in strict accordance with the principles by which his Majesty's councils are guided , and it is only *by a firm and impartial adherence to this system that the peace of the country can be preserved.*

" The Lord-Lieutenant regrets that any circumstance should have occurred by which your lordship

should have been thwarted in carrying into effect this most desirable system of discouraging popular excitement; but his Excellency, after an attentive consideration of the statement made by your lordship, concurs in opinion with you that in the exercise of your discretion it is expedient not to withhold the Commission of the Peace.—I have the honour," &c.

" Signed   " H. HARDINGE."

———

This is an instructive specimen of the " sayings and doings" of the then Government Here is the usual conforming flourish about " the firm and impartial adherence to the system by which alone the peace of the country can be preserved ," followed by the promotion to the Bench of an out-and-out Orange neophyte, who is reported by the lord-lieutenant of his county for disregarding " this spirit ('the firm impartial system') of his Majesty's Ministers ,"—the whole gracefully crowned by the old Eory doctrine of expediency. " It is expedient not to withhold the Commission of the Peace." Undoubtedly ! For Lord Claude was a county member, and his brother, Lord Abercorn, had influence and votes; and the Orange chiefs were staunch and recently reconciled allies True, the discountenancing of Orangeism and all other factions might be the salvation of Ireland ; but votes would be the salvation of power and place So expediency made " firm and impartial" justice kick the beam " *

From the Records of the Irish Grand Lodge, of which Lord Enniskillen was now Deputy Grand Master, we find the utmost activity exhibited at this period in augmenting the numbers of the brethren. Deputies had been sent through the various counties during the previous winter months They returned with the most glowing reports of progress, but with little or no cash. Their services the brethren freely rendered, the use of their good right arms in knocking down a Papist at all possible times, but further they were delicate in moving. We have it from the hon. secretary of the Institution that £200 a year was all that this body of men could be got to contribute to the general fund, though in 1834 that sum was doubled by the extraordinary liberality of the Ulster Orange landlords, whose agents were almost exclusively dignitaries of the institution.

While typhus fever was making fearful havoc amongst the half-fed, ill-clad peasantry, the Orange

* See *Edinburgh Review*, No. CXXVII., for January, 183 page 87.

Association was at this time busy in opposing such schemes as the Poor-law and National Education. Those whom the tide of emigration had left behind were a prey to the scourge of pestilence and famine. "It is in such a state of things," wrote O'Connell, "that the fell fiends of Orangeism exult." Conscious of their supremacy, they sought by every means in their power to initiate the horrors of '98, they wanted by a pretext "to cry havoc, and let slip the dogs of war" Their supremacy was a short lived one. The most was made of it by Sir Robert Peel and his coadjutors in the Government in the hope of strengthening the Tory party, and by the Orangemen in the desire to obtain a firm hold upon the Administration of Irish affairs Numerous Government appointments were made from the ranks of the directorate, and even Lord Reden was offered a place in his Majesty's household. In answer to an address from some of the Orangemen of Ireland the Ministers, in the name of the King, replied that " his Majesty's had been pleased to receive same in the most gracious manner" These words were penned by the Secretary of the Home Department, who in 1827 had admitted the illegality of the Orange Association. Attention was called to this in the House of Commons on the 6th March, when Mr. Sheil moved for papers showing the acknowledged illegality of the Orange Society. This gave rise to a protracted debate upon the Orange system. The members of the Government were charged with secretly countenacing the Orange Societies, a charge which they vigorously denied. In maintaining this charge Lord John Russell ably assisted, much to the confusion of the Tory Ministers. It was admitted in the course of the debate, by Colonel Percival on the part of the Orangemen, that there were tests in connection with the initiatory ceremony, upon which admission Mr. O'Connell followed and showed how by law the organisation was therefore illegal. A speech of a most violent character, recently made by the Recorder of Dublin in Exeter Hall, called for much comment. In the course of it the learned

gentleman had observed "that they would lay their bodies upon their bibles before they would allow the King to touch them, and that their rallying cry would be 'To your tents, O Israel.'" The Irish Orangemen had got their war paint on.

But the tide of reform which came steadily onwards, gathering strength as it came, gave fearful warning that the reign of intolerance was to be a short one. A great upheaval amongst the toiling millions of England sent terror to the hearts of The Orange processions on the July anniversary following (while the committees of inquiry into Orangeism were actually sitting) trebled the number of the preceding year, and the Orange outrages increased in the same ratio. those hereditary task-masters who lived upon the labour of others The new reformation had begun in earnest. The old Tory clique was fast losing its hold upon the cat-o'-nine-tails. In despair they threw themselves into the arms of a conspiring faction— a faction which never allied itself to any Government it did not bring to destruction. Boldly they together faced the storm; desperately they awaited the issue, arm in arm they both went down—pigheaded, obstinate, unrelenting, conditional loyalists to the last.

Under the guidance of Lord John Russell, in the House of Commons, a series of defeats, commencing on the 30th March, awaited Peel and his supporters, and the 8th of April witnessed the dissolution of the Tory Administration, after a brief Parliamentary existence of 6 weeks. With the Tory faction ascendant the Orangemen were content On the downfall of Sir Robert Peel a savage growl was heard from the Orangemen which showed they had been disturbed before half completing their work of plundering desolation. Erect they stood in defiance of law. The long expected hour was at hand. Conditional loyalty bared its arm for the struggle, and not a man amongst them but rejoiced that he had had so little trust in Providence as to keep his powder dry.

CHAPTER XXIX.—THE CUMBERLAND CONSPIRACY.

While on the one hand the Irish Orangemen were, through the aid of numerous gun clubs, arming themselves for some great coming struggle, but vaguely hinted at, they were upon the other exhausting their energies and exposing their plots by their cruel, exterminating practices. Inveterate malice ever defeats itself. Here was its triumph over treason. That triumph saved the Crown to the lady who at present wears it. These Irish were looked upon by their English brethren as a contemptible, silly-headed set, who, unfortunately, could not be done without. When the foolish, boastful old hen goes cackling through the farmyard it reveals the little conspiracy it has been hatching in defiance of law and order in the household; and the freshlaid egg adds to the dainties of the breakfast table: Irish Orangeism was the cackling, ranting, old hen in a way. Had its members been less boastful, more discreet, less intolerant, the plot would have been hatched with probable success; the nest of the traitors would not have been discovered, or discovered only when too late; under the dominion of an Orange autocrat, the worst days of absolutism would have set in; for a decade England might have been a Turkey, with Turkish despotism; then a France, with sewers of blood and tumbling bastiles; and possibly now an America, with American institutions, and American independence. Whether the present generation be indebted to the Irish Orangemen of those days is a vexed question upon which we need not enter. Certain it is they intended not to be our creditors. Much however we owe to the wisdom which regulates most human contrivances, makes the engineer the victim of his own petard, and tumbles the conspirator into the hole he has dug for his neighbours.

While all this was proceeding upon this side of the Channel, there were upon the other a set of cunning, shrewd, and hoary kingmakers, pegging noiselessly away at the very roots of the Constitution. Orangeism in England was quietly eating its way into the strongholds of the State. Into the aristocracy, into the democracy, into the army, into the navy; particularly into the Court and into the camps it crept; its promoters insidiously seeking to instil its treacherous principles into all those institutions which Englishmen were wont to regard as the bulwarks of the Constitution.

William the Fourth was King and *aged seventy-three*. His brother Ernest, Duke of Cumberland, was IMPERIAL GRAND MASTER of the Orange Institution of Great Britain, Ireland, and the Colonies. Ernest was the eldest surviving brother to the King, and, had the Salic law prevailed, the IMPERIAL Grand Master of the Orangemen would have been the legitimate successor of William. But it did not prevail. Failing *legitimate* male issue the young Princess Victoria, then in her "teens," was heir to the Crown of England. A female had not swayed the sceptre since the days of Anne, who came to the throne almost one hundred and fifty years ago. To restrict the English Crown to males only would after all seem but a harmless innovation—surely but a trifling injustice to the legitimate successor. That accomplished the Duke of Cumberland was

the next to reign. Much was at stake recollect. Autocracy was playing its last card against the masses—and that card was up its sleeve. Weak-minded kings had played them falsely before! If a kink had destroyed the Constitution of 1688, what might a Queen not do!! The thing was surely feasible enough!!! Earnest was an Orangeman, and little less than King. The step was a short one. Though a deep it was a narrow gulf which divided "constitutionalism" from treason; and, as they stood upon the brink, the Tempter suggesting the platitude that "kings were made for men"—the Rubicon was passed—and—upon the opposite side, stood the great exclusive loyalists of other days, glowering, in slouch hat and conspirator's cloak, even at that established Constitution which they so pretended to admire.

We have reached a period of our history which, of all others, demands careful, critical, and minute inquiry. The charge is the gravest that can be made. If sustained, it swells the list of rebels to the English Crown and the English Constitution; it brands as traitors two hundred thousand subjects of these realms; judged by a true standard of morality, it places in a much more criminal position than that which the rebels of '98 occupied, a great, unlettered multitude, who, wanting the courage to revolt, sought by traiterous and cowardly designs to secure a baser end—the complete overthrow of the Constitution; it puts beyond the pale of the law a band of conspirators who had no excuse under heaven save loss of monopoly for conspiring; it reveals to us one of the saddest spectacles in the history of a people, where an ignoble few surrounding the Throne led the deluded masses into treason, not to save a nation or assert the rights of a plundered people, but that a despot and a libertine—stealing the precious diadem from the shelf and putting it in his pocket—might mount the steps of that Throne and cheat the scaffold. To read the evidence aright we must endeavour, even at some cost, to form an idea of the times we are treating of. It is not without much difficulty that those of our generation, accustomed as we have been of late years to breathe the cool and temperate atmosphere of political life, can form an adequate idea of the diverse feelings which moved men's minds in the closing days of William's reign. The agitation of the last few years may in some slight sense assist in arriving at an estimate of the turmoil of the political life half a century ago, when all the cherished privileges of a favoured class of idlers defiantly shouted

"No" to the loud demands of a hard-working people just awakening to a sense of their power. "There were thousands," says a celebrated writer—aye and tens of thousands — "who knew little about themselves except that they were very hungry and very miserable." The great uprising of the "hewers of wood" who lived down in the coal mines and iron mines of England, and who came to the surface but to die, had sent the Reformers into the Commons These Reformers did, with what then seemed tardy and unwilling hands the task which had been pieced out to them. Latterly we have come to look upon the slow progress of reform as the necessary result of the inveterate odds that were against them. Between the Lords and the Commons there was a deadly struggle in which the existence of the one, the independence of the other appeared hanging in the balance. Behind the backs of the Commons were the Chartists pushing forward their representatives, urging them to lay rude, unmerciful hands upon all the weeds which precedent had allowed to creep into the Constitution, and monopoly had cherished these Upon the other side were the Lords, legislators from the cradle, who escaped the rule of the nursery, that they in turn might rule a nation, who only laid aside their feeding bottles and their coral bells that they might play with a sceptre and sway the destinies of millions That such a class would bow before the storm was out of question. That they would stop even at treason to secure their privileges was scarcely to be expected. Their fathers had played at chuck-farthing for thrones, knocked sceptres about the ears of lawful kings, and made light about the heads of some of them; while these their sons boasted that they were made of the same stern stuff.

It was a time, in fact, of revolutionary conspiracy; the conspirators, on one hand, being around the steps of the Throne; on the other, around the gates of the workhouse. The peers, opposed to all remedial legislation, expected to undo the Reform Bill. While the Kenyons, and the Rodens, and the Newcastles, and the Wynfords were expecting a speedy restoration of domination in the State, the people were asking themselves, "What will we do with the House of Lords?" and that question which in the present has a living, breathing existence was then breaking upon the people with a faint ray of its necessity and possibility.

It was a time, too, when the moralities were laughed at 'as fit only for old women and the common people. The loose state of society which pervaded the Courts of the Georges, and which had never been looser than during the rule of the last of them, had little improved in the brief reign of William. The young voluptuaries who had accompanied the first gentleman of Europe in his midnight rambles, who reduced the Court to a huge brothel in which all was sin, dazzling gaiety and never-ending revel, were the old roues of to-day, the bad, unrepenting, effete old men, limping about the Court, leering at the ladies—who leered at them in turn—making coarse, brutal, and disgusting jokes, to be laughed at in a measure equal to the dignity and consequence of the old fools who made them. Wicked to the last, they were bent still upon pleasure, and upon that monopoly which ensured it.

Now we have it upon the most reliable authority that the biggest blackguard, the greatest despot, and the coarsest and most brutal of all that jolly senile throng, was no other than H R H. Ernest, Duke of Cumberland, K G., Field Marshal of England, and Imperial Grand Master of the Orangemen of Great Britain, Ireland, and the Colonies.

The Duke of Wellington, whom Ernest hated, once asked George IV. why his brother (the Duke of Cumberland) was so unpopular, and the King replied, "Because there never was a father well with his son, a husband with his wife, a lover with his mistress, or a friend with his friend that he did not try to make mischief between."

Hear Lord Brougham what he says of him, as well as of his character. In his biography, speaking of the schemes which Ernest was hatching against Lord Grey's Government, he remarks—"I had an opportunity of stating, through Sir H. Taylor (private secretary to the King), many of the alarming symptoms.' I refer in particular to one man, whom recent circumstances had made particularly conspicuous—I mean the Duke of Cumberland, against whom personally I had not a word to say. I respect the courage with which he had faced the odious charges made against his reputation, the effect of which courage had been to clear him; I also held him to be a fair, open enemy, and not one who pretended to more liberality than he possessed. He was content to appear what he really was—a rank, violent ultra Tory of the strongest Orange order, and whose principles and propensities were purely arbitrary. He had for many years lived abroad, and there formed his habits of thinking and hi political opinions. He kept himself for some time after his return in the back-ground, knowing how unpopular he was all over England, with the single exception of the universities of Oxford and Dublin, and was putting himself more and more in the popular eye."

"His manners," says Mr. Justin M'Carthy, in his recent great work, "A History of Our Own Times," "were rude, overbearing, and sometimes even brutal. He had personal habits which seemed rather fitted for the days of Tiberius or for the Court of Peter the Great than for the time and sphere to which he belonged. Rumour not unnaturally exaggerated his defects, and in the mouths of many his name was the symbol of the darkest and fiercest passions and even crimes. Some of the popular reports with regard to him had their foundation only in the common detestation of his character and dread of his influence. But it was certain that he was profligate, selfish, overbearing, and quarrelsome. A man with these qualities would usually be described in fiction as, at all events, bluntly honest and outspoken; but the Duke of Cumberland was deceitful and treacherous. He was outspoken in his abuse of those with whom he quarrelled, and in his style of anecdote and jocular conversation; but in no other sense."

With such a voluptuous tyrant reigning supreme over Court circles around the Throne, as the eldest brother of the King, we can readily imagine that the atmosphere was not the purest, especially with a people having all opportunities to sin inclining them to take the key note from the greatest sinner amongst them. From this Court the Duchess of Kent rigidly excluded her fatherless daughter, and that exclusion accounts for the purity which has hung, like an incense, round the Throne during the long and happy reign of Victoria. But go back nigh half a century of our lifetime and judge what must have been the result under such circumstances, and in such a Court, of that seclusion of the heir to the Throne, then a minor. A complete isolation of interest, a want of that first link which connects the Throne with its legitimate heir, the esteem and personal respect of its immediate supporters. That a woman, that a girl, that a child in fact, should succeed to that throne was repugnant to all their cherished notions. Such a girl, unknown and unseen by them, and pure and simple-minded as though she came from behind a convent wall, should dispel the heavy mist of immorality in which those

people loved to breathe, completely overturn the established order of things, and prevent men cradled in crime going down in public iniquity to the grave. It was not in harmony with their wishes. In addition, the suspicion received favour with many reputed possessors of common sense, that the Princess would turn Papist on her accession to the throne, and so general did this belief take hold of the Tory party that the *Times* thought it necessary soon after her accession to warn her that for her Majesty to turn Papist, to marry a Papist, "or in any manner follow the footsteps of the Coburg family," would involve an "immediate forfeiture of the British Crown."

In a Court with "a full flavour such as a decent tap room would hardly exhibit, in a time like the present," it was not simply a question of rule that was involved in the accession of Victoria. It was a question of the curbing of passions which had already grown part of those who indulged them. William was now an old man. Some said he had lost his senses, a feat at no time very difficult. Once it was suggested that he was coming round on the Reform question, it was resolved by those interested in the plot that he *had* lost his senses, and a Regency was proposed, who the Regent was to be being a matter about which there could be no dispute. A similar scheme was on foot during the last days of George IV. Writing to Earl Grey, Lord Brougham uses these significant words:—"You might observe a mysterious statement in the *Times* as if from authority, about the King having come round on the Catholic question. Nobody seems to understand how far this is correct; but certainly, if he is to be brought round, it ought to be tried before the Duke of Cumberland comes, who is fuller of spirits and all mischief than ever; and says he will come if he lives in a coffee-house. In fact, *he wants to start for the Regency under the Orange colours*—making the Brunswick Clubs his handle for the purpose of setting himself up with the country."

The Duke of Cumberland had, in fact, assumed the lead of the ultra-Tory party, ostensibly headed by the Duke of Wellington. "With Kenyon and Falmouth for his supporters," writes Lord Brougham, "and Wynford to back him, he claimed as distinct a place as the Duke of Wellington on the opposite side of the House of Peers. He no longer confined himself to asking questions upon the order of business, &c., &c. It became therefore manifest *that his Royal Highness now thought himself destined to play a great part, and that he was flying at high game."* But that it is proved by documentary evidence, what was that "great part" he had to play—what the, "high game" he was flying at, the story would seem an incredible one

On the 15th February, 1827, the appointment of a Grand Master in the room of the deceased Duke of York, was committed to the care of Lord Kenyon To overcome his reluctance must have been a task of some trouble, for it is not until the meeting of the 17th June, 1828, that we find the Grand Lodge, on the motion of Lord Kenyon, "hailing with heartfelt satisfaction and gratitude the distinguished honour," &c , conferred on the Institution by the acceptance by H R H. the Duke of Cumberland of the office of Grand Master H.R H took the chair upon that day Having once put his hands to the plough he resolved not to turn back. From that day until the dissolution of the society I fail to find a single meeting over which he did not preside

High up in the Grand Lodge of the Orange Society of England there was at this time a certain Lieutenant-Colonel Fairman, who was destined to play a most prominent part in the conspiracy revealed in 1835. He confessed himself before the Committee of the House of Commons "to have been so much *behind the curtains* that he might almost say he was a legislator although never in Parliament" Though Quixotic to the last degree, and professing to have done the State some service, he paid sufficient attention to his own interests to be moved to regret "that he had never been rewarded for it" If not absolutely a very wise man he was possibly of more use than if he had been wiser That he was doing a little trade upon his own account was plain. One of the chief points upon which, in his numerous Orange circulars, he recommended the institution to Protestants is the facility it afforded for securing place and patronage to those within it. He was the obedient tool of the Duke of Cumberland and Kenyon, and was never happy except when he was in a private conference at the private residence of either of them. He saw with the eyes, and heard with the ears of his masters To a tyrant such a man would be extremely serviceable; to a usurper he would be absolutely indispensable. When rumours were spread abroad during the last illness of George IV. as to the necessity of a Regent, Cumberland, Kenyon, and Fairman were at the bottom of it When, again, it was whispered loudly that William IV was insane, it was the invention of the trio. They

kept throughout a steady, even a jealous eye upon the Crown So jealously did they guard it, that when the Duke of Wellington was carrying the Catholic B ll through the House of Commons, a general fear was entertained by the brethren that the Duke of Wellington meant himself to seize the Crown Harriet Martineau, in her "History of the Peace," says—"Men laughed when they first heard this, and men will always laugh whenever they hear it, but that such was the apprehension of the Orange leaders is shown by correspondence in Colonel Fairman's handwriting, which was brought before the Parliamentary Committee of 1835 " The following is an extract of a letter evidently designed for the Grand Master Ernest, and written during the last illness of George IV :—"Should an indisposition which has agitated the whole country for a fortnight take a favourable turn—should the Almighty, in His mercy, give ear unto the supplications that to His heavenly throne are offered up daily to prolong the existence of one deservedly dear to the nation at large, a divulgement I have expressed a willingness to furnish, would be deprived of no small portion of its value Even in this case, an event for the consummation of which, in common with all good subjects, I obtest the Deity, it might be as well your Royal Highness should be put in possession of the rash designs in embryo, the better to design measures for its frustration; at any rate, you would not then be taken by surprise, as the nation was last year, but might have an opportunity of rallying your forces and of organising your plans for the defeat of such machinations as *might be hostile to your paramount claims* Hence, should the experiment be made, and its expediency be established, your Royal Highness would be in a situation to contend for the exercise *in your own person of that office* at which the wild ambition of another may prompt him to aspire." Miss Martineau says who this 'other' of wild ambition is plainly expressed in two subsequent letters. "It was Wellington!" she exclaims, "the devoted Wellington, who perilled his reputation for consistency, and what his party called political honour, over and over again rather than desert his Sovereign. Wellington lived to have this said of him by a man claiming to be a colonel in his own 'perfect machine' of an army!"

In a letter to Sir James Cockburn, giving an imposing account of the institution, Colonel Fairman speaks of the "grovelling worms who dare to vie with the omnipotence of Heaven," and of one of

these "grovelling worms" he writes as follows.—
"One, moreover, of whom it might ill become me to
speak but in terms of reverence, has nevertheless
been weak enough to ape the coarseness of a
Cromwell, thus recalling the recollection to what
would have been far better left in oblivion. His
seizure of the diadem, and his planting it upon his
brow was a precocious sort of self-inauguration."
That the gallant colonel was doing all in his power
to win his colours and bring the question of
Regency within the reach of " practical politics" is
made distinctly evident by the following letter,
dated April 6th, 1830, during the illness of George
IV, and addressed to the editor of the *Morning
Herald*.—

" DEAR SIR,—From those who may be supposed
to have opportunities of knowing 'the secrets of
the Castle,' the King is stated to be by no manner
in so alarming a state as many folks would have
it imagined. His Majesty is likewise said to dictate the bulletins of his own state of health
Some whisperings have also gone abroad that, in
the event of the demise of the Crown, a Regency
would probably be established for reasons which
occasioned the removal of the next in succession
from the office of High Admiral (William Duke of
Clarence had been removed from that office). That
a maritime Government might not prove consonant
to the views of a military chieftain of the most un-
bounded ambition may admit of easy belief, and as
the second heir presumptive is not alone a female
but a minor, in addition to the argument which
might be applied to the present, that in the ordinary course of nature it was not to be expected
that his reign could be of long duration, in these
disjointed times it is by no means unlikely a
vicarious form of Government may be attempted.
The effort would be a bold one, but after
the measures we have seen, what new violations
should surprise us ? Besides, the popular plea of
economy and expedience might be urged as the
pretext, while aggrandisements and usurpation
might be the latent sole motive. It would only be
necessary to make a plausible case which, from the
facts on record, there could be no difficulty in doing
to the satisfaction of a pliable and obsequious set
of Ministers, as also to the success of such an ex-.
periment.—Most truly yours,

" W. B. F."

From these extracts it will be seen that the
lieutenant-colonel was moved by some other motive
than the welfare of the State; nor is it unreason-
bale to assume that within the closed doors of the
lodge rooms the suspicions regarding the motive of
the Duke of Wellington seizing the Crown were
used by him as a powerful lever for bringing
the aims and intentions of the Duke of Cumberland forward without shocking the feelings of the
brethren.

The new Pretender and his right-hand man, Lord
Kenyon, now began to see that Fairman was not
in his proper place; that his selfish enthusiasm
and his obsequiousness could be better utilised;
that he would be extremely useful and more
to be depended upon as Deputy Grand
Secretary of the Orange Institution. Now,
in 1828, and for a considerable period prior to it,
there was a Mr. Chetwoode Eustace Chetwoode,
an Irishman, acting as Deputy Grand Secretary of
the Orange Institution. He seems to have been
an honest, simple-minded man in his way—certainly, one not fit for treasons, stratagems, and
broils Under his supervision as secretar , the
Institution lived out a few years of his exis ence,
when indications began to appear of some
smothered, half-expressed dissatisfaction, existing
amongst the higher members of the Grand Lodge,
with regard to him. He was not the man for the
place, they said, an excuse the first and
most tangible that offers itself to those who
wish to rid themselves of an objectionable official.
Then it was found that he did not keep his mind
to himself. Next the fortunate discovery was made
that the books and accounts were not kept in
proper order, and lastly he was dubbed a " Papist,"
called upon by the Grand Lodge with all seriousness to prove he was not a Papist, and—dismissed.

The Duke of Cumberland was Field Marshal of
England. On the 19th of April, 1832, Lieutenant-
Colonel Fairman, his intimate friend and confidant,
was, after several private interviews at Kew with
Ernest upon the nomination of the Duke, seconded
by Lord Kenyon, elected to the office of Deputy
Grand Secretary of the Orange Institution
of Great Britain, &c. The grand object seems
to have been to win over the army to
their side, and immediately afterwards we find
great efforts put forth to spread the institution in that direction, the General Orders of 1822
and 1829 to the contrary notwithstanding. A new
system was now devised, new pass words invented,
the signs changed, and every means of securing
secrecy resorted to. Three months had only elapsed
after the significant appointment of Col. Fairman,
when we find the Imperial Grand Master issuing
an itinerant warrant or commission—"given under

our Great Seal, at St. James, this 13th day of August, 1832. Earnest, G.M."—to his "trusty well-beloved, and right worshipful brother, Lieut. Colonel Fairman," to make a tour of inspection through the kingdom, and visit Ireland, in order to bring the two systems into unison. This document, given at St. James under the Great Seal of Orangeism, has all the formality and significance of an imperial mandate, and between it and a commission under the Great Seal of the Empire the most striking parallel exists. While Col. Fairman was sent on the home journey, a Mr. Nucella received a like commission for Italy and our garrison in the Mediterranean, while the Grand Mastership of Canada with extensive local powers was conferred upon a Mr. Gowan. The machinery was now set agoing, the liveliest anticipations being entertained that it would produce a full-blown Orange king.

The first precaution that would naturally suggest itself to men engaged in such a desperate struggle would be to provide against discovery through the medium of the dismissed secretary. This is what actually did suggest itself. Accordingly, we find, from the evidence before the Parliamentary committee, that a short time before Mr. Chetwoode was formally dismissed a tyler and messenger of the Grand Lodge named Condell, another man named Osborne, who occasionally acted as tyler to the Grand Lodge, and an Orangeman of the name of George Payne, broke into Mr. Chetwoode's chambers in Lyons' Inn during his absence, and abstracted therefrom all the papers they could lay their hands upon. It is not surprising that many private papers of the former secretary had to be sacrificed, even at the risk of augmenting the danger. The best proof that the Grand Lodge were the instigators of this robbery is to be found in the fact that they produced some of those stolen books before the Parliamentary Committee. Letter-books and a note-book in which the secretary was in the habit of entering all transactions from day to day were missing. On handing over the stolen documents to the Grand Lodge, the robbers were actually paid for their services by Colonel Fairman.

Immediately on Colonel Fairman becoming Deputy Grand Secretary, the ROYAL ARMS were adopted for use on all documents, and from this period we find, on the assurance of Lieutenant-Col. Fairman himself, that "the Grand Committee sat like a Cabinet, or Privy Council," at its periodical meetings, and that its proceedings were conducted with regal pomp and circumstance. His Royal Highness never entered or left the lodge without the mace been borne in state before him; the members and grand dignitaries were bound to attend in their orders and regalia; the rev. functionaries of the Institution in canonicals; his Royal Highness sat behind the mace, whilst the doors were guarded by Condell, the tyler, and Osborne, his assistant; the reports were read aloud, put seriatim from the chair, and approved or rejected, the Imperial Grand Master—still keeping up a striking parallel with Royalty—having an absolute veto upon every proposition.

The three emissaries were now about setting out on their traitorous mission.*

Before starting in June, 1832, upon his tour of inspection, Colonel Fairman had frequent, long, and confidential interviews with the Duke of Cumberland. Lord Londonderry now appears upon the scene. Just before starting upon his mission, Colonel Fairman learned from the lips of the Duke of Cumberland that he (his Royal Highness) had written to Lord Londonderry upon Orange matters. Colonel Fairman, therefore, wrote "with more explicitness than he should have otherwise done" to Londonderry relative to the establishing of orange lodges amongst the pitmen on the estate of the Marquis. After much mouthing about "a Popish Cabinet, and a democratical ministry having given birth to a monster they could not control," he suggests, "by a rapid augmentation of our physical force, we might be able to assume a boldness of attitude which should command the respect of our Jacobinical rulers. . . . . If we prove not too strong for such a Government as the present is, such a Government will prove too strong for us; some arbitrary steps would be taken in this case for the suspension of our meetings. Hence the necessity for our laying aside that non-resistance, and passive obedience which has hitherto been religiously enforced to our own discomfiture." In this letter Colonel Fairman further relates how he was reproached by Lord Longford the day before for "the tameness of the English Orangemen, while the Irish were resolved to resist all attempts on the

* If we take the character of one of those three emissaries from the Irish brethren it would appear that he was one of the most degraded and abandoned characters to be found. Mr. Ryves Baker, the Deputy Grand Secretary of the Irish Orange Lodge, declared him (Ogle Robert Gowan, Esq.), to be so, after he had, with much eulogy and flourish from the Duke of Cumberland, been installed into the G. and Mastership of Canada. The Irish Grand Lodge actually forwarded documentary evidence in support of this opinion, and remonstrated with their English brethren against the appointment, on the ground of Gowan's moral unfitness and of their own jurisdiction over the Canadians. The English Lodge waived their jurisdiction but retained their man.

part of the Government to put them down." This anxiety for laying aside that foolish non-resistance policy, so out of harmony with the gallant colonel's character, this absolute contempt for passive obedience is shown in several letters written to different parties about the same period, and within a few days of his starting upon his tour of "inspection." They will help the reader to form in anticipation an idea of what were the principles he was about to inculcate In a short letter, written on the 30th July, 1832, to Lord Londonderry to supplement his communication of the previous day, he says—"I omitted to mention *than we have the military with us* as far as they are at liberty to avow their principles and sentiments, but since the lamented death of the Duke of York every impediment has been thrown in the way of their holding a lodge" To these communications Lord Londonderry replies "that the moment had not yet arrived," but promising that he would lose no opportunity of embracing any opening that might arise. Lord Londonderry when questioned about this correspondence in the House of Commons admitted it, and stated that he complied with the wishes of the Duke of Cumberland which were made known to him by Lord Kenyon. But the colonels outspoken letter to the Duke of Gordon, in reply to an invitation to pay a visit at Gordon Castle during his tour of inspection, is possibly the most significant of any we owe to his pen. Not only do we find here the doctrines of obedience and non-resistance condemned as unworthy of an Orangeman, with an additional assurance than they would shortly "be assuming an attitude of boldness such as would strike the foe with awe;" but we have the following —"Our brethren in that country (Ireland) are determined to resist all attempts that shall be made by a Whig Ministry to interrupt their meetings or to suspend their processions; but they complain of our not affording them that support which would give vigour to their proceedings, and which would be an *eternal source of terror to the enemy.* Their charges are, I must admit, too well founded , however, the time is fast approaching *when matters will be brought to an issue* A conciliatory course will be laid aside, and an opposite one will be resorted to. But to return to our own society. What we want chiefly now is men of influence *to take the lead in the country.*"

. It was after writing the letters from which the above are extracts that Colonel Fairman was accorded, previous to setting out upon his mission, a final private interview at Kew with the Imperial Grand Master. For three hours according to the admission contained in his own letters, he was closeted with his chief, and after receiving specific instructions he set forth upon his journey through the Three Kingdoms for the great manufacturing house of Cumberland, Kenyon & Co. The letter book of the Grand Lodge was, upon the admission of the writer in the *Edinburgh Review,* "most reluctantly and partially submitted to the inspection of the Committee by Colonel Fairman"* But partial as was that inspection, we are afforded sufficient insight for our purposes For this, however, we are in no way indebted to the generosity of the Grand Committee. The Colonel visited Dublin, and afterwards most of the great English manufacturing towns, and at various stages of his route he reported progress, sometimes by private letter to Lord Kenyon, sometimes by letter to the Grand Lodge. It was while in Manchester that he is alleged to have made in Grand Lodge the treasonable communication respecting the succession to the throne, and the intention of securing it to their Imperial Grand Master, which was subsequently revealed by Mr. Haywood an Orangeman of Sheffield Haywood alleged that Colonel Fairman distinctly intimated to the brethren, of which he was one, that the great crisis for which they were preparing was the accession of Prince Ernest, Duke of Cumberland, Imperial Grand Master of the Orangemen of Great Britain, Ireland, and the Colonies, to the Throne of England. To throw in a sprinkling of heroism and loyalty into their proceedings, and to give the zest of contention to their movements, he would seem to have put the matter before them somewhat in this light—William "insane"; Victoria, "a woman and a minor;" Wellington, "ambitious, and a second Cromwell," Ernest, the King's brother, strong minded, and an Orangeman ; the tide of revolution "a menace to our altar, our throne, and our households," leaving no alternative between vigorous Imperialism and Republicanism ; a *king* (not a queen), therefore, absolutely necessary , and their interests and those of the country pressing to no other conclusion than that ERNEST SHOULD BE KING.

It was after this partial tour, that upon the 24th October of the same year Lord Wynford wrote to Colonel Fairman, expressing himself in the most eulogistic terms on the character and estimable qualities of his Royal Highness Prince Ernest

* See *Edinburgh Review* for January, 1836—page 504

Duke of Cumberland, and explicitly stating that
"The Tories have not been sufficiently grateful to
him," winding up with the following, every word
of which requires to be calmly and deliberately
considered —"As you are so obliging in your last
letter as to ask my advice as to whether you
should pursue the course you have so ably begun, I
can only say that you must exercise your discretion
as to the company in which you make
such appeals as that which I have been reported. When you meet only *sure* Tories
you may well make them feel *what they
owe* to one who is the constant, unflinching champion of the party, and who by his steady course
has brought on himself all the obloquy that a base,
malignant faction can invent." Now, what were
those appeals that shou'd be made only to *sure
Tories*, and the disclosure of which to those who
were not "sure Tories" seemed to be attended by
disastrous consequences? What was it the "sure
Tories" owed to "the unflinching champion" of
their party? Was it something they dare not reveal to the outer world? Was it something beyond the ordinary giving of a political party? If
it was, what was it? Lastly, who was this "constant and unflinching champion" to whom so much
was due, but whose claims to something undefined
were to be mentioned in a whisper? These are
questions which each reader may determine for
himself. Colonel Fairman quoted Lord Wynford
and Lord Kenyon to each other as consulted
by him "*on the propriety of my continuing*
to introduce the Duke's name in the prominent
shape I had previously done"* He notifies the
fact to Kenyon that he had written to Wynford as
to "the advisability of bringing the Duke's name
into prominence in the lodges" and the expression
of Lord Wynford above quoted he interprets into
an intimation of its being "a policy with which he
(Wynford) seemed to agree" The Colonel concludes his letter, dated from Doncaster, by showing
the wonderful popularity he had won for the
Duke, intimating "if he would make a tour into
these parts, *for which I have prepared the way*, he
would be idolized" Following this is a letter
written to the same person (Lord Kenyon) from the
same place and upon the same date—so rapidly
were events moving—in which he said that a subscription of £50 each was talked of to get up an
entertainment for their illustrious Grand Master,
"if they might be permitted to look forward to so
distinguished an honour as a visit from him" He

* See appendix to English Report, No. 13—page 112.

enters into a narrative of the maudlin loyalty of
the old women of both sexes with whom he came
in contact; of how "the *Blue* belles of Yorkshire,"
and the gentlemen as well, actually shed tears at
the mention of the Duke's name—so enamoured
were they of the reputation of that hoary reprobate
whose conversation was "unfit for the lowest pot-
house of our time" In recounting this affecting
scene the worthy and gallant colonel himself
seems, by his own account, to have been unnerved—
so powerful is the excitement of success—for he
says—"By excess of toil my own nerves are so un-
strung, too, that in making to your lordship this
report I am playing the woman." It was truly an
affecting scene; the confidential spy of a pack of
grey-haired conspirators mingling his tears with
the "noble dames of Yorkshire" over the success of
a plot which was to place a bald-headed libertine
upon the throne Time was when noble dames of
high degree, young, beautiful, and fair, risked their
tender necks for a smile from the handsome outlawed Stuart ; when love, romance, and chivalry
lent a charm to plots which meant to secure to a
fool his rightful possessions. But, behold, now all
is changed Into it no single element entered but
monopoly and unvarnished treason. Harriet
Martineau, in treating of this document, seems at
first to think it a good joke, and describes it as a
letter "too absurd to have been penned by the confidential agent of princes and lords on the gravest
political matters," but, breaking into that high
strain of serious criticism which was her wont, she
continues—"It was a grave affair to the interests
of some of the brethren, if we may judge by a
letter of Lord Kenyon's to Colonel Fairman in
January, 1833 'The good cause,' writes his lordship, 'is worth all the help that man can give it,
but our only trust must be in God In the last
two years and a half I have spent, I suspect, in its
behalf nearer £20,000 than £10,000.'"

The reports of Colonel Fairman from Scotland
show in the same sense a desire for "lighting up a
flame" in that part of the country, for the raising
"of our standard," and an anxiety for bringing forward the name of the Grand Master into all prominence with the brethren "On my landing at
Leith, I called my troops together," is his phrase
and having imbued his troops with the seditious
sentiments of the Grand Lodge, he sought for
fields green and pastures new in which treason
might take root and fructify. The Colonel's
visit to these parts led to the opening up of a correspondence with a Mr. Laurence W. Craigie, which

for violent and libellous abuse of the Constitution as then established is unequalled. But Craigie was profuse in his denunciations of more than the Constitution, for it appears that he saw in his brethren much that was condemnatory. For instance—" I detest the idea of publishing the accounts of the Institution to any but the Grand Committee, for *the base villains* who compose some of the town lodges are apt to become presumptuous." Again —"The scoundrels in Donaldson's lodge are *a set of thievish gamblers*, who spend all their money in drink." The secret of this gentleman's loyalty to the cause was contained in a postscript to one of his letters:—" May I remind you of the little matter, which I would request you would attend to in your conference with the Duke of Cumberland"—which "little matter" meant that he wanted employment of some sort in London.

But Mr. L. W. Craigie was not the only person to abuse the brethren. The description of Colonel Fairman himself shows them to be anything but a happy family. Referring to some of those who possibly opposed his seditious purposes, he speaks of "their fell machinations of the most specious villainy;" of his being made "a victim for the appeasement of a vile junto;" of his refusing to be again "immolated upon the shrine of iniquity;" of the "clamours of men indecently murmuring at calls on them for less than a halfpenny a week," while the high dignitaries, with their splendid donations, stood by in silence; on their being allowed fees of initiation, which "were spent in a single night's debauch;" of their "embezzling the funds of their warrants;" and of all the moral depravities of which "perfidious colleagues" could be guilty. These letters probably afford better evidence than any that the Purple party had resolved themselves into a clique.

One of the results of this tour was the determination to issue an address to the Carleton Club. The headings of this address were furnished by the Hon. R. E. Plunkett, which document contains the following:—" The Orange Institution is the only society peculiar to Great Britain and Ireland which already includes individuals of every rank and grade *from the nearest to the Throne* to the poorest peasant.* In this phrase we find the rights of the young Princess Victoria summarily laid aside to make room for the Duke of Cumberland's accession. It is an unblushing acknowledgment of all charges made against them under this head, and a happy illustration of how

* Ibid. No. 14—page 114.

continued concentration of the mind upon a desirable object leads to the ignoring of prior claims and brings that object within the reach of possible accomplishment. The Duke of Cumberland was not the "nearest" to the Throne. The Regency Bill of three years previous had settled the right of succession upon Victoria, with the position of Regent upon the Duchess of Kent, her mother, in the event of the demise of the Crown. "People now began to understand," says Miss Martineau, " the strange proceedings and the violence of the debate about a regency after the accession of William IV. . . . People began to remember how from one occasion to another rumours of the insanity of King William came floating abroad from the recesses of Toryism, till exploded by contact with free air and light." This phrase, signifying that the Duke of Cumberland was *nearest* to the Throne, seems to have been considered too explicit by the Grand Lodge, for we find in the document, as issued to the Carleton Club, the expression is toned down to " the first male subject in the realm," a phrase of almost equal significance when the then question of succession is regarded. In their "appeal to the Conservatives of England," in which we may also see Colonel Fairman's hand, we find such a passage as the following:—" The Church, the dear sister of the State, is exhibited to public view in the mangling embraces of a lustful ravisher," and with the object of inciting greater enmity a postscript is added to this address to the effect that this should be posted "upon all church doors" and in other public places. Little wonder that Harriet Martineau wrote of this infamous production "in one of these circulars the position of the Church in the eyes of Orangemen of the period is described in language too indecent for quotation!"

Recollect that Fairman was not at this time acting upon his individual responsibility. Proof of this is everywhere at hand. "We find the Orange peers continuing their confidence to Colonel Fairman up to the time of the demand of a Parliamentary committee. Lord Roden writes to him about 'our cause.' Lord Kenyon confides to him his views of the comparative influence of some Scotch peers, and observes, 'It is a great pity, too, that the amiable Duke of Buccleuch does not see the immense importance of sanctioning such a cause as the Orange cause.' Lord Thomond writes to him about his subscription in England and Ireland. Lord Wynford reports to him a private consultation between the Duke of Cumberland, Lord Kenyon, and himself about the purchase of a newspaper, and declares it highly probable that "something would soon be done about it by the Carlton Club."

"The gleanings," says the author already referred to, "which might be made from the evidence of the report would afford material for a curious inquiry into the theory of Christianity held by men whose boast by the mouth of Lord Kenyon was, ' Ours is the cause of all friends of Christianity'; and whose most Christian hope was of 'the arrival of a day of reckoning' when certain ' hell-hounds' would be called on to pay the full penalty of their cold-blooded tergiversations."

Possibly a document as significant as any for indicating the future the Orangemen hoped to have in store for their Imperial Grand Master is the address of the brethern of London to his Royal Highness, which we find inserted in the minutes of a meeting held at the residence of Lord Kenyon. In this document the brethren express a hope that his Royal Highness's valuable life might be prolonged *to watch over the destinies of the nation.*

But if we give the Orangemen the right claimed by every British subject of not being convicted from evidence out of their own mouth, we have still manifold proofs that treason to the Monarchy was in the wind. We have besides Lord Brougham's assurance that his Royal Highness was "flying at high game" under Orange colours, and that he "conceived himself destined to play a great part" in the Empire, a further evidence of the greatness of his aspirations.

Writing to the Chancellor in October, 1833, Earl Grey says—" Wellesley writes me that the Duke of Cumberland as Grand Master is giving great activity to the Orange lodges, and if his proceedings are not checked that the Coercion Bill will be rendered nugatory in that part of the country. I have desired him to get an accurate account of *all* that is being done *to be laid before the Cabinet* when it reassembles officially."—Vol. 3, page 309 of Brougham's life.

Brougham to Grey—"The enemy are already at work, I doubt not. There are, I know, flying reports about town in all directions of the King insisting on Lyndhurst ——, and who knows what the Duke of Cumberland may put into certain people's heads."—*Ibid.,* vol. 3, page 315. The blank is a significant one.

At the meeting at which Colonel Fairman was installed as Deputy Grand Secretary the Duke of Buckingham acted as secretary. From the "Courts and Cabinets of William IV. and Victoria," a partial compilation of events of this period by the Duke of Buckingham and Chandos, we find Prince Ernest, Duke of Cumberland, writing to the Duke of Buckingham—" I shall ever be found at my post, but think it better for you, being unwell, to nerve yourself for another occasion, as I know *you* are STAUNCH, and I can depend upon your support." The italics and capitals are the Duke of Cumberland's. What need had Ernest for the support of a brother duke? In what was he to be STAUNCH to him? Wellington was chief of the Tories, and not Ernest. Was it "that other thing" which seemed not to have a name outside the lodge-room, but to be perfectly well understood between the conspirators? Between the Dukes of Cumberland and Wellington there existed a deadly hostility, for Cumberland was the most jealous and narrow-minded of men. The existence of this feud may be inferred from the character of the correspondence published in Wellington's life. To appreciate a high-minded, chivalrous, and patriotic purpose was beyond the scope of the Orange King, and, seeing everyone in a high position actuated by motives similar to his own, he regarded their progress in popular favour as an encroachment upon his own claims.

"Mr. Hume had got hold of these letters of 1830-31, and the members who cheered so loudly on the perplexity of the ministers were aware how the loyal Orangemen had listened to suggestions for making the Duke of Cumberland King to prevent the usurpation of the Duke of Wellington—expecting that William IV. would be superseded on an allegation of insanity, and the Princess Victoria, because she was a woman, and probably still a minor. . . . Such was the Institution—the great conspiracy against the National will and national interests—the conspiracy against the rights of all, from the King on the Throne to the humblest voter, or soldier, or sailor, or Dissenter, or Catholic (for all were excluded from the Association save Protestants), which was discovered by the energy and diligence of Mr. Hume in 1835."—Chambers' Pictorial History of England, vol. 8, page 486 8.

"Not many of George III.'s sons were popular—the Duke of Cumberland was probably the least of all. He was believed by many persons to have had *more than* an indirect, or passive, or innocent share in the Orange plot discovered and exposed by Mr. Hume in 1835, for setting aside the claims of the young Princess Victoria, and putting himself—the Duke of Cumberland—upon the Throne; a scheme which its authors pretended to justify by many preposterous assertions that they feared the Duke of Wellington would otherwise seize the Crown for himself."—Justin M'Carthy's History of our own Times, vol. 1, page 16-17.

From an ably written paper upon this subject, published in the columns of the *Northern Whig* of November last, and coming from the pen of a gentleman of high position in Belfast, remarkable alike for his literary taste and persevering research, we find that "reports of the insanity of King William had been carefully reported, and a -egency suggested, and the propriety of a female ruling as successor over a great nation, and she a minor, was questioned, and the Orange mind was being prepared by the Tory journals for the assumption of power by the earnest, virtuous, loyal and saintly Duke of Cumberland."

Can there be a doubt in the face of this body of testimony that we are dealing with traitors? I incline to the belief that no man of unbiassed judgment, whose opinion is worth the having, can deny the conclusion that the Orange Institution stands convicted of one of the most dastardly and ignoble attempts ever made upon the monarchy in these realms. Some may incline to make light of the danger when the tempest is past. It is difficult, I must admit, to withhold laughter at their absurd vagaries; at the bombastic effusions of Fairman, the turgid patriotism of Craigie. But there was that beneath which might well make the nation grow pale, and induce those who appreciate the merits of Government by a limited monarchy, to send up a loud *Te Deum* that a storm did not break over their heads, which would inevitably have led to despotism, and probably ended in Republicanism.

CHAPTER XXX.—IN THE DOCK.

WHEN Mr. Finn rose in his place in the House of Commons on the 4th March, 1835, to put a question to the Home Secretary respecting Orange addresses honourable members laughed. Honourable members generally do laugh at anything they cannot understand. The gravity of the question did not just then present itself to them. But there remains now no doubt that Mr. Finn and Mr. Joseph Hume both had in their possession documents which but too truly intimated the serious constitutional question with which it was connected. Since the dismissal of the Liberal Ministry, Sir Robert Peel's associates in the Government had deliberately winked at the proceedings of the Orangemen, though more than one of them had from time to time declared them an illegal association. Viscount Cole, Mr. Leicester, and Earl Roden had presented addresses thanking his Majesty "for the exercise of his prerogative," and to those addresses his Majesty was made to reply by their acceptance "in the most gracious manner." A protracted debate followed upon the advisability of giving such an unusual reply to addresses from an acknowledged illegal body of men. Out of this dilemma the Government could only get by assuring the House that they in no way meant to sanction these associations. Mr. O'Connell asserted that he could prove that the lower class of Orangemen still took oaths on their initiation, a statement which Mr. Anthony Lefroy denied, stating "that nothing now was requisite for being eligible other than a reputation of being a good Christian and a loyal subject." There seems to have been a measure of error on both sides. If the administering of the oath had been abandoned there existed a declaration tantamount to an oath, and little less than an oath in its solemnity. But every one with the "reputation of being a good Christian and a loyal citizen" was not eligible. Granted, Catholics could be neither one nor the other; there were numerous dissenters to whom these requisites could not be denied and who were still rigidly excluded. Indeed the House managed successfully to overlook the main point, and the great majority of the members were associates bound by a secret oath. When taken it mattered not. The danger was the same. The illegality in no sense lessened. The English members, though knowing practically nothing of Orangemen, were loud in their denunciation of the encouragement they were receiving from the Government. Mr. Hume, at this sitting, and Lord John Russell on the 6th March, two days subsequent, charged the Ministry with being abbetters of traitors, and affording every approbation to Orangeism it was possible for them to afford. The majority of the Liberal members did not yet understand the meaning of these heated debates. All they saw was that the Ministry were perplexed.

On the 23rd March Mr. Finn, according to notice, moved, as an amendment to the House going into Committee of Supply, "for a select committee to inquire into the nature, character and tendency of the orange lodges, or associations, or societies in Ireland, and to report thereon to the House.". His speech, upon the occasion shows the utmost acquaintance with the doings of the Irish Orangemen. In the course of it he called the attention of the House to the recent formation of an Orange lodge in Newry, styled the "Adelaide Orange Lodge," and the inauguration of which had been publicly announced in the following terms — "Her gracious Majesty has been much blamed for supposed interference in great political matters. Whether or not she shall express herself highly gratified at the high honour which the High Street boys have conferred on her, by making her their patroness, we cannot presume to say. This, however, we can assert, that she neither would fling dead cats and rubbish over the High Street Nunnery wall nor annoy the ladies walking through the grounds by indecent expressions; nor, we are assured, would she have joined in the wrecking of the convent, or lent the weight of her little finger to the crowbar which was used in attempting to force the gate." To show the violence of reverend Orange demagogues he produced some remarkable extracts from the speeches of the then notorious Rev. John M'Crea, a chaplain of the Grand Lodge This clergyman was annoyed at so many Catholic churches then rising in Dublin, and suggested, in the language of Knox, that "to banish the crows they should pull down their nests. He publicly pledged himself to God in one of his Christian lectures to "raise such a spirit that no power on earth or in hell could resist it. Every Popish altar must be pulled down The Popish priest must be banished to the congenial soil of Cherokee, or fall a victim to the righteous indignation of the people, the blood of whose fathers cries to Heaven for vengeance against the sins of many."*

Mr. Maxwell (an Orangeman) seconded the motion for an inquiry. Whether he saw that the House was in a temper for an inquiry, and thought it wise to yield with a good grace; whether he thought his brethren would be equal to the occasion, and could successfully baffle the curiosity of the Committee it would be difficult to say. Possibly neither of those would be a solution. Mr. Maxwell was of the Irish Institution, and was likely one of those

members whom it was thought unwise to let into the secrets of the plot. That he knew little about the institution and its progress in the army was evident from his speech. It cannot be forgotten that the Grand Lodge had before violently opposed all inquiry of the nature now suggested. The Government assented to the proposition with reluctance, and after a debate which shows a widespread suspicion that the inquiry was likely to turn upon a far more important constitutional question than at first imagined, it was agreed to impannel a jury and place the Orange Institution in the dock.

The inquiry having been extended to England, two distinct committees were appointed to inquire into the origin, nature, extent, and tendencies of Orange Associations in Great Britain, Ireland, and the colonies. The committee in Ireland originally consisted of twenty-seven members, of whom thirteen were Conservatives, one or two neutrals, and the remainder Liberals. Amongst the Conservatives were Colonel Verner, Mr. Maxwell, Sir Edmund Hayes, Mr Shaw, Serjeant Jackson, Colonel Percival, Colonel Connolly; the first mentioned three were grand officers of the Dublin Grand Lodge and prominent members of the Orange Institution. During the five months which the committee sat some changes took place. Mr. Shaw, Colonel Percival, Colonel Connolly were exchanged for other Conservatives, as Mr. Spring Rice, Mr. Cutlar Ferguson, and others were replaced by Liberals on the formation of a new Administration. Twenty-two were examined by this committee. Eight of these were grand officers or leading members of the Irish Orange Institution, and, of course, strongly impressed with the virtue of Orangeism, and blind to all its vices, its faults, and its dangerous tendencies. The remainder of the witnesses examined consisted of four officers of police, two lord lieutenants of counties, three magistrates, two lawyers, one physician, and two farmers. They all resided in, or were connected with, the districts where Orangeism was most active, they were of various religious persuasions, but chiefly of the Church of England, and all expressed opinions condemnatory of the Orange Institution.

Lieutenant-Colonel Verner, Deputy Grand Master; Rev. Mortimer O'Sullivan, Deputy Grand Chaplain; Mr. William Swan, Deputy Grand Secretary; Mr. Stewart Blacker, Assistant Grand Secretary; Mr. William Ribton Ward, Solicitor to the Orange Institution; Mr. Hugh Eyves Baker, Deputy Grand Treasurer; and Lieutenant-Colonel William Blacker, all, of course, gave evidence in

---

* The Rev Johnny M'Crea, as he was familiarly called, was high in the esteem of the brethren His sermons against Catholics and the Catholic religion were the most filthy I believe—so fill by as to prevent reproduction For his outrageous and violent conduct at a meeting at the Royal Exchange, in 1831, he won the approval of the Grand Lodge and was presented with a service of plate See append x to Irish Report - page 77 M'Crea was the poet laureate of the Irish Grand Lodge

favour of the institution, basing their arguments upon the belief that the violence of the Catholics of Ireland necessitated its existence. Now, as the point of inquiry was not whether the Catholics had done wrong, but whether the Orangemen had done right, these arguments seem beside the issue. "Admit," says the writer in the *Edinburgh Review*, writing upon this point, "adm.t all the recriminations against the Catholics for violent obstruction of Orange processions, for severe and often savage retaliation of wrongs, for party spirit in the witness box—they seldom reached the jury or the bench—and for all the secret working of their ribbon societies; yet, if proved to the fullest extent, to what do all these charges amount? They make out no case or excuse for the existence of Orangeism. On the contrary, these offences ·of the Catholics are the necessary consequences of the Orange insults and outrages. Thus, the heavier the charges which the Orangemen substantiate against the Catholics, *the stronger is the recoil upon themselves."*

. As the Irish Committee made no report to the House, it is necessary that the reader should have some idea of the character of evidence given and facts ascertained as to the extent of the Irish Orange Institution Those facts, which best indicate the nature and the tendency of Irish Orangeism, have already been brought in chronological form under the notice of the reader.

It was found that the ramifications of Orangeism in Ireland extended far and wide—into the magistracy, army, militia, yeomanry, county and Grand Jury officials, and most positions of trust and emolument—that the Imperial Grand Master alone had control over the entire body; that the "council or military staff" was made up of fourteen Deputy Grand Masters, of whom eleven were peers, twelve grand and thirty-two deputy grand chaplains, and a grand committee of 186 leading gentlemen, magistrates, members of Parliament, and clergymen. These persons, all bound together by a unity of views and known to each other by secret signs and passwords, commanded twenty Grand Lodges of counties, under whose control were placed eighty district lodges, which, again, were in constant communication with, and were responsible for the obedience of, a corps of 1,500 private lodges, whose members, varying from 20 to 250, were estimated at a grand total of 220,000 men, all, as already stated, under the absolute control of Ernest, the Imperial Grand Master, and. "the nearest to the Throne" of England;

all of whom, bound as they were to obedience, he had the power of calling together, so far as practical, at his pleasure. Mr. William Swan, the Assistant Grand Secretary of Irish Orangemen, stated that 30,000 Orangemen were assembled in 1798, and being asked "if 30,000 were assembled in 1798, could not 30,000 be assembled in 1835?" and he answered "yes, three times 30,000, I think." He was then asked, "Is there power in any functionaries of the Orange body to call together that enormous· mass of 220,000 men to assemble thus in one place from all parts of the country?" To this the Assistant Grand Secretary of the Orangemen of Ireland replied, "I think a Grand Master might order it."

Earl Gosford, who attended by permission of the House of Lords, said, in the course of his examination (3535), that he thought Orangeism, instead of being necessary for the defence of Protestantism in Ireland, rather weakened it; that the society was most certainly employed for the promotion of party and political purposes; that beyond doubt it had chiefly been used by persons of rank and considerable property for their own political furtherance and advancement, that it not only was not necessary, but that it was dangerous to the protection of the property and political rights of Protestants in Ireland, and had led to a great deal of lawlessness; that beyond the aristocracy of Ireland, who promoted these societies for their own ends, there was a lower or middle class of Protestants who regretted their existence as an evil, and "that there was no doubt of the fact, if what he had seen of the rules of the society was correct, he could say that their practices differed greatly from the rules in several instances, and that their conduct had been diametrically opposed to those rules in many instances."

Mr. Wm Sharman Crawford, M.P., who was examined, justified the Catholic want of confidence in the Orange magistracy and in the Orange juries (4371), upbraided the successive Administrations for pretending to suppress and at the same time encouraging the Orangemen by placing its leaders in high positions (6067); thought the Protestant Church in Ireland was in no way in danger or requiring the aid of Orangeism (4410), and believed that those societies led to social disorder (4418).

Sir Frederick Stovin's evidence to be sufficiently understood would require to be produced in its entirety. He says (4464-90) he received the greatest resistance from the Orange processions in the execution of his duty; that he was told th professions of Orangemen were most brotherly, but that the results were anything but that (4519); that the Orange Society was certainly not requisite for the support of Protestantism or calculated to give it strength (4627); that it was absolutely injurious, and gave rise to bad blood, as their conduct was the reverse of their professions (4628-30); that drum beating and processions were calculated to insult Catholics (4551), that if Orangeism ceased religious dissension would as gradually cease in the community (4700-3); and that Orangeism existed extensively in the army in spite of positive orders to the contrary, and was calculated to produce the most mischievous effects (4639).

The inspector of police admitted that he could find no trace of a Ribbon Society in the North of Ireland, and never found anyone who could.

Mr. James Sinclair, J P., said he had observed the course of Orangeism with that attention which a magistrate should pay to passing events, and it had been, in his opinion, productive of great evil, nor had he been able to discover any possible advantage from it (4952); that the society was productive of very injurious consequences to the Protestant religion (4967); that some clergymen, principally curates and rectors, of the Protestant Church, violently encouraged party animosity between Catholics and Protestants for their own ends, and that the poor men in humble condition of life who take part in Orangeism for the purpose of selling their whiskey were less to blame than men of education and rank " who do not disgrace themselves by those outrages, but institute and encourage them" (5016).

Mr. Wm Stratton, police-constable, was of opinion that the country would be very quiet but for Orange processions and drum-beatings, which were the natural results of the Institution, and which were calculated to give offence to Catholics.

The Right Hon. the Earl of Caledon thought it would very much tend to the administration of justice if magistrates were exempted from the suspicion, or even the supposition of belonging to a secret society of any nature; that whatever would prevent party processions would be an advantage (5538); that the system must be detrimental to the administration of justice in regard to having jurors with party bias trying cases.

Mr. James Christie, a member of the Society of Friends, was of opinion that the existence of Orangeism produced most injurious effects upon society; that it prevented the development of

trade, fostered party spirit, destroyed the fair administration of justice; that the Orange magistrates did not act impartially upon the bench, and that the suppression of the society would lead to many good results. (5750-71.)

Mr. Robert Mullen, M.D, instanced numerous cases of Orange violence, the packing of juries, and the way-laying of Catholics by Orangemen; that there was no attempt on the part of the Catholics to attack Orangemen, as if such were their disposition they would be all annihilated in ten minutes, armed as they were. (6141).

Mr. Patrick M'Connell, solicitor, detailed in the amplest manner murders and outrages, plotted and contrived in Orange lodges and carried out by Orangemen, and while representing the Institution as leading to the most dire mischief and the most wilful injustice, said he believed there was no such thing as a Ribbon Society in Ireland to oppose it.

Mr. Richardson Bell, Mr. William John Hancock, J P.; Mr. Randall Kernan, B L.; and Capt. David Duff, the other witnesses examined, who were not connected with the Institution all condemned the Orange Society in the same manner, as promoting lawlessness and animosity, and leading to outrage and murder. Captain Duff instanced many cases in which he had received the most violent opposition on the part of Orangemen, represented Orangemen as an armed faction opposed to all law and order, and invariably denominating as "Papists" all persons discharging their duty impartially, whether as policemen or magistrates.

Mr. John Gore, stipendary magistrate, and formerly an Orangeman, condemned Orangeism as leading to bad spirit; condemned Orangeism as opposing the law most violently in the North; condemned the Orange magistracy for not co-operating with the military authorities except to thwart their ends; condemned the administration of justice by them as leading justifiably to suspicion; condemned Orange landlords as playing a double part with the people, and in general made out a formidable indictment against his former brethren.

Such was the evidence for the prosecution. The principle has not yet been recognised in English criminal jurisprudence of hearing parties in their own cause. Notwithstanding the modern tendency to admit it I am inclined to believe that few men desiring to form a fair approximation of the effects of any secret society will seek out the members of it as their informants. The very fact of being members precludes possibility of impartiality. Everything prompts them towards their own justification. Everything leads them to start upon the inquiry with a mind open but o one conviction. But give the Orange witnesses every scope and their evidence, contrasted with the above (from gentlemen whose position well fitted them to form an opinion), simply urges the unsettled state of Ireland at the time as an excuse for their existence, while in reply to the numerous outrages laid to their charge they point, as a set off to others, outrages committed by the Catholics in retaliation.

While the committee were sitting, part of the evidence was communicated to the newspapers. On the 17th July Mr. Hume asked a question in the Commons as to the truth of the report relative to a most violent and disastrous disturbance having taken place at Belfast on the preceding 12th of July, in which many parties lost their lives. Lord Morpeth answered that the report was only too true. Mr. Hume, amid great excitement and much interruption, proceeded to make an important statement, which he said was a question involving not an ordinary individual, but meant that "a person of the highest rank in the country had been guilty of a high crime and a misdemeanour against the State." This statement created the utmost consternation in the House, which ended by Mr. Hume giving notice to move for that portion of the Orange evidence completed to be laid upon the table of the House.

On the 20th July, on the motion of Mr. Wilson Patten, it was ordered that the part of the evidence then completed relating to Orangeism in the army be laid on the table. During this debate, Mr. Serjeant Jackson assured the House, "on the highest authority," that the Duke of Cumberland had never sanctioned lodges in the army, and that the warrants had been signed by him in blank form; Captain Curtis followed, and assured the House that Orange lodges had been formed in his regiment, which was chiefly Catholic, without the slightest knowledge of the officers generally; and Mr. Maxwell stated that he was not aware of the existence of any lodges in connection with the army or militia. [See Appendix for Report of the English Committee.]

Time passed. The committees on both sides of the Channel were placing together, link by link, a chain of evidence of the most overwhelming character. The scraps of evidence which still continued to leak out were sufficient to shew to honest-minded citizens the appaling nature of the conspiracy, and to produce general alarm in the public mind at the mine which had been so noiselessly and so dexterously laid beneath their very feet. So general was the excitement and indignation that the members who had unearthed the plot feared to wait until the labours of the committees had been concluded before moving in the matter, and on the 4th of August Mr. Hume, when that portion of the evidence relating to the army was laid upon the table of the House of Commons, rose to call attention to the Orange conspiracy. He condemned the Whigs for being afraid during their previous term of office to put down the Orangemen said he would have put his heel upon their necks and trampled them to death, and insisted that every military Orangeman, from a field-marshal down to an ensign, should be struck off the army list. If such proceedings were allowed to continue, better, he said, dismiss the army altogether. The yeomanry, who were all Orange, should be dismissed, and every Orange magistrate should be dismissed the Bench. These expressions must have met with general approbation, for we find him immediately afterwards saying "he was glad to find that his opinions were so favourably received. The police are also Orangemen. I would make a clean sweep of them all." He moved the following resolutions, stating that he found it difficult to imagine, even if the warrants were signed in blank form by the Grand Master, how the Duke of Cumberland could be ignorant of the use that had been made of them:—

"1. That it appears from the evidence laid before the House that there exist at present in Ireland more than 1,500 Orange lodges, some parishes containing as many as three or four private lodges, consisting of members varying in number from 16 to 260, acting in communication with each other, and having secret signs and passwords as bonds of union, and all depending on the Grand Lodge of Ireland.

"2. The second resolution described the manner in which these bodies were bound together, and declared 'that the Orange Institution of Ireland is unlimited in numbers and exclusively a Protestant association; that every member must first belong to a private lodge, to which he is admitted under religious sanction and with religious ceremony, carrying a Bible in his hands, submitting to certain forms and declarations, and taught secret signs and passwords.'

"3. That no lodge can be constituted without a warrant of the Grand Lodge of Ireland, signed by the Grand Master and office-bearers for the time being, and having the seal of the Grand Lodge thereto affixed.

"4. That it appears by the laws and ordinances of the Orange Institution of Ireland, dated 1835, that the secretary of each private lodge is directed to report to the secretary of the district lodge; the secretary of each district lodge to report to the Grand Secretary of the county lodge; the Grand Secretary of the county lodge to report to the Deputy-Grand Secretary of the Grand Lodge of Ireland; and the Grand Lodge to hold meetings at stated periods, to transact the ordinary business of the society; and the Deputy-Grand Secretary of the Grand Lodge to communicate half-yearly to each lodge in Ireland, and also to the Grand Lodge of Great Britain.

"5. That Orange Lodges have individually and collectively addressed his Majesty, both Houses of Parliament, the Lord Lieutenant, and others, on special occasions of a political nature, such as on subject of the colonies, the change of the Ministry, the education of the people, the repeal of the Union Catholic Emancipation, and reform of Parliament.

"6. That the Grand Lodge of Ireland has interfered in political questions and expelled members for the exercise of their constitutional and social rights; has interfered at elections, and defended criminal prosecutions, as appears from the evidence and from the minutes of proceedings in the book of the Grand Lodge, produced before the Selec Committee.

"7. That it appears by the books of the Grand Lodge of Ireland, produced by its Deputy Grand Secretary before the Select Committee of the House, that the undermentioned warrants for constituting and holding orange lodges have been issued to non-commissioned officers and privates of the following regiments of the cavalry and infantry of the line at home and abroad; to non-commissioned officers of the staff of several militia regiments; to members of other corps; and to the police (the warrants and regiments are here enumerated).

"8. That such warrants are sent privately and indirectly to such non-commissioned officers and privates, without the knowledge or sanction of the commanding officers of such regiments or corps, and every lodge held in the army is considered as a district lodge.

"9. That the general orders of the Commander-in-Chief of the Forces, addressed in the years 1822 and 1829, to commanding officers of regiments and

of depots, and to general officers, and other officers on the staff, at home and abroad, strongly reprobate the holding of Orange lodges in any regiment as 'fraught with injury to the discipline of the army,' and 'that on military grounds the holding of Orange lodges in any regiment or corps is contrary to order and the rules of the service;' and 'that a disregard of this caution will subject offending parties to trial and punishment for disobedience of orders.'

"10. That these resolutions and the evidence taken before the Select Committee on Orange lodges be laid before his Majesty.

"11. That an humble address be presented to his Majesty praying that he be graciously pleased to direct his Royal attention to the nature and extent of Orange lodges in his Majesty's army, in contravention of the general orders of the Commander-in-Chief of his Majesty's forces issued in the years 1822 and 1829, which strongly reprobate and forbid the holding of Orange lodges in any of his Majesty's regiments; and also to call his attention to the circumstance of his Royal Highness Earnest Duke of Cumberland, a field marshal in his Majesty's army, having signed warrants, in his capacity of the Grand Master of the Grand Orange Lodge of Ireland (some of them dated so recently as April in the present year), which warrants have been issued for constituting Orange lodges in the army."

Mr. Wilson Patten corrected an error in the resolutions in regard to Orange interference in the Colonies, saying that the Colonies referred to only related to the Protestant colonisation of Ireland. Admitting the danger attendant upon the existence of Orange lodges in the army, he moved as an amendment that instead of the resolutions proposed the following be adopted:—"That a humble address be presented to his Majesty praying that he will be graciously pleased to direct his Royal attention to the nature and extent of Orange lodges in the army, in contravention of the general orders issued by the Commander-in-Chief in 1822 and 1829, which strongly prohibits the holding of Orange lodges in regiments, and that his Majesty will be graciously pleased to direct an investigation to take place with respect to other secret societies in the army."

No man seems to have been more alive to the gravity of the question than Lord John Russell, who had to speak for the Government. "He went through this affair with eminent prudence, courage, and moderation," says a contemporary writer. He saw that beneath that eleventh resolution lay a charge of culpability and disloyalty to the Crown, for like to which ambitious men had lost their heads. While objecting to the introduction of the duke's name, he expressed surprise "that when those distinguished individuals saw that the whole discipline of the army might be subverted and destroyed under colour of their high authority they should lose one moment in making known that they should cease to be members of such an association. He could not conceive that the illustrious duke would hesitate for one moment on knowing the use that had been made of those warrants," and with this significant hint to the Duke of Cumberland, he proposed the adjournment of the debate to the 11th August, which was agreed to.

The Duke did not take the hint. Having proceeded so far with the game, he was reluctant to draw back just when he had a chance of winning. He simply wrote a letter to the chairman of the committee, denying "that he had *issued* warrants to soldiers," a statement which might be literally correct, seeing that he had simply *signed* warrants for Fairman, his subordinate, to issue them. He also declared that he had "declined *sending out* military warrants on the ground of their violation of the military orders of 1822 and 1829"—a statement which could also be accurate according to the letter, side by side with the most criminal knowledge of their being sent out by others. How far these assertions were believed by the committee may be seen from the sentence towards the close of the report—" Your committee submit that it would have been very easy for his Royal Highness to have published the document by which, and the time and place where, he issued any order, or made any declaration, against Orange lodges in the army, instead of a general disclaimer." It was manifest to everybody that his Royal Highness had taken refuge in prevarication, a conclusion which was subsequently confirmed when he wrote to the chairman of committee stating that "he had no statement to make," and declining the opportunity offered of vindicating himself.

"Lord John Russell on the 4th had shewn his prudence," says Miss Martineau; "he now on the 11th showed his courage." Mr. Hume having withdrawn the fifth and sixth of his resolutions, thus confining the proposition to the military aspect of the question, Lord John Russell boldly stated in the House that "he did not think the letter written by the Duke of Cumberland was all that was required." He said he did not think the

House would be satisfied with the Duke's statement that he was not aware of warrants being issued to the army, and that any such should be annulled; nor was it, in his opinion, the one he ought to have made. He was *in hopes* that the whole of the charges brought against him—namely, the signing of blank warrants and presiding at the meetings at which the warrants were issued—had all been carried on without his knowledge and consent. If so, he did expect when such underhand practices were discovered the duke would cease all communication with parties who had been guilty of such unwarrantable acts. Not wishing to press the inquiry further, he suggested that the words "which warrants have been issued for constituting Orange lodges in the army" should be omitted from the 11th resolution. The resolutions thus modified were carried by a majority of 183 to 40.

On the 15th the King's address was read to the House, promising the utmost vigilance and vigour in suppressing political societies in the army. Instead of ceasing all communication with the brethren, the Duke issued an edict on the 24th August calling together the Grand Lodge to go through the farce of "annulling" the regimental warrants as well as to correct a glaring "irregularity" which of itself would have rendered the institution illegal. Lodges being prescribed by law, they had adopted the expedient of calling them "warrants," giving power to the possessor to call a meeting of Orangemen anywhere on its production. This shallow trick was exposed, for by the documents it appeared that the meetings were "lodge meetings" pure and simple, and were styled as such.

The English Committee were still sitting and the inquiry proceeded, eliciting such information as to show that the House was, fortunately for the Orangemen, rather premature in their decision. Much more than the existence of Orangeism in the army demanded attention. But first, touching those regimental lodges, it must be remarked that their existence in the army without the knowledge of the leaders and directors of the Institution—their existence in England, Ireland, Scotland, and the Colonies; with Serjeant Keith as proxy in the Grand Lodge; Fairman complaining of how they were persecuted by the military commanders; Nucella, their special commissioner, writing from Corfu and stations on the Mediterranean of his difficulties in promoting Orangeism in the army; the Grand Lodge giving him thanks for his efforts;

the rules and regulations providing for the existence of regimental lodges, and affording actually special facilities to lodges in the army—is one of those problems which plain, common-sense men will be inclined to solve but in one way. Still it must be recollected that Prince Ernest and the Right Hon. Lord Kenyon say they did not know of it. And it must be true. For they both plead ignorance. And both were "honourable" men. As it relates to the statements of one of those "honourable" men it may not be out of place to say that Lord Kenyon in his evidence before the select committee sitting in England, first denied all knowledge of lodges existing in the army; then admitted (2736) that rule 47 (1821), referring to the regulations of regimental lodges, had been inserted with his sanction He then admits (2742) that he became aware of the existence of that rule, and "knowing that lodges in the army were forbidden, it occurred to his mind that no lodges did at the time exist in regiments, and consequently that they could not exist afterwards." But then we find the rules year after year up to 1834 sanctioned and revised by his lordship in which not alone are the previous provisions made regarding regimental lodges, but certain privileges allowed to relieve soldiers from paying regular fees. These rules of 1834 were revised and approved by his Royal Highness the Duke of Cumberland. But the climax was reached when a letter was put into Lord Kenyon's hands, addressed to and endorsed by Lord Kenyon, and coming from the correspondent of a regimental lodge at Dover, enclosing a remittance.

In many letters in Lord Kenyon's hand writing, addressed to Colonel Fairman, it would seem that the promotion of Orangeism in the army was a subject about which they were constantly in communication, and it is little to be wondered at that the Parliamentary Committee could not explain away the flagrant inconsistency between the facts and statements. Writing from Peel Hall on the 28th December, 1832, to Fairman, his lordship says—"His Royal Highness promises being in England a fortnight before Parliament reassembles, and I hope will come well. To him, *privately*, you had better address yourself about your military proposition which, to me, appears very judicious." Again, writing Fairman from Portman Square, on the 13th June, 1833, he says—"The statements you made to me before, and respecting which I have now before me particulars from Portsmouth, are not of my sphere, and should be referred *toties quoties* to his Royal Highness, as military matters of great deli-

cacy. At the same time private intimation, I submit, should be made to the military correspondents, letting them know how highly we esteem them as brethren." Further, on the 10th July of the same year "if you hear anything further from the military districts let his Royal Highness know all particulars fit to be communicated." And, again, on the 27th April following "I think we had better communicate it to his Royal Highness, as he is the only person, except yourself, who can judiciously interfere in military matters connected with the Orange Institution." Why, the Duke of Cumberland and Colonel Fairman were so qualified, is evident from the fact that the one was Field Marshal of England, and the other had been a captain in the 4th Ceylon regiment. Whether Colonel Fairman in those frequent visits which he made to Kew, and during which he was "closeted" at times for three hours with his Royal Highness, communicated upon the subject of the regimental lodges, it is impossible to say. That Lord Kenyon was aware of the movement in the military is established in spite of his solemn and repeated assurances to the contrary.

"Your committee must repeat that they found it most difficult to reconcile statements in evidence before them, with ignorance of these proceedings on the part of Lord Kenyon, and by his Royal Highness the Duke of Cumberland"—see the English Committee's Report in appendix. In diplomatic circles he is vulgar who calls a spade a spade. When the Blue Book was published, however, the great body of the public who perused it found a much shorter name for the representations of these Orange leaders.

It remained, however, for Colonel Fairman, the Deputy Grand Secretary and Chief Engineer of this complex piece of machinery, to carry off the palm. During the course of his examination in its earliest stages he made frequent protestations of his desire in every way to forward the inquiry. It, however, became known to the committee that the gallant colonel kept a private letter-book, in which he entered the great secrets of the Institution, and he admitted that he had that private letter-book in his possession. The letters entered in it were, he admitted (1,073), principally connected with the Orange Institution, but " *there were letters from himself to Lord Kenyon entered in that book, which he considered private, and was not disposed to lay before the Committee.*" Again and again he was questioned as to what it did contain, and again and again he replied in the same vague manner, but always admitting "decidedly" that it contained correspondence relating to the Institution. He considered them strictly confidential, and though it might show many documents in relation to military lodges, "it might also contain letters to Lord Kenyon upon Orange business, interspersed here and there *with references which he would not make known to the Committee.*" He refused to allow the members to read only the public Orange letters, protesting that it would establish a bad precedent *in a country where a man was never expected to convict himself*, but said he might be induced to copy letters relating to military lodges and any letters to the Duke of Gordon, that he considered of a public nature. The examination for that day closed Two days intervened, during which the Colonel had ample time to examine that letter-book. He was again called before the Committee and asked had he got the letter book or the copies of the letters he promised. He had neither. He stated distinctly he refused to produce or copy it. He was asked were the Committee to understand that he would not under any circumstances produce that part of the letter book which *did not* refer to military warrants and his answer was "Certainly not." A few more days intervened during which the Committee reported to the House of Commons the refusal of Colonel Fairman to produce a book which had relation to the subject of inquiry He was called before the House on the 19th August and admonished, but still persisted in h s refusal. Whereupon, the House ordered "that the witness be called in and informed that it was the opinion of the House that he is bound to produce the book which has been alluded to on his evidence." Again, Colonel Fairman was called before the Committee, on the 20th August, 1835. The following was the closing scene —

The committee have assembled agreeable to the order of the House to receive that book which you have been directed to bring, in order to their prosecuting their inquiries Have you brought the book? - I shall endeavour to extort the approbation of the committee though I may incur their hatred. I have not brought the book.

Have you brought the book with you? . I have not.

Do you intend to bring it? I should consider myself the veriest wretch on the face of the earth if I did.

Do you intend to bring it agreeable to the order of the House of Commons or not? I cannot.

Will you? I have already said that I will not, and must adhere to the resolution I have before expressed

Will you or not? I have stated that I adhere to my former resolution.

Will you produce the book—yes, or no? No.

This was a breach of privilege The reader may surmise for himself what that public-private letter' book of Lieutenant-Colonel Fairman, Deputy Grand Secretary of the Orange Institution of England, contained. There is, however, evidence at hand likely to assist him in his calcu lations.

In October, 1835, Mr. Haywood, the Sheffield Orangeman before spoken of, addressed a letter to Lord Kenyon in which we find the following — " Did not his Royal Highness, as Grand Master, and Lord Kenyon, as Deputy-Grand Master, know what their missionary, Colonel Fairman, had done in 1832? Or rather did he (Colonel Fairman) not act under the directions of his Royal Highness or Lord Kenyon; and was he not under their directions *instructed to sound the brethren how they would be disposed*, in the event of King William IV being deposed, which was not improbable, on account of his sanctioning reform in Parliament; and that that being so it would become the duty of every Orangeman to support his Royal Highness, who would then in all probability *be called to the Throne*."

References upon this subject " between my Lord Kenyon and myself" we may reasonably presume the letter book contained Was this, then, " the great crisis" in the history of Orangeism, for which all the brethren were watching and waiting ?

The *London and Westminster Review*, from Jan. to April, 1836, contains an ably-written article, entitled the "Orange conspiracy," in which a circumstantial account of these proceedings may be found by those desirous of proceeding further in the inquiry. Various important letters *not* inserted in the Report of the English Select Committee, are there to be found, which the publishers offered to produce should the Duke of Cumberland be prosecuted. In addition, they publish the following, which is one of the sworn depositions upon which the prosecutors of the Orange conspirators meant to rely :—

" That the deponent, in the autumn of 1832, was sitting in the house at which—— Lodge was held, in——; and that deponent was informed by a brother Orangeman that Colonel Fairman had arrived, that deponent proceeded up stairs to the lodge room, and found that the brethren were all assembled, the night being regular lodge night. That soon afterwards the said W. B. Fairman appeared in the room decorated with the orange sash and robe, and took the chair. That the said W. B. Fairman addressed the meeting shortly, stating that he had been specially appointed by his Royal Highness the Duke of Cumberland to make this tour; and he then produced a scroll of parchment which he read aloud to the meeting, and which purported to be, and deponent believed was, a commission from his Royal Highness the Duke of Cumberland to said W. B. Fairman to make a tour, &c., &c. . . . . : . . . That on the following morning, about nine o'clock deponent went to——, where the said W. B. Fairman was staying, for the purpose of making inquiries of him as to the nature and objects of his tour, on which occasion deponent was with him several hours. That deponent afterwards left the house with Colonel Fairman, and as they walked towards—— the following remarks were made by the said W. B. Fairman (that is to say) :—He, the said W. B. Fairman, drew comparisons between his Majesty William IV. and the Duke of Cumberland, as regarded their attachment to the Protestant Church. That this was a critical time for Orangemen; that they ought to make a stand; that if any 'row' took place would they rally round the Duke of Cumberland? That his Majesty had no right to sanction the revolutionary measures of the Government in passing the Reform Bill; that a 'row' was expected to take place. The result of all this on deponent's mind was that Fairman was sounding him as to whether, in the event of a 'tumult' taking place, the Orangemen would adhere to the Duke of Cumberland in preference to the King.

"That the said W. B. Fairman also related to the deponent the circumstances that preceded and led to the grant of the travelling warrant, which were as follows:—That he, the said W. B. Fairman, having been in the country one day, on returning home he went into his parlour and found two letters lying on his table, one from Lord Kenyon and the other from the Duke of Cumberland; that he went to Lord Kenyon's first, who directed him to go to Kew to his Royal Highness, to which place he accordingly went, and passed several hours with his Royal Highness, when his appointment as grand treasurer and tourist was arranged."

The original of this was at the time in the hands of an eminent attorney. Between the expressions contained in the above and those in the various letters which passed between Colonel Fairman, Lord

Kenyon, the Duke of Gordon and their confederates, there is remarkable similarity. Why the letters, published in this review, and handed by Mr. Hume to the writer, were not published in the Parliamentary report, it would be difficult to say. Mr. Madden, in his history of the United Irishmen, says (at page xiii. of vol. 4), and evidently with more reason than has been hitherto supposed, that "proofs of the existence of that conspiracy (the Orange succession conspiracy) during the time his Royal Highness was Grand Master of the Orange Institution of the Empire, that were considered of too formidable a character by the Government of that day to be published in a Parliamentary report, exist in the hands of the gentlemen by whom that committee was moved for."

On the 20th August the Committee again reported Colonel Fairman's refusal to produce the letter book, and the House of Commons ordered that he be committed to Newgate. But by this time *Colonel Fairman had absconded*. It was next proposed to search his house, but this was not carried out, it being believed, apart from the odium of the proceeding, that wherever Colonel Fairman was concealed there too was the letter book.

It was now resolved that as the case was analagous to that of the Dorsetshire labourers, who had been convicted and sent to penal servitude for similar proceedings, the Orangemen were liable under the same law. The Duke of Cumberland, Lord Kenyon, the Duke of Gordon, Col. Fairman, and others, were to be brought before the Central Criminal Court. Haywood, the Orangeman, had taken fright at Fairman's treasonable suggestions, and made them known. The next move was checkmate. A *coup de main* was resorted to by the Orange leaders. It was resolved to prosecute Haywood for libel, if possible, before the prosecution of the conspirators came off. A favourable verdict would have been an easy matter. Sworn accomplices generally give preference to the oath of the brotherhood, if they have preference for any. But Haywood was to be the principal witness for the prosecution of the Orangemen, and to the committee it was clear that his testimony was borne out by the evidence produced before them. It was, therefore, determined to appoint counsel for his defence. Those retained were Serjeant Wilde, Mr. Charles Austin, and Mr. Charles Buller. For the prosecution the most eminent counsel were retained. The indictments upon both sides were drawn up. The original letters were arranged. All was prepared. The public anxiously awaited the great event when on the one side the brother to the King and his co-conspirators would be placed in the dock on a charge of treason, and when the chief witness for the prosecution would be tried for libel on the other. Thus matters stood when two things happened which rendered further proceedings unnecessary. Haywood burst a blood vessel from excitement and died; and Mr. Hume having an important motion to make in the Com-

mons, and knowing that the House would not entertain it if the subject was at the same time occupying the attention of a criminal court, requested that the prosecutors of the Orangemen would stay proceedings. Events shortly afterwards happened which still further obviated the necessity of placing in the dock those titled traitors

> Who unconcerned could at rebellion sit,
> And wink at crimes they did themselves commit.

CHAPTER XXXI.—GUILTY.

It was late in the session of 1835 when the English Committee on Orangeism (which was the last to rise) completed their labours. The report was not, therefore, presented in time to afford members to examine minutely its interesting details, as well as the evidence furnished by the Irish Committee, and then enter upon a discussion of the question. The subject was regarded in too grave a light to permit of haste; and considering all the bearings of the question, the Whig Government—still inclined as of old to that laxity euphoniously termed "moderation"—were disposed to let the matter drop, if they could successfully put an end to this dangerous conspiracy. No doubt, they were largely influenced towards this disposition by the reasonable belief that once the light of day was let in upon the organisation and the force of public opinion brought to bear upon it, it would become powerless and insignificant. But the fact of such prominent individuals in the State being mixed up with it, for the Orange plot extended much further into the high places of the Kingdom than dared be mentioned, and the fear that extreme proceedings might only defeat the end sought for, largely influenced their decision as well. The discussion upon the report of the English Committee and the resolution thereon were therefore looked forward to with hope, as likely to accomplish the objects of the Administration without any accompanying danger.

But in the interim more than one leading journal in the kingdom had anticipated the verdict. The *London and Westminster Review*, at the close of 1835, had denounced the institution as an illegal conspiracy to alter the succession, showed why the leaders should be placed in the dock, and pointing out that even the organisation itself was contrary to law, from the fact that the same Act which rendered the administering of an oath illegal, also prohibited all tests, declarations, and signs. The *Edinburgh Review*, of January, 1836,

avoided, as it distinctly admitted, all consideration under the graver heading of treason, as the criminal proceedings were then pending. But upon the general question of the tendencies of the institution it sums up its conclusions, in the following which is too remarkable to avoid quoting.—

"Our task is now nearly complete. We have seen enough of 'the proceedings, extent, and tendency of the Orange Institutions of Great Britain, Ireland, and the colonies' to feel satisfied that the existence of this 'oldest, best, and most sacred of institutions' is not for the peace or well-being of the community. It may be objected that many of its proceedings are so silly that they can scarcely be dangerous. But this is a mistake. The Orangemen, and more especially the Irish Orangemen, have had a firm and fierce faith in the truth and righteousness and utility of their pernicious institution. Founded on principles of exclusiveness and insolence, they have believed themselves to be meek and charitable; existing as a privileged minority amongst a conquered and oppressed population, they have considered themselves the injured and offended; combining against, or acting beyond the law, they have thought themselves the most loyal of subjects, and reprobating bigotry, they have been at best but the bigoted persecutors of imputed bigotry. There are many, too, who have entered and used the association as a stepping-stone to power and connection, or who have seen in it an engine well fitted for securing that ascendency in Church and State which has been a fruitful source of ascendency in patronage and pelf to them and their party.

"There can be no doubt that Orangeism has been, and continues to be, hurtful to the very cause and principles *it professes* to support. Our charges against it are—

"That it has rendered Protestantism weaker than it found it.

"That it has fomented hostile and intolerant

feelings between co-sects of the Christian religion.

"That by its annual processions and commemorations of epochs of party triumph it has exasperated and transmitted ancient feuds, which have led to riots, with loss of property and life.

"That in consequence of the civil and religious antipathies thus engendered, the administration of justice in all its departments, whether of the bench, the jury, or the witness-box, has become tainted or suspected.

"That, prompted by the encouragement or remissness of former Administrations, the ambition or presumption of individuals has at length organised an association of nearly half a million of men, held together by secret signs, and an affiliation kept up throughout the empire, contrary to law.

"That this society has strengthened itself by secretly introducing its lodges amongst the privates of more than fifty regiments, both at home and on foreign service, contrary to the known rules and regulations of the army. That gatherings, or demonstrations of physical strength, have been recommended by the executive authorities of the society both in England and in Ireland, and have frequently taken place to a great extent.

"That this association, addressing itself to the religious passions of the multitude, is placed under the absolute command of a prince of the blood, who, as imperial grand master, has, amongst other powers, that of assembling the whole Orange body, as far as practicable, at any given place or time.

"These are grave charges. We have carefully quoted the authorities upon which they are founded."

On the 12th February 1836 Mr. Finn in the House of Commons moved—"That Orangeism had been productive of the most painful effects upon the character and administration of public justice in Ireland and that its prevalence in the Constabulary and peace preservation forces and yeomanry corps of that country, as well as in large bodies of the above description of forces to the gross neglect and violation of their public duty, and to the open daring and lawless resistance of the authority of the magistrates and the Executive Government; that a system of surreptitious introduction of Orangeism into every branch of the military service, in almost every part of the empire in direct violation of the orders issued in 1822 and 1829 by the Commander-in-Chief of his Majesty's forces, and the absolute power and control vested in its governing body, the Grand Orange Lodge of England and

Ireland, in his Royal Highness the Duke of Cumberland, together with the rank, station, influence, and numbers of that formidable and secret conspiracy, were well calculated to excite serious apprehension in all his Majesty's loyal subjects, and imperatively call for the most energetic expression on the part of the representatives of the people of this Empire to *secure a safe, peaceable, legal, and rightful succession to the Throne of these realms.*" He distinctly asserted that the object of the conspiracy was to alter the succession in favour of the Duke of Cumberland, stated that this was the great " coming crisis" for which they were all arming, and argued that it was proved by the report of the Select Committee that the organisation was one of deadly hostility to the great mass of the population, setting law and justice at defiance. Mr. E. Bulwer seconded the motion. As notice had been given by Colonel Verner, member for the County Armagh, for a motion upon the same question, the debate was adjourned to that date, this course being also influenced by the fact that Mr. Hume was upon that day also to move a resolution having the same object in view.

On the 23rd of February Mr. Hume entered into an elaborate criticism of the evidence, which will be found in the pages of Hansard. It is needless to reproduce it. Suffice it to say that he branded the Orange Confederation as an illegal conspiracy; that their assemblage, instead of being restrained, were headed by the magistracy, deputy-lieutenants, and gentry of weight and consideration, and urged that every one connected with it holding a public office should be dismissed. " If," he said, " the Duke of Cumberland persisted in continuing to be head of such a body it was time to consider whether he was to be King or subject—for that was the real question." The evidence, incomplete as it then was before the House, gave reason to suspect "that the individual who had been sent through the Kingdom to forward the objects of the Institution under the warrant of the Grand Master had hazarded speculations on the possibility of the King being deposed and a regency *at the least* established under the Duke of Cumberland during the minority of the heir apparent." Mr. Hume moved "That this House, taking into consideration the evidence given before the select committee appointed to inquire into the extent, and character, and tendency of the Orange Lodges, associations, and societies in Ireland, Great Britain, and the Colonies; and seeing that the existence of the Orange societies is highly detrimental to the peace of the community by exciting discord among the several classes of his Majesty's subjects, and seeing that it is highly injurious to the due administration of justice that any judge, sheriff, magistrate, juryman, or any other person employed in maintaining the peace of the country should be bound by any secret obligation to, or be in any combination with, any society unknown to the laws, and united upon principles of religious exclusion; that even if justice were impartially administered under such circumstances, which is in itself impossible, yet connection with such societies would create suspicion and jealousy detrimental to the peace and good government of this country; that Orange societies, and all other societies, which have secret forms of initiation, and secret signs, and are bound together by any religious ceremony, are particularly deserving of the severest reprobation of the House, and should be no longer permitted to continue, an humble address be presented to his Majesty to direct measures to be taken to remove from the public service at home and abroad every judge, privy councillor, lord-lieutenant, &c., magistrate officer, inspector, &c.; and, in Ireland, every functionary in the justice of the peace who would not, being an Orangeman, quit the society after one month's notice." Sir William Molesworth, an English member who followed, likewise contended that the Grand Lodges in England and Ireland were illegal under the statutes 37, 39, and 57 of George III., and said that the ritual, as then existing, was to all intents and purposes an oath. He likened the case to that of the Dorsetshire labourers, who were not headed, he remarked, by a Prince of the blood. He was sure that sufficient evidence would be forthcoming to obtain a conviction for misdemeanour against its chiefs in any court of justice, and concluded thus:—" Let then, the law officers of the Crown, without delay, prefer a bill of indictment before the Grand Jury of Middlesex against the illustrious Grand Master of the Orange Institution, against Lord Kenyon, the Deputy Grand Master; against Lord Chandos, against Lord Wynford,* not forgetting the prelate of the order, Thomas, Lord Bishop of Salisbury. Thus, the society will easily and quickly be annihilated, and a few years residence on the shores of the Southern Ocean will teach those

* This peer had actually been made an Orangeman while Deputy Speaker of the House of Lords, the mummeries of initiation having been gone through in the Deputy Speaker's private room attached to the House of Lords.

titled criminals that the laws of their country are not to be violated with impunity, and that equal justice is to be distributed impartially to both high and low." Lord John Russell, in a speech characterised more by prudence than by manliness, agreed with all the accusations made against the Orangemen, but, fearing that the removal of all public functionaries connected with Orangeism would create resentment, he proposed an amendment, "That an humble address be presented to his Majesty praying that his Majesty would be graciously pleased to take such measures as to his Majesty seemed advisable for the effectual discouragement of Orange lodges, and generally all political societies, excluding persons of different faiths, using signs and symbols and acting by associated branches" The Orange leaders in the House had nothing to urge in their defence. An attempt was made at the last moment, by appealing to the good nature of Lord John Russell, to get the word "Orange" omitted from the resolution, but without avail. Lord John was determined that the verdict of the nation should be given directly against the Orange conspirators. Mr. Hume, though still maintaining that his resolution was the better of the two, having no object to serve but the abolition of the association, and he accordingly withdrew the original motion, and Lord John Russell's resolution WAS UNANIMOUSLY AGREED TO.

Through the lips of royalty itself came the verdict and sentence of their doom. The address having been presented to the King, his Majesty, on the 25th February returned the following reply:—

"*I will willingly assent to the prayer of the address of my faithful Commons that I will be pleased to take such measures as may seem to me advisable for the effectual discouragement of Orange Lodges, and generally of all political societies, excluding persons of different religious faith, using signs and symbols, and acting by means of associated branches. It is my firm intention to discourage all such societies in my dominions, and I rely with confidence on the fidelity of my loyal subjects to support me in this determination.*"

The Home Secretary transmitted the reply to the Duke of Cumberland, the leader in the conspiracy, and his Royal Highness answered, that, before receiving the communication he had recommended the dissolution of the Orange Institution in Ireland, and that he would forthwith adopt steps for the dissolution of the institution in England.

Was his Majesty depending too much upon "the fidelity of his loyal subjects? Unquestionably he was. The English Orangemen dissolved. The Irish Grand Committee met in Dublin, and after debate published a series of resolutions to the effect that *the will* of the King was not law, and that therefore they were strongly opposed to dissolution. They at the same time passed a vote of thanks "for his conscientious preference of principle to expediency" to Colonel Verner, whom, for some reason unexplained, they presumed to counsel resistance to the King's wishes. The greatest excitement prevailed, for the fear was entertained that the indiscretion of the Irish members might necessitate criminal proceedings against the leaders. The interval between the meeting of the Irish Committee and the 14th of April, the date of the special meeting summoned to consider the question of dissolution, the Orange organs occupied in debating the subject. The *Dublin University Magazine*, ever loud in expressing the virtues of Orangeism, now acknowledged the truth. In its April issue it said "*the organisation of Orangemen was designed simply for the concentration of physical force*—these times demand the exhibition of moral power;" it admitted "that the dangers which menaced Protestantism when these societies were formed were not now exactly of the same character;" said that "for the purposes of political interference the Orange societies were not originally intended, and were never adapted;" hinted that the association "would still remain united in reality;" and counselled dissolution. The result was that the Irish Society was abandoned by all who gave it weight or respectability. The disreputable portion of it threw off their yoke of allegiance, asserted that a Royal proclamation was not an act of the Legislature, and, though formally dissolved, became more secret and more illegal than ever.*

This is what Orangemen of the present day call loyal obedience and a yielding to the wishes of their sovereign !

On the dissolution of the English and the temporary submersion of the Irish Society the public breathed again. A feeling of relief pervaded the community that the English Crown was saved to its rightful inheritor. One year afterwards, a young and virtuous and noble-hearted girl ascended the Throne of England amid the general acclamations of her people; and the hoary reprobate who so longed to wear a crown, who had so long wielded his mock sceptre, exchanged his pasteboard diadem for a real one. The Duke of Cumberland became King of Hanover, the Crown being limited to males, and there was not a law-abiding subject in these realms who did not wish the Hanoverians luck of a bargain of which they soon learned to repent.

* See "Westminster Review" for 1836 page 211.

<hr/>

CHAPTER XXXIII.—SCOTCHED, NOT KILLED—DOLLEY'S BRAE.

IT has been stated by more than one writer, making casual reference to the subject of our story, that Orangeism was non-existant from the year 1836 to 1845. This is an error. The fact is, Orangeism was not dead. Nor was it even sleeping. After Sir Harcourt Lee's advice to the Ulster brethren, "To increase and multiply," and "Keep their powder dry," the lowest classes, particularly in country districts, still remained bound together by the mystic secrets of the local lodges. The guilty thing dragged itself into the dark corners, and there, in the sulks, maintained a miserable existence; with the air of a martyr, it cherished recollections of the "glorious past," when its members were the paid persecutors of the State secretly it bewailed the evil days of reform which made intolerance a crime instead of a virtue. It was a head without a body up to the close of the year 1837. In the month of November of that year an effort was made, but with little success, to creep out of their hiding places into the public thoroughfare. The *Evening Packet* of the 16th November, 1837, contains a report and resolutions of a meeting of Orangemen assembled for the purpose of reviving the Grand Lodge. This report, a summary of which will also be found in the *Dublin University Magazine* for December of that year, disposes of the assertion that the Institution was defunct until 1845. It is headed, "Re-establishment of the Orange Society," at the same time stating that the meeting at 85, Grafton Street, was an assembly "of the members of the Orange Society of Ireland." The object seems to have been he formal revival of the Orange Institution. No names of those present were published, but to the series of resolutions and to the address is appended the name of William Swan as secretary, who, it will be seen, was also secretary before the formal dissolution. Notwithstanding the fact that the Grand Lodge had at their meeting in April, 1836, declared "that the end for which the Orange Institution was originally framed will no longer be served by the further continuance of that Institution." the objects of the Institution declared in 1837 to be such "as heretofore." Up to 1845, however, there was little in connection with the Institution that could induce us to linger over it. The Anti-Procession Act having expired, an effort was made in 1845 to revive them against the wishes of Lord Roden and other noblemen who sympathised with the society. The result was an armed procession in Armagh, where one Roman Catholic was killed and three were wounded, A Mr. Watson, Deputy Lieutenant, residing at Brookhill, presided over an Orange meeting at Lisburn, and, replying to Lord Roden's letter condemning demonstrations, he said their minds were made up, and that they would proceed. The result was the suspension of Mr. Watson. The Orangemen had been too long accustomed to regard party intolerance as a sure passport to Ministerial favour, and they at once made common cause with Mr. Watson, and also with a Mr. Archdale, of the County Fermanagh, who had been suspended on similar grounds. Through the Press they called upon he Orangemen "to make themselves feared," and said that there should be monster meetings held to serve that end. Lord Roden now praised Mr. Watson for having done the very thing he had written to him not to do. Lord Enniskillen, the Marquis of Downshire, Lord Londonderry, and other noblemen of Ulster now placed themselves at he head of hat contemptible band of malcontents who had, as the remnants of an expiring faction, existed since 1836, and the organisation in Ireland again came forth into the light of day. Meetings of Orangemen were held in all the northern counties; the flame of party spirit spread like wild-fire. On the 10th October, 1845, a meeting was held in the Town Hall, Enniskillen—Lord Enniskillen in the chair—for the purpose of receiving and considering the answers of Mr. Napier, Q C., to three questions put to him, as to the legality of openly re-establishing the society. These answers were read, but even the Warder newspaper was not sufficiently in the confidence of the brethren to be allowed to copy the legal opinions. The reporter, however, was assured that the opinions were quite favourable, &c., &c., and this meeting, thereupon, resolved to make public acknowledgement of their existence, protected as they were beneath the spacious name of En-

killen. We are assured by this authority that signs and pass-words were to be discontinued. He was told so. In an address from a meeting of noblemen, amongst whom was Lord Ennis killen, published in the News-Letter, October 24, over Lord Roden's name the Protestants were called upon to unite but warned not "to weaken their union by administering oaths or using secret signs—a system which modern sedition had polluted and the law denounced" While calling upon them to unite, it warned hem "not to seek aid from any source which the spirit of the laws or the Constitution denied." Mark the consistency! A few weeks after this address appeared the Orangemen were called upon by the same Lord to come boldly out into the open day. With a spirit of wild exaltation over a miserable people, a prey to the multiplied horrors of famine and its concomitants, the Institution was formally re established There is reason for belief that it adopted that system which "sedition had polluted"—signs, passwords, and observances, only less sacred than an oath. Lord Enniskillen became its Grand Master; Lord Loden, its Deputy Grand Master.

The rules, as revised by Joseph Napier in 1845, and which were adopted by the Grand Lodge of Ireland assembled at Monaghan in 1849, display great professional skill in the way in which a clever, wily adviser of a political clique can drive a coach-and-four, not through one, but through half a dozen Acts of Parliament But above and beyond all they show the truculency of the Orange Institution. Mr. Madden begins the fourth volume of his "Lives and Times of the United Irishmen" with an address to the people of England, in which he shows up the infamy of this institution. The author re-issued this address in 1861 in pamphlet form, having extended it, and in the extended pamphlet of 1861 (whether it has been published in any of the late editions of his work I have not ascertained) will be found a complete copy of the rules of the Orange Institution as they came from the revising hands of Mr. Napier. Their voluminous character, and indeed their general similarity to the old rules in most respects, prevent their being included in this work. It is sufficient to say that conditional loyalty alone was still promised to the occupant of the Throne and her successors, as the phrase "being Protestant" sufficiently implies; that the association was formed upon the old exclusive basis, the qualification being "the religion of the Reformation;" that an oath was not required upon entering or "any illegal test or declaration," though the absence of all three was very successfully and effectually atoned for; that an Orangeman was bound not to wrong a brother or know of a brother being wronged without giving him due notice; that a brother before being admitted should be found to be "one who would not in any manner communicate or reveal any of the proceedings or counsels of his brother Orangemen, in lodge assembled, or any matter or thing therein communicated to him; and that a Purple man, before being initiated, should be distinctly known to be a man who would not reveal things confided to him, *even to an Orangeman*. To Mr. Napier there were three questions propounded:—1st, whether the Orange Society, retaining its former name, and acting by affiliated branches, could be recognised consistently with the law as it then existed? 2nd. In what manner, if at all, the organisation could be effected; and he was requested to remodel the rules so as to render them conformable with the law 3rd. Was it lawful for a magistrate in the commission of the peace to advise or encourage such reorganisation? Before this small clique of the Irish nobility attached themselves to the remnant of the faction of 1836 they resolved at last to hedge themselves round with the technicalities and quibbles of an astute lawyer. To these questions Mr. Napier replied by reviewing the several Acts which operated against secret societies, and said:—1st—That no oath could in any manner, or under any pretence, lawfully be used or administered; 2nd, that secret signs and passwords, or other secret modes of communication, could be employed; and 3rd, that any test or declaration used should be approved of by two magistrates in the county where it was being used, and should subsequently be sanctioned by the majority of magistrates at Quarter Sessions, and registered with the Clerk of the Peace. A magistrate who approved of the principles of the society might be believed also assist in reorganising it in conformity with the existing law, but "the *propriety* of such a course, like the exercise of any privilege, must be decided by himself for his own guidance." He suggested the "importance of cautioning the branch associations of the old society against any premature or partial revival of combinations which might violate the *spirit* in attempting to evade the *letter* of the law," and concludes his opinion in these words, remarkable because coming from a lawyer of a decided leaning towards a confederacy which had many favours to dispose of:—"I with is

should be understood that I do not mean to express or insinuate any opinion as to the propriety or imprudence of the course upon the legality of which I am requested to advise. Popular confederacies are perilous, because they generally become unmanageable; but allowance of them under a free constitution shows that circumstances may exist which may require such united vigour as they call into activity." With all due deference to Mr. Napier's memory, such "allowances under a free constitution" show nothing of the sort. There being no express prohibition upon the statute books against confederacies of an exclusive kind such as this, does not argue their occasional necessity. It rather argues that it is a free constitution; that men's desires may be as intolerant as their selfish natures will prompt, but so soon as those desires proceed to acts or threats they become responsible to the common law of the country. Why they were not held responsible as often as might be is because the magistrates who administered that common law in most instances took Mr. Napier at his word, and became part and parcel of the confederacy. Little wonder, however, that the reporter of the *Warder* was not permitted to give that precious document to the public, and that it remained hidden in the archives of Orangeism until Mr. Madden laid unholy hands upon it.

But it should be here stated that the 57 of George III., chap. 19, provided "for the more effectual preventing seditious meetings and assemblies." By section 39, this Act is made *not* to extend to Ireland, but under it this "representative" body might in England have been held to be illegal, thus placing the Orange institution in the anomalous position of being tolerated by law in Ireland, and expressly prohibited in England. The legal ingenuity of lawyers identified with the Orange cause here set the existing laws in Ireland at defiance, and placed before the British Parliament the necessity of framing a special measure for their suppression. Mr. Madden quotes upon this question the opinion of a legal gentleman of eminence at the bar who says:—"When English writers in the Press, and English politicians upbraid Irishmen for the existence of such an institution amongst them, they must have singularly short memories for, within thirty years the institution was in full operation in England, and but for a law against it, would be so still. All the Irish Liberals who seek the suppression of the Orange Institution ask is to have the same law in Ireland as in England." The blind folly and prejudice of the Irish Orangemen prevented them from seeing the discreditable position they occupied. The times were exciting, no doubt. But the threat of armed resistance, for this was its true meaning, against the Repealers, who were taught to run from the sound of a gun as did the naked savages of Central Africa, was for that very reason the more cowardly and the more criminal. It was the opposition of brute force to numbers. Certainly the movement which ended in the miserable *fiasco* at Ballingarry was not of a character to leave the English Government in Ireland in need of assistance. Oppression, it is said, makes wise men mad. Oppression and famine, acting upon men who at best were never very wise, certainly who were not selfish enough and too big hearted to display it, as the world goes, had made a handful of men lunatics. But it acted in a directly opposite sense on the oppressors. It made them jubilant. And seeing their countrymen flying before famine and the law, they gave cry, "Halloo, mad dog," and resolved to follow. What a position, now that we look back upon it!

On the 8th July, 1848, Lord Roden addressed a letter, dated 8th July, to the Northern Orangemen, expressing regret that they were not able to make Tullymore Park their place of meeting, "in order that he might have an opportunity of witnessing their numbers." He denied, when afterwards called to account for the consequences, that his letter was an invitation, and said it simply meant that "he would not shut his gates against them," which explanation most readers will regard as a distinction without a difference. Lord Roden was a peer and a Privy Councillor; he was for years a Deputy Lieutenant of the County Down, and custos-rotulorum of another county. Being a man of mature age and full of sanctity, he deserved the compliment of being capable of estimating the results of his acts. The result of the demonstration of Orangemen in 1848 was most unfortunate. "The seed of mischief was now sown," says a writer in the *Edinburgh Review*. "The evil of these exclusive associations is the ill-will which they engender, the resistance which they provoke, and the counter associations which they infallibly call into existence." While life and strength remain no men fit for anything but slavery will submit to be trampled over, or to accept the badge of inferiority sought to be fastened upon them by a rival faction. The Roman Catholic element now determined to celebrate their festival on the 17th of March, the

consequence being the perpetuation of that cursed party spirit which has ever since been the bane of Ulster.

The hint thrown out by Lord Roden to the Orangemen in 1848 did not need to be repeated in the following year. It was resolved to assemble on the 12th of July, 1849, at Tullymore Park and Dolly's Brae, an exclusively Catholic district of the County Down, adjacent to Castlewellan, and a place, for many long years sacred from Orange demonstrations, was to be "taken" on the route. When it became known that the Orangemen had resolved upon this step the utmost consternation prevailed. The legality of the procession became so much a subject of discussion that the assistant barrister at the Newry Quarter Sessions thought it advisable to warn the country that "none but persons duly authorised by law were entitled to assemble in numbers and in public with arms;" the Bishop of Down and Connor besought, by public letter, the Orangemen "to refrain from processions, calculated, as surely they were, to engender party strife," while Lord Massereene hastened to assure his lordship "that the clergy appeared to be the chief promoters of the Orange demonstration." Thus matters stood previous to an event which, for its sanguinary nature, rivalled the bloody disaster of the "Diamond," and which, in more respects than one, resembled that massacre, seeing that it celebrated the awaking, as the Diamond did the inception, of Orangeism. The Dolly's Brae conflict is thus admirably described by one who must be taken as an impartial witness * :—

This spot had already become notorious in the annals of party strife. Thirty-four years ago, in a contest which took place there, a Roman Catholic was killed. His widowed mother soon followed him to the grave; but left her dying injunction, so the story goes, that no Orange procession should ever be allowed to pass that way. After her death her name was given to the hill; and it became a point of honour with the Orange party to march in procession over "Dolly's" Brae, and with the Roman Catholics to prevent them. It is situated about two miles from Castlewellan, on the old road from Rathfriland, which passes through Ballyward, the hamlet of Magheramayo and Dolly's Brae. This road is so bad and hilly that a new one was made a few years ago, which, diverging from the other at Ballyward school-house, about three miles from Castlewellan, takes the level ground to Castlewellan where the roads unite again. The hill road,

* *Edinburgh Review* for January, 1850.

though the shorter of the two, is rarely used—the new one being more level and convenient. So that a procession going from Ballyward to Castlewellan would avoid Dolly's Brae, unless, indeed, they went out of their way on purpose.

The arrangement of the procession and the choice of the route devolved, as before, upon Mr. W. Beers. He was aware that the new road was the natural one—he admits that on the preceding anniversary it had been adopted, and that no collision took place. But he had heard that to pass through Dolly's Brae would be regarded as a triumph by the Orange party; and this motive appears to have outweighed all other considerations in the mind of the magistrate. About the middle of June, according to his own account, he issued his orders through Mr. Jardine of Rathfriland, that the procession should take the Dolly's Brae road, and he was careful to communicate the order to his friend and correspondent—Lord Roden. That there should be no mistake, the rendezvous of the lodge was fixed at Ballyward, near the point of divergence of the two roads, at the house of his brother, Mr. F. C Beers, another magistrate, and in Tollymore Park he himself repeated the order to the Orangemen to return, as they had arrived, by Dolly's Brae.

The consequences of this order were foreseen. After consultation among the magistrates, one of them, Mr T Scott, went to Dublin, and requested that a strong force should be sent down Accordingly, two stipendiary magistrates, two troops of cavalry, two companies of infantry, and a sub-inspector and forty policemen were despatched to Castlewellan and Rathfriland, where the sub-inspector, Mr Hill, was stationed with thirty-four of his own constabulary. In the meantime proof was accumulating that these precautions were not unnecessary. It was openly stated in the newspapers that the Roman Catholics had held a meeting, and were determined to resist the march of the Orange procession through Dolly's Brae, and an anonymous letter was sent on the 9th of July to a magistrate, Mr. George Shaw, Lord Annesley's agent, professing to come from the repealers—"To give you and Moore, and the Beers, and Roden, and Hill, and Skinner, and all other magistret's, with the pig-drovers, the police, and your handful of solgers to meet us on Dolly's Brae on the 12 morning inst, to show your valure," &c. We have quoted the date and some of the words of this epistle that our readers may see the character of the "challenge," which the member for Fermanagh,

in a style of argument savouring rather of Tipperary than Westminster Hall, and with a great contempt for the date of Mr. Beers' order, adduced in Parliament as the cause and justification of the march through Dolly's Brae.

Early on the morning of the 12th, the military and police occupied the pass of Dolly's Brae, and the Ribbonmen, who had begun to collect in great numbers, finding their intentions anticipated, moved off towards Magheramayo; and, after firing and manœuvring in their own fashion, finally posted themselves on the side of the hill above the road The Orange lodges from the Rathfriland district collected at Mr. F. C. Beer's house at Ballyward. The magistrates who had gone to the same place, seeing that the Orangemen were armed and preparing to advance, and perceiving through a telescope that the Ribbonmen had assembled in force to oppose them, became alarmed for the result, and Mr. Scott proposed to Mr. Beers that the procession should go by the level road to Castlewellan. The reply was almost in the same words as those previously used by Mr. Jardine to Mr. Hill—"that no power on earth would prevent the Orangemen going by Dolly's Brae." The magistrates seem to have thought that the only course open to them in such circumstances was to intimidate the Ribbonmen by a display of police and military, and by main force prevent an actual conflict. Accordingly the military were hastily brought up from Rathfriland and the procession was formed, the police and dragoons going in front followed by the Orangemen, many of whom were armed, and at intervals in the line were carts covered with grass and containing fire-arms. Before they reached Dolly's Brae, a negociation with the Ribbonmen had been opened by the party there through the medium of two Roman Catholic priests, and by great exertions a kind of armed truce was established, so that the procession passed on undisturbed towards Tollymore Park.

Lord Roden, on horseback, received the party at his gate and entered the Park at their head. He describes the procession as consisting of fifty lodges, composed of 2,000 men, of whom he saw 300 armed, besides women and children. Refreshments were then served in tents, and there were barrels of beer and bread and cheese for the crowd

Captain Fitzmaurice, the stipendiary magistrate, now applied to Lord Roden, urging him to use his influence with the Orangemen to induce them not to return by Dolly's Brae, saying—"They have had triumph enough now, and why go back and run the risk of bloodshed?" He replied that he feared he had no influence, but would speak to the Grand Master, Mr. W. Beers. He did so, and even suggested—" Would it not be better for them to go that way?" but on receiving from the Grand Master the answer—" Oh, there will be no danger, and it would be impracticable or impossible, as there would be a split," he felt the answer to be so satisfactory that he did not press the matter any further.

The Orangemen having enjoyed the hospitality of Tollymore Park, were summoned by the sound of a bugle round a platform, where Mr. Beers addressed them, requesting them to return quietly by Dolly's Brae. Lord Roden also spoke—he congratulated them on their numbers, told them that it was for the right of private judgment in the study of God's word that Orangemen contended; trusted that they would never forget the preservation of their rights; talked about the magnificent scenery and the coming of the Queen, and inculcated forbearance and love. Lord Roden, but apparently only after the manner of Lord Massereene, "disapproves of processions altogether." He takes some credit for allowing the procession to come to his park, "for then I should have an opportunity of addressing them and requesting them to conduct themselves properly, and by all means to preserve the peace." If Lord Roden felt that his influence would be efficacious in inducing an excited multitude to avoid a breach of the peace it seems extraordinary that when he was requested to persuade them to take the ordinary road homewards, he should have told Captain Fitzmaurice that he had no influence. The peaceful address which he was so anxious to deliver, and on which his adherents now lay so great stress, was after all not particularly successful, perhaps, because, as Mr, Scott tells us, "part of the speech was quite inaudible in consequence of the uproar."

Towards six o'clock the drums of the Orangemen announced to the party at Dolly's Brae the return of the procession, which was about three-quarters of a mile long, armed, as Major Williamson says, to the teeth. The guns in fact had now been taken out of the carts, and Constable Scanlon counted four hundred and twenty-eight stand of arms in the procession, exclusive of those in the hands of the Castlewellan party. In front came Mr. Hill's police, then the Orangemen, next came the dragoons, then another party of police, and last of all the infantry. Mr. Scott makes honourable mention of the Roman Catholic priest, Mr. Morgan, who

exerted himself to the utmost to keep the people quiet. But the excitement, which in the morning had been almost uncontrollable, had now risen to fury. The women and children of the Roman Catholic party collected on the sides of the road, and covered the Orangemen with taunts and execrations. They retorted with the cry—"There's a priest—to hell with the priest—to hell with the Pope!" and in this manner Dolly's Brae was passed.

When the police at the head of the procession reached the place where the Ribbonmen had collected on Magheramayo Hill, they found them in three divisions, numbering about 1,200 men, posted behind some walls the nearest about a hundred yards from the road. On coming abreast of the wall the police halted between the Ribbonmen on the hill and the Orangemen on the road, and remained stationary until the rear of the procession was in the act of passing them. At this critical moment a shot or squib was fired from the head of the procession,* immediately came two shot from the hill, then a volley, and then the firing was general on both sides. Mr. Hill's police charged up the hill and fired upon the Ribbonmen, who soon broke and fled, on which the fire of the police ceased, and they secured a number of prisoners. Nearly two hundred Orangemen also began to ascend the hill and kept up a fire upon the retreating Ribbonmen; and while the rear part of the procession were thus engaged those who were in front broke loose from all restraint in Magheramayo, where there was no opposition, and began to burn and wreck the houses, while some scattered themselves over the fields to complete the same work of devastation. The dragoons now pushed forward and drove the Orangemen onwards towards Rathfriland. By this time a number of houses were blazing, and a party of police were sent to extinguish the flames. Mr. Scott saw two men trying to set fire to a house, he struck one and took the gun from the other. Mr. Tighe, a magistrate, saw an Orangeman firing into the thatch of a house, but never thought of arresting him. Inspector Corry went into six burning houses; from one an old woman was struggling to escape, but the door was partially closed and the blazing thatch falling

* With reference to this point the Review says:—"The evidence is conflicting, whether the squib came from the road or the hill. There are seven or eight witnesses in support of each opinion; but where there is plainly a general leaning towards the Orangemen—the agreement against them of the three commanding officers, Major White, of the Enniskilleus, Captain Fitzmaurice, the stipendiary, and Mr. Hill, the Inspector of Police, is to our judgment conclusive.

in; and she would have been burned to death had he not saved her. A policeman rescued a girl eighteen years old from another Louse. Sub-Constable Fair took a woman out of a house on fire in a desperate state, blackened and wounded Another constable saw an Orangeman strike a woman with the butt end of his gun as she was trying to get away.

"The work of retaliation, both on life and property by the Orange party, was proceeding lower down the hill and along the side of the road in a most brutal and wanton manner, reflecting the deepest disgrace on all by whom it was perpetrated and encouraged. One little boy ten years old was deliberately fired at and shot while running across a field Mr Fitzmaurice stopped a man in the act of firing at a girl who was rushing from her father's house; an old woman of seventy was murdered; and the skull of an idiot was beaten in with the butts of their muskets, Another old woman was severely beaten in her house, while another, who was subsequently saved by the police, was much injured, and left in her house which had been set on fire. An inoffensive man was taken out of his house, dragged to his garden, and stabbed to death by three men with bayonets in the sight of some of his family The Roman Catholic chapel, the house of the Roman Catholic curate, and the National school-house were fired into and the windows broken, and a number of the surrounding houses of the Roman Catholic inhabitants were set on fire and burnt, every article of furniture having been first wantonly destroyed therein." (Mr. Berwick's Report.)

The scenes which took place in the houses are best described in the witnesses' own words.—

Bridget King—I know Pat King who was killed on the 12th of July. He was taking care of his mother on that day. The door was shut, I saw the Orangemen fire at the house They broke in the door. They pulled him over the garden ditch and stabbed him. He died in ten minutes afterwards. He was not out of the house that day.

We condense the evidence as to Arthur Traynor. He was standing near his own house. Had no arms in his hands on the 12th. Was hit with a ball in the cheek. Ran to Mr. F. C. Beers to save his life. Mr. Beers thought him a peaceably disposed man. Ran him among the prisoners where he was handcuffed. No attention was paid to him for four days On the 16th, when under examination before the coroner, it was made known that the ball was still in his face.

On the 17th, this man, who had not had arms in his hands, and was known by Mr. Beers to be a peaceable man, having had his house burned, all his property destroyed, and being himself severely wounded, *was discharged!*

Margaret Traynor—The men with sashes on them fired into my house and burned it and destroyed it; they chased the old woman who is dead into the byre, and followed her. I saw her after they went away; she was drawing breath, but she died in about an hour afterwards. They shot my husband in the cheek and made a prisoner of him. I saw Pat King a killing. They dragged him out of his house. He begged for mercy. He got away from them and ran into the garden. Three of the men made a bounce at him, others following them, they stoned him in the garden. I saw him gather, ing himself up and begging for mercy.

Margaret King—I was in the house when the door was broken, and my uncle, Pat King, killed. The house filled in with Orangemen. One of them hit him on the head with a stone. Three of them then took him down to the low room. I got into a field. One of the Orangemen said—"D—n your soul for a Popish b——h," and knocked me down off the garden ditch with a stone. When I returned to the garden three of them had my uncle down and were stabbing him. I got into a byre and hid in some hay. Some of them came in and stabbed the cow in two places, broke the stake, and let her out. When I could do so with safety I went to my uncle, and got his head on my knee. He lived about ten minutes after that. The dragoons came up just as my uncle was dying. One of them said—"May be he'll come to again" They (the Orangemen) d——d my grandmother, who is an old bed-ridden woman the last year and a half, spat in her face, hit her on the head with a stone, cut her arms, and then smashed a chair on her forehead.

The result of this day's proceedings seems to have been that four Roman Catholics lost their lives, besides a considerable number wounded. And it is particularly to be noticed that only one of these lives was lost in the conflict on the hill. When armed parties are firing on each other bloodshed is the natural consequence; and some allowance may be claimed on account of the excitement of the actual struggle, and the absence of individual animosity. But even this can hardly be said of the little boy, Hugh King, for though shot in the field, he was deliberately singled out, The other three were cases of cold-blooded, delibe rate, wilful murder, where there was neither danger, provocation, nor resistance. John Sweeny, an idiot, was found on the road with his skull battered to pieces Patrick King was dragged out of his cabin, stabbed, and beaten to death. Ann Traynor, a woman seventy years of age, was cruelly beaten, and died soon after. Eight houses, one of them belonging to " Buck" Ward and a half a mile from the scene of conflict, were wrecked and burned , and a great many others, including the Roman Catholic curate's house, the chapel, and schoolhouse, were fired into and more or less injured That three women, one of them badly wounded, were not burned to death in their houses, was solely owing to the timely interference of the police.

So perfectly, in the short space of twelve months, did Lord Roden and Mr. Beers, by re-establishing Orange processions in the County of Down, reproduce the horrors of Maghery and Annahagh. But savage and brutal as was this scene, the events which followed are, to our minds, more deeply disgusting.

On the Monday following an inquest was held on the bodies by Mr. George Tyrrell, the coroner of the district, no novice in these inquisitions. In his charge he informed the jury that this armed procession of 2,000 men was a legal assembly. He admitted that some persons were of a different opinion, but " he believed that he carried with him the opinion of many of the magistrates who sat on the bench." He might, we humbly conceive, have been more positive on this point ; considering that Mr. F. C. Beers was sitting beside him, along with Captain Hill, Lord Roden's agent, and other magistrates who had accompanied the procession. He further instructed them " that the Government so far countenanced these processions that they sent an armed force to protect not only the processionists but to guard the peace of the country." The jury, we must presume, were satisfied with Mr. Tyrrell's exposition of the law and of the policy of the Government; because instead of returning a verdict of wilful murder against those persons known or unknown who had entered a cabin and beaten to death an offending man and an old woman, they simply found that the deceased had died from injuries inflicted by persons unknown in a party procession. The intrepid coroner went so far as to suggest a verdict of justifiable homicide! but this was rather too much ; but the jury confined themselves to the established precedent

Next day there was a magisterial inquiry. Captain Skinner, a magistrate and agent to the Marquis of Downshire, having asserted that " the people ought to be satisfied with justice as it is administered in Castlewellan Petty Sessions," it becomes interesting to observe how even-handed is the justice which an Orange magistrate, and one of the most upright of his class, thinks good enough for " the people," and to test the moral obligation on Roman Catholics to have entire confidence in the impartiality of Mr. Shaw (Lord Annesley's agent), Captain Teigh, Mr. Bill (Lord Roden's agent), and the two Messrs. Beers, who were present on this occasion. We are glad to learn that for firing upon the Orangemen and police twenty of the Ribbon party were committed for trial; but we were hardly prepared to find that for firing upon the Ribbonmen—even when running away in defiance of the orders of the stipendiary magistrate, Captain Fitzmaurice—for murdering three helpless, unoffending Catholics—for burning eight houses—for robbing, wrecking, and injuring a great many more, including a chapel and schoolhouse, all done in broad daylight, in the midst of hundreds of witnesses, in the presence of several magistrates who had actually seized some of the offenders in the act, and who had at their command seventy-five policemen, two troops of cavalry, and two companies of infantry—not a single Orangeman was arrested or molested in any way whatever !

At a subsequent period, when the Government thought it right to interfere, Mr. Ruthven, the Crown Solicitor, tendered informations against a number of Orangemen, and Mr. Berwick attended to advise the magistrates as to the law ; although if any doubt had existed on this point it could hardly have failed to have been dispelled by the discussions which had taken place, and the authoritative opinions which had been expressed in the House of Commons and elsewhere, as well as officially by the Irish Attorney-General. Mr. Keown, the brother of the High Sheriff, appeared, however, as counsel for the Orangemen. Five of the magistrates, under these circumstances, were willing to receive the informations; but the course of justice, which in other parts of Ireland is sometimes arrested by accomplices on the jury, was turned aside at the Castlewellan Petty Sessions by accomplices on the Bench. Lord Roden himself came to the rescue, accompanied, we grieve to say, by three clergymen—Mr Annesley, Mr. Forde, and Mr. Johnston

—who had not attended the previous investigation; and these gentlemen being, according to their own confession ignorant of the law, and preferring to be guided by their own ignorance rather than by the eminent advice at their command, outvoted the others, and refused to accept the informations!

It is painful to say that worse than even this remains behind. We should have thought that, although the madness of party might have led men into unjustifiable actions, and even into an open evasion of the law, yet that the ordinary feelings of gentlemen, and, we must add, of clergymen, might have in this instance occasioned some little compunction and have induced them to cast a veil over these excesses, and to give to the poor Roman Catholic peasantry some thin excuse for bearing with patience their unredressed wrongs. But the victory (for that is the word used by an Orange clergyman, Mr Drew) of Dolly's Brae would have lost half its charms, if any such feelings been allowed to temper the full-blown triumph of the Orange party

On the day week after the burning of Magheramayo, on the second day after the magisterial inquiry which taught the Ribbonmen the precise amount of protection to life and property afforded to them by the law as administered at the Castlewellan Petty Sessions, a grand Orange dinner was given to the hero of the day, the Grand Master of the County Down Orangemen, Mr. William Beers. No pains were spared to do him honour. The Seneschal of Downpatrick gave the use of the Manor Court House; a hundred guests sat down to dinner, Mr. Maxwell, of Finnebregue (another magistrate, by the way) hurried from a Church Education Society to join in the festivity; and the chair was filled by Mr. Keown, the High Sheriff of the county. No cloud seems to have dimmed the gaiety of the evening · no one cared to consider what at that moment was passing in the minds of the villagers of Magheramayo, mourning over their murdered relatives, the poor idiot, the inoffensive man, the young boy, the aged woman, and contemplating the blackened ruins of their cottages, and the ground strewed with the remnants of their little property wantonly destroyed. Or, if such thoughts occurred, they were soon dispersed by the music of "The Protestant Boys," and the triumphant cheering which greeted the "Glorious, pious, and immortal memory." Grace was said by the Rev. Mr. Breakey, who seems to have thought it better to rejoice with those that rejoice, than to weep with those that weep. The High Sheriff gave the toast of the evening, "William Beers, Esq;, our County Grand Master, with nine times nine, and the Kentish fire," and then this gentleman, thoroughly appreciating the taste of his hearers, and encouraged by their sympathy, delivered the following speech, which, remembering the time; place, and circumstances, we think absolutely unparalleled :—

"He thanked them for the high honour conferred upon them by their entertainment of that evening. If consistency to his principles were the cause of it, he did claim that he had been consistent to his principles as an Orangman; but he regretted that he had not done as much for the cause as his feelings had dictated. They had only lately celebrated the anniversary of the 12th of July, and such an anniversary as it would have been, only for the little blot, if blot he could call it. No; it was a treacherous attempt to betray innocent Protestants of the district; he had been well aware of the plots which had been got up against them, but knew that God was with them. There was nothing contemplated by their enemies but murder and treachery—only think of 1,000 men attacking 25. What would have saved them only they had God directing them, &c "

On this oration we cannot trust ourselves to say one single word. The audience, however, seem to have highly approved of it, for it was received, according to the Downpatrick Recorder with loud and continued cheering.

One more incident and we pass from this part of our subject. Where, as in Ireland, the spirit of party is so much stronger than the love of justice, complaints of packed juries are frequent; and however unreasonably, people think it important to have a Sheriff of their own way of thinking. It was therefore an encouraging fact that the Orange dinner was presided over by the High Sheriff; and the vice-chairman, Mr Ellis, Grand Master of the Newry Orangemen, took care to bring it prominently forward, saying that "they ought to be proud to see at their table the first officer of the county;"—a sentiment to which Mr. Keown, as "Chief Magistrate," promptly responded. But it may be doubted whether all this tends to create confidence in the pure administration of justice; and whether a Magheramayo man is to be blamed for distrusting a Sheriff who is brother-in-law of the County Grand Master, presides over an Orange dinner, and is one of those who hail with loud and continued cheers Mr. W. Beers' opinion, that, when committed by Orangemen against Roman Catholics, robbery, burglary, fire-raising, and murder, are only "a little blot, if blot *he could* call it."

Such is the history of this crime, the inaugurating sacrifice of the second reign of Orangeism. It stands not without a parallel. Our narrative has already furnished many a one, but for cold blooded vindictiveness, for deliberate and heartless bloodshed it is unsurpassed. An effort has been made to fix the blame upon anyone, save the real offenders. The blackest crime has seldom wanted an apology, and they have been loudest in their excuses who were the real criminals. It is even so with the Orangemen. It has been alleged that the procession was legal and, therefore, those who obstructed it provoked the contest.

But was the procession legal?

Did not the precautions taken by the Government demonstrate that there were reasonable apprehensions of a breach of the peace?

Has an armed multitude a right to assemble upon the Queen's highway to the terror of her Majesty's subjects?

Did not the the threat "that no power on earth could prevent the Orangemen going over Dolly's Brae," indicate an intention to commit a breach of the peace, and their selecting an unfrequented route clearly showed that they were willing to go out of their way to commit it?

Take it that the squib came from the repealers, and the evidence is in favour of the opposite assumption; did that squib justify a reply with loaded rifles, make the murder of an idiot boy and the bayoneting of a helpless woman heroic acts of self-defence, and the pillaging of humble cabins subjects for glory and congratulation?

Take it that the procession was legal, will we find in that legality a justification for the acts of one set on men, while the actual contest was being carried on by another set of men in another place?

And supposing that the poor idiot was a danger and a menace to that gang of stalwarth murderers, and that they were justified in putting an end to his miserable existence; that the old woman who ran into the byre went thither not for shelter but for some infernal machine which would have hurled destruction amongst the Orangemen, and that, therefore, her assailants were justified in murdering her; let us suppose even that Pat King, unarmed as he was, was so powerful as to be able to kill the three armed Orangemen, and that they had no other alternative but to stab him to death;

take, in fact, any view you like of it, and was not the whole transaction, at least, something to keep silent over?

Supposing it not to be a massacre, but a battle and a victory, can anyone point me out anything of glory in it, or is there a single Orangeman living who took part in that day's bloody work—and if there is his head is hoary, and he must shortly be summoned before his God—is there any one of them who will come forward in his sober moments and say he has not learned to blush for his share of the work, that he does not feel the brand of Cain upon his brow, that he will not shrink from before the Judgment Seat when the soul of that idiot boy or of that miserable woman comes forward as his accuser? And yet, for we live in a truculent time, it has inspired the pen of some village poet, and furnished a drinking song to the Orangemen of today; a song seldom heard in the lodge room save when fanaticism is at his height, when men's minds are debauched with drink and debased by the orations of skilful mountebanks, who hoodwink the ignorant and mislead the prejudiced to their certain advantage. The poet represents "William's sons in peaceful mood," as a matter of course, "homeward all returning," and to rhyme wit "mood" we are introduced to the "viperous brood" who "crept near with passions burning." He then takes the customary licence of the muse, and, contrary to truth, represents the peaceful heroes as having been fired on by "the fiendish Ribbon band the ground with brave blood staining." And next he describes the massacre in true heroics :—

Over the ditch, and up the hill,
Rush'd on the brave pursuers,
Who prov'd to all the world they still
Were takers le s than doers.
The foremost of their little band
Had stretched some of the foemen.
As they, with pike and scythe in hand,
Fled from the Orange yeomen.

* * * * * * *

Come now, applaud with heart and voice,
The heroes in this action;
And in *their* triumph we'll rejoice,
Who crush'd the rebel faction;
To God above all praise we'll give,
For shielding them in danger,
And for the truth we all will strive
'Gainst false friend, foe, or stranger.

And thus it runs through the entire gamut; without honour enough to avoid a crime—without feeling enough to be ashamed of it

CHAPTER XXXIV.—BOYCOTTED.

WE have seen sufficient to show that the administration of justice in the hands of the Orange magistracy was not pure. It could not be pure. We have seen enough to show that the Orangemen, still inspired by the dogged pugnacity of fanatics, were determined to carry on their annual carnivals in spite of the interference of the authorities, or of the more solemn enactments of the Legislature. To enter into the details of the partiality displayed before the bench by Orange partisans would be an endless labour. That a sign from the dock put a prisoner on good terms with the jury and procured his acquittal contrary to evidence, and that the Orange criminal in many cases, if not in most cases, found upon the bench an absolute partizan is best judged by the subsequent action of the Government, recollection being had to the fact that even a Whig Government never moved in the matter except under the strongest compulsion. The Procession Act, 13 Vic., passed in 1850, was based upon Mr. Stanley's Act of 1832, which has already been noticed. In introducing that Act Mr. Stanley had said that the reason why the Bill was directed against Orange Lodges was because the Orange party alone persevered in endeavouring to keep alive religious animosity, which had led to so many fatal consequences. The object of the Government, he said, was to declare by special enactment all such processions illegal, and he called upon the Orangemen, if they were the loyalists that they pretended to be to show it by their actions; to prove they "were not the blind and bigoted partisans of an expiring faction, which would be loyal just as far as it suited their own interests and their own convenience, and who would exert themselves to maintain the peace of the country just so long as that peace could be preserved by the Government placing implicit reliance in them and *in them alone.*"* We now find those words verified to the letter, and abroad over Ulster were scattered the seeds of dissension year after year until in the end it became evident justice under such auspices was a farce that peace an impossibility. We pass over seven years during which every effort was made by the landed proprietors of the North to keep alive that spirit of

faction in the certainty that they would be the first to thrive by it.*

In 1857 Lord Carlisle was Viceroy, and Maziere Brady Lord Chancellor. This Lord Chancellor deserves the honoured place of being the first who gratuitously administered a blow to the Orange faction. Entering upon its period of decline on the compulsory withdrawal from public notice, after the succession conspiracy, the Orange institution had fanned the agitation into a comparatively feeble flame, which flickered until Lord Chancellor Brady all but totally extinguished it. To drive its nominees out of all responsible offices was, at any rate, his aim, and this he, with considerable success, accomplished. The following are important documents touching upon this question which the Irish Orangemen of the present day would desire to see lost utterly in oblivion :—

"TO THE EDITOR OF THE NORTHERN WHIG.

SIR,—The enclosed extract from a letter I have received from the Lord Chancellor, which I have his lordship's permission to make public, is of sufficient moment to warrant my asking you to give it a place in your columns.—I am, sir, your obedient servant,

"LONDONDERRY, Lieutenant County Down.

"Newtownstewart, October, 6, 1857."

"In reference, generally, to appointments to the Commission of the Peace for the County of Down and some other counties in the North of Ireland, I feel obliged, by recent events, to introduce conditions which seem to me imperatively called for, with the view to the maintenance of public tranquility.

"Your lordship is, no doubt, well aware of the success of turbulence and riotous outrage which have so long prevailed in the town of Belfast. Whatever party may have been to blame for the acts which more immediately led to these disgraceful tumults, it is very manifest that they have sprung from party feeling, excited on the recurrence of certain anniversaries which

* See Hansard's debates, Vol. XIII., page 1035.

* Instances have occurred where the bailiffs upon particular estates in the North of Ireland spent their leisure hours at night-time in swearing in Ribbonmen, that they might at the proper time inform upon them, while bailiffs upon the same estates were engaged in stirring up Protestant bigotry against the deluded Ribbonmen.

for years have been made the occasion of irritating demonstrations, too often attended by violations of the public peace, and dangerous, and sometimes fatal, party conflicts. The Orange Society is mainly instrumental in keeping up this excitement; and, notwithstanding the proceedings respecting that association which are now matter of history, and, in consequence of which, it was supposed that it would have been finally dissolved, it still appears to remain an extensively organised body, with but some changes of system and rules, under which it is alleged to be secure from a legal prosecution. However that may be, it is manifest that the existence of this society and the conduct of many of those who belong to it tend to keep up through large districts of the North a spirit of bitter and factious hostility among large classes of her Majesty's subjects, and to provoke violent animosity and aggression. It is impossible rightly to regard any association such as this as one which ought to receive countenance from any in authority who are responsible for the preservation of the peace; and however some individuals of rank and station, who hold her Majesty's commission, may think they can reconcile the obligations of that office with the continuing in membership with the Orange Society, it does appear to me that the interest of the public peace, at least in the North of Ireland, now requires that no such encouragement should be given to this society by the appointment of any gentleman to the Commission who is or intends to become a member of it.

"Intending the rule to be of general application, I think it right to ask from every gentleman the assurance that he is not, nor will, while he owns the commission of the peace, become a member of the Orange Society. I think it right to inform your lordship that in expressing the foregoing opinions and determination, I do so with the entire concurrence of his Excellency the Lord Lieutenant."

Let me explain. The time in which the foregoing letter was written was one of great excitement in the North, a time teeming with events which ultimately placed Orangeism again on its trial with the result indicated. For the previous ten years every Twelfth of July had been attended with more or less of turbulence and outrage. On the 12th July of 1857, the Rev. Dr. Drew came upon the scene, and subsequently a clergyman who yet survives to reap the reward of his insolent and unchristian

bigotry—the Rev. Hugh Hanna, a Commissioner of National Education. Now all was changed. The turbulence of the previous years burst forth under their stimulating sermons into civil war, casual assaults now became open and deliberate massacre, and for the boyish freaks of window-breaking we find substituted pillage and wholesale conflagration. On the 12th July (Sunday) there was a service for the Orangemen of Belfast in Christ Church. As the report of the Commission of Inquiry subsequently pointed out, it was a place dangerously situated between two opposing districts—Sandy Row, the Orange quarter, on one side; the Falls, the Catholic locality, on the other. The Orangemen walked in military style, and though the great body of them abstained from further outward show a minority of them stopped in the open space opposite the church, formed in line, and donned their sashes previous to entering the "House of God." There was then no opposing mob, there being none present save the Orangemen and the constabulary. Inside the church all the brethren wore their scarfs. The Rev. Dr. Drew preached a sermon which in the quiet of his own study he had prepared. The text was taken from Matthew, chap. v., verses 13, 14, 15, and 16, which went to show that the brethren were "the salt of the earth" and "the light of the world," and which conjured them to "let their light so shine before men that they might see their works and glorify their Father, who was in Heaven." For rampant bigotry that sermon of the Rev. Dr. Drew probably stands unparalleled. It is equally remarkable for the falsification of history. This Christian minister having shown the "errors of the Church of Rome," and how the persecution of it was a work to glory in, said, "in the history of the maligned and indomitable Orange Institution, it will be found, when a great part of the aristocratic leaven was withdrawn from it, and by a majority, the leaders consented to its extinction, the *masses held together*; and again in time of treason and expected insurrection, the gentry once more flocked under the folds of the Orange banner. Then a Lord Lieutenant was glad to commit the Castle of Dublin to the special care of Orangemen, and to supply them with arms. * The

* This relates to the '48 movement, and to the arming of the Orangemen of Dublin, reference to which will be found in Madden's History. Lord Enniskillen wrote to the Master of Horse, Major Turner, for arms for the Irish Orangemen, and a sum of £50 was handed by Major Turner to Colonel Phayre (an Orangeman), who gave it to Lord Enniskillen. Arms were procured, and a difficulty arising as to how they could be brought into Dublin—a proclaimed district, Colonel Brown, the head of the police, ordered them in. The question as to who had contributed this sum was left in abeyance.

General of the North of Ireland, at the same time, gratefully accepted the proffered services of the Orangemen of Belfast, while Belfast, in its quietness, remained for days without even a sergeant's guard of soldiers And so, the Lord reigning, it is ever likely to be, Orangemen will by God's help hold together; at least, till laws are honestly and impartially administered, and till our lost ground is regained, and the Parliament is purified [of the Catholic representation of course] and the nation exalted in righteousness. Could we bear in mind the Scripturality and magnificence of Orange principles, the line towards all men which they enjoin, and the purity of life which they inculcate; could we be all that men of such a goodly profession ought to be, in sobriety, unity, and consistent lives, then we need never dispair. By such a confederation all society would be influenced and swayed. The principles of Protestant truth would then stand in victorious array against the detestable machinations of the Confessional, of Jesuitism, and of the Inquisition. The deadly night-shade would wither, and the emblematic flower of loyalty would flourish and gladden all hearts." And then with a violent outburst in which bigotry surpassed itself, having painted the dangers that threatened the land, he came to a close with the following significant quotation —

Hearts resolved, and hands prepared
The freedom of their land to guard.

It could not be otherwise than as it was, and the terrible conclusion must force itself home to all thinking men, that those who, by impartal judges such as the Government Commissioners, were held responsible for the subsequent riots, had actually laboured to produce them.

The night of the 12th was spent in fearful preparations for the morrow, and before the morning sun broke over Belfast, the town was precipitated into a riot, in which all property was transferred from its rightful owners into the hands of two opposing mobs, and in which the lives of all were at the mercy of contending factions. What does it matter now who fired the first shot? Did the murdered, as they lay between earth and—Heaven only knows what fate—did they ask who fired the first shot?—did the maimed, the houseless, and the ruined either ask or care who first struck the blow? The Orange party now came out fully armed into the public thoroughfares, and carried on a war of extermination which it is painful to chronicle. Each lodge had its arms, and every member came well prepared for

the struggle. It was a time in which the constabulary was not as efficient a force as in the present day, and with the cognisance of a partisan and exclusively Protestant magistracy (there was but one Catholic magistrate then upon the Belfast bench), the Orange party pursued their work of destruction unrestrained. Houses were wrecked, passengers in the street shot down with the calm deliberation exercised by sharpshooters. While the Riot Act was read in Sandy Row and the resident magistrate shot at, the paving stones of the Pound were heaped up ready for actual warfare. Patrick M'Giveny, a police constable, attached blame to the superior officers for their glaring partiality, while James M'Intyre, bewailing the inactivity of the police, exclaimed, "It was a shame to see such conduct in the streets of Belfast." In full view of the police houses were wrecked, and the furniture brought out into the street and burned before the doors. This was done in many instances where Catholics resident in Protestant districts did not quit their houses in compliance with the notice.

At this time the Catholic populat on were unarmed, disorganised, and unprepared—as was the duty of all citizens depending for protection upon the power and effectiveness of the Executive —without ostentation, while their neighbours like the braggart of Shakspeare were placing their rapiers upon the table and praying, "Heaven grant we may have no need of them" It was, therefore, resolved to form Catholic gun clubs by some of the most respectable inhabitants of the town, men whose voices were not for war, and the peaceful demeanour of whose lives indicate now as then that all they asked was to live on terms of amity with their neighbours of all religions. It should be marked that the meetings were of no hole-and-corner character. The Catholic residents openly met, charged the local government of the town with being permeated with partiality, and openly resolved to form gun clubs for their defence against Orange intolerance. The formation of these clubs, granting all the necessity claimed for them, had the effect of inflaming the minds of the Catholic population towards resenting the outrages committed upon them, and while it may have tended to massacre reduce upon one side, it at the same time helped to prolong the civil war. A "Protestant Defence Association' was the next and natural issue, and thus both sides stood face to face with each other when, fortunately, active steps were taken to suppress the disturbance. The local forces and constabulary, under the ominous control of such men as Captain William Verner, Captain Thomas Verner, Mr. Getty, and Mr. Thompson, were either unable or unwilling to quell the disturbance, but a great accession of military into the town restored peace, and put the conflict to an end.

It was during the progress of this conflict that a few Protestant and Presbyterian ministers thought it wise to carry out their objectionable proceeding of open-air preaching—not preaching in which the Word of God was inculcated, but in which the rev. lecturers stooped to the baseness of inflaming men's minds against the "abominations" of the Romish religion. The riots which followed are familiar to many men living at the present day, and all, whether of one religion or another, looking now at both cause and results, will agree in the one prevalent opinion that this open-air preaching was not calculated to inculcate peace and Christian charity in the minds of men, but to produce quite an opposite result. That they did produce opposite results is now apparent, and those reverend gentlemen who have lived to look back from a distance upon the work of their early days, must indeed have lived to little purpose, and have failed to acquire wisdom with their years, if they do not regard it with sorrow, and exclaim, *mea culpa, mea maxima culpa.*

But we have entered now upon debatable ground, and possibly it is better, even at the expense of a little consecutiveness in the narrative, if we should be guided by the report of the Commissioners, Mr. David Lynch, Q.C., and Mr. Hamilton Smythe, Q.C., who in September following held an inquiry, under the Commission of the Lord Lieutenant, into those riots. The report, which is an elaborate one, and in which disapproval of the Orange *regime* in Belfast during those days is implied rather than expressed, says :—"In practice it [the Orange Institution] is not as in the letter of its constitution. Lord Enniskillen knows nothing of secret signs and passwords, yet we refer to the evidence of George Stewart Hill and others to show *that they still exist* in the very classes of the society where they are most dangerous. Lord Enniskillen condemned in his evidence the practice of wearing orange scarfs in church ; yet openly and ostentatiously in Belfast these Orange emblems were worn in a parochial church during service. The milder and kindlier men belonging to the Orange confederacy would, no doubt, condemn the preaching of a sermon by a clergyman to a large congregation assembled for religious worship, containing denunciations of a large class of his fellow-men ; yet such a sermon was preached in Christ's Church last July, and afterwards published in the newspaper by Dr. Drew, who is himself a Grand Chaplin of the Orange Society. Lord Enniskillen, no doubt, condemns the violence and outward manifestations of insult to the Roman Catholics exhibited by the Sandy Row mob ; yet it is seen that they are directly the effects on vulgar minds of these celebrations that are kept alive and in offensive activity by the Orange Society. Security against Ribbonism and other secret societies can hardly be needed in Belfast, where the population of Protestants considerably outnumbers the Roman Catholics ; and it can hardly be necessary to imitate the vices of the Ribbon system in order to counteract it. The Orange system seems to us now to have no other practical result than as a means of keeping up the Orange festivals, and celebrating them, leading as they do to violence, outrage, religious animosities, hatred between classes, and too often bloodshed and loss of life. In the midst of conflict, of course, everything is perverted, and these remarks will, no doubt, be denounced by those who live and have their profit in scenes of confusion and riot that mark the conflict ; but the prudent and humane should remember (and the Belfast riots are evidence of the truth) that the war of class is of little moment, comparatively, to the higher orders, many of whom have in it the means of worldly honour and advancement ; but to the poorer and humbler orders it is different ; with them the war is a real one, personal suffering attends it with them, they are maimed in limb, and rendered houseless and homeless often by it ; on them falls the misery of what brings advancement to the more exalted."

The report then proceeds to detail the results of the open air preaching. How the Rev. Mr. (now Canon) M'Ilwine, who was in the habit of "distributing placards of his controversial discourses in language not unaturally considered offensive by the Roman Catholic people for whose sake they were stated to be delivered," published his advertisement during the time the riots were actually proceeding (though the Commissioners state that they had been written beforehand) and announced a series of open-air sermons ; how the Rev. Mr. M'Ilwaine, having ascertained from the magistrates the probable results of these proceedings with commendable good sense, retired from the field, and how the Rev. Hugh Hanna stepped defiantly into the deserted breach, reckless of all consequences, and with the certainty of conflict and bloodshed staring him in the face, called on the Island bludgeonmen to arm, warned them that their "blood-bought and cherished rights were being imperilled by the audacious and savage outrages of a Popish mob," and calmly *wrote*, in his address to the Orangemen of Belfast, "Where you assemble around, leave so much of the thoroughfare unoccupied that such as do not choose to listen may pass by *Call that clearance 'the Pope's Pad'*"

Now that we read those violent and shocking utterances we are only surprised that the results were not even more dreadful than they actually proved. It furnishes, too, a sad and dangerous, but a tempting example, an example which has in our time been faithfully copied by some, those weak-minded men who have a craving for office, emolument, and distinction without the ability or education to win them in honourable contest with their fellow-men. It is little to be wondered at that "the conflict of July was thus more dangerous than before renewed, and the pious and weak-minded of the Protestant inhabitants of Belfast were easily persuaded that the question at the issue was whether Protestant worship was to be put down by violence, while those of the Catholic inhabitants were as easily persuaded that the question now was whether Belfast was henceforth to be proclaimed as a Protestant town, in which Roman Catholics could barely find sufferance to live in a state of degradation;" that "the former class became, by this teaching, almost the supporters of the mobs of Sandy Row, and the latter of the mobs of Pound Street." We have the moral. It would be useless to go into particulars of the narrative. Many persons now living can recall that fearful reign of terror in Belfast. It is sufficient to quote Mr. Hanna's words—"Out of conflict our rights arose, and by conflict they ought to be maintained," to indicate what must have been the state of things with such a body, and with such a warlike fellower of Christ at their head. Pity it is, that those who are so fond of the open Bible should forget the oft repeated advice of their Divine Master, and ignore the inculcations towards peace and Christian charity which adorn every line of its teaching! The Commissioners threw all the blame upon Mr. Hanna, but for whom "matters might easily have passed off without further trouble," and in addition expressed regret that there was but one Catholic magistrate in Belfast

at the same time seeking, but with poor success, to throw a veil over the misdeeds and partiality of the large majority of those who then held the position of justices of peace.

We have seen in the foregoing that the Orange Institution was a subject of inquiry before the Commissioners. Messrs. Lynch and Smythe state that the evidence regarding its constitution was *forced* upon them, and that they, therefore, thought it better to receive it. Whether they had made out a clear case that they did not use signs and passwords may be seen from the report. At any rate, some of its leaders (Lord Enniskillen amongst the number) swore that signs and passwords were not in use. I may possibly be able to account for the great anxiety of the Orangemen to be heard upon this point. I have been assured by a respectable Catholic solicitor in Belfast, whose word I dare not doubt, and who in turn had the information from an Orangeman, that upon the night of the 25th September, 1857, a meeting of the Grand Orange Lodge of Ireland was convened in a public house (the name and number were given, and are now before me), and that then and there the Orange Institution of Ireland was dissolved, the Grand Master being in the chair. It was, my informant proceeds, reorganised in such a way that the Grand Master, Lord Enniskillen, might go into court the next morning and swear there were neither signs nor passwords in connection with the Institution. I do not vouch for the accuracy of the information. I know too well how readily the most exaggerated stories receive credence, and are spread abroad in times of public ferment, but these things bearing upon the matter, and likely to assist the reader, I do know—1st, that such conduct would not be inconsistent with the history of the Institution; 2nd, that Lord Enniskillen was examined on the 26th September, 1857, before the Belfast Commission of Inquiry, and 3rd, that he did deny all such associations such as signs and pass-words in connection with the Orange Institution *as then established*.

The Commissioners declared in their report that the riots of 1857 owed their origin to the insulting manifestations and outrages of the Orangemen on their principal anniversary on the one part and to the resistance of them on the other, of those whom they insulted and assailed, and to the formation of gun clubs by the Catholics in their defence. They recommended that the magistracy and constabulary should be remodelled and rendered independent, of Orange influence and politics

It was after the facts above stated had been ascertained and duly reported to the Lord Lieutenant, that Chancellor Brady issued the order already quoted

The Orange Institution was now for the second time engaging public attention. The leaders in the North, alive to the fate which threatened them, rose up in arms, and everywhere were held meet ngs denouncing the Papists, denouncing the Government, denouncing the Executive, holding out over the heads of the authorities the old but now disregarded threat of constitutional loyalty. Still the blow of the Lord Chancellor was regarded as a fatal one to Orangeism The institution had been of late used for electioneering purposes, and for the securing of favours by aid of the influence which connection with it lent, to persons who would otherwise have pursued to the end a life of honest and honourable obscurity. The honours gone, it was argued with truth that all the respectability would go with them. The *Times*. of October, 1857, declared the Chancellor's letter the death blow of the Irish Institution "Orangeism," it said, "should have expired in the midst of a storm, or on the field of battle—not in the long vacation when statesmen have gone to Scotland to shoot grouse; when all the world is touring in Switzerland, Germany, Norway, and hardly anybody is left at home; when even the news of its death will be a week old before it meets the eyes of the greater part of the legislators. Orangeism had, indeed, lingered so long in the last feeble stage that its death is now hardly felt as an event. It was like the old year at 11 p m. on the 31st December." It then went on to state that there would be a few wild Orangemen who would speak as in the days of George III, that there would always be men who when life was gone would assert that it was not dead It declared that the Institution was dead, indeed, and that had it lived it could only do mischief or go on doing nothing. The Grand Committee met shortly afterwards in Dublin and protested, as the *Times* indicated, that the Institution was not dead, and issued an address signed by Edward Waller, Chairman, commenting upon the situation Referring to their production in a subsequent article the *Times* says, " The Institution, it was expected would die hard. Gameness may be justly predicted to be the quality of an Orangeman. Pugnacity in the face of superior numbers, forms the very essence of his character. He is the descendant of

a victorious race; the propagator of a spreading language, the partizan of a proselitizing religion. His father and grandfather before him were accustomed to regard themselves as the real Church militant, as the salt of the earth, as the few who, in the midst of idolators would not bow the knee to Baal. The present representatives of those who slammed the gates of Derry and charged across the Boyne have not achieved any deeds of heroism. But they are ardent admirers of former prowess If they had only been their own ancestors what great things they would have done for King William or the Hanoverian Georges! . . . If Orangeism is to be abolished, at any rate let it be with something like a spir.t that bites and kicks to the last." The writer then proceeds to ridicule the claim of the Orangemen for all the prosperity of the North of Ireland, says "that the best proof that its time was come was to be found in the Grand Committee denying that they kept alive party animosity," and concluded with the salutary warning that the time had come when " they should undertake to govern Ireland without Orangeism The Protestant as well as the Catholic must be content with the laws of the country. The Orange Society will do well to dissolve itself again, after the precedent of twenty years since, and if, after another decade, public opinion calls for the step, it may again open its lodges and martial its processions.",

But from the *Daily Express*, of Dublin, came the unkindest cut of all. Its connection with the party and with its politics, and the relations existing between its proprietor and the two most eminent men of the Orange party whose politics were advocated in that paper, made its expressions the more remarkable, and gave corroboration to the oft-repeated opinion that some of the ablest leaders of the Institution heartily wished its dissolution. But it goes further, for, condemning the institution as *a secret one*, connected by secret signs and passwords, it suggests a strange inconsistence between the facts and the statement in evidence of Lord Enniskillen The *Express* said "that the institution was identical in essence and form with that which was condemned by a Parliamentary Committee (in 1835) and by the Crown. It is a secret political society, excluding persons of a different faith and acting by associated branches." In a subsequent article the *Express* counsels dissolution as being unfit for an age like the this, and argues upon the religious aspect, that Church of God being divinely ordained for the cultivation of Christian worship, if the Church did not accomplish its object it should be reformed, but that it was blasphemy to say that the Orange Institution, being a human one, could do it. It then asks this pregnant question, " By what right does the Orange Society *impose an oath* to bind the consciences of Christian men ?" The writer in the *Express* must be presumed to have known the workings of an institution with which very probably he was connected, and his opinion upon the existence of an oath must be taken as one of weight. Declaring that the religious object had not been fulfilled, he proceeds to say that equally untenable is the Orange Society as a political institution. Its object, they were told, was to "uphold" the Constitution. He then details how the Constitution should be upheld, and says, " this is the way the Constitution is to be upheld, *not* by arming ourselves, by meeting in secret societies, and by combining against another class of our fellow-subjects. This is the first step to anarchy. It tends directly to the disruption and dissolution of society. It is a libel on the British Constitution to say that it requires to be aided by a perpetual "Vigilance Committee like the Orange Society. . . . The Orange Institution *is* a secret one unknown to the law, antagonistic in principle to the larger portion of the people, and an anomaly which it is utterly impossible to defend. There is one thing connected with Orangeism which we hold to be utterly unworthy of a free country nurtured by Protestantism and the British Constitution, and that is *its secrecy*. What should Protestants have anything to say to one another which they must whisper in private lodges as if they dwelt in a land cursed by despotism and espionage, dogged by *gens d'armes?* Why should honourable high-spirited gentlemen and brave hearted yeomen stoop to the self-imposed necessity of communicating with one another *by secret signs and passwords ?*" *Et tu Brute!* In the death struggle of respectable Orangeism came the blow, from a f iend, which finished its existence.

In this condition, with all the respectability and intelligence of the Three Kingdoms crying them down, and with former friends disowning them, a small clique of gentlemen termed the Grand Lodge, who had not yet derived all the benefits they had hoped for, met in Dublin and resolved to carry their complaint by petition to the head of the Government.

The advocates of Orangeism, on the 18th of February, 1858, waited on Lord Palmerston for the purpose of presenting a memorial protesting

against the [then] recent letter of Lord Chancellor 'Brady.

A report of " the deputation of Conservative members of Parliament and gentlemen, representing the Orange Associations of the North of Ireland," consisting of the Earl of Enniskillen, the Earl of Belmore, Lord Claude Hamilton, M P , Mr Vance, M P ; the Hon. H. Corry, M.P.; Mr G. A. Hamilton, M.P ; Mr. Richardson, M P , Mr. Miller, M P , Mr. Davison, M.P , Mr. Archdall, M.P., Mr. Cairns, M.P ; Mr. Whiteside, M P , &c , appeared in the London morning papers of the 19th of February.

Mr (now Lord) Cairns introduced the deputation to the Premier, and explained to him the purport of the memorial, signed by 2,700 persons, including 32 peers, 38 members of Parliament, 17 baronets, 641 Justices of the Peace, 162 deputy lieutenants, 377 clergymen, 40 barristers, 100 members of the medical profession

Lord Palmerston, in reply to Mr. Cairns' lengthy address in reprobation of Chancellor Brady for the insult offered to the Orange Institution, said—I am clearly of opinion that it would be far better for us to look to the future than to the past ; and what, let me ask, is the object, and what are the prospective advantages of this Orange association? Is it an organisation which belongs to the age in which we live ? Is it not rather one that is suited to the middle ages—(a laugh)— those periods of society when anarchy prevailed, and when one body of people were in the habit of arming themselves to resist some outrage or violence committed by another—and this because they felt that they could not depend upon the Government of the country for adequate protection or security. But this state of things no longer exists, and not being an Orangeman myself, I confess I am at a loss to understand the use of the association in the present age. (A laugh.)

The Earl of Enniskillen — Self-defence, my lord.

Lord Palmerston—Self-defence against what ? (A laugh.) I must really say that I think it is offensive as regards the Government and institutions of the country, to say that the general government of the nation is not adequate to protect individuals from violence.

The Earl of Enniskillen—It is too true, my lord.

Lord Palmerston—Well, I have no intention to say anything offensive to the Orange association ; but I must be allowed to say, that the very foundation on which it rests casts a reflection on the institutions of the empire; and coupled as it is with old recollections of periods when the action of the Government and the authority of the state were less efficient than they are now to protect life and property, I really do submit to the impartial consideration of gentlemen belonging to that association, whether it would not be more in accordance with that spirit of conciliation which I am sure animates every gentleman connected with Ireland—(a laugh)—to dissolve the association, and to put an end to an organisation which cannot answer any practical purpose; to rely for defence upon the action of the executive government, administered by persons responsible to parliament. Should the laws prove defective or inadequate, it were easy to appeal to the legislature for their emendation. I do think that the protection of individuals should be left to the law of the land, and that the formation of private associations for the purpose of supplying defects in the law is not a system suitable to the spirit of the times in which we live. If those who now belong to the Orange association would, upon full consideration, and as a gracious act of national conciliation, resolve that this bond of union is no longer necessary, I am sure that there is nothing that they could do which would more materially contribute to the peace of Ireland and to the obliteration of ancient prejudices. The dissolution of the association would not, I am persuaded, be viewed as an admission of the illegality of the association, but it would be taken as a gracious tender on the part of its members towards effacing former animosities; and I do believe that it would be an important step in the direction of a general union of feeling among both parties, and that by this means it would be of essential advantage to the country at large. In stating this much, I am only submitting my own private views, and as far as my sentiments go. I can but repeat, that nothing could be more desirable for the real interests of Ireland than the complete abandonment of the association.

Mr. WHITESIDE said he was not an Orangeman, but that he would cut off his right hand before he would subscribe to the Brady declaration. He begged the noble lord to reconsider the subject, and withdraw the objectionable letter.

Lord PALMERSTON said that the memorial should have the consideration of the government; but that the deputation coul not expect him to make any further promise.

In a debate in the House of Lords, 15th March, 1858, on the Orange society and the magistracy of Ireland, with respect to the letter of Chancellor Brady, the Earl of Derby said:—This was one of the subjects which had engaged the attention of his noble friend the Lord Lieutenant of Ireland a short time before he left this country, than whom there was no man who would wish to hold the balance more evenly between parties in Ireland. The Earl of Eglinton was no more connected with the Orange society than he was himself; and looking at the entire subject he was of opinion that no matter what may have been the advantages of that society formerly, upon the whole the organisation of the Orange association was rather a misery than a benefit to Ireland. They were, however, of opinion that the letter of the late Lord Chancellor, which laid down an absolute disqualification, was a step beyond what the law required, and although the society was one whose existence they regretted, he thought that the members of it should not be subject to any disqualification.

Three months later, we find Earl Derby, in a discussion on the Belfast riots and the Orange lodges, in the House of Lords, 7th of June, 1858, deploring the disgrace of the minor civil war which had been lately carried on in Belfast, "to the discredit of the inhabitants and the local authorities of one of the largest, the wealthiest, and most commercial towns in Ireland."

Commenting upon this, Mr. Madden says Lord Derby (in referring to the local authorities) evidently alluded to the magistrates in the first place; and of these magistrates of Belfast, Lord Derby must have known there was only one Roman Catholic amongst them; and he must also have known a considerable number of them were Orangemen, and yet his lordship would not disqualify one of that body for the office of magistrate on that account. How is this inconsistency to be explained? Lord Derby repudiates the Orangemen as much as Lord Palmerston, but the interests of party are more potent than the interests of peace and the interests of the Empire, and Lord Derby's party think they cannot dispense with the electioneering services of Orangemen, nor could Lord Derby's administration afford to lose the votes of the Orangemen in Parliament. This is a very lamentable and a pitiable fact—it is what the French call a misère.

The Government was made aware by the report of the Commissioners of 1857 that a most objectionable practice largely prevailed in the Orange Institution in reference to the exclusion of members

The reports of the Grand Lodge meeting in the November of this year showed that a large number of members were expelled for various offences, such as " for marrying a Papist; for voting at an election against a dignitary of the institution;" and, again, " for practice unbecoming an Orangeman ;" an undefined offence, which might mean anything from refusal to join in a riot to the extending by a magistrate of even-handed justice to Catholics and Protestants alike. The records of the fourth day of this meeting in Grand Lodge (the 6th November, 1857, Edward Waller, J.P., D.G.M., in the chair) are made more than ordinarily interesting by a list of some fifty members of the County Derry, all of whom " were expelled for voting against their Grand Master—Sir H. H. Bruce, Bart., at the late Parliamentary election;" while some fifty others in the same county were suspended for seven years " for using their influence against their Grand Master at the election." The reports of this period disclose the most appalling information of the intimidation and evil influence exercised by the leaders of the Institution. So constant was the fluctuation of party power it is not surprising to find that Chancellor Brady's letter was partially ineffective. For this, however, the Government of the day, though wholly responsible, were not solely at fault. The Orangemen had been too long accustomed to the various tricks by which office is attainable to find in this edict any insurmountable difficulty. Of this the best proof is forthcoming in the appointment of Mr. Cecil Moore, Deputy Grand Master of the Orangemen of Tyrone, to the position of Crown Prosecutor for the county in 1858. The appointment had been brought under the attention of Parliament by Mr. Fitzgerald, the late Attorney-General, and by the advice of Mr. Whiteside, Mr. Moore was induced to resign his position in the Orange Association before the matter came under the notice of the House. It is easy to divest oneself of those borrowed dignities which the Orange Institution so lavishly scatter amongst its favourites. Not quite so easy, however, is it to divest oneself of the prejudices which such associations inevitably produce. The appointment, therefore, if objectionable before, had now lost none of its objectionable features—some would be inclined to think they had been augmented.

The stigma, however, was there, and could not be removed. Orangemen could be made public officials, and by back-stair influence might obtain pay and pension, but once in office they had now to kick from under them the ladder by which they had ascended, and to disown those—their associates —whom they had so skilfully befooled. The end attained, the means were soon learned to be despised, and this in turn brought about another and an important change in the history of the Institution. Becoming too disreputable to permit an Administration with the slightest respect for good order or decorum to make it an instrument of Government preferment, a number of needy gentlemen, eager for notoriety as the next best thing to popularity, seized hold of this disused weapon of an ascendancy faction, and, furbishing it, they applied it to their own individual advancement. Such men had to select either to be known as Orangemen or not to be known at all. Their choice was not unnaturally in favour of the former, and how they utilised their position over their brethren we have seen in the expulsions of 1858. If they did not derive immediate benefit, and that was seldom the case, there was always a reward in the patronage of noblemen, to whom, as henchmen, they were useful. Fearful of the advancing wave of democracy which came threateningly on a few of the nobility, who saw no other means of preserving the feudal dominion of their families in Ulster lent it previous to general elections, a sort of left-handed support. By this means these lords and lordlings secured seats in Parliament which would otherwise have been beyond their reach. Perpetuating the old Tory regime of landlordism, they made a few counties in Ulster their strongholds, out of which they looked grimly down upon the rising tide of intelligence and liberal'ty beneath. It is needless to say that, stimulated by these men, the Orange brethren determined to die game. From 1857 to 1860, scenes of riot and bloodshed on a more or less moderate scale ensued. In Derrymacash, Lurgan, on the 12th July, in the latter year they met to hold "a musical festival" in order to avoid the penalties of the Procession Act. The instruments were exclusively made up of drums and fifes. It might have been a matter of accident, but the tunes played at this " Orange musical festival" by the perambulating orchestra of Derrymacash and Lurgan did happen to be party tunes. A few Catholics jeered at them. The Orangemen loaded and fired into the crowd, wrecked the chapel, and left not less than fourteen persons either dead or wounded upon the highway. Mr. Cogan, member for Kildare, on the 20th July called attention in the Commons to this scene in an able and manly speech, and proposed the introduction of a Bill to restrain the use of Orange emblems. This was abandoned on Mr. Cardwell's undertaking, on the part of the Government, that a sufficient measure would be introduced by him. Accordingly, the 23 and 24 Victoria, c. 141, "An Act to Amend an Act (13 Vic., c. 2) to Restrain Party Processions in Ireland" was introduced, and became law on the 20th August, 1860, to remain in force for five years. This Act had chiefly for its object to restrain the use of party emblems. No sooner was it passed than the Orange societies manifested their feelings of loyalty to the throne of Orangedom in a manner not likely to leave a very pleasing impression upon their Sovereign. They outraged all—the Sovereign, the Parliament, the judges of the land, even the dignitaries of the Established Church, with the utmost audacity. Before the Parliamentary Emblems Bill had been a month the law of the land an address was issued to the Orangemen by "A Member of Gwynne's True Blues, No. 728," bombastically calling upon them to arm, and to tell their Sovereign—" Hear, O Queen of yet mighty England! hear, O Monarch of a Protestant and much honoured line! Behold the increasing concessions made to Popery by successive Parliaments, and know that these must end in woe to a Protestant nation;" and exhorting the brethren to "stand ready, if it must come to that, to march to the banks of the ever-memorable Boyne, and there plant the standard of Orange once more, and repeat the deed of our conquering fathers."

While this Orange twaddle was being written by some unknown scribe, the *Downshire Protestant* was boldly throwing off the mask. That newspaper threatened the Government that before they would permit any attempt to interfere with the Orangemen they would crush the English rule in Ireland, and added, "Before the Orangemen of Ireland will submit to be hunted down by Popish law officers, only for being Orangemen, and before the public worship of God on the 12th of July, shall be allowed to be made penal, the persecutors of the loyal Protestants of Ireland must be taught a lesson, and freedom and truth be protected and guarded by 100,000 Orangemen in arms"[*] One would be inclined to laugh at such blustering, conditional loyalty but for the sad results which it has left behind. One of the most painful and disastrous proofs of the evil influence of Orangeism and of the incendiary writings of its infuriated fanatics is to be found in Belfast but a few years later. Unfortunately it has so well earned for itself discreditable distinction that it may well claim the prominence of a separate chapter.

[*] But other and more important individuals were not averse to the appeal to arms. There are in the British museum two octavo volumes, originally from the library of Dr. Drew, and amongst many other matters relating to the Institution, these volumes contain letters of Lord Enniskillen counselling the Orangemen to arm.

CHAPTER XXXV.—'64.

The fearful riots of 1864 in Belfast will live long in the recollection of its inhabitants and of the country at large. Many of the citizens will never recall it but with pain; for through the shades of the past will come back to the wife, the familiar face of the husband who is gone, to the mother, the sweet and laughing countenance of the child, offered an innocent sacrifice to the demon of religious fanaticism; the houseless, the homeless, the ruined in health, in fortune, and in character cannot recollect without regret the events of this sad year. And that large number of respectable and sensible men who have survived the disgraceful struggle in which they had taken more than a passive part, must now look back with shame upon their share of the work, and with thankfulness that they have lived into times of, let us hope, greater toleration. If we are not all that we should be, at last that day is past, when difference in religion justifies a man in cutting the throat of his neighbour.

On the forenoon of Monday, August the 8th, Belfast seems to have been in the absolute enjoyment of entire tranquillity, nor was there any apprehension on the part of the authorities that disturbance was meditated by any part of the population. Others may have had a faint suspicion of it, for it was known so early as eleven o'clock in the morning that the Orangemen of Sandy Row intended to burn an effigy of O'Connell. Why they selected that particular day for offering the insult to their Catholic fellow citizens is explained by the fact that a site for a statue to the Liberator was, in Sackville Street, Dublin, opposite that bridge now known as O'Connell Bridge, upon the same day inaugurated. Such a testimony of veneration to the dead the Orangemen of Belfast could not regard with calmness And so, in the secrecy of the lodgeroom of Sandy Row they resolved—after the regular business was over, let us hope—that Dan O'Connell's effigy should be burned upon the Boyne Bridge, so called by the spirit of faction because of its position between the Orange and Catholic districts—burned on the evening of the day upon which a site for a statue was dedicated to him in he metropolis. It may seem strange that this intention only became known to the authorities late in the evening. The mysterious lodgeroom explains it. That the intention was known to most of the local police, some of whom were likely present in lodge when it was debated, is now beyond question. It was about five o'clock p.m. when Head-Constable M'Kittrick, of the local police, first received a report from Inspectors Duff and Robinson, also of the local force, of this intention to burn the effigy As soon as he received the report, he immediately proceeded to Head-Constable Rankin, then in charge of Albert Crescent Constabulary Barracks, adjacent to the district in which the burning was to take place, and requested him to turn out as many men as possible. The Mayor, Mr. Lytle, who resided in Bangor, had by this time gone home, and Rankin undertook to communicate with the only resident magistrate in town, Mr Orme, who resided within a short distance. It was near six o'clock when Rankin was spoken to, and he experienced considerable delay in getting his men together, owing to its being Assize time. It was consequently n ar eight o'clock in the evening when he reached the Boyne Bridge, having then with him thirty-two of the constabulary and twelve of the local force, under M'Kittrick. In the meantime he had sent for Mr. Orme, who at once attended. The brethren had stolen a march upon them When they arrived upon the scene about 4,000 of the low Orangemen of the district were assembled together upon the bridge, burning the effigy and dancing with fiendish glee around the flames, while others were beating "The Protestant Boys," "We'll kick the Pope before us," and such inoffensive tunes upon the drum of the Sandy Row Orange Lodge. Mr. David Taylor, J P., was, with the police, in at the death, but they confined their efforts to "inducing the people to desist and go home," an effort in which they seem not to have been at all successful. Mr. Orme, R M , arrived when "it was all over," as he himself stated. But Mr Orme was mistaken It was not all over. The effigy having been burned,

a determined effort was now made to pass the bridge and get into the Roman Catholic quarter. This the police opposed. In their opposition they are represented as having been successful, that the Orange mob ultimately dispersed, and that the remainder of the night was spent in quietness. This demonstration, and the occasion and. the object must also be recollected, was made in a prominent position within a stone throw of the Catholic quarter of the town. To the credit of the residents there, it is established upon authority* that they did not openly exhibit any resentment, or by any outward act manifest their displeasure On the evening of the 9th, however, another very extraordinary and far more objectionable scene took place, in which the Orangemen of the previous evening were the chief actors. A vast crowd, numbering about 2,000 persons, assembled on this evening in Sandy Row, for the purpose of "burying Dan O'Connell," whom " they had hanged and burned the night before." They formed into procession, were armed with staves, carried with them at the head of the procession an ordinary coffin, black in colour, *with a conspicuous cross on top;* with drums and fifes playing party tunes, and they themselves indulging in party cries and imp ecations, too long familiar to, and too well understood by the Catholics of Belfast, they proceeded to Friar's Bush Roman Catholic Burying Ground, situate about a mile distant The burial ground is walled in, and the gate was locked. Having arrived at the gate they called out to the sexton, offensively bidding him "open the gate till we bury O'Connell," and at the same time "using some of the familiar party cries of the locality." The sexton and his son, who were licensed to carry arms, were not to be intimidated, and the appearance of a gun at the gate-lodge window sent these sacrilegious ruffians scampering round the most convenient corner. Baulked in their original intention, they now, from a safe point of attack, wrecked the sexton's house, and otherwise indulged their fiendish propensities by actually throwing stones at the crosses adjacent. They then retraced their steps to Sandy Row to seek for some better opportunity of indulging their malignant desires. A small party of constabulary, a constable, and six men had been posted upon the Boyne Bridge to "intercept" the progress of the Orangemen, it being feared that they would at once proceed towards the Pound or Catholic district. The absurdity of

* See report of '64 Commission, page 9.

placing such a mere handful of men to intercept irresponsible ruffians, whose acts during the previous two days plainly showed they were intently and irresistibly bent upon riot, must be apparent to all. At any rate, the six policemen were not able to intercept them, and wanting only an excuse to justify their opposition, the Orange party found a ready one, by alleging that Christ's Church was being attacked. The rioters proceeded towards the Pound, where they wrecked some houses, but a strong force of constabulary coming up under command of Head-Constable Rankin, they were driven back through Durham Street towards the Boyne Bridge and Sandy Row. No arrests were up to this time made, the smallness of the force being alleged as an excuse. The magistrates were not aware of this second attack of the Orange party, but when it became known to them, and acting on the belief that it would be renewed, Mr. Orme and the Mayor determined upon obtaining a reinforcement of constabulary. Sub-Inspector Garraway, upon their requisition, undertook to have and did actually have 150 additional men in Belfast on the following evening. The riotous proceedings of the 8th subsided, as we have seen, into quiet. The attack upon the Catholic quarter was again made on the evening of the 9th. . Quiet again followed, but it was no more an assurance than that of the previous evening that the 10th would not bring another and still fiercer attack upon the inhabitants of the Pound district. All that evening was occupied in the Pound in preparations for defence. That the police force were unable to protect them had been, in fact, acknowledged, nor had the reinforcements yet arrived. Stones were heaped up in the centre of the streets, and every evidence shown that the residents were preparing for a state of actual siege. Nor were they mistaken. In Sandy Row at the very same time similar preparations for attack were being made. The lodge swords were being brought down and committed to the charge of the most distinguished members, rusty old guns were brought out from their hiding place, staves, and clubs—a fearful style of weapons peculiarly the arms of the Belfast Orange mobs—were distributed about with the magnanimity of brothers in arms. At eight o'clock the entire force was mustered in Sandy Row. The signal was given, and a raid of a most terrific character was made into Durham Street. It once past this they were in the middle of the Catholic quarter, where small streets were numerous, and the possibility of dislodging them by a combined

attack more remote. The Pound party met the Sandy Row mob near the end of Durham Street, and here a fearful encounter took place The air was thick with missiles thrown by those in the rear of each faction, while the men in the front rank were engaged in an actual hand to hand combat; the Orange party seeking to advance, the Catholic party to retard them. While they were actually contending Mr. Orme, R M., with all the available force of constabulary, appeared upon the scene. So violent was the struggle that the Riot Act was read, and with difficulty the rioters were ultimately separated into their own districts, each party removing their wounded beyond the reach of observation. While engaged in quelling this riot news reached Mr. Orme, R.M., that the windows of the Methodist chapel on the Falls Road had been broken. Leaving a small force in Durham Street to guard the pass, he proceeded thither, and found that the windows had been broken. Mr. Orme's vigilance was now summoned into activity. Two attacks had been made upon the Catholic quarter, and no arrests were made. The sexton's house had been wrecked, and no arrests made. Houses belonging to Catholics in Durham Street had been wrecked, and no arrests made, but the breaking of the windows of a Methodist chapel—no doubt a-wanten and malicious act—could not be tolerated with impunity. He pursued the Catholic party, now for the first time a Catholic mob, into Milford Street, and five persons were arrested and lodged in the Police Office. These were the first arrests made during the three days' tumult through which we have already passed. The fact of their being so in no way tended to allay the excitement in the Pound quarters, or restore confidence with the Catholics in the police force and the magistracy, the want of which, if not altogether reasonable, was pardonable under the circumstances No further disturbance took place during that night. The Orange party retired to glory in their triumph, and the Catholics to brood in silence over their defeat and the capture of their friends. The long expected reinforcement soon arrived, and there were now in Belfast 210 constabulary, making, together with the local force, about 370 in all for police purposes upon Thursday morning At five p.m. on the 11th the constabulary assembled for duty. All was then tranquil. At seven o'clock the same evening Mr. Lytle, the Mayor and Chief Magistrate of Belfast left for Harrogate to breathe the sea air, an unfortunate preference which had he recollected the proceedings of the previous evenings and wisely construed the ominous quiet which preceded each tumult, he ought not have indulged. Within an hour after the Mayor sailed from Belfast, and almost before he was well outside the lough the town, of which he had taken charge, was again a scene of riot and disorder. Rioting of a serious character took place in Durham Street, where the opposing mobs again came into collision upon the same scene and under exactly similar circumstances as on the previous night.

Work done, opposing parties, full of the excitement of the hour, met at the street corners of their respective localities to discuss the contest of the preceding days. Discussion gave rise to interest interest created excitement; excitement was followed by a desire for a renewal of the conflict upon one side; a desire for retaliation upon the other. Rioting of a serious character again took place. Expecting the customary evening raid upon the Catholic quarter, a number of the Pound party had assembled to guard the "gap" in Durham Street, when an attempt was made to dislodge them by the Sandy Row party. The conflict now assumed a still more serious character than before, and it became with both sides a question of strength as to who would carry the trophy off the field. The shooting was incessant, and, for the first time, the houses in the respective localities were utilized as convenient points of attack. After not less than half-an-hour's free fighting, Mr. Orme and Head-Constable Rankin, with a party of the Constabulary and some local police, interferred. Before we proceed further it must be recollected that the old locals were, of all others, the most objectionable parties who could have interfered as peace preservers. They were, with few exceptions, Orangemen—practically they were an exclusively Protestant corps—with sympathies and prejudices antagonistic to the Catholic population, who had suffered grievously at their hands. The appearance of the "old locals" upon the scene was not calculated to allay excitement. In their presence the riot continued, the residents of the Pound occasionally dividing their attention between the Orangemen and the "locals," while the inhabitants of Sandy Row distributed their favours liberally between the Catholics and the constabulary. Several prisoners were made, who were lodged in the Police Office by the Resident Magistrate. On his return to Durham Street he was again attacked, and was compelled to charge his assailants, driving them to the Boyne

Bridge, where he made twelve prisoners. This assault was so threatening that some of the constabulary who had charge of the prisoners had to take refuge in an adjacent house, which was besieged and wrecked, the constabulary escaping with their prisoners by a back entrance. Then, as now, the Irish constabulary was not in favour with the Orangemen. Out into the open street the brethren came, deliberately knelt, and picked down their men. This species of warfare lasted up to midnight and past it, and at one o'clock on Friday morning, the 12th, the constabulary returned to their quarters, and Mr. Orme to his residence.

The authorities imagined they were dealing with a case of riot of, perhaps, something more than the ordinary character. In this they were mistaken. It is difficult to impress upon the mind of a reader the state of excitement upon that morning of the 12th. The reign of civil war had now absolutely and actually set in in that portion of the town to which the rioting was still confined. Civil authority was upon one side set aside as an unnecessary incumbrance, upon the other, as a broken reed, and each party becoming emboldened by the absolute helplessness of the police force, they now came out boldly into the highway to fight the matter out to the death. It has been the custom of late to regard the riots of '64 as excesses consequent upon the mere casual and momentary excitement of a town mob. The conclusion, though a highly natural one, is erroneous. From the morning of that 12th of August, 1864, to the amnesty which brought the fighting to a close, military manœuvring of a very efficient and fearfully suggestive kind was shown, such as might have rivalled the dreadful science of the boulevards and put to shame the desultory fighting over the street ramparts of Paris. It is impossible to say who commenced this bloody night's work. No doubt, each party will say they expected attack from their opponents. But, begin it who may, at half-past one o'clock upon that eventful morning, word was sent round in both the Sandy Row and the Pound districts that every man was wanting at his post. Out of their beds they jumped, some whole dressed (for not a few expected the summons, and were prepared for it), some half dressed, and many scarcely dressed at all, and from the safety of the blankets they betook themselves to the streets to join in the contest. Looking at it now, we judge it a sacrifice; but then, amid excitement the most intense, with shouts of defiance, and the whizzing of bullets breaking upon the ear, men—Orangemen and Catholic alike, with a wife, a family, or a sweetheart, must have felt that hasty knock at their doors after the hour of midnight, as a fearful summons to duty. I have talked with men, of this party and of that, and thus it was they regarded it. A fearful dread seems to have reigned over the inhabitants of the Pound that some night, not far distant, they would be attacked and murdered or burned in their beds. The reasonableness of the conclusion let each man judge for himself. By two o'clock in the morning both parties were again face to face with each other upon the old battle ground. Firing recommenced and for the first time during the warfare, there seemed an absolute desire for extermination. In the middle of the struggle Mr. Orme and the constabulary, under the charge of Head-Constable Lamb arrived. While they were endeavouring to quell the riot in Durham Street, small contingents were engaged in trials of strength in the adjoining streets, so that their efforts were wholly ineffectual. The locality was in the hands of the two mobs, and they kept it with a perversity which showed that both parties now entirely disclaimed foreign aid. It is customary to regard street mobs as unruly and reckless, and it may be true, as a rule. But here, with, no doubt, the feeling of self-preservation still strong within, we find the utmost caution in both attack and defence. Having thus fought it out for two hours, each party withdrew to its respective quarter, and the constabulary were left occupying a somewhat ignoble position upon the neutral ground in Durham Street, with a few persons as their prisoners of war. The truce was a significant one.

At half-past five o'clock on the morning of the 12th, workers—naturally those who had nothing to do with the morning's fighting, for rioters would be little disposed to work—proceeded to the mills and factories as usual. With the exception of in one place of business, the great majority of the Catholics had to pass to work through Orange quarters, and on their way both males and females were rudely set upon and assaulted. It appears from the report of the Commission that this course of conduct was pursued by one party as well as the other, but from the peculiarity of the circumstances, the Catholic workers, being the minority, and surrounded as they were by the vast milling population in which Orangeism prevailed, were the greater sufferers.

In the mills and warehouses of Belfast the Pro-testants were, without exception, in the ascendant. Those Catholics who wanted to work, and cared not for rioting, would now not get leave to work. The ferment had spread into the business houses and localities, and the few who did succeed in gaining their respective workshops were either rudely thrust out or found the doors closed against them. Civil war was upon that morning openly proclaimed, and the inhabitants of the Pound saw nothing before them now but fighting it out to the bloody end. And fight it they did. "Houses," says the Commissioners, Messrs. Barry and Dowse, in their report regarding this particular period of the contest, "houses of both Protestants and Roman Catholics in several parts of the town were wrecked. Riot had, in fact, become rampant, and authority appeared to be set quite at defiance; the insufficiency of the force at the disposal of the magistrates again enabling the criminals to escape the consequences of their acts." Immediately following this we find detailed an event which had better be left to the descriptive powers of the Commissioners, lest there might be some lingering suspicion of exaggeration:—

"The early part of this day (the 12th) was signalised by an outrage than which nothing more brutal and unmanly was perpetrated throughout the riots—namely, the wrecking of the Bankmore Roman Catholic Female Penitentiary. The title, of course, explains the character of the institution; and considering that its only inmates were women —poor creatures who sought a refuge in which they might atone for evil courses, and ladies, who through motives of the purest charity, undertook the task of their reformation; the fanaticism that could make it the object of attack could be regarded as nothing less than revolting. This institution was twice attacked on the day in question. On the first occasion the windows were broken by the mob. Soon after, by way of retaliation, it is supposed, the windows of Dr. Cooke's church, and those of the houses of several Protestants, were smashed by the opposite party. This seems to have led to a second and more violent attack on the Penitentiary, which the constabulary suppressed with some difficulty, having had to load their carabines before they were able to disperse the crowd."

From the evidence of Dr. Dorrian, who was then coadjutor bishop of the diocese of Down and Connor, we find disclosed the still more dreadful fact that the intention was to burn the Penitentiary, and, of course, its inmates, all of whom were females. His lordship had received information of this intention, and wrote to Mr. Orme, R.M, who upon *that same morning* handed the letter to Sub-Inspector Garraway. "That officer proceeded with a body of constabulary to the locality, but after an hour, seeing no symptoms of disorder, withdrew, *and the wrecking then took place*" The significance of this may be further verified by the fact that upon the same night the bishop's residence, in Howard Street, was attacked, the windows broken, and two clergymen assaulted as they entered the house. All through this day the town was in the utmost state of excitement, acts of violence upon person and property being perpetrated in several localities. In that part of the town to which the fighting was confined, the rioters had it all their own way. Even the local police would not now venture into it except supported by a strong force of constabulary, while the magistrates were for the first time brought to believe that they were face to face with actual civil war. Two hundred additional police arrived, which included a hundred men and two officers from the depot. Mr Coulston, R M., and Mr M'Cance, J P., also arrived to aid Mr Orme, who by this time had gone through more than an average amount of laborious duty. As on the previous days, the evening was spent by the contending parties in seeking to settle the quarrel, and the duel was fought out with reverse and victory alternating upon both sides. The weather favoured the belligerents, for, according to all accounts, those summer evenings of '64 were such as to entice people into the streets, and we have long learned to know, while the law recognises the fact, that there is little difference, and a very short step, indeed, between looking on at and actually engaging in a riot. This is more especially so when both parties are warm sympathisers, as we find it here.

On the following Saturday there would seem to have been somewhat of a lull in the conflict, which the commissioners attributed to the fact of the police force having been augmented to over 400 strong. On Saturday evening the authorities took it into their heads that they would disperse the Catholics who were assembled in the Pound, and accordingly ordered the 8th Hussars to go up the "loney," by which rame the Pound was generally known. They advanced with sabres drawn, officers shouting, and with all the pomp of war, but had only gone about ten yards when they were assailed principally by women from the windows of the houses on both sides of the street, with all the household crockery and what they contained. The Hussars were compelled to beat a hasty retreat (cursing vehemently all the while as troopers alone can curse), amid the derisive cheers of the people, Sunday and Sunday night were comparatively tranquil; but the actual excitement remained to a great extent unabated. The following Monday was the 15th of August, and a holiday in the Catholic Church The report of Messrs. Barry & Dowse says—"That, as a consequence, large numbers of the lower orders of Catholics did not go to work" In this I am inclined to think they are mistaken; being, no doubt, led into error by the practice which, almost without exception, prevails in the South of Ireland in regard to the observance of Catholic holidays. In the North the observance of Chuch holidays is, through pure necessity, confined, more or less, to the attendance at chapel previous to going to work, and it is, therefore, questionable whether the large numbers who remained from work did it through necessity, or as a matter of choice Certainly it was not the custom? I incline to the belief that they remained from work purely and simply because they would not be allowed to work, and the facts justify the assertion From the mills and workshops, on the previous Friday and Saturday, they were driven forth, and the reasonable presumption was that they would not be allowed to resume work upon the Monday morning. At any rate, whether, by choice or necessity, it would seem that herein we have that cause of the renewal of a dreadful reign of terror which prevailed during the latter portion of the previous week. The early part of Monday was quiet, but at half-past ten o'clock in the morning large crowds began to assemble in the vicinity of St Malachy's church, and amongst them were a number of navvies, who were then engaged at the making of the new docks. The riots of the previous days were, of course, the subject of discussion, and moved by a spirit of revenge, with which no peaceably-disposed person can sympathise, they marched in a body to Brown Street, a Protestant quarter, firing shots and shouting defiance as they went. This and their subsequent behaviour were such as to call for the strongest reprobation. On reaching the Brown Street National School, chiefly attended by members of the Presbyterian Church—and then occupied by 444 innocent mortals, who, unless on the principle that the sins of the father descend upon the children, were in no way responsible for the conduct of their elder co-religionists—an attempt, it is said, was made to break open the door. Failing in this the windows were shattered, and even shots fired into the school. After being engaged at this day tardly work for ten minutes they proceeded up the Shankhill Road. The belief that the handful of men who sallied out of the Soho Foundry were sufficient to disperse that large, really terrible and desperate body of stalwart ruffians seems absurd. The sortie was judiciously made as the navvies were retreating, and upon some of the few stragglers. So it is at least evident that much more damage could have been done if they really desired it. Their having been dispersed by the Soho Foundry men is not altogether consistent with the fact that the navvies took as their course a direct route into a densely Orange locality—the Shankhill Road. They were, beyond doubt, a body of men whom few mobs in Belfast could safely, and would willingly, encounter. It appears that so great was the terror inspired by their march through the district that even to the present day the mothers of the Shankhill keep the navvies of '64 as the "bogies" with which to frighten their children. When "the ghost," or " the booh man," or "the sweep" will fail utterly to bring unruly children off the street, the mere mention of " the navvies ! the navvies !" will send them scampering to their mothers' knee.

The intention was to pass into Sandy Row, where a mob from that quarter had assembled, but too ready to encounter them. The opposing parties were every moment increasing, and if lives were to be saved not a moment was to be lost by the authorities. In the nick of time Mr. Orme, a force of constabulary, and a number of cavalry arrived, and succeeded in sundering the mobs, thus preventing what must have been a most disastrous collision.

About ten o'clock on that day a party from the Shankhill made a raid upon the Pound, by way of the Falls Road, but were met by the Pound mob at Milford Street, beside St. Peter's Church, then in the course of erection. Here a very desperate encounter with firearms took place A man named Heyburn who was working at the Church, and who was on the scaffold at the time, was shot dead by the retreating Orangemen.

It was now evident that peace had not been made, and at once additional troops were telegraphed for to Dublin, were sent down that evening. They consisted of two troops of the 4th Hussars and 300 men of the 84th Regiment. The inhabitants of Brown Street now prepared

for an attack upon their Catholic neighbours. Notices were served, doors were hastily chalked, and over an extensive district it was evident that the angel of death had marked and passed where next his blighting hand should fall Immediately on the arrival of the additional troops they were despatched to Brown Street, and, in the midst of great excitement and considerable danger, the district was cleared. Stone-throwing and firing were kept up, however, in the locality, and towards nightfall a Protestant named Murdock was shot. It remained now for the Protestants to retaliate upon the Catholics for the march to Brown Street About six o'clock the same evening an Orange mob assembled in the Sandy Row district, and marched in military order, with guns, staves, and other weapons, for the purpose of wrecking St Malachy's Church. News of their intended visit had reached the Catholic body, and large crowds assembled around it to protect it from sacrilege A regular engagement here took place, in which firearms were used upon both sides. Many of the parties contending received gunshot wounds, and were carried to the hospital. The constabulary and troops arrived before the issue of the conflict was decided, and both parties were dispersed by a free application of the bayonet and the sabre. A Catholic named Heyburn, who died on the 18th, is said to have been shot in the course of this encounter. This fight was one of the fiercest that had yet taken place, and gave painful evidence of the spirit of both parties engaged. The evening was spent in rioting in the disturbed districts. Scarcely a resident in Sandy Row retired to rest, and the continued and regular discharge of firearms gave ominous warning of what would follow. The Catholic mill girls going to work had been maltreated On the morning of the 16th a small party of police was posted upon the Boyne Bridge to afford them protection as they passed to their occupation. The declared intention of the Orange party was now to prevent the Catholics from working in the same concerns with them under any pretence, and, enraged at the interference of the police, the Orangemen of Sandy Row attacked them. The constabulary were a small party, but with muskets, and the hope was entertained that they could be dislodged. About 1,000 of the Orangemen assembled and joined in an organised attack upon the police who were stationed on or adjacent to the Bridge. With stones and other missiles they were beset, some of them having to take refuge in the few hospitable doorways that were opened to afford them shelter. The assault was a most violent and desperate one, and would have resulted in the complete annihilation of the party but for the timely arrival of a strong detachment of constabulary under the command of Sub-Inspector Caulfield. Their forces being now largely augmented they took up their position upon the bridge, but the Orangemen were not to be intimidated. This construction had but recently been christened the 'Boyne Bridge" as indicative of a pass which was not open to the Catholic residents from whose district it divided the Orange quarter Enraged at seeing their sanctuary desecrated by the presence of policemen, seeking to aid the passage of their enemy, the cry of "Take the bridge" was raised upon all sides. A moment's hesitation, and then with steady and well-ordered step they pushed on to drive the police from their position, while stones and brick-bats were flying in all directions A couple of their most expert marksmen where sent forward to the front who discharged their pieces and then gave place to their fellows It must be recollected that this was amid a scene of the most dreadful excitement in which no man's life was worth a minute's purchase Beset as he was with Orangemen upon one side of the bridge and Orangemen upon the other, Caulfield was pushed to the last desperate extremity of fighting the mob upon their own ground. A shooting party was at once ordered to the front from the ranks of the police. The order to load was given. The Orangemen still came fiercely on. "Load," and they loaded. "Ready!" and others their knees they went. Still the Orangemen were bent upon having the bridge, and the wild cry of fanaticism "to hell with the Pope" rent the air, "Present," and true to the ord r, and their duty, they coolly presented One moment more to see if that mad crowd would shrink from their doom, but they halted not. "Fire," and those policemen fired and upwards of twenty persons lay stretched upon the earth In that truly, tragic onslaught John M'Connell and Robert Davidson, both Protestants, met their death.

About the same hour a serious riot took place in Millfield, in the Catholic quarter, in which a Catholic mob and the constabulary were the parties concerned The conflict on the side of the Catholics was chiefly carried on with stones, but so violent was the assault that the police had to fire and several men received gunshot wounds. In the cour e of the day, owing to the violence of the re-

spective mobs, Mr. M'Cance, R.M., had repeatedly to order the constabulary and troops under his command to fire.

It was now nothing more nor less than a species of cruel warfare in which each party sought to exterminate the other, the military and police being in the extremely unpleasant position of being between two fires, while seeking to keep both asunder.

All that day and the following evening Belfast was like a beleaguered city, and so general was the riot in the working localities of the town that it would be useless to seek to combine all into one comprehensive photograph.

In the disturbed districts no one dared venture out, particularly in the evening, whose religious sympathy was not distinctly known to the mob-leaders of the locality, and as the more daring passengers walked the streets, possibly to night work, the dread whiz of the speeding bullet reminded them unpleasantly of their danger. The sharp-shooting tactics were again resorted to, and those skilled in rifle practice stealthily approached the outposts of the enemy, musket in hand, deeming it as much an honour to pick down a straggler in the enemy's quarter as to hit the bull's-eye in a shooting ga'lery. Beyond doubt the military proclivities of each party were now brought into play, and the reg et is that their reckless bravery was not engaged in a better quarrel Fortunately, the arms were of that character which were, from their age and construction, peculiarly adapted for shooting round a corner. The O tholics, as was ever the case in such contingencies, were handicapped. Marshalling and drilling, and arming, and threatening armed resistance had not with them been a political programme—I mean with the Catholics of Belfast—and they found themselves in this respect but ill-matched with their Orange opponents From the tactics pursued by the Orangemen, particularly upon this and the following day, it was clearly seen that the question was now one of absolute extermination, and a number of respectable Catholics prominently connected with Belfast formed themselves into a club for the purpose of providing arms It is not for me to comment upon this movement. There were men connected with it respectable, aye, and peaceable in character, some of whom are still living—men who would willingly hold out the right hand of fellowship to any man of any religion, but who saw, or thought they say, in that complex state of affairs no other means of preserving their existence and the existence of the community with whose welfare they were interested, and I will say with whose prejudices they were identified. There are times when this call to arms is a duty. It is for the reader to say whether, having regard to the evident insufficiency of the police in town, to the threats of the Orangemen, and to the comparative helplessness of the Catholics, that time had now arrived.

Reprisal upon both sides was now alone thought of; and the authorities, and the small garrison of armed men that supported them, were cast aside with that contempt which showed how conscious of superiority were the rioters. The walls were regularly loop-holed, for the purpose of enabling the contending parties to perform rifle practice with greater safety, and, from behind these enclosures, passers-by were cooly shot down if regarded as of the adverse faction. An incident now occurred which, more than all others, indicates the desperate intents of the Orange faction. At about ten o'clock upon the morning of the 16th, the ship-carpenters abandoned their work and, following the example set them on the previous day by the navvies, they marched in a body through the town, armed with those dreadful weapons, which from the nature of their trade they could easily extemporize for use in close conflict. On their way down North Street they halted opposite Hercules Street, an almost exclusively Catholic locality, occupied by butchers. A wild shout was heard from the women of the street, and immediately with cleavers and knives they rushed to the head of the street where the Orangemen were, and after a very short fight, in which one of the ship-carpenters had his arm cloven off by a woman, they hastily retreated. The terror which their passage through High Street communicated can scarcely be described. The shops, at least any of them whose owners still hoped to pursue business under such precarious circumstances, were hastily closed, and the fearful presentiment ran through town that all property would soon be in the hands of faction. This mob marched into Peter's Hill, and on to Brown Street, the scene of the previous day's wrecking, a visitation which in itself bore terrible significance. Here they were joined by large crowds of sympathisers, who urged an immediate incursion into the Pound. This being decided upon, they returned to High Street, determined first to provide themselves with arms. At this time a gunsmith named Neill carried on an extensive business in High Street. Arriving here the mob halted, while some of its ringleaders

went forward and demanded arms. Brooking no delay, a rush was at the same time made for the entrance. Immense stones, crowbars, and the shoulders of a dozen stalwart men were as the "'Open, Sesame,' of the fable." Beneath such overpowering influence, the door now quaked, now gave way, and amid the triumphant cries of a thousand fanatics the shop was entered, the shutters then removed to give easier access, and the store with all its dread implements of death, and all its destructive combustibles, were in the hands of an Orange mob, wild with passion and blind with prejudice. Will they stop at this? must have been the question of the neighbouring traders as they waited in breathless anxiety for the issue. Not likely. The assault upon the gun shop had been too successful not to suggest further pillage. The mobocracy of our big cities hold the reigns of government so seldom that when once in authority they, like the hungry man at a banquet, are not easily content. A hardware shop was next the object of attack. In a like manner the barriers were disposed of, and shovels, scythes, hatchets, and other weapons little less destructive, when wielded by vigorous arms, were added to the armoury of the Orange rioters. Several pawn-offices in the adjoining streets were next visited, and in the same manner entered and pillaged. The gold rings, gold watches, and other jewellery which were carried away were of course neither weapons of offence nor defence. But entering with a comparatively chivalrous intent, it is not hard to see how in the face of such temptations they could scarce keep their hands from plunder. "Where were the authorities at this time?" A very natural question, which I will leave Messrs. Barry and Dowse to answer:—

"The raid here described, and the plundering in the midday of shops in the High Street of Belfast, and this at a time when a force of some 400 constabulary, 300 infantry, and a troop of cavalry were in town, in addition to its regular police, its quota of constabulary, and the men of the depôt battalion ordinarily stationed there are certainly amongst the most astonishing instances of lawless daring that have ever occurred in a civilised community. The robbery took place in no obscure quarter, in the midst of an ignorant and turbulent population, but in the great commercial centre of this wealthy and enterprising town, the property of whose inhabitants was thus proved to be utterly at the mercy of the marauders who perpetrated it. No circumstance could more strongly show how outrage gains strength from impunity, and how necessary it is for authority to be in a position to check with strong arm its first manifestations"[*]

Thus armed, emboldened by success, and fit for the work of slaughter, this gang of desperadoes proceeded in search of the navvies. Fortunately, owing to the concentration of troops in the vicinity in which the struggle was expected, further outrage was for the time prevented. While these scenes were being enacted, the magistrates were engaged in making formal arrangement for "preserving" (rather a misnomer) the peace of the town by dividing it into districts, giving each magistrate a separate charge At this meeting *special constables* were sworn in, and Sir Thomas Larcom was telegraphed to despatch at once 500 additional constabulary, a regiment of infantry, and all the cavalry at his disposal All that evening and night Belfast was given over to mob 'law. Few dared to venture out of their homes, and many Catholics of prominence, likely to be made objects of attack, no longer trusted to the safety of their residences, but awaited armed and ready for a midnight assault. The furniture of many Catholic residents in Sandy Row and on the Shankhill were taken from their houses and burned before their doors, while they themselves took refuge in flight

The conflagration had now spread beyond the limits of Belfast Word was sent to the Orange lodges in the suburbs and in the adjacent towns and villages of Lisburn, Hillsborough, Broombedge, and Lurgan, that the Belfast brethren needed their assistance, and faithful to their brotherly compact, they came.[†] Whether the Catholics derived assistance from outside it is difficult to say. Probably they did not, for wanting the ties which bound Orangemen in life or death, they were more or less thrown upon their own resources. Whether from actual knowledge that Catholic aid was arriving—and the rumour ran like wildfire through the Orange quarters that the Catholics of Dundalk and Dublin were sending assistance—or whether from a fear that the same tactics were pursued by their oppo-

nents as by themselves, a large party or armed men waited the arrival of the five o'clock evening train from Dublin, and an attack was made upon the passengers in the train, who were mistaken for Catholic sympathisers The same night, at ten o'clock, Major Esmond, Assistant Inspector-General of Constabulary, arrived by express train, bringing with him a large force of police. He was accompanied by Colonel Lightfoot, of the 84th Regiment, with a detachment of 217 men. Of this regiment 115 men more arrived the following morning, making in all, with the detachment that arrived on the 15th, 24 officers and 560 men of all ranks then in Belfast of the 84th Regiment.

The rioters were perhaps weary of their day's labour, and the night of the 16th passed over in *comparative* peace, a system of guerilla warfare being alone indulged in. On the 17th the mobs were again on the street, busy at housewrecking. The military and constabulary now, for perhaps the first time, did efficient work, and dispersed them at the point of the bayonet, making numerous arrests. Shortly after mid-day Brigadier-General Haines arrived from Dublin. Under the presidency of the Marquis of Donegall, a meeting of magistrates was held, at which an immediate search for arms in the Pound and Sandy Row districts was decided upon, warrants from Dublin Castle having been received for the purpose This search only resulted in the capture of twenty-one stand of arms, a result in no way surprising, considering how hopeless was the task undertaken.

While this search was being made at one side of the town the most shocking and most inhuman outrage that occurred during the whole progress of the riots was being enacted at the other side. Some navvies, and as it follows as a natural consequence, those who were not implicated in the disgraceful conduct of their former fellow-labourers, went as usual to work upon the slob-lands, at the new dock, that morning. At about three o'clock the workers upon the Queen's Island sallied forth upon them. These navvies were chiefly old men. Tame blood and constitutions weakened by arduous and unrelaxing toil little inclined them towards joining in those wanton exhibitions of ruffianism in which their younger brethren had indulged and were possibly then indulging. But it mattered little to the Islandmen They were "navvies" all the same; and a point was actually gained in their being navvies who wanted the young blood of the Brown Street heroes. The chances of war were this time in favour of the shop

* See report of 1864 Commission, page 12
† After the riot had terminated part as from the district of Hillsborough visited Belfast to see rch for their relatives who came to town during the riots They never found them Some years afterwards I am told that a party of workers were engaged in making excavations for the building of a line of new houses in a street off Sandy Row, and they came upon a number of coffins The builder procured their silence, fearful that his property would be ruined as building ground The coffins remained undisturbed, piles were driven as a substitute for foundations, and beneath a row of humble houses of the artizan class rest, I am assured, the remains of many of those who fell in this conflict.

carpenters, and forgetful of all humanity this multitude of men cast aside the hammer and the adze and issued forth like a pack of hungry wolves upon the industrious mudlarks, who' were at the time knee deep in mire. I have heard that assault described to me by those who witnessed it, described in language simple, ungrammatical no doubt, and adorned here and there with expletives not recognised in police society; and I have come away with the conviction that here, upon the slob-lands of Belfast, in the midst of a populous town, of a big Christian city, with the spires pointing heavenwards to tell that there there is a God and a home; here, where men boast of the open bible and button-hole their Maker, was committed upon that 17th of August, 1864, one of the most dastardly acts that disgraces humanity, an outrage in miniature that out-rivals the massacre of Glencoe, because having neither necessity nor convenience to justify it

Desperate and determined was the onslaught. So perplexing was their situation, the victims were placed completely at the mercy of their savage assailants. No escape was left them. To escape by the land meant to rush into the arms of those very persons who sought their death. To retreat meant to traverse a vast domain of mud, in which suffocation was certain, which was again bounded by the lough which offered no friendly shelter. Placed as they were in that pillory, they were subjected to the fiercest attack with muskets, stones, brickbats, and iron nuts, some of the assailants being so far forgetful of the common principle of fair play, which should hold good amongst rioters as amongst thieves, as to rush into the mud and court a personal encounter with their helpless victims. In order to be as far as possible outside the reach of their pursuers, the navvies retreated into the mud until they were immersed beyond the waist, and now commenced a revolting rifle practice more inhuman than all else. Helpless, and placed beyond the power of self-defence, they were now relentlessly shot down by the island men. George Nolan, who gave evidence upon the point, described the encounter, he said there were between 300 and 400 of the Orange party there, described them as shooting at the navvies in the mud, "as if they were so many wild geese," and said that each volley, of which there were many, consisted of upwards of twenty shots. Some parties who witnessed the attack from the opposite bank of the lough put off in boats, and came to the rescue of the navvies, who were thus conveyed beyond the reach of pursuit. In the meantime, a troop of

cavalry and some police came to the rescue, and drove the Orangemen from their position. Nolan expressed surprise in his evidence that more prisoners were not made—only a few arrests were effected—and said that Mr. Lyons interfered to have one man released who was strapped, a prisoner, to the saddle of one of the cavalry men One man named Fagan, residing in Berry Street, was killed by a gunshot wound in this affray, and it was a well-known fact that he had not in any sense taken part in the previous rioting.

"The entire transaction," say the Commissioners in their report, "indeed, furnishes a sad illustration of the fury that had taken possession of the people" And further, "The state of alarm and excitement into which Belfast was thrown at this period, may be best judged of by the circumstance that on this day, the 17th, a memorial to the Lord Lieutenant, praying to have the town and district forthwith placed under martial law, was laid on the table of the Commercial Reading Room, and obtained the signature of sixty-three persons, including several of the principal merchants and manufacturers of the town The next day, the 18th, an event occurred which appears to us to call for the most serious consideration, as the circumstances connected with it, in our opinion, indicate, even more distinctly than the violence and outrage which we have described, the strong and dangerous influence which fanaticism and party spirit at this time exercised over the population of Belfast."

The event herein referred to was the funeral of M'Connell, who had been shot while engaged in the attack upon the constabulary at the Boyne Bridge. On the 18th there were at least three deceased persons, whose deaths were generally known, awaiting interment. Fear was reasonably entertained by the authorities that the funerals would be made an occasion of party display, if not of party riot. As the report says, the authorities seemed to have altogether overlooked the obvious necessity of forestalling the danger apprehended, by the apparently simple method of preventing any unusual concourse of people at the funerals, and strictly limiting attendance to the friends and relatives of the deceased "*One magistrate, indeed, suggested something of this sort, but no consideration seems to have been given to the proposal.* It is right to say that owing to the exertions of the Roman Catholic clergy, the funerals of those of that persuasion were attended only by near relatives, and passed over quietly."[*] When Fagan, the unfor-

* See report of Commission, page 13, paragraph 7.

tunate navvy, was to be buried, Dr Dorrian had an interview with the person who had charge of the interment, and from that person directly I have received his words. "Now, M'——," he said, "by all means have this funeral as private as possible." And it was private. Four men li'ted the body of the unfortunate man from the hospital bed upon which he expired to a car waiting for it outside; four men accompanied it to Friars Bush Burial-Ground; with their own hands, aided by the sexton, four men dug his grave and silently and mournfully they lowered him into it in the twilight, with nothing save a whispered " Heaven rest his soul !" to break the stillness of that midsummer evening   It was so with the other Catholics who were interred.

Not thus did the Orangemen bury their dead The Mayor waited at an early hour upon the friends of the deceased seeking to persuade them to have a private funeral, but without success.   As a large concourse of Orangemen was expected to be present, and the belief entertained that what should be an occasion of mourning would be made a means of party triumph, a troop of cavalry and a number of constabulary were told off to accompany the funeral   But with irreverent haste the parties having the direction of the ceremony stole a march upon the authorities, and while the magistrates were actually engaged in making the arrangements the procession started.   During the meeting Mr. Lyons, J P., left to procure the attendance of the military, and on his arrival at Albert Crescent Barracks he learned that M Connell's funeral was actually starting.   He left at once for the purpose of accompanying it, informing Mr M'Cance, R M., who had intended going with the funeral, that he would do so.   He ordered up the constabulary and hussars, and when he got up " there were a lot of cars at the corner of Howard Street," which he considered part of the funeral *cortege*   These cars are said to have contained arms and ammunition.   The direct route to the Knock Burial-ground, the place of interment, would have been a straight line from the west end of Howard Street through to Lagan Village.   But had they taken this line Hercules Place would not have been passed, and the display would have lost all its significance.   "The funeral *cortege*," and again we have to make the acquaintance of our friends the Commissioners, lest I may be accused of exaggerating—"the funeral *cortege*, it is right to inform your Excellency, by no means consisted of

persons in a very low rank of life; on the contrary, many of those composing it were stated in evidence to be of respectable station, *including several of those who had been sworn in as special constables*, and who carried their batons openly in the procession.   The numbers who attended the funeral seem to have been between 2,000 and 3,000 persons (rather an unusual number of friends, or even acquaintances, for a person in a low rank in life)   Some of them on foot, walking twelve or fourteen abreast, and a considerable number on cars.   Several, both of the pedestrians and those on cars, carried firearms, and discharged them from time to time."   What a melancholy spectacle !   In the presence of death; when the head is bent, and the heart is softened, and old feuds are forgotten, and a truce is made with all the miserable contentions of a brief existence; when all man's feelings are nerved to the unravelling of a mysterious future, and all his finer faculties are engaged in peering into an impenetrable void--here we have instead—cries of exultation—hissing imprecations that told of bitter enmity -shots and shouts and cheers—to hell with the Pope, and no surrender ; and all that demonstration which told—not alas ! of the triumph of death over one of their kindred— but the triumph of a faction over their next-door-neighbours.

> O judgment, thou art fled to brutish beasts,
> And men have lost their reason !

Mr. W. T. B. Lyons with that officiousness which characterises little men upon great occasions, took control of the military out of the hands of an official who was better fitted for the duty   With an air which Wellington was much too sensible to assume when going to fight the battle of Waterloo he headed the troops and actually led the way amid sympathising cheers into a district which it was his duty to avoid.   Then, when in the midst of a perplexity in which his own presumption had entangled him, he helplessly exclaimed, " Here I am, with her Majesty's hussars, attending an illegal process on—what am I to do ?"   Nothing !   Nothing, Mr. Lyons; but go home and learn to know that nature did not fashion you for a soldier.   Taking advantage of the incompetency displayed by the " military commander," the processionists pushed on through Donegall Place to Hercules Street, hundreds of shots being discharged as they proceeded.   Now, reader — I am placed at a disadvantage.   Probably you are not a Belfastman; likely you have only heard of Ulster as a place where men brain each other for God's sake (for boiled down, that's what it means) and possibly you are not an Irishman at all. But try and imagine two thousand armed men, following a mournful-looking hearse, with drooping plumes expressive of woe; those two thousand fringed by military and preceded by a troop of cavalry, having been led by a magistrate to the very verge of a quarter whose inhabitants the demonstration was intended to offend; imagine those two thousand—"Christians" let us call them, cheering, shouting, and still shooting in order to provoke a combat over the remains. You can't imagine it, unless you had witnessed it. That scene was so inconsistent and so repugnant as to defy description. The idea seems to have been suggested of surrounding and disarming the multitude, but even Lieut. Kennedy's proposal to Mr. Lyons, "to draw up his hussars across Donegall Place," received "no audible answer." Everything practical seems to have been abandoned, and possibly now with reason, for the fear was that if any such attempt were made the inhabitants—"the respectable inhabitants of Donegall Place, who cheered from the windows"—would have afforded to the processionists a means of escape. At the end of Hercules Place the funeral procession halted, and several volleys were fired; but, wanting opponents to encounter, they passed on, 'special constables" and "respectable inhabitants" to the number of between 2,000 and 3,000, and proceeded to bury their dead.

"When we consider the numbers who attended it," say the Commissioners; "when we remember the long line of public streets it traversed, and at a funeral pace moreover; when we bear in mind the universally acknowledged fact that many persons of a respectable class attended it, including special constables, made remarkable by their official staves, openly carried; and when we know that all the circumstances connected with it made it an object of marked observation to everyone—we find it altogether unaccountable that the police should have failed to identify or discover *a single man* of those composing the assemblage. The two chief constables, Green and M'Kittrick, saw the procession turn into Donegall Place; laid hold of the heads of the horses attached to the hearse, and tried to turn them into Chichester Street. They at least were in a position to observe those composing it; but neither they nor one of their men ever discovered a single individual of the crowd. This we cannot but regard as most unsatisfactory; for nothing, surely, should have attracted their notice more than such a for-

midable array of persons openly violating the law by carrying and discharging firearms *in a proclaimed district*, where, as we have before observed, the possession of them without a licence was a crime."

The disturbances in the different quarters were, of course, renewed, and housewrecking and desultory shooting was continued that evening. At night-time a party of Orangemen proceeded to Friar's Bush and sawed down the tree of the large Cross which was there standing, leaving this, the emblem of salvation to all Christian men, levelled to the ground.

On the following day, the 19th, a respectable young man named Halliday was shot down in Millfield, while passing through the street, the assassin being located in Brown's Square. At the funeral on the following Sunday, the Rev. Malachy Kelly and the Rev. George Conway nobly exerted themselves to keep the peace, and succeeded in doing so, by restraining those anxious to join in the funeral procession.

I will now give one more quotation, and it will be the last and not the least interesting one, from the report of the Commissioners. The second paragraph of page 16 begins—

"Such is the melancholy outline which we have to present to your Excellency of these deplorable outrages, which during so many days disgraced a town the most flourishing and prosperous we believe in Ireland. We are sorry to say it is but an outline, and that it would need a vivid imagination to fill up the picture. A few broad facts may help towards its realisation. Dr. Murney, a magistrate, drew up a statistical report (which we publish in our appendix) of the number and nature of the injuries sustained by persons during the riots, so far as he could ascertain them. In this report we find that 316 were more or less injured, of whom 11 died, 9 from gunshot, and 2 from other wounds. *

* In reference to this record the accuracy of which I do not wish to dispute, I can only say I am assured that the system of private burial was largely pursued. In the neighbourhood of Sandy Row (arts regularly called, I am told, at night ue and con eyed the dead to burial grounds in the suburbs. If relatives wished to inter privately it may reasonably be assumed that many suffered and died privately. In truth, the doctors know but little about its results, though the public are at the same time indebted to Dr. Murney for his p aisow; thy effo ts. One incident especially struck me as strange, and even in this note I will relate it as told to me. While the riots were actually proceeding a blustering Orangeman challenged a neighbour as to the want of activity on the part of the brethren; asked why they did not go out and fight, and said with an oath how he would do so-and-so. The person challenged was standing at his own door in Sandy Row, he made no reply, put his hand to the latch of the door, lifted it, and told his friend to look inside. Within that bravado saw the de d bodies of no less than twenty men who had fallen in that days fighting. The story may be an exaggeration, but it carries a certain signifi ance wi h it.

The entire number of gunshot wounds was 93, of which 34 are pronounced " severe." The cases of contusion and laceration were 212; of stabs or incised wounds, 5; and 1 of 'mania caused by fright.' This last case, we think, calls for special notice, as it shows how much mental agony and terror may have been caused during this dismal period to persons of whose sufferings no record is to be found. Dr. Murney tried to ascertain the dates of the injuries, in which he only partially succeeded; but he ascertained that on the 16th, 54 contusions and 40 gunshot wounds were inflicted; on the 18th, 41 contusions and 23 gunshot wounds; these being the two most formidable days of the rioting.

"It may not be out of place for us to remark that, having regard to the irregular and desultory character of the firing, the inferiority of the firearms, and the probable badness of the ammunition, the proportion of the shots that told with any effect was, in all likelihood, very small. If so, 98 gunshot injuries inflicted tell a fearful tale of vindictiveness and of hate. For it is only too probable that they indicate many hundred shots, fired by fellow-townsmen and neighbours on each other, with deadly intent, or at least with the design of inflicting serious injury, and no thought as to whether that injury might not prove fatal. We ourselves saw regularly loop-holed walls, from behind which, doubtless, deliberate aim was taken at the passers-by, if regarded as of the adverse faction.

"The following brief and simple narrative, given us by a Presbyterian clergyman (Rev. Isaac Nelson), of what came under his own observation, gives an insight into the character of the scenes that must have been too common at this melancholy time, and may help to show how impossible it is, by any mere detail of houses wrecked or injuries sustained, to convey a true idea of the misery suffered by the victims, often wholly unoffending, of the outrages committed:—

"For these four—or I shall say three—melancholy nights my Protestant neighbours remained up, wandering round the houses, playing 'The Protestant Boys' and the 'Boyne Water,' and using phraseology which I hope will in future be foreign to our towns. Having taken possession of the highway, they maltreated, in spite of all my remonstrances, every passer-by who would not use certain language. I am speaking of a number of persons with whom I had been to a certain extent acquainted for years, and can state to be most well-conducted and quiet persons. I saw that crowd

come up to the houses of four poor members of the Latin Church. I did not then know myself exactly their religious denomination. I saw the furniture broken to pieces on the floor, and I saw the houses, as you express it, gutted. . . . I hold as responsible for these three or four nights' melancholy proceedings *all who heard and did not oppose them.* . . . The mobs in my neighbourhood not only hunted poor Roman Catholic neighbours out of their houses, but I had to go and beseech them to go and grant so many hours to these poor people to take their furniture out of the place. I had also to go and get horses and carts to remove the furniture, and I had a great deal to do to repress the violence of the mob. . . If I were to tell you, and wanted to work on the feelings of others, I could have sat down and wept when a poor little girl came with a pet canary bird in a cage, when the poor people had been driven from their houses, the children in one direction and the father and mother in another. I had to protect a family in whose house there was a dying person, and I believe that death had actually taken place in the house when they were obliged to vacate. I regret that there was no interference on the part of the authorities, so called, I presume, *quasi lucus a non lucendo.*"

When the riots were at their height Mr. A. J. M'Kenna and a number of influential Catholics met by arrangement an equally representative number of Protestant gentry, and the result of their conference was that each and all of them should exert themselves to get the workers back to their employment as the best means of finishing the riots. "But for this the town would have been in a blaze in a few days," says the person on whose information I have for some of the foregoing particulars relied. This arrangement, with the aid of the large garrison then in town, brought the rioting of '64 gradually to a close. The latter influence must, I am inclined to think, have been a powerful auxiliary. Those who began the fight found to their disappointment it was a game at which two could play; those who held it on were painfully reminded that under some circumstances a third party, the military, could take a hand.

And now, reader, will you again answer the question were the Catholics justified in arming? Were men who are gone, but who have left living, some brilliant memories behind, and were men who are living justified in enabling their co-religionists to defend themselves? The report of that subsequent commission recommended the dissolution of that exclusively Orange force, the local police. Why did they recommend it? In 1857 they were an exclusively Protestant force with seven exceptions, and the Commissioners, Messrs. Lynch and Smythe, "felt constrained to call attention to it." In 1864 they were an exclusively Protestant force—and the Police Committee refused to have a test declaration adopted that they were not Orangemen—an exclusively Protestant force with five exceptions; so that under the regime of Mr. Black, who has earned the reward of his servility and who admitted that he would desire to "uphold" the old fashioned exclusiveness, we find the number of Catholics in the force reduced to five.* What, let me ask, can it have been in quiet times when even in the midst of party conflict Orangemen could be sworn in as "special constables," and when those men could be so forgetful of the duty they undertook as to join in a demonstration as illegal as it was unseemly at M'Connell's funeral?

The Rev. Isaac Nelson, a clergyman, "held responsible for those three or four nights' melancholy proceedings all who heard of and did not oppose them." If we are all but constrained to inculpate those who had no interest at stake, and who, therefore, held aloof from the rioting, have we no word of excuse for the excesses of those who saw in the conduct of the Orangemen a war of extermination, and who had their feelings more powerfully operated upon by seeing their household gods given over to the sacreligious hands of infuriated fanatics? Recall the shocking incidents of that mock funeral procession. O'Connell, the dead tribune of a people, whose memory was rendered still more dear from the ceremonies taking place in the metropolis—ceremonies into which nothing of party was allowed to enter—represented in a begging attitude, with a large wallet by his side to indicate his love for "rents;" the effigy given to the flames amid the wild shrieks of the Orangemen, who sent the Pope to perdition; the mock interment; the real coffin, with its five Roman

* Dr. Dorrian, in his evidence before the Commission, narrate', that one day while the riots were proceeding, he was standing in the public street of Belfast (I thik it was Corn Market) talking to a gentleman, a Protestant, when two rioters went past armed with staves or bludgeons. Just at the corner were stationed two local police, who took no more notice of them than if they were peaceable citizens.

candles placed on the top;* recall the scene at Friar's Bush; the desecration of the crosses; the return journey and its rioting; the ashes of O'Connell pitched into the Blackstaff; the attack made upon the Catholics of the Pound; the attempted entry of the Penitentiary; the wrecking of Catholic houses; the furniture of the Catholic residents strewn in heaps about the highway, and should we blush to say a word in excuse for those whose manly feelings took the place of what would have been ignoble descretion? Let the conduct of the navvies be described as wanton and ruffianly, if you will—and so I have ventured to describe it—have we not all a fearful misgiving that their survivors of to-day can confound us by recalling from that peaceful seclusion, which is the reward of a well-spent and useful life, a great patriarch as their advocate and their witness, by placing Isaac Nelson in the witness-box, and calling upon him to recite in their justification:—

"*I hold as responsible for these three or four melancholy nights' proceedings all who heard and did not oppose them.*"

What—and it is a still more vital question—was the cause of all those disastrous riots of unfortunate, disgraceful '64? Messrs. Barry and Dowse now live as judges in the land, and if they dare answer I would leave the reply to them. I will speak for them. It was Orangeism. During those twenty-one days upon which they sat to investigate the riots they had conclusive evidence bringing home to them the fact that the exclusive Orange bigotry of Belfast had culminated in those disastrous events which cost the town much more money than the estimated £50,000. They had to deal with results, however, and not with causes—a stupid arrangement which men in office have not yet learned to ignore; and if we do not find it expressed upon the pages of their elaborate report, no sensible reader can deny that it is implied there —implied that Orangeism created the riots of '64; and that when the last dread reckoning comes Orangeism, or its promoters, will be held responsible for their consequences.

* The Annual Register of 1864 assures of these particulars.

CHAPTER XXXVI.—FROM '64 TO '74.

The year 1864 inaugurated in Belfast a reign of intolerant party spirit the fruits of which we are reaping in the present. The following year did not pass over without its complement of rioting. July was election time, and the record is becoming so appalling that there is a natural anxiety to shift the responsibility wherever feasible to other shoulders. Let us agree to say, then, that those riots of 1865 were not solely due to the existence of Orangeism, though it is a conclusion, I grieve to say, at which the resident magistrate, Mr. O'Connell, did not arrive after sitting from day to day for whole weeks in the Police Court to hear the numerous charges that were made against those arrested. We will, however, give the benefit of the doubt, if doubt there be, to the Orangemen; say that the immense body of shipcarpenters who took possession of Howard Street Court House on the morning of the 12th, the day of the nomination, was an electioneering mob, and not a gang of Orange rioters, and that the disturbances which followed, and which were prolonged for a couple of days in the Sandy Row and Pound districts, owed much to the election contest then pending. In the provinces we cannot, even though we look for it, find a like excuse. In defiance of the law the Orangemen in various localities marched in procession. The district of Dungannon specially distinguished itself. There the Killyman Orangemen to the number of 5,000 marched into Dungannon in opposition to the police, and wrecked the houses of the Catholic residents.

July had now become a period of increased anxiety to Government, and it was a matter of ordinary routine of office to draft into the various towns and districts of the North large forces of police and military to preserve the peace. In 1866 Belfast was duly garrisoned, and though great excitement prevailed the peace was kept, the Orangemen but stealthily taking an opportunity here and there of insulting their Catholic neighbours. A faction they were now pure and simple, and though occasionally such men as the Prestons, the Hendersons, and the Hamiltons— men who are now magistrates and respectable— might condescend to be present at their convivial tea parties, the gentry and merchants rigidly kept aloof from their annual carnival of the 12th July. There are never wanting, however, a few demagogues so mean as to climb to office from the shoulders of their compeers. Of this character were the Johnstons and the Beers; men who but for their truculency would have pursued to the end the quiet walk of country squireens; who in the latter as in the earlier period of their career would have been wholly engrossed in the honourable struggle of providing for the wants of the day; men, whose poor abilities would have been put to

the stretch, solving the all but impossible problem of making both ends meet.

On the 12th of July, 1836, an Orange demonstration was held a Ballykilbeg, County Down, the demesne of Mr. William Johnston, who now for the first time becomes a necessary quantity in the history of these people. Mr. William Beers took the chair. Large forces of military had been drafted into Downpatrick, as a fear was reasonably entertained that a breach of the peace would ensue. The Chief Secretary wrote to this effect to the inspector of police, who in his turn served the document upon Mr. Johnston. It stated that there was reason to apprehend a serious breach of the peace at what was called "the great Protestant demonstration," to be held at Ballykilbeg, and his Excellency trusted that Mr. Johnston would at once see the propriety of instantly countermanding the meeting, while he (his Excellency) had given strict orders to prevent the assembling of persons under such circumstances as might lead to a breach of the peace. Did Mr. Johnston at once loyally respond to the reasonable request made upon him by the representative of the Queen in Ireland? No. Mr. Johnston wanted to become a member of Parliament, and having his eye upon some snug little place, such as the Inspectorship of Fisheries, he could not afford to be loyal. He accordingly encouraged and promoted the meeting. In his address to the assembled brethren, he said he could not see how his Excellency knew there would be riots, "though he found that the priest of the parish, Mr. O'Kane, on Saturday last entertained the magistrates with an absurd story of a contemplated firing at a huge cross, with a sponge and spear, recently set up in Down chapel yard under the auspices of the Redemptorist Fathers." Mark the mocking tones of this Christian demagogue! Mr. Johnston refused, therefore, to countermand that meeting, but rioting and disturbance followed it, nevertheless; and, if they were not of so violent a character as was anticipated, no thanks are due to the action of Mr. Johnston.

Demonstrations were held the same year in Lisburn, Kilwarlin, Warringstown, Lurgan, Portadown, and Dungannon. In the latter place lodges 178 and 1620, on returning home from a meeting in Killyman suddenly discovered that they had business to call at Dungannon. They accordingly proceeded upon that route. The magistrates, however, had unpleasant recollections of the previous year's doings of the brethren in that town and resolved to prevent them. They first sought to persuade them to take the direct road homewards. Persuasion has no effect upon such men save to make them more conscious of their strength and, therefore, more obstinate. The police and military were then drawn across the road, with fixed bayonets, the magistrates refusing to allow them a passage. The force was a strong one, and nothing was to be gained by fighting their way through. The Orangemen accordingly sat down upon the road side, determined to try the patience of the authorities. It can easily be imagined that in this foolish competition the mob had the advantage. A compact was accordingly made that they should not, if allowed to pass, play any party tunes, and would go quietly through the town, guaranteeing that they would give no insult, and the Orangemen proceeded. It is suggestive of the confidence placed by magistrates in the Catholic inhabitants of Dungannon, whom they must evidently have pre-supposed would not have interfered in that Orange procession, unless grave insult was offered them. It seems strange, however, that no arrests were made, for every man of them, upon that highway, were, at the time, doubly criminal, offending, as they were, against the statute law and the common law of the land.

The 12th July, 1867, should be a memorable date in our history. It marks on the one side a violent attempt made by Orange conditional loyalty to outrage and defy the law, and upon the other a praiseworthy effort made by the Government to uphold it. Party processions were by Act of Parliament not only illegal, but the revision which the statute had undergone on its re-enactment had made it illegal and a misdemeanour to display party emblems, or to parade with bands, banners, or with arms. The aristocratic Orangemen and the big J.P.'s were content with presiding at tea parties in honour of the glorious, pious, and immortal memory, where they aired their eloquence and befooled the smaller fry with bigoted declamations, in which they did not believe. Mr. Johnston, D.G.M. of Ireland, and Grand Secretary of the Orangemen of County Down, now saw an opportunity of striking out a new line for himself, and the democratic section of which he aspired to be the leader. To openly outrage the law was the nearest road to those men's hearts, for of all others the lower classes of the Irish people love their martyrs. Mr. Johnston then aimed at becoming a martyr—and something more. He realised his expectations in the fullest. The celebrated march to

Bangor was, therefore, resolved upon, in order to openly defy the authorities and dare them to put the law in motion against them. There were men amongst them who did throw in their counsels in the opposite side, but enthusiasm and conditional loyalty were at their height, [and moderate men were classed among the "old fogies" and relegated to the tea-drinking section of the brethren. For months before the 12th preparations were made upon a vast scale for the celebration, and even arms and ammunition were procured "should the worst come to the worst." The quotation is taken from an address delivered by a gentleman now living and enjoying a position of independence, in a lodge in Belfast to the assembled brethren a few weeks before the Bangor demonstration came off. In that address (and I have it on the authority of an ex-member of the Institution who heard it) the speaker advised every man to be prepared with arms, but "not to use them unless the circumstances necessitated it." Immense numbers of Orangemen left town upon the morning of the 12th July for Bangor, where they were met by the local brethren. Here they formed in procession, and with guns, with flags (a constable afterwards counted 67), with drums and fifes they marched to Newtownards and back, the musical programme rendered on the route being comprised chiefly of three tunes—"The Protestant boys," "Croppies lie down," and "The Boyne water." At the meeting Mr. William Johnston, Ballykilbeg, spoke. In that speech the future member of Parliament and present Inspector of Fisheries declared that they would not tolerate any longer being told that it was illegal for Protestants on the 12th July, to display Orange flags and beat Protestant drums while it was perfectly legal and perfectly proper for Catholics to march through the streets of Dublin, with their chosen emblems. They, he said, had with them Orange flags, and had played and would play, such tunes as were suitable to them, and they would boldly declare they were [no party procession * They were tired of hole and

*. Mr. Johnston, 't should here be remarked, was indulging a little in the license taken by Orange orators. In fact, he was simply hoodwinking his hearers in order that they might persist in their illegality. The legal question was not simply one of party procession even. The fact forbade processions with party emblems, no doubt; but it also forbade processions with drums and music playing party tunes, and the members of which carried and displayed arms. If the Executive had allowed such processions in Dublin as that of Earl Mulgrave's, it was because they could not rightly characterise them as party demonstrations. They had never allowed demonstrations by armed multitudes, which were manifestly illegal, to go unpunished.

corner meetings; of the gentlemen who assembled at small tea parties, and who implored them for God's sake *to keep quiet* on the 12th July." They would disregard those gentlemen he added, and and would send a voice acro s to the Prime Minister and the Government of England, telling them that they, the Orangemen and Protestants of Ulster, would no longer stand oppression and tyranny. After such plain speaking it was evident that Mr. William Johnston, of Ballykilbeg, had fair prospects of becoming an Orange martyr. The most remarkable, if not the most audacious, incident of the entire day's proceedings was, that they resolved to petition to Parliament against that Act which, at that very moment, they were breaking and defying. Upon the same day the brethren throughout the Province of Ulster were, in a like manner, defying the law, demonstrations being held in most of the Orange centres, some of them being attended with the usual riots and disturbance.

On the 15th August following, the Catholics of Rathfriland and Loughbrickland foolishly resolved to copy the bad example set them by the Orangemen. For the first time Lady Day was celebrated But the Orangemen were ill-disposed to allow to the Catholics the liberty they were seeking for themselves, and riots took place in which some lives were lost In England, the "Murphy riots" were at the same time proceeding, over which many persons lost their lives.

In July, 1867, an Imperial Grand Council of Orangemen met in London and issued an address, in which the public generally cannot be interested

Two months afterwards, on the 4th September, 1867, William Johnston and twenty-five others were prosecuted by order of the Attorney-General for having, on the 12th of July, formed part of an unlawful assembly, for meeting and marching together, firing arms, and displaying arms and other offensive weapons, with banners and symbols the display whereof was calculated to provoke animosity between different classes of her Majesty's subjects. The prosecution was brought, as it may be seen, from the above under the Act of 1850 which was an Act "to restrain Party Processions in Ireland." With the exception of two defendants, who were not identified, all the parties were returned for trial to the Spring Assizes.

Up to this time the public generally, even of the North of Ireland, had known no more about this Mr. Johnston than they did about the numerous Browns, Jones', and Robinsons who directed the

tag rag of the faction. He was now a martyr. Having defied the law the next step was an easy one. He became a hero. And this Mr.—Johnston of somewhere in the County Down became Wm. Johnston of Ballykil beg, the great idol of Orange Democracy, the "People's William" before whom these haters of Popery, superstition, and idolatry, humbly bowed down in worship. His picture was in every window side by side with the great hero of the Boyne, than whom, though he had never drawn a sword, or pulled a trigger in defence of any one right, he was but a shade inferior. It is true he might have handled a sabre as old women do a broomstick. With firearms in his hands he very probably would have proved himself his greatest enemy. But he had broken an English Act of Parliament, and with conditional loyalists the result was the same. So he was hung up is the shop windows, depicted with a grave but heroic countenance, posturing with one hand upon his heart and the other raised aloft in solemn adjuration, in all the gravity of a martyr at the stake; and those "who would have made mouths at him". a few weeks ago, now gave two, three, and even ten shillings " for his picture in little "

At the Down Spring Assizes, on the 23th of February, 1868, Wm. Johnston, with four others, were indicted by the Chairman before Mr. Justice Morr s, the Attorney-General, prosecuting. ,Two of the prisoners pleaded guilty, and the prosecution did not ask for punishment. Mr. Johnston and two others were put on their trial, and from the clearest testimony were found guilty upon the second count in the indictment charging them with marching in procession, accompanied by flags, carrying arms, &c, in a manner calculated to create animosity between different classes of her Majesty's subjects; and upon a third count charging them with unlawful assembly. They were lectured by Mr. Justice Morris, upon the illegality of their proceedings, who said the meeting was ostensibly to petition for a repeal of the very Act which those who planned the procession and formed it were ostentatiously violating. He sentenced each to one month's imprisonment. At the expiration, William Johnston was to enter into personal security to the amount of £500, and procure two sureties of £250 each, to be of good behaviour for a period of two years, or in default of doing so to be imprisoned for a further term of one month. A like provision was made in regard to the other two prisoners, the securities being £50, and two of £25.

All the other prisoners pleading guilty, they

were allowed out on their own recognisances to be of good behaviour.

On Wednesday, the 23rd April following, Mr. Johnston, who refused to give bail "to be of good behaviour" was discharged from prison on the recommendation of the medical officers, having put up in prison within four days of his allotted time. He had utilized the time not spent in picking oakum by writing a mongrel Orange ballad with a refrain of "no surrender": which he generously distributed amongst his devotees after his liberation. Mr. William Johnston, of Ballykilbeg, was now in a fair way to fame and fortune. Had he not marched to Bangor, he would not soon after have been member for Belfast, nor would he now be drawing the respectable salary of £700 a year from Government resources. When the time came, however, the great Orange leader became a representative in Parliament with a party to sell. He had not to wait long until he found a purchaser. The conflict between principle and pocket cannot have been a great one. So, selecting respectability and opulence instead of being the leader of a party who had nothing to bestow, the great William Johnston of Ballykilbeg, the people's William, the hero whose march to Bangor, where there was no foe, was thought as memorable as William's passage of the Boyne in the face of imbecile James and his cowardly troops, the second Prince of Orange, the future author of "Nightshade," ignobly subsided into an Inspector of our Fisheries, leaving his brethren to fight out that great battle against Popery, which very probably in the beginning, as in the end, he thought not worth the winning.

Even in their mistaken triumph they found their defeat. This walk to Bangor was the beginning of a split which has gone on widening and widening, and will go on, so doing until it ends in total disruption. An announcement was made by advertisement in the columns of the *Whig* that a meeting "of the Protestant (Orangemen) of Belfast" would be held in the Ulster Hall on the 4th March. It was in it stated that the Grand Jurors of Down had betrayed the cause (by not breaking their oaths and ignoring the bill against Wm. Johnston). A slip or proof sheet of this advertisement, with a charge to *Whig* upon it having been sent to the *News-Letter*, the latter the organ of the aristocratic Orangemen, took offence and refused to insert it. It was not, they urged, through the medium of their contemporary that they had been accustomed to be inducted into Orange secrets. The *News-Letter* now warned "the Protestants of Belfast" not to hold the meeting; to stop at home from the meeting; that nothing could be more calculated to injure the Protestant cause than the holding of such a meeting, and said a great meeting of the Protestant gentry of the province—the Marquis of Downshire presiding—would shortly be held, for which they should reserve their fire. But the meeting was held, the distinct purpose being, to express sympathy with William Johnston, to form the Workingmen's Protestant Association, and to present a memorial to Mr. Disraeli, for repeal of the Party Procession's Act. The representative of the *News-Letter* was expelled from the hall, but was subsequently recalled, and, on the following day, he presented the readers of that organ with a summarised report of two columns of what was really a significant and important demonstration. On the following night, March the 5th, a demonstration of the aristocratic, or Protestant party, was held in the same hall. Nobody spoke who was not a marquis or a J.P. No vote of sympathy was passed in regard to the incarcerated Mr. Johnston. The *News-Letter* now devoted ten columns of its pages to the reporting of this meeting. It was evident there was a split in the party. Orangeism had ceased to be respectable even in the estimation of those who obtained their influence by it. A few months later found them face to face with each other in two hostile camps contesting the representation of Belfast, Mr. Johnston being the nominee of the Orangemen, Sir Charles Lanyon the representative of the high Tory clique. The Orangemen were victorious. The Protestants were defeated, and from that day to this respectable Protestantism is neither in name nor in interests identified with the Orangeism of Ulster.

From the report of the Grand Lodge, held this year in Armagh, it seems that the brethren were much amazed that the secrets of the lodge were being discovered. The *Whig* had for obvious reasons being publishing reports of proceedings of the Belfast Grand Lodge. The matter was reported to the Grand Lodge of Ireland, and "Brother Charles N. Davis stated that although every effort was made the delinquent was not yet discovered, and suggested that there should be a re-ballot of the County Grand, and stated that there was then in the Room a Brother who held a situation in the office of the *Northern Whig*, and being asked for his name, said it was Jeremiah M'Kenna. Brother M'Kenna being called on, if he knew anything of the author of these publications, replied in the negative, and stated that he was in the commercial department of the *Northern Whig*, and knew nothing whatever of the reporting department. A statement having been made that there were several Orangemen on the staff of the *Northern Whig*, Brother M'Kenna, in reply, said there were fifteen. It was also stated by Brother William Mortimer, that Thomas Henry had said that a certain article affecting the County Grand Lodge would appear in the *Northern Whig*, and that it did accordingly appear. "Moved by Brother Dr. Drew, seconded by Brother James H. Moore, and

'No. 3.—Resolved—Inasmuch as at various times publications have been made of proceedings connected with the Orange Institution, without the sanction of the Grand Lodge, and as it is desirable that persons connected with newspapers, who thus encourage an improper use of our documents, should not be in connection with our Institution; that brethren employed in such printing offices be requested to withdraw from the Institution, pending their employment in such offices'.* But the resolution did not mend matters, for upon the following day the offence was repeated, which led "to stringent and immediate steps" being taken to allow all members to exonerate themselves. In other words, the members were separately *put to their oaths* to say they had no connection with the publication.

The latter part of 1863 gave the Orangemen a new cry. The English reformers, who if they march not in a pace with the ideas of our time, should yet be respected for their boldness in assaulting and taking the bulwarks of monopoly which remained even un'o our day as the relics of a mediæval age—the English reformers resolved that the time had come for disestablishing the Irish Church. Most of, us, who are not children, can easily recall the violent agitation of the Orangemen over that question. "Flaming O'Flanaghan' at many of the Orange meetings stated, amid the applause of the multitude, that they would "kick the Queen's crown into the Boyne" rather than allow the Church to be disestablished. The phrase was an expressive one, and becoming the watchword of the Orange party, it was echoed and re-echoed through all the Orange lodges of the kingdom. But few knew better than

* This is taken word for word from the report of 1863, a document which the brethren believe to be in the exclusive possession of the Institution.

Mr. Gladstone and the Marquis of Hartington that this was all bravado—indeed, both of them so expressed themselves—and while giving Orangemen credit for the desire to kick the crown into the Boyne, they knew too well that the brethren had not the courage to do so. Accordingly, in spite of all their menace and all their bluster, despite the vapouring of O'Flanaghan and the bouncing of the people's William, despite the threats of the "great Imperial Council of Orangemen for England, Ireland, Scotland, and the Colonies," held in London, the Church was disestablished. The Bill received the Royal assent the following year, and the crown rests upon the brows of her Majesty yet.

In 1869, the rules of the institution were again revised, and were printed in book form in the *News-Letter* printing office, every precaution being made to keep them exclusively within the range of the members of the institution. They are present before me in their entirety, but they bear such a similarity to the former rules, that I cannot be tempted into an analysis of them. It is enough to say that they consist of 93 provisions in all; that conditional loyalty ("the succession to the Throne being Protestant"), is still the programme, and that under the qualifications of membership, we find "that the candidate must, to the utmost of his power, support and maintain the laws and Constitution of the United Kingdom." If Wm. Johnston and his Bangor brethren were not dismissed, we may excuse the inconsistency. It is not the first in the history of the institution.

Mr. Johnston this year brought in a Bill to repeal the Party Processions Act, which the Government refused to adopt; nor was it until a considerable time after they were tempted into the rash adventure of yielding to the clamour of demagogues, giving Ulster over to an annual reign of terror, and the Catholics to repeated, deliberate, and wanton insult.

In 1871 we find Orangeism in Canada showing the cloven foot. Riots occurred this year of a desperate character. The Orangemen persisted in walking despite the direct orders of the Government and the objections raised by the Catholics, the result being the loss of about 30 lives. Montreal was again and again the scene of riot, the Orangemen persisting in their demonstration even in the face of opposition from the military and police authorities. An effort had been made ten years previous, on the occasion of the visit of the Prince of Wales to Canada, to secure official recognition of the institution, but the plot was defeated by the firmness of His Royal Highness who would have nothing to do with it, and by the judicious counsel of his advisers. Up to this time as Chambers's Encyclopedia assures us they had but distinguished themselves by the wrecking of convents. From 1871 to 1873 each recurring 12th July (it is needless to dwell upon particulars) was a scene of riot and bloodshed in Canada such as the inhabitants of Ulster had long since become familiar with. In the latter year an abortive effort was made in New Brunswick to have the Institution recognised by the Governor-General of the dominion and Isaac Butt, formerly a member of the Institution, on behalf of 25,000 Irish-Canadian Catholics, presented a petition to the Queen, praying to have the Society discountenanced That petition, showing the experience of Catholics in another hemisphere, tells simply the tale of suffering which Irish Catholics at home have experienced at the hands of the Orange Institution Its expressions will, I am assured, find an echo in every Irish Catholic heart.

Having rehearsed the story of '64, it is needless to dwell at length upon the sad tale of 1872 This year Belfast was again a scene of dreadful riot, in which no man could count either his life or his property his own. Taking every opportunity of celebrating the triumph of faction, it was but natural that the Catholics, now that the Party Processions Act was repealed, would resort to the same devices. It was decided to test the Orangemen whether they would allow that freedom of procession to others which they claimed for themselves. Accordingly the Catholics resolved to hold a meeting at Hannahstown on the 15th of August, at which a Protestant, Mr. Joseph Biggar, was to take the chair. They assembled at Carlisle Circus, and marched to Hannahstown, a few miles distant from Belfast. On the outward journey, the Orange workers having by this time left their mills and workshops, they were savagely set upon at a place known as the Brickfields, which has ever since been the battle-ground of the two parties. Shots were fired into their ranks, and many persons wounded. The presence of a small army, both horse and foot, alone saved them from assault on the return journey. This attack again set the ball rolling, and for a fortnight business was practically suspended in Belfast; the scenes of 1364 were re-enacted; the Catholics resident in Protestant districts had again to fly for their lives; Catholic workers would not get leave to enter establishments where the majority was Protestant; the discharge of musketry

broke the stillness of the midnight air; the assassin picked down his man from behind street corners and out of garret windows, and riot and massacre ruled the town. The ratepayers were again subjected to pay a fine for fostering Orangeism in their midst. Not alone in Belfast, but all over Ulster the same course was pursued. "The Catholics were rebels and shou'd not be allowed to walk." Driven thus to the necessity of asserting their right, they resolved upon walking, and, at the risk of their lives and the loss of many of their companions, they until lately continued doing so. During those periods of party conflict Ulster presented a pitiable scene, in which civilization seemed to be breaking in upon the people rather than achieving its final and ultimate development.

At an inquiry in Magherafelt, in April, 1874, relative to a riot on the 17th March, at Bellaghy and Castledawson, in the County Derry, some facts were elicited worthy of attention. Not only was it there sworn that the Orange Lodge was utilised for the purpose of "getting up" evidence for these inquiries, but it was elicited in the cross-examination of some of the Orangemen *that an oath was taken upon their entering the society;* that secrets were revealed in the lodge room which they dared not disclose even for the purposes of the administration of justice. It was also sworn that there were secret signs and passwords in connection with the institution. Some extracts from the evidence may prove interesting:—

John Martin, in answer to Mr. M'Erlean, swore —I am an Orangeman, and a good one too. In our lodge it was *decided* that we should not interfere with the Roman Catholic procession on the 17th of March. These were fourteen or fifteen in the lodge room when this was *agreed* to.

Tell me, now that we have got so far, do you get in by giving this (Mr M'Erlean here gave three raps on the desk)? Witness gave no answer.

Now, upon your oath, is not the password—"ask and you shall receive, seek and you shall find, knock and it shall be opened unto you"? No answer.

The question was repeated, and witness swore that he would not tell, as it belonged to the secrets of the society.

On the following day the witness was recalled, and on being questioned, said he refused to say how long he was an Orangeman.

Mr. Giausen, J.P.—Answer the question. You should not be ashamed to show your colours.

Witness said he was fifteen years an Orangeman.

Mr. M'Erlean—How far are you advanced in the order?

Mr. Gaussen ruled that the witness was not bound to reveal the secrets of his society

Witness ultimately stated that he was a Purple Orangeman, and on being asked to repeat the oath declined to do so.

Mr. M'Erlean—I suppose I am on dangerous ground when at the Purple Order! (To Witness) —Have you ever taken an oath in your life except in a court of justice?

Mr. Gaussen—He is not bound to answer that question.

Were you at a club called the Brunswick Club, at or near Magherafelt, for the purpose of preventing Catholics obtaining land in this district Question overruled.

Did you ever state that "you would allow your throat to be cut with a rusty sword, and you tongue to be dragged out by the roots, before you would allow a Roman Catholic procession to pass through Bellaghy? Question disallowed

Did you ever see a person three times carried round a room, with his back to the ground, and, if so, for what purpose? Question disallowed.

Were your shoes taken off your feet and your feet and your trousers rolled up? Question disallowed.

Did you, sir, ever, for the purpose of illustrating that text of Scripture where you are told to take the shoes off your feet, as the ground whereon you stand is holy, do this? Did you take the shoes off your feet in any room or place, and was Moses in the burning bush represented at the same time? Question disallowed.

Remember you have admitted to me that you assumed the Purple order; and do you swear that these or similar words were repeated? Question disallowed.

On your oath, sir, though Bellaghy is a proclaimed district is it not impossible to give a man the Purple and other orders without a pistol being fired on the occasion? Question disallowed.

Are there secret signs and passwords in connection with the Institution.

Witness objected to answer.

Mr. Gaussen ruled that he was bound to answer providing he did not tell the secret signs and passwords were.

Witness—There are secret signs and passwords in connection with the Orange Institution and that is all I will tell you.

Is there a secret oath in connection with the Orange Institution

Mr. Gaussen—You are not bound to answer that question.

Did you ever this—"I, A B, swear never to bear reveal, and for ever to conceal, all that is now about to be secretly communicated to me, never to make an Orangeman behind a hedge, or in bye-ways; to assist a brother in distress; never to know of an injury to a brother without communicating it to him" Have you heard these words before, or anything like them?

Mr. Reid, Sessional Crown Solicitor—That is not a legal question in this case.

Mr. M'Erlean said there were magistrates who were Orangemen.

Mr. Gaussen—No doubt. There is nothing to prevent magistrates from being Orangemen.

Mr. Rea—Lord Enniskillen is a magistrate, and he is the Grand Master of the Orange Society.

Mr. Gaussen—It is a recognised society by the Government.

Mr. M'Erlean—I don't say there is a gentleman on the bench who is connected with the Orange Society

Mr Gaussen—There is not one.

Mr. Rea—I have been trying to get into the society during the last five years, and I would not be admitted because I am too good a Protestant.

Mr. M'Erlean—Were you ever beaten with a holey or a knotted rope?

Mr. Rea—I will withdraw my application for admission.

Question overruled.

Martin Davidson, a publican in Bellaghy, and an Orangeman for five years, and Master of Lodge 1,511, was prevailed upon by the Court to answer, and corroborated Martin's evidence by saying— "Of course, there are secret signs and passwords in connection with the Orange Society." He said, in answer to Mr. Rea, that as long as he had been connected with the society there had been secret signs and passwords.

Mr. Rea—I suppose also there are secret oaths in the order.

The Bench ruled that the question need not be answered.

Mr. Rea—When this evidence is laid before Parliament it will read like a Waverley novel.

On being cross-examined as to the facts, this

witness swore that he saw one of the defendants named Dougherty throwing stones at his (witness's) windows. On the previous deposition being produced, it was found that he had stated twice in them *"that the damage was inflicted by some person or persons unknown"* He also admitted that he had been at the Orange Hall getting up evidence, but that nobody told him to go. "He heard two men and a woman in the street saying that Mr. Ward (the attorney for the Orangemen) would be there."

Mr. M'Erlean said the Orange Society was upon its trial. It was for the members of the society to say that the oath he had read was not taken. It might be true Orangemen were not sworn; but there were three orders in the society that were sworn—the Purplemen, the Knights of Malta, and the Black Preceptory—and every one of these orders were illegal. The 37th of George III, cap. 173, made it an offence against the law for any one to take an oath not required by law, to subscribe or assent to any oath or declaration or test not sanctioned by law.

Andrew Kennedy, for about two years a member of the Orange Society, Lodge 96, *Castledawson*, said he did not know that he ever knew an Orange man who had not the signs and pass-words.

Mr. Rea—Is this the first time ever you were sworn in a court of justice? Yes.

Is this the first time ever you have been sworn?

Mr. Gaussen—You are not bound to answer that.

Mr. Rea—Well, of course, the refusal will do as well as if he answered. How often have you been sworn before this day, which you say is the first time you ever were sworn in a court of justice? *I was sworn once.*

About how long ago is that? I don't remember.

Is it a year, or two years, or three years? It might be *about two years* ago since I was sworn.

Was it in Magherafelt, in Bellaghy, or in Castledawson? It was in Castledawson.

Was it before a magistrate? No.

The Chairman—*Well, now, you see,* there's the point, because no one can lawfully administer an oath except a magistrate.

Mr. Rea—Wasn't it as a member of the Orange organisation that the oath was administered? I decline to answer.

Well, is it because it would subject you to a criminal prosecution you decline to answer?

The Court decided that he was not bound to give a reason, and the witness refused to give one.

William Gray, a letter-carrier, and a member of the Orange Society for about eight or nine years, was sworn, and in cross-examination by Mr. Rea, gave corroborative evidence relative to the existence of signs and pass-words, which he believed always came from Dublin, and were given him by the Master of the Lodge.

Were you ever sworn outside a court of justice? (After a pause)—I'll not answer that question.

Were you ever sworn on the Evangelist except in a court of justice or before a magistrate? I don't see that I have a right to answer that question.

The Chairman—Can't you answer the question? Witness—I was once.

The Chairman—Why did you hesitate to tell?

Mr. Rea—Was that in Castledawson or in Bellaghy? It was in *Castledawson.*

Wasn't it about seven or eight years ago? It was *between seven and eight years ago.*

Now, you need not answer this question if you don't like. Wasn't it as a member of the Orange Society that you were sworn—you may decline to answer it if it would tend to criminate you? No answer.

Do you decline to answer it on that ground? I do.

From the above sworn depositions the reader may draw his own conclusions. Recollect the fact that Mr. M'Erlean was at the close sentenced to seven days' imprisonment for alleged contempt of court.

CHAPTER XXXVII.—LEGAL.

THE legal question is one which may be briefly dealt with. According to the present law every club and society is an unlawful combination or confederacy of its members, according to its rules, or according to any previous provision or agreement for that purpose, are required or permitted to take any oath not required or authorised by law; or take, or in any manner bind themselves by any such oath or agreement on becoming or in consequence of being members of any such society; or any society the members of which shall take, subscribe, or assent to any test or declaration not required or authorised by the law, whether that test or declaration be by words, signs or otherwise, either in order to become or in consequence of becoming a member of of such society. To this there is a reservation where the form of test has been approved and subscribed to by two or more justices of the peace of the county in which the society exists, and where it is registered with the Clerk of the Peace Again, any society is an illegal combination if the names of the members, or any of them, are kept secret from the society at large; or where there is a select body so chosen or appointed that the members constituting the same are not known by the society at large to be members of such select body

The 4th George IV, Cap. 87, recites the 50th of George III., Cap 102, which I think I have already quoted, and enacts that every society "now established, or hereafter to be established, of the nature hereinafter described, shall be an unlawful combination and confederacy — viz, every society, association, brotheroohd, committe, lodge, club or confederacy the members whereof shall, according to the rules thereof, or to any provision or agreement for that purpose, be required, or admitted, or permitted to take any oath or engagement which shall be an unlawful oath, or engagement with the intent or meaning of said recited Act, or to take any oath not required or authorised by law, and any and every society, association, &c, the members whereof or any of them, shall take or in any manner bind themselves by any such oath or engagement upon becoming, or in consequence of being members of such society, association, &c, and any and every society, association, &c, the members whereof shall take or subscribe, or assent to any test or declaration not required by law, and any and every society, association, &c, of which the names of the members, or any of them, shall be kept secret from the society at large, or which shall have any committee or select body chosen or appointed in such manner that the members constituting same may not be known by the society at large to be members of such committee or select body, or which shall have any president, treasurer, secretary, or other officer chosen or appointed in such manner that the election or appointment of such persons to such offices may not be known to the society at large; or of which the names of all the members, and of all committees or select bodies of members, and of all presidents, treasurers, secretaries, delegates, and other officers shall not be entered in a book or books to be kept for that purpose, and to be open to the inspection of all members of such

society," &c., &c., "shall be deemed guilty of unlawful combination and confedracy."

From the above it is manifest that the Orange Society is illegal. It is not included in the exception which applies only under this Act and others to be read with it, to Freemasons and Friendly Societies, nor does the reservation in regard to tests secure them from illegality, as the tests of this society are not subscribed to "by two magistrates in the county in which it exists." The administering of an oath by them is illegal under all circumstances. That the Orange Society administers an oath as a rule on the admission of associates is not proven. That certain sections of the society, these being chiefly the lodges which are hidden away in remote districts and situated in localities where bigotry and party strife largely prevail, do administer oath to associate is plainly made evident upon depositions which would hold good in any court of law. If this illegality is inevitable as a natural consequence of the society itself, which I hold it to be, the society is then unlawful, and must be hel responsible for the administration of unlawful oaths under the 4 George IV, Cap 87. But under the same section of this Act it is also evident that the society as a body is rendered illegal by the prohibition of tests, unless those subscribed by two magistrates which it contains. The Act forbids all test's or declarations u ed by persons upon becoming or in consequence of becoming members of such society. What is a test? It is to have some secret mode by which one member can challenge, or make himself known to another without the ordinary means provided by the act—namely, the "book or books" in which the names of the associates are entered. Such a test exists in the Orange Society. The lecturer visits the district lodges periodically, and upon all occasions when a change in those tests, signs, and pass-words are rendered necessary, and personally communicates them to the Master, by whom they are again communicated to the members. It is needless to refer to "the half o five or the fourth of ten," and to the various other means by which the brethren can make themselves known to each other. Tests these are, pure and simple. Say, an Orangeman meets a friend in a public-house, which is too frequently the place of rendezvous. He gives the sign to which the brother responds. The brother thus accosted decides to test the person who has so challenged him, and he accordingly proceeds with a routine of tests prescribed by the society for the purpose, and actually communicated in secret by the representative of the Grand Lodge. By these tests he ascertains if his companion is an Orangeman.' Herein is found illegality under the statute of George IV., already quoted; but the illegality of the society extends further in my opinion. That Act provides "that any society which shall have any committee or *select* body chosen or appointed in such manner, that the members constituting the same may not be known by the society at large to be members of such committee or select body, shall be deemed guilty of unlawful combination and confederacy." In the Orange Society there are such select bodies. The rules themselves plainly provide that Purplemen shall not reveal their secrets to Orangemen; and there is also set apart a district order of tests, signs, and passwords, not alone to keep the inner circle within itself, but to prevent Purplemen from communicating with or being known by Orangemen. The same regulation prevails in regard to the Black Preceptory and other orders. It is therefore evident that not only is it a fact, but that it was the intention to bring that fact into existence, that the Orangemen and Purplemen do not, and cannot know each other. This is illegal under George IV., Chap. 87. By the 2nd and 3rd of Victoria, Chap. 74, the use of all secret modes of communication by signs and passwords amongst the members of any society was prohibited. That Act, which extended the provisions of the 4th of George IV., was continued by the 8th and 9th of Victoria, Chap. 55, and Mr. Napier, in giving his opinion in '45, not only said that no oath could in any manner or under any pretence be lawfully used, but that secret signs and passwords were illegal, as were also the use of a test or declaration,

not sanctioned or already specified. In the face of this distinct opinion the society still held in by its signs and passwords, its tests and its declarations, and, in all probability, it still held on by its oath in some form or other. Those Acts are now obsolete.

By the 27th George III., cap. 15, sec. 6, it is illegal to administer or cause to be administered an oath which is not compelled by inevitable necessity; and the 50th George III., secs. 1, 2, and 3, prohibits "the administering, tendering, or causing to be administered or tendered, or by undue means causing to be taken any oath or *engagement* binding to belong to any society formed for seditious purposes, or to disturb the peace, or to compel any person to do or not to do any act; binding to obey the orders of an unlawful committee or leader; or *to assemble at command*." Of course, it is plain that the Orange Society does fall within the provisions of this Act of George III., as it is undoubtedly tended to disturb the peace, and as its members bind themselves to obey unlawful committees and leaders, and "to assemble at command."

Under 27th George III., the penalty for taking an illegal oath is seven years' imprisonment, to which, I have good reason to fear, many Orangemen are to-day liable.

That it is an illegal association there can be no doubt, and it would soon be declared to be such if legal authorities and our Irish Attorney-Generals, chosen as they have been from that class who sympathises with and finds its interest in the maintenance of political supporters, would choose to be consistent at the expense of expediency, and put those laws into motion that we find upon the Statute Book.

CHAPTER XXXVIII.—ORANGEISM AND THE LAND LEAGUE.

WHEN Michael Davitt, the Fenian, and the felon, rose amid the ruins of a demolished homestead to preach that new doctrine, "the land of Ireland for the people of Ireland," to some thousands of political sympathisers, he little thought he was sounding the death knell of Orange ascendancy in Ireland. It was a result beyond the purpose of the moment. It was a result devoutly to be wished for. But it was a result which could not reasonably seem within reach to the most sanguine expectations. Many national projects some, wild in theory, impossible in practice, had again and again been placed before the country. The warm Celtic blood of the Southerners, which

disdained difficulties, snatched at every new scheme, and eager for something which might help to drive the wolf from the door and save a starving people, joined with their usual enthusiasm in each new movement. The cool-headed Northerners still kept aloof. Finding nothing to appeal to their selfish natures, they bent to the dictates of their leaders—namely, their landlords — with the same meekness which a slave would to a master of whom he found it impossible to rid himself, and whom he thought it his interest to at least, conciliate. The result was to consolidate and unite the Orange party. Though they grumbled and growled by times beneath the hard rule of their task-masters, the system of discipline was such that they dared not rebel. The Orange henchmen, the Orange bailiffs, and the Orange agents met the first murmur of disaffection against the landlords, with a cry, "Are they not our brethren?" and at once the *regime* of the lodgeroom overpowered all natural expressions of feeling. But, in the face of all, it was still dreadfully apparent that the fact of being "brothers" to men whose rent-rolls were counted by the thousand did not any better enable the tenant to struggle against adverse seasons, and that the lip-sympathy which was annually given from Orange platforms by men who crossed from the hells of London, Paris, and Berlin for the purpose, and thereupon took their flight, but ill-compensated for the harshness of office rules and the exacting nature of office cupidity. The question was muttered in whispers between lodge night and lodge night. "If they are our brothers where is the brotherly love?" But the discipline of the order prevailed, the rank and file still suspecting that they had placed at their head a number of men who had their eyes open only to their own interests. The youngest son had now to find a home in Canada, for the facilities for emigration were not withheld them, and the agents boastfully talked of that other home beyond the seas where Orangemen would find a land of plenty. The daughter went next "lovelier in her tears" leaving the rural simplicity of Irish country life for the big cities of America. But still the rent-collector called and could not be paid. The agent then followed, as did also the clergyman to show how it was the duty of all true Orangemen to pay their rent; and to insinuate that non-payment was but the practice of rebels and of Papists. Another son now followed, and then another, and the old couple at home were left to dream over the glories of the Boyne, the gallant defence of Derry, and anon to watch with anxious expectation the arrival of the mail which brought the money orders of America to defray the expenses of non-resident landlords, and keep in luxury those agents who found compensation for their isolation in riotous living.

While this was proceeding in the counties there, was a body of men growing up in the cities who had already seen the game which the nobles were playing, and, though moved by no motives of sympathy for their agricultural brethren, but rather by that desire to share in power, which generally pervaded

the labouring classes of the kingdom at the time they struck against the old *regime*. They saw that Orangeism had too long been the tool of the landlords to secure their rent, and of the nobles to secure their power, and forthwith they set about altering it, never suspecting for a moment that they could not do so without reconstructing it from its foundation; not seeing that they could alone mend it on the principle of the proverbial stocking with the new foot and the new leg. These men were the reformers of '69. Down through their entire history, commencing from that unfortunate day when neighbours were hounded at each other upon the bloody Diamond had the landlords exclusive hold of the reins, no a tightening, now relaxing them to suit the stubborn nature of the team, but withal managing it with the dexterity of a skilful driver, who saw at any moment the possibility of being pitched from the box seat. The wedge was inserted in 1868, and, recollection being had to their tutoring, praise is due to a few unselfish men who followed the leaders of that movement. The Land Act of 1870 placed the farmers of the North in a new position. Though it may not have fulfilled all anticipations respecting it, or filled the pockets of the farming classes, it helped to place them in a position of comparative independence for some time. The professors of Orangeism were soon after confined to the farmers' boys and the labourers upon the holdings of those who were formerly of the brethren. But its failure, in accomplishing the ends intended, again placed the tenants at the mercy of the bailiff, and in the hope [of being in a better position to claim mercy under office rules, the tenants again found it their interest to resume their old position in the society. The result was as unsatisfactory as before. A few bad harvests made the payment of rent impossible, and again the human sacrifices followed as of old. Those who have traversed the Northern provinces between the years of 1870 and 1878 will easily recall the many affecting scenes which they witnessed at the railway stations as sons and daughters took a final leave of relatives and friends, whom they were never more to see upon this side of the grave. The breach went on widening; and at this crisis Michael Davitt—even Davitt, the Fenian and the felon; but Davitt, a fellow-sufferer, with feelings the same, with wrongs the same, hunted by the same cruel race of men, who allowed neither religion nor politics to interfere with their purses— Michael Davitt rose to preach a doctrine for the three provinces, in which he never believed the fourth would have joined.—

· "The land of Ireland for the people of Ireland" ' For a time Ulster remained passive. Some hoped that good might come of it, the majority feared it was a scheme as wild and visionary as many another, and meant that the land of Ireland should be for the Catholics of Ireland. Amongst the starving populations of the South and West the agitation spread like wild-fire. Fearing that it would not stop short of the Boyne, and that if the Ulstermen once tasted of this fruit they would begin to relish it, the Orange Grand Committee met in Dublin and decided that it was time to bestir themselves. These few noblemen and landed gentry, who composed the Grand Committee, had never wanted a few clergymen of the firebrand type, whom they feasted at their tables and who were prepared to befoul their cloth by any menial office if their relations were only allowed to remain unbroken. The clerical dodge had succeeded in the past and the hope was entertained that it would again succeed. Away to their pulpits and their platforms they went to denounce Communism and Popery, Land Leaguers, and Jesuits in disguise. But the hard-headed puritans of the North were but ill disposed to follow the example of the office-runners, who threw up their hats and cried, "No surrender," at the appointed moment. A few, it is true, did follow as they will always follow with "respectability," and on these few the Orange clergymen exhausted all their rabid utterances with some effect. But the time had passed when it was the highest ambition of Protestants and Presbyterians to be Orangemen. The ambition was how to live and the great problem of the day, how it could be accomplished. The wiser and more respectable section, if they quietly acquiesced, occasionally nodded their heads, and muttered there was much to be said on both sides of the question. Still the fire was spreading dangerously in the South. The agents next joined the clergy, and failing alike in their efforts, the word went round, over England and the Continent, that the landlords were wanted at home, for the brethren were likely to became rebellious. Home they flocked in numbers. Some had never seen their estates before; many had seen them at their imajorityonly and had since contended themselves with repocketing their rents. Many had only heard of Orangeism as a profession necessary for agents and bailiffs, and with extreme reluctance now submitted themselves to the mummery's of militia ion. Forth came this happy trio;' the lordling, his agent, and the clergyman, to excite the people to stand at the ramparts of landlordism. The text chosen at the beginning had failed. Could it be possible that it had failed because of not going far enough? they asked themselves, and, without waiting to inquire, they rushed into illegality, stepped upon the dangerous line which marks off civil war from the happiness of social life and the healthiness of constitutional agitation, and called on the brethren at once to arm. The wild utterances of such men—clergymen, be it remembered—as R. R. Kane, the Don Quixote of the party, and William Stewart Ross will long be remembered; and when the present agitation has ceased, and men settle down to their ordinary avocations, at peace under their own fig-trees, the duplicity of one of them will still stand as a monument of shame, and a warning to clerical partizans. Orangemen were called upon to arm, and were furnished with the means by men who refused to expose themselves to similar dangers. But the split of '68 was still there, and widening. Many refused the proffered musket, and told the landlords to keep them and fight their own battles.

The Land Leaguers now determined to meet their opponents upon their own ground, and accepting the challenge that they dared not show face in Ulster, Davitt appeared at a meeting at a place called The Kinnego, but a few miles removed from the memorable field of the Diamond. Here he again enunciated his doctrine, and at the close of the meeting was borne upon the shoulders of six stalwart Orangemen, amid the acclamations of the people. Amongst the first Protestants who stood by Davitt's side was the Rev. Harold Rylett, the clergyman of a small but respectable Unitarian congregation at Moneyrea, which counts every man of them a democrat alike in politics as in religion. Rylett was made organiser, and when Davitt went back into his prison cell, his ticket-of-leave being withdrawn, the Unitarian clergyman was left by Mr. Parnell to complete the work which had been so successfully commenced in Ulster. How it prospered is a matter familiar to all. While one section allied themselves with the old faction in the hope of picking up the crumbs of Emergency Committees and Protestant Defence Associations, the other boldly broke away from their old associations, heedless of the anathema of the Grand Lodge, and joined in a movement which they believed had for its object the benefit of all their class. Those brethren who did ally themselves with the Land Leaguers were not only vigorously denounced, but the paid libellers of the Institution were ready to declare that these men never were Orangemen at all, and forgetful of how much there is in an "if," they inconsistently added, "if they were Orangemen, they were never good ones."

The spirit of the time may well be read in such words as the following, which is an extract from a letter written by an Orange tenant-farmer to one of the Belfast morning papers:—

"What does this lesson teach? — that the mightiest Empire in the world does not require their (the Orangemen's) puny assistance. The Orangemen are kicked and persecuted when they are not required for electioneering purposes, and caressed when they are the useful tools to return a supporter of Tory landlordism to Parliament. If the Orange tenant-farmers ask themselves these questions—What have they gained by being the electioneering agents of Tory landlords? Are their rents any lower than their neighbours? Have Orangemen's widows or their orphan children in the hour of their distress been spared more than those of Catholics? Have both not been equally compelled to pay to the uttermost farthing, and equally mulcted in their tenant-right, and the poorer and more helpless the greater the burden placed upon them? Let all Orangemen cultivate their Orangeism, which means civil and religious liberty, and freedom of Parliamentary election, but let them cut loose from their Tory task-masters and deceivers, and, like true sons of William, become Orangemen in deed as well as in name."

Or from this, an answer to the denial of the statements that some Orangemen took the chairs at Land League meetings in the county of the Diamond:—"Those divines—Ellis, Kane, and other Christian men— feel it their duty to leave the pulpit, and for awhile occupy the platform, in order to save their brethren from becoming the easy dupes of designing impostors. We can hardly conceive it possible, at this enlightened period of the nineteenth century, for men to be so blind as not to comprehend the object these gentlemen have in view, because they are using the same wornout weapon of warfare that landlords always used—namely, the Orange against the Green, and because they know this old fabric is crumbling to the dust, they summon up all their forces and cry aloud from the Diamond Hill, 'It's all Popery!' But the

response is weak, and there are few to answer. In their last moments, like the Prophets of Baal, they say, 'O, people, hear us.' But the people will no longer sacrifice their own interests; and because they are disobeying these instructions we hear a Rev. Kane, Rector of Tullylish; Rev. Ellis, of Killylea; a Mr. Peel, of Armagh, all joined hand-in-hand to represent their fellow-men as traitors to the Orange cause. Why? Because these men feel they can no longer endure the pressure of the landlords' burden; and because they have become associated with anything likely to improve their condition, they must, according to these public teachers, be expelled from that society known as the Loyal Orange Lodge, with which some of them have been connected for more than twenty years. Why, we ask, have these men to be expelled from the lodge when Peel says they never were members? "Mr. Weir and Mr. Marshall are not Orangemen at all," is Mr. Peel's statement at the Diamond. Rev. Mr. Kane says if they are not drummed out he himself will leave the society. We ask the public which of these gentlemen are we to believe—whether Mr. T. G. Peel, who used to be a Methodist preacher, or the Rector of Tullylish, who evidently intends making a name for himself, if not in the pulpit, at least on the platform. We can hardly suppose Mr. Peel to be ignorant of the fact that both Weir and Marshall have been Orangemen for many years; and if their names are not to be found in the returned lists from the society, it does not alter the fact everybody knows. They are Orangemen notwithstanding. If Mr. Peel would look over another class of lists nearer home he would probably find the name of both parties connected with a little subscription. But we will push the matter no further at present. As regards the rector of Tullylish, the public are not ignorant of his inflammatory movements. Is it not a fact that some time ago, on a public platform, the same gentleman said that if a Protestant landlord was shot the blood of two Roman Catholics should flow for it, and is it not also a fact that for this and similar expressions his own bishop, the Bishop of Down, who we all know is a most liberal gentleman, cautioned Mr. Kane, and wrote to him on the subject; but the fatherly counsel of the bishop was set at naught, and he would have none of his reproof. Consequently we are not surprised at his remarks on this occasion. The spirit displayed by Mr. Peel and others towards the Land League movement since its commencement in this county has done more to further its interest than anything else we know of. James Weir will strike his name out of the Kinego Lodge, and when he does so, and takes with him his other brother Orangemen who have joined the League, the remaining body will not be difficult to number. There will be a branch of the League established near Mr. Marshall's, at the Bondhill; and of course the people will join, let Coroner Peel and Rev. Mr. Kane be ever so much excited. Every arrow they shoot will only kill in their own ranks. The wall of landlordism is already crumbling, and a few more Orangemen in the field of the League will speedily cause it to disappear.

WEIR, MARSHALL, & CO.,
Orangemen.

Kinego and the Bondhill.

How strangely would the heroes of the Diamond stare if those words could pierce through that impenetrable space which divides the living from the dead—the men of the Diamond of 1795 from the men of the Diamond of 1881—and tell them of the change that a century had wrought in the minds of men.

Despite all the frantic efforts of the Orange leaders, in the face of the bludgeon brigades of Down and the no surrender cries of Tyrone the land agitation kept steadily progressing, until, within a few months from the time I write, the Land League was enabled to make a firm footing in one of the most ultra-Orange counties of the North, and the appearance of a Land League candidate in Tyrone where greetings everywhere awaited him, where but a year before he would have been received with rotten eggs, told the fanatics and the landlord faction that the reign of Orange ascendency was no more.

Need we go further? Just a word more in my own justification, and we part, never, let us hope, to meet again over the discussion of such a painful subject. Some men whose intelligence command respect think the appearance of this history unadvisable because inopportune. It may tend, they fear, to keep many Orangemen from joining in with the ranks of the people. I think otherwise. The time has passed when the concealment of the truth can benefit any cause or any people. Let each man learn to know himself, should be the maxim, not only of men, but of parties, and as I cannot esteem the man who, on being shown his failings, is too self-conscious to correct them, neither can I esteem a party who, on reading over the errors of the past, determines to persist in them in the future. Nor do I hold in such low estimation many men of this Orange party as to think, when shown how they have been used by persons who were not of them, whose interests and whose motives were alike opposed to their interests and their motives, that they will not, however reluctantly, sever themselves from a society so inimical to the prosperity of their country. It is true it may make some men more bigoted, because it is opposed to every passion and every prejudice which bind them to the tail of a political junto condemned to die; but while the ignorant little boys and mistaken old men withdraw themselves behind the barriers which faction has raised against a people's progress, whatever intellect and whatever respectability still belong to the Orange brethren will come out in the end, I believe, into the open—rank themselves beside the people in the people's march, and, seeing in those hastily-put-together pages the sad records of their fathers' misdeeds, will become more earnest, more patriotic and more energetic, in the hope to blot those records out.

The End.

APPENDIX.

THE BATTLE OF THE DIAMOND.

(SEE CHAPTER VI., PAGE 18.

THE following is an account relative to the fight at the Diamond which will be found in the IV. Vol. of "Grattan's Life," by his son; a book deserving of much more attention from students of Irish history than it has hitherto received.

The account by Lord Gosford may seem almost incredible, and many may imagine that passion and prejudice might have coloured or exaggerated the facts, and that Government would not have permitted any body of magistrates so far to neglect their duties. But in confirmation of what Lord Gosford said, an evidence has of late appeared—an eye-witness of the facts, and whose testimony may be considered impartial, given as it is after a lapse of time, when the anger and fury of the day has subsided, and when truth may fearlessly be told, with a probability of being believed. An officer of the 24th Light Dragoons, whose regiment was sent to the North of Ireland in 1795, thus writes:—

[TO THE EDITOR OF THE GLOBE.]

"Newmarket, October 19, 1839.

"SIR * * * * * * *

"As a cornet in the 24th Light Dragoons, then commanded by the late Lord Wm. Bentinck, I accompanied the regiment to Ireland in 1795. We disembarked at Dublin, and proceeded to Clonmel, from whence, in the autumn of that year, a squadron was suddenly ordered, in consequence of the disturbed state of the country, to proceed to Armagh. To this squadron I was attached. Very shortly after our arrival the Caithness Highlanders, commanded by Sir Thomas, then Major, Molyneux, relieved a regiment of Irish militia stationed at Armagh. The County of Armagh was then in a very disturbed state, arising from the feuds between the Protestant and Catholic population, unhappily too much encouraged by the dominant party; but of these religious dissensions the Orange Societies, fostered and encouraged by the father of the present Colonel Verner, had their origin. The avowed object of the Protestant party was to drive the Catholics out of the country.

"In the course of the following year the whole regiment took up its quarters at Armagh and the neighbourhood. It so happened that I commanded a detachment of the regiment at Loughall, in the very centre of that part of the County of Armagh where the disturbance most prevailed, and not very far distant from the spot where the Battle of the Diamond took place. There I remained several months, and during that period I had witnessed the excesses committed by the Orange party, who now began to form themselves into lodges, and the dreadful persecutions to which the Catholic inhabitants were subjected. Night after night I have seen the rackings and burnings of the dwellings of these poor people. And notwithstanding the active exertions of the Sovereign of Armagh, under whose orders the military frequently scoured the country, our movements were so closely watched that these depredations were continued almost with impunity. When we arrived at a burning dwelling the perpetrators had fled across the country, and their course could only be traced by the fires they left in their progress.

"Many of the Orangemen, however, notwithstanding the secrecy with which they conducted their proceedings, were discovered on private information, and brought to trial.   But most of them, through the influence of their party, escaped, either altogether or with slight punishment.

"In one case, a most atrocious one, a man had been sentenced to death ; this man's sentence was respited, and I well remember the whole country found being illuminated with bonfires on manifestation of the joy of the Orangemen on that occasion   The result was an increased measure of persecution; many poor families were driven from their homes, their dwellings burnt, and themselves obliged to take shelter among their Catholic brethren in Connaught   These outrages were not unfrequently accompanied with bloodshed.

"I may mention one of these dreadful scenes, of which I was myself an eye-witness, during our nightly patrol.   We had already reached a heap of ruins, when a shot was heard, apparently about a quarter of a mile from the fire.   On proceeding to to the spot we discovered a dying man, whom the miscreants had shot in his house in their retreat from the fire.   They had fired through the window into the room where the man was sitting with his family.   The poor fellow died a few minutes after our arrival.

"It is impossible for me to describe, at this distance of time, the horrors and atrocities I witnessed during that period, which Major Molyneux describes as being without disturbance. Indeed, such was the state of the County of Armagh, that our regiment was quartered in the different mansions of the gentry of the county.

"Mr. O'Sullivan states that the Battle of the Diamond broke the neck of the Irish rebellion   It so happened that I was quartered at Market-hill, the house of Lord Gosford, when the rebellion of 1798 broke out, and I can positively assert, and I appeal to the history of those times, that the Catholics had no share in the disturbances of that period, at least in the North of Ireland.

"The rebellion, it is well known, was brought out by the United Irishmen, who were none of them Catholics, and not one of the leaders who were convicted and executed in the Counties of Down and Antrim were of that creed.   On the contrary, when the troops assembled at Castledawson, under General Knox, a most active magistrate, a resident in that town, Mr Shiel, who with his sons were in a corps of yeomanry, and took a most decided part in the suppression of the rebellion, were Roman Catholics.

"An Old Officer of Cavalry.".

JUDGE FLETCHER'S CHARGE.

The following is a summary of Mr. Justice Fletcher's charge at the Summer · Assizes of Wexford in 1814, and will, we think, be read with interest by our readers, dealing as it does, from an impartial standpoint, with the condition of the country at the time. As an exposure of the various jobs that were then perpetrated by the landocracy, the charge is, perhaps, unexampled.   In consequence of its length, much interesting matter has, of course, to be omitted ; but those desirous of perusing it in extenso will find a full report of the charge in the New Monthly Magazine of 1814 — .

Gentlemen,—It is matter of great congratulation that, after a period of thirty years (at the commencement of which I first knew the County of Wexford), I have reason to say, it is precisely in the same situation in which it was then, except as to an increase of wealth and population, and an improvement in agriculture, which has ameliorated its condition and multiplied its resources. The County of Wexford was then a moral curiosity. When other parts of the country were lawless and disturbed, this county had a peasantry, industrious in their habits, social in their disposition, satisfied with their state, and amenable to the laws, cultivating their farms with an assiduity which insured a competency. Their conduct was peaceful, their apparel whole, their morals improved, their lives spent in the frequent interchange of mutual good offices. It was a state of things which I reflect upon with pleasure. Each succeeding circuit showed me wild heaths and uncultivated tracts brought under the dominion of the plough, and producing corn for the sustenance of man. As it was then, so it continued for many years, until those unhappy disturbances, which burst out in this county with such a sudden and unexpected explosion. I knew what the state of things was then, and how that explosion was produced—professionally I knew it; because I enjoyed peculiar advantages of knowledge which other men did not enjoy. For several years I conducted the prosecutions for the Crown at Wexford, and hence I derived an intimate knowledge of those transactions. Besides, I was connected with no party, I was indifferent about party. But here I stop; I willingly draw a veil over the events of those days, and their causes. God forbid that I should tear asunder wounds, which, I hope, are completely and for ever closed.

I have now been absent from this county twelve years (with the exception of one Assizes, when I came here in the King's Commission, but upon that occasion I did not sit, as I now do, in the Crown Court.) I can say, however with the greatest truth, that at no period from my earliest acquaintance with your county, down to the present time, do I remember to have seen it in more profound tranquility, more perfect peace, more complete security, than at present—a state of things indicating a due administration of the laws by magistrates, neither over zealous and too active on the one hand, nor too negligent and supine on the other.

In my circuits through other parts in the kingdom, I have seen the lower orders of the people disturbed by many causes, not peculiar to any particular counties, operating with more effect in some, but to a greater or less extent in all. I have seen them operating with extended effect in the north-west circuit, in the counties of Mayo, Donegal, Derry, Roscommon, &c., &c. These effects have made a deep impression on my mind. My observations, certainly, have been those of an individual. but of an individual, seeing the same facts coming before him, judicially, time after time, and I do now publicly state, that never, during the entire period of my judicial experience, (comprising sixteen circuits), have I discovered or observed any serious purpose or settled scheme, of assailing his Majesty's Government, or any conspiracy connected with internal rebels, or foreign foes. But various, deep-rooted, and neglected causes, producing similar effects throughout this country, have conspired to create the evils, which really and truly do exist.

First—The extraordinary rise of land, occasioned by the great and increasing demand for the necessaries of life; and by producing large profits to the possessors of farms, excited a proportionate avidity for acquiring or renting lands. Hence extravagant rents have been bid for lands, without any great consideration; and I have seen these two circumstances operating upon each other, like cause and effect—the cause producing the effect; and like effect by re-action, producing the cause.

Next, we all know that the country has been deluged by an enormous paper currency, which has generated a new crime, now prominent upon the list in every calendar, the crime of making and uttering forged bank notes. In every province we have seen private banks failing, and ruining multitudes; and thus have fresh mischiefs flowed from this paper circulation. In the next place, the country has seen a magistracy over active in some instances, and quite supine in others. This circumstance has materially affected the administration of the laws in Ireland. In this respect I have found that those societies, called Orange Societies, have produced most mischievous effects, and particularly in the North of Ireland.

They poison the very fountain of justice; and even some magistrates, under their influence, have, in too many instances, violated their duty and their oaths. I do not hesitate to say that all associations of every description in this country, whether of Orangemen or Ribbonmen, whether distinguished by the colour of orange or of green—all combinations of persons bound to each other (by the obligation of an oath) in a league for a common purpose, endangering the peace of the country, I pronounce them to be contrary to law. And should it ever come before me to decide upon the question, I shall not hesitate to send up bills of indictment to a Grand Jury against the individuals, members of such an association, wherever I can find the charge properly sustained. Of this I am certain, that so long as those associations are permitted to act in the lawless manner they do, there will be no tranquillity in this country, and particularly in the North of Ireland. There, those disturbers of the public peace, who assume the name of Orange yeomen, frequent the fairs and markets with arms in their hands, under the pretence of self-defence, or of protecting the public peace, but with the lurking view of inviting the attacks from the Ribbonmen, confident that, armed as they are, they must overcome defenceless opponents, and put them down. Murders have been repeatedly perpetrated upon such occasions, and, though legal prosecutions have ensued, yet, such have been the baneful consequences of these factious associations, that, under

42

their influence, petty juries have declined, upon some occasions, to do their duty. These facts have fallen under my own view It was sufficient to say, such a man displayed such a colour, to produce an utter disbelief of his testimony, or, when another has stood with his hand at the bar, the display of his party badge has mitigated the murder into manslaughter

Gentlemen, I do repeat that these are my sentiments, not merely as an individual, but as a man discharging his judicial duty, I hope with firmness and integrity. With these Orange associations I connect all commemorations and processions, producing embittering recollections, and inflicting wounds upon the feelings of others, and I do emphatically state it as my settled opinion that, until those associations are effectually pulled down, and the arms taken from their hands, in vain will the North of Ireland expect tranquillity or peace.

Gentlemen—That moderate pittance which the high rents leave to the poor peasantry, the large county assessments nearly take from them ; roads are frequently planned and made, not for the general advantage of the country, but to suit the particular views of a neighbouring land holder, at the public expense. Such abuses shake the very foundation of the law; they ought to be checked. Superadded to these mischiefs, are the permanent and occasional absented landlords, residing in another country, not known by their tenantry, but by their agents, who extract the uttermost penny of the value of the lands. If a lease happens to fall in, they set the farm by public auction to the highest bidder. No gratitude for past services, no preference of the fair offer, no predilection for the ancient tenantry, be they ever so deserving; but, if the highest price be not acceded to, the depopulation of an entire tract of country ensues. What then is the wretched peasant to do? Chased from the spot where he had first drawn his breath—where he had first seen the light of heaven, incapable of procuring any other means of existence—vexed with those exactions I have enumerated, and harassed by the payment of tithes, can we be surprised that a peasant of unenlightened mind, of uneducated habits, should rush upon the perpetration of crimes, followed by the punishment of the rope and the gibbet? Nothing (as the peasantry imagine) remains for them, thus harassed and thus destitute, but with strong hand to deter the stranger from intruding upon their farms; and to extort from the weakness and terror of their landlords (from whose gratitude or good feelings they

have failed to win it a kind of preference for their ancient tenantry.

Such, gentlemen, have been the causes which I have seen thus operating in the North of Ireland, and in part of the South and West. I have observed, too, as the consequences of those Orange combinations and confederacies, men, ferocious in their habits, uneducated, not knowing what remedy to resort to, in their despair, flying in the face of the law, entering into dangerous and criminal counter associations, an endeavouring to procure arms, in order to meet, upon equal terms, their Orange assailants.

Gentlemen, I say it is incumbent upon you to vindicate the state of your county; you have ample materials for so doing, you know the roots of those evils which distract the country, they are to be found in those causes which I have now stated.

But, gentlemen, is there no method of allaying the discontents of the people, and preventing them from flying in the face of the laws? Is there no remedy but Act of Parliament after Act of Parliament, in quick succession, framed for coercing and punishing? Is there no corrective but the rope and the gibbet? Yes, gentlemen, the removal of those causes of disturbance which I have mentioned to you, will operate as the remedy. I should imagine that the permanent absentees ought to see the policy (if no better motive can influence them) of appropriating, liberally, some part of those splendid revenues which they draw from this country—which pay no land tax or poor's rate, and of which not a shilling is expended in this country! Is it not high time for those permanent absentees to offer some assistance, originating from themselves, out of their own private purses, towards improving and ameliorating the condition of the peasantry upon their great domains, and rendering their lives more comfortable?

For my part, I am wholly at a loss to conceive, how those permanent absentees can reconcile it to their feelings or their interests to remain silent spectators of such a state of things; or how they can forbear to raise their voices in behalf of their unhappy country, and attempt to open the eyes of our English neighbours, who, generally speaking, know about as much of the Irish as they do of the Hindoos. Does a visitor come to Ireland to compile a book of travels, what is his course? He is handed from one country gentleman to another, all interested in concealing from him the true state of the country; he passes from squire to squire, each rivalling the other in entertaining their guest; all busy in pouring falsehoods into his ear, touching the disturbed state of the country, and the vicious habits of the people.

Such is the crusade of information upon which the English traveller sets forward, and he returns to his own country with all his unfortunate prejudices doubled and confirmed—in a kind of moral despair of the welfare of such a wicked race, having made up his mind that nothing ought to be done for this lawless and degraded country. And, indeed, such an extravagant excess have these intolerant opinions of the state of Ireland attained, that I shall not be surprised to hear of some political projector coming forward and renovating the obsolete ignorance and prejudices of a Harrington, who, in his Oceana, calls the people of Ireland an untameable race, declaring that they should be exterminated, and the country colonized by Jews; that thus the state of this Island would be bettered, and the commerce of England extended and improved

Gentlemen, I had an opportunity of urging some of these topics upon the attention of a distinguished personage, I mean Lord Redesdale, who filled the high office of Lord Chancellor here some years ago. I was then at the bar. His Lordsh'p did me the honour of a visit, after I had returned from circuit, at a time when many an alarm, of one kind or another, floated in this country. He was pleased to require my opinion of the state of the country. I averred that I thought it was as tranquil as ever it had been; but I did ask his permission to suggest certain measures, which, in my opinion, would go very far in allaying the discontents of the people. One of these measures was a reform of the magistracy in Ireland; another was a commutation of tithes, if it could be satisfactorily effected; a third was the suppression of the home consumption of whiskey, and the institution of a wholesome malt liquor in its stead. I requested his Lordship to recollect that Hoga-th's print of "Gin-Alley is an unerring witness to testify what the English people would now be if they had nothing but a pernicious spirituous liquor to drink. A man who drinks to excess of a malt liquor becomes only stupefied, and sleeps it off; but he, whose intoxication arises from those spirituous liquors (which we know are too often adulterated by the most poisonous ingredients) adds only fever to his strength. Thus the unfortunate peasant in Ireland is maddened, instead of

being invigorated; and he starts out into acts of riot and disturbance, like a furious wild beast let loose upon the community. I took the freedom to add, " Reform the magistracy of Ireland, my Lord. You have the power to do this; and, until you do it, in vain will you expect tranquillity or content in the country." His Lordship was pleased to lend a courteous attention to these opinions; and I do believe that his own natural judgment and good inclination would have prompted him to measures beneficial to Ireland and honourable to his fame.

Gentlemen, this subject brings me to a consideration of the magistracy of the country. Of these, I must say some are over-zealous—others too supine: distracted into parties, they are too often governed by their private passions, to the disgrace of public justice, and the frequent disturbance of the country.

Here let me solicit your particular attention to some of the grievous mischiefs flowing from the misconduct of certain magistrates. One is occasioned by an excessive eagerness to crowd jails with prisoners, and to swell the calendars with crimes, Hence, the amazing disproportion between the numbers of the committals, and of the convictions, between accusation and evidence, between hasty suspicion and actual guilt. Committals have been too frequently made out (in other counties) upon light and trivial grounds, without reflecting upon the evil consequences of wresting a peasant (probably innocent) from the bosom of his family, immuring him for weeks or months in a noisome jail, amongst vicious companions. He is afterwards acquitted, or not prosecuted, and returns a lost man, in health and morals, to his ruined and beggard family. This is a hideous but common picture.

Again, fines and forfeited recognizances are multiplied through the misconduct of a magistrate. He binds over a prosecutor, under a heavy recognizance, to attend at a distant Assizes, where, it is probable that the man's poverty or private necessities must prevent his attending. The man makes default, his recognizance is forfeited; he is committed to the county jail upon a green wax process; and, after long confinement, he is finally discharged at the Assizes, pursuant to the statute; and, from an industrious cottager, he is degraded, from thenceforth, into a beggar and a vagrant.

Other magistrates presume to make out vague committals, without specifying the day of the offence charged, the place, or any other particular, from which the unfortunate prisoner could have notice to prepare his defence. This suppression is highly indecorous, unfeeling, and unjust; and it deserves upon every occasion, a severer probation of the magistrate, who thus deprives his fellow-subject of his rightful opportunity of defence There are parts of Ireland, where, from the absence of the gentlemen of the country, a race of magistrates has sprung up, who ought never have borne the King's commission. The vast powers entrusted to those officers, call for an upright, zealous, and conscientious discharge of their duty.

Persons there have been of a sort, differing widely from those I have described These men identify their preferment with the welfare of the church; and if you had believed them, whatever advanced the one, necessarily promoted the other Some clergymen there may have been, who, in a period of distraction, perusing the old testament with more attention than the new, and admiring the glories of Joshua (the son of Nun), fancied they saw in the Catholics the Canaanites of old; and, at the head of militia and armed yeomanry, wished to conquer from the promised glebe. Such men, I hope, are not to be now found in that most respectable order, and, if they are, I need scarcely add, they should no longer remain in the commission.

Gentlemen—I must further admonish you, if you are infested with any of the Orange or Green associations in this county, to discourage them—discourage all processions and commemorations connected with them, and y u will promote the peace and concord of the country; but suffer them

to prevail, and how can justice be administered ? "I am a loyal man," says a witness, that is, "Gentlemen of the petty jury, believe me, let me swear what I will.' When he swears he is a loyal man, he means, "Gentlemen of the jury, forget your oaths and acquit the Orangeman" A truly loyal man is one who is attached to the constitution under which we live, and who respects and is governed by the laws, which impart more personal freedom, when properly administered, than any other code of laws in existence ' If there are disturbances in the country, the truly loyal man endeavours to appease them. The truly loyal man is peaceful and quiet. He does his utmost to prevent commotion, and, if he cannot prevent it, he is at his post, ready to perform his duty in the day of peril, But what says the loyal man of another description—the mere pretender to loyalty? "I am a loyal man in times of tranquility; I am attached to the present order of things, as far as I can get any good by it; I malign every man of a different opinion from those whom I serve; I bring my loyalty to market" Such loyalty has borne higher or lower prices, according to the different periods of modern times. He exposes it to sale in open market, at all times, seeking continually for a purchaser.

Such are the pretenders to loyalty, many of whom I have seen; and incalculable mischiefs they perpetrate. It is not their interest that their country should be peaceful; their loyalty is a "Sea of troubled waters."

REPORT OF THE SELECT COMMITEE (ENGLISH) OF THE HOUSE OF COMMONS OF 1835.

THE Select Committee appointed to inquire into the Origin, Nature, Extent, and Tendency of Orange Institutions in *Great Britain* and the Colonies; and to report the evidence taken before them, and their opinion, to the House—have considered the matters to them referred, and agree to the following report ·—

Your committee have examined Lord Kenyon, the Deputy Grand Master of England and Wales; Lieutenant-Colonel Fairman, the Deputy Grand Secretary and Deputy Grand Treasurer; Mr. Chetwoode, the late Deputy Grand Secretary; Mr Nucella, Commissioner to the Continent, and several other persons, officers and members of the

Orange Institution of Great Britain. The Duke of Cumberland, the Grand Master of the Empire, communicated to the committee that he had no statement to make to them, as appears by the annexed correspondence. The Duke of Gordon, the Deputy Grand Master of Scotland, was summoned, but being on the Continent did not attend.

Your committee have also examined several of the books and papers belonging to the institution; but they regret that their inquiries have been much narrowed by Lieutenant-Colonel Fairman withholding the Book of Correspondence since February, 1834, and also the numerous documents of the institution remaining in his possession; your committee are, however, of opinion, that the oral and documentary evidence which they have obtained (without reference to the evidence taken before the Committee on Orange Lodges in Ireland) is amply sufficient to prove the existence of an organised institution pervading Great Britain and her Colonies to an extent never contemplated as possible; and which your committee consider highly injurious to the discipline of his Majesty's army, and dangerous to the peace of his Majesty's subjects.

ORIGIN.

The Letter-book of the Loyal Orange Institution laid before your committee commences only with the year 1808, although Orange Lodges were held in England before that time, by warrants under the Grand Lodge of Dublin. The correspondence with Mr. Verner, of the Grand Lodge in Dublin, shows in what manner the first Grand Lodge was established in England. It was formed in Manchester in 1808, under Samuel Taylor, Esq,, of Moston, as Grand Master; and warrants, to hold lodges under the English institution, were then first granted. The Grand Lodge of England, continued to hold its meetings in Manchester, granting new warrants, and exchanging English for Irish warrants to all who sought for them and were qualified to receive them, until the year 1821, when it was removed to London; and the first meeting (as appears by the minutes) was held at Lord Kenyon's on the 27th of April, 1821, his lordship, as Deputy Grand Master, in the chair.

But, in order to lay fully before the House the nature, extent, and tendency of the Local Orange Institution of Great Britain, your committee consider it requisite to explain the constitution, rules, and ordinances under which the lodges are constituted and conducted.

NATURE OR CONSTITUTION.

The Loyal Orange Institution of Great Britain is unlimited as to numbers, and exclusively a Protestant association, its affairs are directed by a Grand Master, a Grand Secretary, a Grand Treasurer, a Deputy Grand Master, a Deputy Grand Secretary and a Deputy Grand Treasurer, a Grand Chaplain and Deputy Grand Chaplains, a Grand Committee and Grand Officers constituting the Imperial Grand Lodge in London.

IMPERIAL GRAND LODGE.

The Imperial Grand Lodge meets in the metropolis on the third Thursday in February; on the 4th of June, and at such other times as shall

be appointed by the Grand Master or the Deputy Grand Master. No regulation, resolution, or rule of the Orange Institution can be at any time rescinded, altered, or amended without notice of the intention to move or rescind, alter or amend the same, being given at the regular meeting of the Imperial Grand Lodge previous to such motion; and no complaint, proposition, matter, or thing can be considered or discussed in the Imperial Grand Lodge until the same shall have been submitted to the Grand Committee, unless the Grand Master or Deputy Grand Master, or dignitary presiding, shall be of opinion that inconvenience or injury would arise from its postponement. The order observed and attention given to all proceedings of the Grand Lodge may be judged of from the fact that the Grand Master never enters the lodge or leaves it without the mace being carried before him; that, during the sittings of the lodge, the mace is always placed on the table before the Grand Master; and that a member of the lodge styled a Tyler is stationed outside the door. Every lodge is opened and closed with prayers, the forms of which are printed in the rules and ordinances of the institution.

The Imperial Grand Lodge is held in Portman Square, London, at the house of Lord Kenyon, the Deputy Grand Master of England and Wales; and the Duke of Cumberland, when in England, has always, since he accepted the office of Grand Master, presided at such meetings. The business is generally prepared some days previous to the meeting by the Grand Committee and the Deputy Grand Secretary; and is submitted to the meeting of the Grand Lodge, as a report, in due form; there being a rota of business always prepared and placed at the same time before the Grand Master or chairman. The report of the Grand Committee and the resolutions prepared by them are read through in the first instance, and then put separately from the chair; such resolutions, being seconded and put to the assembly, are decided by show of hands; and the resolutions, when agreed to, have often the initials of the Grand Master affixed to them. The minutes of the proceedings of every meeting of the Grand Lodge are submitted, after the meeting, by the Deputy Grand Secretary to the Deputy Grand Master, for his examination and correction; and are afterwards printed, as appears by the following extract from the minutes of a meeting of the Grand Lodge, 27th April, 1821: —"Resolved—That no communication, written or printed, of the proceedings of the Grand Lodge be made without the special orders of the Grand Lodge, Grand Master or Deputy Grand Master." The Deputy Grand Secretary officially signs all those circulars, and copies of them are generally sent to each dignitary of the institution, to the Deputy Grand Masters of districts, and to masters of separate lodges at home and abroad.

CONNECTION OF IRISH AND ENGLISH ORANGE LODGES.

The connection of the Orange Lodges of Ireland and Great Britain is shown by the following rule:—

"Rule 12—The members of the late or present Grand Orange Lodge of Ireland are honorary members of the Imperial Grand Lodge of Great Britain.

"Proxies from masters of lodges and from dignitaries are admitted to the Grand Lodge meetings."

The grand committee, consisting of thirty-six members, all of them being grand officers of the institution, are appointed by the Imperial Grand Lodge, with power in the Grand Master and Deputy Grand Master to add to their number; the duty of this committee is to watch over the affairs of the institution while the Imperial Grand Lodge is not sitting, to decide all applications or appeals, and to exercise such other powers, conformable to the rules of the institution, as the exigencies of the different cases coming before them shall require. Five members are competent to act; and six members are annually nominated in the room of six retiring, but who are re-eligible. Lieutenant-Colonel Fairman states that the grand committee, whenever the Deputy Grand Secretary finds it necessary to call on them for advice, meets to deliberate and advise, in the same manner as a Cabinet or Privy Council; all the acts of the grand committee are submitted to the scrutiny and concurrence of the Imperial Grand Lodge at its ensuing meeting.

DEPUTY GRAND MASTERS.

The Deputy Grand Masters of counties, cities, and boroughs, sending members to Parliament, are appointed by the Imperial Grand Lodge. The Deputy Grand Masters of districts are appointed by the Imperial Grand Lodge on the recommendation of the brethren of the districts. The Masters of Warrants are annually elected by their respective members, subject to the approbation of the Imperial Grand Lodge, in which they are represented by the Deputy Grand Masters of districts. And each Deputy Grand Master of a district convenes a meeting of the several masters in his neighbourhood, at which he presides, once every

six months, or oftener if necessary, to discuss the affairs of the institution. Each master of a lodge is directed, at each regular half-yearly meeting, to present a correct report of the state of his warrant (or lodge) to the Deputy Grand Master of the district, who makes his return to the Imperial Grand Lodge on or before the 24th days of May and December respectively. Besides the district lodges there are isolated lodges—that is, such lodges as, by reason of distance or any other circumstances, cannot be conveniently attached to any particular district; and all these may communicate with the nearest Deputy Grand Master of any district. And at each regular half-yearly district meeting the Deputy Grand Master collects, and transmits to the Deputy Grand Treasurer or to the Deputy Grand Secretary of the Imperial Lodge, the returns, with the fees, dues, and all moneys received on account of the institution. Every member of the institution, from the rank of Grand Commissioner downwards, must first belong to some specified lodge. No lodge can be constituted except by warrant from the Grand Lodge, under the signature of the Grand Master, and with the seal of the Grand Lodge; and all members of the Imperial Grand Lodge are members of every other lodge in Great Britain.

RULES AND ORDINANCES OF THE LOYAL ORANGE INSTITUTION.

Your committee call the attention of the House to the fact that the rules and ordinances of the Loyal Orange Institution in Great Britain, and of the Grand Orange Lodge in Ireland, are nearly similar; the rules of the former having been first formed from those of the latter; the objects of both institutions are also nearly analogous; the same signs and passwords are used by the members of both institutions; members of lodges in Ireland are admitted into lodges of the Loyal Orange Institution in Great Britain, and also in the colonies, and vice versa; the systems of England and Ireland were assimilated in 1831-2*; and the new system of lectures, secret signs, and passwords has of late years been adopted by all Orangemen in the United Kingdom and in the colonies; and the ordinances declare that "its whole institution is one neighbourhood, within which every Orangeman is at home in the farthest parts of the world."

PASSWORDS AND SIGNS.

The system of signs and passwords adopted by

---

* Grand Lodge Minute Book, 4th June, 1832. For reasons at once satisfactory and obvious, the Grand Lodge have judged it necessary to alter their passwords, and to assimilate the English and Irish lectures in both orders.

the Orange Institution in Ireland on its revival, 15th September, 1828, was framed by the Deputy Grand Secretary of England, and is now in use in Great Britain and Ireland. The English Orange Institution originated from the Irish; and in 1828 the Irish was revived from the English; and the same signs became common to both countries.

FEES.

All members must be ballotted for, and (with the exception of soldiers and sailors who may be admitted without any charge) are required to pay to the Imperial Lodge for initiation 3s each. Those who attain the Purple Order pay 2s more. The annual contribution of not less than 2s from each member is collected by the master of the lodge, who remits every half year all moneys he receives to the Deputy Grand Treasurer of the Imperial Lodge. Fees are paid by the grand officers, varying from £5 by the right reverend the prelate of the institution to 5s by masters of warrants.

OATHS.

Much controversy has existed about the taking of oath at the initiation of members. It has been distinctly proved to the committee that every member admitted prior to 1821 took a particular oath, as appears by a copy of the rules and orders, printed in 1800, and delivered in by Mr. Chetwoode, as follows:—

"Obligation of an Orangeman.

"I, A B, do solemnly and sincerely swear, of my own free will and accord, that I will, to the utmost of my power, support and defend the present King George the Third, his heirs and successors, so long as he and they support the Protestant ascendancy, the Constitution and laws of these kingdoms, and that I will ever hold sacred the name of our glorious deliverer, William the Third, Prince of Orange; and I do further swear that I am not nor ever was a Roman Catholic or Papist; that I was not, am not, nor ever will be an United Irishman; and that I never took the oath of secresy to that or any other treasonable society; and I do further swear, in the presence of Almighty God, that I will always conceal, and never will reveal either part or parts of what is now to be privately communicated to me, until I shall be authorised so to do by the proper authorities of the Orange Institution; that I will neither write it nor indite it, stamp, stain, or engrave it, nor cause it so to be done, on paper, parchment, leaf, bark, stick, stone, or anything, so that it may be known; and I do further swear that I have not, to my knowledge or belief, been proposed and rejected in or expelled from any other

Orange Lodge, and that I now become an Orangeman without fear, bribery, or corruption. So help me God."

HIS ROYAL HIGHNESS THE DUKE OF YORK.

His Royal Highness the Duke of York accepted the office of Grand Master of the Loyal Orange Institution in England, as appears by his letter of 3rd February, 1821; but being informed soon afterwards that "the law officers of the Crown and other eminent lawyers were decidedly of opinion that the Orange Association, under the oath administered to their members, was illegal," he withdrew himself from the association.

OPINION OF COUNSEL AS TO THE ORANGE INSTITUTION.

The Loyal Orange Institution under Lord Kenyon, the Deputy Grand Master for England, submitted, in December, 1821, a case for the opinion of Mr. Serjeant John Lens and other counsel as to the legality of the Orange Institution, under the alterations proposed to be made in the rules and ordinances, leaving out the Orangeman's oath, but retaining the oaths of allegiance. 1st William and Mary, c. 1, s. 8; oath of supremacy, 1st Anne, c. 22, s. 1; and of abjuration, 6 Geo. 3, c. 53; retaining also secret signs and passwords, and certain religious ceremonies at the initiation.

The committee refer to the case and opinions thereon, and have to observe that the Orangeman's oath appears to have been, from that time, left out of the rules and ordinances; and certain religious forms, as prescribed in the Ritual, are stated to have been substituted, and to be now invariably used on initiation of members; besides the administration of the oaths of allegiance, supremacy, and abjuration, which everyone must also take.

WARRANT FOR LODGE.

To evade the law the word warrant was substituted for lodge; the original form was to grant a warrant to hold a lodge in a particular house or place; and, by the alteration, it was given to the person to hold a lodge wheresoever he pleased. It has been a rule that Irish warrants cannot be acted upon in England, or English warrants acted on in Ireland; and a new warrant is therefore given in exchange, as a matter of course, on application.

LODGES IN IRELAND IN 1825 UNDER THE LOYAL ORANGE INSTITUTION.

It is particularly deserving of notice that when the Grand Orange Lodge was discontinued in Ireland in the years 1825 to 1828 the Loyal Orange Institution of England issued warrants, under which lodges were held in Ireland; and the objects and intentions of the law were thus frustrated.

GRAND ORANGE LODGE PROCEEDINGS.

The effect of the religious ceremonies and forms has been to enforce, with the apparent obligation of an oath, secresy on the members admitted; as the Deputy Grand Master of England and Wales, and all the Orangemen examined by the committee (with one exception) refused to communicate the secret signs and passwords of the institution, and it appears that a disclosure of the system by a member would subject him to expulsion.   The committee are, however, of opinion that the object and effect of these religious ceremonies cannot be better comprehended than by reading the following extracts from the Ritual of the Purple Order :—

RITUALS.

(Ritual of the Introduction to the Purple Order)

When a brother is to be introduced the tyler shall first enter the room, after him two Purplemen, then the two sponsors of the brother, each bearing a purple rod, decorated at the top with orange ribands, and between them the brother himself, carrying in both hands the Bible, with the book of the Orange rules and regulations placed thereon. On his entering the room a chaplain, or in his absence a brother appointed by the Master, shall say—

"We have a strong city; salvation will God appoint for walls and bulwarks   Open ye the gates, that the righteous nation which keepeth the truth may enter in. Thou wilt keep him in perfect peace whose mind is stayed on Thee ; because he trusteth in Thee. Trust ye in the Lord for ever, for in the Lord Jehovah is everlasting strength.—Isaiah xxvi, 1, 2, 3, 4

The Master shall then say—Friend, what dost thou desire in this meeting of true Orangemen ?

The Brother shall answer—Of my own free will and accord I desire admission into your loyal association.

[Then the sponsors shall bow to the master, and signify the same, each saying—I, N. M. vouch for all these things]

Master—What do you carry in your hand?

Brother—The Word of God.

Master—Under the assurance of these faithful Purplemen, we believe that you have also carried it in your heart. What is that other book?

Brother—The book of our rules and regulations.

Master—Under the like assurance, we trust that you have hitherto obeyed them in all lawful matters. Therefore, we gladly advance you into this order. Purplemen, bring to me our brother.

[He shall then be brought by the two sponsors before the master, the tyler retiring to the door, and the two brothers standing one at each side of the centre of the table]

During this the chaplain or brother appointed shall say—

"In that day shall the branch of the Lord be beautiful and glorious; and the fruit of the earth shall be excellent for them that are escaped out of Israel   And the Lord will create upon every dwelling place of Mount Zion, and upon her assemblies a cloud and smoke by day, and the shining of a flaming fire by night; for upon all The Glory shall be a defence "—Isaiah iv., 3, 5.

[The brother shall then kneel on his right knee, and the master shall invest him with a purple sash and such other decorations as may be convenient]   Then the chaplain or brother appointed shall say—

"Behold the stone which I have laid before Joshua.   Upon one stone shall be seven eyes · behold I will engrave the graving thereof, saith the Lord of Hosts, and I will remove the iniquity of that land in one day "—Zec. iii, 9.

[Then the master shall communicate, or cause to be communicated, unto the new Purpleman the signs and passwords of the order.

And the chaplain or brother appointed shall say—

"Seek Him that maketh the seven stars and Orion, and turneth the shadow of death into the morning, and maketh the day dark with night ; that calleth for the waters of the sea, and poureth them out upon the face of the earth, The Lord is his name."—Amos, v. 8.

"He that hath an ear, let him hear what the Spirit saith unto the Churches."—Revelations, ii. 29.

[After which the brethren shall make obeisance to the master, and take their seats; the certificate of the new Purpleman being first duly signed and registered]

Signed by order of the Grand Lodge,

W. BLENNERHASSETT FAIRMAN, D.G.S.

POWER OF THE GRAND MASTER.

By the laws and ordinances of the Loyal Orange Institution, the Grand Master of the Empire is the chief and supreme head; his office is permanent and uncontrolled; no particular functions or duties can be prescribed to him, as his powers and authority are discretionary, illimitable, and absolute; and, to him the honour and welfare of the institution are implicitly confided, t is declared in the report of the Grand Lodge on 18th February, 1834, "that implicit obedience to the commands of the Grand Master, due subordination to the Grand Lodge and the constituted authorities, and unreserved conformity to the laws and ordinances of the institution, are duties imperative on Orangemen."

His Royal Highness Ernest Augustus Duke of Cumberland is now the Grand Master of the Empire, being equally the supreme head of the Loyal Orange Institution in Great Britain and of the Grand Orange Lodge in Dublin, thus connecting all the Orangemen in the United Kingdom and the colonies. The same powers are vested in the Deputy Grand Master, either by delegation from or in the absence of the Grand Master. His Grace the Duke of Gordon is Deputy Grand Master for Scotland, and Lord Kenyon Deputy Grand Master for England and Wales; and it is stated by the Grand Secretary that Lord Kenyon "is probably better informed than any other man with the working of the institution."

ORANGE LODGES, HOW CONSTITUTED.

The Orange Lodges are held under warrants from the Grand Lodge of the institution, which are always signed by the Duke of Cumberland as Grand Master of the Empire, and are also generally signed by some of the grand officers of the lodge; but his Royal Highness has also power to grant on his sole responsibility, and without any other signature warrants to any person to constitute lodges within or without the kingdom. The itinerant warrant granted to Lieutenant-Colonel Fairman, the Deputy Grand Secretary, under which he made two tours of inspection in Great Britain, and the warrant for foreign countries granted to Edward Nucella, Esq., to hold and to establish lodges in Malta, Corfu, and other places out of England as he might think proper, have been laid before the committee, and copies of them are hereafter annexed in proof of the exercise of the unlimited power of the Grand Master in matters respecting the spread of Orangeism.

ITINERANT WARRANT.

By that commission or itinerant warrant, dated the 18th of August, in the year 1832, the Duke of Cumberland, as Imperial Grand Master, by virtue of the authority vested in him by the code of laws and ordinances of the 30th March, 1826, nominated "his trusty, well-beloved, and right worshipful brother, Lieutenant-Colonel Fairman, Master of the Metropolitan Warrant; Member of the Grand Committee, Deputy Grand Master of London,

Acting Deputy Grand Treasurer, and Deputy Grand Secretary of the institution, to make a visitation, or tour of inspection of the kingdom; to perform, settle, and terminate every matter of business in anywise connected with the society or its affairs, or tending to promote its prosperity or welfare, with a dispensation and power to enable that dignitary and officer to communicate to the brotherhood the signs and passwords of the new system; to teach the lectures in both Orange and Purple Orders; to open new lodges, and to suspend or expel contumacious and refractory members, subject to a ratification of his proceedings by the Grand Lodge."

Lieutenant-Colonel Fairman, under the above authority, made two visitations or tours of inspection of the kingdom at the expense of the Grand Lodge, assembling and visiting the lodges at Birmingham, Wolverhampton, Manchester, Sheffield, Bolton, Wigan, Chowlent, Burnley, Bolton-le-Moors, Preston, Blackburn, Bury, Middleton, and other places. He visited the established Orange lodges at those places and in their neighbourhood, and exerted himself also to form new lodges wherever there was a prospect of success. At Edinburgh and in other places in the West of Scotland, as stated elsewhere, he visited the old and established some new lodges, thereby giving life and activity to Orangeism in that country. Lieutenant-Colonel Fairman had the power and authority of initiating any person when travelling in the country, or under certain circumstances, by virtue of the special commission; he has often initiated persons at his own house; he granted to Private Wilson, of the 6th Dragoons, at Sheffield, a military warrant in the spring of 1834, which, he said, was the only warrant he ever had granted to a regiment. [Here follows a copy of the warrant granted by "Ernest," Imperial Grand Master, to Lieut.-Colonel Fairman.]

THE OSTENSIBLE OBJECT IS RELIGIOUS.

The ostensible object of the institution is to support the Protestant religion and Protestant ascendancy, and to protect what they consider the rights of Protestants. Lord Kenyon declares the institution to be essentially religious, although he admits that its acts have not always strictly preserved that character. In Lancashire some funds have been collected for the assistance of decayed brethren, and thereby given, in some degree, the character of benefit or benevolent societies to Orange lodges. The Imperial Grand Lodge, however, has never sanctioned such an object, having stated in the ordinances of 1834 that benefit clubs are excrescences which the institution takes no notice of whatever, and will not recognise; but they will not prohibit them, provided they do not interfere with any of the rules of the institution.

QUALIFICATION OF AN ORANGEMAN.

If the objects of Orange lodges were to be judged of by the moral qualification required by any person before he can be admitted a member there would be little objection to them. The qualifications are stated in the rules and ordinances, and the following are some of the chief requisites:— "Every person to be qualified to be an Orangeman should love rational and improving society, regarding with affection the Protestant established religion, and sincerely desiring to propagate its precepts. Wisdom and prudence should guide his actions; temperance and sobriety, honesty and integrity, direct his conduct; and the honour and glory of his King and country be the motives of his exertions." But your committee are of opinion that the character and proceedings of the Orange Society ought not to be tried by a mere reference to their professions, inasmuch as the conduct of that society and the results which have ensued from their measures, are at variance with the ostensible objects held out by their rules and ordinances.

Your committee find that the Orange lodges have a decidedly political character, and that almost all their proceedings have had some political object in view.

It appears by the correspondence that the institution has been considered by some Orangemen a source of patronage, and there are various applications from the brethren for the influence and assistance of the dignitaries of the Imperial Grand Lodge (which influence and assistance appear frequently to have been used) to procure licences for public-houses, pensions in the artillery, and situations in the police and in the docks; and these applications appear to have increased to such an extent that the Deputy Grand Secretary intimates in the printed circular of the proceedings of the Imperial Lodge, held on the 16th April, 1833, "that the duties of the Deputy Grand Secretary are so irksome and onerous as compels him to notify that his labours will not admit of the additional toils imposed by applications for patronage and places which are pouring in upon him daily. To so oppressive an extent have such importunities been carried as to be sufficient to engross the whole attention of one individual to read (far less to in-

vestigate the merits of) memorials and petitions, with the prayers of which neither the illustrious Grand master of the Empire nor the Deputy Grand Master has the power of complying. The Deputy Grand Secretary has to remind the brotherhood that it never was intended the institution should be rendered thus subservient to the personal views and private ends of the interested."

NUMBER OF LODGES UNDER THE LOYAL ORANGE INSTITUTION.

The committee have found considerable difficulty in ascertaining the number of Orange lodges holding under the Loyal Orange Institution of Great Britain, as Lieutenant-Colonel Fairman, the Deputy Grand Secretary, declared that he had no register of the lodges made up to the present time; he stated that there were about 300 lodges in activity, although he had kept no general register; but had noted the list of new warrants granted, and of old warrants renewed, on separate slips of paper, which were sometimes entered on the minutes of the Grand Lodge, and at other times omitted; and, therefore, he could not give the exact number. Mr. Eustace Chetwoode, who who had been (for about ten years) Deputy Grand Secretary, previous to Lieutenant-Colonel Fairman, stated that there were in his time about 800 lodges in Great Britain and the Colonies; and he delivered in a printed list of 297 lodges, corrected, in manuscript, up to 1830—thirty of which, as afterwards stated in this report, were lodges held in the army and artillery; with the number of the regiment or corps printed in the list opposite the number of the lodge. The committee directed Mr. Colwill, the assistant-secretary to Lieutenant-Colonel Fairman, to make out a register of the existing lodges, as far as they appear to be now entered in the books of the institution, amounting, as will be seen by the appendix, to 381 warrants, of which 293 are belonging to 47 districts, and 93 warrants, are unattached to any districts. It appears by reference to the books of the secretary of the Grand Lodge laid before the committee, and from which the assistant-secretary made out the list, that there are 47 districts, with a Deputy Grand Master appointed to each—viz., in the Ayr district 10 lodges are entered on the books, in Bradford 18, in Cambridge 3, in Glasgow 12, in Liverpool 13, in Leeds 14, in Rochdale 12, in Woolwich 9, &c.; the 93 lodges unattached, are in the army, in the Colonies, and in isolated places.

NUMBER OF ORANGEMEN IN GREAT BRITAIN.

There is no correct list of the number of Orange-

HISTORY OF ORANGEISM.—APPENDIX. 283

then belonging to the London Orange Institution; and it is impossible for the committee to form a correct opinion thereon, from the contradictory statements before them. The Deputy Grand Secretary would not, or could not, state any specific number. Mr. Cooper, a member of the Grand Committee, who had taken an active part in the affairs of the institution, stated that he had met in a lodge in Cockspur Street 200 masters holding warrants; that the number of Orangemen in London might be 40,000, and that these, if any emergency should occur, might be assembled by the Grand Lodge; that if all the dormant lodges were called into activity there might be 120,000 to 140,000 Orangemen in Great Britain. Other witnesses could give no estimate, and your committee can hardly believe, from all the evidence before them, that the numbers are so great as have been stated by Mr Cooper.

Any number of brethren, not less than five, may meet and transact Orange business in any part of Great Britain, under the authority of a Master's warrant, provided that a dignitary, or a Deputy Master, or a committee-man, be amongst them.

LODGES IN THE ARMY.

In the earlier years the applications to the Loyal Orange Institution, from the militia and the other regiments which had been in Ireland, were chiefly for the exchange of Irish warrants, which they had received in Dublin, for English warrants; and the letters will show that they were very numerous. In the circular of the proceedings of the Imperial Grand Lodge of the 4th June, 1833, there is the following notice:—"All Irish warrants now in operation in Great Britain should be immediately exchanged for English warrants, by an application to the Deputy Grand Secretary, to whose office the former ought to be sent without delay." And Mr. Chetwoode informed the committee that he never hesitated to exchange English for Irish warrants to regiments, or to any part of the army, and never made any inquiry or hesitated to grant them. It is, however, stated by him that he had an impression that all military warrants had been granted in Ireland to non-commissioned officers and privates, with the previous sanction of the commanding officers, although he never saw any note or certificate to that purport to warrant that belief.

LETTERS.

Your committee have selected some letters received from the non-commissioned officers and privates in the army, and also the answers to them, which will satisfy the House that the grand officers

of the Loyal Orange Institution have given assistance and encouragement to keep up and to establish lodges in the army, although these officers were made acquainted with the orders of the commander-in-chief, forbidding the attending or holding them in regiments, and notwithstanding they were informed that some commanding-officers had actually suppressed the lodges in conformity with the general orders. Major Anderson, commanding the 50th Regiment, destroyed warrant No 53, which was held in that corps, and thereon a letter was written to Henry Nichols, of the Light Company, dated May 27, 1830, requesting a new warrant. Major Middleton, of the 42nd Regiment, also prohibited the holding of the lodge in that regiment at Malta. It will also be seen by the letters from New South Wales, and the letters to Corfu and other places, that the general orders of the Commander-in-Chief were explained by the Deputy Grand Secretary to the soldiers with whom he corresponded, as being intended, not really to suppress the lodges, but merely to hold out only a semblance of doing so.

Your committee inserts a list of military warrants issued to the following regiments to hold lodges under the Loyal Orange Institution, and which was extracted from the printed register of 1830, presented by Mr. Chetwoode; and, if the regiments and military corps holding warrants under the Grand Lodge of Dublin, as stated in the evidence before the House, are taken into account, it will be seen how large a portion of the army has been at different times imbued with Orangeism.

No.
30. 13th Light Dragoons.
31. Royal Sappers and Miners, 7th Company.
33. 24th Regiment of Foot.
58. 95th or Rifle Brigade.
64. 35th Regiment.
65. Royal Artillery Drivers.
66. 43rd Regiment.
67. Royal Artillery.
77. Royal Horse Artillery.
84. 42nd Foot (Highlanders).
87. 59th Foot.
94. Rifle Brigade, 2nd battalion.
104. 42nd Regiment.
114. Rifle Brigade.
120. 31st Foot.
125. 7th Dragoon Guards.
131. 16th Light Dragoons.
165. 51st Light Infantry.
181. 6th Foot.

190. 6th Dragoon Guards.

204. 5th Dragoon Guards

205. Royal Artillery, 4th battalion.

232. Royal Artillery, 7th battalion.

238. 67th Foot.

241. 29th Foot.

243. Royal Sappers and Miners.

248. Royal Artillery, 5th battalion.

254. Royal Artillery, 6th battalion.

258. 94th Foot.

260. 17th Foot.

269. 1st Royal Dragoons.

204. 6th Dragoon Guards.

The following are extracts from the account book, entitled, "The Grand Orange Lodge Treasurer" of moneys received from military lodges—viz :—

[Here follow extracts of an interesting character.]

COLONIES.

It will be seen by the correspondence between non-commissioned officers and privates in different regiments of the line, and of the artillery at Bermuda, Gibraltar, Malta, and Corfu, and the Deputy Grand Secretary of the institution, that Orange Lodges have not only been held in regiments in these Colonies with the knowledge of the grand officers of the institution, but that the soldiers have been encouraged by them to hold such lodges under the *most suspicious circumstances* The books of the institution show also that money has been received from them from time to time for the warrants, and there are a great many letters demanding the dues owing to the Grand Lodge by the members of these lodges; and it is difficult to comprehend how all this could be done, and continued for so many years, without the knowledge of the grand officers of the institution in London, to whom, it may be fairly presumed, that the books of the secretary and treasurer have been always accessible.

NEW SOUTH WALES AND VAN DIEMAN'S LAND.

New South Wales and Van Dieman's Land appear to be deeply imbued with the system of Orangeism. Your committee refer to several letters which have come before them, and which will explain the progress of the system there; but your committee consider it of importance to place prominently before the House one letter dated January, 1833, in which it appears that the then Deputy Grand Secretary of the institution in London induced the writer, a soldier, to disobey the orders of his commanding officer, and did actually exchange an Irish for an English warrant

to hold a lodge in the regiment, contrary to the orders of the Commander in-Chief, and at the time he knew that the military orders were in force against such grant :—

"Sidney, 13th January, 1833.

"SIR AND BROTHER,—I beg leave to lay before you the following account of 260 Loyal Orange Association, who are increasing rapidly in the 17th Regiment at present; our number of members at present is seventy-three regular good members; our fund is not strong at present, for we allow our sick 1s per week, and our entering charge is only 2s 6d. We held a number from the Benevolent Orange Systery of Ireland in 1828, but I thought better to exchange the same, which I did in 1829, shortly after I was ordered to embark for New South Wales.

I was ordered, previous to embarkation, if I had or held a warrant of the Orange system, to send it back to the Grand Lodge, which I did not think proper to do; this, I must own, was direct disobedience of orders to my commanding officer; but I wrote to Mr. Chetwoode Eustace, then Deputy Grand Secretary, and he informed me not to be the least afraid, for no harm would be done me. I knew there was an order issued in 1829 prohibiting Orange lodges in the army, but this was only, as I believe, to satisfy our most bitter enemies; but if our beloved Sovereign was depending on them for the support of his Crown he would find the result; but I hope God will keep them from further power, for they are getting too much in power, both in the army and public. I am of opinion that if Orange lodges were established in this country it would increase the welfare of the community, for there are numbers of free respectable inhabitants and discharged soldiers would support the same; but we are not allowed to make inhabitants Orangemen under our warrant as a military one, but if there was a warrant granted to me, I am assured it would increase rapidly, as I intend to stop in this country by purchasing my discharge, when I shall make communication to you on the same.

"WM. M'KEE, Corporal 17th Regiment.

"God save the King.

"N.B.—Direct to Corporal Wm. M'Kee, H.M. 17th Regiment, Sydney."

EFFORTS TO SUPPRESS LODGES IN THE ARMY UNAVAILING.

When every endeavour on the part of Government to put an end to Orange lodges in the army has been met by redoubled efforts on the part of the Orange Institution not only to uphold but to increase them, evidently violating the military law; and aggravating its violation by concealing from the officers of the different regiments, and from the Commander of the Forces—from all, in fact, but Orangemen the fixed determination of fostering their institution. When soldiers are urged in official letters from the Deputy Grand Secretary of the society to hold meetings, notwithstanding the orders of the Commander-in-Chief to the contrary, but with instructions to act with caution and prudence, it is surely time for Government to take measures for the complete suppression of such institutions.

COMPLAINT AGAINST THE GOVERNMENT.

In a letter, dated 30th July, 1833, addressed to the master of a lodge at Portsmouth, Lieutenant-Colonel Fairman writes :—"It is a lamentable thing that the Government is so shortsighted, or so wilfully blind, as not to encourage Orangeism in the army, which would operate as an additional security for the allegiance and fidelity of the soldier on all occasions; but the Ministers of the present day are holding out premiums for disloyalty to subjects of every class."

UPPER AND LOWER CANADA.

Although, by an arrangement between the Grand Orange Lodge in Dublin and the Loyal Orange Institution of Great Britain, the lodges in Upper and Lower Canada are to be under the Irish jurisdiction, yet considerable correspondence has passed between the soldiers and non-commissioned officers of the army there and the Deputy Grand Secretary of the Loyal Orange Institution in England; and strong encouragement appears to have been given at one time by the Imperial Grand Lodge in London to the establishment of new lodges and to the extension of Orangeism amongst the troops in those provinces. Your committee refer to the correspondence with those colonies for the state of Orangeism there, and they refer to extracts in the reports of the proceedings of the Grand Lodge in London for further information on that subject.

Meeting of Grand Lodge, 8th January, 1827.—A letter from Sir Harcourt Lees, Bart., was read to the meeting, "strongly recommending the object of Brother John Montgomery West's mission relative to the organisation of the Orange system in the Canadas to the serious consideration of the Grand Lodge as a subject of great and material importance."

"A letter was also read from Alexander Matheson, Esq., of Perth, in Upper Canada, in which he

states 'that many thousands of Orangemen at present in the Canadas are without any regular lodge.' The benefit that would result from a regular system to those provinces and to the rising generation would be incalculable.'"

ORANGEMEN IN POLICE.

Although there are police in London entered in the returns of some of the Orange lodges, your committee have not been able to learn the numbers of Orangemen now in the police.

CLERGY OF CHURCH OF ENGLAND.

Your committee have to observe that the clergymen of the Church of England appear to have engaged, to a considerable extent, in the affairs of the Orange Institution. The Right Reverend Thomas, Lord Bishop of Salisbury, is Lord Prelate and Grand Chaplain of the order. There are also twelve or thirteen Deputy Grand Chaplains of the institution. Some clergymen have warrants as Masters of lodges, and conduct their affairs. No dissenting clergymen in England, and only two clergymen of any persuasion in Scotland, appear to have joined the institution. The reverend functionaries of the institution are directed to appear in the Grand Lodge in canonicals; their insignia consist of a purple velvet scarf with gold binding, gold fringe at the ends, and lined with orange silk.

DEMONSTRATIONS OF PHYSICAL FORCE.

In the printed report of the proceedings of the Imperial Grand Lodge, on the 4th of June, 1835, amongst the notices for circulation to the Orangemen of Great Britain and the Colonies, there is the following paragraph, copied from the proceedings of the Grand Lodge of Ireland :—

"The Grand Lodge of Dublin thought proper to thank their Orange brethren for having assembled in large numbers in one place, to the number of 75,000 Orangemen, at Hillsborough, and the Loyal Orange Institution of England, in the same circular, calls the attention of their Orange brethren by republishing the resolutions of the Grand Lodge of Dublin, as follows:

"And lastly, we beg to call the attention of the Grand Lodge, and through them return our heartfelt thanks and congratulations to our brethren through various parts of Ireland, who, at the late meetings of the three thousand in Dublin, five thousand at Bandon, thirty thousand at Cavan, and seventy-five thousand at Hillsborough, by their strength and numbers, the rank, respectability, and orderly conduct of their attendance, the manly and eloquent expressions of every

45

Christian and loyal sentiment, vindicated so nobly the character of our institution, against the aspersion thrown on it as 'the paltry remnant of an expiring faction.' And we ardently hope that our brethren in the other parts of the kingdom who have not yet come forward will do so, and not forget the hint given to us in our Sovereign's last most gracious declaration, 'to speak out'"

In the letters from the Deputy Grand Secretary to the Marquis of Londonderry and to the Duke of Gordon and others there is a general reference to the advantage of increase of numbers, of boldness of attitude, and even of physical force, to support the views of the Orange Institution.

(Copy.)

" Cannon Row, Westminster,
30th July, 1832.

"MY LORD MARQUIS,—In my letter of Saturday I omitted to mention that we have the military with us as far as they are at liberty to avow their principles and sentiments; but since the lamented death of the Duke of York every impediment has been thrown in the way of those holding a lodge The same observation that was applied to the colliers might be attached to the soldiery. As Orangemen, there would be an additional security for their allegiance and unalterable fidelity in times like the present, when revolutionary writers are striving to set them up to open sedition and mutiny. In trespassing thus upon the attention of your lordship I am not so presumptuous as to suppose that anything urged by me could influence your conduct, but understanding the Duke of Cumberland has communicated with your lordship on this subject, I felt it my duty to put you in possession of certain facts with which you might not be acquainted.—I have the honour to be, my lord marquis, your lordship's very respectful and obedient servant,

" W. B. FAIRMAN.

"To the Marquis of Londonderry"

Extract of letter to the Duke of Gordon.

" Cannon Row, Westminster,
11th August, 1833.

"Our institution is going on prosperously, and my accounts from all quarters are of the most satisfactory kind. By our next general meeting we shall be assuming, I think, such an attitude of boldness as will strike the foe with awe; but we inculcate the doctrine of passive obedience and of non-resistance too religiously by far.—I have the honour to be, my lord duke, your Grace's most devot d and respectful servant,

"W. B. FAIRMAN."

In June, 1833, Lieutenant-Colonel Fairman writes to Lord Longford in these words:—"We shall speedily have such a moral and physical force, I trust, as will strike with terror and sore dismay the foes of our country"

It appears, by a paper endorsed by Lieutenant-Colonel Fairman that he had received on the 8th June, 1834, from Randel E. Plunket Esq., M P (Grand Master of County Meath, Deputy Grand Master in Ireland, and member of the Grand Committee of the London Orange Institution), the draft of an address to the members of the Carlton Club, to be printed and circulated in the name of and by the Orange Institution. The following is the first paragraph:—"The Orange Institution is the only society peculiar to Great Britain and Ireland which already includes individuals of every rank and grade, from the nearest to the Throne to the poorest peasant." The draft was modified among other alterations, the expression, " nearest to the Throne," was changed for the term "the first male subject in the realm;" the address was then widely circulated. Mr. Plunket, in a letter of the 5th July, 1834, to the Deputy Grand Secretary, says:—"In the general tenor of the appeal I fully acquiesce, every word of it must find an echo in every loyal breast." He further adds—"That the physical strength of the Orange Institution, as its last resort, should be explained by a short address." The Orange body is capable of being rendered eminently 'available at elections," and Mr. Plunket adverts to "its peculiar and almost unique application to purposes of communication between persons of all grades and to large bodies, whether the intent of such application be for insuring an election or strengthening the hands of a Governor, &c.," and he continues, "Conservatism is inferior to Orangeism, as it is solely, and almost selfishly political. I cannot consent to lose your valuable exertions by identifying you with the politics of the Carlton Club. I should fly at higher game, and endeavour to make the members of the Carlton Orangemen."

Your committee could not keep out of sight the incidents that took place in Ireland at that gentleman's election by the interference of large bodies of armed Orangemen, as detailed in the evidence on the table of the House.

EFFORTS FOR EXTENSION IN ENGLAND.

The following paragraphs of the address to the members of the Carlton Club and the Conservatives of England, as circulated, are worthy of attention:—

"The day has passed when a debate and a vote of either House could settle, even for a time, a vital question. To restore that day a large portion of the community must be bound in union for the support of the institutions of the country. Their ostensibility would give *physical weight* to those spirited and truly patriotic members of both Houses who should have the moral courage to oppose the will of bold innovators and the rash measures of wild experimentalists. Where then, is this union to be found? Where is the nucleus around which may be arrayed the advocates of our social system who are now disheartened, passive lookers-on at the march of Radicalism since they are without leaders on whom they can rely?

"Such an union, such a nucleus, has (to a very limited extent in England)) some years existed, and requires only to be well understood and adopted by the Conservatives generally, to become so expanded as to present the happiest means not only of preserving the vessel of the State from wreck, but of carrying her in safety clear of all rocks, shoals, and shallows which at present peril her navigation; that union, that nucleus, noble lords, gentlemen, and fellow-countrymen, is 'The Royal Orange Institution.'

"This is the only society peculiar to Great Britain and Ireland, which already includes persons of every rank and grade, from the first male subject in the realm down to the humblest individual.

"It is not an occult society; it is not one of concealments; it is not bound by oaths, although every member has either taken, or is willing to take, the oaths of allegiance and supremacy; but it is a society, every member of which pledges himself to support to the utmost of his ability, and by all legal means, our Protestant establishment, and ancient institutions in Church and State.

"It is governed by a Grand Master, the first prince of the blood, who, with the aid of noblemen and gentlemen, eminent for loyalty, wisdom, and sound discretion, will be able (when the institution shall become more extensively ramified) to muster, in every part of the empire, no small portion of all that is sound in the community, and thus present in every quarter a phalanx too strong to be overpowered by the destructives, which will give a moral as well as a known physical strength to the Government of the King, and will enable it to set at defiance the tyrannous power that has been so madly called into existence."

Your committee submit that such publications indicate the importance which is attached to the increase of numbers in the Orange Institution with the view to the effects likely to be produced by a display of physical force.

POWERS OF THE IMPERIAL GRAND MASTER.

In the printed proceedings of the Grand Lodge, 4th June, 1833, the Duke of Cumberland is reported to have stated that "if the Grand Lodge have not confidence in the Grand Master it is better perhaps that I should know it; but if it have confidence its members must be aware that it is my wish to simplify the proceedings of the institution as much as possible. 'Individual opinion is not to be consulted upon vital and important arrangements, involving the welfare and best interests of the institution.'"

It must always be kept in mind that the power of calling out the members of all the Orange lodges in Ireland rests with the Grand Master and his deputy, on the application of twelve members of the Grand Committee; that the same person is Grand Master of Great Britain and of Ireland having the same powers, which are stated to be uncontrollable and arbitrary, of bringing together large bodies of armed and unarmed men, to make a demonstration of physical force, which might prove highly dangerous.

ACTIVITY OF THE LOYAL ORANGE INSTITUTION.

The activity of the institution may be judged of from the declaration of Lieutenant-Colonel Fairman, that he has been in the habit of receiving a multiplicity of communications from all parts of the world, and that he now has a cartload of correspondence in his house at Lambeth.

TENDENCY OF ORANGEISM TO INTERFERE, &c.

The obvious tendency and effect of the Orange Institution is to keep up an exclusive association in civil and military society, exciting one portion of the people against the other; to increase the rancour and animosity too often unfortunately existing between persons of different religious persuasions—to make the Protestant the enemy of the Catholic, and the Catholic the enemy of the Protestant—by processions on particular days, attended with the insignia of the society, to excite to breaches of the peace and to bloodshed—to raise up other secret societies among *the Catholics in their own defence, and for their own protection, against the insults of the Orangemen*—to interrupt the course of justice, and to interfere with the discipline of the army, thus rendering its services injurious instead of useful when required on occasions where Catholics and Protestants may be

parties. All these evils have been proved by the
evidence before the House in regard to Ireland,
where the system has long existed on an extended
scale, rendered more prejudicial to the best in
terests of society by the patronage and protection
of so many wealthy members high in office and in
rank taking an active part in the proceedings of
these lodges, though in Great Britain in a more
limited way.

The Orange lodges have also interfered in various
political subjects of the day, and made Orangeism
a means of supporting the views of a political
party, to maintain, as they avow, the Protestant
ascendancy. The Orange lodges have addressed
his Majesty, and individuals, on special occasions
of a political nature—have patronised and supported, by subscriptions, votes of thanks, &c., parts
of the public Press which advocated their opinions
and views in politics—have interfered in the course
of justice by subscriptions to defend and protect
parties of Orangemen, and to prosecute the magistrates for interfering with them (as in the case of
Liverpool in 1819, when the Mayor of Liverpool
interrupted the Orange procession on the 12th of
July in that year), and have also interfered with
the elective franchise by expelling members of
their body, as at Rochdale, in 1835, for voting for
the Liberal candidate. The following are some of
the many instances recorded in the minute books
and in the printed circulars of the society, and will
support the statements of your committee,—

At Moston, committee meeting, 11th August,
1819. Resolved—"That an immediate subscription be entered into by the Loyal Orange Institution to defray the great expense attending the late
prosecution in Liverpool, which expenses amount
to a serious sum of money in consequence of the
great number of witnesses and the exertions required to collect evidence for the support of the
prosecution; the amount of expenses attending the
prosecution and amount of property destroyed are
upwards of £200.

7th August, 1820—Resolved at a special meeting
of the committee in Manchester, "That from the
conduct adopted by Sir John Tobin, Knt., Mayor of
Liverpool, towards the members of the institution,
when walking in procession in that town on the
12th July last, and seizing and illegally impri-
soning Mr Tyrer, the committee deems it highly
necessary for the honour of the institution that Mr
Tyrer should immediately adopt proceedings against
the mayor, unless a proper explanation and

apology be made by the mayor to Mr. Tyrer for
such outrage."

Committee meeting, 13th October, 1819, Manchester—Thanks to Lord Kenyon for his subscription towards the prosecution in Liverpool, and to
the lodges who have subscribed and transmitted
their subscriptions for the same purpose.

Committee meeting, 26th July, 1823—The following resolution, recommended to the Grand
Lodge by the Grand Committee, "That the several
Deputy Grand Masters and Secretaries constantly
report to the Grand Committee the increase or de
crease of our enemies and their proceedings, as
well as the increase or decrea e of our friends, with
any suggestions for the good of our constitution in
Church and state, and that brothers who reside
where either Popery or disloyalty prevail be especially on the alert."

NEWSPAPERS.

At an annual meeting of the Grand Lodge in
Manchester, 26th and 27th June, 1820, it was resolved, "That this meeting strongly recommends
to the notice of all lodges the newspaper called the
Hibernian Journal, published in Dublin, by our excellent brother, John Burke Fitzsimmons, Esq., as
the only paper which has avowed spiritfully, and
undauntedly maintains the Orange principles in
defiance of all Popish attempts to stifle the swelling chorus of loyalty to our King, and sincere attachment to our glorious constitution."

Meeting at Lord Kenyon's, 27th April, 1821—
Resolved—"That the grateful thanks of this meeting be given on behalf of the Loyal Orange Institution of Great Britain, to the proprietors and editors of the True Briton and the Hibernian Journal,
for the constitutional part which they took on the
introduction into Parliament of the late Bills for
the destruction of the Protestant religion and
glorious constitution of this country."

At a meeting of the Grand Lodge, 16th June,
1823—Thanks were given to the editor of the
John Bull, Sunday Newspaper, "for his advocacy
of constitutional Orange principles on a recent occasion."

16th June, 1823—Thanks to Sir A. B. King,
Bart.—"For the gentlemanly, firm, and conscientious conduct he displayed at the bar of the House
of Commons during his examination on the subject
of oaths and constitution of the Orange Society,
whereby we have considered him to have completely
established its entire confidence with the true
principles of our glorious constitution."

Thanks to Mr. Secretary Peel were given for his

support of Protestant principles.

"That D. G. M. French do ascertain what Orangeman of warrant No. 60, authorised attendance on the Birmingham Political Union, and that he transmit the list of Orangemen who so attended and who have not sufficiently testified regret and contrition for such un-Orange and improper conduct."

Thanks moved by the Duke of Gordon in the Grand Lodge, on June 4, 1823, to the editors of *Edinburgh Evening Post, Glasgow Courier,* and other papers.

THE COMMITTEE CANNOT RECONCILE THE IGNORANCE OF THE GRAND OFFICERS OF THE EXISTENCE OF LODGES OF THE ARMY—BOOKS REGULARLY KEPT.

Your Committee, in reviewing all the facts brought before them, and taking into consideration the mode in which they have been proved, are unable to reconcile those facts with the ignorance professed by the Imperial Grand Master, the Deputy Grand Master of England and Wales, and by other grand officers of the institution, of the existence of lodges in the army.

The books of the institution have been from time to time neglected;* the evidence of every witness proves that the Deputy Grand Secretary and Grand Committee prepare the business for the Grand Lodge; and that every proposition for its deliberation is considered by the lodge in the order entered on the *Rota;* and a report of the proceedings of every Grand Lodge, detailing the business therein transacted, is printed and circulated soon after the meetings, to every grand officer of the Grand Lodge, and generally to every Master of a lodge. All these forms induce your committee to place reliance on the documentary evidence, which may be classed under the following heads—viz:—

MILITARY WARRANTS.

There have been minutes of the proceedings of the Grand Lodge kept, with some interruptions since 1819; and in them there are entries respecting the military brethren, the granting of warrants and the demanding and the receipt of money from various lodges in the army. The following are examples of such entries—viz:—

At a meeting of the Loyal Orange Institution, Manchester, 25th June, 1819—"Resolved that a warrant be granted to brother Brew to hold a lodge in the 6th Regiment of Infantry."

26th and 27th June, 1820. Meeting at Manchester—Resolved, "That all military lodges on their arrival in Ireland shall communicate with the

* No minutes of the proceedings of the Grand Lodge are entered from 1829 to 1831.

Grand Lodge of Ireland, but must transmit their returns regularly to the Grand Lodge of England."

6th March, 1821, Manchester—Resolved, "That Sergeant Hill, of the 4th Dragoon Guards, be again admitted as a member of the institution, in consequence of the charges originally made against him having been proved to be malicious and false."

16th June, 1821. Half-yearly meeting at Lord Kenyon's—Resolved, "That Brother William Bridgeman, Master of lodge 131, lately held in the 16th Regiment, be required to account to the Grand Lodge for his conduct on pain of expulsion;" at the same meeting warrants were granted to Faithful Hall, 11th Regiment of Foot, Thomas MacKean, 10th Light Dragoons, and to Henry Gray, 2nd or Coldstream Guards, to hold lodges in their respective regiments.

25th March, 1823. Meeting of Grand Lodge at Lord Kenyon's—Resolved, "That warrants be granted to John Sempleton, schoolmaster sergeant, 3rd Regiment of Guards." And at this meeting there is a separate resolution—"That no distinction in numbers be made between military and civil warrants."

At a meeting of the Grand Lodge in Lord Kenyon's, on the 29th September, 1823, Deputy Grand Master Stockdale in the chair, it was resolved, "That our military brethren holding warrants, regularly notify to the Deputy Grand Secretary their change of quarters, that the necessary communications may be preserved with the Grand Lodge."

Meeting of Grand Lodge 15th June, 1827—Lord Kenyon in the chair. "John Gibson (military) Woolwich," attended the meeting and was appointed a Deputy Grand Master.

And at the first meeting of the Orange Institution of Great Britain after the Duke of Cumberland became Grand Master, held at the house of Kenyon on the 17th March, 1829, the Duke of Cumberland in the chair, the report of the Grand Committee was read, received, and confirmed, and the following resolutions were unanimously adopted;—

"That *new warrants* be granted."

No. 66, to Samuel Morris, musician, 43d Foot, Gibraltar.

94, to Hospital-Sergeant Charles O. Haines, 2nd Batt. Rifle Brigade, Malta.

104, to Private James Bain, 42nd Foot, Gibraltar.

114, to Corporal John Parkinson, 2nd Batt. Rifle Brigade, Devonport.

248, to R. Lawrence, 5th Batt. Royal Artillery, Gibraltar.

At a subsequent meeting in the same place, on the 4th June, 1832, where the Duke of Cumberland also presided, the report of the Grard Committee and their resolutions were read before the grand lodge The tenth resolution is to the effect that "several additional letters were laid before the Grand Comm ttee, containing complaints against Mr. Chetwoode;" among these were letters from the following non - commissioned officers and privates :—

Bermuda—Sergeant Charney, Nov. 2, 1831.

Corfu—Hospital - Sergeant Haines, 2nd Batt. Rifles, April 15, 1832.

Dublin—Brother Nichole, 50th Reg. May 12, 1832

Malta—Brother M'Innes, 42nd Reg. Highlanders, 1st May, 1832.

Quebec— —— Inglis, 24th Reg

By the report of the proceedings of the grand lodge, held on the 16th of April 1833, the Duke of Cumberland being in the chair, it appears that the proceedings of warrant 233, Woolwich (being a *military warrant, Boyzl Artillery, 9th Battalion*) were read, and Brother John Gibson *(military)* of the said warrant was *examined*, and it was resolved that Charles Nimens *(a private in that batta ion)* should be suspended from membership, with right of appeal through the Grand Committee to the next grand lodge.

LETTER BOOK.

2nd. In the letter-book of the Institution, from 1808 to the latest period, up to which Your Committee have been enabled to obtain evidence, there are copies of letters addressed by the Deputy Grand Secretary of the institution to non-commissioned officers and privates in regiments, and in detachments of artillery at home and abroad (copies of some of which are annexed in the Appendix) all sent by the Deputy Grand Secretary for the time, in the name of the grand lodge. There is also a mass of letters from soldiers belonging to lodges in the army, some of them addressed to Lord Kenyon, which his lordship admitted he must have seen, although he did not at first recollect them , these letters embrace a large portion of the army, and will be seen in the Appendix.

DUES FROM MILITARY LODGES — DEPUTY-TREASURER'S LEDGER OF CASH RECORDS.

3rd. There are regular entries of the names of the regiments and the corps of artillery, and to others, in the ledgers from 1820 to 1824; the number of the warrants granted to each of them,

the amount of dues owing by them to the Grand Lodge, and the amounts received from to time from them ; all these accounts are kept by the Deputy Grand Treasurer, and once a year, or oftener, the accounts of the institution were balanced and laid before the Grand Lodge, and in these printed accounts entries from lodges in the army also appear. In the accounts published and circulated within the last three years to every member of the Grand Lodge, there are many entries also of the names of the privates and non-commissioned officers from whom money was received—viz :—

Dues received from the following military lodges from the account submitted to the Grand Lodge, 4th June, 1835

Woolwich, 133—13, dues to March, 1833, £0 15 6
„ 206—1st Royal Dragoons, ... 2 8 0
Gibraltar—53rd Regiment, for new warrant, ... 1 11 6
From Malta—Fusiliers, granted by Commissioner Nucella, for new warrant, ... 3 9 0
Dover 114—Dues from June, 1832, 1st Rifle Brigade, ... 1 0 0

ALPHABETICAL REGISTER OF MILITARY.

4th There is a reg ster in which some thousand names are alphabetically entered, with the number of the lodge they belong to, and of these some hundreds are entered as military, and opposite to them the number of the regiments they respectively belong to.

LIST OF THE LODGES.

5th. There exists a register printed in 1826, and made up in manuscript by Mr. Chetwoode to 1830, of all the lodges under the institution having the names of thirty regiments or corps opposite the numbers of the warrants they held, and many of the printed circulars announced that those printed registers of the lodges were on sale at 2s each. An extract of the registers of military lodges is given in another part of the report

PRINTED REPORTS.

6th In the printed circular reports o the proceedings of the Grand Lodge, at which his Royal Highness presided, there are entries of the warrants granted to regiments by that Grand Lodge; for instance, it appears from the minutes of proceedings of the meeting of the Grand Lodge at No. 9, Portman Square, on the 17th February, 1831, the Duke of Cumberland, Grand Master of the Empire, in the chair, that the issuing of twenty-four warrants to hold new - lodges was approved, and three of them are thus inserted—viz.:—

No. 254 to Samuel Heasty, 6th Battalion Artillery.
258 to James Smith, 94th Foot.
260 to Private Wilson, 17th Foot.

PROXY FROM MILITARY LODGES.

There are also entries (1947) of Sergeant Wm. Keith having attended two meetings as proxy for the 1st Regiment of Dragoon Guards, warrant 269. And by a resolution at a meeting of the Grand Lodge on the 15th February, 1827, "No person can be received as proxy in the Grand Lodge who is not of himself qualified to sit and vote therein.

NO FEES TO SOLDIERS.

7th. In the laws and ordinances of 1821, 1826, and 1834, there is an apparent encouragement held out for the initiation of soldiers and sailors to be Orangemen by the remission of the fees of admission.

On the 4th of June, 1834, there is the following entry in the printed report of the proceedings:—

"The laws and ordinances of the institution, as revised by the Grand Committee, and submitted to the inspection of his Royal Highness the Grand Master, and his lordship the Deputy Grand Master of England and Wales, were approved and confided by his Royal Highness to the final supervision of Lord Kenyon."

And it is difficult to understand how either of them could be ignorant of the following law—viz:—

Rule 41st. No person can be admitted into this institution for a less fee than 15s, nor advanced into the Purple order, after a reasonable probation, for less than extra fee of 5s, except soldiers and sailors, when the fee of admission shall be at the discretion of the meeting.

This rule was entered in the manuscript laws submitted to Mr. Serjeant Lens in 1821, also in the copy of 1826, and is to be found in the last copy revised in 1834.

FOREIGN WARRANT TO BROTHER E. NUCELLA.

8th. A warrant was granted in 1832 to Edward Nucella, Esq., to visit established lodges on the Continent of Europe, and in Malta, and the Ionian Islands, and to establish others where he could, as follows:—

(Copy).

No. Foreign Warrant.,   Granted
this 10th day of August,   1832.

BY VIRTUE OF THIS AUTHORITY,

Our well-beloved Brother Orangeman, Edward Nucella, Esq., of South Lambeth, in the County of Surrey, is nominated and warranted to the office of Worshipful Master in the Orange Institution, and appointed to perform the requisites thereof beyond the realm of Great Britain.

Given under our seal at London.

(Signed)

CHANDOS, Grand Secretary.
ERNEST, Grand Master.

Seal, King William III.   Seal, King William III

PUBLICITY.

Mr. Nucella was informed, before his departure from England, that there were military lodges in Malta, and he stated to the committee that it was publicly known in that island that Orange lodges were held in the regiments there. He was known in Malta as the agent of the Loyal Orange Institution, and the soldiers and non-commissioned officers visited him as such, and he attended their lodges. He wrote several letters from Malta and the Ionian Islands to the Deputy Grand Secretary describing his proceedings; these letters were read by the Grand Committee—were read in the Grand Lodge when the Duke of Cumberland and Lord Kenyon were present, and the thanks of the Grand Lodge were given to Mr. Nucella for his zeal—Mr. Nucella stated in his letters that he had granted two warrants—viz., to the 7th and 73rd Regiments, to hold lodges; and these were afterwards approved of by the Grand Lodge, and the dues for the same were entered in the account of the regiment, kept in the book of the Grand Lodge as received. On the 4th of October, 1833, he writes, "I find only two out of four battalions of regiments and companies of artillery stationed in this island—viz., 42nd Highlanders (the head lodge) and the 94th are sitting under warrants, the former, No. 104, Master John M'Kay; the latter, No. 258, Master Frederick Spooner; the two other regiments, the 7th and 73rd, are sitting under precepts." On the 30th October, 1833, he sends a list of the members of lodge No. 258 in the 94th Regiment, and of No. 194 lodge in the 7th regiment; he states "that Major Middleton, of the 42nd Regiment, had put down the lodge No. 104 held in that regiment," and he details his expostulation with the major for so doing. In his letter from Corfu, 26th November, 1833, he states that he had been prevented by Lord Nugent, the Civil Governor, from establishing a lodge there; and he mentions with astonishment the orders of the Commander of the Forces prohibiting the soldiers from holding or sitting in any lodge whatever. In his letter of 7th February, 1834, he mentions that he had granted to Captain M'Dugall, paymaster of the 42nd Royal Highlanders, the warrant No. 193 Z lodge for having been an Orangeman for thirty years, and that he had raised him and the Deputy Master, Ensign and Quartermaster Hickman, of the 73rd Regiment, to the dignity of the Purple order. "All this," he adds, "subject to the approbation and confirmation of the Grand Master of the Empire, whom you, of course, make acquainted with the whole, and also the Grand Lodge." Mr. Nucella never thought of concealing his mission as Commissioner appointed by the Orange Association; but, in every letter, and in his evidence, seems proud of that duty; his warrant was hung up openly in his chambers all the time he was in Malta. These letters were read in the Grand Lodge at different times. Notice of them was made on 4th June, 1833, by Lord Kenyon, in very favourable terms, and at another time the following entry appears —

"The zealous exertions of Brother Nucella, M.D.C. and Grand Commissioner on the Continent for the advancement of the institution as detailed in his letters from Italy, Malta, and the Ionian Islands, afforded high gratification, and called forth the unanimous approbation of the Grand Lodge."

Your committee call particular attention to the proceedings of Mr, Nucella, as he was sent under a foreign warrant of the Duke of Cumberland, Imperial Grand Master, to Malta and other places, and that warrant could not have been signed blank; he reports to the Deputy Grand Secretary his progress, and the state of Orange lodges in the regiments from time to time—his letters are read in Grand Lodge—notice of them taken in the printed reports; and, finally, he received from the Deputy Grand Secretary the following letter of thanks from the Imperial Grand Master:—

(Copy)
"ORANGE INSTITUTION.
"Cannon Row, 6th June, 1834.
"MY DEAR SIR,—It affords me no small portion of pleasure to forward you an extract from the last report of the Grand Committee, which was confirmed by our illustrious Grand Master in Grand Lodge. My time has been so engrossed as well in preparing for that meeting as in presiding at

Grand Committees, since another of which, on finance, will be held to-morrow, that I have scarcely had one moment which I could call my own. This must serve as my apology for not offering you my respects in person, which I shall seize the first opportunity of doing; in the meanwhile, begging you to accept my best wishes for the restoration of your health, I have, &c.
"(Signed)
"W. BLENNERHASSETT FAIRMAN.
"To Edmond Nucella, Esq.

"Having heard read the highly interesting, important, and valuable communications of Brother Nucella, M.G.G., &c., from Corfu, Malta, and other remote places, of various dates, as also one of this morning from Vauxhall Place, on his return to England after an absence of two years, during which he had been making a tour no less extensive than useful, your Grand Committee beg to offer him their warmest congratulations and their most cordial welcome on returning to his native land. The acceptable proofs he has afforded on all occasions of his unremitting zeal to promote the objects and to extend the principles of our institution have been such as cannot fail to ensure him the approbation of the grand lodge. In bearing this testimony to his merits the committee would be guilty of great injustice were they not to recommend him strongly for some especial mark of honour for the heavy claim he has established on the gratitude of the high dignitaries and of the brotherhood in general. They cannot close this well deserved tribute of respect for him without expressing their regret at his indisposition, with their best wishes for his recovery.
"W. B. F, Chairman."

9th. Lieutenant-Colonel Fairman states that soldiers from the garrison in the Castle were admitted in their regimentals to the lodges he held in Edinburgh whilst on his tour of inspection; that he granted a new military warrant to the 6th Dragoons at Sheffield; and, as a matter of course, he and his predecessor, the former Deputy Grand Secretary, exchanged many old Irish military warrants for English ones without inquiry. At Rochdale it was publicly and generally known that the military belonged to the Orange Associations. In Malta the existence of Orangeism in the army was generally known by officers and men, and Mr. Nucella was recognised by them openly as a Commissioner from the Duke of Cumberland, the Imperial Grand Master of the Loyal Orange Association of England. Mr. Nucella remonstrated, with the commanding officer of the 42nd Regiment on the subject of his suppressing the lodge in that regiment; and he afterwards attended the meetings of other military lodges there, although he knew they were being held contrary to the order of the commander of the forces.

Your Committee therefore submit to the House these details, as some of the many proofs which have been brought before them, of the manner in which the Orange Lodges in the army have, from time to time, come under the notice of the Grand Committee and of the grand lodge; and, when it is also known that, at almost every meeting of the grand lodge since his appointment, the Imperial Grand Master and the Deputy Grand Master for Great Britain have been present your Committee must repeat that they find it most difficult to reconcile statements in evidence before them with ignorance of these proceedings on the part of Lord Kenyon and by his Royal Highness the Duke of Cumberland.

SCOTLAND.

The two tours of inspection in 1833 and 1834 by Lieutenant-Colonel Fairman under his itinerant warrant was intended to extend the Orange system in England and in Scotland, and, with the patronage of the Duke of Gordon as Deputy Grand Master of Scotland, great expectations were formed of the extension of Orangeism from these tours. It appears by the evidence that the Deputy Grand Secretary assembled the established lodges in Edinburgh, where some of the military (cavalry and infantry) were admitted in their regimentals, and that he gave them every assurance of support from the Loyal Orange Institution of London; but the Committee have been unable to ascertain what number of Orangemen were at that time in Edinburgh. The Deputy Grand Secretary spent some weeks in the north with the Duke of Gordon, but it does not appear that there are any Orange Lodges north of the Firth of Forth. At Glasgow and in the West of Scotland Orange Lodges have been established for many years, and Lieut.-Colonel Fairman in 1833, visited these established lodges, and also formed the Gordon Lodge in Glasgow, under the patronage of the Duke of Gordon. By the evidence of Mr. Motherwell, the Deputy District Master, that lodge has not flourished, and may only be noticed as having sent addresses to Colonel Blacker on his dismissal from the magistracy in Ireland; and to Colonel Verner for having resigned the magistracy in disgust at Colonel Blacker's dismissal. An address was also

sent at the same time to Mr. Judge Smith to thank him for an address he had delivered to the Grand Jury, as they supposed, in support of Orangeism. There are Orange Lodges at Airdrie, Port Glasgow, Ayr, Kilmarnock, Girvan, Paisley, Neilston, Johnston, Maybole, Stranraer, Glenluce, Wigton, Dumfries, Castle Douglas, Kircudbright, &c., and Lieutenant-Colonel Fairman visited all these places, assembling the lodges at each place and infusing into them as much new life and activity as possible. He was received at Airdrie and other places with processions and honours as the representative of the Imperial Grand Lodge. The account of the proceeding of Lieutenant-Colonel Fairman in Scotland is published in the proceedings of the Grand Lodge, 4th June, 1833.

Copy of the proceedings of the Grand Lodge, 4th June, 1833:

"A vote of thanks having been passed to the editors of the *Glasgow Courier* and *Edinburgh Evening Post* for their exertions in the Orange cause, Deputy Grand Secretary observes thereupon 'that as the noble duke who is Deputy Grand Master of Scotland (Gordon) was not present at the last grand lodge I will now take the liberty of assuring his grace that such a fire has been kindled in North Britain as must speedily burst into a conflagration not easily to be extinguished.' Brother Thompson, Deputy Grand Master for Neilston, stated at the same meeting that having had the pleasure to attend Colonel Fairman during a part of his last mission in Scotland, 'he could testify it had been the means of infusing new life and vigour into those districts of the institution, that a firm basis was thus laid for great accession of strength to the lighting up of a flame of Orangeism in the North' which all the efforts of its opponents would never be able to smother."

It is particularly worthy the consideration of the House to consider what is meant "by lighting a flame of Orangeism which all the efforts of its opponents will not be able to smother," and your Committee direct their attention to the evidence of Mr. Cosmo Innes, a Deputy Judge Advocate of Scotland, for an explanation.

NUMBER OF LODGES IN SCOTLAND.

Your Committee has been desirous of ascertaining the exact number of Orange Lodges and of Orangemen now existing in Scotland, but without success. Lieutenant-Colonel Fairman, in his evidence (1863 to 8), stated the number of lodges at some of the towns he visited, but withheld the general return of Scotland, on a plea that he had no correct register. A reference must, therefore, be had to the return prepared from the books of the institution by Mr Colwill, the assistant to the Deputy Grand Secretary, from the entries of the district cts, and of the lodges in each of the seven districts in Scotland, amounting to 41 lodges, besides seperate lodges too far distant to be under the Deputy Grand Master of any of these districts. If the evidence of Mr. Motherwell, the editor of the *Glasgow Courier*, is referred to (3324) the lodges in Glasgow do not appear to be in a very flourishing state, as ho, as District Master, has suspended some of them from communication with the Grand Lodge in London, for offences and disobedience of various kinds; and the Gordon Lodge, which was to embrace a higher class of members, seems at present at a low ebb.

TENDENCY OF ORANGEISM

To show the tendency of Orange Lodges in the West of Scotland, the whole of Mr Innes's evidence must be read Mr. Innes was deputed by the Lord Advocate of Scotland, the law officer of the Crown, to proceed to Airdrie, Glasgow, and other places in the West part of Scotland, to inquire into the nature and extent of the riots that had taken place in July last in several parts of that country and their causes; he stated to the Committee that the existance of Orange Lodges had been the cause of those riots, some of which had been attended with loss of life and the subsequent execution of the offender, and that some of the late rioters were now waiting their trial. It will be seen that the meeting and procession of the Orangemen at one time led to the riot and breach of the peace; that at another time the Catholics became the agressors, having met and proceeded in great numbers with the determination of preventing any Orange procession which they expected to take place; and on another occasion the inhabitants of the town were brought forth to put down the riots between those two parties and to drive them from the town. Your Committee observe that in Mr Innes's opinion those breaches of the peace, alternating from one party to the other, are expected to continue as long as that cause remains. Mr. Innes states, an authority on which your committee place confidence, that the existence of the Orange lodges, their meetings, processions, and proceedings, have roused an opposition on the part of the Catholics to protect themselves from the insults offered by the Orangemen, and that secret societies have been formed for that purpose, by which the members can be called forth at any time

when occasion shall require their meeting to protect themselves against the insults of the Orangemen or to be revenged upon them; that the meeting of Catholics on the Green at Glasgow, before they marched to Airdrie, where they expected the Orangemen to walk in procession, was assembled by that means, and, from the proofs already mentioned, although Mr. Innes has been unable to procure any copy of the rules of those societies, he is satisfied that the delegates of no less than twenty-four of these societies, which he calls Riband Societies, having secret oaths and signs, previously met together to arrange the meeting and procession to Airdrie. The opinion of Mr Innes, after all the informa ion he has become officially possessed of, is that it will not be possible to restore the West of Scotland to tranquillity, and to prevent breaches of the peace occur.ing occasionally, unless measures are taken to put down the Orange lodges and Ribandmen, and every other secret society. Whether the existence of Orange longes has produced the Riband lodges, or the Riland lodges has produced the Orange, appears to be of little consequence. It is notorious that the Orange lodges exist, under the patronage of men high in rank in England, Ireland, and in Scotland, and the countenance given, in consequence of all the orders of the Orange Institution being issued by, and under, the authority of such men as his Royal Highness the Duke of Cumberland, as Imperial Grand Master, and of his Grace the Duke of Gordon, as Deputy Grand Master for Scotland, will be found to have a greater effect on the poor and the ignorant, of which the Orangemen there chiefly consist, than might be expected. When we see an emissary despatched for two successive years to extend Orangeism in that country, under the special and extraordinary commission of the Duke of Cumberland, bearing his sign and seal, with powers to propagate Orangeism, to form lodges, to dismiss members, or to pardon offences of Orangemen how, and when, he pleases, it appears time for Government to interfere. When that emissary is entertained and countenanced for weeks as an inmate of Gordon Castle the influence of the peer may be by the ignorant transferred to the emissary in everything respecting Orange lodges in that country. There are various ways of enlisting men in a cause, and when it is seen by the reports of the proceedings of grand lodges that such men as the Duke of Cumberland, the Duke of Gordon, Lord Kenyon, Lord Wynford, peers and members of Parliament, are united by a the same secret signs and passwords, and seated in the same room with a poor pensioner of one shilling a day, or any Orangeman, whatever his state in society may be, allowance must be made for the sacrifices that may be made by such persons, to be able to call the duke, or any other Orangeman, his brother; with permission to apply whenever in difficulty or distress, for the assistance of such wealthy and influential men.

As a proof of the baneful effects of the existence of Orangeism in Scotland, Mr. Innes states one example where a lodge of pitmen lately expelled from their body all the Catholics who had previously lived and worked together with them in peace and harmony.

Your committee will only add that the mischievous effects of Orange lodges shown, though on a small scale in Scotland, may be expected wherever such a system is upheld and promoted by men of high rank and by influential members of society; a reference to the evidence before the House of the working of Orangeism in Ireland, on the broadest scale, and after many years continuance, will completely bear out that opinion.

Your committee, in looking for a corrective to those evils which disturb both civil and military society so much, and which threaten the most serious consequences to the community of the United Kingdom, if allowed to continue, do not contemplate that any new legislative enactment is necessary, the powers of the law being at present, in the opinion of your committee, sufficient to protect the country from all such associations, bound together, as the Orange lodges are, by a religious sanction, with secret signs and passwords, by which the fraternity may be known to each other in every part of the world. It appears only to be necessary to enforce the existing laws against all such offenders, whether belonging to Orange lodges, to Riband lodges, or to any other society having secret signs and bonds of union.

GENERAL ORDERS OF 31ST AUGUST, 1835.

Your committee have been much pleased to receive a copy of general orders issued by General Lord Hill, the Commander of the Forces, and dated Horse Guards, 31st August, 1835, forbidding all officers and men in the army from attending Orange lodges, by whomsoever, and wheresoever held, which order your committee most anxiously hope will put an effectual stop to the spread of Orangeism in the army. The following is a copy of the order:—

"GENERAL ORDER.

"Horse Guards, 31st August, 1835.

"Lord Hill has reason to apprehend that the orders prohibiting the introduction of Orange lodges into the army have not been duly communicated to the non-commissioned officers and privates, or, if communicated, that they have not been sufficiently explained and understood.

"His lordship now refers commanding officers of regiments to the confidential circular letters of the 1st of July, 1822, and 14th of November, 1829, upon the foregoing subject; and declares that any officer, non-commissioned officer, or soldier, who shall hereafter institute or countenance an Orange lodge, or any other meeting or society whatsoever, for party purposes, in barracks, quarters, or camp, shall be brought to trial before a general court-martial for disobedience of orders.

"His lordship, moreover, peremptorily forbids the attendance of either officer or soldier at Orange lodges, by whomsoever or wheresoever held.

"The present order is to be read to the troops periodically on the parade with the articles of war.

"By command of the Right Honourable General Lord Hill, Commanding-in-Chief,

"JOHN MACDONALD, Adjutant-General."

Your committee, anxiously desirous of seeing the United Kingdom and the Colonies of the Empire freed from the baneful and unchristian influence of the Orange societies, recommend the early attention of the House to that important subject, with a view to the immediate removal from office of all public servants who shall continue, or become members of any Orange lodge, or of any other association bound together in a similar manner.

LETTERS OF THE DUKE OF CUMBERLAND OF 24TH AUGUST AND 5TH AUGUST, 1835.

Your committee think it proper to notice that his Royal Highness the Duke of Cumberland, the Imperial Grand Master, in his letter of the 24th August, states that "owing to the acknowledged indiscretion and negligence on the part of the Deputy Grand Master, and a like indiscretion and negligence on the part of other officers of the Orange Institution, many grants of warrants or renewals of former grants have, without the knowledge of his Royal Highness, and contrary to his declared determination, been issued from time to time in contravention of the order of the late illustrious commander-in-chief, his Royal Highness the Duke of York; and his Royal Highness the Duke of Cumberland "therefore declares that all warrants held by persons in his Majesty's service must henceforth be considered null and void." Your committee submit that these are important admissions, and they call the further attention of the House to the letter of his Royal Highness, dated 5th August last, addressed to the chairman of the committee on Orange Lodges, in which he says "he knows of no Orange lodge in any regiment." It is satisfactory to know that one result of the inquiry by the committee of this House has been to bring to his knowledge, and to convince his Royal Highness, that Orange lodges did, *and do* exist in many regiments of the army; and that he has presided, as Imperial Grand Master, over an institution which has for many years been acting in contravention of the orders of commanding officers of corps and of the Commander of the Forces. Your committee submit that it would have been very easy for his Royal Highness to have published the document by which, and the time and place where, he issued any order, or made any declaration, against Orange lodges in the army, instead of a general disclaimer.

ORDERS OF THE COMMANDER OF THE FORCES,
WHETHER CONFIDENTIAL OR NOT.

It has been alleged by some of the officers of the Orange Institution that the orders of the Commander of the Forces of 1822 and 1829 were merely confidential recommendations, and not general orders published from the Horse Guards. Your committee are desirous of removing that error by referring to the evidence of Major-General Sir J. Macdonald, the Adjutant-General of the army, who, on the 6th of August, stated to the Committee on Orange Lodges in Ireland that the confidential circular letter of July, 1822, was embodied in the edition printed in that year of the General Regulations and Orders of the Army; that it is the duty (27) of the colonel or commander of every regiment to have one of those books; that every regimental officer (31) is directed to supply himself with a copy of it; and that every regimental orderly-room ought to have a copy (31). Of the orders of the Duke of York, Sir J. Macdonald adds, no officer ought to be ignorant.

THE DUKE OF CUMBERLAND AS IMPERIAL MASTER.

Your Committee further submit whether an institution presided over by the brother of his Majesty, having peers and members of Parliament as office-bearers, having lodges extended to almost every part of the United Kingdom and also to the Colonies, should be allowed to continue, particularly when lodges are established in so large a portion of the army at home and abroad, having apparently the countenance of a field-marshal at their head.

NUMBER OF ORANGEMEN IN THE UNITED KINGDOM.

The number of Orangemen in Ireland is 220,000, as stated by the Deputy Grand Secretary for that country, and these chiefly with arms in their possession; and if the Orangemen in Great Britain and the Colonies amount only to half that number the House will judge how dangerous such an association, bound together by religious ceremony and sanction almost equal to that of an oath, might become under possible circumstances of the country. A great political body thus organized in the ranks of the army and in every part of the British Empire is a formidable power at any time and under any circumstances; but when your Committee look to the political tendency of the measures of the Orange Societies in England and in Ireland, and particularly to the language contained in addresses to the public, and in the correspondence with the grand officers of the institution, and consider the possible use that might be made of such an organised power its suppression becomes, in their opinion, imperatively necessary.

ORGANISATION AS A CORRESPONDING SOCIETY.

The nature of the organisation of the institution and the dangers from its existence will appear when the House is informed that the master of every lodge is required to meet the Deputy Grand Master of his district every half year and deliver to him a return (a copy of which will be seen annexed) of the number of members and of the proceedings of the lodge during the preceding half year, he is required also to collect and to pay at the same time the dues of his lodge. The returns and cash are then sent by the Deputy Grand Master of the district to the Deputy Grand Secretary in London, who lays the accounts and returns before the Grand Committee for their examination, and that Committee reports thereon to the Imperial Grand Lodge whatever may have occurred of importance in the last six months worthy of their consideration. Lodges communicate sometimes direct to the Grand Lodge, and the Grand Lodge sends copies of all its proceedings and orders periodically to every district master and to every lodge throughout the empire.

Your Committee think it right to place before the House the words of the statute, the 39 Geo. 3, C. 79, regarding corresponding societies. Section 9—"Any society composed of different divisions or branches, or of different parts, acting in any manner separately or distinct from each other, or of which any part shall have any distinct president, secretary, treasurer, delegate, or other officer, elected or appointed by, or for such part, or to act in any office for such part, &c." And in conclusion your Committee submit that it will be for the House to consider whether the present organisation of Orange Lodges, in connection with the Imperial Grand Lodge, comes within the words of that statute; and if so whether the law officers of the Crown should not be directed to institute legal proceedings without delay against the grand officers of all Orange Lodges.

September, 1835.

LEGAL.

(See Chapter xxxvii.; page 263.)

Since the foregoing pages were written, and after that portion of the volume bearing upon the legal aspect of the Orange Institution had passed through the Press, the Atlantic cable transmitted to this country the following brief but significant corroboration :—

"ORANGEISM DECLARED ILLEGAL.

"Montreal, Friday.

"In the case of Grant v. the Mayor of Montreal, for unlawful arrest while attempting to hold an Orange procession, the Court decided that the Orange Society is illegal under the laws of the Dominion."

The accounts that have since come to hand through the Canadian newspapers confirm this statement, so that, at least in one part of her Majesty's dominions, we have the Orange Association declared illegal.

The dispute out of which the proceedings arose took place as far back as 1878. On the memorable anniversary, the 12th July of that year, there was a demonstration at Montreal to commemorate the battle of the Boyne. The Mayor of the city, however, took steps to prevent the display. The District Master who headed the party was arrested immediately on his emerging from the Orange Hall, with him five of his fellow ring-leaders. All the others were surrounded and beleagured in their hall until they were glad to get out, and to be allowed to proceed to their homes under protection from the hostile crowds that had assembled. They were marched out in small bodies between lines of armed soldiers and thus escorted out of danger. It was the Mayor who ordered the arrest of the District Master and his five brethren, thus setting an example which it would be well to have imitated more generally elsewhere. But in return for this act of kindness, and for which a vote of thanks ought to have been passed to him, he was proceeded against in the Civil Courts for 10,000 dollars damages for illegal arrest. The case was heard in 1880, and the suit was dismissed by the Superior Court, but upon the technical grounds that the plaintiff had not given the Mayor as defendant the full notice as required by law. The case was taken to the Court of Appeal — as might be expected where such mighty interests were at stake — and on five judges of that High Court not only sustained the previous decision, but, what was eminently more satisfactory, they went much further, and deciding on the merits of the suit, declared that by virtue of chap. x. sec. 6 of the Consolidated Statutes of Canada, the Orange Order "is an illegal body, and its members may be prosecuted and found guilty of misdemeanour for the reason that the Orange oath enjoins secrecy." The judgment is final.

Lightning Source UK Ltd.
Milton Keynes UK
UKHW021907040822
406875UK00003B/100